THE FOUNDING OF SPANISH CALIFORNIA

ANTONIO MARÍA BUCARELY Y URSÚA, VICEROY OF NEW SPAIN,
1771–1779.

From M. Rivera Cambas, *Los gobernantes de México*, Vol. I, opposite page 422.

THE FOUNDING

OF

SPANISH CALIFORNIA

THE NORTHWESTWARD EXPANSION
OF NEW SPAIN, 1687–1783

BY

CHARLES EDWARD CHAPMAN, Ph.D.

OCTAGON BOOKS

A DIVISION OF FARRAR, STRAUS AND GIROUX

New York   1973

Reprinted 1973
by special arrangement with The Macmillan Company

OCTAGON BOOKS
A DIVISION OF FARRAR, STRAUS & GIROUX, INC.
19 Union Square West
New York, N. Y. 10003

Library of Congress Cataloging in Publication Data

Chapman, Charles Edward, 1880-1941.
    The founding of Spanish California.

    Originally presented as the author's thesis, University of California, 1915.

    Reprint of the ed. published by Macmillan, New York.

    Bibliography: p.
    1. California—History—To 1846.   I. Title.
F864.C46   1973   979.4   73-9760
ISBN 0-374-91438-9

Manufactured by Braun-Brumfield, Inc.
Ann Arbor, Michigan

Printed in the United States of America

PREFACE

THE present study owes its form to two principal ideas, which seem at first sight only distantly related, but which in fact merge into one. In the first place, I have endeavored to trace those influences that were at work prior to the nineteenth century whose tendency was to preserve Alta (or American) California, perhaps also Oregon and Washington, for ultimate acquisition by the United States. In the second place, I have aimed to give in detail an account of a Spanish experiment in colonization, although the narrative is limited to a comparatively brief span of years, and is still further narrowed in scope by treatment from the standpoint of governmental interest, rather than from that of events or experiences in the lands referred to. The problem of colonizing the Californias (considered as extending from Cape San Lucas indefinitely northward) was one of such extreme difficulty that it was manifestly impossible of successful accomplishment without an extraordinary effort on the part of those attempting it. After permanent establishments had been formed by the Spaniards in Alta California, a still more extraordinary effort would have been required to develop them into a populous province. Nothing but a sequence of fortunate events — such as discoveries or inventions that would have helped to overcome the difficulties of communication, and the finding of gold, which would have made the region attractive to settlers — could have enabled Spain to achieve the establishment of strong colonies in Alta California without great expenditure of treasure and of effort. Noteworthy inventions facilitating communication, and consequent growth of population, were not to come, however, until well into the nineteenth century, while the discovery of gold was

v

almost certainly destined to come only as a result of an increased population, before it could become in turn a cause for yet further growth. Gold lay back from the coast, up the river valleys, whereas the early settlements were founded, as it was natural they should have been, in a narrow strip along the coast. Until population should become great enough to induce men to seek new lands in the interior, the gold was likely to remain undiscovered. These considerations make it clear that the two ideas above referred to are in reality, as stated, only different aspects of one idea: the difficulties of colonization from the Pacific were so great that in the absence of exceptional exertions by Spain, or in default of fortuitous events extraordinarily favorable to her, the era of populous settlement was inevitably postponed until the way to California was opened to colonists from across the continent.

This will appear more clearly if we consider for a moment the difficulties that lay in the way of colonization from the Pacific. The Californias were nearly the farthest from western Europe of any of the lands of the earth. Merely to reach the Pacific required a voyage of unusual length. Once there, the storms of that ill-named ocean had to be encountered; and especially was this the case for the voyage northward from Cape San Lucas. Furthermore, there was the danger of uncharted seas and little known shores; nautical information was not at all what it is to-day; ships' crews and officers were often of an inferior character; pirates not infrequently lay in wait; and ships themselves were small and frail. Other difficulties, which arose from the nature of the land and inhabitants of the Californias, combined with the preceding to deprive these of communication with the outer world by sea. The Indians of that region were on such a low plane of culture that they had almost nothing which could serve the needs of white men. The food products which California now yields in such abundance did not exist in any part of the Californias when the early voyagers came there. Not only were there no agricultural products capable of sustaining a white population, but there were no domestic animals, and none of the utensils required by civilized men, wherefore everything that was needed had to be brought from without. Supplies inevitably dwindled, and this precluded a long stay by the early explorers. What was perhaps worse, was that the sailors contracted scurvy, owing to a lack of fresh supplies, and died in such numbers that it was rare indeed when a vessel could return to Europe from a voyage to the Pacific with as many as half its original crew. Even the short voyage along the peninsula of Baja California was in many cases equally fatal. Finally, although men could in some cases overcome extraordinary difficulties and reach the Californias, they did not at first bring women with them, and therefore any establishments they formed lacked for a time a very necessary element of permanence.

From this review it is evident that a base of supplies, near at hand, was required, if settlement of the Californias under normal conditions, without the influence of unusual forces, was to be realized. This meant that colonists who approached by land, maintaining communication with well-settled communities behind them, would have the best chance of acquiring the Californias. This narrowed the contest to the Spanish, English, French, and Russians. The French were ousted by the English in 1763, and the English advance towards the Pacific broke into two columns with the establishment of the independence of the United States. Curiously enough these four peoples succeeded in acquiring portions of the Californias, although the Spanish part was cut down to Baja California, after Mexico had succeeded to Spain's claim, and the Russians voluntarily withdrew, after the sale of Alaska to the United States.

It was thus that matters ultimately worked out; but there was at least one diversion from the normal progress of events. That was due to an extraordinary effort on the part of Spain, as a result of which Alta California was occupied by the Spaniards in 1769, and so developed, in the face of such difficulties as have been named, that by the founding of San Francisco in 1776 the Spanish settlements were rescued from impending failure and placed on a permanent basis. The leading names associated, respectively, with these great achievements are those of the *visitador* Gálvez and the viceroy Bucarely. Their work proved to be a piece of extreme good fortune for the United States. At a time when the Russians and English, particularly the latter, were pressing onward with a prospect of settling Alta California, it enabled the land to be held temporarily by Spain and Mexico, until the American movement acquired the impetus that carried it to the Pacific coast in the early forties of the nineteenth century.

Spain's capacity for great effort in Alta California seemed likely to continue. Bucarely had plans under way, the successful accomplishment of which would have advanced the colonies far beyond the stage of mere permanence into that of populous development. And here, indeed, was danger to the future prospects of the United States; for a populous development of Alta California must almost certainly have involved discovery of gold, and a consequent haste of settlement before the United States could have been ready to make good her interests in the region. It is well to bear in mind, too, that the Spaniards have been among the most expert seekers of precious metals in the history of modern times; the rush of miners to Arizonac and Cieneguilla, referred to in this volume, shows what might have happened if they had been the discoverers of Alta California's gold. It must be remembered, also, that the United States did not extend beyond the Mississippi until 1803, did not acquire frontage on the Pacific until 1819, and did not make great progress in colonizing the Oregon country until after 1840.

Bucarely was not permitted to carry out his plans, however. Through Gálvez's agency the Californias were taken from his command and placed under a new government of the frontier provinces of New Spain. Teodoro de Croix, whom Gálvez chose to rule the new government, proved incompetent to carry out the projects for the development of Alta California, which depended for their success on the maintenance of an overland route from Sonora, already opened by Bucarely. Croix founded some weak establishments on the California side of the Colorado River at its junction with the Gila, opposite Yuma, Arizona, but in other respects neglected the problems affecting the route. The result was that the Yuma Indians rose against the Spanish establishments in 1781 and destroyed them. The Yuma massacre closed the overland route to Alta California, and with it passed Alta California's chance for early populous settlement. It meant that gold was reserved for discovery until 1848. That discovery at that particular time was yet another bit of good fortune for the United States, for it insured the development of the region when the United States had just become possessed of it.

Four dates, then, in the history of California are of more than passing significance in the history of the United States, to wit, 1769, 1776, 1781, and 1848; particularly the last three. They had a bearing on the acquisition and, in the case of the last, on the retention of California by the United States. The effect on Oregon and Washington of the events marked by the first three dates may be gathered from that of the discovery of gold in 1848; after the first rush for the gold fields was over, Oregon and Washington shared in the development that was transforming California. And the significance of the events connected with the dates just mentioned may be even greater in the future than now, if frontage on the Pacific becomes a vital factor in the history of the United States, as the interests of other peoples around that ocean continue to develop.

For the reasons given, it would seem worth while to relate the story of Spain's attempts during two centuries and a half to occupy the Californias. As a corollary the history of Spain in its broadest aspects is of great import. If logical proportions alone were considered, a large share would be allotted in this study to that history. The space cannot be given, but its lack may in a measure be met by emphasis at this point. It was an important factor in

American history that Spain followed an imperialistic policy in Europe, seeking possessions in Italy and in the Low Countries, or their retention, once they had been gained. This involved her in almost continuous war, requiring troops and heavy expenditures. Spain herself being unable to provide enough funds, she resorted for them, after the discovery of America, in large measure to her colonies. Receipts never equalled the need, however, with the result that as little revenue as possible was expended by her in the colonies, whose affairs were regarded as less important than her policy in Europe. Had she been content or able to restrict herself to the Iberian peninsula and her colonies, there might have been funds available for the benefit of the latter. If more funds had been applied to the founding of settlements in Alta California, an object which Spain so ardently desired that even as things were, she was willing to go to some expense to accomplish it, an early development of that province, with all the consequences above indicated, might well have been realized. It is perhaps, a far cry from the Italian conquests of Pedro III of Aragon (1276–85) to the acquisition of California and other territories by the United States, but there is ground for asserting that the connection exists.

To treat in detail of the entire history of Spain's undertakings in the Californias would require many volumes, wherefore it has seemed best to put the greatest stress on the vital period in the history of Spanish settlement in Alta California from 1773 to 1776, when Bucarely was transforming the weak establishments of earlier years, and placing them on an enduring basis. It has further seemed necessary, since the tale is for the most part new, to introduce a vast amount of documentary detail, in order to drive home the conclusions that have been formed. The portion of this study most intensively treated is preceded by a discussion in seven chapters of projects bearing on the advance of the Spanish conquest overland toward the Colorado and Gila rivers, from 1521 to 1773, with some reference also to the occupation of the two Californias before the mainland conquest had reached those rivers. This portion of the present volume was presented as a doctoral thesis in May, 1915, at the University of California, in substantially the same form as it appears here, under the title *Preliminaries of the Spanish advance from Sonora to California, 1687–1773*. Then follows the principal part of the work, to which are added two concluding chapters, showing that Spain did not, after 1776, continue her extraordinary efforts to develop Alta California.

In a subject like that treated in this work, it is impossible to avoid touching upon a variety of subjects that cannot be carried to a conclusion. Among topics of such a nature that appear in the present study are the following: Spanish colonial administration in its various phases; the story of the Spanish advance from Mexico City to Sonora, and along another line to Nueva Vizcaya; events taking place east of Sonora in Nueva Vizcaya, for they in fact had a bearing upon Sonora affairs, and northwestward advance; the part played by the regular and secular clergy in the conquest; the part played by military and civil authorities; the importance of the civilian population, especially miners, involving discussion of the use and treatment of Indians by the whites; the inter-relations of the elements just named, and, in particular, conflicts between them; Spain's chronic fear of foreign encroachment on her dominions of the Pacific; the occupation of Baja California and progress there; the early voyages to Alta California; the Manila galleon and Pacific commerce; the wars with the Seris, Apaches and other Indians in Sonora; the internal development of Sonora; the Department of San Blas; the expeditions of 1769 to Alta California; the reforms of Gálvez in Baja California and Sonora; the northwest voyages in the last quarter of the eighteenth century; the internal development of Alta California; the attempts to open a route between New Mexico and Alta California; a detailed study of the Anza and other expeditions, in themselves, aside from external factors to which they were related; the *comandancia general* of the frontier provinces; life in

Alta California in the later Spanish period and under Mexico. Most of these topics, as far as they come within the period 1760 to 1786, may be studied with a fair degree of adequacy by use of materials included in my *Catalogue* (see bibliographical notes).

An explanation may be made of some of the methods that I have adopted in the mechanical construction of the volume. The opening paragraphs of each chapter after the first consist of an interpretation and summary of that chapter. Thereafter comes a recital of details gleaned from the documents with but little accompanying comment.

In names of persons modern spelling has been used for the Christian name, and the form employed by the individual himself, when known, for the *apellido*, or family name of the father. Accents have been used, whether employed by the person in question or not. Thus, "José" for "Josef" or "Joseph," "Bautista" for "Baptista"; "Bucarely" for "Bucareli," "Roxas" for "Rojas"; "Garcés" for "Garces," and "Gálvez" for "Galvez." So many Indian tribes are mentioned for which I can find no present-day equivalent, that I have followed Spanish spelling of the eighteenth century in all cases, even when the tribe is easily identified now under another name. Thus, "Cocomaricopas" for "Maricopas," "Quiquimas," for "Quigyumas," and others.

In the nomenclature of places difficulties arise owing to changes in names and boundaries of provinces, and to the practice of transferring the name of a particular place to another site, although the last-named practice is not likely to cause confusion in the present work. In the case of provinces, the writer has usually employed the modern names designating states of the United States or Mexico, as for example "Sinaloa" and "Sonora," instead of one name for both, or either or both with Ostimuri, which was at times regarded as a separate district. The same rule is observed in such cases as the following: "Pacific Ocean" for "South Sea"; "Colorado River" for "Río del Tizón" and other names; "El Paso" for "Paso del Norte." This rule has a number of exceptions. "Arizona" does not appear, the region south of the Gila (the only one in Arizona which enters the account) being regarded as part of Sonora, usually under the name of its northernmost portion, "Pimería Alta." "Moqui" is retained because always referred to as separate from New Mexico. The terms "Californias" and "California" appear so frequently in the documents in connection with Pacific coast regions from Cape San Lucas northward, that a distinction has been made. "Baja California" has been used to denote the peninsula; "Alta California" for the modern American state; and "Californias" for both, also including in some cases the far northwest. "Nueva Vizcaya" has been employed rather than "Chihuahua" and "Durango," partially because those two states do not accurately describe the limits formerly assigned to Nueva Vizcaya. Similarly, "Nueva Galicia" is used for Guzmán's conquests. "New Spain" is preferred to "Mexico," not so much because it was Nueva España to Spaniards, as to avoid confusion with Mexico City. It is a temptation to say "Provincias Internas," as do the documents, for the northern tier of provinces from Sonora to Texas. That phrase has been avoided, however, and "frontier provinces" used instead. The word "Gulf" often appears instead of "Gulf of California," there being no other gulf with which confusion is possible. The "Colorado River" refers to the river of that name emptying into the Gulf of California, unless special notice is given that the Colorado of the east is meant. Accents have been employed where they would be used in modern Spanish, except where the place name is of very frequent usage in English, in which case the accent is dropped. Thus, "Querétaro" with the accent, and "Mexico" without; "San Jose" and "Santa Barbara" when referring to those places in Alta California, but "San José" and "Santa Bárbara" when concerned with regions farther south. The accent is retained in "Panamá," although that case is near the line, and also in "Santa Fé," New Mexico, — possibly with some failure of consistency.

The selection of maps for insertion in the text has been based only partially on their value for illustrating the narrative. If already published and easily accessible, they have been omitted. An attempt has also been made to include such maps as would indicate all, or nearly all, of the place names referred to in the text. Aside from these reasons the determining factor for inclusion or exclusion of maps has been their importance as affecting this account. In order that technical matter may not interrupt the narrative I have often used such phrases as "this letter," where "a copy of this letter" would be the technically accurate phrase.

Spanish terms have rarely been retained, but there are three notable exceptions. An *expediente* means all of the documents in an official file of papers on a given case. A *testimonio* is an *expediente* of a special type. It is a copy of an *expediente*, physically bound together by sewing, and usually with a title describing the contents. As used in this work it refers nearly always to certified copies of original files, or *expedientes*, in Mexico, sent to Spain with a letter of the viceroy and perhaps other documents. It thus forms only part of the *expediente* as found in Spain. The term *ministro general* or *ministro general de Indias* is used to denote an office which was undergoing changes, in name as well as in functions, in the period covered by this work. Julián de Arriaga and José de Gálvez, who held that post in the period most intensively covered, were certainly officials of more consequence than was the Council of the Indies of their day. They dominated the Council, and were apart from it. Hence, it would not be proper to say "Council of the Indies," when *ministro general* is meant. Usually, it is possible to avoid use of the latter term by employing the official's name, but it seems worth while to call attention to an office which, so far as I know, has not yet been adequately treated in an historical work.

To Professor H. Morse Stephens I am greatly indebted for instruction, advice, and encouragement during the past eight years. This volume is the first to be completed of several in preparation as a direct result of his prescient leadership in promoting the study of the history of the Pacific coast. I wish in the second place to make acknowledgments to the patriotic Californian order, the Native Sons of the Golden West. Acting under the inspiring leadership of its Grand Presidents this order is contributing liberally to the encouragement of historical study by supporting annually two Travelling Fellowhips in Pacific Coast History. The very preponderant bulk in this volume of materials from the Archivo General de Indias of Seville, Spain, selected during two years while I was privileged to hold one of these fellowships, measures my debt to this fraternity. My stay in Seville was made both more agreeable and more profitable than it might otherwise have been by the exceptionally kind treatment and efficient service that I received at the hands of the officials of the Archivo General de Indias. Especially do I thank the scholarly and courteous chief of that archive, Señor Don Pedro Torres Lanzas, and I acknowledge with gratitude the many favors accorded by Señores Verger and Jiménez Placer, both now deceased, and by Señores Llorens, Navas, and Lafita, all of them of the archive staff during the period of my residence in Seville. Since my return, Mr. Clarence M. Hunt, editor of the N. S. G. W. organ, the *Grizzly Bear Magazine*, has aided me in innumerable ways in connection with the publication of this volume.

I wish in particular to acknowledge the aid and encouragement of Dr. Herbert E. Bolton, chairman of my doctoral committee, from whose vast knowledge of the entire field of North American colonization I have profited greatly. The first chapter and a half have had the advantage of his rigid criticism, and I have often consulted him with regard to the later portions of the volume. To him also I owe my access to the large body of materials discovered and procured by him in Mexican archives. To Mr. Herbert I. Priestley, Assistant Curator of the Academy of Pacific Coast History, I am deeply indebted for repeated favors and able criticism, rendered doubly valuable by his intensive knowl-

xvi PREFACE

edge of Spanish colonial administration and of the field
covered by my work. Many others have given me help,
in some cases by valuable advice, in others by supplying
me with materials that I desired, and in still others by criticism of different chapters. A few of those who have thus
aided me are Dr. David P. Barrows, Dr. Francis S. Phil-
brick, Dr. Eugene I. McCormac, Dr. Frank A. Golder,
Dr. William L. Schurz, Mr. Champlin Burrage, Mr. Gordon
C. Davidson, Mr. Karl C. Leebrick, Mr. Charles W. Hackett, Mr. Colin B. Goodykoontz, Mr. Frederick J. Teggart,
and Mr. George L. Albright, the last named a student in
my seminar.

BERKELEY, January 5, 1916.

CONTENTS

xviii   CONTENTS

PAGE

XVI. Bucarely's Difficulties in Maintaining the Department of San Blas, 1775–1777 368
XVII. The Incompetent Rule of Croix, 1776–1783 . . . 386
XVIII. The Aftermath, 1783–1822 417
Bibliographical Notes 437
Appendix I. Table Showing Total Receipts and Disbursements of the Real Caja of Guadalajara in Each Year from 1743 to 1781 455
Appendix II. Specimen Tables of the Real Caja of Guadalajara Showing Receipts and Disbursements, Item by Item, for Each of Two Years . . . . . . facing 456
Appendix III. Diaries of the Anza Expeditions . . . 457
Appendix IV. The Echeveste-Anza Calculation of the Probable Cost of the Second Anza Expedition 461
Appendix V. Resolution of the Junta of December 16, 1774, Concerning Authorization of a Second Expedition by Anza to Alta California 467
Appendix VI. Gálvez's Order of March 6, 1779, Directing Croix to Give the Californias Preference in His Attention 469
Appendix VII. Table Showing the Population by Districts of Sinaloa and Sonora in 1781 470
Index 471

MAPS

FACING
PAGE

The Sánchez Map of Pimería Alta and the Colorado-Gila Country, 1751 36
Russian Map of 1773 of Siberia and the North Pacific . 224
The Crame Map of the Isthmus of Tehuantepec, 1774 . . 231
Map of 1777 of Garcés' Travels, 1775–1777 364
Font's Map of 1778 of the Regions Visited by Garcés . . 366
Spanish Settlements of Alta California 434

INTRODUCTION

THE peculiar fascination of the history of Alta California, that is of the northern part of the two Californias, which is now the State of California, is to be found in the fact that in it, and in it to a greater extent than in the other States carved out of Spanish North America, can be traced a story of Spanish romance, Spanish exploration, and Spanish administration in a country where was later to be established a vigorous American State. While most of the older American States boast of the romantic beginnings of settlement from England, while Louisiana grew out of the ambitious designs of great Frenchmen, a certain group of southwestern States, such as Texas, and Arizona, and New Mexico, as well as California, trace their origins to the Spaniards of New Spain. American civilization in the United States is so thoroughly an outgrowth of English individualism and English law that students and readers of the history of the United States are apt to forget the contributions made by the Dutch in the New Netherlands, now New York, by the French in Louisiana, and by the Spaniards in the larger area of the Louisiana Purchase and the Mexican Concession. Douglas Campbell made an attempt to estimate the influence of Dutch institutions in North America, though it has generally been held that he considerably overshot the mark, and no doubt attempts have been made and will be made to estimate, and perhaps to exaggerate, the influence upon both local and general American civilization of the French in Louisiana, and of the Spaniards in Florida and the Louisiana Purchase. Whenever the time comes to work out in detail the extent of these influences, a serious contribution will be made to the history of institutions. It will probably be found that the actual influence of non-English institutions has not been very great, but that, on the other hand, the traditions of early exploration and settlement have helped to create a peculiar fund of local sentiment. If it be true, as seems to be generally held at the present time, that the spirit of nationality is not so much the outcome of identity of race, or language, as the product of historic traditions sung by poets and taught by historians, it can be asserted with equal probability that the enthusiasm of State loyalty in the United States is the result of the early history of each individual State. While New England is generally regarded from the outside as a historic unit, some modern scholars have tried to trace a distinct difference in the civilization of New Hampshire and Massachusetts, or of Rhode Island and Connecticut, from the particular conditions of their first settlement. To the outsider, New England is just New England, but to those who reside within the New England States, a sort of State loyalty, differing only in degree from the national spirit in the states of Europe, is clearly to be seen. The same thing is true with regard to the Southern States. A very short residence in Virginia or South Carolina will make manifest that in those two States is a marked State loyalty and State consciousness which sets them apart from the other Southern States, each of which, nevertheless, has its own sentiment of a distinct State civilization. Even in the Middle West, which has been more recently settled, and which cannot boast of any romantic colonial memories, there is yet a local historic pride which differentiates the citizens of Ohio from the citizens of Indiana, and the citizens of Wisconsin from the citizens of Minnesota. State pride, based upon State consciousness, has been the outcome in these modern States, not simply of different sources of population, not simply of different political traditions, but of the complex spiritual influences which make up in a nation or in a state, as in a family, the abiding and characteristic sentiment of a united community. Hitherto, the great tendency in the United States has been, consciously and unconsciously, towards the desire to create

a national spirit. The vehement belief in the unity and
indivisibility of an American nationality, which was forged
amidst much bloodshed in the great Civil War, or War
between the States, has induced leading American historians
to dwell upon the history of the United States as a united
whole, and has led its most famous statesmen and orators
to insist upon the unity of the nation. No one would be so
foolish as to deny this prevailing trend of public sentiment
in the United States, but, at the same time, there exists, so
clearly that no one may ignore it, the local sentiment of
State pride, based upon State traditions, which runs side
by side with the larger national spirit.

The view set forth in the preceding paragraph is so obvious
that it needs no further demonstration. Every one who
lives in the United States recognizes that there is a New
England temperament and a Rhode Island temperament, as
there is a New England pronunciation of words; every one
realizes that there is a Southern spirit as well as a Southern
accent; every one knows that in the Middle West there
is a sharp contrast between Kansas and Illinois; the characteristics of Louisiana and the charm of New Orleans differ
from the characteristics of New England and the charm of
Boston; and the latest school of American historical writers,
especially in the Middle West, has shown that it is necessary
to go beyond Professor Turner's epoch-making *Significance
of the Frontier upon American History*,[1] and points out that
every one of the States that has developed in the West has
its own character and its own temperament.[2] Who, that
has lived in Utah, can have failed to observe the influence
of the Mormon tradition? And, to come at last to the pre-
cise subject of this introduction, who that has ever visited
California has failed to feel that the Californian differs
from the people of other States?

It is usual, and not wholly untrue, to declare that the peculiar temperament of the people of California in their

[1] American Historical Association, *Report*, 1893.
[2] See, for instance, "Kansas" by C. L. Becker in *Essays in American history*, dedicated by F. J. Turner, New York, 1910, pp. 85–112.

attitude towards life is due to their descent in large part in central California from the sturdy and adventurous pioneers who were led to that beautiful land by the rush for gold. Bret Harte has fixed in literature certain types of the first gold miners in California, and, though his idealistic treatment of these earliest settlers has been much criticised, there still remains the fact that in San Francisco and Sacramento and in the old mining counties the pioneers were men and women of a strikingly free, daring, and individual character. But, after all, the entire population of modern California is not descended from the gold miners. The great territory of Southern California is just as conscious of California ideals and as proud of them as the descendants of the pioneers themselves. Whence comes, then, the characteristic California loyalty to a mode of living and a mode of thought that differs from that prevalent in other States? Disciples of Buckle would doubtless assert that environment due to climate has shaped the nature and the sentiments of the people of California. Disciples of the economic interpretation of history might declare that the difference is entirely due to economic conditions, in the old cattle ranches, the old grain ranches, and the orange groves of to-day. And yet these explanations are as inconclusive as the similar explanations of the characteristics of nationality in European countries. It is something more than climatic conditions, or economic development, or descendance from the gold seekers, that makes the people of modern California a distinctive community with a distinctive civilization, with a creative aptitude for literature and art, and with a sort of personality that is everywhere recognized. Consciously, in these latter days, an effort has been made in California, as to a greater or less degree in the other States of the United States, to bring together a body of historical tradition to explain and create a California State pride and a California State individuality. This spirit quickly invades the minds of new settlers in the State, whencesoever they come. If a brief residence in California is enough, as it is, to make a loyal Californian, even though the vast majority of the

people of California have no direct affiliation with either
the early Spanish settlers or the enterprising gold-seeking
American pioneers, it is clear that something is being done
to create a California nationality. The California organization of the Native Sons of the Golden West was deliberately
founded to maintain an interest in the history of California,
and that part of the population which is immigrant and not
native has shown itself ready to aid the Native Sons in their
generous attempts to give life and truth to California
history.

There are two romances which lie at the back of the consciousness of California pride in the State of California;
one is the romance of Spanish exploration and settlement,
the other is the romance of the gold diggers. The first
romance has been twined around the name of Father
Junipero Serra and the history of the Franciscan missions
in Alta California. Mission architecture, mission furniture,
the study of mission sites, and the restoration of mission
buildings all bear witness to the sincere desire of the modern
residents in California to seek a common interest in at least
one side of the Spanish settlement of Alta California. For
some years, one of the most popular demonstrations of the
interest felt in the Franciscan missions has been the success
of the San Gabriel Mission Play, which has been witnessed
by thousands, and has stirred the sensibilities of the casual
tourist as well as of the resident or the native son. Cele-
brations in honor of Don Gaspar de Portolá, the Spanish
captain of dragoons, who led the first expedition by land
northward from San Diego, have been held in San Francisco.
The study of California history, introduced into the California schools, among the new settlers of the south, as well
as among the descendants of the pioneers in the north and
central parts of the State, has, hitherto, always begun with
the story of the Franciscan missionaries. And yet the establishment of the missions is but an episode in the Spanish
settlement of California, and a new school of California
historians is arising, and is attempting to cover the story of
the Spanish settlement in a more thorough fashion and to

show the forces that lay behind the movement of New Spain into Alta California.

The publication of Doctor Chapman's book is an evidence of the new spirit with regard to the foundation of Spanish California, developed among younger historians. All earnest students of California history acknowledge the enormous debt of gratitude they owe to Mr. Hubert Howe Bancroft, for the treasury of information with regard to California brought together in his colossal work. Mr. Bancroft undertook the task of writing California history upon a stupendous scale. He realized his opportunity. Seeing that California was first brought to civilization through New Spain, he collected sources of information, not only upon the history of Alta California, but also upon Central America and Mexico. The large way in which he conceived his work led to the gathering of the unequalled collection of primary sources which now forms the glory of the Library of the University of California. All was grist that came to his mill, and he absorbed such great collections of material as the Squier Collection on Central America, and the library of the Emperor Maxmilian. Professor Langlois of Paris, the recognized master of historical bibliography, in an article published so long ago as 1891 in the *Revue Universitaire*, under the title of *H. H. Bancroft et Cie*,[1] drew the attention of European scholars to the remarkable work accomplished by Mr. H. H. Bancroft. Mr. Bancroft was not a native son of California, but came from Ohio, and yet it is to him that California historians owe their greatest debt of gratitude. Professor Langlois wonders at the grandeur of the ideas of this bookseller and publisher, without academic training, who conceived the possibility of collecting all the accessible sources on the history of California civilization, and who then formed an organization not unlike that of the old Magdeburg Centuriators in the sixteenth century in Europe to collate and interpret them. "Mr. Bancroft and Company," to translate the title of Langlois' article, brought

[1] This article is reprinted in *Questions d'histoire et d'enseignement*, par C. V. Langlois, Paris, 1902, pp. 243–274.

forth thirty-nine large volumes of Pacific coast history, based upon his own collection of original sources. This is not the place to criticise, even if the desire existed, the stupendous work of Mr. H. H. Bancroft, and, as the years go by, the value of his vast collection is being more and more appreciated. Every generation writes its own history of the past, and modern historians may not agree with all Mr. Bancroft's views, especially with regard to the attitude taken by him upon certain phases of Spanish and Mexican California, but the collection of sources that he made will be forever the mine in which future California historians must dig for information. To the same epoch of historical composition, belongs the *History of California* by Theodore H. Hittell, published in 1885, an admirable book composed upon a smaller scale than that of Bancroft's more elaborate work, and confined more strictly to the history of Alta California. These remarkable books were representative of the period in which they were written, and both of them laid a considerable amount of emphasis upon the Spanish settlement of California. But historians, like histories, get out of date, and new men arise to take up the task of interpreting the past where their predecessors left off. Among the more recent histories, especial weight should be laid upon the books of Mr. Irving B. Richman, whose *California under Spain and Mexico* appeared in 1911, and of Mr. Zoeth S. Eldredge, whose *Beginnings of San Francisco* appeared in 1912. Both of these books, and especially that of Mr. Eldredge, are real contributions to a knowledge of the early history of California. But more remained to be done; for however wide-reaching had been Mr. Bancroft's net, he had failed to gather in all the sources upon the romantic history of the Spanish settlement of California. It was known that vast quantities of material were preserved in the great collection of public records known as the *Archivo General de Indias* at Seville in Spain. Here has been collected all the official correspondence from Spanish America with Spain. Mr. Bancroft had obtained copies of some of the most necessary documents, but it was quite certain that hidden away and unindexed among the masses of state papers there must be many more that would explain in detail the settlement of Spanish California.

The difficulty that presented itself was how to prepare students of California history to work among these great stores of official documents, and how to maintain them during a residence at Seville. The University of California made ready to undertake the task by calling to its Faculty an acknowledged master of modern history. Professor Herbert E. Bolton, who had done admirable work in the University of Texas, who had made himself familiar with the treasure houses of Spanish documents in Mexico, and who had finished his well-known *Guide to Materials for the History of the United States in the Principal Archives of Mexico*,[1] was the very man to train California historical scholars. His wealth of knowledge of Spanish American history, together with his practical experience in dealing with Spanish official documents, made it possible to deal adequately with the materials preserved in the Bancroft Collection, and to prepare for further investigation at the fountain head in Spain. At this moment, came providentially most generous aid from the local California society, devoted to the study of California history, and organized as the Order of the Native Sons of the Golden West. At the critical moment, when a school of young California historians was foreshadowed in the work of Professor Bolton, the Native Sons of the Golden West came forward with a subsidy of $3000 a year for the maintenance of Travelling Fellows, who were to reside in Spain and devote themselves to a search for documents on the history of Spanish California. The first fruits of their generosity are to be seen in Doctor Chapman's volume, to which this is a general introduction. Other volumes are now in hand, and during the next few years a series of monographs on the early history of Spanish California may be expected which will supplement the historical work accomplished by such pioneers as Bancroft and Hittell, and by such modern historians as Richman and Eldredge.

[1] Published by the Carnegie Institution of Washington, D. C., in 1913.

It is now time to turn to the actual contribution made by Doctor Chapman to the history of Spanish California. It has already been said that the attention of the people of California with regard to their Spanish predecessors had been at first almost entirely devoted to the Franciscan missions. Not until the publication of Mr. Eldredge's book had sufficient weight been laid upon the fact that the Portolá expedition and the foundation of the missions would have had but little effect if this movement had not been followed up by the Anza expedition, which resulted in the foundation of the Presidio of San Francisco in 1776. But behind the expeditions of both Portolá and Anza, lay a long story of the development of the movement of New Spain towards California Alta. With the story of this preliminary movement and its growth into the Anza expedition, Doctor Chapman's book deals. It is a sincere and valuable contribution to history, and it sets forth not only the facts of the northwesterly landward movement towards California from Mexico, but also the motives which underlay that movement, and the reasons which had delayed it until the latter part of the eighteenth century.

The history of California becomes part of the general history of civilization with the establishment of the Presidio of San Francisco in 1776. Up until the eighteenth century, the Pacific Ocean had been a Spanish lake, traversed by the Manila galleons carrying their annual freight between Manila and Acapulco. But in the eighteenth century other European nations began to enter the Pacific Ocean. The Russians, having moved across Siberia, crossed into Alaska and began to work their way down the northern Pacific coast of America. French traders, even before 1715, had made their way up the Pacific coast of South America. An English squadron, under Commodore Anson, broke into the Pacific Ocean in 1740 and captured one of the Manila galleons. The mystery of the Pacific Ocean attracted European public opinion; possibilities for commercial expansion into the South Sea were widely discussed; exploration of the ocean was undertaken, most conspicuously in the famous voyages of Captain Cook; and Spain felt that she must protect the entire Pacific coast, if she was to maintain the monopoly of the Pacific Ocean itself. But could the coast of Alta California be occupied from the ocean? Could the Pacific coast of Alta California be held through the command of the sea? This problem had long been in the minds of Spanish officials in New Spain.

Nothing is more interesting in Doctor Chapman's book than the evidence he has gathered to show that the problem of the occupation of Alta California grew naturally out of the northward expansion of New Spain. Just as the expansion of Rome was the natural and inevitable sequel of the history of the Roman Republic; just as the conquest of each new Roman province, whether civilized or uncivilized, led inevitably to further advance; just as the United States moved irresistibly westward across America, and Russia eastward across Siberia; just as the history of the British Empire in India bears witness to the steady movement in search of a scientific military frontier; so the Spanish officials in Mexico City witnessed, sometimes almost with despair, the inevitable expansion of New Spain. A certain school of historians, like a certain school of statesmen, have lamented the expansion of the great empires of the past and of the present. Now and then, desperate efforts have been made to check an expanding movement and to declare that the final frontier has been reached. But the best intended efforts to check expansion from policy have been vain in the past, as in the present. Growth is a law of life. Stagnation means death. Although Spain, in the eighteenth century, was too exhausted at the heart to be capable of covering efficiently a further area in America, yet the demand for movement was felt in the extremities of Spanish America, and the Christian missionaries pressed onward and onward in their pious fervor. The viceroys of New Spain tried to hold back both missionaries and pioneers and to set limits to the irresistible advance. Augustus and Tiberius endeavoured to check the growth of the Roman Empire, and to fix strategical boundaries, but in vain. English statesmen, in the middle of the nineteenth century, tried to stop the development of the British Empire, and furiously resented the onward movement of the Australians into New Guinea, of the Anglo-Indian statesmen into Afghanistan, and of the great empire builders, like Goldie, and MacKinnon, and Cecil Rhodes, in Africa. Spain, in America, could not stand still so long as the road was open, any more than Russia, in Siberia. It was forced into expansion.

The most valuable part of Doctor Chapman's book is his development from the original sources, still buried at Seville, of the northward expansion of New Spain. He has done full justice to the hardships that faced the advancing missionaries and settlers, but he has also seen the difficulties that beset the Spanish officials, and has concentrated attention upon the importance of the views held by, and the work done by, the Viceroy Bucarely and the Visitor-General Gálvez. The importance of the work of Gálvez has never been adequately recognized, but a most valuable and interesting monograph, based upon the original sources, has been written upon him by Mr. H. I. Priestley, which is about to be published by the University of California. Gálvez saw the danger presented by the incursion of other European states than Spain into the Pacific Ocean. He realized that the political and commercial situation in Europe was going to affect the Pacific Ocean, and would sooner or later press problems upon the Pacific coast. With feverish activity, he labored for an immediate advance, and since an overland advance was for the moment impossible, for the reasons Doctor Chapman has set forth, the first movement to the northward to Alta California was undertaken along the coast line in the famous expedition under Don Gaspar de Portolá. But the missions and presidios in Alta California could not be maintained by coast communication. An overland route had to be developed.

The middle chapters of Doctor Chapman's book deal with the problems that faced the officials of New Spain after the Portolá expedition. The European situation in the Pacific Ocean was becoming more defined; the Russians

and the English were particularly active. King Charles III
of Spain developed a strong anti-English attitude, which,
combined with the Family Compact made with the French
king, induced him to take part in the American War of Independence upon the side of the American Colonies. The
Viceroy Bucarely, with calmer judgment, but with less
feverish activity than was displayed by Gálvez, made ready
for the Spanish occupation, through an overland route, of
Alta California.

Doctor Chapman's hero in the third part of his book is
Don Juan Bautista de Anza. Mr. Zoeth Eldredge, in the
volumes more than once referred to, has brought out very
clearly the momentous character in the history of Spanish
California of the great Anza expedition, which culminated in
the establishment of the Presidio of San Francisco. From
this point of view, Mr. Eldredge's book is excellent and conclusive. But Doctor Chapman's book brings out a point
that does not clearly appear in Mr. Eldredge's volumes,
namely, the fact that Anza's expedition was the culminating
feature of a long attempt at the northwest expansion of
New Spain. The work of Anza did not suddenly leap into
prominence; it was the outcome of a long series of movements
and of the natural development of frontier policy. Anza
himself inherited his interest in the movement of expansion.
Like certain officers on the northwest frontier of India, his
entire life had been spent as an officer and an official upon
the frontier. Like Colonel Warburton,[1] his life had been a
frontier life. His father had been killed in a fight with the
Apache Indians upon the frontier. He knew the Pimas and
the Yumas and the frontier tribes, whose territories he was
to traverse, as Warburton knew the Afghan frontier tribes.
It was with a full consciousness of the danger of his mission,
and with a full experience as to the organization that was
needed, that he set forth at last in 1775 upon his epoch-
making expedition from Sonora to San Francisco. The details of the great march can be read alike in Mr. Eldredge's

[1] *Eighteen years in the Khyber*, by Colonel Sir Robert Warburton, London,
1900.

Beginnings of San Francisco and in Doctor Chapman's volume. The two accounts supplement each other, though, as has been said, the point of view and of departure of the two authors differs greatly.

This introduction, written at the request of Doctor Chapman, is not intended to contain a summary of the result of his researches in the documents bearing upon the history of the Anza expedition, which he has discovered at Seville. The truthfulness of his work, his patient examination, analysis, and transcription of new documents, are made clear upon the pages of his book, in the carefulness of his citations and in the valuable appendices. His volume belongs to the class of historical works based upon the consultation of primary authorities, which is now forming so creditable a feature of modern historical work in the United States. The careful reader need have no hesitation in accepting his conclusions, for he has shown what Gibbon, in his famous preface, declared to be the only merits which an historical writer may ascribe to himself, namely, "diligence and accuracy." That such a volume should be the first fruits of the generosity of the Order of the Native Sons of the Golden West gives hope of an even more valuable harvest to follow.

Instead of giving a summary of Doctor Chapman's contribution to the knowledge of the preliminary steps towards the Spanish occupation of Alta California, it has seemed more fitting in this introduction to try to explain wherein its largest value lies. First and foremost, an attempt has been made in a few sentences to indicate wherein the occupation of Alta California is connected with the general situation in Europe with regard to the Pacific Ocean in the eighteenth century. The writer of a monograph is apt to be so interested in his particular field that it is most necessary that the effort should be made to show the connection of all studies of local history with the trend of general history. Some day, some historian of large vision, and with a grasp like that of Gibbon of a wide field of history, will bring out the general story of the expansion alike of states, of nations, and of civilizations. Local histories and specialized histories of all kinds are apt to be too specialized and not to pay sufficient attention to general considerations. But further, it seemed worth while in the opening paragraphs of this introduction to say something upon the importance of such detailed work as Doctor Chapman's as illustrating the growth of State loyalty and State consciousness// The people of California are very proud of the traditions of their State, even if the vast majority of them are either themselves recent immigrants, or, at the most, only in the second or third generation from pioneer settlers. Yet all alike have absorbed and now express the traditions of the old Alta California under Spain and Mexico, and they feel that their State is no common land, but boasts of a romance and a charm that other States cannot rival. While some may boast of climate, and some of citrous fruit, far back in their consciousness, in their pronunciation of old Spanish names of places, in their love for the old mission buildings, and their pride in the picturesque careers of Franciscan missionaries and of Spanish *hidalgos*, of gold seekers from all parts of the world, and of a courageous folk, who undauntedly built up the ruined city of San Francisco, the chief bond of that California loyalty which they instil into their children, and which they themselves cherish with the enthusiasm that an Englishman or a Scotchman, a Frenchman or a German, feels for his historic nationality, is based upon the historic traditions of the land in which they live. Doctor Chapman's book is, upon the one hand, a witness to the love that Californians feel for their historic traditions, and, on the other hand, a worthy contribution towards a broader view of the Spanish statesmen and pioneers, and towards a better and more detailed understanding of that Spanish background against which is now reared one of the proudest and most self-conscious States of the United States of America.

H. MORSE STEPHENS.

BERKELEY, CALIFORNIA,
March 6, 1916.

THE FOUNDING OF SPANISH CALIFORNIA

CHAPTER I

THE SPANISH ADVANCE FROM MEXICO CITY TO PIMERÍA ALTA, 1521–1687

THE discovery of America in 1492 marked the beginning of a struggle, in which Spain was to play a leading part, for possession of the new world. Spain acquired a base in the West Indies, and thence went forth to the conquest of the mainland. One line of effort led her to the Isthmus of Panamá, where the Spaniards established themselves by 1510. As their foothold there became more secure they began to extend their rule northward. Before they had gone very far, they met another stream of conquest coming south, for in 1519 Cortés had landed on the Atlantic coast of Mexico and had begun the war which in two years resulted in the overthrow of the Aztec power. The capture of Mexico City in 1521 gave Spain a new base of operations for conquest. By 1522, Cortés had reached the Pacific coast, establishing a settlement at the Port of Zacatula, and a few years later the lands south of Mexico to Panamá were taken. There remained a vast ever-widening area to the north, not yet subjected to the Spanish crown.

The sixteenth century was the era of the Spanish *conquistadores*. These men led expeditions which made a permanent conquest of large areas, and developed a preliminary knowledge of nearly the whole field subsequently occupied. They were followed, perhaps in the wake of other expeditions, by soldiers, missionaries, and civilians, all of Spanish blood. The civilians were for the most part miners, a smaller number engaging in stock-raising and other pursuits characteristic of frontier life.[1] This was a second phase of the conquest. Eventually, in a portion of the field, there came a third phase, when settled orderly government appeared, the military moving on, secular clergy replacing regular, and civilians entering in greater numbers and engaging in a greater variety of occupations. This was the final stage, when the particular region ceased to partake of the attributes of a frontier province. In all three stages the white people, although a very small minority, were the ruling class. As a rule the Indians were not driven away or killed, as in the English colonies, but, although strictly ruled and virtually enslaved, were allowed to remain.

Northward expansion from Mexico City may be said to have followed three principal lines: northwestward to Sonora and the Californias; up the central plateau through Nueva Vizcaya to New Mexico; similarly, but branching

---

[1] Not much has been written concerning the importance of the civilian element in Spanish conquests. Some small attention has been paid to the military, but the greatest space by far has been assigned to the religious, certainly after the era of early conquests. This is because but little use has thus far been made of any but printed sources, and because these are in most cases writings of the religious themselves, who were bent upon telling of the achievements of their order; see the list of works cited in connection with this volume. The laws themselves operated to discourage any but religious publications, from fear lest the subject population read anything which might tend to diminish their belief in Catholic Christianity, and thus weaken the bonds by which Spain ruled them. No books pertaining to the Americas could be printed unless previously approved by the Council of the Indies (Recop., lib. I, tít. XXIV, ley I). No books of romance of profane or fabulous subject-matter were allowed to be sent to the colonies (ibid., ley IV). Religious in Spain were to inspect books carried by ships going to the Americas (ibid., ley VI), and government officials in the colonies were to do the same, delivering forbidden books to the proper religious authorities (ibid., ley VII). Great care was also enjoined to avoid circulation of books by heretic pirates (ibid., ley XIV). As Bancroft says, "religious teachers guided public taste, and strove to obtain a circulation for their own productions," and "Since every work had to pass through the hands of censors, notably the rigid inquisition, it became almost necessary to give a pious tinge to the pages in order to secure permission to publish, and above all to suppress whatever savored of acquaintance with works not favored by the church." Bancroft, Literature of colonial Mexico, in Essays and miscellany, 486.

The story of the civilian is in large measure gone beyond recall, but a rich harvest nevertheless awaits the investigator who will use the unpublished materials which exist in such stupendous quantity in the Archivo General de Indias.

off to run through Coahuila into Texas. A fourth line, basing in early days on Tampico, and, later, on Mexico City and Querétaro, ran to Nuevo León and Nuevo Santander (Tamaulipas), and slightly into Texas. This was hardly so important as the others. It is the purpose of this work to direct attention to the first-named movement, and to only its latest phases with any degree of completeness. Yet, all four were closely related, — so much so, that we shall often be forced to take into account what was happening to the east of Sonora. All went ahead at relatively the same rate of progress, except the much shorter fourth movement. Military and exploring expeditions made side trips that crossed different lines of advance. All were related by the problem of Indian warfare, especially against the Apaches, who were wont to appear in all sections, often going from one to another according as resistance to their raids was strong or weak. All were threatened by foreign aggressions from the northeast, for the Colorado River of the west was believed to be a route making the western provinces almost as accessible to the French or English as those in the east. Some or all of the regions along the four lines of advance were at different times under the same political rule, or served as a field for the same body of religious, or were part of the same diocese. Finally, all of these regions had much the same internal problems, political, economic, and social, and all were under the viceroy, or, in the latest period, under the *comandante general*. Despite these unifying factors, not much space can be given to the northward movement as a whole. Before proceeding to a consideration of northwestward advance, however, it is worth while to give an idea of the sweep of the other lines of conquest.

Naturally, the line of advance through Nueva Vizcaya to New Mexico was most closely related, because nearest, to the movement through Sonora. The same Indian wars often affected both. The Jesuits were in western Nueva Vizcaya as well as in Sinaloa and Sonora until 1767. Sinaloa and Sonora were included in the government of Nueva Vizcaya until 1734, and formed part of the same diocese under the bishop of Durango until 1779, when a bishopric was created for Sinaloa, Sonora, and the Californias. The first great name in the history of Nueva Vizcaya is that of Francisco de Ibarra, who set up a government there in the middle of the sixteenth century. By the end of that century the line of settlement had reached southern Chihuahua. Next there was a gap, beyond which lay New Mexico, settled by the Oñate expedition of 1598. By the close of the seventeenth century the line of settlement had approached or reached the Río Grande; for example, the presidios of Pasage, Gallo, Conchos, Janos, and Casas Grandes were already in existence. In the eighteenth century there were many changes in presidial sites, the general movement being to suppress the more southerly presidios, and establish new ones toward the Río Grande. Similarly the missions advanced, and the region behind them was gradually yielded over to the secular clergy. In 1767, according to statistics compiled by Bishop Tamarón, Nueva Vizcaya had a Christian population of 120,000 divided evenly between Chihuahua and Durango, its northern and southern divisions; but while Durango had 46,000 civilized people, there were but 23,000 in Chihuahua.[2] Meanwhile, New Mexico had enjoyed great prosperity until 1680, when all was destroyed by an Indian revolt, and the land was not reconquered until over a decade later.[3] Thenceforth, the land was held, but little further advance was made. By the end of the eighteenth century there may have been 20,000 civilized people in the province, and 10,000 Christian Indians.[4]

Along the Coahuila line Parras and Saltillo in southern Coahuila were occupied by the end of the sixteenth century, although these two settlements were under the government

[2] The term "civilized people" is used for what Spaniards called *gente de razón*, including those of white or mixed blood or even negroes. In fine, all but Indians were included.

[3] Hackett, *The revolt of the Pueblo Indians of New Mexico in 1680;* and *Retreat of the Spaniards from New*

Mexico in 1680, and the beginnings of El Paso.

[4] For a good summary of the Spanish advance through Nueva Vizcaya to New Mexico until near the end of the seventeenth century, see the introductory part to Hughes, *The beginning of Spanish settlement in the El Paso district.*

of Nueva Vizcaya until 1785. Coahuila never enjoyed
striking prosperity. By the close of the seventeenth century
Monclova was the most northerly presidio, while the missions had passed on to the Río Grande. Early in the
eighteenth century the presidios reached that river. The
total Christian population of Coahuila in 1780 was about
8000, of whom 2000 were Indians. The addition of Saltillo and Parras in 1785 doubled the population. The most
interesting portion of this line is the Texas extremity. In
the sixteenth century there were voyages along the coast,
and overland incursions from New Mexico and even from
Florida, but no settlements. Between 1685 and 1688 La
Salle made a disastrous attempt to found a French colony
in Matagorda Bay. This incident, joined to tales of fabulous wealth in the land of the Tejas in eastern Texas, induced the Spaniards to send an expedition in 1689 under
Governor León of Coahuila, which led, in the next few years,
to the establishing of missions east of the Trinity.[5] These
failed, but on the renewal of French activities, this time
from New Orleans, several missions and a presidio were
founded in eastern Texas in 1716. In 1718, establishments
were made at San Antonio, not far from Coahuila. In
1721, a presidio was placed near the coast at Espíritu Santo,
and the eastern settlements (which had been destroyed by
the French) were reëstablished and strengthened. Between 1745 and 1763 several new posts were founded,
notably in northern Texas, but the northernmost of these,
on the San Gabriel and the San Sabá rivers, were soon
abandoned. By the cession of Louisiana to Spain in 1762
the French peril, the dominating note in Texas history up
to that time, was removed, and the eastern settlements were
given up. In a few years, however, many of the Spanish
settlers returned to eastern Texas.[6] In 1782 there were
only 2600 civilized people in Texas, and 460 Christian
Indians.

The beginnings of Nuevo León date from its colonization

[5] Bolton, *The Spanish occupation of
Texas, 1519–1690.*

[6] Bolton, *Texas in the middle eighteenth century.*

by Carabajal, late in the sixteenth century. Nothing else occurred that need be noted here until 1748 when Escandón, coming from Querétaro, achieved an almost bloodless conquest of Nuevo Santander. His work was remarkable by reason of the number of settlements formed by him, rendering the conquest as thorough as it had been quick and peaceful. Unruly Indians were soon conquered or went elsewhere, and this part of the frontier enjoyed unusual prosperity.

The first great conqueror after Cortés along the line leading northwestward to Pimería Alta was Nuño de Guzmán. In 1529, he set out from Mexico City with an army of five hundred Spaniards and perhaps ten thousand native allies, and by 1531 he had passed through Jalisco to Sinaloa, reducing the country along his line of march. At one stroke, over half the territory between Mexico City and Alta California had been traversed and made known to the Spaniards, and much of it remained definitely conquered. Contemporary with this conquest were the first northwestward voyages, made under the authority of Cortés, one of whose ships reached Baja California, probably at La Paz, in 1533. Cortés himself founded a settlement there in 1535, but it did not endure, being withdrawn in 1536.

The romantic adventures of Álvar Núñez Cabeza de Vaca became known at this time, and aroused enthusiasm anew for northward explorations. Núñez had been a member of the ill-fated Narváez expedition to Florida in 1528. After several years of wandering and vicissitudes he had crossed the continent, going by way of Texas, Chihuahua, and Sonora, to the Spanish settlement of Culiacán, Sinaloa, which he reached in 1536. He told of substantial cities to the north, of which he had heard, but which he had not seen. His story was confirmed by the Franciscan, Marcos de Niza, who crossed Sonora and Arizona to New Mexico in 1539. There, from a distance, he saw one of the seven cities of Cíbola (Zuñi), really a wretched native town, but which to his inflamed imagination seemed larger than Mexico City. Meanwhile, Cortés had equipped a sea expedition under Francisco de Ulloa to seek the fabled wealth of the north. Ulloa set sail from Acapulco in 1539, following the coast of the mainland to the mouth of the Colorado River. Descending the gulf along the coast of Baja California, he came to Cape San Lucas, and went up the western shore to a few leagues beyond Cerros Island. He had proved Baja California to be a peninsula; previously it was believed to be an island. Two centuries had to elapse, however, before its peninsularity became definitely recognized. In the next year, 1540, Coronado led an army by way of Sonora to New Mexico, and from there went on to Kansas in a vain search for the reputedly rich province of Quivira. The principal expedition returned to Mexico in 1542. Meanwhile, two supporting parties had made the first direct approaches to Alta California by way of the Colorado River. A fleet under Hernando de Alarcón left Acapulco in May, 1540, to coöperate with Coronado's expedition. Alarcón reached the mouth of the Colorado, and ascended the river in small boats, but seems to have stopped short of the Gila. Seeing nothing of Coronado's expedition, he returned to his ships, and sailed back. Late in the same year, Melchor Díaz, with a part of Coronado's forces which had been left behind in Sonora, set out to coöperate more directly than Coronado with Alarcón. He reached the Colorado, and crossed it, probably at some point south of the Gila. Finding that Alarcón had departed, the expedition returned.

Interest in northwestward exploration now shifts to sea voyages up the coast of the Californias. The most notable were the following: that of Cabrillo [7] and Ferrelo, 1542–43, to the vicinity of the present Oregon-California line; Drake's voyage of 1579, including a stay of several weeks at Drake's Bay, a voyage of which the Spaniards had information; the annual voyages, after 1565, of the Manila galleons,

[7] Cabrillo is referred to in López, 281, as the pilot Juan Rodríguez, without mention of the name Cabrillo. The full name being Juan Rodríguez Cabrillo, it would seem more fitting to call him Rodríguez, as López did, that being the family name, and Cabrillo in all probability the name of his mother.

which passed near the California coast, en route to Acapulco, in particular the voyage of Francisco Gali, who in 1584 sighted Cape Mendocino; that of Cermeño from Manila in 1595, resulting in shipwreck at Drake's Bay, named San Francisco by Cermeño; finally, the most famous of this series, that of General Sebastián Vizcaíno in 1602–3, from which dates the story of Monterey's excellence as a port. This was the last notable voyage to Alta California until 1769. As a result of these voyages the general trend of the California coast became known, all ports of importance having been discovered, except the most important of all, that of San Francisco Bay, and all of them, Monterey in particular, being deemed worthy of eventual occupation, lest some other power seize them. The name "Californias" was extended northward from the peninsula, no northern boundary being set, unless it were the vainly sought Strait of Anian (as it came to be called), an imaginary body of water through the continent uniting the Atlantic to the Pacific. Alta California was known to have a considerable native population; but a more intensive knowledge of the land, its real wealth and productive possibilities had not in fact been obtained, although they had been guessed at by writers about the Californias, who added many tales of fabulous wealth. These factors, although not of equal weight, and of greatly varying interest at different times, were a standing incentive to further northwestward exploration, and to the settlement of Alta California, when the authorities at Mexico should find occasion to undertake such an enterprise.[8] It is noteworthy that the natives of San Diego,

[8] A detailed description of the California coast appears in González (or as writers have usually called him, Cabrera Bueno), Navegación especulativa y práctica. Though not published until 1734 it may be taken to represent Spanish experience over a period of nearly two centuries preceding that date. It is a technical work on navigation, but one of its five parts is devoted to descriptions of sailing routes, and of lands along these routes, though always from the standpoint of the navigator. The routes treated are that of the Manila galleon and off-shoots, even to Spain around South America on the one hand, and to various parts of Asia on the other. The route from Cape Mendocino south to Acapulco is described in eleven pages (302–13). From this it appears that the Spaniards had a detailed and fairly accurate knowledge of the coast. González's language would imply that the region between Cape Mendocino and Monterey must often have been sighted by the galleon. According to him also, the galleon must usually

Catalina Island, and Ventura told Cabrillo that there were other white men in the interior. The Indians of the Bay of San Quentín and of San Diego told like stories to Vizcaíno. They probably were referring in the first instance to the Coronado expedition, possibly to its offshoots, the Alarcón and Díaz expeditions, and in the second, to Oñate's expedition, then in New Mexico. These statements might well have induced belief in the existence of a practicable route to the Californias from Sonora.

The Oñate expedition, just referred to, set out from San Bartolomé, Chihuahua, in 1598, to conquer New Mexico, and achieved its object. In one of its ramifications this expedition extended Spanish knowledge of the lower Colorado River country. In 1604–5, Oñate marched westward along Bill Williams Fork to the Colorado, descended the latter to its mouth, and then retraced his steps to New Mexico. According to Bancroft, this journey had been unknown to nineteenth century writers before himself.[9] There is no doubt, however, that this and other notable expeditions referred to in this chapter were well known to Spaniards of the eighteenth century.[10] Hence, mention of them here is appropriate; they were a factor affecting the question of a route from Sonora to the Californias. Oñate reported that a strait existed between the Californias and the mainland.[11]

have seen the coast from Monterey south. After describing the bay and even the land at Monterey, González says: "This port is in 37° north latitude and is a good port for relief of the ships from China (the galleon) on account of its being the first land that they see (reconocen) when they come to New Spain."

[9] Bancroft, Ariz. and New Mex., 157.

[10] Both the Coronado and Oñate expeditions were referred to quite casually, as if they were well-known facts, in a letter to the viceroy in 1737 by Anza's father, a presidio captain in Sonora. C–178. This letter was considered by the authorities in Mexico and Spain at that time, and again in 1772, with relation to proposals of the Anzas, father and son, for opening a

route to the Californias by way of the Colorado and Gila rivers. Numerous other references might be given.

[11] Renewal of the belief that California was an island may not have been due to Oñate so much as to certain memorials of Nicolás de Cardona. It has been traced by Bancroft to Ascensión, a friar on the Vizcaíno expedition of 1602–3. The earliest writing now extant of Ascensión on the point is his memorial of October 12, 1620, in which he implies that the Californias had recently been discovered to be an island. Referring to the Gulf of California, Ascensión says: hasta agora se ha entendido que aquella era ensenada ó seno grande que allí hiciese la mar, y no mar corriente y seguida como lo es. In Colección de documentos inéditos relativos al descubrimiento, conquista y

From Oñate's time until late in the century Spanish explorations northwestward seem to have been confined to Baja California and the Gulf, and very little was accomplished. As far as memorials and governmental plans went, the Californias held a prominent place in the seventeenth century. Friars petitioned for a mission field there; navigators and traders offered to get information about the Californias, cartographical and otherwise, and to found settlements, all at their own expense, in return for which they asked a license to fish for pearls, usually to the exclusion of others; and the government was continuously desirous of occupying the territory as a defensive measure. Many voyages were made to the eastern shore of the peninsula, the greater number of which, it seems probable, have not thus far been made known. The real object of the voyagers was not to found settlements, but to seek pearls; the terms of the contract were but a lure to get the more remunerative advantage of the license. When at length it seemed clear that nothing of consequence would be

organización de las antiguas posesiones españolas de América y Oceanía, VIII, 537–74 at 546. The recent discovery to which Ascensión referred was probably that of Juan de Iturbe in 1615, and not Oñate's of a decade before. Iturbe was in charge of a vessel engaged in the pearl-fisheries, in pursuance of a contract obtained from the king by Tomás de Cardona and others in 1611 (not 1610, as Bancroft says). C–20. Iturbe went to the head of the Gulf, and believed he saw a strait to northward. This voyage led to a number of memorials by Nicolás de Cardona, of which I have seen nine, between the years 1617 and 1643. The earlier ones were probably known to Ascensión, or at least the results of the Iturbe voyage. But perhaps the most important of the Cardona memorials as affecting resumption of belief in the insularity of the Californias is a manuscript in the *Biblioteca Nacional,* Madrid, entitled *Descripciones, Geographicas, E hydrographicas de muchas tierras y Mares del norte y sur, en las Indias, en especial del descubrimiento del Reyno de la California . . . por el Capp^{an} y Cabo Nicolás de Cardona . . . dirigidas al Exmo Sr D. Gaspar de Guzman, Conde de Olivares, Duque de S.*

Lucar la Mayor, Sumiller de Corps de su Mag^d Gran Canciller de las Indias. The document is dated June 24, 1632, Madrid, and is signed with the name and rubric of Nicolás de Cardona. Part of the document, the "*Relación,*" appears in *Colección de documentos inéditos relativos al descubrimiento, conquista y organización de las antiguas posesiones españolas de América y Oceanía,* IX, 30–42. The most significant part, however, namely forty-two maps with individual descriptions, has not yet been published. These maps, which are most graphically represented, must have carried a great deal of weight as affecting geographical beliefs. Some of the documents noted in my *Catalogue* show that attention was paid to the Cardona memorials, e.g. a *real cédula* of March 15, 1635, adding one of the Cardona memorials to the *expediente* arising out of the *cédula* of August 2, 1628 (cf. *infra,* note 12), so that the viceroy might inform himself about the Californias, and call for memorials from others who might wish to discuss that subject. C–37. Photographs of the entire Cardona manuscript of June 24, 1632, are in the Academy of Pacific Coast History.

accomplished by private initiative, the government resolved to assume the expense. The Otondo expedition resulted, a colony being founded in 1683, which failed, however, after an existence of two years. This was the most successful attempt until 1697, when, at length, a permanent settlement was made.[12]

The age of the *conquistadores* along the northwestward line had passed, but the work in its second and third phases had been steadily proceeding. Guzmán founded a settle-

[12] Very little historical work has been done with regard to explorations and discoveries in the Californias in the seventeenth century. Bancroft skimmed through a few documents, and nobody has added much to what he said. The following documents of my *Catalogue* might serve as a convenient starting point for further investigations in this field : C–15, 17, 20, 21, 24, 26, 27, 30–63, 65, 66. Ten of these are great *testimonios*, and the rest, for the most part, memorials of individuals, and royal decrees. As an example of the materials that go to make up a *testimonio*, the documents of C–27 may be cited, omitting oaths taken by notaries :

1. 1628. [Aug.] 2. The king, by Andrés de Rocas, to the president and *oidores* of the *Audiencia* of Mexico. This recites Vizcaíno's voyage of 1602–3 to Alta California, and alludes to the slight knowledge that Spain still had of that land. The *Audiencia* is ordered to obtain reports about it from Fray Antonio de la Ascensión and others, and to advise the king in great detail as to the best manner of making further discoveries, in case it is deemed wise to make them.
The other documents are the requested memorials, as follows :
2. 1629. May 20. Ascensión to the *Audiencia*.
3. 1629. June 8. Ascensión.
4. 1629. May 5. Juan López de Vicuña.
5. 1629. May 25. Juan López de Vicuña.
6. 1629. May 27. Gonzalo de Francia.
7. 1629. June 15. Martín de Lezama.
8. 1629. June 23. Lope de Argüelles Quiñonel.
9. 1629. July 3. Juan de Iturbe.
10. 1629. July 30. Henrique Martínez.

11. [1629.] — Sebastián Gutiérrez.
12. [1629(?).] — Alonso Ortiz de Sandoval.
13. 1630. Dec. 22. Conde del Valle.
14. 1632. Mar. 22. Ascensión.
15. 1632. Sept. 30. Esteban Carbonel de Valenzuela.
16. 1632. Nov. 19. Diego de la Naba.
This is one of the smaller *testimonios*, aggregating 157 pages, but it must be remembered that the size of the page used (31 by 21½ centimetres) and the practice of writing *testimonios* without leaving much margin or wide spacing enabled the scribe to get as much on a page as we might expect to-day on the average-sized page of print. Among noteworthy features of the testimony is the fact that Nicolás de Cardona is not referred to as commanding expeditions which he himself claimed to have led ; Juan de Iturbe is named as commanding them, and Cardona is not even mentioned.
As examples of the larger *testimonios* C–39–41 may be cited. The three aggregate 1888 pages, all concerning proceedings against Francisco de Vergara and Francisco Esteban Carbonel. Vergara had been authorized by the viceroy, the Marqués de Cadereita, to engage in pearl fishing, and make discoveries in the Californias, but he transferred his rights to Carbonel. The case arose over the following charges against Carbonel: that he was a Frenchman ; that he had Frenchmen with him, some of them from New France, who said that a strait through the continent existed ; and that he had secretly been building a very large boat on the Río Santiago. It was thought that he planned to seek the strait, sail through to France, and thus open to that country a passage to the Spanish possessions of the Pacific.

ment as far north as San Miguel de Culiacán, Sinaloa, in 1531. By 1550 an *audiencia* for the government of Nueva Galicia, the name of Guzmán's conquests, was established; this was located for a time at Compostela, but soon afterward moved to Guadalajara. López, writing between 1571 and 1574, said that there were as many as 1500 Spaniards in Nueva Galicia, which at the time included most of New Spain north of Mexico City.[13] There were thirty-one or thirty-two settlements, of which fifteen or sixteen were mining camps. Guadalajara was the largest place, with a Spanish population of 150. The only settlement in what later became Sinaloa was San Miguel de Culiacán with about thirty Spaniards. There were no Spaniards in Sonora.[14] An increase in the population of Sinaloa came in 1596, when the presidio of San Felipe de Sinaloa, the first in that province, was established, with a garrison of twenty-five men. Meanwhile, the Franciscans, Dominicans, and Jesuits had been making converts, so that the region south of Sinaloa had become Christian, nominally at least, by the end of the sixteenth century, and, after futile revolts, was definitely reduced to the Spanish crown. The erection of a bishopric in Michoacán in 1537 may be regarded as a first step in the third phase of the conquest. So, despite the scant white population of Nueva Galicia, that part of it lying south of Sinaloa was fast losing the characteristics of a frontier province.

Up to 1591 not many conversions had been made in Sinaloa,[15] but in that year the Jesuits reached there, and the real work began. Father Zapata's report of 1678 shows that by that time Sinaloa had been thoroughly reduced. The province had been Christianized, and had a white population of 600. In addition, there were many more of part Spanish blood; at San Felipe de Sinaloa alone there

13 The provinces as he named them were those of Guadalajara, Xalisco, Zacatecas, Chiametla, Culiacán, Nueva Vizcaya, Cinaloa, Cíbola, Tuzán, Peñón de Acuco, Llanos de las Vacas, Quivira, and California. Only the first six named had Spanish settlements in them. California was correctly described as a peninsula.
14 López, 260–82.
15 López, 276, says that there were over 2000 peaceful Indians at San Miguel de Culiacán, and these represent, very likely, the number that had been converted.

were 1200 of Spanish or mixed blood. The missionaries and civilians were supported by two presidios, Fuerte de Montesclaros having been added in 1610. The occupation of Sonora did not begin until early in the seventeenth century, the successful military campaigns of Diego Martínez de Hurdaide paving the way. The Jesuits took charge of mission work, and made rapid progress. By 1678 there were twenty-eight missions in Sonora, serving seventy-two villages with a combined population of about 40,000. There were perhaps 500 people of Spanish or part Spanish blood, a large proportion of them engaged in mining.

The conquest had been carried almost to the limits of modern Sonora by way of the Sonora valley. This route led the Spaniards somewhat inland, leaving a large stretch of coast to the south and west as yet unoccupied. In this district were the Seri Indians, destined to cause trouble during the greater part of the eighteenth century. Northeast of the Sonora valley was a little-known region whence was to come an even more terrible enemy — the savage Apaches. Due to the hostility of these two peoples, Sonora was destined to remain a frontier province. Until near the close of the seventeenth century another district of Sonora, offering less difficulties than the other two, though by no means an easy field for conquest, remained open. This was the region between the Altar and Gila rivers, known as Pimería Alta, beyond which to the northwest lay Alta California. A beginning was made there by the entrance of the Jesuits in 1687. Thenceforth, by comparison with earlier years, the Spanish advance overland was to be very slow and increasingly difficult.

CHAPTER II

EARLY PROJECTS FOR ADVANCE BY WAY OF THE COLORADO
AND GILA RIVERS, 1687–1752

THERE is abundant evidence that an advance, at least as far as the Colorado and Gila rivers, was officially planned for three-quarters of a century before the Anza expedition of 1774. This raises the questions why such an advance should have been considered desirable by Spain, and why it was so long delayed. It is the purpose of this chapter to give evidence which shall answer both questions, although much will be said regarding them in later chapters as well. Causes for such an advance may be summarized, in inverted order of their importance, before proceeding to the proof, with an indication, also, of what was accomplished in the period covered by this chapter.

Conquest in itself would not have induced such a movement. The most cursory examination of the documents would satisfy one as to that. Conquests involved expenditure, and it will appear clearly that Spain was often unwilling to go to expense, even where prospects of a good return were promising. Mere vainglory of conquest was, therefore, no reason at all for an advance. Nor was the fabled wealth of the north any longer a sufficient lure, as in the past, to cause an expedition, certainly not in the eighteenth century. Too many times the marvels of the north had failed to materialize. Nevertheless, this incentive plays a part in the documents,[1] although not seriously considered by governmental authorities.

Conversion of Indians to Christianity is constantly alleged as an object of prime importance. Writers who have used but one or two documents are apt to be misled in

---

[1] For example, in C–178.

consequence, and to assert that Spain's conquests were actuated primarily by Christian motives.[2] Unquestionably this was the principal motive of the missionary orders, but was hardly at all a motive of the government.[3] It was merely a means to an end, just as were presidial troops and settlements, not itself an end; the government did not undergo expense for missions, unless it had some other object in view. As an agency, missions were very important; for example, to pave the way for a proposed conquest, to hold the more securely an already conquered territory, or to take steps toward providing a labor supply for existing or future Spanish colonies.[4] Much was accomplished by the Jesuits in this era, notably the conversion of large parts of Baja California and Pimería Alta, together with journeys of exploration and pastoral visitation to the Colorado and Gila.

Definite discovery of wealth might induce governmental expenditure for a conquest. Stories of wealth had to be very convincing, however, before the government would take a hand, and save in the case of mineral wealth in gold or silver, it probably would not move even then. Gold and silver mining meant an increase in royal revenues; for example, by the royal fifth exacted on products of precious metals, or by the sale of quicksilver. An official advance might then follow an earlier one on the part of Spanish miners. Tales of mineral wealth were frequent in this era, and often the government displayed interest, but the only striking discovery was that of the Arizonac mine.

A second cause for frontier advance was the fear lest some

[2] For example, see Guppy, *Solomon Islands*, 194. In stating "the principal object" of the Mendana expedition which discovered the Solomon Islands in 1567, Guppy says: "It was for the propagation of the Christian faith amongst the peoples of the unknown islands of the West that this expedition was dispatched from the shores of Peru."

[3] Englehardt, I, 142–43, says: "The kings, indeed, desired the conversion of the Indians to Christianity, and frequently declared this to be the chief aim of the conquest; nevertheless, the object for which alone expenses were incurred was political." Again, II, 6: "The men who presumed to guide the destinies of Spain then, and as a rule ever since, cared naught for the success of Religion or the welfare of its ministers, except in so far as both could be used to promote political schemes."

[4] *Ibid.*, II, 4: "The experience of two centuries in Lower California had demonstrated that, while soldiers might defend the country against foreign enemies, they could not transform savages into loyal subjects."

other European power might occupy lands that would threaten those already possessed by Spain. Many documents will be adduced, and more might be, to show that Spain's fear of foreign enemies in the Pacific was constant. Whatever other countries did or planned to do, Spain was unceasingly distrustful. Mere unauthenticated reports of foreign aggression were enough to cause the government to go to considerable expense in this period, whereas the most exaggerated guesses at the wealth of unoccupied lands failed to induce the expenditure of a *peso*. There were many projects of conquest on this account, but they got no farther at this time than foundation of presidios within territory already occupied, although this was a forward step by no means to be despised. What might have happened, if definite proof of foreign aggression had been received, is a question, but such proof was never obtained. Suspicion there was, always. In this period it was directed primarily against the French.

It was necessary that the two last-named factors, but especially that of foreign aggression, should be combined with another, if they were to result in important action; a man must be found of sufficient energy and ability to carry plans into execution. Leaders, like missions, may be regarded as an agency of conquest, rather than a cause, but on them depended in more than usual degree whether undertakings should be executed, the causes being always existent. Hindrances to conquest were such that none but an extraordinary leader, with such scant means as Spain was willing to supply, could hope to succeed. No such individual appeared at this time.

Indian wars were a continual factor tending to check the Spanish northwestward advance. The Apaches began their raids into Sonora before the close of the seventeenth century, although Chihuahua to the east was their principal object of attack. The presidio of Corodeguache de Fronteras was established in northeastern Sonora as a check against them. Janos and Casas Grandes in Chihuahua were founded to coöperate with it. In 1695, there was a serious

revolt of the Pimas in Pimería Alta. In 1696–97, Indians
of the eastern Sonora missions were in revolt. The year
1699 saw the beginning of Seri wars in the region between
the Yaqui and Sonora rivers.

Yet, toward the close of the seventeenth century and in
the early years of the eighteenth, not a little was done in
the way of exploration and reports with regard to an
advance to the Colorado and Gila rivers. These events
were very closely related to the affairs of Baja California,
some mention of which may first be given. After repeated
failures a permanent settlement had been made in Baja
California in 1697, success being attained by the Jesuit
order under the leadership of Father Juan María Salvatierra. By the terms of their contract the Jesuits were to
have entire control over the province, spiritual, economic,
civil, and even military. Through the institution of the
pious fund,[5] supplemented by government aid, Baja California did not suffer greatly from lack of funds under Jesuit
rule, although there were several occasions when abandonment of the missions was narrowly averted. Its development, however, was greatly hindered by three factors :
opposition by the Jesuits to development of a sort that
would bring in many Spanish settlers, or lessen their own
authority ; sterility of the peninsula ; and difficulty of the
voyage across the Gulf. The ground for Jesuit opposition
was that Spanish settlements would interfere with conversions. Aside from that, however, the other two factors
were enough in themselves to prevent a great development
of the peninsula. For eight hundred miles it stretches
out, a mountainous, arid waste, — unfit for mining, stock-
raising, or agriculture, in Spanish colonial days, on any
but a modest scale. Baja California could not serve as a
base of supply for more northerly lands. Rather it stood in

[5] The pious fund had its origin in
1697 in sums given by private individuals for propagation of the faith in
the Californias. It was managed by
the Jesuits until their expulsion in
1767, after which it became a branch
of the *real hacienda*, retaining, however,
its original characteristics as regards

objects and mode of accumulation, *i.e.*
by gifts. For a summary of its history
down to the present day, for the Mexican government still owes an annual
sum of $43,050.99 to the Catholic
authorities of Alta California, see
Englehardt, I, 595–99. Cf. chap. V,
n. 78.

c

need of aid, which had to come by sea, unless a land route could be found. The severity of storms in the Gulf, and the likelihood of shipwreck were such that, despite the shortness of the voyage, a land route was desirable, even though involving a detour around the head of the Gulf.[6] Father Eusebio Kino of the Jesuit order had served in Baja California during Otondo's unsuccessful attempt of 1683–85 to found a colony there; and he never ceased, thereafter, to be interested in the Californias. It was Kino who inspired Salvatierra to make the attempt which led to the Jesuit entry into Baja California in 1697. After exploring the Gila and Colorado valleys, Kino became interested in the northern lands as well, hoping to reach Monterey. He trusted that the Manila galleon might be ordered to stop there and send goods overland to Sonora; and he grew to believe that a settlement should be founded on the Colorado River, to serve as a base for operations against the Apaches and Moquis, and for the conquest of the Californias and the lands between Sonora and New Mexico. Yet, aside from his missionary zeal for conversions, the development of a supply-route from Sonora to Baja California may be regarded as his most immediate object, and this too was keenly desired by Salvatierra. This project was the result of Kino's explorations in Pimería Alta.

[6] In 1768 it took Gálvez forty days to go from San Blas to Baja California, a voyage of less than a hundred leagues. In the same year the *San Carlos* and the *San Antonio* required nearly three months for the voyage, after which they had to be careened and repaired. Gálvez felt that voyages to the Californias should be made at particular seasons so as to avoid dangerous storms. After referring to difficulties of Alta California voyages on this account, he said that it was worse yet in the Gulf, owing to the added danger of shipwreck, for there were many islands there. Gálvez, *Informe*, 141–47; also C–1834. Writing to the viceroy on this subject, September 8, 1768, Gálvez said that voyages to the peninsula had always been difficult on account of storms. He suggested that, in future, they should be made by going outside the cape, as the Philippine galleon did without encountering storms, and the return made by crossing to the coast of Sinaloa and following down the coast. C–1075. Gálvez's statement is borne out by the facts. Instances need not be multiplied here; one has only to note voyages mentioned in Bancroft, *N. M. St. & Tex.*, I. Otondo's voyage of 1683 may be cited as an illustration of what often happened. Otondo spent over two months trying to get across the Gulf, and then did it in one night, although it took him three days more before he was able to approach the coast. The Jesuits lost five vessels between 1712 and 1717, and yet another was wrecked but saved. These are but a few instances of the many mentioned in the same volume of Bancroft.

In 1687 Kino had established the mission Dolores on one of the upper branches of the Sonora River, the initial step in the advance across Pimería Alta. In the next quarter century he and his companions pushed the frontier of missionary work and exploration from this outpost to the Gila and lower Colorado rivers. By 1695 Kino had established a chain of missions up and down the valley of the Altar River, San Ignacio, Tubutama, Caborca, Cocóspera, Santa María Suamca, and others. In 1691, accompanied by Father Salvatierra, he began his expeditions in the valley of the Gila, going as far as Tumacácori, an Indian village on the Santa Cruz. Three years later he descended the Santa Cruz to Casa Grande. In 1697 he went again to Casa Grande, accompanied by a guard of soldiers from Fronteras under Captain Bernal. In the following year he went to the Gila, and returned across Papaguería, by way of Sonoita, Caborca, and the Altar valley. In 1699 he went to Sonoita, continued northward east of the Gila Range, and reached the Gila River, which he ascended to Casa Grande.

Kino had come to America in the belief that California was a peninsula, but, under the influence of current teachings, had accepted the doctrine that it was an island. During his last journey to the Gila, however, he had been given some blue shells, such as he had seen on the western coast of Baja California, and nowhere else. He now reasoned that California must after all be a peninsula, and that it might be possible to find a land route over which to send supplies to Salvatierra's struggling missions. To test this view was the principal object of his later explorations. In 1700 he for the first time descended the Gila to its junction with the Colorado. In the following year, accompanied by Salvatierra, he tried to reach the head of the Gulf by going up the coast from Sonoita. Failing in this, he went to the Gila junction, descended the Colorado nearly to its mouth, and crossed over on a raft. In 1702 he again descended the Colorado, this time reaching the Gulf. He had now proved, to his own satisfaction at least, that California *no es ysla*, *sino penisla.* Meanwhile, Kino and his companions had pushed the missionary frontier to the Gila. In 1700 he founded the mission of San Javier del Bac, and within the next two years those of Tumacácori and Guebavi, all in the Santa Cruz valley and within modern Arizona. Kino's exploring tours were also itinerant missions, and in the course of them he baptized and taught in numerous villages, up and down the Gila and Colorado, and throughout Pimería Alta.

Kino's work and his reports aroused new interest in northwestward expansion. The map which he made of his explorations, published in 1701, was not improved upon for more than a century. The principal writing of Father Kino was his *Favores Celestiales*, which constitutes a history of his life-work on the frontier. It was written at the mission Dolores at different times within a period embracing more than a decade. The first part was finished in December, 1699, and was carried to Rome in 1701 by the Jesuit procurators Bernardo Rolandegui and Nicolás de Vera.[7]

It was just about at that time that governmental interest in the Californias began to reawaken. This cannot be traced directly to Kino, but the inference that his memorials were the moving cause of action is so strong that it cannot reasonably be doubted. Burriel says that no attention was paid in Madrid to the earliest reports of the settlement, but that affairs took a new turn on the accession of Philip V, who as a result of private advices brought the matter before the Council of the Indies. Royal orders followed, dated July 17, 1701, that all possible aid should be given the new establishments; that the royal treasury should pay 6000

---

[7] The foregoing sketch of Kino's work was written by Professor Bolton, who based it on Kino's *Favores celestiales*, a manuscript volume which is still unpublished. After the middle of the eighteenth century little advance was made in the history of Father Kino's achievements until a few years ago, when Bolton discovered and identified this rare manuscript. For an account of the discovery, identification, and contents of the work see Bolton, *Father Kino's lost history, its discovery, and its value,* in Bibliographical Society of America, *Papers,* VI, 9–34. Richman, in his *California under Spain and Mexico,* gives a chapter based on Bolton's translation of the manuscript.

pesos a year toward their maintenance; that reports be called for, giving information as to the nature of the land, the means of advancing the conquest, communication with the mainland, the state of the missions of Sinaloa, Sonora, and Nueva Vizcaya, and whether these might aid the Jesuit establishments in the Californias.[8] It will be noted that Kino's project of a supply-route was prominently to the fore, and it is likely that Rolandegui and Vera furnished the "private advices." They had just passed through Spain.[9] Further action was taken in 1703. In that year, says Burriel, Fathers Rolandegui and Vera presented a memorial to the king about the Californias.[10] This was reviewed by the Council of the Indies on June 16, the king himself being present. In consequence, there were enacted five decrees on September 28, 1703, the most important of which was one directed to the viceroy. Besides adding 7000 *pesos* to the annual charge of the missions against the royal treasury, ordering the purchase of a boat, and making other provision for the missions, the king called for a *junta* in Mexico in order to provide for establishing a presidio of thirty soldiers, to be placed as far north as possible on the Pacific coast of the peninsula, to serve as protection to the land, and as a way-station for the Manila galleon, the presidio captain to be chosen by the viceroy. Pearl-fishing was to be encouraged, and settlers sent from New Spain.[11] A *junta* was held, June 6, 1704, at which all agreed that the royal wishes should be fulfilled, although the matter of the presidio was left to be discussed with the missionaries and others.[12]

The Jesuits eventually got the additional sum of money, but the rest of the decree was blocked, largely by their own action. Their objections appear in a memorial of Salvatierra to the viceroy, May 25, 1705. "One ship, he

[8] Burriel, *Noticia*, II, 62–64.

[9] The Kino manuscript carried by Rolandegui and Vera was received at Rome in December, 1701. *Favores celestiales*, part II, chap. 1.

[10] Burriel says that they had just come from Mexico, but unless this was a second visit the statement is in error. It is probable that the matter was associated with their names by reason of their former visit, and that they were not present on this occasion.

[11] Burriel, *Noticia*, II, 139–41.

[12] *Ibid.*, II, 141, 152.

said, could not adequately perform the service required, nor was the liberal allowance of 13,000 *pesos* sufficient to make ends meet. He did not wish pearl-fishing to be encouraged, as it led to trouble with the natives. Nor did the Jesuits desire the presence of Spanish settlers to breed dissensions. As to a presidio on the western coast, it would be an unnecessary expense, as the missions would soon be extended there. The suggestion that the garrison officers should be appointed by the government was very ill-advised, since only by this power of appointment could the padres restrain the natives and soldiers." [13]

In ensuing years there were a number of decrees which, like those already mentioned, evinced the royal will to develop the Californias. Especially notable is one of January 29, 1716, for which Alberoni, then dominant in Spanish politics, is said to have been responsible, although it is likely that he was influenced by the memorials of Kino, whose ideas appear in the decree. The decree itself was like many another, asking information as to the progress of conversions in the Californias, referring to the great importance of promoting spiritual conquest there, and ordering the viceroy to fulfill a decree of July 26, 1708, requiring him to take steps in that regard. At the same time orders were given to promote the advancement of the Sonora missions; and verbal instructions were issued to the viceroy to explore the Pacific coasts and to found colonies and presidios there. In addition to these colonies Alberoni planned "in like manner to advance the Spanish domain with new settlements in the vast unknown territories to the north of Sonora from the Gila and Colorado rivers onward." The last-named settlements might send their products to the new colonies on the coast, and receive in exchange what they needed. These regions were not to rely on New Spain and Europe for trade, but were to develop commerce with the Philippines, which islands he designed to be the centre of the trade of the orient.[14]

[13] Bancroft, *N. M. St. & Tex.*, I, 419. The memorial is inserted entire in Burriel, *Noticia*, II, 154–66.   [14] Burriel, *Noticia*, II, 287–94.

Alberoni was not left in peace to work out his ideas. A few years later, after a stormy career in power, he found himself an exile from Spain. The viceroy called a *junta*, however, to act upon the decree of 1716, announcing that he proposed to found at least one colony on the west coast of the Californias. All present approved, with one exception, Father Romano, the Jesuit procurator, who asserted that the peninsula was too sterile to maintain such a colony. Other Jesuits were of the same opinion, and the matter was dropped for the time being. Another decree of 1719 urged furthering the conquest, holding as especially important the occupation of west coast ports up to Monterey, and ordering the viceroy to take action. There was another decree to the same effect in 1723, and others of later date. These at least show a desire of the government for an advance to the northwest. The chief result in Baja California of the decrees, however, seems to have been the growth of the royal subsidy. This, at length, reached some 30,000 *pesos* a year. The Jesuits remained in authority.

From Kino's time on, the project of a settlement on the Colorado plays a prominent part in memorials and governmental plans. Enough documents have been found to show that interest was continuous, although the event had to wait. This was one of the keynotes in the documents already referred to with relation to Baja California. The same idea appears in those concerning Sonora. Father Campos fell heir to Kino's ideas. In 1715 he wrote to Viceroy Linares that Indians of the north were coming to his mission to have their children baptized, and suggested that he be sent to their country to administer the sacrament. He also proposed that the territory between Pimería Alta and Moqui be taken from the Franciscans, to whose jurisdiction it then belonged, and given to the Jesuits; the latter, he said, were nearer than the former who were in New Mexico, and moreover the Indians did not like the Franciscans.[15] Campos seems to have made the visit that

[15] Cited in Rebolledo to Vizarrón, Apr. 11, 1737, in C-1872.

he suggested, a number of times.[16] Bancroft says that the
Jesuits were not so much interested in getting to Moqui
as they alleged; that was merely a pretext to enable them
to get missions and a presidio in the lower Gila valley.
These obtained, they had in mind the ultimate occupation
of the Californias or of the territory northeastward, according as events should decide. The Jesuits were partially
successful in their petition; in 1719 the king granted to
them the Moqui field, but the missions and the presidio
were not founded. In 1725 there was a royal order authorizing expeditions from Pimería Alta to New Mexico,
but none were made in consequence.[17] A few years later
royal funds were forthcoming. Several Jesuits were sent
from Europe and assisted to their stations at state expense.[18]
Three of them came to northern Sonora, and were escorted
to their posts by the captain of Fronteras, Juan Bautista
de Anza, father of that Anza who was later to discover the
route from Sonora to Alta California.[19] Abandoned missions, such as Santa María Suamca, Guebavi, Tumacácori,
and San Javier del Bac, were reëstablished; and Jesuit
visits to the Gila were resumed.

Shortly afterward occurred an event which seemed likely
for a time to lead to vigorous governmental action in northwestward advance, and the papers in connection with it
were also used, several decades later, when authority was
given for the Anza expedition of 1774. In 1736 a most
remarkable silver mine was discovered at or near a place
called Arizonac, or Arizona, just south of the border of the
present-day state of Arizona. The more usual name for
the mine at that time was *Bolas de Plata*, or *Planchas de
Plata;* because the precious metal was found in balls or
nuggets of almost pure silver. These were on or near the
surface, and were of immense size, some of them weighing
a ton or more. Accounts differ, but there are several stating

[16] See *infra* note 85.
  In 1723 Campos wrote to the
viceroy describing the country as far
as the Gila. Bolton, *Guide.*
  [17] Stated in Bishop of Puebla to the
king, Apr. 16, 1737, C–182.

[18] Rebolledo to Vizarrón, Apr. 11,
1737, in C–1872.
  [19] For his work on this occasion
Anza won encomiums, not only from
Jesuit writers, but also from the king
of Spain. Alegre, 245–46.

that the largest nugget weighed 3500 pounds; one of the reputed finders, Fermin, spoke of a 4000-pound nugget, and said that there were many of about 500 pounds. There was an immediate rush of miners to the spot. Captain Anza of Fronteras interfered with them, claiming that the *bolas* belonged properly to the king. According to law, one-fifth of the silver accrued to the king if the discovery were a mine, but if a hidden treasure, the king was entitled to all. Anza claimed that if not a hidden treasure, it was at least a *criadero*, or growing-place of silver, and therefore belonged to the national treasury. The viceroy reversed Anza's decision, but the royal decree of 1741 sustained the Fronteras captain. It is doubtful whether Anza could have held back the miners, if the mines had proved to be extensive. Cavo intimates that Anza's interference was not very effective anyway, the greater part of the wealth going to the discoverers,[20] and Anza himself stated that he had difficulty in saving any for the king.[21] Although the region was rich in mineral wealth of the ordinary type, the *bolas* seem to have been but a superficial deposit,[22] and nothing is heard of them after 1741. Nevertheless the *bolas* incident did lead to an official consideration of northwestward conquest by way of the Colorado and Gila rivers, and to some action by the government. The *bolas de plata* were a definitely proved item of wealth, which was infinitely more important than, for example, a fabled mountain of gold. Where so much silver had been found, there was good reason to expect that more existed.

In a letter of January 7, 1737, to Benito Crespo, bishop of Puebla, Anza tells of the discovery of the *bolas*, and says that this should prove an impetus to further advance of the Spanish conquests. He urges Crespo to use his influence to bring about such action.[23] On January 13, 1737, Anza reported to Viceroy Vizarrón what he had done

[20] Cavo, 271.
[21] C-177.
[22] For a brief history of mining in Sonora, see José Francisco Velasco, *Noticias estadísticas del estado de Sonora* (Mexico, 1850), 185–205. Portions of the Velasco work were translated to English by William F. Nye under the title of *Sonora* (San Francisco, 1861).
[23] C-177.

in relation to the *bolas*.[24]   The next day he wrote again proposing an expedition to the north with himself as leader. He quoted a number of the reports of early explorers, and reviewed the evidence for belief in the wealth of the north. The vast ruin on the Gila known as the Casa Grande and an even greater one in Chihuahua, built, he thought, by Aztec kings in the course of their migration southward,[25] were mentioned by him in support of this belief.   Indians of the Gila had told Jesuit visitors of the existence of quicksilver in the north.[26]   Anza had something to say too of the island California, of the strait through the continent, and of the Seven Cities, Gran Teguayo, and Quivira, and as usual, the vast number of Indians awaiting conversion was adduced as an argument for an expedition.   His project was to make discoveries toward the Colorado River, paying visits to the tribes of that river and the Gila as a preliminary to founding a settlement on the Colorado, this to be a base for further discoveries.   The expedition should consist of fifty or sixty soldiers and a hundred friendly Pimas. Funds might be obtained from pious persons, while he himself was willing to provide horses, cattle, mules, and articles as gifts for the Indians.   As the Apaches were a constant source of trouble, and Seri uprisings no inconsiderable difficulty, most of the troops should be drawn elsewhere than from his presidio, Corodeguache de Fronteras, as this had to play a large part in meeting these dangers.[27]

Anza's proposal was seriously considered by the governments of Spain and New Spain, being discussed in connection with the question whether the *bolas* were mine or treasure.   A few of the documents used may be considered here, and a reference given to the rest in a note.[28]   On April 11,

[24] He had first heard of them on November 13, 1736.   Anza, *Declaration*, Nov. 15, 1736, in C–192.

[25] For an account and bibliography of the Casa Grande see Garcés (Coues ed.), I, 89–101.

[26] Lack of quicksilver was one of the prime causes for the slow development of Sonora.   The miners needed it in order to extract precious metals from ores.   Cf. n. 63.

[27] C–178.

[28] The following that bear on the subject were not used by me: C–185, 186, 191–93, 199–201, 203–5, 207–8, 212.   Three of these would seem to be of particular value in a detailed study of this period.   C–191 is the original of a communication from the Council of the Indies to the king, October 5, 1737, giving its opinion on the matters arising from the discovery

1737, the *fiscal*, Juan Olívar Rebolledo, to whom Anza's
petition had been referred by the viceroy, delivered his
written opinion. He referred to various earlier expeditions,
among others to a voyage up the Gulf of California by
Guillermo Estrajort in 1730 or 1731.[29] This had led to a
doubt whether California were an island, as had been
supposed. Rebolledo thought that an expedition such as
Anza proposed would make that point clear, and give information of the lands and peoples of the Colorado River
and thence to Moqui. He therefore recommended that
Anza be permitted to go, taking with him, besides the force
proposed, a man skilled in the use of instruments for determining latitudes, and Father Campos, if the latter wished
to go, to instruct natives in the catechism.[30] Among papers
received by the viceroy were certain memorials from one
José de Messa, written from Guadalajara in July and August, 1737. Messa told of the mineral wealth of the Arizonac mine, which he claimed to have discovered. Stories
of its wealth had not been exaggerated, he said. Moreover,
Indians had told him of great riches in gold, silver, pearls,
and quicksilver farther in the interior. He spoke of the
multitude of Indians ripe for conversion, naming especially
the Pima, Pápago, and Seri tribes. In his opinion an extension of Spanish conquests beyond Sonora would be of great
service to God and the king.[31]

It was not until September 15, 1737, that the viceroy
wrote to the king of the *bolas* incident and Anza's project,
his letter of that date[32] being based on the Messa memorials,
which he enclosed. Meanwhile, the authorities in Spain
had already heard of the matter from another source.
Anza's letter to the bishop of Puebla had borne fruit, for
the latter had written to the king on April 16, 1737. It

of the *bolas* and Anza's proposed expedition, a manuscript of 22 pages.
C–192 and 193 are great *testimonios*
of respectively 263 and 124 pages.
Both are certified copies, dated 1738,
of files of papers in Mexico on this
subject matter.

[29] An Englishman called Guillermo
Estrafort (William Strafford?) was

pilot on Ugarte's voyage of 1721 to
the head of the Gulf. This may have
been the individual to whom the
fiscal was referring. Probably, too,
the 1721 voyage was meant, and not
1731 as stated. Estrafort kept a
diary of the Ugarte voyage.

[30] In C–1872.

[31] C–184.   [32] C–187.

seemed to the bishop a propitious moment for fresh conquests. There was reason to believe that great mineral wealth would be found on the other side of the Gila and Colorado. Nobody had yet gone beyond the above-named rivers.[33] The bishop's letter and the two of Anza, for the latter had sent to the bishop a copy of his letter to Vizarrón, were considered by the Council of the Indies. The *fiscal* gave his opinion, September 18, 1737, that a *junta* should be called in Mexico to consider the advisability of the proposed conquests beyond the Colorado and Gila.[34] The Council concurred, embodying the recommendation of the *fiscal* in its decree of September 27, 1737.[35] Much the same procedure was ordered in a royal decree of June 13, 1738. The viceroy was reminded of a report made by Benito Crespo when, as bishop of Durango, he had just completed a diocesan tour in 1731. Crespo had gone from Pimería Alta by way of El Paso to New Mexico. He had stated that it was easy to get to the Colorado and Gila rivers, as had been proved by repeated trips there, but had regarded such journeys as a needless expense, believing that settlements there could not be maintained. He had thought that an advance to territories of the Pimas of the Gila was feasible, as these people, being natural enemies of the Apaches, might be expected to welcome them. Moqui probably was not far away, according to the bishop, but was on the other side of a very deep river which only an occasional Indian had been able to cross.[36] Proceeding, the royal decree ordered the viceroy to call a *junta* of practical, intelligent men to consider Anza's proposal, examining former projects and reports, and getting the advice of missionaries and others then in service. A full account was to be sent to the king for his decision in the matter.[37]

The expedition was not in fact made, and no materials have yet come to light stating reasons for abandonment of the plan, but they may be inferred with a fair degree of certainty. A series of Indian wars had broken out in

[33] C–182.
[34] C–188.
[35] C–189.

[36] The Grand Canyon of the Colorado?
[37] C–202.

Sonora. In 1737 the Pimas of the coast revolted and took refuge in the Cerro Prieto, an almost impregnable mountain stronghold in the vicinity of Guaymas; the Cerro Prieto was to play an important part in the history of Sonora from that time forth. On this occasion Anza subdued the Pimas. He was unsuccessful, however, with the Apaches, who continued to be troublesome, losing his life in a battle with them in 1739. In 1740–41 the Mayo and Yaqui Indians were in revolt against the mission system. Probably quite as important as these events, even more than the death of Anza, was the fact that the *bolas* proved to be only a superficial deposit. They were at length adjudged to have been buried treasure. Yet, if no striking advance was made at this time, the *bolas* incident was not without result; something was done to clear the way. Two presidios were established in 1741; Pitiqui as a protection against the Seris, Pimas, Yaquis, and Tepocas, at modern Hermosillo; and Terrenate in the vicinity of the Arizonac mine as an outpost against the Apaches. In 1745 there were at these two presidios and at Fronteras, with also a garrison at Buenavista, a total of 183 soldiers, not enough to overawe the Seris and Apaches who gave much trouble, but, as matters went in the frontier provinces, the establishing of two presidios must be regarded as a considerable step in northwestward advance.

Meanwhile, the Jesuits of Sonora and Baja California were continually petitioning for the occupation of the Colorado-Gila country, and were displaying not a little activity in exploring that region. After 1736, frequent trips to the Gila and Colorado were made by Fathers Ignacio Keller and Jacobo Sedelmayr. Journeys of explorations became even more frequent after 1741 as a result of a royal decree in that year awarding the Moqui field to the Jesuits, — another step, it would seem, in the projected northwestward conquest. It now behooved the Jesuits to reach their charges, Moqui being regarded as not far beyond the Gila. In journeys made between 1743 and 1750 the most prominent name is that of Father Sedelmayr. On one occasion he seems to have gone up the Colorado as

far as Bill Williams Fork, and on another he descended the
Colorado nearly to its mouth. These and other Jesuit
expeditions failed of their purpose if they were intended to
prove the nearness of Moqui, but if, as Bancroft asserts,
the real object was to interest the king in founding establishments on the Colorado and Gila rivers as a preliminary
to a further advance, they were decidedly successful. One
noteworthy statement of Sedelmayr, much quoted in later
years, was that the Indians had told him that the Colorado
flowed to the west, a little north of where he had gone.
This led to conjectures that there might be a branch of the
Colorado emptying into the Pacific, possibly the Carmelo.
These Jesuit explorations also had some effect upon the
much broached project of uniting the Sonora missions to
those of Baja California by way of the Colorado River.

An Indian revolt occurred in Baja California in 1734,
which was not suppressed until two years later. Questions
arising out of this revolt have a bearing upon the proposed
land route in the official correspondence of the next decade.
Meanwhile, war broke out between Spain and England in
1739, which, coupled with Anson's appearance off the Pacific
coast of Mexico in 1742, tended still more to direct attention
to the Californias and the Sonora coast. The Marqués de
Aysa, president of the *Audiencia* of Guadalajara, took steps
to get information with regard to the islands and pearl-
fisheries off the coast of Sonora, and about the ports and
mineral wealth of the coast.[38] In a letter to the king of
January 21, 1743, he proposed that these places be occupied,
and settlements made, utilizing for that purpose criminals
and other disturbers of the peace in Nueva Galicia.[39] In the
same year the matter of the Baja California revolt came
before the Council of the Indies, which approved the steps
taken by the viceroy, authorizing such expense as had been
incurred.[40] The *ministro general*, Fernando Triviño, began
also to make inquiries with a view to forwarding the spiritual and temporal conquest of the Californias.[41] The

[38] C–236.
[39] C–242.
[40] C–243, 245–46.
[41] C–240, 244–46, 253.

Jesuits renewed their petitions, and the viceroy, the Conde de Fuenclara, recommended, June 25, 1744, that the king send as many Jesuits as possible for use both in their colleges, and in converting the natives of Sinaloa, Sonora, and the Californias.[42]   All of these matters came to a head in the royal decree of November 13, 1744, directed by Triviño to the viceroy.   The keynote of it is the necessity for occupying the Colorado River country.   The gist of the decree follows:

In considering questions arising from the Baja California revolt of 1734 the *fiscal* of the Council of the Indies had made a report, May 12, 1744, declaring that the retention of Baja California was a matter of great importance.   The Council therefore recommended the founding of Spanish settlements, as well as the encouragement of the Jesuits in their work of conversion.   It also proposed that Jesuit missionaries should enter Baja California from the north, since it had been discovered that the Californias were joined to the continent.   In this way the reduction of the peninsula would be simplified, the Indians being hemmed in on both sides.   There should be two missionaries in each of the frontier missions, one to travel among the heathen and to make converts, and the other to be in charge of the mission. This applied not only to the missions of Baja California, but also to those of Pimería Alta.   When on journeys to visit outlying tribes the missionaries should be furnished with a military escort.   Thus, the Jesuits of Pimería Alta could reduce the Cocomaricopas and Yumas of the Colorado. As these Indians were well disposed, it might be possible for the Jesuits from Pimería Alta to found a mission on each bank of the Colorado, thus securing communications on both sides of the river.   They might then proceed southward to the missions of the peninsula.   The escort could be secured by dispensing with the presidio of Pitiqui.   As these proposals were expected to produce many benefits to the royal dominions, among others the freedom of Philippine commerce, the viceroy was directed to take immediate

[42] C–259.

steps to put them into effect.   Furthermore, the viceroy
was to consult with the Marqués del Castillo de Aysa, who
had proposed, January 21, 1743, that two ships of war should
be maintained on the Pacific coast, both to protect that
region, and to promote the pearl-fisheries of the Gulf; and
that the Islas Marías [43] should be settled, so as to prevent
some enemy's ship from hiding there to wait for the Manila
galleon.   The first proposal merited particular attention,
said Triviño, but the second required more consideration.[44]
Sixteen years later the Council stated that the decree of
1744 had been enacted with a view to checking foreign
aggression from the direction of New Mexico.[45]   Develop-
ments of the next few years following the 1744 decree make
it probable that this was after all the most prominent factor
in the minds of the authorities.

Triviño asked reports of various individuals who might
throw light on the matter.   Of the replies received [46] only
one will be considered in any detail, that of the Jesuit Provincial of New Spain, Father Escobar, November 30, 1745.
Escobar was assisted in drawing up his memorial by the
man who knew the Colorado River country better than
any one else, Father Sedelmayr, who had just returned from
his journey of 1744 to Bill Williams Fork.   Escobar stated
that the proposed colonization of Baja California was impossible because of the sterility of the land.[47]   As it was, the
missions already occupied could not exist without the products sent to them from Sinaloa.   The region about Monterey was more fertile, but would be difficult to reduce by
an advance from Baja California, owing to the [intervening]
barrenness and the lack of laborers.   Therefore, he proposed a conquest of Pimería Alta, which was easy of access,

[43] Otherwise Tres Marías; off the
coast of Tepic at the mouth of the
Gulf.

[44] In Burriel, II, 502–17; Natural
and civil history, II, 165–73.   Except
for page 513, the latter omits what
appears from the bottom of page 511
of the Noticia to the end of the document.

[45] C–1455.

[46] Among other replies not noted
here was one by the bishop of Durango,
June 19, 1745, giving his opinion concerning the lands about Pimería Alta,
and what Spain might do there.   C–260.

[47] This was true, but it is probable
that the traditional objection of the
Jesuits to Spanish settlements near
their missions had something to do
with Escobar's argument.

and, in the region of the Colorado and Gila rivers, fertile; for, just as the lower part of Baja California could not exist without products from Sinaloa, the upper part would be unable to exist without those of Pimería.[48] Such a conquest would facilitate that of Moqui, in case it did not succeed by way of New Mexico, and it would be a check upon the Apaches. To achieve it, the number of Jesuits would have to be increased, the Gulf explored again, as the authorities in Mexico were not yet certain that the Californias were joined to the mainland, and a presidio of a hundred men established on the Gila in Apache territories. It would not be safe to do away with the presidio of Pitiqui, as in that event the Indians of that vicinity, the Yaquis, Seris, and others, might rise in rebellion. Brilliant results were predicted by Escobar if his plan were adopted: the suppression of the Apaches; the conquest of Moqui and intervening territories; conquest of the tribes of the two rivers; the opening of a field for conversions beyond them; and, above all, the facilitation of a passage to the Californias.[49] Early in 1746 Sedelmayr himself wrote a report, but as it expressed much the same views as the Escobar memorial, it may be omitted here.[50]

The voyage of Father Fernando Consag in June and July, 1746, was one result of this renewed interest in the northwest. Consag went to the head of the Gulf, and definitely proved the peninsularity of the Californias.[51] Moqui

---

[48] There is hardly a doubt but that Escobar referred to the upper half of the peninsula. The phrase is "California alta" in Burriel, but the distinction had not yet been made of applying *alta* to the California now part of the United States. Only the lower part of the peninsula had been occupied; hence *alta* might well be the upper part. Cf. notes 49, 54, and especially 84.

[49] C–263. The above, however, was taken from Burriel, *Noticia*, II, 537–42. It is probable that the last remark refers to the peninsula; the one preceding it doubtless refers in part to the American state of California.

[50] Sedelmayr "gives a résumé," says Bancroft, "of what had already been

done, a full description of the country and its people as observed by himself and others and his own ideas respecting the territory and tribes not yet seen. He presents as motives for the foundation of the missions the fertility of the soil; the great numbers of Indians awaiting salvation; the mineral wealth awaiting development; and the desirability of a new base of operations from which to protect the old missions, to reduce the Moquis, to check the Apaches, to learn if California is an island, to push the reduction up to Monterey, and to solve the great geographical mysteries of the far north." Bancroft, *N. M. St. & Tex.*, I, 538.

[51] C–266, 272.

D

appearing to be much nearer to the Franciscans in New Mexico than to the Jesuits in Pimería Alta, the decree of 1741 was reversed in 1745, Moqui being reawarded to the Franciscans. This did not lessen interest in the Colorado-Gila region, although the death of Philip V in 1746, and the arrival of a new viceroy, the elder Conde de Revilla Gigedo, in the same year may have tended to delay action. A *junta* had been held, prior to Revilla Gigedo's arrival, about the general subject of conquering the Californias. Its recommendations were considered by the Council of the Indies, along with the Escobar memorial and the reports of Consag's voyage,[52] leading to the royal decree of December 4, 1747.

The decree of 1747 quoted in full that of November 13, 1744; stated that the preceding viceroy, Fuenclara, had begun to receive reports, and take other action in pursuance thereof; remarked that the king understood that Revilla Gigedo, because so recently installed in office, had been unable to give much attention to it; and cited with approval Father Escobar's memorial. Revilla Gigedo was to proceed, without awaiting fresh royal orders, to do what he thought advisable to carry out the decree of 1744, always bearing in mind, however, the state of the royal treasury, so that he might not cause needless expenditures. He was ordered to devote himself in particular to reducing the Seris, also the Pimas Altos and Pápagos, and to check the hostilities of the Apaches.[53] The document is interesting in that it states the necessary preliminaries to the discovery and use of a land route to the Californias: the conquest of the Seris and allied tribes; the repulse of the Apaches; and the occupation of the Colorado-Gila country. Thence, Spaniards might go to New Mexico, or to Alta or Baja California; but the prime concern then was that the decree might bring about the reduction of the peninsula, Baja California.[54]

[52] For papers considered by the Council of the Indies see C–274, 276–79, 335.
[53] C–283. The above account, however, was taken from Burriel, *Noticia*, II, 501–20. The *Natural and civil history* does not contain the 1747 decree. The special recommendation to reduce the Seris and other tribes was the principal suggestion of the *junta* called by Fuenclara.
[54] Richman, 59–60, says of this decree that it "sanctioned for the

The decree was not without results so far as Sonora was concerned. José Gallardo was sent there in 1748 as *visitador*,[55] having to deal primarily with the question of conquering the Seris. Governor Vildosola had neglected work on the presidio of San Pedro (Pitiqui), and, as a result, that part of the province was in a defenceless state. Such, at least, was Gallardo's report.[56] Vildosola was relieved from office, being succeeded by Diego Parrilla who arrived in 1749. He was instructed by Gallardo to attack the Seri strongholds of the Cerro Prieto and Tiburón Island. The Seris were to be exterminated, or at least removed from Tiburón Island to the mainland, where they might the more easily be punished. Gallardo himself removed the presidio of Pitiqui to San Miguel de Horcasitas, regarded as a more effective site against the Seris. He also planned in 1749 to make explorations himself toward the Californias by way of the Colorado River, doubtless hoping to reach Baja California, as ordered in the decree, but was prevented from so doing by Apache wars. He left orders, however, that presidio captains should visit the more distant missions from time to time. In 1750 Governor Parrilla made his campaign against the Seris, and reported a complete success. Events were to prove, however, that the troublesome Seris were far from being conquered.

Further action was soon taken by the authorities in Mexico and Spain. A *junta* was held in Mexico in 1751, and a meeting of the Council of the Indies in 1752 to consider the affairs of Sonora. The documents from which these bodies drew their conclusions throw great light upon

reduction of the Californias the exact plan of Kino. Pimería Alta (the scene of Kino's labors) was to be occupied; a presidio was to be established on the Gila river; and Alta California was to be entered by way of the Arizona desert." This statement seems intended to convey the idea that the present American state of California was to be entered. The word "California" or the "Alta California" of Burriel may have misled Mr. Richman. There is nothing about an advance to Monterey in either decree.

[55] "Whenever unsatisfactory reports came in concerning any governor or magistrate, the India Council, or its higher representatives, at once despatched a visitador to hold investigation and submit the result, although at times he had power to carry out reforms and penalties on the spot." Bancroft, *Mex.*, III, 521. Employment of the words "whenever," "any," and "at once" may be objected to, but otherwise the above definition of a *visitador* will serve.

[56] C–286–87, 290–91.

the history of Sonora and northwestward advance, and some of them will therefore be dealt with at length. The decisions were based primarily upon five representations written in Mexico City by Fernando Sánchez Salvador, a captain of cuirassiers in Sinaloa and Sonora.[57] Four of these memorials are dated March 2, 1751, and are addressed to the king;[58] the fifth, May 15, 1751, is addressed to the *junta* in Mexico.[59] On the latter date Sánchez directed another letter to the king,[60] enclosing documents tending to sustain his proposals. Most important of these is the map.[61] It was considered to be of sufficient moment to be called to the attention of the foreign office, due to Sánchez's remarks about the proximity of the French, being forwarded October 5, 1751, to José Carbajal y Lancaster by the Marqués de la Ensenada.[62] Numerous other documents were used, both in Mexico and in Spain, but the Sánchez memorials and the map tell most of the story.

The first memorial urged that the same methods of government be employed in Sinaloa and Sonora as in other provinces, which could be brought about by secularizing the missions of Sinaloa where that step had not taken place already, and those of the Mayo and Yaqui districts of Sonora, putting religious instruction in charge of the secular clergy, and civil affairs in the hands of the government. The Jesuits might be used on the frontier. One of the principal reasons for this suggestion was that the Indians could then be taxed; as matters were, those north of Culiacán, Sinaloa, paid nothing. The second suggested that the unruly element of Sinaloa and Sonora be sent to the Tres Marías

---

[57] His rank appears in C–292. Although he is called Salvador in Bancroft, it seems better to say Sánchez, that being his *apellido*, or father's name. The documents usually refer to him as Sánchez, but occasionally as Salvador.

[58] C–308. See also C–307, the remitting letter.

[59] C–310.

[60] C–311.

[61] The date is given as 1757 in Torres Lanzas, I, no. 206, but it should be 1751. This may be proved, not only

by its presence in the Sánchez *expediente*, but also by internal ᴠvidence. Neither Tubac not Altar appears, but San Miguel (Horcasitas) is entered. The two former were founded in 1752, and the last named in 1751. Clearly, therefore, the map is of the year 1751. Although drawn by Don N. N. Anbile. Sánchez ought to be considered the real author, for the map represents his ideas, and was made, no doubt, under his direction.

[62] C–316.

The Sánchez Map of Pimería Alta and the Colorado-Gila Country, 1751.

Islands, and that a presidio be placed there to guard them.
Unruly whites, as well as Indians, should be sent there, but
Sánchez referred more particularly to the latter. The
Seris, Pimas, Apaches, and others were mentioned as
possible malcontent tribes, but the Apaches deemed most
apt to merit removal to the islands. The third recommended
better provision for bringing about agricultural development, and, even more, gold and silver mining. Missions
should not be allowed to monopolize the best agricultural
lands, and the price of quicksilver should be reduced, so
that mining might become more profitable.[63]

Sánchez's chief interest was in his fourth memorial, to
which the first three were but preliminaries. In this he
advocated establishing strong settlements on the Colorado
and Gila rivers, coming to this conclusion largely because
the French were said to be extending their settlements westward. They were in the vicinity of northern New Mexico,
he said, and did not need to advance much farther to reach
the Carmelo River on the Pacific Ocean. The proposed
settlements would serve three purposes: first, that of checking penetration by France to the Pacific coast; second, as
a base of operations for conquering the Indians of the
Colorado-Gila region; third, it would conduce to the occupation of "the richest and most abundant land that this
vast kingdom contains," for whereas Baja California was
lacking in water, the region to the north, according to
[González] Cabrera [Bueno], from the Carmelo to the south,
had a luxuriant growth of trees, and good sites for settlement, the Indians, too, being most tractable. Sánchez
referred to a westward branch of the Colorado flowing into
the sea between Monterey and Point Concepcion which he
believed to be the Carmelo. This should furnish an easy
route to the coast. For the better execution of his project
he recommended a new viceroyalty with its capital either
at San Juan de Sonora, or at some point in Chihuahua, with
jurisdiction over Sonora, New Mexico, Nueva Vizcaya,
and the regions of the Colorado River.

[63] The government maintained a monopoly on the sale of quicksilver. Cf. n. 26.

Sánchez's fifth memorial, addressed to the *junta* at Mexico, was similar to the fourth one to the king, but with some additions. Two hundred soldiers should be located on the Colorado, he said, and families sent there for the formation of three or four strong *villas*.[64] Sonora could not provide these settlers, as it needed all it had; they should come from Sinaloa, Nueva Vizcaya, and Mexico. Climate, rich mineral wealth, and numerous Indians were mentioned as attractive features of the Colorado River region. Once established there, communication should be opened with New Mexico by way of Moqui. Just as soon as peace was secure in the Colorado settlements, a detachment should be sent to explore a route to the sea at the point where the Carmelo emptied, and it would not have far to go, for the Colorado emptied in 33° 30', and the Carmelo in a scant 36°. A settlement on the Carmelo would be useful. The Manila galleon might have recourse to it in case of trouble, and news of its coming might be received much earlier than at the time. Such a settlement might also give information of the presence of foreign enemies in that neighborhood. Sánchez regarded his proposal as of particular importance as a means to check French encroachments on Spanish territory. He referred to the crafty methods of French conquest, as by sending to America their men and women of low morals to marry Indians. By such methods they had made the French language universal, and had conquered at such a rapid rate that they surrounded the Spanish possessions from Texas on the east to New Mexico on the north. In course of time they hoped to possess themselves of the Spanish colonies; they were already very near the Sierra Madre,[65] and if they ascended that, they would find the

[64] The *villa* in Spain was a town having special privileges, especially as regards civil and criminal jurisdiction, as distinguished from the *aldea* or unprivileged town. It goes back to the eleventh century, the *villas* or *concejos* being in the frontier districts facing the Moslems, privileges being granted as an inducement to settlement. Perhaps because the meaning of the word was so well understood, it is not defined in the laws of the Indies, but is merely distinguished from the *ciudad*, or city, by having fewer local officials (*Recop.*, *lib.* IV, *tit.* VII, *ley* II). Book four of the *Recopilación* has several titles which deal with the settlement and government of cities and towns in the Americas.

[65] That is, the "mother range," a descriptive term to indicate the principal mountain chain.

Pacific before them. It was quite possible that they might
come upon the sources of the Colorado or the Carmelo. In
this connection it was well to bear in mind a suspicious
French action in 1740, when ten Frenchmen with Indian
guides arrived in New Mexico near Albuquerque, saying
that they had come on foot from the lakes with the intention of making a settlement. It was likely, said Sánchez,
that they were a scouting party from a much larger force,
and that they hoped to discover where the Spanish were
carrying on their conquests.[66]

Among other documents before the Council in its consideration of the Sánchez memorials, were letters from the
viceroy dated July 10,[67] August,[68] and October 29,[69] 1751.
Those of the first and third date treated of hostile Apaches,
dealing for the most part with presidio and mission conditions in Nueva Vizcaya, but there were references to northeastern Sonora as one of the regions where the Apaches
committed depredations. The letter of August 6 pointed
out the Seris and their neighbors as the disturbing factor
that "for over a century" had proved a hindrance to further
exploration of the Gila and Colorado rivers, and to establishing communications between the Californias and the mainland. This obstacle was now of less account, thought the
viceroy, for by Governor Parrilla's campaign of 1750, the
Seris had been reduced in numbers to a thousand. In his
first answer to the Council, January 16, 1752. the *fiscal*,[70]

<hr>

[66] This may have been the event which influenced the royal decree of 1744.

[67] C–313–14.

[68] C–315.

[69] C–317.

[70] The *fiscal* was an exceedingly important official of manifold functions in Spanish administration. As referred to in this work the *fiscales* of the Council of the Indies and *Audiencia* of Mexico were officials to whom matters were referred for a report. The *fiscal* would draw conclusions from documents bearing on the case, summarize their contents, and give an opinion as to the course of action to pursue. In most cases that the writer has seen, although not in all, opinions of the *fiscales* were followed

verbatim, this being especially noteworthy in the case of the *fiscales* of the Council. The *fiscal* was a lawyer, but did not confine his advice to legal matters. It will be noticed that he had become something quite different from what the laws originally intended. The *fiscal* of the *Audiencias* of Lima or Mexico, for example, was supposed to be a kind of prosecuting attorney, having a special care for the royal interests in financial and legal matters as against possible usurpations by other officers of the king. By the close of the eighteenth century he had become in effect the first servant of the viceroy. The same thing had occurred in Spain, where the *fiscales* occupied a similar relation to the Coun-

José de Goyeneche stated that most of these projects had already been suggested by the Council on May 12, 1744, and approved by the king. Therefore no action ought to be taken until the decision of the *junta* in Mexico was received. But in view of the fertility of the Colorado-Gila country, the ease of reducing Indians there, and especially the danger from the French, he was of the opinion that Sánchez's proposal of conquest and settlement was of sufficient importance to demand the principal attention of the viceroy. The French seemed to be desirous of occupying a port on the Pacific, a contingency which must be averted. He approved of secularizing the missions, because the Indians had been gathered into settlements and converted, in which case the laws provided that secularization should take place, and that the Indians should pay taxes to His Majesty. In conclusion, he approved of the proposal to lower the price of quicksilver as an aid to the miners of Sonora.[71]

The fourth proposal of Sánchez came before the Council again in its meeting of March 13, 1752, to consider Sonora affairs. The Council thought that it would be quite natural for the French in their westward advance to descend the Colorado to the Gulf, and by its branch, the Carmelo, proceed to the Pacific. Once in possession of Monterey they would dominate all that coast of the Californias, and it must be remembered, said the Council, that Monterey was only 350 Spanish leagues from Acapulco.[72]

On May 15, 1752, Goyeneche delivered his second answer to the Council. Referring to the proposed establishments on the Colorado, he said, "The conquest which has been made of Tiburón Island, and the dislodgment of the Seri Indians [73] are of great importance, for by occupying, as they were, the territory through which the route to the Colorado River lay, they rendered it difficult to make settlements there, as appears from the map of Don Fernando Sánchez.

cil of the Indies. For their functions as enacted by law, see *Recop., lib.* II, *tít.* V, for the *fiscales* of the Council; and *Recop., lib.* II, *tít.* XVIII, for the *fiscales* of the *Audiencias.*

[71] C–325.
[72] C–335.
[73] The supposed conquests by Parrilla in 1750.

These natives having been suppressed, the way remains without hindrance." This conquest, along with measures that the viceroy had taken in Nueva Vizcaya would result in catching the Apaches between two Spanish forces,[74] thus not only checking them, but also making it possible to conquer, dislodge, or punish them. Thanks were due the viceroy for this achievement, but at the same time he should be requested to forward the determination of the *junta* with regard to Sánchez's proposals. Of these projects Goyeneche said that they "seem to him to be so important, especially that of the prompt conquest and settlement of the Colorado River, because of the grave damage that may be occasioned to the kingdom of New Spain and its provinces by any post of vantage that may advance the French nation, that it will be fitting to charge the viceroy to devote his primary attention to the conquest and settlement which Don Fernando Sánchez proposes, inasmuch as by the conquest and dislodgment of the Seri, Tiburón, Carrizo, and Salinero Indians the way to the Colorado and Gila rivers has become free."[75]

After quoting the correspondence leading to the decree of December 4, 1747, and citing two royal decrees of August 19, 1606,[76] with regard to making a settlement at Monterey, the Council pointed out the dangers that would result from a French advance to that port by way of the Colorado and Carmelo rivers. The French would then dominate the Pacific, and threaten Spanish trade with the Philippines. The question whether Spain should occupy Monterey was then considered. If done, Monterey would serve as a place of refreshment for the galleon, for it had a good port, the lands were fertile for every kind of crop, and good for cattle, and the natives were docile. It would also be a place of refuge in case of storms.[77] While these deliberations were going on, news was received from the viceroy which gave a new turn to affairs. On January 16, 1752, he wrote that the Pimas of Pimería Alta had risen in

---

[74] In that the Seris could no longer make a diversion.

[75] C–330.

[76] C–15, 16.

[77] C–335.

serious revolt in the preceding November. A *junta* held
in Mexico had decided to procure peace by despatching a
squadron of fifty men to that region, but with instructions
to deal gently with the Pimas, lest they form a pact with the
Apaches and Seris. Peace established, this troop was to
advance to the Colorado and Gila in order to open communication with the Californias.[78] This letter seems to
have been received at the same time with another by the
viceroy of February 10, 1752. The latter[79] enclosed a *testimonio* giving a full account of what had happened and of the
measures taken.[80] Commenting on these events the *fiscal*
recommended, June 26, 1752, that action on Sánchez's
proposals be postponed until Sonora should be restored
to peace,[81] and such was the decision of the Council.[82]

Consideration of the subject went on in Mexico, however,
another *junta* being held in 1752. Among the documents
considered was a memorial of Father Sedelmayr, June 25,
1751, signed also by other Jesuits of Pimería Alta. The
document recites that the Jesuits had become discouraged
because of the lack of attention paid to their previous memorials, but they were taking fresh hopes, due to the peace[83]
and to "news of the zeal" of the viceroy. Consequently,
they were urging an advance to the Gila and Colorado
rivers, a region of vast lands, mighty rivers, great fertility,
and withal, easy to govern. After reducing the peoples
there, they could proceed to other important ends, such as
the conversion of *superior California.*[84] Moreover, the

[78] C–324.
[79] C–326. See also C–327.
[80] C–321.
[81] C–334.
[82] C–335. This document is a long report by the Council of the Indies to the king, July 7, 1752, citing most of the documents mentioned above in connection with the Sánchez memorials, and stating the action of the Council. For a summary of proceedings to June 15, 1752, see C–332.
[83] Another reference to Parrilla's campaign of 1750.
[84] Richman quotes this document to show that Pimería was to be "a base of operations" not only to Moqui but also "northwestward as far as

Monterey." There is no warrant for this statement except the phrase *superior California*, which, as has been shown, referred to the upper part of the peninsula. Sedelmayr speaks of *superior California* as a sterile land, lack of provisions in which might be remedied by sending them *via* the mouth of the Colorado River. This then was the oft-mentioned plan of supplying Baja California by an over-land route. Besides, Alta California would not have been called a sterile land, because belief in its fertility was general. Finally, why send provisions from the Colorado-Gila country to Alta California *by way of the mouth* of the Colorado?

first-named reduction would be necessary before Moqui could be reconquered, besides which the Colorado-Gila lands were better and more populous than those of Moqui. The natives of these rivers desired Christianity, as had been made clear to Sedelmayr during his visit of 1744, and if they had missions among them, the Spaniards would soon get to know of other peoples farther up the Colorado. Perhaps they were not far distant from the most westerly conquests of the French, who were said to be seeking this same Colorado River. At least eleven or twelve missions would be necessary, because of the great number of Indians. There also should be a presidio of more than the usual number of soldiers, which should be located on the Gila, not far from Apachería, as a check against the hostile Apaches. This done, it might be possible in a short time to transfer the presidio of San Miguel de Horcasitas to the Gila, provided the Seris should remain subjected.[85]

On December 16, 1751, the Marqués de Altamira, *auditor* of the *Audiencia* of Mexico, addressed a voluminous memorial to the *fiscal* of that body with regard to this matter. It is especially noteworthy here as evidence that the attention of the authorities had been focussed upon the Colorado-Gila country. Nearly one-third of the memorial is concerned with a review of the frontier situation from eastern

[85] Sedelmayr and others to the viceroy, June 25, 1751, Tubutama. The signers and their stations were: Jacobo Sedelmayr, *visitador* of Pimería Alta, stationed at Tubutama; Gaspar Stiger [of San Ignacio]; Tomás Tello of Caborca: and Juan Nentuig of Saric. It will be observed that the surnames of these Jesuits are spelled differently than in Bancroft, with the single exception of Tello. The above is the way they themselves wrote them. Bancroft's surmise that Nentuig was located at Saric proves to have been correct.

This letter contains an intimation that Fathers Campos and Adam Guilg were among the Jesuits who engaged in northward exploration, a fact that the writer had not seen mentioned elsewhere. Cf. n 16, *supra*. Sedelmayr refers to the Colorado and Gila regions as places which by various journeys since 1694 Kino, Campos, Guilg, Keller, and he himself had known, explored, managed, and dealt with [*habíamos conocido, reconocido, manijado y tratado*]. Adam Guilg is the Adan Gil of Bancroft. At probably about the same time, although the letter is not dated, Father Felipe Segesser wrote to the viceroy, the letter being signed also by Carlos de Roxas, Nicolás de Perera, and José Fora, the last named not mentioned in Bancroft as among the Sonora Jesuits. This letter definitely includes Campos with those who made journeys to the Gila and Colorado rivers. The document, however, is little more than a transcript of the one written by Sedelmayr and the Jesuits of Pimería Alta, taking up the same subject-matter in the same order, but in less detail. Both documents are in Arch. de la Secretaría de Gobierno, Chihuahua, *Siglo* XVIII, *Legajo* 8.

Texas to Pimería Alta and Baja California. Concluding this part, Altamira said that it was necessary to consider this whole frontier as no less worthy of attention than the Californias and the region of the Gila and Colorado rivers. By paying attention to one part of the field as if there were no others equally worthy of consideration, or more so, would mean that such measures as might be taken in the matter of reductions would be defective, and that but little or no progress would be made. To the question of advance by way of the Colorado and Gila he devoted the remainder of the memorial. He recommended a number of missions and settlements, and a presidio in the Colorado-Gila region. These establishments would result in the conquest of the natives, would serve as a nucleus for an advance to the Californias, and in time might lead to the opening of communication with Moqui and New Mexico.[86]

The much planned advance to the Colorado and Gila did not come at this time. Much was done, however, which tended toward it, such as the transfer of the presidio at Pitiqui to Horcasitas in 1751, the founding of Tubac and Altar presidios in 1752, and the preparation of general campaigns against the Apaches along the whole northern frontier, all of which matters were related to the problems which produced the Sánchez memorials. The way was not clear for expansion of the quiet, normal kind. Sonora was a seething hot-bed of Indian war and attendant evils. Thus the Pima revolt may be regarded in a double light; as causing the postponement of an advance to the Colorado and Gila, and as hastening measures which would in fact conduce to that end. As these events relate to the subject-matter of the next chapter, discussion of them will be reserved until then. Enough has been said here to indicate the continuous desire of the government for an advance to the two rivers, showing also that it was not great enough to bring about fulfillment of the project, unless there should be some powerful impelling cause, or the way of advance be easy.

[86] In ibid.

CHAPTER III

OBSTACLES IN THE WAY OF AN ADVANCE, 1752–1765

THE revolt of the Pimas of Pimería Alta broke out in November, 1751, headed by an Indian chief named Don Luis. All of the missions, villages, mining camps, and ranches in the northwest were speedily destroyed. Governor Parrilla and the presidio captains rushed troops to the scene in 1752, and the revolt died as suddenly as it had begun. Two missionaries and perhaps a hundred other whites had been killed. In the next twenty years, plans for an extension of the frontier by way of the Gila and Colorado rivers were secondary to the question of establishing good order in Sonora, a necessary preliminary to further permanent advance. The principal prerequisites to good order were: an adjustment of the differences between the religious and secular authorities; the subjection or annihilation of the Seris, and the repulse of Apache raids; and a sufficiently great increase in the white population of Sonora to develop its resources, in order to render its retention permanent, and to ensure a commensurate return to the central government for the expense of its reduction.

One of the purposes of this chapter will be to show the status of these problems in the period elapsing between the suppression of the Pima revolt and the coming of José de Gálvez as *visitador* of New Spain. A second object will be to account for Spain's failure to cope with the situation. Third, it will be shown that plans for northwestward advance were at no time given up, although they failed to result in great accomplishment, for the same reasons as those mentioned in the preceding chapter.

Most of the missions of Pimería Alta were reoccupied in 1752, after the Pima revolt had been suppressed, but prosperity did not return. Decline was fostered by a bitter controversy that broke out between the Jesuits and Governor Parrilla as to the causes of the outbreak. Father Keller said that Parrilla was at fault for flattering Don Luis, the revolt following as a natural consequence of the latter's conceit. Parrilla claimed that the Jesuits had ill-treated the Indians intolerably oppressing them with work and punishments. Many Indians and white settlers, probably the majority, supported Parrilla's charges, although others took the Jesuit side, the arguments depending usually, perhaps, on the interests of those making them. Many of the Indians did not like the restraints of mission life; the whites wanted secularization, which would give them a chance to appropriate the mission lands, and virtually enslave the Indians; and secularization, if possible, was also in the interests of the government, as the Indians would then have to pay tribute. The dispute dragged on, resulting in many great *testimonios* that came before the Council of the Indies for consideration. Not until September 27, 1759, was the case declared officially at an end,[1] the Jesuits being exculpated.[2] Whatever may have been the merits of the controversy, the Jesuits became less and less influential in Sonora. Few neophytes were obtained from this time forth. Indian women and children, and old and infirm men resided at the missions, but others rarely came in, unless impelled by hunger or by fear of the Apaches. At other times they remained in the mountains, or aided the Seris in stirring up trouble.[3] Meanwhile, complaints against the Jesuits continued.

The Seris, as well as the Pimas, had given trouble in 1751, continuing from that time until 1771 in almost constant war with the Spaniards, taking refuge when hard pressed in the Cerro Prieto. Apache campaigns also occupied attention along the entire northern frontier from Sonora to Texas.

---

[1] C–460.
[2] C–459.
[3] Among documents that bear on the dispute arising out of the Pima revolt of 1751 are the following: C–322, 324, 326–27, 334–40, 345, 348–53, 356–65, 367–71, 379, 382, 384, 388, 393, 398, 402–5, 438, 440–41, 450, 453, 458–60.

Expeditions against the Apaches accomplished little, as they could never be brought to a general engagement. About the only result worth noting is the conclusion that Moqui might be reached by way of the upper Gila, if such a route were desired, a project considered in connection with the plans for conquest toward and beyond the Colorado and Gila. This conclusion was arrived at because the Apaches had blankets supposed to have been made by Moquis. Often the Apaches took advantage of expeditions against them to raid the country about the presidios, thus deprived of its usual guard. "It is impossible to estimate the damages suffered in Sonora," writes Burriel, "especially since the death of the brave Captain Anza, in villages, settlements, farms, roads, pastures, woods, and mines, many of which have been abandoned on that account, although very rich." [4] Even the mission Indians could no longer be controlled, the Jesuits fearing to discipline them, lest they provoke revolt. General lawlessness prevailed.

Internal conditions of Sinaloa and Sonora are well illustrated by the statistics of population obtained by Bishop Tamarón while on a diocesan tour from 1759 to 1763. At that time there were in the two provinces 32,000 of Spanish or mixed blood, and 31,000 Indians professing Christianity, of whom 25,000 lived in missions. There were fifty missions, most of them in Sonora. The number of unconverted Indians was very large, but no estimate of them was made.

The greater part of the white population lived in Sinaloa. White settlements [5] were the rule there, the exceptions being a few Indian villages along the coast, where there was not the inducement of mineral wealth to draw the Spanish settler. There were some considerable towns in Sinaloa. San Felipe de Sinaloa had a white population of 3500; Fuerte, otherwise San Juan de Montesclaros, 1886; Rosario 2459; San Sebastián 2500; Culiacán 2216; and

---

[4] Burriel, *Noticia*, II, 556.
[5] The term "white settlements" is intended to include all elements of the *gente de razón*. The "white settle-ment" of Mazatlán, for example, was composed of mulattoes. Cf. chap. I, n. 2.

Mazatlán 966. These places had nearly half the total white population of the two provinces. Secularization of missions had taken place in most of Sinaloa, although the Jesuits were more numerous than secular clergy, but they usually served as parish priests, the mission system prevailing but little. Much of this change came as a result of the Sánchez memorials, having occurred prior to the Tamarón visita.[6] There were probably not many unconverted Indians in Sinaloa, or if there were, they caused no trouble.

In Ostimuri, as that part of Sonora below the Yaqui was then called, conditions were almost as good as in Sinaloa. Alamos had a population of 3400 of white or mixed race; Bayorca 1004; Río Chico 1400; Trinidad de Plata 715; and Soyopa or San Antonio de la Huerta 300. All of these were mining towns. Farther north, in the mountain districts near the Sonora valley, there were a number of mining towns at considerable distances from a presidio, such as Arivechi, Sahuaripa, Nacori, and Arispe. In northeastern Sonora, where the Apaches were wont to make raids, most of the white population was grouped around presidios there and near by in Nueva Vizcaya, there being 484 at Fronteras. Near the coast, where the Seris and their allies were numerous, and precious metals not plentiful, there were no whites. The case with Pimería Alta was a little better, due to the existence of gold and silver. There were eight missions, Suamca, Guebavi, Bac, Saric, Tubutama, Atí, Caborca, and San Ignacio, and three presidios, Terrenate, Tubac, and Altar. Subsidiary to these were a number of visitas, villas, and reales de minas. In the mission districts there

---

[6] In addition to documents already cited in connection with the Sánchez memorials the following may be referred to: C–341, 348, 355, 379, 381, 383, 397. These documents are for the years 1753 to 1755, dealing with the cession of twenty-two Jesuit missions to the secular clergy under jurisdiction of the bishop of Durango. The Jesuits objected to the cession, saying that the Indians were opposed to it, and that they had threatened to withdraw to the mountains if deprived of their missionaries. The government overruled these objections, and the viceroy was able to write, March 9, 1755, that the twenty-two missions had been secularized. This relieved the government of an annual expenditure of over 7000 pesos, the amount required by the missionaries for wine, oil, and other articles used in administering sacraments, and rendered the Indians liable for tribute.

were 4223 Indians and 348 whites, the latter being at the mining camps of Guebavi, Santa Bárbara, Buenavista, Arizonac, and Santa Ana. At the presidios there were no Indians, but there were 1117 whites, including garrisons of fifty men at each presidio. All of the white settlements of Pimería Alta were within easy reach of presidios, without which they could not have existed.

From the above it will appear that Sinaloa had undergone adjustment to white rule, removing it from the status of a frontier province; that a great part of Sonora, including all prominent mining regions, except Pimería Alta and the northeast, was in a fair way to become adjusted; that northeastern Sonora, Pimería Alta, and the coast regions were far from such adjustment; that the line and progress of conquest depended largely upon the existence of mineral wealth. Thus it seems that the situation in Sonora was not hopelessly bad, if only the government would exert itself to conquer the Seris and repulse the Apaches, but this it did not do for a long time. As a result Spanish settlements were abandoned, and to many it seemed that Sonora might be lost. The authorities in Mexico and Spain were memorialized by a vast horde of officials and priests as to the most effective methods for saving the province. In 1763 Father Lizazóin reported that it was in a fair way to become depopulated, and urged steps to prevent it, laying stress on the mineral wealth to be obtained there, should good order prevail. He suggested two new presidios as additional checks against the Indians: at Guaymas against the Seris and Pimas, and at Babispe against the Apaches. The anonymous author of the *Descripción Geográfica Natural y Curiosa de la Provincia de Sonora*, writing in 1764, recommended that the Seris and Pimas Bajos be transported; mining and agriculture might then revive. Pedro de Aragón, September 6, 1765, recommended concentrating on Ostimuri, and establishing a presidio south of the Yaqui River. These three memorials were only a few out of many, and although similar views were held in high quarters, they probably exhibited more pessimism than the facts war-

E

ranted.[7] The official correspondence of the time shows that affairs were bad enough, but it was not so despondent in tone as were letters of the religious, and of private individuals.[8] It must be remembered that affairs were probably as bad, or possibly worse, along the frontiers of Nueva Vizcaya, where the Apaches caused far more trouble than in Sonora, the problem of restoring peace being one of a long frontier, and not of a single province. As regards the matter of a permanent advance to the Colorado and Gila rivers, the situation was worse in 1765 than in 1752. The other two objects of this chapter involve a consideration of the general policy of the Spanish government for the period under review.

The establishment of Bourbon rule in Spain in 1700, although carrying in its train a number of disastrous wars, was accompanied by sincere efforts for regeneration of the country. Spain's object in this period was not primarily one of aggrandizement, but rather to make herself so strong that she could ensure retention of what she already had. Subordinate to this was the natural desire for the recovery of what had been taken from her, and for the removal of certain onerous restrictions upon her freedom of action, as, for example, those resulting from the *Asiento* treaty with England.[9] At every turn in the accomplishment of these

[7] Yet, at a later date, in a private letter to his brother, May 29, 1767, Viceroy Croix wrote that Sinaloa and Sonora were almost deserted by reason of Indian invasions. If the Indians could be defeated, and the provinces repopulated, they would yield more treasure than the rest of the kingdom, he said, for they were the richest provinces in New Spain in gold and silver. Croix, *Correspondance*, 207. Conditions in 1767 were not materially different from what they were in the period covered in this chapter.

[8] The three memorials quoted are cited from Bancroft. Among other documents about internal conditions of Sonora are the following: C-495, 499, 501-3, 511-13, 518-21, 524, 527-28, 530-31, 546, 549-50, 560, 564, 569, 590, 596. These are for the most part official correspondence for the years 1761 to 1765, of governors Cuervo and Pineda, Viceroy Cruillas, and Arriaga, the *ministro general*.

[9] One of the results of the War of the Spanish Succession was Spain's grant of the *Asiento* treaty to England in 1713. By its terms British subjects were allowed to sell 4800 slaves a year in the Spanish colonies for thirty years. They might also send one ship a year of five hundred tons burden with goods for the annual fairs at Vera Cruz and Porto Bello. These privileges were used by the English as an entering wedge for smuggling. They were set aside on the outbreak of war in 1739, and at the conclusion of peace, England surrendered her rights for the unfinished term of the treaty (the four years lost by war), upon Spain's payment of an indemnity of £100,000.

policies Spain found herself confronted and threatened by
England. Five times, in little more than the first half
century of Bourbon rule, Spain and England were opponents in war.[10] Through violations of the *Asiento* treaty,
England was breaking down Spain's monopoly of its colonial
trade. English imperialism was a constant menace as
against Spain's retention of her colonies. British subjects
trespassed upon Spanish domains, as in the case of the
dye-wood cutters in Honduras, and were sustained by their
own government. Gibraltar and Minorca were held by
England, a standing affront to the national dignity of Spain,
and a danger to the peninsula itself. The British government supported Portugal in the latter's claim to the Sacramento region of the Río de la Plata in South America.
British vessels claimed a right to search Spanish ships on
the high seas, and even seized some of them.

One obvious way to a successful issue of these contro-
versies was the building up of a strong army and navy, but
this required more money than Spain's revenues supplied.
To get it Spain pursued two courses: the wise one of economic regeneration at home, so that, by attainment of greater
wealth, greater amounts in taxation might be levied; and
the unwise policy of bleeding the colonies, by exacting great
sums from them, without attempting in equal measure their
development. The primary intention in the latter case
seems to have been to get the greatest amount of revenue
possible, not ultimately, but at once, at least so far as was
commensurate with retention of the colonies. This is
not the place to treat in detail of the results of this policy,
temporary or ultimate. Suffice then to say that Spanish
revenues were increased, the economic wealth of Spain developed, and an army and navy created. But the need never
caught up with the danger. The resources developed under
Ferdinand VI were wasted by Spain's brief participation in
the Seven Years' War. Whatever funds Spain got, she
constantly needed more. It was for this reason that José
de Gálvez was sent to New Spain in 1765, for that vice-

[10] To wit: 1701-13, 1718-21, 1727-29, 1739-48, 1762-63.

royalty produced far more revenue than the other Spanish colonies.[11] More yet was wanted.

It is now time to consider how this policy affected the region of which Sonora forms a part. Materials have been found in the Archivo General de Indias by the writer showing the receipts and disbursements of the *Real Caja* (royal treasury) of Guadalajara for each year from 1743 to 1781. This was the principal *real caja* within the jurisdiction of the *Audiencia* of Guadalajara, and until the arrival of Gálvez the only one dealing with the region west of the central plateau of Mexico. Gálvez founded a *real caja* at Alamos, June 1, 1769.[12] Later there was another at Rosario. Figures of the *Real Caja* of Guadalajara may be used, although with reservations, owing to lack of information as to the extent of its jurisdiction and the inter-relations of different *cajas reales*, as some evidence that Spain did not make a supreme effort to put down the Indian wars. The means for so doing were at hand, had the authorities not considered other matters as of more consequence. For the entire period, 1743 to 1781, an average of 86 per cent of the receipts at the *Real Caja* of Guadalajara were sent to the *Real Caja* of Mexico, or in later years, to that and other *cajas reales* of the viceroyalty. Not only is this the average for the entire period, but about the usual percentage for each year. From amounts remitted, however, should be deducted sums sent back for maintaining the presidios of Sonora. This in some cases was about half of the total remitted to Mexico, but certainly after 1761 was always less than that, falling to a general average of about one-third.[13] Sums remitted to Mexico grew steadily greater. In the decade from 1743 to 1752 the average annual remission amounted to 222,663 *pesos*. In the next decade, ending 1762, remissions had jumped, despite disorder in Sonora, to

[11] Wilhelm Roscher, *The Spanish colonial system* (tr. ed. by Edward Gaylord Bourne. New York. 1904), p. 40.

[12] C–1271. See also C–1290.

[13] The annual cost of a presidio ranged from 18,000 to 25,000 *pesos*, but was in most cases about 20,000. In 1771 the annual fund for each of the six in Sonora was 20,665 *pesos*, except Horcasitas which got 24,065, the added amount being for the governor's salary. C–1760.

an annual average of 263,285 *pesos*. The very next year, 1763, the year of Lizazóin's despondent memorial, the amount sent to Mexico was higher than it had been in previous years, certainly since 1743, no less than 372,497 *pesos*. In the years that Gálvez was most prominent in his reforms of *real hacienda*, 1765 to 1769, it was more than that in each year, reaching the high-water mark of 477,209 *pesos* in 1766, a figure that was never surpassed in the thirty-nine year period considered here. From 1770 on, receipts were lower, though averaging well over 300,000 *pesos* a year, but Guadalajara was then sharing activities with Álamos and Rosario.[14]

Had these sums been applied for the protection and development of the regions from which they were collected, a stronger establishment or even additional conquests might have resulted. Probably, however, the greater part of the funds, after deducting the presidial *situados*, found their way to Europe. Certainly this was the case at a later time,[15] and it may confidently be assumed to have been so in the period under review. It is, therefore, a reasonably safe conclusion that Spain failed to cope with the situation in Sonora, because it would not go to the expense, or rather reduce its profits, in order to apply a remedy. There being no definite foreign danger from the direction of Sonora, no discoveries of unusually rich mines, and no man of such exceptional ability as to be able with the means at hand to bring order to Sonora, it was left without great assistance from the government in its problems of development.

Whether or not an advance to the Colorado and Gila

[14] For financial operations of the *Real Caja* of Guadalajara outlined above see *legajos* 104-3-9 and 104-3-21, Archivo de Indias, Seville. The writer has prepared a table showing results for the entire period from 1743 to 1781, which appears as Appendix I. Sample *estados* or tables for a single year, showing receipts and disbursements, item by item, will follow as Appendix II.

[15] Between 1785 and 1790 the average amount of receipts a year for the entire viceroyalty of New Spain was 10,747,878 *pesos*. The largest item of expense was the amount devoted to *situados* of presidios, 3,011,664 *pesos*. Yet there remained for remission to Spain, after deducting costs of carriage, 5,843,438 *pesos*, over half the total receipts. Fonseca and Urrutia, I, *Estados* 1 and 2, between pp. XXXVIII and 1.

rivers might have resulted, but for the Pima Revolt of
1751, this event did not cause the government to lose interest in the project. Investigations as to the causes of the
outbreak were often linked with questions or proposals
as to the advisability of an advance. The same subject
came up in considering Indian difficulties along the frontiers
of Nueva Vizcaya. Presidios were established in Sonora,
primarily with a view to clearing the way to the Colorado
and Gila; for that reason mention of their establishment
has been reserved for this part of the chapter.

On June 18, 1751, the viceroy, urged to this course by
Parrilla and Gallardo, authorized the transfer of the presidio
of Pitiqui to San Miguel de Horcasitas. Lands were allotted to settlers in hopes that the region might ultimately
be defended by its inhabitants, allowing the presidio to be
moved to a more advantageous site for northward conquests,[16]
but the hoped-for removal did not occur. In August of the
same year steps were taken to clear the way of Apaches.
The captains of San Felipe de Sinaloa, Fronteras, and
Terrenate were ordered to make a general campaign
against them.[17] In 1752 the presidio of San Ignacio de Tubac was founded, and a garrison placed at Altar which soon
became a presidio. Tubac, at least, was to aid against the
Apaches, and both were intended to serve not only as a
check against the Pimas Altos, but also as bases for extending the conquest to the Colorado and Gila, once the
Seris and their allies should be suppressed.[18] Campaigns
were also made in Nueva Vizcaya, and presidios founded
in accord with the general plan for crushing the Apaches.[19]
Even there, the ideas of Sánchez were operative, the object

[16] Referred to in Amarillas to Arriaga, Jan. 13, 1758. C–444. See also the voluminous *testimonio*, C–433.

[17] C–366.

[18] Anza is authority for this statement. Anza to Bucarely, Mar. 7, 1773. In C–2113. Bancroft has a reference to a presidio at Bayorca. *N. M. St. & Tex.*, I, 554, note 6. This would seem to be an error.

[19] The subject of these wars cannot be taken up here. The following is a partial list of the materials that might be used, over half of them being great *testimonios*: C–372–75, 377, 394–95, 399–401, 418, 420, 431, 437, 448, 451, 454–55, 477–78, 489, 493, 571–74, 597. These are dated 1754 to 1765, but refer to campaigns begun in 1751, as well as to those made between the above dates. They do not include some documents used in another connection in this work, but which also refer to the Apache wars.

being to defend the frontier against the French. All of
these activities seem to have grown out of the events which
produced the Sánchez memorials.

Sánchez's fear of a French approach to the Pacific by
way of New Mexico, against which the Colorado-Gila establishments were to be a check, seemed confirmed when
two Frenchmen were apprehended in New Mexico in 1753.
While this event was still being discussed, a French settlement on the Trinity River, Texas, was discovered in 1756.
French deserters from New Orleans, and French traders
from the same place were a source of worry. These events
were not regarded lightly, but occupied the attention of
the highest authorities in Spain, and were taken up diplo-
matically with the court of France. The captured Frenchmen were condemned to death, but had their sentence
commuted to imprisonment. Strict orders were given to
the viceroy not to permit Frenchmen or other foreigners
to enter Spanish dominions, and the attention of the governors of New Mexico and Texas was especially directed to
this injunction. The documents used on this subject run
to the year 1761, when the Family Compact between France
and Spain was signed. In 1762 France ceded its territories
west of the Mississippi to Spain, and its other continental
possessions, in the next year, to England. This, of course,
meant an end of danger from the French. As regards
northwestward advance it is significant that the Sánchez
memorials were used in dealing with these events; if Frenchmen were in New Mexico, that was regarded as threatening
the Pacific, and Texas was considered but a step from
New Mexico.[20] The direct heir of Sánchez's ideas was
one Pedro de Labaquera, but as his memorials dealt with
the whole question of northwestward advance, of which
fear of the French was but a part, and as they were
written as a time when the French were no longer con-

[20] As to French aggressions, 1753 to 1761, see C-344, 354, 380, 386, 389, 391, 411-13, 415, 421, 427-29, 434-35, 468-69, 472, 492, 496. Bolton, *French intrusions into New Mexico, 1749-1752* (manuscript), gives a summary of French aggressions not only for the region and period named, but also for the entire Texas-New Mexico frontier in the first half of the eighteenth century.

sidered dangerous, it is more appropriate to take them up in another connection.

One of the most important documents in the history of northwestward advance is the *Noticia de la California* of Father Andrés Burriel, published anonymously in Madrid in 1757. The body of the *Noticia* was taken from the manuscript of Father Miguel Venegas, written in Mexico, 1739. Venegas in turn had been indebted largely to the unpublished work of Father Tarabal.[21] Burriel began his work at Toledo in 1750, employing additional materials as well as the manuscript of Venegas, writing the important appendices, and making the map, which, like the book, is usually ascribed to Venegas. Early in 1754 the work was completed. Then followed a period of two years before authorization to print was granted, not only that of the government being required, but also that of the Jesuit order. Burriel, writing May 3, 1754, to Father Pedro Altamirano, the Jesuit *procurador general de Indias*, enjoined that his own name was on no account to appear, saying that most of the work was Venegas', anyway. "Aside from that," he added, "affairs of considerable delicacy are touched upon, and it is well that I, an employe of the king,[22] do not appear, while we do not know how they will be received." Many of these *cosas bastante delicadas* were stricken out in course of various official readings before publication; for example, remarks which seemed in any way to reflect upon the government for its delays or failures to execute royal decrees were expunged, to the bitter regret of Father Burrial.[23]

The book is in a sense a defence of the Jesuits, and a plea for the extension of their missionary field. Before it was published, many Jesuit missions of Sinaloa and elsewhere

[21] Tarabal came to Baja California in 1730 when thirty years of age. He was charged by the provincial with the duty of writing a history of the Jesuit missions of Baja California. That he did so is testified to, not only by Venegas, but also by Clavigero, who saw over twelve volumes of his manuscripts at the Jesuit college of Guadalajara.

Bancroft, *N. M. St. & Tex.*, I, 455.
[22] As an archivist in Toledo.
[23] For the facts of this paragraph, see Real Academia de la Historia, *Boletín*, LII, 396–438. Additional documents, 1754 to 1756, having to do with the grant by the Council of the Indies of leave to print, are C–387, 409, 416–17, 419.

had been secularized, as already noted. Competition of
other orders had to be met, and Jesuit mission work, just
then much criticized, to be defended. Whatever the ultimate objects, the arguments of Burriel were convincing, and
their effect upon northwestward advance was such, that the
book merits considerable space here.

The *Noticia* deals with Baja California, and is divided into
four parts, as follows : a description of Baja California and
its people; a history of the peninsula up to the coming
of the Jesuits in 1697, noting repeated attempts to settle
it, all ending in failure; a history of the peninsula, and of
related events occurring on the Sinaloa and Sonora coast,
from 1697 to 1752 ; and a series of appendices commenting
on documents relating to Baja California, with the idea of
showing why this "most disagreeable, barren, and wretched
country in the world" should be a matter of so much concern to the Spanish crown and to the Jesuits. Parts one and
two need not be considered here. Only a little need be said
of part three. The Jesuits had planted a number of missions in Baja California southward to the cape, and north
to a point between 27° and 28°, about due west of the
Yaqui River in southern Sonora. One project constantly
in their mind, as has been shown, was to advance to the
Colorado and Gila rivers, and there to meet their brethren
from Sonora, the Sonora Jesuits being possessed with the
same idea, and likewise entertaining projects of further
advance to Moqui and Alta California. The junction of
the Colorado and Gila may be said to have been the goal
of the Jesuits on both sides of the Gulf. So far as Baja
California was concerned, this advance was designed merely
as a means of preserving the peninsula, by getting the products of Sonora; the peninsula was not regarded as headquarters for general northward advance. The royal decree
of December 4, 1747, had furthered this aim of a connection
between Sonora and Baja California. Finally, says Burriel,
"On both sides, in Pimería and California, there are the
most ample gateways for spreading the gospel. To the
north side of both are vast lands, inhabited by infidel nations,

who never heard of the most sweet name of Jesus, through whom alone are salvation and eternal life." [24]

The introduction to part four is particularly important on the question of northwestward advance. It was because of the location of the peninsula, said Burriel, that the conquest of this barren land had been preferred to that of any other American country; if the peninsula were unoccupied, the whole western coast of New Spain, "from Acapulco to the Colorado River," would be unsafe. This was not due to any great danger from savages, but pirates might locate there, as in the past, and upset trade. Moreover, "What would be the consequence if some European power should erect colonies, forts, and presidios on the coast of California?" Then again, for the safety of any northward extension of the frontier the Spanish missions must be connected with those of New Mexico, and extended beyond the Gila and Colorado to the farthest known coasts of the Californias, that is, to San Diego, Monterey, and Aguilar's River in 43°. The Colorado and Gila and the lands beyond, especially Monterey and Mendocino, were too far from Mexico to be supplied by land; therefore, maritime communication was necessary. Thus the peninsula must be occupied, if further advance were to occur. Possession of the peninsula was also necessary for retention of the Philippines. They could not be held, were it not for the commerce between Manila and Acapulco by the annual galleon. The trade of this galleon would be attended with less loss of life, if there were some port in the Californias where the voyage might be broken. Equally important, however, was the danger to this trade, if a foreign nation should possess the Californias. The Russians had extended their territory eastward to the Pacific, and had even touched North America, as in 1741, when they landed in 55° 36'. If the Californias were abandoned, the Russians might be expected

[24] Burriel, *Noticia*, II, 563; *Natural and civil history*, II, 212. As an example of the translation in the *Natural and civil history*, compare the following with the translation given above. The author refers to infidel nations "who never have heard of Christianity, and the glad tidings of salvation it offers to the human race."

to extend their possessions to the southernmost extremity
of the peninsula. Similary, there was danger from the
English who had repeatedly tried to reach the Pacific by
way of a strait north of America, or from Hudson Bay, such
an attempt being made as late as 1753. Should they succeed, the Spanish dominions of the Pacific would be in
danger. Newspapers had told of an English project to
make settlements north of the Californias, by expeditions
coming from the East Indies. One had only to note how
the English took Jamaica, Georgia, and other places to
realize that they might do the same in the Californias.[25]

Burriel should not be construed as urging the substitution
of Baja California for the Colorado-Gila country as the base
for an advance to Monterey. Rather, he was thinking of
the direct sea route from New Spain to Alta California,
for the security of which the peninsula had to be occupied.
In speaking of the distance from Mexico as necessitating the
sea route, he must have had in mind only such things as
had to come from Mexico, notably manufactured articles.
Settlers (if desired), domestic animals, and food supplies
might reasonably have been expected to be procurable nearer
at hand, although the last named had in fact to come by
sea in later years. Burriel hoped to accomplish his aims by
extending Jesuit rule; it is unlikely that he contemplated
any such radical departure from Jesuit policy as would have
been involved in establishing presidios and settlements
under secular authority. It is clear too from part three of
his work that he favored the old Jesuit ideas of an advance to
the Colorado and Gila, and thence to Baja and Alta California and Moqui. The three last-named regions should be
regarded as ends of branch lines of northwestward conquest, looking back to the Colorado-Gila junction as a base.
Special circumstances, primarily fear of foreign colonization, led to the occupation of the two California ends before
the intervening regions, but that should not be allowed to
obscure the fact that Sonora was the real key to northwestward progress of a permanent nature.

[25] Burriel, *Noticia*, III, 1–19.

Burriel concluded his introduction by saying that his object in this fourth part was to show what was already known of the coasts of the Californias,[26] the intimation being that further exploration and extension of the frontier should follow. In quoting Walter's account of Anson's voyage to the Pacific, 1740 to 1744, during which Anson captured the Manila galleon and learned its route, Burriel used that event as an argument for occupying Alta California. Walter had stated that the voyage from Manila could be made in much better time by going north as far as 40° or 45°, instead of keeping south of 30°; by the more northerly course one could take advantage of the trade winds. Burriel agreed, but stated that it would necessitate a Spanish settlement at San Diego, Monterey, or Cape Mendocino.[27] Other considerations conduced to the same end. The Walter account was only one of many writings in foreign tongues, Russian, German, French, and English, mentioned by Burriel as having been published in recent years with relation to discoveries in the Pacific, or projects therefor.

Publication of the *Noticia*, 1757, directed attention more than ever to the Californias, and especially so, it may be assumed, because of the reception which the work got in foreign countries. A translation into English promptly appeared at London in 1759. Within a short time this was in turn translated to Dutch, French, and German in the years 1761, 1767, and 1769–70, respectively. Later there were yet other translations. The complacent view taken in the preface to the London edition might well have stirred misgivings in the minds of Spanish authorities. The reader will be able to learn, says the editor in his preface, "that the discovery of a northwest passage, is far less problematical there, in the opinion of those, who, from their situation, are the ablest judges, than it is here, and that the dread of seeing the English form an establishment in the

[26] In a letter of May 3, 1754, to Father Altamirano, he put it that his object was "to justify the expenses for the maintenance of California, which, wretched land that it is [i.e. the peninsula], are well worth while." Real Academia de la Historia, *Boletín*, LII, 403.
[27] Burriel, *Noticia*, III, 212–17.

remoter parts of this country, . . . is held by those who
have the best means of knowing, to be a very probable
thing. Lastly, he will see it made plain to a demonstration,
that while the Spaniards have the hard task imposed on
them, of settling, improving, and fortifying the very wildest,
and worst parts of this country; the English, if they should
ever think of making any attempt, may seat themselves in
a pleasant climate, fruitful soil, and in regions well peopled,
from whence they may, with certainty, command the most
valuable branches of commerce that have been hitherto
discovered." [28]   At the same time, reports began to come in
that the Russians were making discoveries in the far northwest. An account of these appeared in German at St.
Petersburg in 1758, in the third volume of Müller's, *Sammlung russischer Geschichten*. This part was translated to
English, and published at London in 1761 under the title
Voyages from Asia to America. A second English edition
appeared in 1764, and a French edition in 1766. Torrubia's
brief work in Italian, *I Moscoviti nella California*, was
published in 1759. Official reports of Russian discoveries
were forwarded from St. Petersburg by the Spanish ambassadors there, by the Marqués de Almodóvar in 1761,
and the Vizconde de la Herrería in 1764.[29]   It would have
been strange if the Spanish government did not feel a measure of apprehension.

Meanwhile, other individuals both public and private
had memorialized the government concerning conditions
in Sonora and projects for northwestward conquest, and
occasionally these were followed by action on the part of
the authorities. The transfer of Pitiqui to Horcasitas in
1751, the founding of Tubac and Altar in 1752, and the
general campaigns against the Apaches along the entire
northern frontier of New Spain have already been noted.
Father Altamirano, cognizant of Burriel's work on the
Noticia, and eager like him for an extension of the Jesuit
field of effort, wrote to the king in 1752 urging that more

[28] Burriel, *Natural and civil history*,
I, last page [unnumbered] of the trans-
lator's preface.
[29] C–442, 494, 545, 561.

effective measures be taken than had hitherto been the case for the reduction and conversion of the Californias.[30] Father Juan Antonio Balthasar, Jesuit *provincial* of New Spain, in a long memorial to the king, August 15, 1753, concerning the Pima revolt of 1751, had much to say about the general subject of further conquests. He gave an account of Jesuit labors in Baja California, Sonora, and the region toward the Colorado and Gila, referring to the Sánchez projects for an advance.[31] Viceroy Revilla Gigedo had written to the king on the same subjects a month before, July 3, 1753, laying particular stress on the Sánchez proposals.[32]

In this year the Seris were tolerably quiet; so letters were sent to Governor Arce y Arroyo (1753–55), asking whether the presidio at Horcasitas might be dispensed with. Arce reported to Mexico in due time, and his memorials were, on February 28, 1754, ordered sent to the *fiscal*, but were not in fact acted upon for a year and a half, due to a change of *fiscal* at this time. Arce was relieved early in 1755 by Juan de Mendoza. By this time the Seris were more troublesome, so that Mendoza wrote to the Marqués de Amarillas, successor of Revilla Gigedo, on August 31, 1755, asking permission to subject them. Permission was granted, and in the following year a campaign was undertaken. It was not successful. When the news came to Mexico a *junta* was called, which decided that San Miguel de Horcasitas should be retained, without diminution of its garrison, for the Seris were cutting every route northward, and needed to be held in check. Governor Mendoza was authorized to take fitting action against them at the expense of the royal treasury.[33] On February 15, 1757, Mendoza wrote three letters to Amarillas in which he told of the campaign against the Seris, urged provision for additional troops and presidios in Sonora, and advised an extension of Spanish conquest to the Colorado and Gila. In one of them he

[30] C–331.
[31] C–352. For the opinion of the *fiscal* of the Council of the Indies, see C–382.
[32] C–348.
[33] For the *testimonio* of the proceedings of the *junta* concerning Mendoza's campaign, see C–432.

reported having gone into the interior so far as to explore the banks of the two rivers, and stated that his campaign had involved an expense of over 3000 *pesos*. A *junta* was called to consider Mendoza's projects, and, mindful of expense, it decided against them, holding that the time had not yet come for conquest of the Indians of the Colorado and Gila, and that the royal treasury must not be burdened by erecting new presidios. Such was the situation when on January 13, 1758, Amarillas wrote of it to the *ministro general*.[34] The *expediente* was referred to the *fiscal* of the Council of the Indies, who on July 31, 1758, advised approving what had been done in the matter.[35]   The following year, September 27, 1759, a royal order approved the action of the viceroy and the several *juntas*, both as to the suppression of Indian wars in Nueva Vizcaya, and the handling of Sonora affairs bearing upon Seri wars and projects of frontier advance, — with one striking reservation. Despite the *junta's* decision against conquering the Indians of the Colorado and Gila, the viceroy should be very much on the alert, said the royal order, lest foreign nations approach that region as there was reason to fear that they might.   Even the least lack of care in that very important matter might result in the establishing of communications by a foreign power with the Colorado and Gila, and that would have fatal consequences to Spain.   The viceroy was instructed, therefore, to take all such measures as prudence might dictate, and to report the results of his action.[36]

At about this time, probably in 1760 or 1761, four interesting memorials were directed to the king by Pedro de Labaquera. From internal evidence of the documents it is clear that Labaquera was in Spain, when he wrote them, but he had long been a resident of New Spain, he said, having been in Nueva Galicia for twelve years as lieutenant

---

[34] C–444. The writer has seen no other reference to Mendoza's expedition to the Colorado and Gila. The Spanish in Amarillas' letter is *asentando haver internado hasta reconocer las márgenes de los Ríos Gila y colorado.* Judging from a letter by Anza to Bucarely, March 7, 1773 (in C–2113), there is room for doubt whether the expedition was in fact made. Cf. p. 153.

[35] C–449.

[36] C–461.

captain-general. One of the documents is a petition for
certain privileges, and the other three, which probably
accompanied the first named, are recitals respectively of
conditions at Cape San Lucas, at the Colorado and Gila
rivers, and in Apachería (the region northeast of Sonora),
with suggestions for their betterment. The effect of these
memorials is hard to determine, as they do not appear in a
file with other documents, nor has the writer seen any reference to them, but clearly they reached the authorities in
Spain; otherwise they would not have appeared in their
papers.[37]

In his petition, Labaquera referred to the *bolas de plata*
mines of 1738 as evidence that that part of Pimería Alta
must contain veins of precious metal, much of it in the
form of treasure, all of which by law belonged to the king.
He asked permission to explore the country around Arizonac at his own expense, and that a presidio be erected
there under his command, to be supported out of royal
duties from mines and discoveries of treasure. As recompense he wanted half the net proceeds of virgin silver,
or treasure, after the expenses of the establishment had been
deducted.[38]

With regard to Cape San Lucas, he stated that English
pirates landed there in 1686, a Dutch ship came in 1746,
and the Manila galleon always stopped there. In 1750
at that point Manuel de Ocio discovered a vein of silver
which for a time yielded well. The falling off, he thought,
might be more apparent than real, because of illicit arrangements that the settlers might have made with the galleon,
something that it was difficult to prevent. These mines

[37] The papers of *legajo* 104–6–13,
in which these memorials appear, are
for the years 1760 to 1768. The
latest date mentioned in the Labaquera documents is 1754, a reference
to the publication of the *Apostólicos
afanes*. This reference is made, not
as if to a new book, but casually, as
if it were already well known. Danger
that the French might come overland
to the Colorado and Gila and threaten
Spanish possessions is discussed in
one document, which could not have
been the case in 1763, when France
had lost her own colonies, and probably
would not have been alleged in 1762,
when Spain and France were allies in
war against England. Either 1760
or 1761 would therefore seem to be
the year in which they were written
and more likely the latter; lack of
action on them may have been due to
knowledge by higher officials that the
Family Compact had been arranged,
that treaty being made in 1761.
[38] C–483.

might be made a source of profit, but they were even more
a danger, serving to make Cape San Lucas a desirable conquest for foreign powers. Yet, in all of the Californias
there were but sixty soldiers, few of whom were at the cape.
Mineral wealth being there, it should be developed, if only
to cause an increase in population to such a point that Cape
San Lucas could be defended in case of a foreign attack.[39]

Of the Colorado River he told what was known as a result
of explorations by Kino, Sedelmayr, and Consag, and said
that further exploration was necessary, for three reasons.
There was reason to believe that the source of the Colorado
was not far from French territory, and if the French should
descend the Colorado, the possibility of further expansion
by Spain in that promising region would end. In the second
place, it should be ascertained whether the Colorado in
fact connected with a certain Río Amarillo, of which the
Indians told Sedelmayr; this might be an arm of the sea,
or a strait, and if so, it was important to know it, as the
English were reawakening to the idea of discovering a
northwest passage to the Pacific; precautions ought to be
taken to avoid dangers which were to be feared on that
account. Finally, an exploration would prove whether it
were desirable to establish a settlement on the Colorado as
a base for reduction and conversion of the Indians. The
expedition should be made in boats, which ought to proceed as far as possible, not only up the Colorado, but also
along such rivers, bays, or straits as might be found.[40]

The remaining memorial is in some respects the most
interesting of all, showing a keen knowledge of frontier
conditions, in accounting for the failure to conquer the
Apaches. The Apaches, when attacked, habitually retired
to the mountains which were inaccessible to the presidial
troops. This was due not merely to the fact that the
latter were cavalrymen, but to the nature of the soldiers
themselves. Most of them were mulattoes of very low
character, without ambition, and unconquerably unwilling to travel on foot, as was necessary in a mountain

attack. Moreover, their weapons carried so short a distance that the Apaches were wont to get just out of range and make open jest of the Spaniards. Furthermore, some presidial captains were more interested in making a personal profit out of their troops, arising from the fact that part of the latter's wages was paid in effects, than they were in subjecting the enemy, nor did the various captains work in harmony when on campaigns. Continuance of the Apaches in Apachería was in the highest degree prejudicial. Not only were they a hindrance to conquests toward the Colorado, and in the direct route between Sonora and New Mexico, but also they endangered regions already held by Spain, leading subjected Indians, either from fear or from natural inclination, to abandon missions and villages, and, whether in alliance with the Apaches or by themselves, to commit the same kind of atrocities as the Apaches did. Labaquera recommended that two hundred mountain fusileers of Spanish blood be recruited in Spain, equipped among other things with guns of long range, and despatched to New Spain for service against the Apaches. These men, under a disinterested leader, would quickly subject the Apaches, and might then be given lands in that region. Being of a higher stamp than the presidial soldiers they would be eager to develop their lands, and would be a permanent source of strength to that country.[41]

It seems natural to expect that official attention to projects of conquest in the Colorado-Gila region would be very slight after 1761 for a few years, despite Spain's intention to develop communications ultimately by that route with the Californias and New Mexico. From the time of signing the Family Compact in 1761 Spain was preparing to engage in the war against England, and in 1762 to 1763 she did take part. The alliance with France withdrew the pressure occasioned by the supposed nearness of the French to the sources of the Colorado; no other definite situation arose to compel an advance; and the actual, immediate interest of the war demanded all that Spain had. The same reasons

[41] C–486.

for an advance existed, but it could wait, as it already had done for so many years; true, the French danger was gone, but, as Labaquera pointed out, Spain had now to consider the English. Governmental attention to Sonora until 1765, if the documents seen by the writer are a fair criterion, directed itself more to questions of defence against Indian outbreaks, which have already been considered, than with aggressive or indirectly defensive measures of conquest. Some straws show that the wind still blew in that direction, as, for example, the satisfaction with which the news was received of the defeat of the Indians of San Luis Gonzaga, Baja California, in 1763, and the resultant progress in conversions;[42] similarly, the governmental inquiry of 1764 as to the status of the rental of pearl-fishing rights in the Californias.[43]   In February, 1766, Father Wenceslao Link of San Francisco de Borja, Baja California, set out with a large party from Borja with the intention of going by land to the Colorado River. He came within some twenty or thirty leagues of the river, as he believed; but the difficulties of the route, and the exhaustion of the animals forced him to turn back.[44]   These events were in line with Spain's ideas for protecting and developing the Californias. Of more consequence was the establishment, late in 1765, of the presidio of Buenavista, north of the Yaqui River, as an additional check against the Seris. At about this time, in August, 1765,[45] José de Gálvez reached Mexico, and took up his work as *visitador* of New Spain. The effects of his *visita* were to be of tremendous import; in one of its ramifications it led to real accomplishment in the long-planned northwestward advance. To the progress made in this matter under his influence, the next chapter will be devoted.

[42] C-533, 542, 558.
[43] C-540, 544, 562.

[44] Bancroft, *N. M. St. & Tex.*, I, 473.
[45] Gálvez, *Informe*, 118.   C-1834.

CHAPTER IV

ACHIEVEMENTS OF JOSÉ DE GÁLVEZ, 1765–1771

THE coming of José de Gálvez marks a turning-point in the history of northwestward advance. Prior to his arrival there had been nearly a century of memorials and plans, and something had been done to strengthen the line of advance already held, but beyond that not much had been accomplished. In Gálvez the long-needed, forceful, energetic man had appeared, and he proceeded to put into effect a series of measures, touching every phase of northwestward conquest, that were fairly bewildering both in number and results. True, his work was in large measure not destined to endure, partly because of his own mismanagement after he became *ministro general*. Furthermore, if the occupation of Alta California in 1769 be excepted, most that he did with relation to the proposed conquest was indirect, even though leading inevitably to direct action. Finally, his work most likely would have been in vain, had it not been for the exceptional ability of Viceroy Bucarely, the man who carried it on. For these reasons a detailed recital of his acts is unnecessary here ; they were rather of the nature of preliminaries to the real overland advance, although exceedingly important.[1]

From the Pima revolt of 1751 to the suppression of the Seris, twenty years later, northwestward advance by way of Sonora trembled in the balance. For the greater part of this period it looked as if the frontier might recede toward

[1] The need for detail is still less, in view of the fact that a history of the Gálvez *visita* by Mr. Herbert I. Priest-ley, Assistant Curator of the Academy of Pacific Coast History, is now in press.

Mexico, rather than advance toward Alta California, owing to the hostility of the Indians, and to the government's inability, or unwillingness, to spend enough to cope with the situation. That Sonora was not lost was due very largely to the efforts of the *visitador*, José de Gálvez. He it was who organized the expedition under Elizondo which in 1771 restored peace to the greater part of Sonora, by suppressing the Seris and their allies. The royal order for expulsion of the Jesuits, too, was carried out under his direction, in 1767, an event having important effects in Sonora. Gálvez also instituted a number of administrative reforms tending to the same end, although he was cut short in this work by illness. In the closing years of the Elizondo campaign rich mines were discovered, notably Cieneguilla in Pimería Alta, which meant a sudden increase in population. This gain in population seems to have been retained permanently and added to, because the mines continued to yield richly. Thus, Sonora, far from being a financial burden, was able to produce a surplus for the royal treasury.

The result of all these things was the temporary establishment of good order in Sonora, making possible a farther advance of the frontier. Only one prominent disturbing factor seemed to remain, — the Apaches had not been subdued. They affected but one part of the province, however, the northeast. Steps were taken, notably by the Marqués de Rubí, which led, subsequently, to the *reglamento* of 1772, a measure calculated to prove effective against the Apaches, although it did not in fact do so.

Meanwhile, plans for an advance of the frontier were not forgotten. The question of occupying the junction of the Gila and Colorado rivers as a base for approaches to New Mexico, Moqui, Alta and Baja California, was several times discussed, but was invariably postponed until the disorders in Sonora might be overcome. In all of these plans the route of advance was to be by way of Sonora; without aid from Sonora and the more populous provinces behind it, a permanent advance on a large scale was regarded as difficult or impossible.

The history of Baja California in this period does not indicate a change of base from Sonora to Baja California. The overland expeditions of 1769, and the use of the peninsula by Gálvez as a base of supplies for Alta California, represent only temporary ideas, — exploration of the land, support of the sea expeditions, and aid to Alta California until such time as a Sonora route should become possible. Meanwhile, the real base for both Californias was on the mainland at San Blas, established by Gálvez with that object in view. As noted before, the sterile peninsula represented the end of one line of advance, rather than a fresh starting-point, and so too in the case of Alta California. In the meantime, until overland communication could be established, both were dependent upon the sea route from San Blas for certain things that they needed.

The occupation of the Alta California extremity in 1769 was due in a measure to a fear of the supposed aggressions of a foreign power, Russian activity in the Pacific having been reported. The danger was not greater, however, nor believed to be so, than on many previous occasions. Moreover, Gálvez seems already to have planned expeditions to Monterey, before he had heard of the Russian aggressions. Thus, it is to the initiative of the *visitador*, impelled by permanent rather than temporary motives for such expeditions, that we may ascribe the occupation of Alta California, although it is probable that his action was hastened by the reports of Russian action. The sea route from San Blas was employed, because, for the moment, a land route was not available, and in any event occupation by sea would be quicker.

Meanwhile, important explorations bearing upon the selection of an overland route were undertaken by the Franciscan missionary of Bac, Father Francisco Garcés, but as they seem rather to belong to the subject matter of a later chapter, their discussion will be postponed. This chapter will deal, therefore, with plans and measures bearing upon problems that were in their nature preliminary to an overland advance to and beyond the junction of the Gila and Colorado rivers.

As the *visita* worked out, Gálvez was practically ruler of New Spain during his stay, rather than the actual viceroys, Cruillas and Croix ; certainly was this true in the case of the latter.[2] His primary object was to procure an increase of revenues to the government of Spain, but to accomplish this he employed constructive measures to develop the land, as well as the purely destructive ones of increased taxation. Until 1768 he was engaged primarily in matters of *real hacienda* in the central regions of the viceroyalty, although taking measures even then that affected the outlying provinces. In 1764, the king ordered the viceroy to devote himself to restoring peace in Sinaloa and Sonora. Thereafter, various *juntas* were held in Mexico, resulting ultimately, in 1768, in the sending of an expedition under the command of Colonel Domingo Elizondo. In the work of preparation Gálvez played a large and probably the most important part. He began as early as the close of 1765 to seek for funds other than those of the royal treasury, with which to finance the reduction of the disturbed provinces, the government being unable, or unwilling, to expend money on it. He wrote to Captain Lorenzo Cancio of Buenavista, saying that he could get nothing from the royal treasury, but that he expected to obtain contributions from merchants. In this he was successful, the *Consulado* of Mexico and merchants of the Jalapa fair contributing considerable amounts. Gálvez wrote again to Cancio, July 22, 1766, saying that he planned to conquer Sonora, and to establish thirty Spanish settlements in southern Sonora on the Yaqui. Replying,

---

[2] As regards Croix this may be deduced not merely from the official acts of Croix and Gálvez, but also from the former's private correspondence with his elder brother, the Marquis d'Heuchin of Prévoté, near Lille, France. In this Croix appears as an amiable man, not fond of hard work, nor markedly ambitious, although by no means inefficient. His favorable disposition to Gálvez also appears in several of these letters. In a letter of May 20, 1769, he said that he had so much to do as viceroy that he rejoiced to see the time pass, bringing him nearer the end of his term. Croix, *Correspondance*, 218. In a letter of January 25, 1771, he spoke of asking permission to retire from New Spain on account of advanced age, ill-health, and the immense work which he had to do. He had heard news of the possibility of war between France and England, and foresaw, much to his regret, a terrible increase in labor (*un terrible surcroît de travail*). *Ibid.*, 224. Other citations to the same work might be adduced in support of this estimate of Croix.

October 31, Cancio stated that the Yaqui region was less in need of settlers than other parts of Sonora. It would be better to reënforce old settlements or reoccupy abandoned ones. First, however, it was necessary to conquer the Seris and Pimas, who were the real stumbling-block in the way of progress.

Since 1766, wars with the Seris and Pimas had not been prosecuted with much vigor by either side. Everybody was waiting for the coming of Elizondo's expedition. The Indians were somewhat in fear of what might happen to them if they continued to resist. The white population, settlers, religious, and military alike, looked forward to the expedition as the solution of their difficulties. One of these elements was suddenly removed from the scene before the arrival of Elizondo. In 1767 the Jesuits were expelled from all Spanish dominions. This action came so suddenly in Sonora that, for a time, there were no religious to take their places. In the following year the Franciscans of the college of Querétaro took charge of the missions of Pimería, the Jaliscan Franciscans were given the rest of Sonora, and Sinaloa was put in charge of secular clergy. Henceforth, the religious were to exercise only spiritual jurisdiction. This was limited in the case of the friars to the Indians, the white people being subject to secular clergy, no matter how far away from the parish of their spiritual advisers. The new arrangement seems to have been very unsatisfactory to the clergy, who complained that the Indians were no longer amenable to religious instruction, and that the whites were too free from moral restraints. Yet, whether due to this change or not, substantial advantages seem to have followed. For a while at least, there were no more revolts by Christianized Indians, a matter in no small degree conducive to ultimate good order in Sonora. Again, whatever may have been the motives of the settlers in checking the powers of the missionaries, one great element of discord that had divided Sonora for years, strife between the religious and civil elements, was now tempered, though not removed. Whether the Indians themselves gained or lost

by the expulsion is not the concern of this work. There
remained the hostile Indians and the need for settlers.
Meanwhile, Gálvez continued to manifest interest in the
frontier provinces. He offered to go there himself, as soon
as the military expedition should be successful, and found
settlements.³ Arriaga asked Croix, July 20, 1767, to call a
junta that it might consider Gálvez's proposal.⁴ The *junta*
rendered its decision on January 21, 1768, holding that
settlements were necessary, not only in Sonora, but also
in Nueva Vizcaya and the Californias, if the best results
from the Elizondo expedition were to be obtained and the
frontiers extended. The work was too important to be in
charge of anybody but Gálvez.⁵ Croix was of the same
opinion,⁶ and Gálvez announced his willingness to undertake
the task.⁷

Croix and Gálvez had drawn up, independently of the
junta, a most elaborate plan for a separate government of
the frontier provinces. It was enclosed in Croix's letter of
January 26, 1768, to Arriaga, but although forwarded as his
plan, was also signed by Gálvez, who had shared with Croix
in drawing it up,⁸ and was probably the one primarily responsible for it.

The idea was not a new one. Several times in the preceding three decades similar plans had been proposed, in some
cases for the coast regions of Nueva Galicia, and in others
for the provinces of the northern frontier. In such plans,
foreign danger and the difficulty of administration from
Mexico, owing to distance, were the moving factors. It
came up in Nueva Galicia as a result of Anson's expedition
to the Pacific, 1740 to 1742, Anson having appeared off
that coast.⁹ The question was raised again in 1750. A

³ Referred to in Croix to Gálvez,
Jan. 23–24, 1768, A.G.I., 103-3-23.
⁴ C–842.
⁵ Plan of the *junta*, Jan. 21, 1768,
A.G.I., 103-3-23.
⁶ Croix to Arriaga, Jan. 26, 1768,
A.G.I., 103-3-23.
⁷ Gálvez to Arriaga, Jan. 26, 1768,
C–940.
⁸ Gálvez, *Informe*, 150. C–1834.
⁹ The Marqués de Aysa, president

of the *Audiencia* of Guadalajara,
governor and captain-general of Nueva
Galicia, was very active in taking precautions against Anson. He pointed
out the danger of leaving the Islas
Marías unoccupied, as they might be
taken by a foreign power, and serve
as a base of operations, or at least as
shelter, in which foreign ships might
await the coming of the Manila galleon. Sánchez and others later made

royal decree of October 31 in that year referred to the coming of two Dutch ships to Nueva Galicia to trade in 1747, and stated that it had involved considerable expense to bring the matter to the attention of the viceroy. The decree questioned whether the viceroy were not too far away from Pacific coasts to deal effectively with similar arrivals of foreign boats, and asked whether that part of Nueva Galicia should be put under a government by itself.[10] A *testimonio* on the subject was made up at Guadalajara,[11] but a new government was not formed. Sánchez's recommendation, in his fourth memorial of March 2, 1751, for a separate viceroyalty of the northern provinces has already been noted.[12] In December, 1760, a separate government of the frontier provinces under the jurisdiction of the *Audiencia* of Guadalajara was planned,[13] but it did not go into operation. We may now consider the Croix-Gálvez plan of January, 1768.[14]

The opening paragraphs (1–7) stated general reasons why the plan should be inaugurated. Although Sonora and Nueva Vizcaya were very rich, Spain had not preserved order in them, due to the excusable neglect of the viceroys, because of their distance from the city of Mexico, and the pressure of other business. The present viceroy, desirous of restoring prosperity to the distant provinces, as well as of enlarging the Spanish domain and extending the Catholic faith, was proposing a *comandancia general* with exclusive jurisdiction over Sonora, Sinaloa, Nueva Vizcaya, and the Californias, the *visitador* joining in this proposal. The latter had already been authorized to proceed to those

the same point. Aysa's efforts were not too greatly appreciated, the Marqués de Ensenada writing him, June 8, 1743, that the considerable expense which he must have undergone ought not to be repeated, except in case of extreme danger to those coasts, a danger which no longer existed in view of the retirement of Anson. In fact, however, Aysa's expenses had been met by private gifts, and not by sums taken from the royal treasury. For the correspondence on the entire affair, 1740 to 1744, see C–213, 217, 219, 224–25, 228, 231–32, 239, 241, 249, 254, 256.

[10] C–295.
[11] C–343.
[12] *Supra* p. 37.
[13] Referred to in the Croix-Gálvez plan. Cf. *infra* n. 14.
[14] Croix and Gálvez, Jan. 23–24, 1768, A.G.I., 103–3–23. Croix signed on the 23d, and Gálvez on the 24th. A translation made from a copy of a copy in the Mexican archives, or from a copy of the draft, appears in Richman. It differs in arrangement from the plan as sent to Spain, the one followed here, but otherwise is substantially the same.

provinces and reorganize them, with a view to facilitating erection of such a government as the one here set forth, in which the *comandante* was to be practically independent of the viceroy. If the plan were adopted, these vast, naturally rich provinces might in a few years equal or even surpass those of New Spain.

Next (8–11) came the inevitable plea for the project as a necessary safeguard against foreign attack. Such a government would avert dangers from foreign powers who now had the opportunity and the keen desire to establish a colony at Monterey, or at some other port on that coast. France and England had for two centuries been trying to find a passage to the Pacific from their colonies on the Atlantic. Russia was penetrating Spanish coasts in the northwest. Besides, the Spanish government knew that England would not rest, now that it had taken the colonies of France, until it should push forward its discoveries as far as the Lake of the Woods, whence a great river flowed westward. If it reached the Pacific, or should prove to be the Colorado, then the English were near New Mexico, and not far from the Pacific. The Spanish court knew too, from books published in Europe, how the Russians were encroaching upon Spanish coasts, they being already engaged in the fur trade on an island reckoned to be about eight hundred leagues west of the Californias. Again, since Anson's voyage in 1743, the English and Dutch from the East Indies had been acquiring knowledge of Pacific coast ports, especially those of the Californias. It would not be difficult for one of these three nations to plant a colony at Monterey, a port with excellent facilities for an establishment. Thus, Spain's possessions in the Pacific might be invaded and exploited as were those of the Atlantic.

Regarding projects of conquest (12–13), the memorial stated that Spain should take precautions at once by despatching vessels to Monterey to plant a colony there. Later, the government of the *comandancia general* could develop the settlement, and establish others on that coast, for there were good harbors there, and the soil was productive. A *comandante* on the ground might also secure a considerable extension of the frontiers of Sonora and Nueva Vizcaya in other directions.

Concerning the choice of a capital (14–16), the governor should not reside at Durango, as the plan of 1760 had suggested, because that was too far from Sonora, and farther still from the Californias, which at the time needed his presence; even in Nueva Vizcaya the place for the governor was at San Felipe de Chihuahua on the frontier, an important mining centre. The new capital should be in Sonora, and some central settlement ought to be established immediately on the Sonora frontier, at or near the Gila River. Meanwhile, the government should be set up at the mission of Caborca, that being farthest toward the frontier, or else at the junction of the Colorado and Gila rivers. It would then be almost equi-distant between the Californias and Nueva Vizcaya, enabling the *comandante* to travel to either with equal facility.

Then follow miscellaneous provisions (17–20). There should be a mint at the new capital, to avoid the necessity of transporting ores to Mexico. There should also be a bishopric there for Sinaloa, Sonora, and the Californias. That would advance the conversion of the natives, who were very numerous. The expense would not be great as the lands were fertile, and, if placed under cultivation, would yield abundantly. The royal treasury would be more than repaid, because of the mineral wealth of those provinces.

Coming finally to questions of government (21–26), — the *comandante general* should be independent of the *Audiencia* of Guadalajara, and have a salary of 20,000 *pesos*. This and the salaries of the *intendentes* of separate provinces, proposed in another plan, would be more than repaid, especially by the royal fifths on gold and silver, for these metals abounded in Sonora and the Californias. There would be a great saving in presidios, for the frontier settlements would guard against the Indians. The present presidio system was ineffective; for example, there were six presidios in Sonora which was invaded more often than any other province. This was because they were nothing but settlements for the enrichment of the captains and their backers. A garrison of five hundred troops, stationed at the capital in Sonora and in frontier settlements, replacing the presidios, would save so much that the salaries of the *comandante general* and the three *intendentes* could be paid, the frontiers in fact protected, and the Spanish domain extended. If more troops should be required for the advancement of conversions and discoveries, they would be easy to get, when the great advantages of these provinces should become known, for they were undoubtedly richer in mineral products than any that had been discovered in North America. The three *intendentes* of Nueva Vizcaya, Sonora, and the Californias were to be directly subordinate to the *comandante general*.

It is worthy of note that the land route by way of Sonora was regarded as the permanent method of approach to the Californias, the sea route being a temporary expedient. Northward advance by way of Baja California was not even considered. Archbishop Lorenzana, to whom the Croix-Gálvez plan had been submitted for an opinion, wrote to Croix, January 27, 1768, approving it. He reviewed frontier extension since the time of Cortés, and said that still more was possible, as nobody knew how long the Californias were. A *comandancia general* would certainly help to advance the frontier.[15] A *junta* had also favored establishing the *comandancia general*.[16] Upon receipt of the plan Arriaga forwarded it to the Duque de Alva, president of the Council of the Indies, asking his opinion.[17] Alva replied, July 13, 1768, approving it and calling attention to the importance of the provinces involved.[18] Meanwhile, he had drawn up an elaborate report, June 4, 1768, discussing the plan in more detail. He approved generally of proposals which involved an extension of the faith, but advised modifications of this

---

[15] Lorenzana to Croix, Jan. 27, 1768, A.G.I., 103-3-23. On the following day the Bishop of Puebla, to whom also the plan had been submitted, wrote to Croix saying that he agreed with Lorenzana.

[16] Croix to Arriaga, Jan. 26, 1768, A.G.I., 103-3-23.

[17] Arriaga to Alva, Jan. 26, 1768, A.G.I., 103-3-23.

[18] A.G.I., 103-3-23.

particular plan.   Settlements should be made in Sonora
to overcome the lamentable conditions there, and Monterey
should be occupied, but settlements on the Gila should not
be made unless at its junction with the Colorado.   He was
somewhat sceptical of the wealth of the provinces, thought
that the capital should be at Durango, and believed that a
bishopric of Sonora ought not to be established until the
settlements had been founded.[19]

Although the plan did not go into effect until 1776,
Gálvez's activities of 1768 and 1769 in Sonora and the
Californias were directed with a view to its enactment, and
but for his illness in 1769 more might have been accomplished
at the time.   Gálvez's immediate object was to pacify the
lands to be embraced by the *comandancia general*.   It
must be borne in mind that Elizondo's expedition and subsequent campaigns were directed to the subjugation not
merely of Sonora, but also of the entire frontier considered
as an unit.   This feature had been brought out in the decision of a *junta*, January 8, 1767, although the war in Sonora
had received primary attention.[20]   Troops raised in accordance with that decision, those destined to accompany
Elizondo, were enlisted for an expedition to Sonora and the
frontiers of Nueva Vizcaya.[21]   Gálvez, writing to Arriaga,
May 27, 1767, said he had received gifts of 300,000 *pesos*
for the campaign, but as he had learned that the war against
the Apaches in Nueva Vizcaya, Coahuila, and New Mexico
was less pressing than that against the Seris and Pimas of
Sonora, he would undertake to subjugate Sonora first.[22]
Croix's letter of July 16, 1767, to Arriaga is even more
specific.   He said that the expedition was designed to bring
peace not only to Sonora, but also to the other frontier
provinces, and that as soon as the first-named object had
been attained, it would proceed to New Mexico and Nueva
Vizcaya.[23]   Such, indeed, had been the orders of Julián
de Arriaga three months before.[24]   Other documents to the

[19] A.G.I., 103-3-23.
[20] C-735.   [21] C-712.
[22] C-811.   Acknowledged   by   Arriaga, Oct. 21, 1767.   C-880.
[23] C-840.
[24] Arriaga to Croix, Apr. 20, 1767.
C-775.

same effect have already been quoted in connection with
the plans of the *junta* and of Croix and Gálvez in January,
1768. In the following month plans were made for the
journey which Gálvez was to make to the Californias,
Sonora, and Nueva Vizcaya, he to visit them in the order
named.[25] Such too is the tenor of Gálvez's letter of February
26, 1768, to Arriaga, with regard to the mission with which
he had been charged;[26] and, similarly, Croix's letter to
Arriaga of February 29, 1768.[27] On May 18, 1768, the
Audiencia of Guadalajara informed the king that the
inhabitants of Guadalajara had made a free gift of 3000
pesos for the expedition to Sonora and Nueva Vizcaya, and
an exploration of the Californias.[28] On the same day,
Gálvez ordered Diego Fernández to visit the silver mines
of the Islas Marías, the Californias, Sonora, Sinaloa, and
Nueva Vizcaya, and to arrange their affairs in accordance
with royal orders.[29] While this order does not relate to the
expedition, it shows a tendency to treat the region involved
as an unit. Squarely on the point are letters exchanged
between Lope de Cuellar and Gálvez in 1769. The former
wrote, June 20, of his march to Janos, Nueva Vizcaya, and
gave his opinion that no peace should be made with the
Apaches, for as they occupied territories from the Gila
River to Texas, a treaty with one group would not be
recognized by the others.[30] Gálvez replied, July 4,
ordering Cuellar to continue the campaign against the
Apaches, doing what he could until Colonel Elizondo,
after suppressing the revolts in Sonora, might advance by
way of the Gila to his assistance.[31] A summary for the
Council of the Indies, September, 1769, of notices received
from Mexico refers to what Gálvez had done to subject the
Apaches, and punish the Seris, Pimas, and other tribes
in Sonora, Sinaloa, Pimería Alta and Baja, and the frontiers
of Nueva Vizcaya.[32] Other evidences might be adduced,

[25] C–954.
[26] C–956.
[27] C–961. Acknowledged and approved by Arriaga, Sept. 20, 1768.
C–1080. In reply, Jan. 3, 1769, Croix reiterated that he would put into effect the plans resolved upon in February, 1768 (cited *supra* n. 25). C–1167.
[28] C–993.
[29] C–994.
[30] C–1305.
[31] C–1317.
[32] C–1365.

but perhaps it will be sufficient to point out that in 1776 when accounts were made up, the expeditions to Sonora, the Californias (including the founding of San Blas and the occupation of Alta California), and Nueva Vizcaya, were treated as one general project, and not separately.[33]

The unity of the frontier had long been understood by the Spanish government, certainly since early in the eighteenth century. Between 1724 and 1728 the presidios of the entire frontier had been inspected by Pedro de Rivera, sent for that purpose as *visitador*. Teodoro de Croix's long memorial of October 30, 1781, cites a long list of documents from 1735 on, dealing with the question of placing frontier presidios with a view to the defence of the whole line.[34] Something approximating real accomplishment, however, began to appear in the Gálvez era, though independently of the *visitador*. In 1765, the Marqués de Rubí was commissioned to make an inspection of the presidios of New Spain.[35] He took up his work in January, 1766,[36] and did not complete it until early in 1768. With the exception of the Californias, he traversed the entire frontier from Texas to Sonora, even the New Mexico salient, making detailed investigations of each post visited by him, and inspecting lands with a view to a new alignment of the presidios.[37] In his report to Arriaga, dated April 10, 1768, he made recommendations for the better location of the presidios from Sonora to Texas, urging that a line of seventeen be formed, dropping seven presidios and two provincial companies then in existence.[38]

[33] C–3254, 3319.
[34] C–4430, at paragraph 417.
[35] The only establishments called "presidios" were those of the frontier provinces.
[36] C–622.
[37] Abundant materials for a history of the inspection by the Marqués de Rubí appear in my *Catalogue*. See especially C–731, which refers to fifty-one subordinate entries. Of these, one is Croix's instruction of July 18, 1771, for the formation of a line of fifteen presidios; another, a chart of July 23, 1771, showing the forces of the presidios at the time, and as they would be under Croix's *reglamento;* the other forty-nine are *testimonios*

relating, most of them, to Rubí's inspections of presidios, but including some reports of a more general nature. These are by no means all of the Rubí documents in the *Catalogue*. Among others the most important of a general nature, both sent direct to Arriaga, are the one cited in note 38, and a chart, dated April 3, 1768, sent by Rubí to Arriaga, specifying the number of officers and soldiers in the frontier provinces, the number of horses, the time when each presidio was founded, the annual expense for each presidio, and the authority approving the commission of each captain then in charge of a presidio. C–974.
[38] C–977.

This was eventually to bear fruit in the establishment of such a line, the decree coming in 1772, at which point the problems which occasioned the recommendation of a line of presidios will be discussed in greater detail. This is perhaps a good place to accord recognition to a man who has hardly received the credit that is due him. If more was accomplished in northwestward advance in the period of Gálvez and, later, of Bucarely than at other times in the eighteenth century, it was owing in no small measure to the man who was then *ministro general de Indias*, Julián de Arriaga. He had been promoted to the post in 1750 or 1751.[39] Gálvez, Rubí, Bucarely, and others carried out his ideas, and while they often acted wisely on their own initiative, he sustained them in their measures. While it will require much further work to determine his place in history, negative evidence of his importance appears in the change for the worse that occurred, certainly as regards the problems of northwestward advance, after his death in 1776. Yet he was succeeded in that year by a man who had been one of his most efficient workers on that very problem, Gálvez himself.

Gálvez's interest reached beyond the immedia   problem of establishing order in the frontier provinces. It is probable that as early as 1767 he had made up his mind to occupy Monterey, before the occurrence of the events usually alleged as causing the expeditions of 1769. The determination of this point is involved in another, the idea which lay back of the founding of the Department of San Blas. In the instruction which Viceroy Croix left to his successor, September 1, 1771, he said that Gálvez had some ships built to facilitate transporting Elizondo's troops to Sonora, and for that reason had established a shipyard at San Blas. The boats were used for the Sonora expedition, and later for the one which went to San Diego and Monterey.[40] Croix's instruction for a settlement at San Blas, January 11, 1768, stated that after having taken the measures necessary for

[39] Bernard Moses, *The Spanish de- London. 1914), II, 354.
pendencies in South America* (2 v.   [40] Croix, *Correspondance*, 289.

G

the pacification of Sonora and the other frontier provinces, it had been deemed indispensable to found a port for the advantage of boats employed on such expeditions and in commerce with that region, and for the preservation and advancement of the Californias.[41] Before this time, in December, 1767, we learn that Gálvez was already ardently at work on plans for the department, having charged one Rivero with the duty of establishing a port there.[42] Gálvez had come from Spain at a time when many books were being circulated concerning foreign interest in the Californias,[43] and the direction of his mind toward Monterey appears strongly in the Croix-Gálvez plan of January 23–24, 1768, noticed above. The *Audiencia* of Guadalajara in reporting Gálvez's passage through that city referred to his project of exploring the Californias,[44] which would indicate that Gálvez had spoken for such a project while there. It was not until the day after he left Guadalajara, namely, on May 5, 1768, while on his way to San Blas, that he received mail from Croix telling of Russian explorations in the Americas.[45]

In a letter dated November 31 [sic], 1767, the Vizconde de la Herrería had written to the Marqués de Grimaldi, Spanish minister of state, that the Russian empress was not desisting from her attempt to establish communications with the Pacific coasts of America, and was preparing expeditions.[46] The papers were forwarded to Julián de Arriaga, who wrote to Croix, January 23, 1768, that the Russians were planning to found settlements on the North American coast, or had done so already, as some believed. He bade Croix order the governor of the Californias to exercise vigilance to observe these attempts, frustrating them if possible.[47] This letter, it will be observed, did not order an expedition to Monterey, as has usually been stated, but it was sufficient to give an active man all the authority that he needed.

[41] C–930.
[42] Extract from a letter of Rada to Arriaga, Dec. 27, 1767, in C–908.
[43] Cf. pp. 60–61.
[44] C–993. The phrase is *Peninsula de California* which was habitually used interchangeably with the *Cali-* *fornias* to connote Baja and Alta California combined.
[45] Juan Manuel de Viniegra, June 10, 1771, Madrid. A.H.N., *Estado, Leg.* 2845.
[46] C–888.
[47] C–938.

Gálvez afterward said that Croix directed him to despatch an expedition to Monterey in the ships that had been constructed to carry troops to Sonora,[48] which statement is confirmed by Croix. Croix's letter is not at hand, but his instruction of 1771 to Bucarely tells the nature of it. He thought that the Russians might occupy Monterey, and directed Gálvez to make an expedition by sea toward the threatened port. In view of the difficulties of a maritime expedition and because of his desire to explore the Californias, Gálvez sent two expeditions, one by sea, and the other by land.[49]

Soon after receiving the news from Croix, Gálvez on May 13, 1768, reached San Blas, where he busied himself for twelve days establishing that department. On May 16, he called a *junta* to discuss the details of an expedition to Monterey, such as the boats to be used, the best season for a voyage, and the route to be followed.[50] On May 20, he wrote to Croix of his plans for the expedition. He had determined upon it as a result of the news of Russian encroachments, he said, and in pursuance of discussions that he had formerly had with Croix.[51] On the same day he recommended that care should be taken along the coasts of the Pacific, because of the pretensions of the Russians,[52] and urged that settlements be made on the Islas Marías, lest that group serve as a place of refuge for enemies' ships, in which they might await the Manila galleon, or whence they might attack mainland ports.[53] Of Gálvez's other acts at San Blas nothing need be said, beyond the fact that he put the establishment on its feet.[54] Croix heard from Gálvez in time to write to Arriaga, May 28, 1768, of the proposed expedition,[55] and the announcement met with favor, Arriaga writing to Croix, October 18, 1768, that the king was eagerly awaiting news of it.[56]

[48] Gálvez, *Informe*, 141. C–1834.
[49] Croix, *Correspondance*, 290.
[50] C–990.
[51] C–1002.
[52] C–1001.
[53] C–1000.
[54] For materials not only concerning

Gálvez's activities at San Blas, but also for its history in detail to the end of the eighteenth century, see my *Catalogue*. Several hundred references will be found there.
[55] C–1014.
[56] C–1100.

It seems clear from these documents that Gálvez intended, all along, at least to explore Alta California. It is equally clear that Croix did not contemplate anything more than a naval expedition at the time, and did not plan to occupy the province. The royal order did not even call for an expedition. Finally, the Department of San Blas from its inception served primarily as a supply-depot for the Californias, its relation with Sonora being of hardly any account in comparison. The Russian encroachments were simply in the long chain of permanent, continuing causes for an advance of the Spanish frontier, and were not reported as more pressing at this time than had been the foreign aggression of other periods. The real cause of advance was that a man of energy had appeared, José de Gálvez, who achieved what others had for a long time planned. Contemporary reports of aggressions, however, may have had the effect of accelerating his plans, but not more than that.[57]

The story of the occupation of Alta California need not be told, other than to review the outstanding facts. In 1769, five expeditions were despatched, two by land up the peninsula, and three by sea. A junction of four of them was effected at San Diego, one of the ships having been lost. From there the commander in chief, Gaspar de Portolá, proceeded northward in search of Monterey, and actually visited that port, but failed to recognize it from the description of González Cabrera Bueno. Pushing on, he reached and discovered San Francisco Bay, after which he returned to San Diego. The year 1769 saw a mission established at San Diego, and a garrison was left there which eventually became a presidio. In 1770, Portolá again marched north from San Diego. This time he convinced himself of the identity of Monterey, and a mission and presidio were

[57] It may be wondered why such a self-centred man as Gálvez certainly was should give so much credit to Croix. They were friendly, to be sure. Furthermore, he could not ignore or belittle the viceroy's part. Possibly another reason for his generosity was that it was not yet certain, when he wrote his 1771 report, that the Alta California establishments would be a success. Gálvez was capable of making himself appear to be the instrument of the viceroy in case of failure, while sure at the same time of receiving the major credit in case of success, as actually happened.

founded there.   Great hardships had been endured in making these small beginnings, and but for the capable preparations of Gálvez, and the courageous leadership of Portolá,
ably seconded by the efforts of the Franciscan missionary,
Father Serra, and of others, it is doubtful if the result could
have been other than failure.[58]   It had required a remarkable effort to gain a foothold at all, but even more striking
endeavors were to be necessary if the new lands were to be
held.   The battle for permanent establishments had only
begun.

As the Indian wars of Sonora rendered communication
with Alta California from that province temporarily out of
the question, Baja California became important for a time,
although in less degree than San Blas, as an aid to San Diego
and Monterey.   Events in the peninsula are also of interest on the old grounds of its defensive importance against
foreign attacks and of its own need of an overland supply-
route.   Moreover, it is certain that at this time Baja
California was believed to be very rich in precious metals,
an opinion prevailing that the Jesuits had wilfully concealed
the fact.   We may therefore pay some attention to Gálvez's
activities in the peninsula.   As regards its supposed wealth
we may note a memorial by officials of the *Real Caja* of
Guadalajara, October 8, 1765, which stated that there were
two mines in Baja California, and might be more, if quicksilver for extracting ores could be had, and if persons of
expert mining knowledge might be sent there.   The land
was worth being developed.   Gold mines were being discovered; pearls were found in many places; the soil was
fertile; and there were great numbers of cattle.   Yet the
inhabitants were for the most part Indians.   Eight years
before, in 1757, they had made the same suggestions to
Viceroy Amarillas, but got no reply.[59]   On February 25,
1766, Arriaga forwarded this memorial to the Council of
the Indies.[60]   Croix's letters to his brother show that reports

---

[58] An idea of the difficulties attending the Portolá expedition is given in
chapter five.

[59] C–593.
[60] C–628.

of this character were believed. In a letter of December 29, 1768, he remarked that the Californias, which had always passed for a sterile country, would be able from 1769 on to maintain themselves without costing the king a *sou*. Judge what a profit the Jesuits must have had, he said, and yet they had drawn a subsidy from the king for many years on the pretext of the land's sterility.[61] Again, January 25, 1769, he mentioned Gálvez's work in the peninsula, saying how pleased the king would be with that province, because of its pearls, gold, and silver, a wealth which the Jesuits had in great part concealed.[62]

Gálvez's characterization of Baja California,[63] and the measures that he took while there show that he had Burriel's idea of the importance of the peninsula from the standpoint of the defence of New Spain.[64] He seems to have held the same opinion about occupying the entire coast, including Alta California, as appears from some correspondence concerning the Bay of San Bernabé near Cape San Lucas. Miguel Costansó was sent there, and made a careful examination of the port in the bay, recommending measures for the protection of the site in a report of September 1, 1768,[65] accompanying it with a map of the bay.[66] Writing to Croix, September 8, 1768, Gálvez told of his own visit to Cape San Lucas, which he described as the key to Spanish possessions in that part of the Californias. He had decided to place a Spanish colony there, he said, and added that there ought to be a colony and presidio in every good port of the lands about to be reduced to Spanish control.[67]

Little need be said of his other measures in Baja California. Gálvez found the peninsula in a very bad condition. Its population had fallen away, until it consisted of but 7888 of all races. This necessitated reducing the missions from fifteen to thirteen, but a new one was added in the north, San Fernando de Velicatá, to facilitate expeditions to Alta

[61] Croix, *Correspondance*, 216.
[62] *Ibid.*, 217.
[63] Gálvez, *Informe*, 139–40. C–1834.
[64] In many respects, as, for example, in his desire to occupy Monterey, Gálvez seems to have been influenced by Burriel, though he later characterized the *Noticia* as grossly inaccurate. C–4189–90.
[65] C–1066.
[66] C–1068.
[67] C–1076.

California. For the same reason he increased the garrison
of the peninsula, and provided ships for northward voyages.[68]
Nor did the expected wealth of the peninsula materialize.
In Croix's instruction of September 1, 1771, to his successor,
Croix said that the Californias were not so rich as people
had believed. It would be necessary to encourage agriculture, mining, and pearl-fishing, and would be well to
employ men who could rouse the Indians from their habit-
ual indolence.[69]   In fine, Gálvez did not, and could not,
succeed in making Baja California a permanent storehouse
for advancement of the settlements in Alta California;
the need for an overland connection with Sonora was, if
anything, made only more evident. In Gálvez's mind, as
appears from his plan of January, 1768, Sonora was the
centre from which all lines of advance were to radiate. In
his own words, one of his reasons for going to the peninsula
was to occupy his time pending the advancement or conclusion of the campaign in Sonora.[70]   This view is confirmed
by one of his letters, written while he was yet in Baja California. Upon receiving notice of a royal order asking
reports as to the advisability of establishing a mint in the
frontier provinces, he wrote to Croix, August 15, 1768, that
he was in favor of it, but it should not be in Durango or
Guadalajara, as had been proposed, but in Sonora, so as to
be at the most convenient point of resort from the mines
of Sonora, Sinaloa, and the Californias.[71]

The great expedition under Colonel Elizondo had reached
Sinaloa in February, 1768. In May headquarters were
established at Guaymas, and Elizondo was ready to begin
the campaign. The military details need not be mentioned.[72]
The war centred about the Cerro Prieto,[73] and it was three
years before the conquest was complete, so vigorous was
the resistance of the Seris and their allies, the Pimas and
Sibubapas. The conquest was not as thorough, however

[68] Gálvez, *Informe*, 142–46. C–1834.
[69] In Croix, *Correspondance*, 291.
[70] Gálvez, *Informe*, 140. C–1834.
[71] C–1051.
[72] Heretofore materials for the study of the campaign itself have not been
available in great quantity, but by use of documents cited in the *Catalogue*
the story in detail may now be learned.
[73] For maps of the Cerro Prieto see C–1150, 1207.

as it has been regarded.[74]   Had it in fact brought lasting peace to Sonora, the history not only of that province, but of Alta California as well would have followed a very different course. But, taken with other events which will be mentioned presently, it seemed to be final at the time, and was followed by a few years of actual peace. An advance to the Colorado and Gila now appeared to be possible; the way had been cleared. Thus, the Elizondo campaign was of considerable importance as affecting the problem of communication between Alta California and Sonora.

Other events had occurred in course of the campaign that tended toward the stability of Sonora, and therefore toward northwestward advance. Gálvez came to Sonora in May, 1769. Two months later, he was stricken with a severe illness, but he had shown all his characteristic activity in the meantime. He established a royal treasury at Álamos, lowered the price of quicksilver, and did may other things calculated to improve mining, agricultural, and commercial conditions in Sinaloa and Sonora, as well as to provide revenue. He wished to secularize the missions of Sinaloa and many of those of Sonora, but, unable to obtain a sufficient number of parish priests, he gave over Sonora to the Franciscans of Jalisco and Querétaro, and Sinaloa alone to the secular clergy.[75] What he might have done, had he retained his health can only be conjectured, but it is likely that he would have taken steps looking to the long-planned advance to the Colorado and Gila. That the progress of the Alta California settlements was near to his heart is proved by the best of evidence. On August 22, 1769, he wrote to Croix about his illness, saying that he expected it to be his last, reiterating his feelings of personal friendship for Croix, and commending his subordinate officers to the latter's attention. Yet, the greater part of the letter concerns the expeditions to Alta California, Gálvez urging Croix, in what he believed to be his death-bed message,

[74] Bancroft, N. M. St. & Tex.,I, 680, says, "The danger of attacks from savages having been averted from most parts of the country, the people entered upon an indolent uneventful career." [75] Gálvez, Informe, 148–50. C–1834.

to aid and protect the new establishments that were being founded there.[76] Over two months before, June 10, 1769, he had proposed to Croix that the Indians of Tiburón Island be brought to the mainland, and reduced to a mission,[77] thus to remove another stumbling-block in the way of northwestward conquest, for the Indians had used this island, like the Cerro Prieto on the mainland, as a place of refuge, whence they might attack Spanish posts in Sonora. Gálvez later said that he and Croix had taken steps after the former's return to Mexico City to promote measures looking to the exploration of routes from New Mexico and Sonora to the Californias, but that both returned to Spain before they found time to put their plans into execution.[78]

Coincident with the termination of the military campaign occurred an event which served better than bullets to make for peace. While pursuing a band of Indians in 1771 a detachment of Elizondo's army discovered the rich gold placers of Cieneguilla, near Altar. Vast quantities of gold were found near the surface. There was an immediate rush to the scene, over two thousand men reaching there within a few months of the discovery. Official reports were quite on a level with rumor in their enthusiasm. Between April 24 and May 13, 1771, Elizondo[79] and Pedro Corbalán[80] wrote to Croix, and Corbalán[81] and Father Manuel Gil Samaniego[82] wrote to Gálvez of the immense wealth of Cieneguilla and of other mines discovered in the same neighborhood. Croix in turn, June 27, 1771, reported to Arriaga,[83] who gave orders to Croix's successor, Bucarely, November 23, 1771, that he should take measures to maintain the peace achieved by Gálvez and Croix, and to facilitate the successful operation of the newly discovered mines.[84] Unlike the Arizonac mine of other days, Cieneguilla continued to yield richly for a decade, and other mines in the neighborhood did so for the rest of the century and later. At about

[76] C–1356.
[77] C–1294.
[78] Gálvez to Arriaga, Mar. 8, 1774. C–2566.
[79] C–1725.
[80] C–1731.
[81] C–1735.
[82] C–1738.
[83] C–1752.
[84] C–1810.

the same time, other mines were discovered elsewhere in Sonora, that of San Antonio de la Huerta on the Yaqui being especially rich. This was the most flourishing place in the province between 1772 and 1776. The royal revenues from Huerta and Cieneguilla were sufficient at this time to support the province, according to Captain Anza.[85]

Statistics are not at hand to show the exact effect of these discoveries upon the population of Sonora, but Bancroft furnishes some figures worth noting. In 1769 there was a white population of 970 in all Pimería, exclusive of the soldiery, of whom but 178 were in Pimería Alta, as compared with 1315 in Pimería Alta alone at the time of Bishop Tamarón's diocesan tour of a few years before, showing how population had declined as a result of the wars. The discovery of the Cieneguilla mines in 1771 had brought a population to that one place of more than double the number for all Pimería two years before, and fifty per cent more than for all of Pimería Alta as it was in Tamarón's day. Even by 1770 Pimería had become a paying investment to the government. In that year revenues exceeded expenditures by $77,277.[86] Prosperity seems also to have come to the regions farther south, if amount of revenues is any criterion. The troubles of Sonora as regards Indian wars were not at an end, but from this time forth it seems to have had a sufficiently great population to ward off actual dangers, if not the fear of them.

With the pacification of Sonora, Elizondo and most of his troops returned to Mexico, abandoning the original plan for a descent upon Nueva Vizcaya. This was not because there was no need for such a campaign; on the contrary,

[85] Between January 1, 1773, and November 17, 1774, no less than 4832 *marcos* of gold from Cieneguilla were accounted for at the royal treasury of Alamos, from which the royal revenues amounted to 72,348 *pesos* 4 *tomines*. Cavo, 317. Mayer, I, 248–49. This is not an exact indication of the wealth of Cieneguilla. Fully a third part had been removed by robbery or other unlawful act. Cavo, *supra*. The greater purchasing power of money in that day must also be borne in mind. As late as 1792 both Cieneguilla and Huerta were yielding appreciable amounts in excises collected for the royal treasury, respectively 686 and 4186 *pesos* in that year.

[86] This probably means *pesos*. Bancroft, Mayer, and others frequently render *pesos* as dollars. A *peso* is worth half a dollar, but if purchasing value at that time were considered, a dollar would be nearer the mark.

along the whole line from Sonora to Texas, the Apaches were as hostile and bold as ever. Although Apache attacks in Sonora were confined to the northeast, that was sufficient, however, to interfere seriously with the best of the north-westerly routes, — by way of Tubac to the Gila, and down that river to the Colorado. Of the obstacles impeding an advance in 1752 all but the Apaches had been cleared away. But for them, granted need for a route and a leader of energy, the long-planned advance might now have been expected. The need had long been felt, and with the occupation of Alta California became more pressing. Moreover a man was to appear, a greater than Gálvez in many respects, and certainly a more noble character, the new viceroy, Antonio María Bucarely y Ursúa.

CHAPTER V

ALTA CALIFORNIA'S NEED FOR AN OVERLAND ROUTE, 1769–1773

THE general, long-operative reasons for an advance of the Spanish frontier by way of the Colorado and Gila rivers have been discussed in preceding chapters, and in the last chapter it has been pointed out that by the establishment of comparative good order in Sonora, such an advance had become possible. On May 2, 1772, Juan Bautista de Anza, captain of the presidio of Tubac, proposed that he be allowed to seek an overland route from Sonora to Alta California. On September 13, 1773, he was authorized to make the expedition, and early in 1774 he did so. Before tracing the course of official action on this proposal, it is necessary to take into account several other contemporary factors. These were: the character of Bucarely, the new viceroy; the condition of affairs in the Californias; status of the other frontier provinces; the events which led Anza to make his proposal; and the events tending to promote its favorable reception by the viceroy. The third and fourth factors will be reserved for the following two chapters. The fifth will be taken up in a measure in chapter seven, but so far as it related to danger of foreign aggression, its discussion will be postponed until chapter ten, where the subject is treated in detail. In this chapter some idea will first be given of Bucarely's character, although it is expected that the documents used later in this work will more amply show him forth. Evidence will be submitted also to show that Baja California could not be counted upon to sustain the new establishments, nor to serve as a fitting route for transmission of supplies brought there from San Blas, having much ado to take care of itself. Most of the chapter, however, will deal with conditions in Alta California.

Alta California's greatest need, if it were to be retained or its full possibilities developed, was a good overland route from New Spain. It lacked manufactured articles, food even (for civilized people could not live on what sufficed for the Indians), and perhaps most important of all, permanent settlers and domestic animals. There were no Spanish families, and no Spaniards, beyond an occasional straggler from San Blas, except the men of the garrison and the missionaries. There were few food animals, and fewer beasts of burden, not enough of either to supply needs. The province could be kept alive at great expense by receiving what it required by sea direct or by way of the peninsula, but either route was a long one, at the mercy of an enemy's navy, and impracticable (unless at great expense, by increase of the marine department) for the sending of families and domestic animals in sufficient number to establish the settlements on a strong basis. As a result the new establishments were maintained at a loss, not with the idea of developing their wealth in great degree, but primarily to prevent occupation by a foreign power. With settlements as weak as those of Alta California there was constant danger that the province might be lost. There were numerous Indians, unwarlike indeed, but showing scant desire for conversion to Christianity and subjection to Spanish rule. Nor were there enough Spanish troops in the entire province to have resisted a determined attack by a single ship's crew of a foreign power.

These dangers led to suggestions for their remedy by the internal development of Alta California, and by opening a route from Sonora. Thus, at least, the expense of maintaining the province might be reduced or might even cease; the Indians could be fed, that being the most effective means to their conversion and subjection; and finally, the province might become populous enough to resist internal revolt or foreign attack. Bucarely acted promptly to relieve the immediate needs of the colony, but its life was still hanging by a precarious thread until, in 1774, his measures of an enduring nature began at length to make their influence felt. One other matter in Alta California occupied the attention of the authorities during this period. A vast bay had been discovered in 1769 which might prove to be a good port. Unexplored and unoccupied, it might fall into foreign hands, and endanger the Spanish Empire. How good a port it was the Spaniards did not know, but deemed it wise to find out, and to possess themselves of it. Thus, the formation of establishments on San Francisco Bay, to which they were referring, was one of the aims of the period.

Antonio María Bucarely y Ursúa succeeded the Marqués de Croix as viceroy on September 23, 1771. Early in the next year the *visitador*, José de Gálvez, returned to Spain, leaving Bucarely in entire control. In him the viceroyalty was to find one of the ablest rulers it ever had. As concerns Alta California, if Gálvez founded the new establishments, Bucarely was to save them from failure. The new viceroy "was a native of Seville, and related to the most noble families of Spain and Italy, being on his paternal side a descendant from a very distinguished family of Florence, which boasted among its connections three popes, six cardinals, and other high officers of the state and church ; and on the maternal, the Ursuas were related to several ducal families. The knight entered the military service of his country as a cadet, and rose by gallantry and honorable service to be lieutenant-general. He had distinguished himself in several campaigns in Italy and Spain, in engineering work, and as the inspector-general of cavalry. Lastly, he was called to be governor and captain-general of Cuba, where he again rendered valuable services to the crown, which were rewarded with the promotion to the viceroyalty of New Spain.[1] Nor was this the only reward. He was

[1] Bucarely's name and titles, as they appear in a document of March 9, 1776, were as follows: El Bailío Fr D. Antonio Maria Bucareli y Ursua, Enestrosa, Laso de la Vega, Villacis y Córdova, *Caballero Gran Cruz y Comendador de la Bóbeda de Toro en el Orden de S. Juan, Gentil Hombre de Cámara de*

not only permitted to grant offices to twelve of his friends and attachés, a privilege that had been withheld for some years from his predecessors, but was given by royal order of January 22, 1777, an increase of $20,000 a year above what had been the viceroy's salary, making it $80,000, as a mark of special favor." [2] Numerous instances, besides those just mentioned, prove the esteem in which he was held, both for his abilities and for his characteristics as an honorable man. On one occasion the merchants loaned him $2,500,000 with no security except his word; at his death the king ordered that there should be no *residencia*, or examination into his conduct while in office, "a course" says Bancroft, "unprecedented in the history of royal representation." [3] Rivera says: "The period during which Señor Bucarely ruled was an uninterrupted sequence of peace for New Spain; it seemed as if Providence wished to reward the virtues of the viceroy by scattering upon his subjects everything that contributed to their well-being; he was one of those men whose memory will never be erased from the heart of Mexicans. His administration is a clear example of what this land was able to be, when a man of integrity and intelligence resolutely undertook the difficult task of developing its elements of wealth." [4] In fine, for ability and high character Bucarely stands out as one of the greatest men in the history of New Spain. Far from being a narrow bureaucrat, he was capable of a broad point of view which grasped both the patent and the underlying problems of the entire viceroyalty. A well-developed sense of perspective was one of his most marked traits, enabling him to see matters as they were, but not checking

S.M., con entrada, *Teniente General de los Reales exércitos, Virrey Gobernador y Capitán General del Reyno de Nueva España, Presidente de su Real Audiencia, Superintendente General de Real Hacienda y Ramo del Tabaco, Juez Conservador de este, Presidente de su Junta, y Subdelegado General de la Renta de Correos en el mismo Reyno.* Garcés (Coues ed.), I, 56. Although his name was written "Bucareli" in print, he himself signed this document and all others that I have seen "Bucarely." Coues holds that the "y" is a flourished "i," but as it certainly formed a perfect eighteenth century "y," I have adopted the form "Bucarely." Bucarely's full signature included the "Ursúa," after which he placed his rubric; thus there can be no confusion with the rubric in that case.

[2] Bancroft, *Mex.*, III, 370–71.
[3] *Ibid.*, III, 373.
[4] Rivera, I, 422.

him, however, from taking measures to circumvent ills which to him did not appear greatly threatening. His letters show him to have been a simple, straightforward, unselfish, clear-thinking, sincerely religious man, without a shadow of conceit or pretence, and even without great personal ambition except to perform his duty to the full. Finally, he was keenly interested in the problems that he encountered and was an indefatigable worker, and these facts, joined to the rest, make clear why he achieved such success in the face of difficulties that would have proved insuperable to a less capable ruler.[5] Between 1771 and the close of 1773, he got acquainted with conditions in the Californias, made timely remissions of supplies, and decided upon the main lines of his policy.

It is difficult for a Californian of to-day to think that his state could ever have been lacking in food supplies. Yet that was the case for a number of years after the occupation of Alta California in 1769. The land and climate were suited to agricultural wealth, but the richest land cannot be developed without man, animals, or machinery to do the work, or without a market for its products. In all of these prerequisites Alta California was ill provided or entirely lacking. As for manufactured articles the province lacked everything from a plough or a smithy's forge to a piece of cloth or a nail. The only remedy for this condition was by importation of goods, which in this period had to come from New Spain by way of San Blas.

Failure of the new settlements due to a lack of food supplies was narrowly averted at the outset. There is abundant evidence to this effect in the various official diaries and accounts of the 1769 expeditions.[6] One of the best brief accounts, however, is a narrative by Portolá several years after the event, being dated at Madrid, September 4, 1773. The official documents confirm the statements of the Por-

[5] My opinion is based upon a reading of several hundreds of his official letters, besides some private correspondence with General O'Reilly.

[6] Many of the diaries and contemporary accounts of the Portolá expedi-tion have already been published both in Spanish and in English translations in volumes one and two of the *Publications* of the Academy of Pacific Coast History.

tolá narrative, but the latter has the advantage of having been told without restraint. For that reason, perhaps, it gives a more graphic idea of the difficulties encountered than would be the case in the other documents, which, it must be remembered, would have been written in full knowledge that they might be read by Gálvez, who had set his heart upon this conquest, and would not be pleased with remarks that seemed to disparage it. The Portolá account is in the form of intimate remarks to a friend, the word *amigo* (friend) appearing several times in the document. Until they had passed the last peninsula mission, said Portolá, the expedition experienced no hardships worthy of notice, but he found it necessary to make provision for the future by taking nearly all the supplies that the missions had, just as Gálvez had done in the south in order to stock the ships. Yet Portolá lacked even sufficient provisions to reach San Diego, and had to resort to hunting and fishing. Furthermore, his party had to go without water for several days. Arrived at San Diego they learned of the horrors of the voyage experienced by those who had come by sea.[7] Portolá held a *junta* which decided to send back the *San Antonio* to San Blas for supplies and men, leaving the *San Carlos* and the sick, with a few others, at San Diego, while Portolá marched on in search of Monterey. Portolá took with him the small number of "skeletons" whom the scurvy, thirst, and hunger had spared sufficiently for the march. Alta California certainly made no appeal to these early explorers. All that there was to covet in that disagreeable country, said Portolá, ironically, was rocks, underbrush, and rugged mountains covered with snow. Moreover, he and his men did not know where they were, and their food supplies had given out. Thus, although they could not feel certain that they had reached Monterey, they were checked, not by the Russians, but by hunger, and resolved to return to San Diego. Upon the return they would have perished, but for eating twelve of

---

[7] Aside from delays from storms, most of those on board got scurvy, and over half of them died. Only two of the three ships reached San Diego; the third was never heard from.

H

the mules.[8] Finally, they reached San Diego *oliendo á Mulas*. The *San Antonio* had not yet returned,[9] but after almost nine months' absence it at length arrived. Most of the crew had died of scurvy, but despite that fact Portolá and his men received "very particular consolation" from the cargo of maize, flour, and rice. During the absence of the *San Antonio* they had had to subsist on geese, fish, and other food given to them by the Indians in exchange for clothing, with the result that some of the Spaniards had hardly enough clothes left with which to cover themselves. Now that provisions had come Portolá again decided to seek the port of Monterey. The *San Antonio* was despatched by sea, and Portolá led a force by land. After erecting the establishments at Monterey, Portolá took ship for San Blas.

Referring to the hardships that he had endured in Alta California, he remarked that the unfortunate Spaniards who remained there were suffering as much as he had suffered. In his opinion it would be virtually impossible to send aid to them by sea, and even more difficult to do so by land,[10] unless at the cost of thousands of men and immense quantities of money. The Indians were docile enough, but as for mines or other kinds of wealth, he and his men had not seen them, their first care being to find meat to keep from dying of hunger. Finally, even if Monterey were moderately well fortified, and if through strange caprice the Californias were coveted by the Russians, there were many other ports where they might land and establish themselves without any opposition.[11]

The crucial moment in the Portolá expeditions had come after Portolá's return from San Francisco to San Diego, prior to the reappearance of the *San Antonio*, from Jan-

[8] Without salt or other condiment, says Portolá, we closed our eyes and assailed the filthy mule (oh misery!) like hungry lions.

[9] It had sailed for San Blas in July, 1769, and was again at San Diego late in March, 1770. Portolá had returned from the north two months before.

[10] It is not clear whether Portolá was referring to the Baja California route, or the as yet undiscovered route from Sonora.

[11] The document appears in the Juan Manuel de Viniegra screed concerning Gálvez's acts as *visitador* in New Spain. A.H.N., *Estado, lejago* 2845. Both Viniegra and Portolá call it a conversation, and the former said that he wrote it at the order of Pedro Rada, a high official of the Indies department.

uary to March, 1770. A story has sprung up that Portolá might have abandoned Alta California but for Father Serra. The latter is said to have prevailed upon the commander to delay his departure, with the result that the *San Antonio* was sighted the very day before Portolá planned to leave. If this is true, then Serra is to be credited with having saved the Alta California establishments in their first hour of need. It seems probable, however, that this is an injustice to Portolá. There is no doubt that Serra wanted to stay, and that Portolá was not enthusiastic over the new country, but the commander in chief was a soldier whose every action in 1769–70 seems to show an intention to carry out his orders and hold the country to the last moment compatible with the safety of the forces under his command. In his diary sent back from San Diego in February, 1770, he tells of the lack of provisions, on which account he held a *junta* which resolved "in order to make it possible to hold this port longer" that Rivera should take a strong force and go back to Baja California, whence he was to return with the cattle intended for San Diego mission. "The remainder of the expedition," decided the *junta*, which must almost certainly have expressed Portolá's views, "was to hold this important port." [12] It is even more clear from Costansó's narrative that Portolá did not wish to abandon Alta California, except as a last resort. Speaking of the possibility of abandonment because supplies were so low, Costansó says: "lest he should incur such discredit, the commander gave orders that the captain of the presidio in California with forty men, should continue the march to the peninsula, to obtain from its missions all provisions he could, and to bring the cattle, which, as was said in the beginning, had been left at Velicatá, being too weak to continue the journey. This wise measure [not only] aimed at the present conservation of what had been acquired by reducing the increased number of consumers of the available provisions, [but also] provided for the future subsistence, even if the relief by sea — so important for the suc-

[12] Portolá (Smith and Teggart, ed.), *Diary*, in A.P.C.H., *Publications*, I, 81.

cess of the desired enterprise of Monterey — should fail to arrive. This detachment set out for the purpose mentioned on February 10, 1770."[13] Both accounts are confirmed by a writing which would certainly have insisted upon Serra's claim to the principal credit, if it had been regarded by anybody at that time as his due, namely, a long memorial of February 26, 1776, to the king by the religious of the Franciscan college of San Fernando, Mexico, telling of the achievements of the *Fernandinos* in Alta California from 1769 to 1776. The San Diego crisis is described in substantially the same terms that Costansó employed.[14] Finally, Palou's life of Serra, a work published in 1787, from which comes the story of Serra's part in saving Alta California from abandonment, is not in fact inconsistent with the accounts just mentioned, except perhaps by literary emphasis. A letter by Serra to Palou, February 10, 1770, is inserted in which nothing is said about Portolá's having an intention of abandoning the conquest, although abandonment is mentioned by Serra, without complaint, as a possible contingency. To be sure, he remarked that he and Father Crespí intended to remain in any event.[15] Then follows Palou's chapter telling what Serra did to prevent the abandonment of San Diego. Reduced to its essentials it amounts to this. Portolá set March 20 as the date for a return to Baja California in case provisions should not arrive beforehand, and from the date of Portolá's announcement all were talking of the expected departure. These words were like arrows in the heart of Serra, who not only was determined to remain himself, but is said to have persuaded Vila, commander of the *San Carlos*, to undertake a voyage to Monterey after the withdrawal of Portolá. On March 19, however, the long-absent *San Antonio* was sighted, and although it did not make port until four days later, all thought of abandoning San Diego was at once given up.[16] It comes to no more than that Serra himself

13 Costansó (Engert and Teggart, ed.), *Narrative*, in A.P.C.H., *Publications*, I, 149.
14 C–3156.

15 Palou, *Vida*, 90–94.
16 *Ibid.*, 94–97. Substantially the same account appears in Palou, *Noticias*. II, 254–55.

intended to stay whether the expedition should depart or not. Other than this the chapter is mainly psychological as to what was passing in Serra's mind, except for the Vila incident. In any event, what Serra and Vila or Portolá might have done is swallowed up in the fact that Portolá did remain. In fine, there seems to be no just reason for depriving Portolá of the credit that by common consent is assigned to the commander of an enterprise, unless there are circumstances which compel a different attribution. Serra and others played their parts with abundant courage — their fame is secure — but to Portolá goes the credit for holding Alta California in 1770, — and indeed, the province was saved by a very narrow margin.

The early settlements consisted of the garrison at San Diego, the presidio of Monterey, founded in 1770, and the missions, founded respectively at San Diego in 1769, Monterey in 1770 (moved to Carmelo in the following year), and San Antonio and San Gabriel in 1771. Conversions came very slowly, the friars assigning as one of the principal reasons the lack of food supplies, which were regarded as a highly effective spiritual argument. In 1772 provisions got so low that the settlements were again in danger, Monterey and San Antonio being almost wholly dependent on gifts of the Indians, and much the same condition existed in the southern missions. Fages managed to relieve the necessity by engaging in a three months' bear hunt. At length, two boats from San Blas reached San Diego. Monterey and San Antonio subsisted on bear meat for a time longer, but were presently relieved. The province had for a second time been saved by the timely arrival of supplies.

The founding of the mission of San Luis Obispo, shortly after the arrival of the supply ships, in 1772, seems to have had some connection with the question of provisions, this being in the region of Fages' successful bear hunt. The natives were so grateful for the killing of the bears that they willingly aided the mission with their labor and their seeds, and on the latter the mission was frequently dependent for food. In a letter of December 2, 1772, to Fages, Bucarely approved of the site selected, not only because the land was good, but also because of the plentifulness of game.

As regards domestic animals, perhaps more emphasis was placed upon a need for beasts of burden, but food animals were also in demand. Some animals were obtained at the outset from Baja California; in 1769, Rivera brought along two hundred head of cattle and nearly an equal number of horses and mules, but these were only for purposes of the expedition, and were to be restored to the Baja California missions. In the course of a year, more were taken, much against the objection of some of the Franciscans. On July 20, 1770, an official of the Franciscan college of San Fernando wrote to Croix that five hundred head of stock in all had been taken, and if they were not given back, the peninsula Indians could not be fed.[17] Two years later, the Franciscans gave up the peninsula to the Dominicans, but retained Alta California; so the animals were not returned. Enough of these animals survived the difficult northward marches to give hope for the future from their natural increase. The colony was far from being relieved of anxiety, however, and greater projects were hindered by the necessity of providing for bare subsistence. Under date of November 29, 1770, in his diary of an expedition to San Francisco Bay, Fages explains that he turned back without reaching his goal [Drake's Bay], because of his "anxiety . . . for the camp, the cultivation of the land, and the raising of stock."[18] For various reasons,[19] increase in the number of stock was slow. Nor could Alta California depend upon San Blas or the peninsula for its animals. The animals could not come by sea, because there were not boats enough, nor was there a sufficient marine establishment at San Blas to allow of that mode of shipment.[20] Baja California could not supply the more northerly province, for despite the fact that it had been settled for three-quarters of a century, it could hardly

[17] Richman, 400, n. 34.
[18] A.P.C.H., *Publications*, II, 152–53.
[19] For example, a lack of male animals.
[20] Some idea of the difficulties of the Department of San Blas in these respects will be given in chapter XVI.

raise enough animals or agricultural products for its own subsistence.

As the insufficiency of Baja California as a source of supply played a prominent part in the plan for opening a route from Sonora, it requires notice here. Detailed proof of the sterility of the peninsula is hardly necessary, as it is a well-known fact.[21] Diaries of the northward marches to Alta California show that even as a route, entirely aside from the difficult voyage across the Gulf, Baja California was not a satisfactory medium between Mexico and the new establishments. So barren and dry was this land that water was not to be had for days at a time on the marches, necessitating its carriage for both men and animals. Furthermore, the Indians of northern Baja California were hostile to the Spaniards, as is attested in various documents. One such is the memorial of February 26, 1776, of the religious of San Fernando. Some sites for missions between Velicatá and San Diego might be found, they said, if the natives could be made to maintain peace. From the first they had had little affection for the Spaniards, and had repeatedly shown hostility to parties passing that way. Despite the Indians' audacity no Spaniard had lost his life, but many Indians had been killed.[22]

For a general description of the peninsula a letter of Father Rafael Verger to Manuel Lanz de Casafonda, June

[21] One of the most notable works on the Californias from the standpoint of criticism of the Baja California part, is the *Nachrichten* attributed to Jacob Baegert, first published in 1772. Baegert had spent many years in the peninsula as a Jesuit missionary, and was inspired to write his own work in order to correct what seemed to him the flagrant errors of Burriel's *Noticia*, or rather the French translation from the English translation, which was the only edition that he had seen. Baegert's criticisms are most strikingly portrayed in his first appendix entitled *Falsche Nachrichten von Californien und den Californiern*, 313–31. His opinion may be summed up in his own words, as follows: "Aside from its pearls, its three different species of fruit, the fact that it nearly always has a clear, sunny

sky, and that in the shade at least it is not too hot but always very cool, California has pretty well nothing which merits to be praised, valued, or envied by even the poorest inhabited country on this globe." Putting it in positive form, he said, *California solo est arido, sterili atque deserto.* Baegert, *Nachrichten*, 313–14. Although published in 1772, it is doubtful if it had any immediate effect on Spanish opinion of the peninsula, not only because it might take some time for the contents of a German work to become known, but also because the works of Jesuits at that time, so shortly after their expulsion from Spain, would not be regarded by Spanish officials as trustworthy.
[22] C–3156.

30, 1771, may be quoted. The former as Father Superior of the College of San Fernando, Mexico, was the one to whom the Franciscans of the Californias were subject. Casafonda was at that time *fiscal* of the *Audiencia* of Mexico. Summing up the experience of his order in the peninsula, since entering there in 1768, Verger said that the Baja California missions never had been, were not, and never would be substantial foundations. Some, but for the impoverishment occasioned by providing for the expeditions to Alta California and other burdens placed upon them, might have been able to clothe the Indians, badly to be sure, and to give them food, but most of the missions never could have done so. The soil was fertile, yielding in some cases an hundredfold, on which account many had been led to believe that Baja California was a terrestrial paradise, when in fact it was a wretched, unhappy land. This was because there was very little good land, and because the rain did not come at the right times for crops. Thus, only such crops were raised as could be produced by irrigation, and as hardly any water was to be had, not much land could be sown. In many years locusts ate the entire crop.

Nor was Verger enthusiastic over the prospect in Alta California. The foundations there could on no account be approved, he said. They would result in the sacrifice of many lives, a loss of many ships, and the expenditure of an excessive amount of money, and perhaps nothing would be gained, despite what was said of the docility of the natives. The College of San Fernando had in no way agreed to founding so many missions at one time, and had sent missionaries only because compelled to do so. The whole undertaking was unsound, and unless God worked miracles, success could not be expected.[23]

In a long memorial to Casafonda of August 3, 1771, Verger took up, in more detail, matters concerning the missions of the Californias. As this is a good exposition of conditions, and as it tends to counterbalance the more optimistic (although not inaccurate) accounts of Father

[23] B.M., Ms. vol. 13974, Sec. G.

Serra, which will presently be quoted, it will be considered
here in some detail. The memorial drew in most part for
its facts on letters of Ortega, an officer at San Diego, and of
Fathers Crespí, Palou, and Serra, then in the Californias.[24]
When the Jesuits were expelled from Baja California,
said Verger, their place was taken for a time by military
commissaries who killed the mission animals and wrought
havoc generally. The situation became worse as a result
of the expeditions of 1769 to Alta California, many beasts
being taken which were never replaced. The Franciscans
of San Fernando had succeeded to the spiritual control of
the missions, April 6, 1768, and to temporal authority over
them by order of Gálvez, August 12, 1768. Gálvez had
also enacted other measures for the benefit of the missions
and Indians, but had subsequently revoked some of them,
and there was no certainty that others not revoked would
be enforced. For example, Gálvez had compelled Indians
to serve the king in salt mines and in other tasks without
pay, which was worse treatment than was accorded to
slaves; the latter, at least, got food and clothing. Verger
was telling these things so as to show that it would not be

[24] The letters referred to, all in B.M.,
Ms. vol. 13974, Sec. G, were the following:
    1. 1769, June 9, San Diego, Crespí
to Palou.
    2. 1769, July 3, San Diego, Serra
to Antonia Valladolid (?).
    3. 1769, July 3, San Diego, Serra
to Antonia Valladolid (?).
    4. 1769, Nov. 24, Loreto, Palou
to Juan Andrés.
    5. 1770, Jan. 10, Loreto, Palou
to Juan Andrés.
    6. 1770, Jan. 23, Loreto, Palou
to Juan Andrés.
    7. 1770, Feb. 6, San Diego, Crespí
to Palou.
    8. 1770, Feb. 9, San Diego, Ortega
to Palou.
    9. 1770, Feb. 10, San Diego, Serra
to Antonia Valladolid (?).
    10. 1770, Mar. 16, Loreto, Palou
to Juan Andrés.
    11. 1770, June 11, Monterey, Crespí
to Juan Andrés.
    12. 1770, June 12, Monterey, Serra
to Juan Andrés.

    13. 1770, June 30, Monterey, Serra
to Antonia Valladolid.
    14. 1770, July 5, Monterey, Serra
to Antonia Valladolid (?).
    15. 1770, Aug. 15, Santa Ana, Palou
to Juan Andrés.
    16. 1770, Oct. 10, Santa Ana, Palou
to Juan Andrés.
    Juan Andrés was the Father Su-
perior at San Fernando preceding
Verger; Antonia Valladolid was a nun.
The letters of Serra to the latter, and
the last two of Palou to Juan Andrés
are mere fragments. Crespí and Ortega
treat of routes, places, Indians, and
conditions generally in Alta California.
Palou deals with mission affairs of
Baja California, and especially with
Gálvez's measures. Serra discusses the
expeditions to Monterey, conditions in
Alta California, and prospects for
founding new missions, of which he
was earnestly desirous. This did not
accord well with the wishes of Verger
who says of Serra in his memorial of
August 3, 1771, *es preciso moderar algo
su ardiente Zelo.*

the fault of the college, if the missions should fail altogether, or not advance.

He then proceeded to complain of the scant funds assigned to the *Fernandinos* in comparison with those granted to others, despite the greater present needs of the Californias. Each Jesuit had received five hundred *pesos* a year, whereas the *Fernandinos* were receiving from two hundred to three hundred and fifty, the higher amount going to those in Alta California, but Palou had written that the pay of the last named was to be cut to two hundred and seventy-five *pesos*. Gálvez would claim to have founded many missions, and to have taken measures to insure their permanence. In a few years they would fail, and the missionaries would be blamed. The missions of Baja California were already as good as dead, and those of Alta California were missions in name only. The latter were assigned only a thousand *pesos* as the amount for their foundation, which was absurdly little (*más parece función de Dⁿ Quijote*). Yet this had to serve for everything, — tools, pots, buildings, cattle, and other things for places two hundred to three hundred and fifty leagues from one another, and eight hundred from Mexico, whence most things had to come, unless a way should be opened from Sonora, for there was nothing in Baja California. Along the Gulf of Mexico, where the problems were much simpler, a great deal more was assigned for founding missions, including an allowance for presents to the Indians.

Verger was opposed to the kind of establishments that were being made in Alta California, but made suggestions in case they were to be maintained. The good will of the Indians must be obtained, if they were to subject themselves to the Catholic faith, as, for example, by making promises to protect them against their enemies. This would require enough troops to enable the Spaniards to fulfil such promises, and to provide adequate security against reduced Indians. These were dangerous because of their free type of life, the bad conduct of Spanish soldiers, and the incitement of priests of native religions for whom the introduction of Christianity meant loss of position. Thus, a sudden rebellion might put an end to everything. If the Indians should not receive Christianity, more troops would be required. With this in view, articles to attract the Indians should be sent, as, for example, tobacco. Agricultural and pastoral laborers were needed, but this meant the sending of yet more soldiers to guard animals and crops. It would be well not to attempt a too rapid development at one time, because of the correspondingly greater expense and the greater number of soldiers and laborers required. The latter class was quite essential for the continuance of the colonies, the only alternative being to transport food supplies from Sonora.

Verger then gave instances showing the danger of revolt by the Indians, and made specific recommendations to meet that contingency. Between Velicatá and San Diego, the Indians had threatened the Spanish march, he said, and in one instance there had been a fight in which ten Indians were killed. They were not peaceful, as Serra had reported, but had not molested a later expedition, because they had learned of the Spanish establishment at San Diego, and were awaiting a better chance. On August 15, 1770, a revolt occurred at San Diego resulting in the loss of several lives. Serra reported that no Indians were killed, but in fact three were, and two died later. Previous to this the San Diego Indians had tried to rob the Spaniards. At another place, at the lake of tar [the La Brea ranch], two Indians were killed in an encounter with Spanish soldiers. What the San Diego Indians had done, others might do, and perhaps they might be even more likely to do so, as elsewhere in Alta California they were more able and proud than the Indians of San Diego. It was noticeable that the Indians of Alta California had not promised to obey the church, and only one village between San Diego and Monterey, a village near the lake of tar, had offered lands. There was doubt, even in that case, it being probable that the Spaniards misunderstood the Indians, as neither people knew the other's language. Thus, a greater military es-

cort for the missions was necessary, the presidios of San
Diego and Monterey should be maintained, and another in
between would be eminently desirable. As it was, there
were but eighteen soldiers at Monterey of whom only the
seven *soldados de cuera* could take the field. There were
twenty-eight *soldados de cuera* at San Diego, none too many
because of the cows and mules there to be guarded. The
mission of San Diego was already in its third year, but, as
Father Paterna had written to Verger, it was not yet worthy
of being called a mission. As for five missions that had
been ordered erected between Velicatá and San Diego,
nothing had been done, for, *¡gracias á Dios!* there were no
soldiers, mules, or horses, for them, and Palou had written
that there were no mules in Baja California to carry them
provisions.

Verger recognized that in accordance with the royal decree of October 15, 1733, founding the college, the College
of San Fernando was obliged to send missionaries at command. He was merely recording his opinion that the
present settlements were injudicious, and that not so many
missionaries should be sent as Gálvez had asked for, namely
forty, because it was inadvisable to found so many missions
at one time, in view of the unwillingness of the Indians to
accept Christianity. He was opposed to wasting royal
funds or pious gifts under the gilded title of propagating
the faith and extending the king's domain. It was well
enough to found missions, but it ought to be done with
an understanding of the meaning of the verb to found,
which did not mean to paint pretty pictures (*pintar per-
spectivas*). It should not be said, however, that the college did not want to spread the faith ; on the contrary, its
missionaries had gone forth to their unspeakable labors
rejoicing.[25]

Several other letters of Verger to Casafonda may be
cited as cumulative evidence of his point of view, based
upon letters received from missionaries in the Californias.
On August 27, 1771, he laid renewed emphasis on the cost

25 B.M., Ms. vol. 13974, Sec. G.

in boats and men for maintaining the Alta California establishments. Voyages to San Diego and Monterey were exceedingly difficult because the winds were usually contrary, and because of the danger of shipwreck on the many uncharted rocks and islets. Crews were wont to get sick, and skilled navigators were few; if the pilot got sick, there might be no one to take his place. The short voyage to Baja California was also an exceedingly hard one, because of the storms in the Gulf. In that same year a sloop and four launches had been lost, and the *San Carlos*, which left San Blas on February 2, had not reached Loreto by June 29, and might prove to have been lost. Unless the king had special reasons for establishments at San Diego and Monterey, it would be better to let the conquest proceed at the normal pace.[26]

Writing next day, Verger said that the missions in the Californias were all "appearances" without solid foundation, the mere shadow of great works, and afterward, when by their failure the truth should become known, blame would be cast upon the missionaries, who would be charged with the responsibility therefor. The rest of this letter concerned Baja California, treating graphically of the status of the missions, the wretchedness of the Indians, the failure of crops due to locusts, the lack of animals, and want of church utensils. Matters were better under the Jesuits, he said, because the government supported them better than it was then supporting the *Fernandinos*.[27]

On September 27, 1771, Verger wrote that, contrary to what had been alleged, his college would welcome a grant of missions in Baja California to the Dominicans, for the field was too large for the *Fernandinos* alone. All that he asked was that the division be made in such a way as not to hinder the communication of *Fernandino* missions with Sonora, and that a separate route for spiritual conquest be assigned to each order. Verger was beginning to believe, due to the continued docility of the natives, that the Alta California missions might be rendered permanent, although

---

[26] B.M., Ms. vol. 13974, Sec. G.   [27] *Ibid.*

he was unwilling to put too much faith in Indian peaceful-
ness. The land seemed to be good. Monterey, however,
had proved to be, far from the excellent port it had been
reputed, hardly a port at all. Similarly, the wealth of
Baja California in pearls had been greatly overrated.[28]

In Palou's *Noticias* there is printed a memorial of December, 1771, by Verger to Bucarely concerning the needs
of Alta California. Its most notable suggestions were that
the mule drove be increased, so that Alta California could
be supplied with provisions from Baja California or Sonora
in case of need, and that two boats with provisions for the
presidios and missions for a year and a half should be sent
forthwith. It also pointed out the lack of laborers, urging
that converted Indians be sent to work on the lands, and
to assist in tasks at the missions. Bucarely replied that he
would take fitting action on Verger's requests.[29]

In his letter of January 23, 1772, Verger spoke of desertions by soldiers of San Diego as threatening the continuance of that settlement, although in these instances the
deserters had returned. The *San Carlos* had at length
reached Loreto on August 23, after a voyage of nearly seven
months from San Blas. It had been blown nearly to Panamá by storms. The proper season for voyages was June
to September, or at most May to October. He reiterated
his support of the royal order for placing the Dominicans
in the peninsula, saying that Gálvez and Croix were the
ones who objected to that course, not the college.[30]

Such were the views of Verger, which may be regarded
as accurately representing affairs in the Californias. Even
his pessimism was warranted by the conditions, despite
the fact that he was to prove a false prophet. It should
be noted that Baja California could not be looked to for
supplies of any sort for the new establishments. On the
other hand, Verger several times mentioned the possibility
of a supply route from Sonora as a solution of the ills of
the Californias. Another feature worthy of emphasis is

28 B.M., Ms. vol. 13974, Sec. G.   30 B.M., Ms. vol. 13974, Sec. G.
29 Palou, *Noticias*, I, 127–31.

his reference to the cost of maintaining Alta California, especially the cost in boats. It was this that held back the advancement of the conquest to a permanent basis, necessitating the finding of land routes. Attention may also be called to his remarks reflecting upon the Indian reputation for docility and the consequent need for soldiers, an important factor calling for the opening of an overland route for a satisfactory solution. These remarks are strikingly confirmed in two documents of later date, a memorial by Pedro Fages, November 30, 1775,[31] and another by the religious of the College of San Fernando, February 26, 1776,[32] both of which will be taken up in more detail in a later chapter.

Verger's opinions are borne out also by contemporary official reports. The two Californias were then under one government, the capital being at Loreto, Baja California, where the governor, Felipe Barry, resided. Pedro Fages, the lieutenant-governor, was stationed in Alta California at Monterey. In letters of July 21 and 23, August 27 and 30, 1771, Fages told Barry that he was about to found missions at San Gabriel and San Buenaventura, and consequently needed more men and horses. Barry sent twenty-one soldiers, five mule-drivers, and sixty-three horses, which were all that he could spare, but Fages asked for yet more soldiers and horses. He was much troubled because of the frequency of desertions. On one occasion nine soldiers and a mule-driver had taken provisions and fifty horses, and started for Sonora, but later returned. Then five soldiers took forty-nine horses, and set out for Sonora. They, too, changed their minds, and took refuge in San Diego mission, where they were protected by the missionaries from the wrath of Fages. He wrote that he had no confidence in any of his men. Commenting on these letters in his own to Bucarely of October 24, 1771, Barry said that there were only eighty-two soldiers in all the Californias, of whom fifty-one were with Fages. He asked that forty more be sent to him, as also four or five hundred mules and two hundred

[31] C–3042.   [32] C–3156.

horses, the animals being required to transport provisions, and as mounts for the troops. As things were, nothing was being done, for he lacked the means with which to work.[33] Bucarely informed Arriaga, November 26, 1771, that he would send eighteen more soldiers, enough to give the Californias a total of a hundred, and that he had ordered Barry to punish those soldiers who deserted repeatedly. These were temporary steps, as the Californias were about to be divided between the Franciscans and the Dominicans, when more enduring measures would be taken.[34]

Fages continued to ask aid of Barry, especially in horses, mules, and cattle. The latter wrote Fages, January 7, 1773, that he had forwarded thirty horses and forty mules, which were all that he could get together in the peninsula, but he sent no cattle. Prior to the cession of Baja California by the Franciscans to the Dominicans, the latter agreed that the former might take some of their animals to Alta California. But when confronted with the actual conditions of the peninsula, they contended, as had certain Franciscans in 1770, that the animals could not be spared, although acknowledging their previous agreement. Bucarely at first inclined toward the Franciscans, ordering Rivera to take the animals to Alta California.[35] Later, he changed front, and the Dominicans were allowed to keep them. Clearly, no help in this respect was to come from Baja California.[36]

The *Puerto* of San Francisco had long been known to the Spaniards, but by that name they meant the modern Drake's Bay. What we now call San Francisco Bay was discovered by Portolá in 1769, taking the name of the *Estero* of San Francisco. For several years thereafter, expeditions in that direction aimed to get around the *Estero* in order to reach the *Puerto*. The distinction seems to have been lost sight of in Mexico, possibly because the name and location were

[33] C-1792.
[34] C-1813. For Arriaga's acknowledgment see C-1915. C-1820 is another letter from Barry, much as before, reported by Bucarely to Arriaga in C-1910.

[35] Bucarely to Rivera, Nov. 3, 1773, A.G.P., *Californias*, 66.
[36] Late in 1776, after many animals had already been brought from Sonora, a supplementary lot was ordered sent from Baja California. C-3070, 3300, 3455.

so nearly the same. Very soon the name San Francisco became understood as connoting the site of the present city and bay of that name. Scarcity of provisions and the consequent necessity of returning to San Diego had prevented an exploration of the bay by Portolá. Thenceforth, however, the project of exploring and occupying the new port was constantly in the minds of the authorities and missionaries, until it was achieved in 1776 by the founding of San Francisco. Rivera, who had accompanied the Portolá expedition, wrote to Croix, March 2, 1770, that the newly discovered port, if deep enough, might prove better than that of San Diego. Moreover, it was a good site for settlement, as it had timber and firewood, running water, good lands, and numerous Indians.[37] Doubtless, he was considering the availability of the Indians as laborers, in referring to their numbers as an advantage.

News of the achievements of the 1769 expeditions had hardly been received in Mexico, when orders were sent by Croix, November 12, 1770, to explore the port of San Francisco and to found a mission there to secure it from foreign occupation. This order was not received until May, 1771. Meanwhile, Fages had paid a brief visit to San Francisco Bay in November, 1770, but had made no extensive exploration.[38] From the first, Serra was most eager to establish a mission there, but Fages regarded it as impossible, owing to his lack of troops for mission guards. Serra would not be satisfied, and voiced his complaint in a long letter to the viceroy, June 18, 1771. He stated that Santa Clara mission[39] had not been founded because Gálvez had objected, due to the lack of escort. As for San Francisco, the viceroy had ordered an exploration of its port beforehand, but Fages and Pérez, the latter being captain of the *San Antonio*, had decided that there were not enough people for the attempt to be made by land, and that it would occasion too great a delay to the *San Antonio*, if made by sea. Serra wished to see the mission placed there

[37] A.G.P., *Californias*, 66.
[38] Fages, *Diary*, in A.P.C.H., *Publications*, II, 141–59. Also C–1583.
[39] This refers, not to the later mission of that name, but to a site south of Santa Barbara.

I

as soon as possible; there would be no delay on his part.[40] This letter must have reached Mexico at about the time that Bucarely became viceroy, or only shortly before. Its statements are confirmed by Fages, who wrote to Croix that he could not found the mission at San Francisco until he got more soldiers.[41] Exploration of the port of San Francisco was also urged by Father Verger in his petition of December, 1771. "They say that Monterey is not a port, and that San Francisco may be a very good one; but there is need of exploring its entrance and [ascertaining] its depth." [42] Knowing Verger's objections to making new settlements, we may conclude that he was recommending exploration rather than a too early attempt at settlement. At length, in March and April, 1772, Fages made an overland expedition to explore the *Puerto* of San Francisco, but failing to get around the *Estero*, returned. He made no examination of San Francisco Bay, and its merits remained unknown.

The aftermath of the San Gabriel revolt illustrates another problem that the viceroy had to consider. Serra asserted that the revolt was due to the mismanagement of Fages, charging that he had not taken steps to prevent outrages by soldiers against native women. In other words, the old feud between friars and soldiers was already in evidence in Alta California, the missionaries believing that they should have wider powers than the lay authorities were willing to give them. Thus, every untoward incident might be cause of mutual recriminations. Whatever may have been the merits of the case, these disputes were a factor to reckon with. A similar situation existed in Baja California. Writing to Arriaga, July 26, 1772, Bucarely said that the discord between the governor and the missionaries was so great that it was difficult for him to learn the truth, as each side appeared to found its representations on a sound basis. He hesitated to take measures, lest they prove mistaken and irremediable, but was seeking information from various sources. He had asked

[40] A.G.P., *Californias*, 66.   [41] *Ibid.*   [42] Palou, *Noticias*, I, 128.

further reports from the Father Superior of San Fernando, and had inquired the amount of funds supplied to the Californias by the royal treasury, what the pious fund paid, and the expense of the Department of San Blas, all with a view to ascertaining the exact cost of the Californias, and to enable him to take fitting measures.[43]

The leading facts as regards the status of the Californias, and opinions concerning them have now been traced up to the time when Bucarely received Anza's petition to explore a route to Monterey from Sonora. The logic of events and conditions pointed to a need for such a communication, if the new settlements were to be maintained. Meanwhile, steps had been taken which emphasized that need. Measures having to do with the grant of a mission field in the Californias to the Dominicans had also been taken which emphasized the importance of having a route to the Californias from Sonora.

As far back as 1760 a royal decree of April 17 in that year, had granted Father Juan Pedro Iriarte's petition for a mission field in New Spain for twenty-five of the Dominican order.[44] By another decree, February 18, 1768, more missionaires were granted, including ten who were to serve in missions from which the Jesuits had been expelled.[45] The necessity of filling places left vacant by the Jesuits imposed a demand upon other orders that they could not supply, and the Father Superior of San Fernando, the archbishop of Mexico, Viceroy Croix, and others joined in petitions for more missionaries, which resulted in a grant of forty-five to the College of San Fernando by a decree of September 2, 1768.[46] The same day the Council of the Indies reported to the king a new petition of Iriarte's, a proposal now being made for the first time that the Dominicans be assigned a field in the Californias. Iriarte wished to go alone, or with others of his order, to the western coast of the peninsula, stating that there were many natives there and many good harbors. It was a known fact, he

[43] C–1995. Acknowledged by Arriaga, Nov. 11, 1772, C–2060.
[44] C–470.
[45] C–952.
[46] C–1070.

said, that foreign enemies had taken shelter in them in times of war, a danger which he thought could be avoided, if he were allowed to convert the Indians of that coast between 25° and 28°. The Council was uncertain about the proper course of action on this petition, suspecting that it was an entering wedge for an extension of Dominican rule to Cape Mendocino, stated to be in 41° 30.′ All presidios and missions thus far erected in the Californias had been on the side of the Gulf, but the Council realized the importance of the spiritual and temporal conquest of other parts of the Californias as against the possibility of foreign establishments; if the latter were formed, it would be a mortal wound to the entire coast of New Spain, and would cut off trade with the Philippines. The Council had planned to avoid this danger by its decrees of May 12, 1744, and August 22, 1747, when it proposed that the Jesuits should enter the Californias by way of the Colorado River, but nothing had been accomplished at that time. It recommended that Iriarte's petition be referred to the viceroy and the archbishop of Mexico,[47] and this was done in an order of November 4, 1768. Croix's reply, April 22, 1769, stated that it would be impossible to assign a field in the Californias to the Dominicans, as it would lead to quarrels between them and the *Fernandinos* to whom that territory had been given upon expulsion of the Jesuits.[48] The archbishop, however, writing May 22, 1769, said that such a great territory as the Californias ought not be given to the Franciscans alone, as they might resist measures that would be desired in future. So the Dominicans should be given a field there, and secular clergy placed in towns that were more advanced in a settled type of life.[49] Gálvez opposed Iriarte's petition. Not only was there no multitude of natives between 25° and 28° on the west coast of the

[47] C-1069. This document contains a definite statement as to the northern boundary of the Californias, placing it in 36° at the mouth of the Río Carmelo. Thus Monterey was deemed beyond it. This may account for the name Monterey (or *Establecimientos de Monterrey*) often applied to Alta California during the early period of settlement. More likely, however, this was merely an instance of careless phraseology in framing the document. A few years later the boundary was extended indefinitely northward. Cf. *infra* n. 59.

[48] C-1237.
[49] C-1253.

Californias, he said, but there were not any at all between
31° and Cape San Lucas nor on the adjacent islands. As
for danger from foreigners, permission had already been
granted to establish nine new missions between Velicatá,
the northernmost mission of Baja California, and Monterey, where a presidio was also to be placed. These would
hold back foreign encroachments, especially those of the
Russians who had lately been active in their designs. There
was no room for the Dominicans, as the Franciscans had
all the desirable territory. The former might be used on
the Sonora frontier.[50] Gálvez expressed the same views in
his *Informe* of 1771 to Bucarely. Let the Dominicans be
assigned missions in Sonora, he suggested, leaving the Franciscans of the College of Querétaro to found five missions
farther on, among peoples of the Gila and those at the confluence of that river with the Colorado.[51] Father Juan de
Dios de Córdova, Dominican *provincial* in Madrid, recommended, January 17, 1770, that Iriarte's petition be granted,
making a point of the necessity for conquests in the Californias as a check against foreign encroachments, for which
purpose decrees aiming to secure the peninsula had been
passed in 1744, 1747, and 1752, without anything being
done.[52] The *fiscal* on February 6, 1770, advised the Council to permit the Dominicans to enter the Californias, but
in separate regions from those of the Franciscans,[53] and so
it was proposed by the Council in its recommendation of
March 2, 1770, to the king. Reference was made in this
document to the decree of 1744 ordering the Jesuits to seek
routes to the Californias by way of the Colorado River.
This was still recommended as desirable on the part of their
successors in Sonora.[54] A royal decree in the terms suggested
by the Council, was sent to the viceroy, dated April 8,
1770,[55] being modified later, November 16, 1770, by another
stating that the viceroy might employ the Dominicans

[50] Gálvez to Croix, June 10, 1769,
C–1284. This was forwarded to Arriaga by Croix, July 29, 1769, C–1348,
and sent by the former to the Council
of the Indies, January 1, 1770, C–1434.

[51] Gálvez, *Informe*, 145.
[52] C–1441.
[53] C–1447.
[54] C–1455.
[55] C–1460.

elsewhere, if he thought best.[56] Croix, however, made no
use of the Dominicans who had already been sent to New
Spain, which drew forth a protest from the archbishop of
Mexico to the Council, dated February 28, 1771. He
doubted if the Dominicans provided for by the recent
decrees were going to be used in the Californias, because
Gálvez was opposed, but urged that the decrees be fulfilled.[57]
A new decree was enacted, September 21, 1771, expressly
ordering that the Dominicans be given stations in the
Californias.[58] Bucarely had called a *junta* to consider the
matter, before the last-named order was received, but it
had come prior to the determination of the matter. Various decrees and reports were examined, among them being
a petition of the Franciscans of Querétaro that they be
allowed to erect five missions along the Colorado and Gila
rivers. A decision was reached in May, 1772, that the
Dominicans should have the peninsula, and the *Fernandinos*
Alta California. The former were to have up to a point
just short of San Diego, and thereafter proceed to the east
or east-northeast toward the Gulf and the Colorado River,
or yet farther in that direction, but without prejudice to
such other orders as might precede them. This division was
being made with the consent of the Father Superior of the
Fernandinos. The latter were to have a field extending
indefinitely northward.[59] Various consequences of this division of the Californias will be taken up later in another
connection. For the present only one may be noted, which
was expressed by Gálvez in criticizing the division. Was

[56] C-1579. So the Council had advised, C-1514, upon advice of the *fiscal*,
C-1504.
[57] C-1712.
[58] C-1782.
[59] Proceedings of the *junta*, C-1602,
forwarded to Spain by Bucarely in a
letter of May 25, 1772, C-1959. The
boundaries named were accepted by
the Council of the Indies in a *consulta*
of May 11, 1775, C-2906, and thus became the first definite boundary between Alta and Baja California, and a
new expression as to the northern
boundary of the former. The language employed by the Council in the

first case is that the Dominicans were
to proceed *hasta llegar á los confines de
la Misión de Sⁿ Diego en su Puerto,
poniendo la última en el Arroyo de Sⁿ
Juan Bautista qᵉ finalizaría cinco leguas
más adelante de una Punta que saliendo
de la Sierra Madre, termina antes de
llegar á la Playa, donde podrían torcer
al Leste con poca inclinación al Les-
Nordeste con qᵉ salían al fin del Golfo
Califórnico y Río Colorado*. As for
the northern boundary the *Fernandinos*
were to go *hasta donde pudiesen estender
sus Conquistas Espirituales*. Cf. *supra*
n. 47.

it proper, he asked, to deprive Alta California establishments of the support which they needed from the peninsula? Was it wise, in view of their importance, to force them to rely solely on the boats from San Blas?[60] Wise or not, it had been done. Clearly, however, the discovery of a good route from Sonora had become all the more desirable.[61]

The division having been made, some sort of *modus vivendi* had to be devised, and this could be done only with a knowledge of conditions. For several years the matter of a *reglamento* for governing the Californias, a temporary one to begin with, to be followed as soon as might be by a permanent *reglamento* was a matter much in the minds of the authorities in Mexico and Spain, but what to do was a question. Prospects in the Californias were none too favorable. In a letter to Arriaga, February 24, 1773, Bucarely wrote of the Alta California establishments that discord between Fages and the missionaries was so great, and desertions of soldiers so oft-repeated, that a deplorable situation had resulted, and the early ruin of the settlements might be expected.[62] He had done all that he could to remedy matters, urging the religious and Fages and Barry, who also quarrelled with the missionaries, to greater harmony, and he had forwarded supplies, but without appreciable results. Affairs of San Blas also required attention, the port itself showing signs of filling in. Until matters there were arranged, and until such time as he could learn the causes of disputes in the Californias, there was not likely to be any good news from that province.[63]

Most important of the reports received from men who had been in the province were two from Father Junípero Serra, president of the Alta California missions. Serra had reached Mexico in February, 1773, having made the trip

[60] Gálvez to Arriaga, Dec. 18, 1773, C-2454.

[61] For a summary of the documents concerning division of the Californias, with subsequent action to May 11, 1775, see the recommendation of that date by the Council of the Indies, C-2906.

[62] Among other letters of Bucarely bearing on desertions of the military are three to Fages, Oct. 14 and Dec. 2, 1772, and May 26, 1773. A.P.C.H., *Prov. St. Pap.*, I, 75–85.

[63] C-2177.

from Alta California largely with a view to securing the
removal of Fages. Bucarely asked him to prepare a memorial setting forth his views as to the needs of Alta California.
Serra's memorial of March 13, 1773, was the response to
this request. In it he embodied thirty-two suggestions,
most of which are worthy of record here, for the light they
throw upon conditions in the new settlements. A store
should be established at Monterey, he said, so that the
soldiers would not have to deal with the far distant one at
Loreto; in that case, they would be better satisfied, and
others would be induced to go there. It would be well to
send thirty to forty more soldiers, some of them married;
with but two families at each mission, other persons would
soon begin to marry. Each mission ought to have from four
to six men to serve as laborers, cowboys, and mule-drivers,
thus providing for the planting of crops and the general
advancement of the province. The men could be sent by
sea from San Blas. Indian families might also be sent from
Baja California to serve as laborers, and to show the Alta
California Indians that the Christians approved of marriage; thus far there had been no Christians with wives
in Alta California. A forge and a smith were needed at
San Diego and at Carmelo, Monterey being the only place
in the province thus far to have them, and iron was required for the forges. Two carpenters were wanted, one
for the northern and the other for the southern missions.
The commissary of San Blas should be instructed to be
more careful about the condition of provisions sent to Alta
California. All the missions were in very great need of
mules, especially the inland missions, with which to transport provisions from the ports; the only mules in the
province were those of the presidio of Monterey, and they
were likely to become extinct because they were being employed in somewhat unnecessary labors, and because of
thefts by deserters who took them away, and by natives
who ate them. Above all, asses and mares should be
sent, for procreation of more mules, or the province would
never be free from trouble because of its lack of pack-

animals. Cows destined for the proposed San Francisco and Santa Clara missions should in the meantime be kept at the existing missions, rather than at the presidios, so that there might be milk for Christian converts, the only aliment that the missionaries had been able, thus far, to give them. Since the departure of Pedro Prat, Alta California had been without a doctor; it needed one. Some reward ought to be given to soldiers who should marry native women, — for example, two cows and a mule, or whatever might be deemed best.

The above shows the lack in elements of permanence of the Alta California settlements at this time, and the need for families and animals. The memorial laid even greater stress upon the relations between missionaries and soldiery, and sought that Fages be relieved of his command.[64] Most of Serra's requests were granted, either at this time or not long afterward, but, for the present, discussion of the action taken may be postponed. The interest here is his description of existing conditions.[65]

Serra's proposals formed an important document before Bucarely and the *junta* in their work of preparing a *reglamento* for the Californias and San Blas, but they did not contain all the information that Bucarely desired. In a letter to Arriaga of May 27, 1773, Bucarely said that the reports thus far received had not served to clarify the situation in the Californias; so he had ordered steps taken to form a permanent *reglamento*. "No subject of the many that this very vast government produces has given me more to do than the regulation of the Department of San Blas and the *Peninsula de Californias*."[66] One of the docu-

[64] Serra's complaint against Fages came at a time when it was apt to be heard favorably. Shortly before, December 2, 1772, Bucarely had written to Fages remarking upon the latter's failure to give an account of conditions at the presidio and missions, and requesting him in future to report all that occurred. A.P.C.H., *Prov. St. Papers*, I, 76-77. Reference to "the presidio" meant Monterey, for San Diego was not so regarded at the time.

Serra's request for the removal of Fages was granted.

[65] For the whole *expediente*, C-2103. Serra's memorial is in Palou, *Noticias*, III, 37-66; also the resolution of the *junta* concerning his proposals, III, 67-82.

[66] C-2278. The term *Peninsula de Californias* continued to be used to include both Californias, even after Alta California had been settled.

ments sought by Bucarely to help in that regard was another
from Father Serra, who was asked to draw up a report on
the state of the missions in his charge. This he did, basing
the report, completed May 21, 1773, on his recollection of
conditions as they were when he left in September of the
preceding year, together with such news as he had received
since departure.[67]

His opening paragraphs concerned the military needs of
the missions. Because of the vast number of Indians,
sentinels were necessary at night, four men and a corporal
being required, each with a three-hour watch, except the
corporal, who escaped duty. If there should be but five
men, they would have that duty every night, and could not
be counted upon to assist the missionaries during the day,
as for example when they went to wash clothes, to seek a
stray cow, or to do other similar tasks. The use of Christian Indians for purposes of defence had been impossible
thus far, because most of those baptized were children, and
the few men converts had to absent themselves in order to
get food by hunting. The missions were therefore at the
mercy of the Indians, if they should be tempted to make an
end of them. He had previously suggested an establishment of a hundred soldiers, but now submitted that the
number could be cut down to eighty, if the founding of the
proposed new missions should be postponed, although he
hoped that one of the two, San Buenaventura, might not
be delayed. With the exception of fifteen soldiers at the
presidio of Monterey, the soldiers should be distributed
among the missions, the largest number, fifteen, to be at
San Buenaventura, if that were founded.

The greater part of the memorial dealt with mission
conditions proper. In this respect it agreed substantially
with a later report drawn up by Father Francisco Palou
on December 10, 1773, the latter constituting the first of a
series of annual reports concerning the Alta California missions. Both Serra and Palou covered the same ground,
giving a history of each mission, stating the progress each

[67] For the memorial, C–2108.

had made in conversions, and in material welfare as regards site, domestic animals, crops, and other details. Palou's report, being made on the ground, with the advantage of mission records, is the more complete and the more specific, but is so nearly like that of Serra that the two may be treated together, despite the difference in date. Palou will be followed here, with some additional comment from Serra.

The principal features of the situation may be presented by two tables, adapted from the two in Palou. The first covers the religious achievements of the missions from their foundation to December, 1773.

MISSION	BAPTISMS	LIVING	MARRIAGES
San Diego	83	76	12
San Gabriel	73	71	0
San Luis Obispo	12	11	0
San Antonio.	158	150	18
San Carlos de Monterey	165	154	32
Totals.	491	462	62

From this it appears that after nearly five years of mission work, remarkably slight progress had been made in view of the great number of Indians in the vicinity of the missions, and in comparison with the rapidity of conversions by Spanish missionaries in other fields. Results, when analyzed, seem even more slender than the figures show. Serra stated in his March 13 memorial that most of those baptized were children. At San Luis Obispo there were as yet no adult converts. Such men as were baptized could not always be kept at the missions, going away occasionally for days and weeks at a time, said Serra. There had been only sixty-two Christian marriages in the whole period, which Bancroft regards as representing the total number of adult converts. The San Diego Indians had persistently resisted conversion, although the mission was already in its fifth year at the time of Palou's report; matters there were showing signs of improvement, however.

It was almost as bad at San Gabriel, then in its third year, while San Luis Obispo, founded in September, 1772, had accomplished almost nothing in a populous field. Conversions at San Carlos had come for the most part in its first year, after which there had been few, said Serra, but by the time of Palou's report they had become more numerous.

The failure to win converts at San Diego and San Gabriel was partly accounted for by the early revolts at those missions, caused at the latter place, says Palou, by the improper conduct of a Spanish soldier, although Serra ascribed it to the excessive precautions of Fages. The most important reason for the lack of conversions, according to both Serra and Palou, was the scarcity of food with which to attract the natives to the missions. On that account, said Serra, they had abstained from making more converts at San Carlos until a more fitting time, for they had nothing but milk to give the Indians, and very little of that. Palou said that there was not enough to eat at San Carlos for those who were already Christians, because of the failure of the crops, and because the supply ship had not come. At San Antonio the Indians had rather to assist the missionaries with food than be supplied by them. Palou felt certain that conversions at San Antonio would be rapid, if the mission might maintain and clothe its converts, for the Indians had been quite friendly. The difficulty at San Luis Obispo was the abundance of foods that the natives were able to procure, for which reason, said Palou, it would not be easy to reduce them to living at the mission. San Gabriel hoped to have large crops with which to make gifts to new Christians, and to attract other natives, having already obtained promising crops of grain, vegetables, and various kinds of melon. At the other missions agriculture had not thus far proved successful. It was almost impossible to grow grain because of the difficulties of irrigation. San Diego lacked a sufficient rainfall. Yet, Serra and Palou were optimistic as to the future of the missions.

No estimates of the number of unconverted Indians were

made, but the number must have been very large, only a small proportion of the Indians having been converted.[68] The unconverted Indians had no agriculture, but lived chiefly on acorns, pine nuts, and certain wild seeds; they hunted for hare, rabbits, squirrels, and occasionally for deer, while those who lived near the sea caught fish.[69] The missionaries at San Diego had sent to San Blas for a canoe and net, that their Christian converts might assist the mission by fishing.

The second table in Palou gives an account of the live stock at the missions, as follows:

	Cows	Sheep	Goats	Pigs	Asses	Breed-ing Mares	Colts	Horses	Saddle Mules	Pack Mules
San Diego	40	64	55	19	4	17	3	9	4	18
San Gabriel	38	30	12	20	0	4	1	6	2	14
San Luis	41	0	0	5	0	4	0	5	2	14
San Antonio	38	0	0	30	0	4	0	5	2	9
San Carlos	48	0	0	28	0	4	0	5	2	10
	205	94	67	102	4[70]	33	4[71]	30	12	65

From this it appears that San Diego was best off in number and variety of animals, with San Gabriel a good second. The northern missions had a few cows and pigs, but little else. The explanation is that the original supply of animals came from Baja California, there being none in

[68] Henry K. Norton, *The story of California* (Chicago, 1913), 1, in a chapter entitled "California in 1540," says: "The number of Indians at that time living within the boundaries of the present state has been estimated at 700,000." While this estimate is almost certainly too high, possibly ten times too much, Alta California certainly had a considerable native population. When the Spaniards came in 1769, there may have been 15,000 Indians along the route that they took between San Diego and San Francisco. Fages said that there were more than twenty villages between San Diego and Monterey along or near the route followed by the Spaniards. They were particularly numerous along the Santa Barbara Channel, where there were some towns of over a thousand Indians,

and, according to Fages, chiefs capable of mustering six hundred warriors. Memorial of Pedro Fages, Nov. 30, 1775, C–3042. The last statement makes one wonder if Fages' estimates were of the men alone. If so, then the total population would be much greater than the estimate just given and the danger to the Spanish establishments was correspondingly greater.

[69] Bancroft, *Native races*, I, 322–442, gives a most vivid, and far from flattering account of the California Indians. A more wretchedly bestial, lazy, or filthy race could scarce ever have existed than they. Among other things he shows that vermin and reptiles were among their articles of food.

[70] Two were she-asses.

[71] Three of the four were fillies.

Alta California, and none coming by sea; so the southern missions got a start over those in the north, being nearer the source of supply. There had been scant increase in animals over the original number brought from the peninsula, but this does not allow for those that had died or were eaten. In the case of San Diego, at least, there had been a noteworthy increase. That mission had obtained eighteen cows from Baja California, and the number had increased to forty. Included in the list of horses was a stallion apiece at each mission. San Diego had also one colt and one jack. At every mission there was excellent pasture.

These figures, to be understood, must be considered in relation to other factors. Food-animals, while not numerous enough to serve as a material argument of the benefits of Christianity, might be expected in time to increase to considerable proportions. Three things, however, might prevent: animals for breeding purposes were not plentiful; there were not enough men to watch the herds and flocks; and the unconverted Indians showed a fondness for meat, and an inclination to indulge that appetite without permission of the Fathers. The same drawbacks applied also as regards pack animals, as may be seen from Serra's memorial of March 13, and over a year later from a letter of Palou, April 22, 1774, to Father Verger.[72] In all Alta California there were less than one hundred and fifty such animals. Serra laid particular stress on the need for them, and Palou's letter pointed out that more horses and mules and every kind of cattle for breeding purposes must be brought, if the missions were to become permanent.

The principal drawback, although not expressed in the Serra and Palou reports, which were dealing with mission conditions, was a lack of settlers with families. Laborers without families would tide over affairs only temporarily, leaving them at their departure or death as bad as before. Serra's memorial of March 13 had urged the sending of families, so that a permanent population might develop.

[72] M.N., *Doc. Rel. Mis. Cal.*, v. 2.

Thus far, there was not a white woman in Alta California, but three soldiers at San Carlos and three more at San Antonio had married native women. The missions reported that they had farming, masons' and carpenters' tools, but a total lack of workmen. San Diego had acquired a forge, but had no smith. Architecture was of the simplest. A stockade enclosed the wooden mission building, and another surrounded the soldiers' barracks. Roofs were of mud, later changed to tule, when it was found that mud roofs were not proof against rain. At San Diego and San Antonio there were some adobe structures.[73]

To the preceding facts but little need be added. To support these distant establishments in a populous Indian country, covering approximately five hundred miles from Monterey to San Diego, there were but sixty soldiers, eleven missionaries, and an occasional mechanic in the service of the government. Clearly, Alta California was not on a very substantial basis. During the period that Verger was writing his pessimistic memorials of 1771–72 it is not likely that the government would have authorized such an expedition as Anza wished to make, and not even as late as February, 1773, if we may judge from Bucarely's letter of the 24th, for it seemed more than likely that the establishments would have to be abandoned. In the course of the year 1773, however, a change occurred, for something, although little enough, had been accomplished. Even Verger's opinion seems to have become more favorable. On November 5, 1773, he wrote to Bucarely of news that he had received from Alta California, telling of good crops and numerous conversions.[74] There was already a growing hope for the future.

This summary of conditions in the Californias preceding the Anza expeditions may be brought to a close with a reference to the cost of the establishments from the founding of San Blas to the end of the year 1773. Complete figures are not at hand, but the most important of them,

[73] For the Palou report, C–2446; also in Palou, *Noticias*, III, 228–54.   [74] C–2425; reported to Arriaga by Bucarely, Nov. 26, 1773, C–2441.

those of the Department of San Blas, are available. The beginning of the department may be dated January 11, 1768, when Croix issued an instruction for the guidance of its commissary, or head.[75] Operations to the end of 1773 are clearly presentèd in two reports of July 20, 1774, by Francisco Hijosa, the commissary. One of these deals with the history of San Blas both before and after its establishment on a new basis in 1768, giving not only local items, but also much that bears upon its principal *raison d'être*, supplying the Californias.[76] The other concerns the town of San Blas and the officers of the department.[77] They show that between March 1, 1768, and December 31, 1773, the department had given aid to Baja California to the extent of 207,006 *pesos*, 6 *reales*, and 10 *granos*, and to Alta California, 250,753 *pesos*. These figures did not include the cost of goods sent from Mexico to each of the Californias, nor such sums as were supplied from confiscated goods of the Jesuits and from the pious fund.[78] Hijosa complained that the amounts supplied to Baja California should have come from the two last-named funds. The department itself had cost 112,542 *pesos*, 7 *reales*, 4 *granos*, resulting in a total expenditure of 570,302 *pesos*, 6 *reales*, 2 *granos*, an average of about 100,000 *pesos* a year. As an offset the salt mines of San Blas had yielded about 25,000 *pesos* a year. Bucarely forwarded these reports to Arriaga, December 27, 1774, giving high praise to Hijosa for his manage-

[75] C-930.
[76] C-2679.
[77] C-2680.
[78] The pious fund at this time was a special branch of *real hacienda*, consisting of free gifts of individuals for furtherance of mission work in the Californias. It was managed, however, by government officials, and portions were occasionally diverted to other objects. Protests against such diversions were made, leading to directions that they must not occur again, or that such an one was to be permitted "for this once only." In a decision by the *Real Tribunal de Cuentas* of Mexico, July 27, 1773, it is stated "that the said pious fund of California . . . ought to be employed only in payment of allowances (*sínodos*) to missionaries, troops, and ships of the same *Peninsula*, and for the establishment of the missions of San Diego and Monterey, and not diverted to other objects." Quoted in a decree of the Council of the Indies, Dec. 16, 1776, C-3394. Engelhardt, II, 655-60, has an appendix on the unlawful use of the pious fund in connection with the expeditions of 1769 to Alta California. "San Diego and Monterey" was employed to indicate all of the establishments of Alta California. "Monterey" alone was often used to connote Alta California, as also were "the new establishments," "northern California" and "new California." Cf. chap. II, n. 5.

ment of the department.[79] These figures help to explain
the importance that was attached to the Californias. They
were a drain on the treasury, but despite that and other
burdens involved in their retention, the government never
slackened in its desire to keep them, so great was their
strategic importance as against foreign attack.

[79] C–2785.

CHAPTER VI

THE need for an overland route to Alta California has just been pointed out. As such a route must come from Sonora or New Mexico, we may now consider whether there was anything to prevent the opening of a route from one region or the other, bearing in mind the significant dates with regard to Anza's proposal, May 2, 1772, when he asked to be allowed to make an expedition, and September 13, 1773, when his petition was granted. As between New Mexico and Sonora, the latter was more likely to prove the better starting-point. That Anza was not authorized to go until late in 1773 was due in part to Bucarely's uncertainty concerning the affairs of the Californias, and partly to fear that Sonora was not entirely pacified, but also in great degree to the continuance of Apache wars along the frontier from northeastern Sonora to Texas; these wars might have threatened communications with Alta California, had a route been open. New Mexico, like the Californias, was in a measure separated from the problems of the frontier line, but, aside from its distance from the Californias, affairs there were less favorable than in Sonora. Although the Apaches confined their attacks in Sonora to its northeastern corner, that region was constantly exposed, because internal revolts might draw off attention from its defence. Moreover, Apache attacks interfered seriously with the best of the northwesterly routes, down the Santa Cruz to the Gila, and by way of the last-named river to the Colorado. Steps were taken in accord with Rubí's suggestions to remedy the frontier situation, but with little effect in the period under review. They formed a basis, however, for hopes of the future.

Following Elizondo's conquest an effort was made to develop the wealth of Sonora, thus to insure retention of the province. Early in 1771 a proposal was made to form a stock company to exploit the mineral wealth of Sinaloa and Sonora, and the government showed interest in it, which is noteworthy, although the plan was soon given up.[1] Nevertheless, rich discoveries were frequently reported. Governor-intendant Pedro Corbalán [2] wrote from Álamos, September 24, 1771, of the finding of new mines at Aygame,[3] which occasioned correspondence between Bucarely and Arriaga, the latter suggesting appropriate methods of examining into the truth of similar reports.[4] Of most importance, however, were the already existing Cieneguilla mines, which were a matter of great concern to the government. Bucarely wrote to Arriaga, July 26, 1772, that he was taking steps to learn the true status of the Cieneguilla placers.[5] Pedro Tueros, the officer in charge at Cieneguilla, reported, December 1, 1772, that the mines were producing scantily. He planned to induce the Indians to work another part of the camp in search of gold, for if no new placers were found, the Indians might desert, — a matter of moment, as they constituted three-fourths of the workers.[6] Bucarely ordered the governor of Sonora to prevent the abandonment of the work and of the territory already settled.[7] A little later, better news came from Cieneguilla. Tueros wrote to Pedro Corbalán, January 14, 1773, that although gold was less abundant than formerly, more than 7000 men were engaged in mining it. Moreover, new placers had been found which promised extraordinary wealth. This information was passed on to Bucarely, and by him to Arriaga, March 27, 1773.[8] Soon afterward, reports of an encouraging nature from the *Real Caja* of Álamos were received. For the year 1772 the royal fifth had been taken

[1] C-1720, 1729, 1807, 1841, 1926, 1983.

[2] Corbalán as governor-intendant of Sinaloa and Sonora exercised a superior authority to that of Mateo Sastre who was governor of Sonora.

[3] C-1783.

[4] C-1802, 1922, 1992.

[5] C-1993. Approved by Arriaga, Nov. 7, 1772, C-2058.

[6] C-2074.

[7] Bucarely to Arriaga, Feb. 24, 1773, C-2178.

[8] C-2204.

from 4857 *marcos* of gold,[9] whereas 1854 *marcos* had already
been presented in the first four months of 1773,[10] an advance
over the average for the preceding year.[11] On the whole,
therefore, the situation as regards mineral production in
Sonora, and the consequent maintenance there of a large
population, was satisfactory, and prospects were improving.
Meanwhile, there had been rumblings of internal revolt
in Sonora, as well as Apache forays. Although Elizondo's
troops had been withdrawn after the pacification of Sonora
in 1771, the original plan of proceeding to conquer the
Apaches was not entirely given up. The presidio captains
of Terrenate, Tubac, and Fronteras were ordered, late
in that year, to unite at San Simón, and proceed with a
force from Janos against the Apaches. The captains asked
for reënforcements, provisions, and equipment before attempting the campaign, but were informed by Corbalán
that he could send no troops from Altar, Pitic, or Buenavista, for he needed all that he had to enable him to watch
the Pimas, protect Cieneguilla, cover the port of Guaymas,
and check Yaqui uprisings. Nor could he send provisions, as
they were scarce, due to a dry season. He did issue orders,
however, that settlers should sell equipment and provisions
to the captains at reasonable prices. Here the matter might
have rested, but Bucarely took measures to see that the
captains got the needed supplies without damage to Sonora.[12]

The campaign seems not to have been made, however,
due in a measure, perhaps, to an outbreak of the Pimas in
December, 1771. A body of these set out to conquer the
recently reduced Seris, wishing to induce them to take up
arms again. The uprising was checked in an unusual way.
Gifts of horses were promised by Spanish officials to the
Seris, if they would attack the Pimas, whereupon the Seris
killed ten of the twelve Pimas who had started the trouble.
The affair pleased Bucarely, who reported it to Arriaga,
February 24, 1772, as a proof of the loyalty of the Seris.[13]

[9] C–2246.
[10] C–2247.
[11] Reported to Arriaga by Bucarely,
July 27, 1773, C–2334.

[12] C–1778, 1799, 1895, 1908, 1969.
[13] C–1909. Also on this subject,
C–1821, 1969.

Later, the Sibubapas committed some robberies in the
vicinity of Buenavista. Writing of this to Arriaga, August
27, 1772, Bucarely spoke of the variety of opinions in regard to governing Sonora, some recommending exceedingly
harsh penalties for such risings as that of the Sibubapas.
He was getting reports preparatory to calling a *junta*.
Meanwhile, he had ordered Governor Sastre to reduce the
Sibubapas, but to use force only in case other means failed.[14]
By April 26, 1773, Bucarely was able to report that the Sibubapas, as also the Seris, were at peace.[15] Disturbances had
occurred in another quarter, however. The Tiburón Indians had been transferred from their island retreat to the
mission of Carrizal on the mainland. In March, 1773,
they rebelled and killed Father Gil, president of the Sonora
missions.[16] Soon afterward, the Sibubapas again left their
missions, but on proof that it had been from lack of the
necessities of life and not with the idea of rebellion, Bucarely
gave orders to provide them with agricultural tools, seed,
and provisions, with the condition that they should eventually be paid for.[17] He also took measures which tended
to root the Seris more firmly in their settlement at Pitic.
If they should continue to sow the fields, he wrote to Arriaga,
March 27, 1773, they could begin to sustain themselves by
the middle or end of June, thus relieving the royal treasury
from the expense of supplying rations. A *Queretarano*
Franciscan was to be sent, and by his management the
permanence of the settlement on a self-supporting basis
should be assured. All crops were to be in his control for
distribution according to needs.[18] Writing again, six months
later, Bucarely said that he had increased the fund available
for mission work among the Seris, the more effectually to
attract them to the faith.[19]

The keynote to the situation, even in Sonora, was the
war against the Apaches. In Nueva Vizcaya it had gone

14 C–2010.
15 C–2237.
16 C–2229. For measures taken by
Bucarely, C–2218.
17 Bucarely to Arriaga, Sept. 26, 1773,

C–2389. Approved by Arriaga, C–2508.
18 C–2203.
19 C–2390. Approved by Arriaga,
C–2509.

on without ceasing, seeming victories having slight result. Thus, after hearing of some victories on the Chihuahua frontier, Bucarely warned Hugo Oconor, in command there, to take special pains to avoid surprises and exposure of the troops to the danger of being defeated in detail, for the Apaches were wont to take advantage of carelessness.[20] It was this practice of the Apaches that made an unit of the whole frontier in a military way. Bucarely expressed this clearly in a letter of February 24, 1773, to Arriaga. It would be easier to keep the Indians of Sonora in subjection, he said, if the Apaches might first be beaten. Nueva Vizcaya had recently been strengthened; therefore, an attack in Pimería Alta might be expected, and indeed the Apaches had already made a raid at Tubac. Governor Sastre had ordered forty-eight men from Terrenate and thirty from Tubac to reënforce Captain Vildosola of Fronteras in order that a campaign might be made toward Janos, and Bucarely had supplemented this order by directing Vildosola to arrange his movements to accord with those of the Chihuahua expedition, so that the Apaches might be beaten simultaneously on both frontiers. In case of need ten or twenty men were to be detached from Altar, Buenavista, and Horcasitas, provided those presidios were left with forces enough to check the Piatos, Pimas, Seris, and Sibubapas, and to pursue the evildoers, bandits, and vagabonds, with whom Sonora was infested. Full success could not be expected until the new line of frontier presidios should be established and the new *reglamento* become effective. By the latter, one hand was to direct all military operations of the frontier provinces, and it would then be more easy to bring about coöperation in warfare against the Apaches.[21]

In expectation of a vigorous campaign in Nueva Vizcaya, Governor Sastre formed a cordon of troops on the Sonora frontier, to oppose the Apaches when they should be driven

[20] Bucarely to Arriaga, Aug. 27, 1772, C–2007.

[21] C–2175. Bucarely wrote again, April 26, 1773, about measures taken against the Apaches, C–2230. This letter is substantially to the same effect as C–2175.

from Chihuahua. He waited some time, but the Apaches did not come, for, as he wrote to Bucarely, January 14, 1773, the Spanish forces in Nueva Vizcaya had not played their part. Indeed, Oconor had not even written to him, he complained. His men were getting sick, and his horses useless on account of the excessive cold, so that he expected to have to retire soon.[22] A week later Sastre wrote to Bucarely that it was not advisable to invade Apachería, as events were proving that the presidial troops were inadequate to defend their own territories. In proof of this he cited two attacks recently made at the presidios themselves. One of these was at Tubac on October 17, 1772, at midday, when more than a hundred horses were taken by the Apaches. The other was at Terrenate, where they got 264 horses. These disasters were ascribed by Sastre to a failure to place patrols to watch the avenues of the enemy's approach despite his orders to do so; otherwise, the Apaches would have found the troops under arms, and no disaster would have followed. At Horcasitas, Altar, and Fronteras, his orders had been obeyed, and there had been no trouble.[23] These two letters caused Bucarely to admonish Oconor, April 21, 1773, telling him that the Apaches must be checked, or the ruin of the frontier provinces might result. The work was difficult, but difficulties must be overcome. The Indians did not seek opposition, but rather took advantage of carelessness and weakness, on which account, resistance to them must be prepared everywhere. New Mexico alone of the frontier provinces did not suffer from Apache attacks,[24] but Nueva Vizcaya was being desolated by some three hundred Apaches, and the troops seemed unable to prevent it. In Sonora the situation was even worse, not only due to the Apaches, but also because of the danger that the Seris and other recently subjected tribes might

[22] C–2137.

[23] C–2140. Juan Bautista de Anza commanded at Tubac, and José Antonio de Vildosola at Terrenate. There seems to have been bad feeling between Sastre and Anza, as is instanced in several of the documents of this period.

[24] By this remark Bucarely meant that Apache wars were less serious in New Mexico than elsewhere. In letters of nearly the same date, January 27, and April 26, 1773, Bucarely refers to Apache depredations in New Mexico. C–2149, 2231.

rise again. Affairs were much the same in Coahuila. Bucarely asked Oconor if he had enough troops to chastise the enemy and at the same time make the changes of presidio sites required in order to form the frontier line, and he ordered him to open correspondence with the various provincial governors, and to inform them whenever he planned to make a campaign, so that there might be a combined movement. Meanwhile, he was to send to Bucarely diaries of his own operations, and letters about everything that came to his notice, so that Bucarely could have ample data on which to base his measures.[25] Reviewing these matters in his letter to Arriaga of April 26, 1773, Bucarely summed up the situation as follows : If we do not promptly and simultaneously check the Indians in all of the provinces, and establish the line of frontier presidios, we may have success in some provinces where we have plenty of troops, but cannot avoid damage in others, for the Apaches flee from opposition, and attack where resistance is weakest. Because of the vast extent of our territory it is exceedingly difficult to cover all ways of ingress and egress, wherefore we must await the completion of the line of presidios, and then wage unceasing campaigns. For the present, it is too much to expect the soldiers to do, for they have the additional burden of building the new presidios ; so, additional troops will be sent. Oconor's task as *comandante inspector* is a hard one, since he has to cover the whole area in person or by his orders, and owing to the tremendous distances, he cannot be sure at the time of giving his commands that his measures will prove beneficial.[26]

Several references have been made to the proposed formation of a line of frontier presidios as a means of combating the Apaches. This traces directly to the inspection by the Marqués de Rubí, 1766–68, to which reference has already been made. On April 25, 1770, Arriaga ordered Croix to take such measures as were fitting to protect the interior provinces in accord with the plan and other documents of Rubí, and with the requirements for bringing about peace

[25] C–2219.   [26] C–2233.

with the Indians.[27] Croix thereupon drew up a detailed
instruction for the forming of a line of presidios from Sonora
to Texas, those of the Californias not being considered as
part of the plan. The instruction is dated July 18, 1771,
and was intended to go into effect on January 1, 1772.[28]
That date, however, was much too early, for the instruction
had called for the suppression of six existing presidios, and
for a change of site of many that were to be retained. A
junta was held, April 2, 1772, in which it was decided that
sites should be explored for new locations of presidios, and
the needs of the frontier in relation to Apache warfare determined,[29] Bucarely giving appropriate orders to carry out
the *junta's* decision.[30] Before anything of importance had
been accomplished the matter was taken up in Madrid, with
the result that a formal *reglamento* was drawn up, signed by
the king September 10, 1772, for the line of presidios about
to be formed on the frontier of New Spain. Among the
more noteworthy terms of the *reglamento* were the following:
 There was to be a line of fifteen presidios from Altar in
Sonora to Espíritu Santo in Texas, these being, as nearly as
possible, forty leagues apart, but with due regard to habit-
ableness of site and the necessities of defence. There were
to be other presidios not part of the line, as Santa Fé in
New Mexico, San Antonio de Bejar in Texas, Buenavista
and Horcasitas in Sonora (although it was planned to suppress the two last named, as soon as the Indians should be
sufficiently reduced to a peaceful mode of life), and also
various garrisons or "flying squadrons," while the Californias were to continue on a separate footing, the viceroy being
ordered "to sustain and aid them by every means possible."
The line was to be established by an official to be called
the *comandante inspector* (or in this document, *inspector
comandante*) of the military rank of colonel at the least,
directly under the orders of the viceroy, but if a *comandancia*

[27] C-1468.
[28] C-1759. The gist of this document appears in an *estado*, or chart,
made by José de Gorráez, July 23, 1771,
C-1760.
[29] C-1850, a *testimonio* including not

only the decision of the *junta*, but also
some of the documents upon which it
was based.
[30] Referred to in Bucarely to Arriaga,
Apr. 24, 1772, C-1941.

general of the frontier provinces should be erected, he was to be under the *comandante general*. He was not to be governor of a province or captain of a presidio, but was to rule over all, changing his residence according to the needs of the service, and seeing to it that the terms of the *reglamento* were enforced. He was to review the presidios each year, but might do this through two *ayudantes inspectores*, who were to have the rank at least of captain. He was not only to erect the new line of presidios, but also to have the determination and direction of military campaigns. He might grant a truce or even negotiate the preliminaries of peace, although in the latter event peace would not be binding and permanent without sanction of the viceroy. His salary was to be 8000 *pesos* a year, and that of each *ayudante inspector* 3000 *pesos*.[31]

Hugo Oconor became the first *comandante inspector*, being appointed the day of the decree,[32] and going forth to take up his duties on December 4, 1772.[33] Bucarely set to work to prepare an instruction supplementary to the *reglamento*. On February 24, 1773, he wrote to Arriaga that he had completed it, and hoped to put the *reglamento* into effect by July 1, 1773. This would not be possible in all places, because of the vast extent of the frontier provinces, and of certain measures that had to precede the placing of the presidios. Oconor must first dislodge the Taraumares from the Bolsón de Mapimí (where a situation existed parallel to that of the Seris and the Cerro Prieto of Sonora in former years). Vast regions had to be explored, presidial sites chosen, and all of the presidios inspected. Bucarely was facilitating matters by arranging that the work to be accomplished in New Mexico, eastern Texas, Nuevo León, and Nayarit be done, not by Oconor, but by others.[34]

The instruction to Oconor is dated March 1, 1773. For the purpose of showing frontier conditions it is quite as important as the *reglamento* itself. It begins with a pre-

[31] C–1843. Also in Arrillaga, *Recopilación* for 1834, 139–89.
[32] Stated in Oconor to Croix, July 22, 1777, C–3606.
[33] C–2077.
[34] C–2180.

amble giving a history of the conquest of New Spain, in particular of the frontier provinces, and praises the Marqués de Rubí and viceroys Casa-Fuerte (1722–34) and Croix (1766–71) for correcting abuses there, propagating the faith, and taking other action redounding to the glory of Spain. Then follow the instructions in seventy-six paragraphs. These supplement the *reglamento* by emphasizing certain phases of the work, and by giving directions as to the way in which it was to be carried out. Oconor's principal duty was to establish the line of presidios, but he was also to give special heed to campaigns against the Apaches and to reviewing presidios. Attention was directed also to paragraphs in the *reglamento* tending to the suppression of graft by presidial captains, who were prohibited from having a hand in the sale of goods to their troops. In arranging the line of presidios Oconor was to begin in the east and proceed westward. Nueva Vizcaya and Coahuila having been strengthened, it was quite likely that the Apaches would attack Sonora, wherefore Oconor was to take with him enough troops to be able to chastise them. Until the four Sonora presidios provided for in the *reglamento* could be placed at their new sites, the "flying company" of Sonora was to be retained in service. The presidios of Horcasitas and Buenavista were also necessary until the Seris, Tiburones, Pimas, and Sibubapas should become definitely settled in missions. The value of Rubí's work was such that Oconor was to have Rubí's report with him wherever he went, that document being described as *esencialísimo*. Former presidio sites, left vacant by the removal of the presidios to the new line, were to be occupied by Spanish and Ópata settlers. While some soldiers were to be employed in building presidios, others could be used for campaigns, aided in this respect by the flying squadron of José Antonio de Vildosola, the garrisons of Horcasitas and Buenavista, and, if hostilities should have ceased there, by some of the troops from Nueva Vizcaya and Coahuila. In case of insurmountable difficulties in obeying these directions, Oconor might make provisional orders, submitting them to

Bucarely, however, for final decision. Weekly reports of occurrences in the frontier provinces were to be made by the *comandante inspector* to the viceroy.[35] In forwarding this, Bucarely wrote a long letter to Oconor. As to Sonora he reiterated that Apaches fleeing from Nueva Vizcaya might endanger Pimería Alta. Some subjected Indians of Sonora were also showing signs of bad faith, and it would be necessary to watch them, although some of the settlements, those of the Seris in Pitic, the Tiburones in Carrizal, and the Sibubapas in Suaqui, were proceeding happily. These three tribes were a very important consideration. They occupied the best lands of Sonora, and their continuance at peace would result in benefit to the province, and a saving to the public treasury, as for example by the suppression of the presidios of Horcasitas and Buenavista. Oconor was charged to devote himself with zeal to maintaining peace in Sonora.[36] At the same time Bucarely took measures in support of the *reglamento*, giving appropriate instructions to the governors of Nueva Vizcaya, Sonora, Coahuila, Texas, and New Mexico, ordering the extinction of the presidios of Nuevo León and Nayarit, and providing for the payment of expenses by the *cajas reales* of Durango, Álamos, Potosí, and Guadalajara. These measures were referred to in Bucarely's letter to Arriaga of March 27, 1773.[37]

Bucarely's letter of February 24 (already cited)[38] and the above of March 27, 1773, were forwarded by Arriaga to the Conde de O'Reilly for his opinion, respectively on May 24 [39] and June 23, 1773.[40] O'Reilly was then the leading military authority in Spain, and also a very great personal friend of Bucarely. He reported favorably in both cases, holding that Bucarely's measures were very well taken,[41] whereupon Arriaga apprised Bucarely of his own approval, in replies of August 6 [42] and August 20, 1773.[43]

[35] C-2186.
[36] C-2185.
[37] C-2199, enclosing C-2185, 2186, 2195, 2196.
[38] C-2180.

[39] C-2270.
[40] C-2296.
[41] C-2324 and C-2352.
[42] C-2346.
[43] C-2356.

Bucarely's instruction had referred to the prohibition placed upon presidio captains from selling goods to their soldiers. This touched upon an evil that was ever present in Spanish colonies, — graft. There is plenty of evidence that it was general along the frontier. To this must be ascribed, in some measure, the failure to stamp out Indian wars, and, as a corollary, the failure to establish an effective route to the Californias. Graft of presidial captains in the sale of goods to soldiers was referred to in one of the Labaquera memorials, as already noted.[44] A royal decree of May 12, 1760, ordered a *junta* to be called in Mexico to regulate the prices of goods at the presidios. The order seems not to have been fulfilled; so, on June 23, 1764, Arriaga ordered Cruillas to call the *junta*, which was to arrange that prices should be the same as those current among merchants of the provincial capitals nearest the presidios.[45] On March 17 of the next year Cruillas wrote that he had called the first *junta*,[46] which drew a sharp reproof from Arriaga, August 1, 1765, for the viceroy's delay in a matter that had been recommended to him as so important.[47] Cruillas replied, October 23, 1765, defending himself,[48] but no evidence has appeared to show that the abuses at the presidios were remedied. They were one of the matters to engage the attention of the Marqués de Rubí in course of his inspection. In a letter of February 21, 1767, he forwarded to Arriaga a file of papers treating of the irregular conduct of some presidio captains, who tyrannized over their troops in the matter of prices and goods furnished them.[49] Arriaga replied, July 24, 1767, that steps were being taken to check that evil.[50] We have seen that Croix and Gálvez stated that the Sonora presidios served principally to enrich captains and their backers.[51] In his instruction to Bucarely of September 1, 1771, Croix said that the officers of presidios had for a long time occupied the

[44] *Supra* p. 66.
[45] C–555.
[46] C–582.
[47] C–591.
[48] C–598.

[49] C–705.
[50] C–845.
[51] Croix and Gálvez, *Plan*, Jan. 23–24, 1768, A.G.I., 103–3–23.

position of merchants, paying their troops in goods and merchandise, and making a great profit for themselves.[52] In the *reglamento* of September 10, 1772, the whole matter is taken up in detail. Of the fourteen titles preceding the instruction for placing the line of presidios, eleven deal with the correction of abuses in the management of presidios. The first paragraph of title one may be translated as follows: "In order that the presidial troops may not in future suffer such damage as heretofore, receiving salary in effects charged at excessive prices, when my royal treasury was paying them in specie: I prohibit this practice from the first day of next year, with an express declaration that those who now are and in future shall be governors and captains of interior presidios are not to take any part whatever in the purchase of the provisions and supplies of their garrisons, under penalty of deprivation from office, and of remaining incapacitated from obtaining other employment in my service; but, on the other hand, they shall take care very particularly that the quality of these effects be good and their prices equitable." Paying the troops, as well as the gathering of rations, horses, clothing, trappings, and other effects needed by the soldiers and their families was to be in charge of an *habilitado* (paymaster), who was to be a non-commissioned officer, owing his appointment as *habilitado* to an election in which the soldiers themselves had some voice, one vote in five, or in some cases one in six. His principal duties may be summed up by saying that he was to procure the necessary goods and to sell them as cheaply as possible, for which he received two per cent to cover expenses.[53] Bucarely's remarks on this matter to Oconor in his instruction of March 1, 1773, have already been alluded to. Abuses continued, however. *Habilitados* began to delegate their powers to private individuals, and to buy goods from a single shop, rather than from those which gave the best prices. These practices were pro-

[52] Croix, *Correspondance*, 291.
[53] C–1843. In Arrillaga, *Recopi-*   *lación* for 1834, 139–89, especially 140–71.

hibited in 1777.[54] Another practice growing out of the
reglamento of 1772 was that the captains and their sergeants
or other subaltern *habilitados*, combined to make an unfair
profit out of sales to the presidial troops. That seems to
have been a prime factor in the revolt of the garrison of
Terrenate against its captain in 1774. On that occasion
the *habilitado* had gone bankrupt, and the enraged soldiery
beat him nearly to death. Captain Vildosola was for a
time suspended from command, and the case dragged itself
out to the year 1782.[55] Not only the spirit of the *reglamento*
but also the letter of the law was disregarded in some instances. Bucarely's letter of October 27, 1775, said that
Captain Tovar of Terrenate was keeping a public shop, and
was also addicted to drunkenness, whereupon Bucarely
ordered his removal, on Oconor's recommendation,[56] and
Gálvez approved,[57] but Tovar was killed in an Indian fight
before the order could take effect. This state of affairs
tended to the continuance of Indian wars, for disorder was
in the interest of dishonest captains and their backers,
preventing competition with them by stock-raisers who
lacked the advantage of presidial troops to protect their
animals.

As New Mexico figures in this work, both as an objective
of a route from Sonora by way of the Colorado-Gila junction, and as a starting point for a route to Alta California,
brief notice may here be given of the state of affairs there.
Pedro Fermin de Mendinueta was governor at this time.
"In 1771 he announced the conclusion of a treaty with the
Comanches on the 3d of February; and the viceroy, replying
with thanks, called for a report on the condition and needs
of the province, which was furnished in March, 1772.
Mendinueta declared that the force of 80 soldiers at Santa
Fé was not sufficient to protect so broad a territory, raided
by savage foes from every side. True, there were about
250 men capable of bearing arms among the settlers, besides the pueblo Indians; but these were poorly supplied

[54] C-3558, 3613, 3705.
[55] C-2676, 2489. 4330, 4541. Besides these, there are numerous others
on the same case.
[56] C-3019.
[57] C-3167.

with weapons, and could not leave their homes unprotected to engage in distant campaigns. The governor's proposed remedy was a new presidio at Taos, and an enforced law requiring the Spaniards to live in compact pueblos like the Indians." [58] No very important change occurred as a result of the *reglamento* of 1772. The province was hardly developed to such a point that it could take up projects of further conquest. Aside from its scant white population it had too many Indian enemies to contend against. The Apaches were not so troublesome there as in Nueva Vizcaya, but they made attacks from time to time. The most persistent was the Comanches. The peace of 1771 with them was little more than a temporary lull in warfare, for in 1773 we find Bucarely writing to Arriaga, January 27, that fresh irruptions of the Apaches and Comanches had occurred in New Mexico,[59] and again, on April 26, of instructions that he had given to Mendinueta to check the depredations of those tribes.[60]

Thus we may conclude that the situation in the frontier provinces, while bad, was hopeful. Sonora and New Mexico were in an uncertain state, and the latter had too scant a population to achieve much in the way of conquest toward the Californias. The seriousness of the Nueva Vizcaya situation had a definite effect upon measures affecting Sonora. Still, as compared to the warfare prior to the suppression of the Seris, a distinct advance had been achieved, and the new *reglamento*, it was confidently believed, would solve the whole problem. The moment was a fairly favorable one, therefore, for attempting to discover a land route to the Californias, of which those regions were greatly in need.[61]

[58] Bancroft, *Ariz. & New Mex.*, 259.
[59] C-2149.
[60] C-2231.
[61] Naturally the question of expense was an important one in the plans for the line of frontier presidios. By the *reglamento* of 1772 it resulted that 387,617 *pesos*, 4 *tomines* were necessary for the annual expense of the presidios. At Bucarely's order Juan

Crisóstomo de Barroeta drew up a plan, in which it was provided that this sum should be charged against the following *cajas reales:* Durango, 194,671 *pesos*, 2 *tomines;* San Luis Potosí, 148,051 *pesos*, 2 *tomines;* Guadalajara, 34,900 *pesos;* Álamos, 9,995 *pesos*. Barroeta to Bucarely, Apr. 27, 1773, C-2244.

CHAPTER VII

GARCÉS AND ANZA, 1769-1773

SOME indication has been given of the need for an overland route to Alta California, and the situation in the frontier provinces has been reviewed in order to discover why an expedition was not authorized sooner. This chapter will treat directly of Anza's petition to make such an expedition, without considering outside factors, up to the official authorization of September, 1773. Although Bucarely's interest in the Californias appears clearly from what has been said already, and from the content of this chapter, the immensity of his work for the new settlements will appear in greater measure in later chapters. Much that he did was contemporaneous with the course of Anza's petition, but discussion is postponed, because the subject-matter overlaps into a period beyond September, 1773.

The immediate causes of the Anza expedition of 1774 and of the selection of the route are closely associated with the name of Father Francisco Garcés, a Franciscan of the College of Querétaro. His explorations of 1770 and 1771 indicated that routes existed to both Alta California and New Mexico, and that the natives of the Gila and Colorado were friendly and desirous of conversion. Juan Bautista de Anza was a meritorious officer of Sonora. For a number of years he had been interested in seeking an overland route to Alta California, just as his father had before him. In 1769 he asked permission of Gálvez to make the attempt, but was not permitted to do so. On May 2, 1772, he again proposed such an expedition, but owing to fears that the war in Sonora might again break out, and that an expedition such as Anza proposed might stir up the Indians of the country traversed, the *junta* was not willing to recommend it until further reports should be obtained. While these were being awaited Father Serra arrived in Mexico. His reports showed clearly that Alta California was in need of an overland route. More reports having been received a *junta* was again called. Bucarely, meanwhile, had received notices of foreign aggressions in the Pacific, and these influenced the decision in favor of the expedition. On September 9, 1773, a *junta* recommended that Anza be licensed to make the exploration that he had proposed, and on the 13th Bucarely so decreed. The long-planned advance by way of the Gila and Colorado rivers was to come, at last.

The Franciscans were eager to make a good showing in Pimería Alta, to which they had succeeded in 1768, following the expulsion of the Jesuits. Therefore, there came a renewal of northward explorations and of projects for converting the Indians of the Gila, and even those as far away as Moqui. Preëminent among the *Queretaranos* of Pimería Alta was a man whose achievements should be written large in the history of exploration, Father Francisco Garcés. Although his principal object in his journeys of exploration was the saving of souls, for in him apostolic zeal burned with an ardor comparable with that of his great predecessors in the Franciscan order, his results were of vast importance from the standpoint of exploration and of plans for frontier advance. Garcés took up his ministry at San Javier del Bac in June, 1768. In August, he started on the first of his tours of exploration going through Papaguería to the Gila. In 1769 he seems to have made an unimportant tour as chaplain. In 1770 he went forth again, between October 19 and November 2, covering from Bac to and along the Gila, and the return to Bac. On this journey he travelled among the Pimas Gileños and Opas, both of whom gave him a friendly reception. He reported that the Pimas Gileños were particularly worthy, and were clamorous for the missionaries that Garcés had promised, when he visited them in 1768. They were far from being a savage people, had good fields of wheat and maize, and knew of God. The Opas were a much ruder, if equally kindly people. This exploration added fresh evidence of the accessibility of Alta California from Sonora, for the Pimas were much excited over accounts of people seen in the west, the previous year; these they described in such a way that Garcés realized that they were referring to the soldiers of the 1769 expeditions to Alta California. The accessibility of Moqui was attested by the presence of blankets of Moqui make, the Indians also stating that they had obtained them in trade with other Indians, who had bought them from the Moquis. In concluding his diary of this journey Garcés urged the conversion and conquest of the Pimas Gileños. They were neighbors of the Apaches, and only four or five days from New Mexico; they ruled Papaguería, and were a valiant people. Conversions there he deemed to be a hundred times more important than in the west,[1] because commerce with New Mexico might be obtained through that region, and the Apaches might be checked from extension westward.[2]

A much more important journey was made by Garcés from August to October, 1771, and the information that he gained had a great influence on the opinion of the *junta* which eventually recommended Anza's first expedition. This journey, too, more than any other, helped to determine the route of the subsequent expedition. The details

[1] In summarizing this diary the *junta* understood this to mean west of New Mexico, i.e. *asegurando que las conquistas y fundaciones que se hagan por aquellas partes serán más apreciables que las que se extablezcan p.ʳ el Poniente del Nuevo México.* Resolution of the *junta,* Sept. 9, 1773, in C–2113.
[2] Garcés, Diary [Nov. 2, 1770], in C–2113. This diary was not in fact written until on or shortly before March 8, 1773, when Garcés forwarded this and his 1771 diary, in response to orders from Bucarely. The opinions, therefore, may be based upon his later experience, as well as upon the journey of 1770. Yet this later account is preferable to the original, because it

was the one actually used by the *junta* in coming to its conclusions. Garcés said that he had sent his original diaries of this and other *entradas* to the president of the College of Querétaro, but believed that they could not be understood because of his bad handwriting. Garcés to Bucarely, Mar. 8, 1773, Tubac, in C–2113. A letter of Bucarely of April 26, 1773, says of this diary that it was very difficult to understand, and he doubted whether it would serve as a guide to the *junta* in its attempt to decide whether Anza should be authorized to open an overland communication from Sonora to Monterey. C–2234. Garcés' letters made up in large measure for the confusion of his diary.

of the diary as to Garcés' route might well have been very confusing to the *junta*, due to the fact that Garcés mistook the Colorado for the Gila. In reality he went through Papaguería to the Gila, reaching it just above its junction with the Colorado whither he was desirous of going; he went on past the junction of the rivers, without realizing that he had done so, and then travelled west and south along the Colorado thinking that he was on the Gila and would in that way reach the junction; he crossed the Colorado, believing that he was crossing the Gila, and came upon a vast lagoon, which he took to be the Colorado; he returned to the Colorado and ascended almost to the junction again, without realizing how near he was to the place that he sought; thence he returned through Papaguería. During his wanderings he visited and named many of the villages west of the Colorado and reached the very canyon by which Anza's expedition was to make its way through the mountains. He had also journeyed west of the Gila Mountains in Papaguería, being the first known explorer to take that route, along which he later guided Anza.[3]

The parts of Garcés' diary that weighed most with the *junta* [4] were those dealing with the conditions that he found. In Papaguería there was but little water, which had caused the Indians to refrain from asking for missionaries, although they desired them. In succeeding days, Garcés had passed through lands almost devoid of water, and occasionally through others where there was too much; at one time, when in fact along the eastern bank of the Colorado, he had travelled for several days through swamps. West of the Colorado, or of the Gila as he thought, he found great scarcity of water; he was at that time in the Colorado Desert. Despite these bad conditions, the Indians had good crops of maize and wheat, squash and melons. The

[3] Herbert E. Bolton, *The early explorations of Father Garcés on the Pacific slope*, in *The Pacific Ocean in history*. I had reached the conclusion independently that Garcés mistook the Colorado for the Gila, but Bolton shows in detail Garcés' exact route in his journey of 1771.

[4] Resolution of the *junta*, Sept. 9, 1773, gives a summary of Garcés' diaries. In C-2113.

natives were of powerful physique, and were most kind to Garcés, listening eagerly to his promises of missionaries. The various tribes were hostile to each other, being always at war, despite which fact their numbers were very great. Garcés also got much information tending to prove the existence of routes to Alta California and New Mexico. The *junta* made no note of the facts mentioned by Garcés in its summary of the diaries, but as it had already commented upon them in connection with other documents, they may be chronicled here. While at San Jacome [5] Garcés was told there were men to the west garbed like himself, and others up and down the river. Shells which the Indians wore in their ears had been procured seven days to the west, where two of their number had been and had seen missionaries. The missionaries of New Mexico were seven days to the east, the Indians said, but only four days from San Pedro, near the junction. They spoke of other white men, who wore a different kind of clothing from that of the friars, which agreed with a story, of which Garcés had heard, told to the Pimas Gileños by a slave who had escaped from the Apaches. Garcés met Indians who had seen a compass such as he carried, — proof that they had seen other white men. He also saw many of the painted shawls of Moqui, and garments of black wool and horsehair, a significant fact, because these Indians had no cattle or horses themselves to furnish the raw material for these articles of wearing apparel. They told Garcés that they got them from the Opas, who lived on the route to Moqui. [6]

Bucarely had already begun to consider establishing communication between Sonora and Monterey, before Anza presented his petition. An *expediente* giving an account of Garcés' journey [7] had been sent to him by Pedro Corbalán, and Bucarely forwarded it to Arriaga, March 25, 1772. [8] The Corbalán *expediente* included a letter from Father Esteban de Zalazar to Fathers Perfecto and Mariano de Buena raising conjectures whether Monterey might not

[5] An Indian village west of the Colorado and below its junction with the Gila, named San Jacome by Garcés.

[6] Garcés, *Diary*, Aug. 8 to Oct. 27, 1771, C–1765. Also in C–2113.
[7] C–1806.
[8] C–1931.

be reached by way of the Colorado and Gila. In a letter to Governor Sastre, March 18, 1772, Bucarely asked Sastre to give his views on the matter.[9] Juan Bautista de Anza, like his father and grandfather before him, had followed a military career in the frontier provinces. With regard to his early life little has yet appeared beyond the fragmentary references in Bancroft.[10] Taking these with a report by the Marqués de Rubí, February 21, 1767,[11] Anza's petition of 1770 that he be confirmed as captain of cavalry,[12] and several other documents not used by Bancroft, a fairly complete summary may be obtained. His grandfather had served thirty years at Janos as lieutenant and captain, and his father twenty years in the same capacities at Fronteras, acting also as temporary governor of the province at one time. In the latter capacity he had merited and won general approval, especially by breaking up an Indian conspiracy in 1737. In that year one Arisivi, an Indian, claimed to be a herald of Montezuma, saying that the latter had come back to life to restore the Mexican Empire. Anza's father hanged Arisivi and several of his followers, which ended the revolt. His connection with the *bolas de plata* incident and his death at the hands of the Apaches have already been referred to. The Anza who now enters the account was born at Fronteras in 1735, and entered the service in 1753, taking part thenceforth, as he put it in 1770, in continuous warfare against the Apaches, Seris, Pimas, and Sibubapas. For the first two years he was a volunteer at Fronteras, serving at his own expense. On July 1, 1755, he became a lieutenant at that presidio. He is mentioned as taking part in a campaign under Captain Gabriel de Vildosola against the Apaches in 1758. On February 19, 1760, he was promoted to the captaincy of the presidio of Tubac, but, owing to the death of Viceroy Amarillas, the appointment had never been confirmed.

[9] Cited in Sastre to Bucarely, Oct. 19, 1772, C–2037. Also in C–2113.
[10] An account of Anza's life appeared in the San Mateo *Leader* of December 2, 1909, but it is so inaccurate as to proved details that it leads one to believe that it was a case of mistaken identity.
[11] *Exttracto de la rebistta de inspección*, Tubac, in C–706.
[12] C–1421.

Bancroft refers to a campaign by Anza in 1760 against the
Seris, and to another of 1766 against the Apaches. One of
Anza's principal achievements was the subjecting of the
Pápagos, a tribe of over three thousand Indians, on which
occasion he killed their chief with his own hand. He had
made many campaigns in southern Sonora, against the
Seris and others of the Cerro Prieto, and according to Rubí,
was the one who contributed most to reducing the Suaquis.
In the military operations of Elizondo, Anza was a conspicuous figure. A letter of his to Fray Juan Sarove, a Carme-
lite of Zelaya, May 18, 1769, tells of an attack by him on
the Cerro Prieto a few days before.[13] A detail of the troops
of the Sonora campaign, made by Elizondo, October 16,
1769, shows that there were four divisions, Anza serving in
that commanded by Captain Diego Peyrán. Of the 255
men under Peyrán, Anza commanded 55.[14] That same
month he was one of three commanders engaged in an attack
on the Cerro Prieto. He is also mentioned in the monthly
reports of events sent by Elizondo to the viceroy.[15] In his
petition of 1770 Anza says that he had twice been wounded,
that he had been in fourteen general engagements and many
lesser ones, that his troops had killed 115 persons, captured
109, and taken over 2500 cattle.

Bishop Tamarón, who was at Tubac in 1763, states that
Anza was a married man, his wife being the sister of one
José Manuel Díaz del Carpio, chaplain of the post.[16] Of
his character and abilities the writer has seen many documents giving praise of the highest kind. Even Father Font
(with Anza on his second expedition to Alta California),
who entertained a deep dislike for Anza, never hinted that
he was other than an able, courageous officer. Governor
Sastre seems to have made several veiled thrusts at Anza.
This is all that the writer has found in derogation of Anza,
prior to the Yuma disaster of 1781, while on the other hand,
there are numerous documents in which he is given the
warmest praise, even by Teodoro de Croix, who, after 1871

[13] Santa Cruz de Querétaro, K, No.
11, Leg. 14.
[14] C-1384.
[15] For example, in C-1250.
[16] A.P.C.H., Tamarón, Visita, 113.

was most bitter against him.   One such document especially
worthy of note is the already mentioned report by the Marqués de Rubí.   After recounting Anza's services Rubí says
that "by reason of his activity, valor, zeal, intelligence, and
notable unselfishness he is an all-round good officer (*un
Completto ofizial*), worthy of being distinguished by His
Majesty in remuneration for his services, and as a stimulus
to others."   More directly to the point were Rubí's remarks in praise of Anza as a result of the former's inspection
of Tubac.   Not only Anza's accounts, but also the declara-
tions of his soldiers, showed that he had never done anything prejudicial to his troops, but, on the contrary, had
always treated them liberally; he had actually reduced
prices for them, displaying a generosity which, according to
Rubí, was very rare in the frontier provinces.   Because of
Anza's just administration many people had come to live
at Tubac, to the great advantage of all that section, a fact
which might in future permit of transferring the presidio
to a more advanced point, affording greater opportunity
for discoveries and for reducing the Apaches.

Anza's petition of 1770 for the full rank of captain was
recommended by his immediate chiefs, Juan de Pineda and
Domingo Elizondo, as also by Viceroy Croix.[17]   The matter
was referred to General Alejandro O'Reilly, who replied,
that as the command of a presidio was a very lucrative
one, it ought not to be given too freely, but only as an exceptional reward.   He therefore recommended telling Anza
that his petition would be borne in mind, and would be
granted, if he continued to merit the viceroy's approval.[18]
O'Reilly's recommendation was adopted verbatim by Arriaga,
who wrote to Croix to that effect, October 2, 1770.[19]   So for
the time being Anza's petition was denied.

Anza seems to have been interested for many years prior
to his proposal of 1772 in projects for an advance by way

[17] Croix to Arriaga, Apr. 29, 1770,
C-1473.
[18] O'Reilly to Arriaga, Sept. 27,
1770, C-1549.   O'Reilly's remark would
seem to indicate that graft on the part
of presidio captains was a quasi-recog-
nized institution.   He could not have
been referring to a captain's salary,
which was small.
[19] C-1553.

of the Gila and Colorado rivers. He and another officer planned to make an expedition to the Colorado River in 1756, and Governor Mendoza was to follow with a large force, but soldiers who had accompanied the Jesuits on previous expeditions gave such accounts of the difficulties to be encountered that the idea was given up.[20] Garcés alludes to Anza's having made such an offer in the time of the Jesuits, saying that it was due to the *visitador* of that order that the project was without effect.[21] Anza also proposed an expedition to Gálvez in 1769, similar to the one which he suggested to Bucarely in 1772. This has hitherto rested upon the following direct evidence: Palou, after mentioning the earlier proposal of Anza's father, says: "The said captain, Don Juan Bautista de Anza, was in accord with the desire of his deceased father and just as if the latter might have bequeathed the idea in a clause of his will, he [Anza of Tubac] made an offer to the very illustrious *visitador general* to make an expedition at his own cost from the region of the last presidios and frontiers of Sonora to the great sea, with a view to meeting with the expedition going in search of the said ports [San Diego and Monterey]. He did not succeed in his designs because the *visitador* did not deem the said expedition necessary at that time." [22] Additional evidence may now be given. Both Anza and Gálvez were in the Cerro Prieto district in the fall of 1769, and Anza speaks of meeting Gálvez at that time, and of telling him, as well as Elizondo and the governor, that he had news from the Pimas Gileños proving a route to Alta California by way of Sonora. The Pimas had heard from Indians west of them of the 1769 expeditions to Alta California.[23] A Gálvez report to Arriaga of March 8, 1774, spoke favorably of Anza's proposal to Bucarely. He and the Marqués de Croix had favored such a plan after Gálvez's return from

[20] Stated in Anza to Bucarely, Mar. 7, 1773, in C–2113.

[21] The Spanish is: *atendo también dho capitán (segun me dixo) havia procurado hazer este gran servicio en tpõ de los Pes. Jesuitas por cuio visitador no tuvo efecto.* Garcés to Bucarely, Mar.

8, 1773, in C–2113. This may possibly be a confused reference to Anza's proposal of 1769.

[22] Palou, *Noticias*, III, 154–55.

[23] Anza to Bucarely, May 2, 1772, in C–1872.

Sonora, he said, but they had departed from New Spain before being able to put it into execution.[24] A number of reasons can be imagined why Gálvez did not authorize an expedition at that time, even granting that Anza offered to do so at his own expense. Every available man was needed against the Seris, and Anza's withdrawal would have taken away a number of troops. Moreover, expeditions at the leader's expense in fact involved much governmental expenditure, as in the case of Anza's expedition of 1774, which was made on those terms. Furthermore, Gálvez's illness might have interrupted the project. Finally, Gálvez might have wished to await the result of the other expeditions to Alta California, to see whether the land could be held, before authorizing a new one. Gálvez's own words would imply that he did not refuse his consent, but postponed it.

Anza was well acquainted with Garcés' achievements, the latter's mission of Bac being only a few miles north of Tubac. During Garcés' 1771 tour Anza wrote him a letter, and it reached him in the midst of his wanderings west of the Colorado,[25] — evidence of the friendly disposition of the Indians. At length, on May 2, 1772, Anza wrote to Bucarely asking permission to attempt the discovery of a route from Sonora to Monterey. Anza's letter was mainly an argument that such a route could be opened with less difficulty and at less cost than had been supposed. He had learned from the Pimas in 1769, independently of Garcés, of their having heard from Indians west of them of the 1769 expeditions to Alta California, and Garcés' diaries had confirmed this news. Garcés had referred to the docility of the Yumas in the vicinity of the Colorado and Gila junction, and also to the peaceful character of the Pimas Gileños. The Yumas had asked to see Garcés' compass and glass instrument for making a fire, and also to see other instruments which he did not have, which proved that there must be a route to Alta California or to New Mexico; nobody from Sonora had visited them, and none of the

Yumas had come there, because their enemies barred the
way. Garcés saw a blue ridge, which he thought might
be the one seen by the soldiers who went to Monterey in
1769, and he and Anza were convinced that the distance
to Monterey was less than people had believed. Concluding, Anza asked permission to attempt an expedition to
Monterey, taking with him Garcés and twenty or twenty-five
soldiers of his presidio, which number would be sufficient,
he thought, for the undertaking.[26] The *fiscal*, Areche,
seems to have understood this last statement as an offer
by Anza to pay the expenses of the expedition, except for
the use of the soldiers,[27] and that interpretation was accepted by Anza.[28]

By a decree of August 26, 1772, Bucarely referred Anza's
petition to the engineer Miguel Costansó for an opinion,
the latter having accompanied the expedition of 1769 to
Monterey,[29] and Costansó returned a very important report,
September 5, 1772. He estimated the distance between
Tubac and Monterey as 180 leagues in a straight line. The
Pimas might have heard of the 1769 expeditions, he said,
as the Indians certainly did communicate with each other.
He himself had seen implements at the Santa Barbara
Channel, such as knives, pieces of sword, and other things,
which had come from Spanish soldiers in New Mexico, not
brought directly, but passed from hand to hand, as the
Indians were too hostile to one another to stray far from
their native land. A pass would have to be found through
mountain ridges between the Colorado River and the Pacific
Ocean; the mountains were certainly extensive and rough,
but if the Indians crossed them, Spaniards could. Pioneers'
tools, such as levers, spades, and pickaxes should be carried,
however, and two soldiers should be brought from San
Diego to serve as guides, once the expedition should approach the Pacific. The utility of such a route was un-
questionable. Lands in the north of Baja California were

[26] In C–1872.
[27] Areche to Bucarely, Oct. 12, 1772,
in C–1872.
[28] Anza to Bucarely, Mar. 7, 1773,
in C–2113. It is possible that Anza may
have said this in another letter, although
Areche did not refer to any other.
[29] In C–1872.

too poor to give even the slightest aid in products to San Diego and Monterey, and from Loreto, farther south, it was three hundred leagues to San Diego, by a hard road, which rendered help difficult. It was a long, arduous voyage from San Blas, and the boats were too small to permit of transporting families. Thus, Spaniards in San Diego and Monterey must remain unmarried. On the other hand, Sonora produced every kind of grain and fruit, and the distance was not excessive, wherefore provisions and families might be sent from Sonora, giving the new settlements greater solidarity than they then had.[30]

The Anza letter and Costansó's report were referred to the *fiscal*, Areche, who reported, October 12, 1772, recommending that the expedition be authorized, since Anza was to undergo the expense. Garcés should go, too, and the tools suggested by Costansó should be taken. Anza was entitled to praise for suggesting the expedition, for it would be a great advantage to have a better route than the slow, arduous ones by way of San Blas or Loreto. It would help the missions and presidios of Alta California, and those of Sonora as well, by giving the latter a market for its products. If Alta California were as fertile as claimed, it could become populous, if families were sent to develop it. This would reduce the burden on the royal treasury in maintaining the new establishments, a very great one with no better routes than the two maintained at the time. The only objection to the project was the withdrawal of troops from Tubac, they being needed against the Apaches, but this could be overcome by transferring the twenty-three soldiers at Altar, supplying their places until Anza's return by use of militia. Anza should be instructed to treat the Indians with kindness, for the better security of the route, if discovered. He should be assured that in the event of success the king would be asked to give him a suitable reward.[31]

A *junta* was called for October 17. In addition to the Anza, Costansó, and Areche documents Bucarely ordered

[30] In C–1872. [31] In C–1872.

those of Anza's father, Rebolledo, and the king, of 1737–38, on the same subject, to be submitted to the *junta*.[32] The *junta* decided, October 17, 1772, that more information was necessary. The following were its resolutions: Garcés' opinion should be asked, and a copy of his 1771 diary should be sent for; the *expediente* should be sent to Governor Sastre, and his opinion asked, whether Anza's undertaking would disturb the peace of that government; Anza should be thanked for the zeal which his proposal indicated; and a copy of the papers should be sent to the king.[33] Bucarely concurred in the decision, and wrote presently for the reports requested, writing at length also to Arriaga, October 27, 1772, reciting the course of Anza's petition and forwarding a *testimonio* on the matter.[34]

Before Sastre had time to receive the papers sent to him at the *junta*'s order, he had replied to Bucarely's letter of March 18, in a communication dated October 19, 1772, making suggestions based upon the reports of Garcés' explorations of 1768, 1770, and 1771. He advised establishing three missions in Papaguería, the desolate region between Sonora and the Colorado. There were no religious there, although the Pápago Indians were Christians, due to their habit of bringing children to the missions for baptism. There was plenty of pasture in Papaguería, but the land was almost useless for crops or for cattle, because of the scarcity of water. Three missions would be practicable, however, and would serve a good end, as that land was a refuge for vagabonds and bad Indians, under no legal or spiritual restraint whatever. Sastre supported Garcés' proposal for five missions among the Pimas Gileños, for the land was rich, the Indians wanted missionaries, and they were enemies of the Apaches. He also called attention to Garcés' good reception among the rude Ópatas. Referring to Garcés' 1771 journey, he noted the friendliness of the Indians, and the supposed proximity of New Mexico. Garcés

[32] Bucarely, *Decree*, Oct. 13, 1772, in C–1872. The documents of 1737–38 have already been considered in chap. II.

[33] In C–1872. The same documents of C–1872 appear with later proceedings on Anza's petition to form C–2113.
[34] C–2045.

thought New Mexico to be only ten or twelve leagues from
Pimería Alta, whereas it was a journey of forty days by
the route then in use.[35] Furthermore, New Mexico and
Monterey were not more than a month's journey apart, in
Garcés' opinion. Garcés had already applied to his president, Father Juan Crisóstomo Gil de Bernabé, in August,
1772, for permission to seek a route to Monterey from
Pimería Alta. Such an attempt, said Sastre, would result
in great advantage, if successful.[36] Father Zalazar, commenting upon Garcés' explorations, had intimated that the
Indians would not let Garcés go through their lands, but
Sastre believed that he would be successful, and should be
permitted to try his project. If the eight new missions
were founded, they should have two missionaries each. All
of his proposals might be accepted, said Sastre, without
endangering the peace of Sonora.[37]

Bucarely acknowledged Sastre's report, January 13,
1773,[38] and sent a copy of it to Arriaga, two weeks later.
In the letter to Arriaga, he told why he had called the
junta. Garcés' explorations, he said, "promise the rich
fruit of a very abundant multitude of souls, disposed to be
included in the body of our holy religion. This . . . and
the fact that the discovery of a way of communication by
land with the port of Monterey may be accomplished, obliged
me to hold a *junta* . . . to decide upon the petition presented
from the presidio of Tubac." He did not at that time favor
establishing the missions proposed by Sastre.[39]

Anza's petition was at this stage when Junípero Serra
arrived in Mexico, in February, 1773. Richman, by emphasis at least, would make it appear that Serra played the
principal part in causing the expedition to be authorized.
Serra's glory as a missionary is sufficiently great, without
the need of foisting upon him every other meritorious action
in the early history of Alta California. It is the popular

[35] By way of El Paso.
[36] Sastre makes no mention of Anza's proposal of which he may not have known, but it is almost certain that Garcés knew of it. The latter's re-

quest, therefore, may have been with a view to accompanying Anza.
[37] C-2037.   [38] In C-2113.
[39] C-2152. Acknowledged by Arriaga, May 12, 1773, C-2254.

belief that Serra conquered and held the province, since his
name is the only one that is generally known. Nevertheless,
as regards the Anza expedition, there is hardly a doubt that
it would have been authorized, without Serra's presence in
Mexico. Aside from the fact that conditions warranted it,
the *fiscal* and *junta* both advised it, the former's advice
being given before Serra arrived in Mexico. Nor were the
memorials of Serra presented to the *junta* which considered
Anza's proposal, its resolution being based on other documents, although members of the *junta* as individuals knew
of the Serra documents, as they had served in a *junta* that
considered them. Serra's primary concern in Mexico was
to settle the relations between the religious and the military
in Alta California, not the question of a Sonora route, and
the matter of a route from Sonora seems to have been discussed by him only after his opinion had been asked by
Bucarely.[40] That he advised the expedition, is no reason
for assigning him the credit for its authorization any more
than to the many others who did the same. Yet, although
the Serra documents were not before the *junta*, although
Serra did not dwell at length on the matter of overland
routes, and although he seemed to prefer an expedition from
New Mexico, rather than one from Sonora, his memorials
must have had a very great influence, because they so clearly
portrayed Alta California's local needs, which naturally
called for an overland route as one of the remedies. After
Garcés and Anza, perhaps comes Serra in the list of those
entitled to credit, although it will not do to underrate the
advice of Costansó and Areche, nor even that of Sastre.
Most entitled of all, however (and it is believed that this
will appear in the course of this work), was the viceroy.[41]

[40] Palou, *Vida*, 185.

[41] Richman states that Serra's memorials suggested that "supply routes be
explored, first, from Sonora, and then
from New Mexico," but does not intimate that Bucarely had first asked
his opinion on those points. Coming
to a consideration of the immediate
preliminaries of the expedition, he says:
"but what of Serra's representation in
favor of explorations for supply routes
to Alta California by way of the present
Arizona and New Mexico?" The documents considered by the *junta* prior to
Serra's arrival in Mexico are then
briefly reviewed, when Richman says:
"It was with the Anza project at this
stage that (February–March, 1773)
Bucarely was waited upon by Serra.
Garcés' diary of the *entrada* of 1771 was
examined, and on September 17, the
captain of Tubac was authorized to

Serra did not relate his remarks directly to Anza's proposed expedition, except for one paragraph in his March 13 memorial, in which he said that it was well worth undertaking. There should also be a westward expedition from Santa Fé, he said, opening communication between Alta California and New Mexico. The discovery of a route from New Mexico would be especially conducive to spiritual conquest.[42] The March 13 memorial made several references to voyages from San Blas to Alta California. Shortly afterward, it was proposed by the *Tribunal de Cuentas* of Mexico to dispense with the Department of San Blas, in order to cut down expense, and to depend upon mule trains to convey supplies to Alta California.[43] This called forth a protest from Serra, April 22, 1773, an important document as evidence of the insufficiency of the peninsula as a supply route to Alta California. Says Serra, "First, to carry the said provisions by land is not only difficult but also practically impossible; second, supposing that by applying our energies it might be done in all security, it would necessitate

make a military reconnoissance to the establishments of Monterey." In a note Richman adds: "The influence of Serra in securing a determination of the matter is mentioned by Palou (*Noticias*, vol. III, p. 155). Direct evidence of it is furnished by Arriaga in a dispatch to the Viceroy, dated March 9, 1774, which refers to a letter from Bucarely of date Sept. 26, 1773, wherein the latter had said that *Haviendo oydo al Presidente de las Misiones de San Diego y Monterey, Fr. Junípero Serra, que apoyó el pensamiento de Anza, convocó V.E. á Junta de Guerra, etc.*" The quotation from Palou is accurate, but something further may be said of the direct evidence. The statement (which is from a summary of Bucarely's letter, not the letter itself) is only part of the whole, the whole reading as follows: *consiguiente á los anteriors avisos sobre la proporsión q^e hizo el Capⁿ del Presidio de Tubac . . . Da V.E. con testimonio en carta de veinte y seis de Sep^{re} llegados los informes pedidos, y haviendo oydo V.E. al Presidente de las Missions de Sⁿ Diego y Monterrey Fr. Junípero Senrra q^e apoyó*

el pensam^{to} de Anza combocó V.E. á Junta de Grra y Hazd^q etc. In other words Serra's report was only one of several, and may have been specially mentioned because the only one not included in the *expediente*. Again, Richman: "by the success of Anza (a success due in part to the presence of Serra in Mexico, in the spring of 1773) the work of Portolá was made sure of completion." As a climax to his chapter entitled "San Francisco founded" with second title "Sonora to the Sea," Mr. Richman has "the venerable Junípero Serra" gazing at San Francisco Bay, the implication being impossible to escape, that he was the one primarily responsible for bringing to pass all those events which had produced the Anza expeditions and the settlement of San Francisco. Richman has erred, not by directly incorrect statements, but by literary over-emphasis of Serra's share.

[42] In C–2103. Palou, *Noticias*, III, 41–42.

[43] Referred to in Gálvez to Arriaga, Mar. 8, 1774, C–2566.

much more expense than at present; third, by this project we would certainly lose the best thing of all, the very commendable disposition to accept the faith which the natives in all that land have." In proof of the first point, he said that both Californias were in dire straits for mules. Many had been taken from the missions of Baja California, when Gálvez sent the expeditions to Monterey, the plan being to replace them by shipments from Sonora, but, owing to the difficulty of shipment or to some other reason, not even one had been replaced. Although the deficiency had been supplied to some extent by breeding, that method had never proved sufficient to stock the peninsula, because of the land's sterility; in the past, it had been necessary to depend on mules sent from the opposite coast. There was also a great scarcity of mules at Monterey. Figuring on the basis of supplies recently sent to California, it would take fifteen hundred mules to carry them, and would require not less than a hundred muleteers. How was it possible to get that number of mules across the Gulf to Loreto, he asked, when not even a few could be transported in the space of three years? And if they could be obtained, what would there be for them to eat in Baja California? For his part, said Serra, he never expected to see the successful establishment of a supply route up the peninsula. The rest of the memorial may be briefly noted, Serra advancing strong arguments in support of his second contention, and saying as to the third, that the passing of these mule trains in charge of men of questionable morality would have a bad effect upon the Indians along the route, and would operate against conversions.[44] This must have weighed heavily with the venerable Father-President, but it does not seem that his arguments on the first two points were on that account an overstatement. At any rate, whether due to Serra or not, the San Blas establishment was retained.

At length, the reports requested by the *junta* of October 17, 1772, began to find their way to Mexico. Sastre's

[44] A.P.C.H., *Prov. St. Papers*, I,91–103.

M

reply, January 21, 1773, was noticeably different in tone from his previous letter. Anza ought not to take any troops with him, he said, but should be accompanied by Garcés alone, thus avoiding the danger of arousing the suspicions of the Indians at the sight of troops, which positively would be the result if they were with him. Referring to his October 19 letter he repeated his comment on Garcés' achievement of 1771. If New Mexico were so near Pimería Alta and only a month's journey from Monterey, all that was necessary was for Garcés to explore the route from New Mexico to Monterey. Anza might be permitted to make an expedition also, provided he went alone.[45]

Anza was in the field on the Apache frontier when Bucarely's letter of October 28, 1772, written in accordance with the resolution of the *junta*, came to him. He wrote from there, January 22, 1773, that he must get permission from Sastre to go to his presidio, before he could answer Bucarely's questions, because his papers were there. Meanwhile, he was quite certain that the Indians en route to Monterey would welcome an expedition such as he had proposed. In his opinion, too, it would not cause trouble among the Indians already subjected, nor among those between the Spanish settlements and the Colorado whom it was planned to reduce ; rather, it would give them pleasure.[46] At length, March 7, 1773, Anza wrote to Bucarely from his presidio of Tubac. First he discussed Jesuit visits to the Gila and Colorado, and the comparatively slight results arising from them. Yet, one poor religious [Garcés] had made this journey alone in a very few days, taking only as much as one horse could carry, and living among the Indians. This proved that they were incapable of doing harm, if treated with the kindness that was the due of their simplicity. The late Antonio de Olguín, lieutenant of Terrenate, who went on the last Jesuit visit to the two rivers, had told Anza that it was due to ill-treatment that the Indians had attempted to steal the horses of that expedition, and yet, at every Indian village the natives had asked for ministers.

45 In C–2113.   46 In C–2113.

According to Olguín and the soldiers, the Jesuits made explorations in a faulty manner, from which it resulted that no exploration was made of the lands on the other side of the Colorado. Anza said that he did not believe anything that the Jesuits had written or said, because their statements were contradicted by those who accompanied them.[47] Garcés, however, was a man of integrity, and his reports were the most fundamental on the subject.

Knowing little about the lands occupied by the Dominicans on the other side of the Colorado, Anza could not say whether they would be prejudiced by the founding of missions at that river from the Sonora side. However, even if the Quiquimas and Yumas, the only tribes there that were definitely known, should prove to be in Dominican territory, it seemed to him that that order would suffer no harm by the establishment of missions on the east bank of the river; rather, it would help the Dominicans, because it would be easier to carry provisions and other necessaries to them by that route than by sea. As matters were, they must have their needs supplied at particular seasons, or wait a long time. This route would establish the commerce of the peninsula upon a better basis, as well as that of San Diego and Monterey.

Some persons said, continued Anza, that he had proposed this expedition in order to disturb the peace of the provinces.[48] On the contrary, it would help them, as it might result in an extension of their trade to New Mexico, and there would also be traffic with Indians, although of less account. Great good, temporal as well as spiritual, would come to the Indians by the establishment of missions, because they would have to live at peace, instead of destroying one another like wild beasts, as under existing conditions. The Indians along Anza's proposed route were lacking in arms and in courage, and were not apt to cause trouble any more

[47] This was only shortly after the expulsion of the Jesuits, when everything that they had done was represented in an unfriendly light. It seems strange, however, that not a single Jesuit document should have been used in the deliberations leading to the Anza expeditions.

[48] This probably referred to Sastre, who had opposed Anza's project on that ground. The "provinces" means Sinaloa and Sonora.

than the Pápagos and Pimas Gileños had done, when
their territories were traversed. The last named were
better armed and more warlike than the others, but they
allowed Spaniards to live among them and render them
[religious?] service at any time. Because of this docility
of the Indians, missions and presidios were not yet necessary
among them. Since the suppression of the Pimas [Bajos]
and Seris, the presidio of Altar had had little to do, and
could for a time supply all needs. Tubac was just then
busily engaged with the Apaches, who might hinder an
advance to the Colorado and Gila, but the campaign then
being waged against them would lead to their suppression,
it was hoped. Once the Apaches were conquered, the troops
of Altar and Tubac could be used for more advanced establishments, and the soldiers of Horcasitas and Buenavista
might in like manner be employed, as the original reason
for founding those presidios, to check the Seris and their
allies, was no longer operative.

Anza's concluding paragraphs bring out the difficulties that
he had to face in the way of jealous rivals, of whom, doubtless, the most prominent was Sastre. His remarks, however,
were couched in the usual diplomatic style that distinguished
him in all his writings. He mentioned no names, but was
probably aware that Sastre had belittled his plan. The
data furnished by Garcés and himself would be enough,
he said, to enable Bucarely to make a decision. He himself had no other concern in the undertaking than a desire
to serve Their Majesties, for whom he would meet death,
if necessary. Difficulties might be expected through the
efforts of rivals, who always opposed such undertakings
when they did not propose them. If Bucarely should
decide to authorize the expedition, Anza asked three
favors : that he might be directly under Bucarely's orders,
"the better to be understood," by which he probably meant
that he did not want to be under Sastre ; that the governor
be ordered to furnish such assistance as Anza should need,
for all of which, with the exception of the troops, Anza
would gladly pay out of his own pocket ; and that he

might go to Mexico upon his return, to deliver his report
in person.[49]

At about the same time, March 8, Garcés wrote to
Bucarely enclosing his diaries, which have already been
treated elsewhere. A copy of the 1771 diary was sent to
Arriaga by Bucarely with his letter of April 26, 1773.[50] In
his letter Garcés recited a number of reasons why Anza's
undertaking was worthy of approval. Inasmuch as Garcés
could not get his own projects carried out,[51] he was supporting Anza's, which seemed to be more favorably viewed.
Anza was the right type of man, for his "zeal in the service
of both Majesties is well proved . . . the said captain is
exceedingly affable, patient, liberal, well-beloved by the
Indians, punctilious in matters of the service, and with
no improper habits of life." Again, Anza had "a sufficient
fund of discretion to resolve any unforeseen incident . . .
and the manners to meet European people or those of other
quality." For Garcés to go alone would be difficult, if
not impossible. The Indians that Garcés saw were exceedingly docile, and he had heard that they were poorly armed ;
moreover, Anza proposed to go with a considerable force,
which would obviate any possible danger. The news that
came in 1769 to these Indians about white people to the
west of them, accounts of which Garcés also received in
his 1770 and 1771 journeys, indicated that a route existed.

The expedition would not prejudice the Dominicans,
but on the contrary would help them. Their conversions
must begin with the Indians nearest the mouth of the Colorado, the Quiquimas, who were terrible enemies of the
coast Pimas as also of the Yumas and their allies, through
whose territories Anza proposed to go. The Yumas and
other tribes would be charged by Anza not to fight against
the Quiquimas, and peace would certainly prevail if a mission each were to be placed among the coast Pimas and
the Yumas. The Dominicans would then require less of a
mission guard, as the Quiquimas could have no other enemies

[49] In C–2113.
[50] C–2234.
[51] For the conquest and conversion
of the Pimas Gileños.

than the tribes named. The ability to control the Indians on both sides of the Colorado would be advantageous to both sections, making rebellion less likely in each place, and aiding in the work of conversions. Every step in aid of conversions ought to be taken, lest neighboring tribes be lost, or the Pimas of the coast revolt again. The Pimas would never have risen in the past, had they not been supported by their numerous relatives. If ministers had been placed in Pimería and along the two rivers sixty years before, at an annual expense of ten or twelve thousand *pesos*, the king would not then have to maintain two hundred soldiers, and the conquest would have advanced much farther.

The march to San Diego would not be too difficult, if the bad stretch between Sonoita and the Yuma country were avoided, but, for the journey to Monterey, Garcés would advise going farther up the Colorado, and searching for a pass through the mountains. After giving further evidence to prove the existence of a route, in particular the presence among the Indians whom Garcés had visited of articles which must have come from the Pacific shore of the Californias and not from the Gulf, Garcés went on to say that he did not regard Monterey as very far distant, and that the tribes along the way would probably be friendly to one another, which would enable Anza, by means of gifts to obtain interpreters to accompany the expedition. Tobacco was recommended as a gift particularly pleasing to Indians. With that and a preliminary notice of the coming of the expedition, by sending Garcés ahead, no fear of the Indians needed to be entertained. It was only necessary to tell them that the king was sending an expedition to visit them, because they were good people, and that would win their affection. If there were the least likelihood of danger, Garcés would not favor this proposal. He himself had gone without escort in his journeys, nor would he have consented to go with a very few soldiers or with a commander in whom he had no confidence, but the present case was different, — all the more so in that Anza had made the offer of his own free will.

To maintain the route to be discovered by Anza would not cost much, as there were already three presidios suited to the purpose, — Horcasitas, Buenavista, and Altar. If the expedition were authorized, orders for it should be sent sealed and without appeal, for in lands so remote from the capital as Sonora it was possible for interested persons to prevent useful undertakings. Finally, he recommended the surrender of the missions of Pimería Baja by the Franciscans, who should proceed to the new fields. The missions given up by them should not be secularized, but should be left to other orders, the Indians continuing free from taxation.[52]

On June 14, 1773, Bucarely referred to Areche the Anza and Garcés letters, the latter's diaries, and the previous file of papers on Anza's petition.[53] Areche replied, August 14, 1773, that he had nothing to add to his previous report, but suggested that these documents, including Sastre's letter of January 21 be cited before the same *junta*, that it might resolve whether the expedition should be authorized or not.[54] Prior to the *junta's* decision Bucarely got word that the English and Russians were pushing to the northwest coasts of North America, and it will be shown in a later chapter that Bucarely's opinion was influenced by the news. It is possible, however, that Anza's expedition would have been authorized anyway. The *junta*, at least, made no mention of foreign danger, and if convinced of the practicability of the route, the docility of the Indians, and the security of Sonora, perhaps also of the sound basis of the Alta California establishments, seemed certain to recommend the expedition.[55] It is possible, too, that Bucarely might have favored Anza's proposals on the long-standing ground of foreign danger without the spur of contemporary reports.

[52] In C–2113.
[53] In C–2113.
[54] In C–2113.
[55] It is possible that the members of the *junta* did not know of the supposed foreign activities at the time. Some evidence of this, although over two months later than the authorization of the expedition, is Bucarely's

letter to Arriaga of November 26, 1773. In it he asked permission, for the sake of secrecy, to dispense with consent of the *junta* for expenditures by him to check foreign encroachments. C–2430. The failure to mention the particular emergency in the documents before the *junta* is an indication to the same effect.

By a decree of September 1, 1773, Bucarely added to the *expediente* considered previously by the *junta* and recently by Areche several documents already discussed in this chapter and one other,[56] the last named being a letter from Arriaga to Bucarely, May 12, 1773, acknowledging Bucarely's of January 27, and giving approval for what had been done thus far.[57]   On September 9, 1773, the *junta* met for the second time to consider Anza's petition.[58]   After summarizing, quoting, or making brief reference to the documents before it, the *junta* made its resolution in the following terms:

"Having read the documents named, and having considered the whole matter referred to, it was resolved by unanimous agreement: That it was a useful and proper thing to discover a route by way of the Gila and Colorado rivers to the new establishments of San Diego and Monterey, according to the terms that Captain Don Juan Bautista de Anza proposes; That for that purpose he may take twenty volunteer soldiers of his own choice, who will make use of their arms only in the unavoidable event of having to defend themselves, comporting themselves toward all Indians along the route with the greatest kindliness and moderation, so that they may be well disposed to the Spanish, and to this matter the said Captain Anza will give every careful attention, on account of its great importance in the service of God and the king; That to replace the soldiers that have to accompany him, an equal number may be recruited to serve for the time that

---

[56] In C–2113. The documents referred to were: Sastre's letter of Oct. 19, 1772; Bucarely's to Sastre, Jan. 13, 1773; and Bucarely's to Arriaga, Jan. 27, 1773.

[57] C–2254. Also in C–2113.

[58] The following men took part in this meeting: Bucarely; Domingo Valcárcel, member of the Council of the Indies, *decano* of the *Audiencia* of Mexico, *auditor*, etc.; Felix V. Malo, second *subdecano* of the *Audiencia* José de Areche, *fiscal;* Juan de Barroeta; Santiago Abad; Pedro Toral, who signed with his mother's name, Valdés; Juan Gutiérrez; Fernando Mangino; and Juan de Arce. Valcárcel, Malo, Areche, and Barroeta belonged to the viceroy's council. Valcárcel, Barroeta, Abad, Valdés, Gutiérrez, Mangino, and Arce, besides Bucarely, held offices connected with financial administration. With the exception of Malo, all of these had been present at the *junta* of October 17, 1772. Two others at that *junta* were not present at this: José del Toro, of Bucarely's council, *subdecano* of the *Audiencia*, and holding administrative offices connected with taxation; and Fernando Mesia, the treasurer.

it takes for this expedition, and for that, compensation
will be made by the royal treasury; That he shall be accompanied by the Reverend Father Francisco Garcés, whose
advice, on account of his wide experience, shall be taken,
for the success of the expedition, in the contingencies that
may occur, and the said Reverend Father Garcés may be
accompanied by another religious agreeable to him and of
good conduct; That the said captain make no establishment, directing his route to the latitude of Monterey, and
from there give an account to His Excellency the Viceroy
in minute detail of all that shall have occurred in the journey,
so that the latter may form a judgment and give the orders
that are fitting; That once the discovery is accomplished,
the said captain may come to this Court to inform His
Excellency of what he shall deem fitting, as he [Anza] proposes; That orders on the subject be sent directly to the
said captain, and that the latter may give an account
directly to His Excellency of what happens; That, to render
the assistance which he needs and asks for, suitable orders
may be given to the *comandante inspector* and to the governor
of the province, His Excellency making such arrangements
as he may deem proper for the happy outcome of this exploration, from which so many advantages may result, if it is
successful, for the greater protection of the new establishments of San Diego and Monterey; That transcripts of
the proceedings may be drawn up, of everything that may
be necessary, [one] for the record in the *Real Tribunal de
Cuentas* of this special, although small expense, [another] to
go to the captain, and [another] to give an account to His
Majesty." [59]

Four days later Bucarely decreed that the resolution of
the *junta* be executed,[60] and on September 26, 1773, he
wrote to Arriaga that he had granted Anza's petition, enclosing a *testimonio* of what had occurred.[61] No further
official action was necessary, although in theory the royal
approval ought to be obtained. On March 9, 1774, Arriaga
wrote to Bucarely, reciting the latter's instructions to Anza,

[59] In C–2113.   [60] In C–2113.   [61] C–2388.

and adding: "The king being informed of what has been referred to . . . has been pleased to approve everything done in this matter." [62]   On that day Anza was nearly across the Colorado Desert; by the time of its receipt in Mexico he must have been near Tubac on the return march. [63]

[62] C-2567.

[63] The facts recited in the last paragraph serve as a reminder of the inadequacy of our knowledge of Spanish colonial institutions, which, indeed, is apparent to anybody making a study of the field or a portion of it, whether he deal with a narrative or an institutional subject. In the present instance the questions suggest themselves, Who was primarily responsible for the authorization of the Anza expedition, and What proportionate share in it did various officials or governmental agencies have? It is believed that enough documents will be cited in later chapters to leave no reasonable doubt as to the answer to the first question. But if the present work were to stop here, one could not answer that question with certainty, and in any event one could not answer the second query without a wider knowledge of Spanish colonial institutions than we now have. The trouble is that institutional studies have employed inadequate materials. The laws of the Indies have been the basis, supplemented by such other source material as exists in print. Only a small percentage of this material is helpful to show the actual workings of colonial administration. The Spanish have always been adept at making laws which they straightway proceed to disregard or use only when they fit the case in hand. Materials in print are an infinitesimal fraction and by no means a good selection of those which exist in manuscript. Better institutional studies might be written, if investigators would use the official materials to be found in the Archivo de Indias, tracing an institution, for example, through a given period, illustrating it by a definite piece of narrative. In that way we may learn eventually just what were the functions of the greater governing agencies, and of the lesser ones as well.

The present study is not an institutional one, but some remarks may be ventured in order to call attention to governmental procedure in a given instance. The method of transacting official business may be gathered from noting the course of documents referred to in this and succeeding chapters. For example, Anza's petition went to the viceroy, the *fiscal*, Costansó, Sastre, the *junta*, Arriaga, and the Council of the Indies. The *expediente*, or file of papers, for this one matter alone was so long that it could not be read carefully in a single day. Nor is there anything exceptional in its length. Many other matters might come up the same day of equal voluminousness. Spanish officialdom encouraged long, full reports, often complaining because some document, which the reader may think verbose enough, was not sufficiently detailed in information. The number of reports that might be called for in a case involving the widest range of official connection is amazing. For example, Lacy's reports of Russian aggressions passed through the hands of Grimaldi, Arriaga, and Bucarely before action was taken, and would normally have gone to Areche and the *junta*, but for Bucarely's request for permission to dispense with the consent of the latter. Before action was completed a series of letters, reports, instructions, and diaries would be written by captains of ships, governors of provinces, commissaries, religious, and others that would fill volumes. All of these would go into the *expediente* and might come up again *in toto* upon some similar occasion. The size of the *expediente* would be swollen to double or treble its proportions, because of the practice of making what almost amounted to a copy of the letter being answered and inserting that in the reply, that being required by law. If copies sent to different persons could be brought together, the papers would again be multiplied in volume. It becomes clear why the government had to rely on its bureaucracy. No one man could possibly read all the documents on a given matter without neglecting everything else. It was the usual rule for the viceroy to accept the decision of the *fiscal* or of the *junta*. Even then, execution depended very largely upon minor officials, especially in distant provinces, where the wishes of the viceroy were often disregarded, under color of some plausible excuse.

By law the greatest authority rested with the king, aided by agencies around him, such as the *ministro general, Consejo de Indias, Casa de Contratación,* and *Contaduría General.* A second stage of authority was that of the viceroy, having many aids, but also many checks, as by the *audiencia,* the *junta,* and others. Third came the vast horde of provincial and local officials, of which the central figure, though handicapped in turn, was the governor of a province. Such was the law, and such perhaps the practice as regards veto power or negation of action, but as regards positive acts the deciding factor in a given case might be, and usually was, perhaps, some official in the third grade of authority. The intent of the law would be carried out if men in the second and first ranks displayed exceptional industry and ability, and then only, as a rule, in matters of wide scope in the case of the vice-regal government, and of very wide scope in the case of the royal government.

A capable viceroy was in a peculiarly good position to do effective work, being near enough to the thing to be done by the lower grade of officials, far enough away from the group above him, and able to dominate those around him. The Anza petition is a good test case. It was opposed unavailingly by Governor Sastre of Sonora. Arriaga might have interposed his veto, but could not have caused the expedition; for many years he had backed the principle of such an overland advance, but no expedition had been made, although Arriaga was an exceptionally able *ministro general.* Of the group around Bucarely the *Audiencia* of Mexico contributed nothing as such, although the *junta* was in part composed of its members. They might also be members of the viceroy's council; three members of the *audiencia* taking part in the *junta* of September 9, 1773, were also in the council; another member of that *junta* was in the council, but not in the *audiencia.* (*Supra* n. 58.) It is also well to remember that the *fiscal* of the *audiencia* had in fact become a servant of the viceroy. (Cf. chap. II, n. 70.) Credit for granting the petition lies either with the *junta* or with Bucarely for no other governmental agency, other than those mentioned and disposed of, intervened.

The *Junta de Guerra y Real Hacienda* of the viceroyalty was a very important institution in the period covered by this work, one upon which little or no information can be obtained in clear form in printed works. Its consent was necessary for the expenditure of royal funds, and it was often called to deliberate whether a given project should be ordered or not. But it was not an insuperable legal obstacle to a viceroy. On November 26, 1773, Bucarely wrote to Arriaga asking for permission to dispense with the *junta's* consent to expenditures undergone with a view to checking Russian aggressions, alleging the desirability of secrecy as the reason for his request. (C–2430.) He was permitted to expend money on his own responsibility. (Revilla Gigedo, *Informe,* par. 47, April 12, 1793, Mexico. C–5613.) The *reglamento* of 1786 was put into effect without the previous assent of a *junta.* (Revilla Gigedo, par. 61.) A royal order of April 14, 1789, empowered Viceroy Flores to make expenditures with regard to the occupation of Nootka and the exploration of the Russian establishments in the northwest without the necessity of asking permission of a *junta.* (Revilla Gigedo, par. 92–93.) Thus, viceroys dispensed with the *junta's* authority either with or without royal consent. More important than the viceroys' legal rights, however, was the actual authority that they were able to exercise as a result of their relations with individuals of the *junta.* Members of the *junta* were, as a rule, men holding administrative positions under the viceroy, often being, as already noted, members of his council. Moreover, membership in the *junta* was not always the same, men skilled in the subject discussed often being called, presumably by the viceroy. The number at a *junta* varied. At the Anza *junta* of 1772 there were eleven present, there were ten in 1773, and twelve in 1774. There seems to have been a difference, however, between a *junta de guerra y real hacienda,* such as those called with relation to Anza's projects, and such a *junta* as that which on January 21, 1768, authorized Gálvez to proceed to the frontier provinces to carry out reforms. In the former case most of the members had offices having to do with financial administration; in the latter, there might be few or none. Those at the above-mentioned 1768 *junta* were: Viceroy Croix; Archbishop Lorenzana; Gálvez himself; Toro and Santaella of the *audiencia;* Cornide, *asesor general* of the viceroyalty; Panes, a military officer; and Vasante, superintendent of the customs house of Mexico City. The *junta de guerra y real hacienda* which met in May, 1773, to consider Serra's petition had practically the same membership as the Anza *junta* of September 9, 1773. Especially noteworthy in this connection is the case of Fernando Mesia who was present at the *junta* of 1772 concerning Anza's request, absent in 1773, as also from the Serra *junta* of that year, and present again in 1774. (*Infra*, chap. XII, n. 70.) Anza's second expedition was ordered by Bucarely on November 28, 1774, without consulting the *junta*, which was called, however, on December 16, when it recommended certain details, treating the expedition itself as one already decided upon. (In C-2496.) The day before, Bucarely had already written to Rivera that the expedition was coming. (A.P.C.H., *Prov. St. Pap., Ben. Misc.*, II, 20–25.) In fine, it can hardly be doubted that a viceroy could dominate the *junta* if he so desired. Finally, Bucarely took a keen interest in Anza's project. This may be deduced, not only from his official correspondence, but also from private letters written by him to General O'Reilly. (A.G.I., *legajo*, 88–5–17.) Therefore, it would seem that Bucarely is entitled to the chief credit for authorizing the first Anza expedition.

CHAPTER VIII

APPROACHES OF THE RUSSIANS AND THE ENGLISH TO SPANISH POSSESSIONS OF THE PACIFIC NORTHWEST

DANGER of encroachments by foreign powers has been given prominent notice in preceding chapters as a principal cause for frontier advance in New Spain in the eighteenth century. Between 1773 and 1776 this factor was to be more than usually operative, or certainly more than usually a cause of action, under the guiding hand of the great viceroy, Bucarely. It affected every other phase of activity related to northwestward advance, and in many cases, certainly as regards the Spanish voyages of discovery, it was the direct cause of what occurred. It seems worth while at this point, therefore, to treat of this factor by itself. It may be viewed in three ways, considering: first, approaches through the centuries of nations who most threatened New Spain between 1773 and 1776, giving an idea of the actual danger; second, the foreign policy of Spain between 1763 and 1779, in an attempt to acquire a view in proper perspective of Spain's attitude concerning the problems of colonial defence, in particular her attitude concerning the defence of the indefinitely extending Californias; third, a detailed account of what Spain thought and did between 1773 and 1776 to meet foreign aggressions in the far northwest, without reference to Spain's other concerns in that period. To this factor of foreign danger three chapters will now be devoted, one for each of the three viewpoints indicated.

To appreciate the significance of any period in the history of our Pacific coast, it is well to review the age-long approaches to this coast of the nations of the earth. The

full meaning of the past or of contemporary events was not
fully understood at any given time, but in telling what occurred at a particular moment, some attempt should be
made to indicate it. We find that it is not true that the
course of empire lies ever toward the west; rather, this
"old conception of a westward line of advance gives place
to another view — that of civilization spreading east and
west from some original seat in eastern Asia, traversing the
world in opposite directions, and drawing at length to a
new focus on this opposite side of the globe."[1] Spain,
England, France, and finally the United States of America
made approaches by land from the Atlantic coast. Russia
came by land, sea, and land again, east and south. Sailors
from all of these countries, and the Portuguese and Dutch
as well, made voyages at one time or another, whether
around Africa and Asia or around South America, to the
western coasts of the Americas prior to the close of the
eighteenth century. Some say that Chinese had visited
these coasts as early as the fifth century,[2] and the Japanese
government was certainly investigating possibilities of
commerce with New Spain in the opening years of the
seventeenth century, going so far as to send a commission
to that kingdom.[3]

The Seven Years' War marks the beginning of a more
determined advance upon the part of European powers.
That war was fought in America and Asia as well as in
Europe, being largely the result of colonial rivalries. Peace
had hardly been made in 1763 when Europe set forth to
seek new colonies, going naturally to the Pacific Ocean,
where the possibilities seemed greatest. France and England sent out voyages to the south Pacific. In the far
northwest of North America, however, Russia and England
were the ones that threatened Spanish supremacy. Therefore, we may devote this chapter to their approaches to

[1] Teggart, *The approaches to the
Pacific coast.*
[2] The principal exposition of this
view is Edward P. Vining, *An inglorious
Columbus*, New York, 1885.

[3] Zelia Nuttall, *The earliest historical
relations between Mexico and Japan*,
in University of California, *Publications, American Archæology and Ethnology*, v. 4, no. 1 (Berkeley, 1906).

the Pacific coast, remembering, however, that Spain had felt misgiving at the approach of other peoples in other days, if not in the time of principal interest here, in order that we may estimate the greatness of the problem with which she had to contend.

The Russian approach was largely in the hands of Cossacks, the underlying causes being their yearning for new homes where they might enjoy personal freedom and the commercial stimulus of the fur trade.[4] The first step was taken in the reign of Ivan IV (1533–84), when the outlaw, Yermak Timofeief, led a band of Cossacks across the Ural Mountains in 1578, and conquered a Tartar kingdom on the Ob River. Thenceforth, the Cossacks made rapid strides across the continent. Ten men could conquer a kingdom, whether due to the superiority of their weapons or to other causes does not matter here. Tobolsk, Tomsk, Yenesseisk, Irkutsk, Yakutsk, and finally Okhotsk on the Pacific successively became centres of their endeavors and supply stations for the next point to the east. In fifty years they had reached Yakutsk, over half way, and eleven more years sufficed to reach Okhotsk, where an establishment was made in 1639. From Yakutsk they went southward up the Lena River to Lake Baikal, where silver mines were found, but here their rush was checked, the Manchu Tartars being too powerful for them. In 1646 they reached the land of the Chukchis in the extreme northeastern part of Asia, and were rewarded by rich finds of mammoth ivory. The Chukchis, however, were not pleasant neighbors, and were able to maintain their independence of Russia to the close of the eighteenth century. In 1648–50 one Simeon Deshnef is said to have sailed along the northern coast of Asia and south through Bering Strait, but if the voyage was actually made, it had no great effect, and its geographical

---

[4] Bancroft, *Alaska*, 14–15. Bancroft has as much as is required here for the principal events of the Russian advance, but the best and most recent account in English of the Russian progress to the middle of the eighteenth century is Golder, *Russian expansion on the Pacific*. The spelling of Russian names in this and succeeding chapters follows Bancroft.

import remained unknown.[5] By 1706 Kamchatka, the last Siberian land to be taken, had been overrun. Arrived at the Pacific the conquerors wondered what lay beyond. There were evidences of a great land not far to the east; strange trees drifted ashore; the swell of the ocean was not great; and the Chukchis told stories of a rich eastern continent, — and well may it have seemed rich to them, when the comparatively agreeable west coast of Alaska is contrasted with the bleak and stormy Siberian shore. The Russian government became interested in the "American Siberia" as early as 1710, and attempts were made to reach it by way of the Arctic Ocean along the north coast of Siberia, and surveys were made of the Kurile Islands. This, it may be noted, was during the reign of Peter the Great (1682–1725). Peter also planned expeditions which were to proceed from Kamchatka to see whether America and Asia joined, and to make discoveries along Pacific shores from Japan to the American continent. It fell to the lot of Vitus Bering, a Dane, to execute the major part of his commands, and to the reigns of his successors to see them carried out.

The expeditionaries had first to make the overland journey across Siberia, which they started to do in 1725. Arrived at the Pacific, Bering left Okhotsk in 1727, and in the following year sailed through Bering Strait. He then returned to St. Petersburg, where he recommended further voyages to discover trade routes to America and Japan, and to explore the northern coast of Siberia. Plans were made on a large scale, and the expeditions were authorized in 1734, but it was six years before they got under way. Bering commanded one ship, and Alexei Chirikof the other, but the two at length became separated. On July 15, 1741, Chirikof discovered the American coast just above 55°. He then sailed northwest and west, passed the Aleutian Islands, and after much suffering reached Kamchatka in October, 1741. Chirikof made another voyage in 1742, but did not reach America. Bering, meanwhile, had

[5] Golder, 67–95, doubts the authenticity of the Deshnef voyage.

sighted the American mainland above 58° on July 16,
1741. The return voyage was one of terrible hardship.
The voyagers were obliged to winter on Bering Island,
where their commander died, and the survivors did not get
back to Kamchatka until August, 1742. Incidentally,
they brought back some furs of the sea otter, and this it
was which proved the impulse for a fresh series of Russian
voyages.

Between 1743 and 1767 a number of voyages by private
individuals were made as far as the Aleutian Islands in
search of furs. The year 1764 marks the beginning of a
new period of imperial interest, when plans were made
which resulted in the Krenitzin and Levashef expedition.
Secret instructions were given, but the object seems to have
been to verify the reports already received from the fur-
traders, and to obtain as much further information as possible. The Krenitzin-Levashef voyage took place during
the years 1766–69. The expeditionaries encountered great
hardships and got no farther than the Aleutian Islands, not
reaching the mainland. Levashef at length got back to
St. Petersburg in 1771. Special notice should be taken of
this voyage as the principal one under imperial direction
in the period of most interest here. We have seen that
the Spanish ambassador to Russia in 1764 reported that the
Russians were engaged in projects affecting the northwest
coasts of North America, and his letters were revived,
nearly a decade later, and notice of them sent to Bucarely.
This expedition may also have been the foundation of the
exaggerated reports from St. Petersburg of the Conde de
Lacy, which will be dealt with in a later chapter. In the
same period came the books by Müller and others to which
reference has already been made. Private expeditions
continued, however, and it is impossible to say how much
they entered into the rumors heard by the Spanish ambassadors. These voyages, too, seem to have reached no
farther than the Aleutian Islands. Not until 1783 did the
Russians make a direct attempt to extend their fur trading
operations to the Alaskan mainland, for the sea otter was

N

disappearing from the Aleutian Islands. In that year an expedition was made under Potap Zaïkof, but was a failure. In the same year Grigor Shelikof organized a company to make a fur trading settlement, and this was made in 1784 on the Island of Kadiak, the first Russian settlement in North America. This occurred several years later than concerns us at present, but it is a proof of the actual danger to Spain several years before.

English approaches to the Pacific coast were along a number of lines, but may be reduced roughly to two : from the Atlantic coast westward, in most part overland, but in some degree by sea, as represented by the attempts to find a northwest passage; the direct approach by sea in the Pacific itself, around South America, eastward from southern Asia, and even across the Isthmus of Panamá. The former was the earlier and more formidable movement, but the latter was first to arrive and the one which in fact gave more trouble to Spain down to the close of the eighteenth century. We may therefore take up the latter series of approaches first.[6]

English entry of the Pacific by way of the Isthmus of Panamá passed through two principal phases. The first came in the latter half of the sixteenth century during the reign of Elizabeth, when English sailors plundered Spanish towns and ships, although their countries were nominally at peace. Drake and Hawkins are the typical names. The second phase came in the seventeenth century, when the men engaged tended to evolve from a shadowy British allegiance into unqualified pirates. Sir Henry Morgan is the outstanding figure of this period. Just at the close of the century, also, came the unsuccessful attempt to found a Scotch colony at Darien. This marks the end of English activity along this line of approach to the Pacific.

Another line of advance to which little space need be

[6] This portion of the chapter has been based in large measure upon a paper by Karl C. Leebrick entitled *English voyages to the Pacific coast during the eighteenth century*, supplemented by Bancroft's works. Mr Leebrick's manuscript was the winner of the James Bryce Historical Essay prize at the University of California in 1912.

given, because it did not in fact get near the Americas, is the British advance around Africa to southern Asia. This may be said to have begun with the chartering of the British East India Company in 1600, the English government granting to that company rights of trade from the Cape of Good Hope to the Straits of Magellan. A voyage to the East Indies was made in the very next year, and in little more than a decade the company had already established a post in India. As early as 1637 English ships had appeared on the coast of China and for the next century and a half they carried on an intermittent trade with China. Spain had little to fear from England in this period from the direction of the East Indies, because of the English conflicts in India with the Portuguese, Dutch, and French, especially with the last named. Once the English overcame their opposition, however, they loomed up as a danger to the Spanish colonies. The capture of Manila in 1762 by an English expedition from India was a significant indication of the reality of this danger. We have seen that the Croix-Gálvez plan of January, 1768, referred to the possibility of English and Dutch voyages from the East Indies to the Californias. Not until the last fifteen years of the eighteenth century, however, was this fear realized, when numerous English ships made the voyage from China to Nootka and the coasts of the far northwest.

The pioneer of English voyagers around South America to the Pacific coast was Francis Drake. After plundering the Spanish coasts he made a brief stay in Alta California in 1579, and then sailed across the Pacific, eventually getting back to England. His voyage showed how weak was the Spanish control of the Pacific, and it was never forgotten by the Spaniards, who likewise realized how much they had to fear from the presence of an enemy's ship. A fresh lesson was not long in coming. In 1587-88 Thomas Cavendish repeated Drake's voyage, capturing a rich Manila galleon near Cape San Lucas in 1588. The seventeenth century was the age of buccaneers, whether virtual or real, and some of them seem to have rounded South

America. One expedition, with a semblance of governmental authority, left Virginia in 1683, turned South America, and joining with buccaneers who had crossed the Isthmus of Panamá engaged in operations against the Spaniards, 1684-86. Cook, Eaton, Davis, Harris, Swan, Wafer, Cowley, Townley, Dampier, and the Frenchman Grogniet were among the leaders of this enterprise. Swan and Townley got as far north as Mazatlán.

The first four decades of the eighteenth century were marked by English voyages in which commercial objects were most largely to the fore, the promoters getting clearance papers from the government. Once in the Pacific, these voyagers acted much as had their predecessors, the buccaneers, plundering the Spaniards. The voyages were different in that the government required records to be kept, many of which were published, and in the general endeavor to advance knowledge of the Pacific coasts, men of science often accompanying the expeditions. The first of this series of voyages was headed by Dampier, who left England in 1699 with a fleet of five ships. The expedition subsequently split up into four separate voyages, owing to the inability of different officers and men to agree with Dampier. Dampier got as far north as the coast of New Spain in 1704-5 before pursuing his voyage around the world. Clipperton and Funnel got back to England by a similar voyage. The expedition had been a financial failure, but some Bristol merchants were persuaded to make another venture. The new expedition set sail in 1708 under the command of Woodes Rogers. Three years later it got back to England with an immense profit, largely the result of having captured the Manila galleon off Cape San Lucas in 1709. After this encounter Woodes Rogers took the usual route around the world. Many companies now sprang up, but they were unable to equal the success of Woodes Rogers. The Shelvocke-Clipperton voyages which were along the coast of New Spain in 1721 are the most noteworthy. The voyages, even when unprofitable to British merchants, cost the Spaniards enormous losses, both in property taken

or destroyed by the English, and in precautionary measures. They also vastly increased English knowledge of
the Pacific and its shores. Spain's sense of danger may
well have been enhanced by the vast literature about English voyages, and the popular interest in them in England.
A new era begins with the outbreak of war between England and Spain in 1739. The departure is marked by the
fitting out of an expedition at government expense, a formal
naval enterprise, under the command of George Anson.
Anson took the customary route around the world, in the
years 1740–44, in the course of which he cruised the western
shores of New Spain. Failing to encounter the Manila
galleon he crossed to the Philippine Islands, and took one
there. Although he did not make a profit, and lost most
of his men, he had caused an immense expense and great
loss to Spain. Furthermore, among the papers taken in the
captured galleon were those which revealed the Spanish
secrets of the Pacific. There were sailing directions for the
South American coast and the trans-Pacific routes, with
charts showing islands, shoals, landmarks, harbors, and the
like. The Pacific was no longer a closed sea.

After the Seven Years' War a new type of voyage begins.
The semi-piratical voyages of the past were no longer in
accord with public morals, nor was there the excuse of war.
Voyages for scientific objects and discovery began therefore to be sent out, with instructions not to interfere with
the ships or territory of European peoples with whom
England was at peace. The impetus came from France,
who having lost her colonies by the peace of 1763, was
eager to replace them by new discoveries. The English
quickly followed the French lead by the voyages of Biron,
1764–66, and Wallis and Carteret, 1766–69. These voyages went around the world by way of South America and
the south Pacific, and made no discoveries requiring notice.

Then came the most important voyages of all, and especially interesting here, as they fall within the period of
principal interest in this work, the three voyages of Captain James Cook. The first voyage occupied the years

1768–71. One object was to observe the transit of Venus, the Island of Tahiti being selected as the place at which to do it. Cook followed the path of Biron, Wallis, and Carteret. After the observation had been taken at Tahiti, Cook proceeded westward and made extensive explorations in New Zealand and Australia. Upon his return to England he was commissioned to go again to the south Pacific to determine whether a great southern continent existed there, about which speculation had been rife for two centuries. The expedition took place in 1772–75, and the myth of the southern continent was exploded. Perhaps a more important fact here is that in all his voyage he lost but four men, and only one by sickness. This was the result of special preparations by Cook. Before his time it was usually the case that from forty to seventy-five per cent of the crew were lost. Cook's methods were published, and were followed by later voyagers. It meant that the terror of the seas had been banished, and in a very great degree made Spain's retention of power in the Pacific so much the less secure.

Cook's third voyage left England in the year 1776, and, as will be pointed out in a later chapter, caused the Spanish government no little anxiety. One of its objects was to attack another long-standing myth, that of a practical water passage through or around North America. Cook was commissioned to approach this problem from the Pacific side. He was also to get information of the coast, and was secretly instructed to take possession for England of all lands not hitherto discovered or visited by Europeans. En route he discovered the Hawaiian Islands in 1778, a group destined to occupy an important place in later voyages of the eighteenth century. He reached the North American coast in about 44°, and proceeded northward. Some furs were picked up from the natives for mere trifles, and were later disposed of in China at such good prices as to open the eyes of merchants to the possibilities of the fur trade. The result was a swarm of European vessels, particularly English ships, on the northwest coasts in the last fifteen years of the century. To return to Cook, he continued northward, and passed through Bering Strait, but was obliged by the ice to turn back. While wintering in the Hawaiian Islands in 1779 he was killed in an affray with the natives. The expedition proceeded under the command of Captain Clerke. Clerke also passed through Bering Strait, but was forced back by the ice, as Cook had been, and, soon afterward, he made his way around the world to England.

To sum up, it is clear that English exploration in the Pacific was gathering momentum. Each new discovery and each advance in the science of navigation or other form of knowledge brought the Spanish empire of the Pacific just so much nearer a fall. To this must be added not only the activities of the Russians, but also the voyages of the French, Dutch, and Portuguese.[7] Furthermore, there were foes attacking from the Atlantic side, stripping Spain bit by bit of her colonies, and expanding into the unoccupied lands that brought them nearer to the Pacific coast. A little reflection on these factors will enable one to appreciate the problem which Spain had to face.

One other factor remains to be considered, that of the English advance across the North American continent. The westward progress of what was to become the United States had reached the Mississippi by 1776, but the American movement did not represent a threatening element as regards Spain's possessions in the Pacific until after the purchase of Louisiana in 1803. Until then the political and geographical barriers were too great for the United States to be a danger. The Spanish government did contemplate the possibility of Americans crossing the Mississippi and

[7] The great volume and importance of French voyages in the eighteenth century is shown in Erick W. Dahlgren, *Les relacions comerciales et maritimes entre la France et les côtes d'Ocean Pacifique* (Paris, 1909), and the same author's *Voyages français de la Mer du Sud avant Bougainville* in Nouvelles Archives des Missions Scientifiques, v. 14, 422–568 (Paris, 1907). These works were extensively used, along with additional matter, in the James Bryce Historical Essay of Mr. Tracy B. Kittredge, *French voyages to the Pacific cost during the eighteenth century*, winner of the prize in 1913 at the University of California. Unfortunately no Dahlgren has yet appeared for Dutch or Portuguese voyages, nor have they yet been made the subject of a Bryce Essay contest.

encroaching on New Spain, but not on the Pacific northwest. The course of events in Canada, however, and particularly the activities of the Hudson's Bay Company, were factors which threatened the far-flung coast of the Californias, and were so regarded by Spain.[8] One must think back to the voyages of the Cabots, followed by a procession of English mariners seeking a northwest passage, — Frobisher, Davis, Hudson, Baffin, James, and others, — if he is to get this subject in proper focus.   France, however, was first to get a foothold in Canada, and soon afterward her colonists began to realize profits in the fur trade.   Two Frenchmen, Groseilliers and Radisson, paved the way for England's sharing in this trade.   Dissatisfied with the rewards accorded them by the French, they temporarily entered the service of some Englishmen who were interested in exploiting the fur trade of Hudson Bay, and in 1668 they started English fur trading operations in that region.   The venture was a success, and led to the chartering of the Hudson's Bay Company in 1670.   The company was granted a monopoly and the proprietorship, with civil and criminal jurisdiction, of all Hudson Bay lands not actually possessed by a Christian prince.   Down to the Treaty of Utrecht the company was in almost continual war with the French, who did not recognize its right to the territory.   The treaty of 1713, however, gave to England all lands embraced by the waters emptying into Hudson Bay and Strait.   The region acquired was not definitely known, but, at all events, the attacks of the French now ceased.

The trade in furs was a very profitable one.   Perhaps for this reason the company decided to let well enough alone, and adopted a policy of secrecy and restriction.   All but servants of the company were kept away from the territory, and the founding of settlements and even the making of discoveries were discouraged.   The discovery of a strait communicating with the Pacific had been one of their char-

---

[8] The brief account given here is based on Bryce, Willson, Laut, and Burpee. Mr. Gordon C. Davidson of the University of California, whose work on the North West Company is in course of preparation, gave me valuable aid in revising this part of the chapter.

ter objects; yet they were charged with opposing a search
for it, until forced to make the attempt. Likewise, agriculture and mining were not encouraged. As a result, after
a century of existence the company had in 1770 but seven
posts, all close to Hudson Bay, with a total population of
about two hundred men, all company servants. This
exclusive policy had not passed without criticism. The
most notable critic was a certain Arthur Dobbs, who
devoted a large part of his life to attacking the company
because of its failure to find a northwest passage. As a
result, several expeditions were made under the auspices
respectively of the company in self defence against Dobbs'
charges, of the government, and of a private concern, the
last-named being financed by popular subscription. This
activity took place for the most part between 1737 and 1747.
Parliament manifested interest by offering £20,000 as a reward to the discoverer of the passage, but the passage was
not found. It is noteworthy that in the last of these expeditions one of the boats was named *California*, and the
forming of a settlement in the Californias was contemplated, if the strait should be found, to serve as the base
for a vast Pacific trade. Failing to find a passage, Dobbs
now sought a charter for a new corporation, charging the
Hudson's Bay Company with failure to extend their settlements to the interior. The case came up in 1749, and
Dobbs' petition was denied. The matter is of no small
importance. A new company would undoubtedly have
stimulated exploration, and might have resulted in much
earlier penetration by a British enterprise to the Pacific
coast, with consequences that stir the imagination. From
another standpoint the Dobbs controversy is important.
It attained considerable publicity, a number of books being
written in the course of it. These came to the notice of
Spain, and were a cause of forebodings on her part.

Twenty years later the company at last awakened to the
desirability of interior exploration. The great name is that
of Samuel Hearne. Hearne's first journey came in the year
1769. He was sent out by the company to obtain infor-

mation of the interior; in particular, he was to reach a certain river said to abound in copper ore and fur-bearing animals. This journey was a failure, and in another of 1770 he again failed to reach the river of copper. In December of the same year, he started a third time, and on this occasion was successful, reaching the river since called the Coppermine in July, 1771, and descending it to its mouth in the Arctic Ocean. Not until June, 1772, did he get back to the company's posts on Hudson Bay. The Hearne explorations were followed by a new policy on the part of the company, which began thenceforth to push its trading operations inland. Not much progress had been made, however, by the close of the year 1776, which marks the end of the period of principal interest dealt with here. That the Spanish government may well have been alarmed, however, is proved by the remarkable westward progress of the company and its rivals in the last quarter of the eighteenth century.

An important rival had sprung up in the Scottish merchants of Montreal, themselves the successors of the French since the Seven Years' War. Before that war had ended the Scottish merchants were pushing into the region of the Great Lakes, and not long afterward penetrated as far as the Saskatchewan River. Gradually these men drew together, and in the winter of 1783–84 the North West Company was formed, an organization which was to accomplish vast results in the way of exploration. These companies were yet another powerful force in motion against the tottering Spanish Empire.

These, then, were some of the actual dangers to Spain's Pacific possessions. The Portuguese, Dutch, and French, however dangerous they may have been prior to 1763, were not a factor in the north Pacific between that date and 1776. They therefore have virtually been left out of this account. The Russians were a real danger, but the English, among whom should be included the American colonists, were in fact the most threatening force. It is now time to see how Spain viewed the situation.

CHAPTER IX

DIPLOMACY OF THE REIGN OF CHARLES III (1759–1788)
FROM WAR TO WAR WITH ENGLAND, 1763–1779

HAVING gained an idea of the actual danger that threatened Spain in the Pacific northwest, we may next attempt to acquire perspective by tracing the leading phases of Spanish diplomacy in the reign of Charles III, before taking up the more specialized topic of Spain's activities against foreign aggressions in or near the Californias. The object is to show what Spanish ministers thought concerning England and Russia, and not so much what those countries did or did not do to merit Spain's opinion. This chapter, like the preceding, is intended as background material for the seven chapters following this. Events from 1763 to 1773, therefore, appear in less detail, although considerable space is given to the Falkland incident. The stress falls between 1773 and 1776, and the story is carried to 1779.[1]

It will be found that Spain's foreign policy in this period was primarily directed toward meeting the possibility of war with England. Russia, though a dangerous opponent in the Pacific, gave Spain hardly any concern in Europe. Troubles there were with Portugal and Morocco, but that which made them cogent factors, especially in the case of Portugal, was the relation which England bore to the situation. To oppose England the Family Compact between the crowns of France and Spain was brought into being, and it continued to be the basis of Spain's foreign policy throughout the period. Spain seems to have been faithful to the intent of this treaty, but France was in-

---

[1] Danvila has been my principal source, with valuable supplementary material from Doniol. Rousseau proved useful as a convenient, although often scant, summary of these two, with additional information based on English documentary materials. Occasional references to other writers have also been made.

187

clined to be lukewarm when the compact did not serve
her purposes, and enthusiastic when it did, using it also
as a plea for specially favorable commercial treatment of
France by Spain. At the time of the Falkland affair in
1770–71, and several times between 1773 and the close of
1776, Spain was ready and even eager to fight England, but
France repeatedly declined. Late in 1775, however, a
change in the Spanish attitude began to be perceptible,
which became marked after 1776. This was due primarily,
it would seem, to the American Revolution, which engendered a belief that Spain's participation in the war would
be fatal, whatever the event; victory, which would also
result in the independence of England's colonies, meant
the presence of a dangerous neighbor in America, and the
eventual loss, perhaps, of Spain's colonial empire; defeat
meant the same danger at the hands of England. In all of
this period one Spanish statesman was consistently for
war, Aranda, who from 1773 on was ambassador to France.
Grimaldi, minister of state, was favorable, but cautious,
desiring to make sure that the time was ripe. Floridablanca,
who succeeded him in 1777, believed in preparation for war,
but in maintenance of peace, if possible. Charles III was
successively of the opinion of his two ministers of state, although perhaps somewhat more inclined to peace than either.

The danger point marked by the diplomatic correspondence of the period, in case of war with England, was not
the Pacific coast, but especially the West Indies and the
near-by coasts of the mainland. Down to the close of the
Falkland affair, whatever anxiety there was for Pacific
ports concerned South America. After 1773 affairs in the
Pacific do not seem to have been important enough to occupy a prominent place in diplomatic correspondence.
That they should have done so, it is easy now to see, but
that Spanish statesmen failed to note the inevitable danger
resulting from the age-long approaches of European nations
to the Pacific is not hard to understand in view of their
more immediate concern for the West Indies.

There are many reasons why Spain should have regarded England as her principal European opponent during the reign of Charles III (1759-88). Charles himself is said to have harbored a feeling of resentment against that country, dating from the time when he was king of Naples,[2] although it is doubtful whether he allowed this feeling to dictate his political action. In any event there were reasons of state for an anti-England policy, irrespective of any personal spite that Charles may have felt. These have already been reviewed in an earlier chapter.[3] They come to this, that England was endeavoring to break down the monopoly maintained by Spain in her colonial trade, and that throughout the middle of the eighteenth century England was markedly imperialistic, especially so after the advent to power of William Pitt. Englishmen smuggled goods into various parts of Spanish America, and the English government added colonies to the British Empire at the expense of both France and Spain. Spain lost Florida in 1763, and might look back to a loss in earlier years of Gibraltar and Minorca, Jamaica and the Atlantic coast strip of North America, the southern part of which, at least, Spain had regarded as rightfully Spanish. It seemed perfectly clear that England would pick up more colonies when an opportunity should present itself. Incidents of temporary import were continually occurring to accentuate the hostility engendered by these disputes of a permanent kind, often closely related to the latter.

The basis of the foreign policy of this period was the Family Compact of 1761 between the crowns of France and Spain, an offensive and defensive alliance directed primarily against England. The first trial of arms had resulted in failure, England achieving a great triumph in

Addison, 26-27, refers Charles' hatred of England to the following incident. During the War of the Austrian Succession, Charles got together an army of 12,000 Neapolitans to fight on the side of Spain against Austria. After his little army had departed for the field, an English fleet appeared off Naples and threatened to bombard the city unless the Neapolitan troops should return, and Charles was obliged to withdraw them. According to Addison he was not of the type to forget or forgive such humiliation. Charles' hatred of the English is noted by other writers as well, e.g. Danvila, IV, 110, 157.

[3] In chap. III.

the Seven Years' War. Neither of the Bourbon monarchies regarded the peace of 1763 as conclusive, however, but rather looked upon it as a truce until such time as their land and sea forces should be ready again.[4] This idea was largely at the bottom of Charles' policy of economic regeneration, as already pointed out, in order that revenues, and hence the sinews of war, might be produced. This it was that lay back of the *visita* of José de Gálvez in New Spain.

Spain was particularly alarmed by the strength of England's position in the West Indies, the possession of Jamaica and Florida by England being looked upon as endangering not only Spain's hold of other islands of the West Indies, but even the security of New Spain and other mainland colonies.[5] Pretexts for trouble were not lacking. Englishmen had obtained a right to cut wood in Honduras, but did not observe the restrictions placed upon them. Spain refused to pay the ransom that had been exacted by the English at the capture of Manila in 1762.[6] The Sacramento disputes went on. French settlers in Louisiana resisted the transfer to Spain, and it was believed that the English had instigated them to do it. Not only in Spain but also in America steps were taken with a view to the possibility of war. In 1764 Cruillas, viceroy of New Spain, complained that he had no troops with which to resist an invasion except one regiment at Vera Cruz and a few scattered companies of regular troops and militia elsewhere. He recommended that capable officials be sent from Spain and that recruiting be authorized.[7] Tanucci, who had been Charles' principal adviser in Naples, and who continued to have an interest in his welfare after Charles became king of Spain, displayed deep interest in Spanish-American affairs in this period. Reforms in the Americas, he wrote, in December, 1764, were the most important question that the king had to confront. He repeated this opinion in several letters of the year 1765, saying that Spain ought to reor-

[4] Danvila, IV, 104; Addison, 51-52.
[5] Danvila, IV, 82-86; Ferrer del Río, I, 450-51.
[6] Rousseau, II, 55-59, 66, 81.
[7] Zamacois, V, 596.

ganize its navy and fortify its ports in the Americas, for the English fanaticism for conquest was increasing. His letter of August 16, 1766, to Squillace speaks, however, of the greater need for reorganizing the fleet. Although the fortification and garrisons of America were too weak to withstand a siege, they could nevertheless keep up a defensive war without great danger of being lost.[8] Nor was the Spanish government unmindful of danger in the Americas, despite its preoccupation over the internal affairs of Spain.[9]

The principal diplomatic interest down to 1771 concerns the events leading to the expulsion of the English from the Falkland Islands in 1770, and the subsequent warlike preparations of England and Spain. Peace was hardly established in 1763 when two English warships were prepared for a secret mission under Biron as commander. News of it was published in Holland in May, 1764, whence the Spaniards learned of it. Biron left England in July, 1764, and touched at one of the Falkland Islands in January, 1765, at a place called by him Port Egmont. He applied the name Falklands to the group, and took possession for England. He did not form a settlement, but went on around the world, reaching England again in 1766. His act cannot be said to have given England title to the Falklands, for the islands had been discovered as early as the sixteenth century by Spanish navigators and had been visited by Spaniards as recently as 1763.[10] A French expedition under Bougainville had preceded the English in the Falklands, and had formed a settlement on one of the islands in 1764. The expedition seems to have been despatched without the knowledge of the Spanish court, which first got news of it from America, the French ships having put in at Montevideo. The news was not well received in Spain, and inquiry was made of the French court concerning the objects of the expedition. A reply was made that the ships had gone in search of a deserted island, to facilitate passage of Cape Horn by French navigators. An accident had forced them to put in at

---

[8] Danvila, IV, 92, 111.
[9] Ibid., IV, 111.
[10] Altamira, IV, 58. Other accounts say that the islands were discovered in 1686 by the English captain Cowley, e.g. Rousseau, II, 59.

Montevideo, but they had no intention of trading with Spanish America. They had found an island to their purpose, one of the Maluinas or Falkland group.[11] That the Falklands were regarded as strategically important by Spain appears from a confidential letter of Grimaldi to an intimate friend, August 6, 1764. Spain ought to prevent the French establishment, he said, as it might later prove an obstacle to the passage of Cape Horn. A Spanish settlement should be made at the Bay of San Julián on the mainland [opposite the Falklands], for the Falklands and San Julián were the keys to Spain's kingdoms in that part of the world. If they were occupied, and if the viceroy of Peru would take action to cover the principal points of his kingdom and to fortify two or three essential ones, those kingdoms would be unconquerable by forces coming from Europe, and illicit trade could not be carried on. The French were soon asked to withdraw, lest the English be tempted to follow their example and settle there. Choiseul agreed, provided Spain herself wished to make a settlement.[12]

In April, 1767, the islands were formally delivered to Spain by the French. Sometime before, an English expedition had reached Port Egmont and had made a settlement. In December, 1766, the English governor had visited the French colony and protested against it, claiming that the islands belonged to England, and the dispute was renewed by the Spanish and English governors after the transfer by France to Spain. Each ordered the other to withdraw, the Englishman setting a time limit of six months.[13] The affair was reported to the Spanish government, which sent an order to the captain general of Buenos Aires, February 23, 1768, to expel the English by force. At least one Spanish minister was for war, the fiery Aragonese, Count Aranda,

[11] Danvila, IV, 93–94. Some such place was believed to be necessary to allow of a break in the voyage. Boats were so poorly constructed then and so slow that they usually had to stop for repairs after making so long a voyage as from Europe to Cape Horn. Moreover, food supplies by that time would be greatly diminished, fresh vegetables all gone, and the crew in sad straits from scurvy.

[12] Danvila, IV, 94–96.

[13] Altamira, IV, 58; Rousseau, II, 60–61; Danvila, 111–12. These accounts all vary somewhat in details.

president of the Council of Castile. The English government was informed of Spain's proposed action in the Falklands, and France was sounded to see whether she would live up to the Family Compact.[14] It was not until December, 1769, that the Spanish were able to find Port Egmont. A fleet was sent from Buenos Aires, and the port surrendered on June 10, 1770.[15]

The news reached Europe at a time when the English government was irritated against Spain on other grounds. By a decree of June 24, 1770, Charles III had prohibited the importation and consumption of English muslins, thereby causing serious lost to English shippers.[16] This and the Falkland incident were enough to cause Parliament to vote funds in preparation for war. Aranda headed the war party in Spain, but Lord North and Grimaldi, respectively chief ministers of England and Spain, were at first less inclined to fight, but as the year 1770 drew to a close, Grimaldi had changed his mind. The English were making excessive demands for satisfaction, as well as for the restitution of Port Egmont. Furthermore, it was believed that the leading French minister, Choiseul, stood ready to bring France in on Spain's side, although according to Rousseau that conclusion was unwarranted. So, expeditions were prepared, fleets united, and the respective ambassadors withdrew. War seemed inevitable, when an unforeseen event occurred, changing the whole aspect of affairs. This was the fall of Choiseul, who was succeeded in power by D'Aiguillon of the party of peace. It was on this occasion that Louis XV calmly disregarded the Family Compact, saying, "My minister wanted war, but I do not." Spain, therefore, had to yield as gracefully as possible, and on January 22, 1771, the Spanish ambassador signed a declaration at London disapproving the removal of the English colonists and promising to restore Port Egmont, without prejudice, however, to Spain's claim of sovereignty.[17]

These events occurred during the time that the Marqués

[14] Danvila, IV, 112–17.
[15] *Ibid.*, IV, 96–97, 103.

[16] Ferrer del Río, III, 67.
[17] Becker, 37–39 ; Rousseau, II, 55–81.

de Croix was viceroy of New Spain. His views are worth noting. Writing to his brother, April 28, 1771, Croix said that he did not yet know whether war had been declared, but he was putting the kingdom in a state of defence. He did not think that New Spain was in any great danger; any English attack on the Spanish colonies would be directed against Porto Rico or Campeche, he thought.[18] His instruction to Bucarely, September 1, 1771, noted Vera Cruz as the most important port of New Spain, and the key to the kingdom.[19] Acapulco would be open to attack, but such an event was unlikely because of the length of the voyage necessary to reach there. The Manila galleon would be able to defend the port, and, moreover, the country was mountainous and thinly populated, not an inviting point to occupy.[20]

A new factor was now to appear to affect the diplomatic relations of Spain and England, the latter's quarrel with her American colonies. George Bancroft intimates that as early as 1769 Spain favored England rather than the colonies, because of the danger that a near-by independent republic would represent, and his view has been followed by other writers, or else nothing has been said by them at all.[21] The first intimation of Spanish hostility to England comes when Spain began in 1776 to contribute funds to the Americans. In fact, Spain's preparations for war were going on for a half decade preceding that year, although in the earlier years without reference to England's colonial troubles.

Spain might justly have abandoned the Family Compact after the Falkland incident, but her hatred and fear of England were too great, although for a time, the compact suffered partial eclipse. Not only the Falkland affair, but also the fall of Choiseul, its proponent in France, weakened it. Charles III saw that in future he could count only upon his own forces, but he continued to increase and equip

[18] Croix, *Correspondance*, 224.
[19] *Ibid.*, 286.   [20] *Ibid.*, 287.
[21] Bancroft's remarks are on a page headed 1769. No date appears in the text, but the impression given is that the Spanish fear of America was expressed as early as 1769. Bancroft, III, 337.

them. Toward the close of the year 1772, we find him making inquiries as to the state of the English military and naval forces.[22] Furthermore, an apparent return to the Family Compact is noticeable by 1773. Late in that year we find the warlike Aranda become Spanish ambassador to France, and his influence at once began to make itself felt. In November, 1773, Aranda conferred with D'Aiguillon about the European situation, and reported the result to Grimaldi. Reference to the partition of Poland had been made, but this was of only passing interest to Aranda. But as regards England he told D'Aiguillon that that country was making exceptional naval preparations with a view to imposing its law upon all opponents, and he urged that France prepare for war, as Spain was doing. D'Aiguillon refused to see anything alarming in the situation, but later made plans in case war should break out, as for example to burn the Portsmouth navy yard. The French army and navy were in a fair state of readiness, so far as Aranda was able to learn. He recommended that the Bourbon kings garrison the principal points of the East and West Indies, in which case it would matter little if the English should occupy indefensible points, as the latter could not hold them without being much weakened. Besides, the English had to reckon on the need of protecting the British Isles, and would not send many men far away. D'Aiguillon was interested in the course of the Russo-Turkish War, and hoped it might continue long enough for Sweden to reorganize her forces. He suggested Sweden as a good base from which to attack the north of the British Isles, and also noted the value of Sweden as a check against Russia. Aranda reported this much, without noteworthy comment. Aranda's conversations with D'Aiguillon were warmly approved by Charles III. Grimaldi's letter to Aranda of December 27, 1773, stated that Spain was continuing her naval preparations with the greatest ardor, and hoped to get the fleet in such shape that it could go to sea quickly; it would be important in a war with

[22] Danvila, IV, 377–78.

England to strike at once, for the English type of government did not permit of uniting its fleet with such rapidity as Spain could employ.[23]

Warlike negotiations seem to have given way to other matters in the first half of the year 1774. Louis XV thought of marrying again, and the possibility of his choosing a Spanish princess for a time held the stage. Later, he gave up the idea, and talk of it had hardly come to an end when Louis was taken sick and, on May 10, he died. Matters were then halted until a new government could get under way. There was a change of ministry and a period of uncertainty as to its attitude. Vergennes succeeded D'Aiguillon as minister of foreign affairs, but as he was at the time ambassador to Sweden, it was not until July that he was ready to take up his duties at the French court. Indications in the meantime, however, were that France would stand by the Family Compact, or so at least the king and his ministers said. This possibility gave England no small concern, according to the Spanish ambassador in London. Choiseul returned to the French court, and that, too, was regarded as a favorable symptom by Spain.[24] In this period occurred an incident which might have precipitated a war if both Spain and England had not been uncertain as to France's attitude. An English ship took possession of Viegues or Crab Island, only two leagues from Porto Rico, despite the protest of the Spanish governor of Porto Rico. The issue remained in doubt for a time, but, on June 18, Grimaldi was able to inform Aranda that the English force had abandoned the island.[25]

Vergennes was at his post by July, 1774. His early correspondence, both with the king and with French ambassadors at other courts, shows that he was an enthusiastic and ardent supporter of the Family Compact, although we shall see that this enthusiasm was tempered in moments of crisis by a clear view of what most favored France, and at all times by a desire to see France profit commer-

[23] Danvila, IV, 386–90.
[24] Ibid., IV, 390–401.
[25] Coxe, V, 7–8; Danvila, IV, 393, 399.

cially. In his instructions of July 22, 1774, to Baron de
Breteuil, ambassador to Vienna, Vergennes outlined the
status of French foreign policy upon the accession of Louis
XVI to the throne. Of France's engagements the most
important was that of the Family Compact with Spain, he
said. It was necessary, not only in case the situation in
England's American colonies should offer a chance to attack England, but also for a more immediate object upon
which the rest depended, that of giving France an opportunity to build up her army and navy again. The compact rested on the strongest ties of blood, amity, and political interest, and fulfilled admirably the double purpose
of opposing superior forces to the English navy, and of
tempering England's penchant for attacking France, because of her unwillingness to break with Spain. Spain, however, was not equally desirous of avoiding a break, because
of England's profits, licit and illicit, in Spanish trade, and
because Spain had in every way to dread the superiority of
the British forces in North America. Thus, the common
enemy, England, was the most dangerous and most powerful
opponent of the two crowns. There were other objects of
the pact, but Spain was not expected to enter into these
any more than she might desire; it is noteworthy that
these other objects included relations with Sweden, Poland,
and Turkey, as against Russia. In fine, the Family Compact should be considered as the basis of Louis XVI's foreign policy.[26] To Ossun, the French ambassador at Madrid, Vergennes wrote, the same day, that he was ready
upon all occasions to give the most unequivocal proofs of
his desire to maintain it.[27] Much to the same effect were
his words to the king, December 8, 1774, on which date he
presented a memorial on the political situation of France
with relation to the different powers. England, he said,
was dangerous, because more jealous of the prosperity of
her neighbors than solicitous for developing her own, and
because the British ministry, despite friendly assurances,
was ready to unite party sentiment in England by stirring

---

[26] Doniol, I, 22–26   [27] *Ibid.*, I, 13–14.

up a war against France. The Family Compact was the surest means of holding England in check.[28] Aranda was favorably impressed by the situation at the French court. He wrote a long letter to Grimaldi, August 5, 1774, in which he discussed the king and queen and the leading ministers. Maurepas, then seventy-three years old, had reëntered the Council of State, and was the king's principal adviser. He was a warm partisan of the agreement with Spain. Vergennes was a man of no party, thinking only of the interests of the service. Turgot had become secretary of the navy, but would have a hard task as his predecessor, M. de Boines, had left that department in confusion.[29] In another letter, the same day, Aranda referred to the surprise caused by the unexpected peace concluded between Russia and Turkey, resulting in advantages to the former. There was some fear lest Russia might renew its pretensions to Finland against Sweden.[30] It is worthy of remark that the Russo-Turkish War had endured from October 6, 1768, to July 21, 1774; also, that the fear of Russia in North America does not seem to have filled large enough place in the diplomatic correspondence to have caught the attention of Danvila, Rousseau, or others who have devoted their works to the diplomacy of Spain in this period. That such a fear existed will be shown in the next chapter, but it seems to have been comparatively unimportant.

The British ministry reached the same conclusion as Aranda with regard to the adherence of France and Spain to the Family Compact, and consequently planned to occupy Spain with other affairs, so as to separate her from France, or at least to turn her from following a common policy.[31] Two matters were at hand of which they might avail themselves, the disputes of Spain with the sultan of Morocco, and her quarrels with Portugal over boundaries in South America.

By a treaty of the year 1767, satisfactory relations be-

[28] Doniol, I, 19.
[29] Danvila, IV, 401–4.
[30] Ibid., IV, 404.
[31] Doniol, I, 26.

tween Spain and Morocco had been established, including the recognition of Spain's right to her establishments on the North African coast. Late in 1774, however, the sultan announced that he could no longer tolerate Christian posts in his empire, and he commenced the siege of Melilla, a Spanish town there. The ensuing military operations need not be followed, except to note a battle before Algiers in July, 1775. On this occasion General O'Reilly, reformer of the Spanish army and a man of tremendous reputation, suffered a crushing defeat with a loss of nearly three thousand men in killed and wounded.[32] When the news came to Spain there was a great outcry against O'Reilly, as also against Grimaldi, who already had many opponents of the nationalist element, Grimaldi being an Italian. What is more to the point here is that England was believed to have inspired the sultan of Morocco to attack Spain. This is the opinion of Fernán-Núñez, himself a participator in the O'Reilly expedition.[33]

There was a much stronger case against England on the charge of inciting her ally, Portugal, against Spain over South American affairs. Certainly England supported Portugal's exaggerated claims.[34] Boundaries between the Portuguese and Spanish colonies of the Río de la Plata had never been settled satisfactorily, resulting in perennial disputes in that region, especially concerning the province of Sacramento. One of the principal causes of trouble at this time was the policy of the Portuguese minister of state, Pombal, who was desirous of making conquests in South America, and who was willing to go to any length in bad faith to achieve his end, relying upon the support of England, in case Spain should declare war. The course of events may first be traced, after which, a discussion of their place in Spanish diplomacy may be resumed.

Pombal secretly sent orders to Portuguese officials in the

[32] Rousseau, II, 84–89.
[33] Fernán-Núñez, I, 246–47.
[34] Ibid., I, 279 ; Ferrer del Río, III, 138–39 ; Doniol, I, 26. Another viewpoint appears in Coxe, V, 8–9. Coxe speaks as if Spain were the aggressor, instigated by the French court, but admits that the Portuguese minister, Pombal, "was eager to extend the domains of Portugal in the new world."

Sacramento region to seize desirable Spanish territories. When news of the seizures came to Europe he would pretend that it was false, or that nothing more than inconsequential affrays between Spanish and Portuguese soldiers had occurred. He promised to order his troops to desist from such actions, and asked Charles III to do the same. The latter did so, but Pombal, on the contrary, continued to order hostilities and to send reënforcements, hoping to secure posts from which it would be difficult to dislodge the Portuguese by the time that his duplicity could no longer be concealed. Not only did he deceive Charles III for awhile, but he misled the English ministers as well, pretending that Portugal was a victim of Spanish ambition.

A change in the situation came as a result of the American Revolution. By the close of the year 1775 England was so busily engaged with her colonies that she was far from desiring war in Europe, and restrained Portugal. The British Cabinet announced that it would take no part in the Spanish-Portuguese quarrel, provided Spain should make no attempts against Brazil or Portugal itself. Pombal now made peaceful overtures to Charles III, hoping to delay Spain's sending of troops to South America, as had been proposed, but the proofs of Pombal's perfidy were so clear, that he was no longer believed. An expedition set sail from Cádiz in November, 1776, the fleet being under the Marqués de Casa Tilly, and the troops commanded by Pedro Ceballos. En route to Buenos Aires the Portuguese island of Santa Catherina, off the coast of Brazil, was captured. Then followed the seizure of the Portuguese fleet, and the reconquest of Sacramento.

Meanwhile, fortune played into Spain's hands in another respect. On February 23, 1777, José I of Portugal died. His wife, María Victoria, who became regent, was a sister of Charles III and an opponent of Pombal, whose fall from power occurred immediately. In October of that year a treaty was signed between Spain and Portugal, entirely favorable to the former. The much-disputed Sacramento colony and the other lands occupied or claimed by Portugal were recognized as belonging to Spain, while Santa Catherina and other parts of Brazil recently conquered by Ceballos were restored to Portugal.[35]

Ossun had reported to Vergennes, July 7, 1774, that war between Spain and Portugal was a possibility, due to the latter's aggressions in South America.[36] The situation was far from pleasing to Vergennes, who feared that Spain might desire to conquer Portugal, and thus bring on, not only war with England, but a general European war, lest Spain's conquest result in too great Bourbon strength, upsetting the balance of power. Naturally, he was eager to learn the attitude of England, and asked Garnier, his ambassador in Lisbon, to learn what he could on that point. Vergennes believed that England would not openly come to Portugal's aid, but that she would do so surreptitiously.[37] At the same time he was not neglecting to use the Family Compact for France's commercial advantage. Writing to Ossun, September 13, 1774, he charged him to say that France was eager to reorganize her finances and her navy, as Charles III had suggested, but commercial prosperity was a necessary prerequisite, and that depended upon finding a market outside her own borders. Spain might, therefore, grant certain commercial favors to France, and at least put her on an equal basis with England, mentioning the case of prepared leathers on which the duty was twice as high against French goods as against those from England.[38]

England's attitude toward Spain in the affair with Portugal was not long in doubt. Lord Stormont, British ambassador to France, told Vergennes that Spain was getting ready to attack Portugal, not only in America, but also in Portugal itself, and that England could not look upon such preparations with indifference. Writing of this to Grimaldi, September 30, 1774, Aranda said that he was answering other foreign ministers at Paris with regard to the alleged plans of Spain, saying truthfully that he knew

[35] This account of the Sacramento dispute was taken from Rousseau, II, 100–9.

[36] Doniol, I, 27.
[37] Ibid., I, 28.
[38] Ibid., I, 36–37.

nothing of them.[39] Whereas Stormont's manner with Vergennes had been brusque, in order to intimidate France, Lord Grantham at Madrid had made similar inquiries with politeness, in order to keep Spain from coming too strongly to France's support. Vergennes was not easily frightened, however. Stormont had demanded that France should check the hostile designs of Charles III, whereupon Vergennes replied that he could not intervene, not having heard from the two countries of their differences, and that he had no reason to believe that the intentions of the Catholic King were less sincerely pacific than those of England.[40] Similarly, Grimaldi expressed surprise at Grantham's representation, saying that it was not Spain but Portugal which was making warlike preparations. Writing of this to Aranda, October 15, 1774, Grimaldi remarked that England had said nothing while Portugal was sending troops, ships, and munitions to South America, but when there seemed a likelihood that Spain might do so, she affected astonishment, and was even bold enough to assert that Spain was forming an army on the Portuguese frontier. One might believe that England was in an agreement with Portugal to draw Spain into a war, if it were not that the British ministry sincerely desired and even needed peace. So, very likely, Pombal was deceiving the English ministers.[41] Ossun's report to Vergennes, October 6, 1774, was in substantial agreement with this. He believed that Grimaldi and Charles III desired peace, but that they would fight in a just cause. If Spain should attempt to retake the posts in South America which the Portuguese had seized, it might lead to war.[42] Vergennes' reply shows that France might have abandoned the Family Compact again in case of a rupture. Vergennes believed that Portugal was the aggressor, and that Pombal was endeavoring to draw the English into it. He said that there was a possibility of an English fleet's being sent to Brazil, which was as important to England as if it were her own, and as the

[39] Danvila, IV, 404–5.
[40] Doniol, I, 29.
[41] Danvila, IV, 405–6.
[42] Doniol, I, 29–30.

British navy had a taste for plunder, such an event might cause war. He had told Stormont that peace might be maintained if England would cause Portugal to stop sending war material and troops. If England desired peace, he continued to Ossun, France had no choice but to agree. Louis XVI was devoted to the Family Compact, but the finances were in disorder. They must be restored, and the navy put in shape, things which would take France several years, and until then France could give no effective aid to Spain. This much was told to Ossun in confidence, and he was not to let it be known to the Spanish ministry.[43] Meanwhile, Vergennes renewed his plea for commercial advantages with Spain, or at least that France be allowed privileges equally with England, the common enemy of the two crowns.[44] To Aranda, however, the impression was given that France stood back of Spain, both in the affair with Morocco and in that with Portugal.[45] And so she did,—in sympathy.

As the year 1774 drew to a close, England's dispute with her American colonies began to loom on the diplomatic horizon, although its importance was not yet grasped. In England it was looked upon as a Whig device against the Tories, and opinion at the French court naturally followed that of London, its advent being welcomed on the ground that England would be kept busy enough to prevent her attacking France. At least one British minister, however, Lord Rochford, saw early in 1774 that the matter was serious. The Boston rioters were descendants of Cromwell's Puritans, he said, implying by that, that they would fight. His remarks were duly quoted to the French court in Guines' report of June 13, 1774.[46] Spain was preoccupied with the Portuguese difficulty, especially because of England's favorable attitude toward Portugal. Grimaldi wrote to Aranda, December 5, 1774, asking him to sound the French ministry to see if France would stand by the Family Compact in case of war; the matter was urgent, as news

[43] Ibid., I, 31–35.
[44] Ibid., I, 38.
[45] Danvila, IV, 406–7.
[46] Doniol, I, 38–40.

had come from Buenos Aires that the Portuguese were planning an assault on the port of Santa Tecla. Aranda's reply, December 19, 1774, advised against open preparation for war, but suggested that the Spaniards in America should be induced to resist the Portuguese. Then, if it came to war, the French would not "have the face" (*no tendrán cara*) to withhold their aid.[47] About at this time Pombal seemed to have relented, being advised, no doubt, of the difficulties in the way of England's sustaining Portugal. Vergennes, who wished to retain the Family Compact for an occasion when it might redound to France's advantage, wrote to Ossun, January 3, 1775, praising him for not having told Charles III of France's need for peace, and adding that the king of Spain must not be allowed to believe that France would not have come to his aid in case war had broken out.[48]

By December, 1774, it became clear that England's American troubles were something more than passing riots. Garnier, who had become *chargé d'affaires* in London, wrote Vergennes, December 19, 1774, that it was the most important event since the English Revolution. He suggested that France help the Americans in secret, as America might withdraw her commerce from England and offer it to other nations, in the event of a quarrel with England. On January 27, 1775, he announced that England was preparing to send General Gage with 9000 men to put down the colonists, and sounded a warning that she might seize the Antilles in the flush of success, or as a recompense for defeat, if the colonists should be victorious. Her seemingly pacific intentions should not allow the French court to be caught unprepared. Vergennes was much impressed by Garnier's warning. Writing to Ossun, February 7, 1775, he urged him to rouse the Spanish court to the importance of England's despatch of troops to America. Although they might be intended solely for use against the colonials, unforeseen events, such as a change of ministry in England, might bring about a new destination for them dangerous to the establishments of France and Spain in that part of the world. France was taking precautions against unforeseen attack, and hoped that Spain would do so, too. Writing again, February 14, he stated that England's difficulties would prevent her from assisting Portugal, but the danger of war with England was even greater, because of the magnitude of her efforts, and it behooved France and Spain to fortify themselves, lest the recoil fall upon their colonies when least expected. "I am not calm, I assure you, sir," he said, "in seeing the English carry such great land and sea forces to America." Ossun's letter of February 20, 1775, said that Charles III and Grimaldi agreed with Vergennes, and had told him that Spain was doing everything possible to put the Americas in a state of defence. Spain now had a navy of forty-four vessels, and artillery and munitions were being prepared for ten or eleven thousand men who were to be ready to embark without delay. Havana, Porto Rico, and the kingdom of New Spain had been fortified ; there was a colonial militia with Spanish officers in those places and in Cumaná, Caracas, and Buenos Aires, and there were Spanish regulars in all of the places named, except Cumaná and Caracas, and also in Cartagena, Panamá, and Portobello.[49]

Meanwhile, Escarano in London had been impressed, much as Garnier had been, by the danger to Spain's colonies resulting from the presence of English troops in America. There were 11,736 British soldiers there, he wrote to Grimaldi, March 6, 1775, and it would be easy to attack Spain's possessions, both because they were near, and because England had so many transports at hand. He was of the opinion that England could not defeat America with its "three million souls guided by the enthusiasm of liberty, and accustomed to live in a kind of independence," a people "who had given so many proofs of valor." If the opposition should overthrow the Tory ministry, it would mean war with Spain, as that would bring Chatham (Pitt), Richmond, and Shelburne into power. Even with a well-in-

[49] *Ibid.*, I, 40–46.

tentioned ministry, it was not certain that England would
not seek a pretext for a rupture, and employ her forces
without warning against some of the less well fortified Spanish colonies. She could avail herself of Spain's quarrel
with Portugal for a pretext. Escarano suggested that it
might be well to intimate to England, that she must withdraw her troops and ships from the Americas, when her
quarrel with the colonies should be adjusted. Lord North
wanted peace, but his position in power was very precarious.[50] In referring to Chatham, Escarano was mentioning
the bugbear which disturbed the peace of mind of both
France and Spain, especially of the former. The great
English imperialist was ever ready for war, and was regarded at the French court as especially hostile to France.

Danvila holds that France and Spain were by this time
resolved to fight England. It was only necessary to increase their forces, and to seek an opportune occasion.[51]
Aranda and the French ministry were making plans of campaign as early as March, 1775.[52] Writing to Grimaldi,
March 30, 1775, Aranda advised that Spain take an attitude of open hostility to England. He had just seen Maurepas, Vergennes, and Sartine, and they had informed him
that the French fleet was in better shape than people thought.
Aranda told them that he believed that France and Spain
together could destroy England, and reminded them of the
insecurity of treaties with England, because of her system
of changing ministries, involving also the possibility of a
change in policy. If the French and Spanish navies were
ready, it would be better to break with England, he had
said. By putting the essential points in the Americas in
a state of defence beforehand, it would matter little if the
English should make attacks elsewhere. The French ministers had shown themselves agreeable to his proposals.
Even the peace-loving Charles III and Grimaldi seemed
ready to fight. The latter wrote to Aranda, April 25,
1775, applauding his warlike proposals, but suggesting

[50] Danvila, IV, 378–80.   [52] Ibid., IV, 447–48.
[51] Ibid., IV, 412.

that it would be well to ask England for an explanation
with respect to her considerable forces in America, and to
request that she disarm, as soon as peace should be made
with her colonies. He enclosed a letter to Escarano to that
effect, but it was not to be forwarded to him, unless the
French court should approve. This would have meant war,
perhaps, but Vergennes did not approve of presenting such
a request. What is more surprising, Aranda agreed with
him, although only because he favored another pretext for
a rupture.[53] While this correspondence was being carried
on, Spain's naval preparations were going on apace, the
maritime expedition against the Barbary Coast peoples
serving as an excuse.[54] Grimaldi told Ossun, wrote the
latter to Vergennes, April 24, 1775, that the British ambassador had taken good care not to evince the least anxiety in that regard, and if he had done so, that he, Grimaldi,
bearing in mind England's colonial troubles, would have
been disposed to tell him that Spain was not obliged to render an account of her conduct to England. Grimaldi was
much impressed by the danger from England in America,
and felt that the Bourbon crowns should spare no effort to
maintain and improve their navies. Spain had made considerable progress, although much remained to be done, and
she regretted that France was still behindhand, despite the
application and good-will of her king and ministers.[55] That
Grimaldi's fears of an attack on the French and Spanish
colonies had some basis is confirmed by a remark of Lord
Rochford of the British Foreign Office. Two campaigns
would suffice to restore order in America, he said, and the
spirits of both the English and the Americans could be
appeased by an attack on the hereditary enemy, France.[56]
This remark seems to have been made in July, 1775.
Aranda sensed such a possibility, and said that England,
knowing the real hostility of France and Spain, was already
thinking of declaring war upon the House of Bourbon.[57]
    At about this time, the Spanish authorities began to be

[53] *Ibid.*, IV, 409-11.
[54] Doniol, I, 47 ; Danvila, IV, 409.
[55] Doniol, I, 47.

[56] Rousseau, II, 111-12.
[57] Aranda to Grimaldi, Aug, 7, 1775, in Danvila, IV, 416.

impressed by an idea which may well have been a cause of their delay in declaring war. The idea seems to have been expressed first in Aranda's letter of July 24, 1775, to Grimaldi. An attempt was being made, he said, to get the English ministry to concede as much as possible to the colonists. An independent America would be a menace, as her population was increasing and, consequently, she needed lands, and would be more apt to seek them in a region with a temperate climate like New Spain than by going north. So the Americans might eventually dominate North America, or might help Spain's colonies to become independent too. There would also be danger if England should defeat the Americans, because the latter would probably join in England's wars as in the past. He urged a more firm control by Spain over Cuba, San Domingo, and Porto Rico, not alone because of their richness, but also because they were the key to the continent, and easier than other places to defend. Louisiana he regarded as exposed in any event, both because of America's expanding population and because it was the nearest of the temperate lands. Grimaldi replied, August 7, 1775, that the king realized the truth of Aranda's remarks, and the wisdom of his suggestions. Spain had too scant a population to settle all of the colonies, and the latter were too extensive to be defended equally well at all places. Grimaldi thought it might be desirable to invite French settlers to San Domingo and Porto Rico. As for Louisiana, the king thought it best to leave it alone. The English would be able to raise great armies against that section, and if Spain should develop it, it might serve only as an inducement for the English to come and attack it.[58]

At this time also the Portuguese question again raised its head, on account of the continued Portuguese aggressions in South America. As we have seen, Charles III was at length aroused to order an expeditionary force sent from Spain. Aranda was asked by Grimaldi in another letter of August 7 to request France to intervene at Lisbon

[58] Danvila, IV, 414–17.

to bring about an amicable end of the dispute by causing
Portugal to withdraw her troops, and Aranda's reply, August 20, stated that France was willing to do as requested.
Aranda and Vergennes proposed that the same plan be
followed in England to get that country to check Portugal,
but principally to discover by her answer the real intent of
the ministry, for it was clear that England and Portugal
were working in agreement. Meanwhile, said Aranda,
let troops be sent to South America, and others stationed
on the Portuguese frontier; England could not land an
army, as she was having all she could do to find troops
enough for her war with the colonies. Not long afterward
the Portuguese question seemed to be approaching a favorable stage. The Portuguese ambassador had shown a
disposition to settle the matter amicably, wrote Grimaldi,
September 15, 1775; so, French intervention would be
unnecessary.[59]

From the beginning of the year 1776 Vergennes was fully
decided on war with England.[60] Aranda, naturally, was as
warlike as ever, and suggested an invasion of Ireland, and
establishing an independent country there. This plan met
with Vergennes' approval, but was less warmly received in
Spain, on the ground that it might result in England's vast
forces in America falling suddenly upon the Bourbon colonies. Aranda recognized that England would probably
attack Spain whether successful or defeated in the war with
her colonies, either to satisfy her ambition, or to recover
from her losses. Louisiana and San Domingo were most
in danger, he said. Havana and Porto Rico could be defended. The best thing to do would be to make military
preparations at once, despite what England might say.[61]
Vergennes tried to frighten Charles III with these dangers,
but the latter's reply asking ten or twelve thousand French
troops to defend French San Domingo found Vergennes less
impressed by the American danger. He declined to send
the men, as it would amount to a declaration of war, which

[59] *Ibid.*, IV, 417–21.   [61] Danvila, IV, 447–53.
[60] Rousseau, II, 113.

P

was inopportune. What better can we ask, he said, than
what England is doing against herself? She was generous
enough to spare the Bourbon courts the pains and expense
of destroying her.[62]

In June, 1776, Spain took a fresh step in the virtual war
against England, making a beginning of contributions to
the Americans. France had begun this practice shortly
before. The reason for their doing so, despite the fear of
an independent America, may be found in a letter of Aranda
to Grimaldi of June 7. It was necessary to make such contributions so that the English and Americans might weaken
each other, destroying the former, and putting the latter
in a state where they would listen to reason, that is, as
dictated by the Bourbons, at the beginning of their independence.[63]   In September Vergennes presented a memorial
to Aranda which was warlike enough in sound. The principal point seemed to be that war against England ought
soon to be declared, before England should make an attack on France and Spain. Spain's attitude is expressed
in Grimaldi's letter of October 8, 1776, to Aranda. The
war was inevitable, and England herself would declare it
as soon as she found a favorable occasion. It would therefore be an indubitable advantage to begin several months
before England planned to do so, especially if she were still
occupied with her colonies. If she were about to make peace
with them, the danger to the French and Spanish colonies
would be great, especially to the latter. Spain was ready,
however, to adopt the policy that France thought best,
although, to be sure, it was uncertain whether the present
was the most fitting time to begin the war. If undertaken,
Spain hoped, among other things, to conquer all or part of
Portugal. This frank statement found Vergennes less
enthusiastic. Aranda's letter of November 9, 1776, called
attention to the difference between Vergennes' words of
September and those of November. Moreover, France was
unwilling to have Spain conquer Portugal, as the other
European powers would object. Charles III seems not to

[62] Rousseau, II, 114–15.   [63] Danvila, IV, 454–59.

have been so disappointed as Aranda, saying that the decision for war ought to be one of free choice, and he himself believed that the right moment had not yet come. Aranda presented a paper to Vergennes and Maurepas in December, however, urging them to declare war. There was nothing to fear from Austria, Prussia, or Russia. On the other hand, there were the oft-mentioned dangers to the colonies of France, and especially of an English attack on San Domingo. Aranda was not successful in making France take a determined stand, but continued his efforts throughout the year 1777.[64] Still, as Danvila says, Spain and France were virtually at war with England from 1776 on. They were aiding the Americans with supplies and funds, were making plans for hostilities, and were carrying on their military and naval preparations.[65]

The diplomatic situation, as far as it affected Spain, has now been given in some detail to the close of the year 1776. For the purposes of this work an equal amount of detail is not necessary after that year, because it marked the end of the tremendous activities in New Spain in northwestward exploration. A brief review down to the outbreak of war with England in 1779 should therefore suffice. After war was declared, naturally it was the principal interest of Spain to 1783, when peace was concluded, a date beyond which the principal limits of this volume do not pass.

Early in the year 1777 Grimaldi was succeeded by Floridablanca, whose policy appears in a memorial by him dated March, 1777. The most immediate advantages that Spain could get from a war with England, he said, would be to expel her from Florida, and to destroy the British establishments in Honduras. France might regain Canada, and the right to fish in Newfoundland, as well as a profitable trade with the insurgent colonies. But neither country ought to think of war until there were considerable forces of troops and ships in their islands of the West Indies, and Spain ought immediately to send as many naval vessels as possible to Havana. If the rebellious colonies should establish their independence, Spain ought to contrive to keep them divided in interests, so that there might not grow up a formidable power near Spanish America.[66] Clearly there was no enthusiasm in Spanish governmental circles on behalf of the Americans. This appears also from the cold reception accorded Arthur Lee, the American representative, who about this time appeared in Spain.[67]

The surrender of Burgoyne at Saratoga caused an entire change in the course of diplomatic procedure. The British government began to make offers with a view to conciliating the colonists. The French ministry acted quickly to prevent a reconciliation ; for reconciliation would mean a loss of the commercial favors which France hoped to obtain, and might also mean a war of England and the colonies against France. Therefore, on December 16, 1777, France declared herself ready to enter into a treaty of commerce and alliance with the American revolutionaries, specifically stating that her willingness was due partially to a desire to diminish the power of England by separating her from her colonies. On February 6, 1778, a treaty was signed.[68]

All of this was done without any official notification to Spain. Aranda had soon learned of it unofficially, although he did not find out the terms of the agreement, and he sent word to Spain. Charles III immediately called for the opinions of his leading ministers. France should be asked to explain the nature of her pact, said Floridablanca, in his memorial of January 22, 1778. The first thing for Spain to do, however, was to assure the safety of the fleet coming from Vera Cruz, and that of the naval vessels and troops returning from Buenos Aires, while more troops should be sent to Havana and Porto Rico. War ought to be avoided if possible, in view of the inconstancy of Spain's allies. England seemed disposed to be on good terms with Spain, and even with France, were it not that the latter's imprudent actions and insatiable desire to get the

[66] Danvila, IV, 494–96.   [68] Danvila, IV, 502–4.
[67] Rousseau, II, 118–19.

world's commerce for herself had caused England to be suspicious. In fine, he recommended continued preparation, as if the war were inevitable, but that it be avoided as long as possible, as it could not be favorable to Spain under existing circumstances. This opinion of Floridablanca's not only manifests his displeasure, which was shared by Charles III and others, at France's proceeding to such important measures without consulting her ally, but also shows that Spain was beginning to comprehend the selfish use that France was making of the Family Compact; France was striking for herself, not for France and Spain. Not until March 4, 1778, did Vergennes give Aranda a copy of the treaties made with the Americans, and not until March 19 did the French government give an official notification to that of Spain. From this time forth Spain felt at liberty to pursue her own policy irrespective of France. The Spanish ambassador in London was advised that Spain's attitude toward England would depend upon the latter; Spain neither wished war nor feared it.[69] Floridablanca had several stormy interviews with Montmorin, who had succeeded Ossun as French ambassador to Madrid. He accused France of compromising Spain when the fleet from Vera Cruz and the squadron from Buenos Aires were at the mercy of the English, alluded to France's unwillingness to make war in October, 1776, when Spain was ready, and gave his opinion that the present, far from being the best moment for the Bourbons to make war, was for Spain the most fatal. He recognized that Aranda was of the French opinion, but decidedly he himself was not. When, in April, Montmorin asked that D'Estaing's fleet be permitted to touch at Cádiz, Floridablanca replied that he thought it extraordinary that France should ask aid of Spain, after having acted contrary to Spain's advice. Did he take the Catholic King for a viceroy of the king of France?[70]

Charles III now began to attempt the part of mediator. He hoped to get Gibraltar and Minorca as the price for

[69] *Ibid.*, IV, 504–18.   [70] Rousseau, II, 119–23.

bringing about peace. In May, Escarano suggested to one of the English ministry that Gibraltar would be a fair equivalent for Spain's services, but was told that the price was high, and that in any event affairs had probably gone beyond the point where mediation would serve; England wanted no more from Spain than that she remain neutral. This was the reply of Lord Weymouth, who rather brusquely thanked Charles III for the magnanimity of his offer. Such an answer was not calculated to be pleasing to the Spanish ear, as Floridablanca very plainly intimated to Lord Grantham. England had had a chance for peace, he said, and declined it; the chance would not return. To add to Spain's displeasure England's conduct on the sea gave cause for complaint, and even the coasts of the Iberian Peninsula were plundered by some Englishmen. Nevertheless, Charles still hoped to fill the rôle of arbitrator, and all the more so when news came of French naval successes against the English. British replies, however, were at no time more courteous than Weymouth's answer to Escarano had been. Charles got Louis XVI to submit terms upon which he would make peace. The latter required an acknowledgment of American independence, the recall of England's land and naval forces, and other conditions of less note. Weymouth haughtily rejected them. On November 14, 1778, Grantham delivered a note saying that England could have no understanding with France until that country withdrew her support from the Americans. At the same time, a proposal by Spain for a twenty-five or thirty year truce between England and her colonies was rejected. However, Charles III still endeavored to mediate. He offered Weymouth an indefinite armistice, to be guaranteed by a general disarmament. He had not consulted Louis XVI before making this offer, but Vergennes did not disavow his act. Again, however, the Spanish king's proposals were arrogantly rejected.[71] To make matters worse England had delayed her reply from January to March, 1779, and English ships had continued

[71] Rousseau, II, 123–35.

to attack those of Spain.   Charles III renewed his offer of
a suspension of hostilities, this time in the form of an ultimatum, April 3, 1779.   England again delayed, and in the
meantime planned attacks on Nicaragua and the Philippines.   On May 28 the ultimatum was rejected.   The
Spanish ambassador left London, and on June 23 war was
officially declared.[72]

[72] Altamira, IV, 66–67.

CHAPTER X

ACTIVITIES OF SPAIN AGAINST FOREIGN AGGRESSIONS IN THE PACIFIC NORTHWEST, 1773-1775

SPAIN was more and more threatened by the activities of other European nations in the Pacific northwest, but, although she was not fully awake to the danger, if we may judge by the history of her diplomacy in the reign of Charles III, nevertheless she did not disregard it. On the contrary, she played no small part in the discoveries, explorations, and conquests of the period, urged on, as usual, by the necessity of defending what she already possessed, and enjoying leadership of an exceptional character in accomplishing these tasks. It has been pointed out that her policy of defence had led to plans for fortifying her American possessions, especially those in the West Indies and those bordering on the Gulf of Mexico and the Caribbean Sea. The Argentine coast, the Falkland Islands, and the coasts of the viceroyalty of Peru had also commanded attention. Thus far, Spanish efforts may be regarded as part of a conscious, general policy. A Spanish writer has implied, although he does not specifically state, that the northwestward expeditions, both by land and sea, were part of the same plan,[1] but the conjecture does not accord with the facts. The Pacific shores of New Spain were on an independent footing. An European war would involve the other lands named, more particularly the West Indies, but was not regarded as greatly endangering Pacific North America. Of this the correspondence of Viceroy Croix, already quoted, is evidence. In this chapter it will appear that action was taken by Spain on the basis of foreign encroachments in

[1] Fernández Duro, VII, 153, 160-61.

the Pacific, as she understood them, irrespective of the state of European politics. Yet, there is a larger unity embracing all of Spain's colonies, even if there were no general plan, namely, the search of European nations for colonies, and the counter-attempts of Spain in self-defence.

England and Russia gave Spain concern in the Pacific northwest between 1773 and 1776, the former much less than the case merited. Even in the case of Russia, despite the great number of documents about her encroachments, Spain was not much afraid. To a certain extent this period is one of particular emergency as regards the Russians, but, in the main, Spanish activities may be ascribed to permanent reasons for combating foreign danger, with the added fact of a capable man to direct the work. To the supposed danger of Russian encroachment were due the Pérez voyage of 1774, and the Heceta and Bodega voyages of 1775. These were only the most direct manifestations proceeding from the same cause. Among other steps taken, related in a measure at least to the Russian peril, were the Crame exploration of the Coatzacoalcos River in the Isthmus of Tehuantepec, the Anza and Rivera expeditions to Alta California, and the founding of San Francisco, the general endeavor to develop Alta California and keep it well supplied, and even the formation of a *reglamento*, or mode of government, for the Californias. Only the Crame expedition will be taken up conclusively in this chapter, but some of the other events will be alluded to because of their relation to the plans against the Russians.

In this chapter, then, there appears not only a discussion of foreign approaches to Spain's Pacific colonies viewed from a third and concluding standpoint, but also a resumption of details concerning governmental attention to this region. In the latter sense it stands forth as the first to be treated of a group of activities from 1773 on, and is so placed because it is the key to the other events,—the impulse to action arising from foreign danger. The other events have to do with the government's interest in local problems of the Californias, and its attention to questions bearing upon the opening and use of an overland route to Alta California. These have been reserved for later chapters, although contemporary with the events related here. Because of their close historical connection, it will be well to note in advance some of the most significant dates, before proceeding to the matter of this chapter.

On July 23, 1773, a provisional or temporary *reglamento* for the Californias, to which Bucarely had devoted much time for several months, received official sanction by his decree. On August 17, instructions were issued to Fernando Rivera y Moncada, who was to lead some soldier-settlers to Alta California up the peninsula, and succeed Fages in command of the new establishments. On September 13, the first Anza expedition was authorized, as we have seen. In January, 1774, Anza's expedition left Tubac, Sonora, and discovered a route to Alta California, returning to Tubac in May. Rivera left Loreto, Baja California, in March, 1774, and got to Monterey in May. A second Anza expedition was authorized in November, 1774. With this were to go settlers and domestic animals, both greatly needed in Alta California. Anza left Tubac in October, 1775, conducted the settlers and animals to Alta California, and was back in Sonora by June, 1776. In September, 1776, a settlement was made at San Francisco by some of the colonists who had accompanied Anza. Late in the same year Garcés proved the existence of a route from Alta California to New Mexico.

A turning point in Bucarely's activities in behalf of the Californias seems to have come at about the time when progress began to be made toward forming a provisional *reglamento*, in May, 1773. Up to that time he had been acquiring information, while attending as best he could to the needs of the province, although with slight expectation of a successful issue of the Alta California establishments. To be sure, he continued to call for reports, and on May 27 wrote that he was as much in the dark as ever, but, from this time forth, his measures began to be effectual. There was no more talk of abandoning Alta California, although that contingency was with difficulty avoided. Between 1773 and 1776 he brought the Alta California establishments out of the realm of uncertainty, and placed them on an enduring basis.

Some indications of Spain's fear of English aggression in the northwest prior to 1773 have already been given, notably the Croix-Gálvez plan of January, 1768, but in the period embraced by this chapter very little evidence on the point has come to light, as compared with the bulk of material concerning the Russians. Yet Bucarely's original consideration of the problem of foreign danger seems to have sprung from news of an English project. In a letter of June 26, 1776, he reviews his acts undertaken with a view to circumventing foreign encroachments, and says that his first measures were due to the king's apprehension, early in 1773, over reports that an Englishman named Bings was undertaking a voyage to the North Pole, with a view to reaching the Californias, if possible. This was responsible for instructions given by him at that time with the aim of safeguarding the Californias against the entry of foreign ships.[2] The instructions referred to were those given to Rivera, August 17, 1773, as follows: "The admission of foreign boats into the American ports of the king's dominions is absolutely prohibited by the laws of the Indies, and it is commanded in many royal decrees and orders that this prohibition be observed; and there are also repeated decrees that commerce is not to be permitted, even in Spanish ships, on the coasts comprised in this viceroyalty, except in the ship from the Philippines, which comes to Acapulco, and the boats in the ship-yard of San Blas for the support of old and new California." All other ships Rivera was to detain if his forces should permit, making prisoners of the expeditionaries, and giving an account to the government in Mexico. Then followed instructions for guarding against surprise, when the Philippine and San Blas boats entered Alta California ports, lest an enemy's ships might be mis-

[2] A.G.P., *Cor. Vir.*, series I, v. 12, No. 2296.

taken for them. In the same document it is stated that the settlers should have arms to aid in defending the Californias if necessary, and Rivera was to make a complete inventory of the artillery, munitions, and arms in the province. The exploration and occupation of the port of San Francisco were also recommended.[3] The Mexican historian, Rivera, says that the instructions to his namesake were also related to reports of Russian aggressions,[4] which was probably the case, since Bucarely had known of them for some time before the date of his instruction to Rivera, and they were considered to be at least as pressing as the report about Bings. Rivera goes on to say that Bucarely was ordered to exercise great vigilance over Pacific coast ports, especially over Monterey, taking the action which the viceroy in fact embodied in his already mentioned instructions. He was to assert that this was done in accordance with provisions to that effect in the laws of the Indies, and not to manifest that it was done by express royal order.[5]

The danger of English interference in the northwest seems not to have been taken very seriously. Writing to Arriaga, September 28, 1774, Bucarely characterized the fears on that account as absurd.[6] Other references to the same effect appear in the correspondence about the Russians. True, this view of the matter underestimated the danger, — this was the period of Hearne's explorations for the Hudson's Bay Company, of activity by the Scottish merchants of Montreal, and of voyages by Cook to the south Pacific, — but nevertheless, it represented the Spanish attitude.

Apprehension about the Russians at this time was due to the reports of the Conde de Lacy, Spanish ambassador to Russia, who, late in the year 1772, scented danger from the Russians. Writing to Grimaldi, on October 22, 1772, of Russian explorations toward North America from Kam-

[3] C-2350. Other aspects of the instruction to Rivera are considered in chap. XI, and to some extent in chap. XIV.
[4] Rivera, I, 428.
[5] I have found no reference to an actual Bings voyage. Bucarely said that Bings was undertaking (*emprendía*) it, and Rivera that he was arranging (*arreglaba*) it. The only fact of importance here, however, is that Spain felt some apprehension.
[6] C-2732.

chatka as a base,[7] he also enclosed an order of the Russian
government of September 5, 1770, calculated to inspire misgiving in Spain. The order stated that the Russian government had received notices that a foreign power [unnamed]
was planning an attack on the port of St. Peter and St.
Paul, Kamchatka, with a view to threatening Russia's
hold on that country. The order called for precautions
by the officials there, the gathering of powder and flour,
and the use of an army of 15,000 men. If English ships
should appear, however, they were to be received with
honors and friendship, and be given such assistance as they
might need.[8] As regards the 15,000 men there was an element of absurdity in this document which makes one doubt
its authenticity. Nor can it have frightened Grimaldi, for
he does not appear to have forwarded a copy to Arriaga.
On February 7, 1773, Lacy wrote again. He had learned,
he said, that a Russian naval officer, Chirikof, had continued
to make explorations in Kamchatka and North America
between 1769 and 1771, and Chirikof and his secretary had
visited St. Petersburg early in 1772. They were sworn
to secrecy by the government, and the former had been
sent back to make another voyage. Several Russians had
said that very important discoveries had been made, but
there had been so much secrecy that Lacy could learn
nothing certain, beyond the fact of Chirikof's voyage.[9]
A copy of this letter was sent to Arriaga, who was instructed
to ask Bucarely to take fitting measures.[10] Arriaga acknowledged receipt of this letter on April 11,[11] and on the same
day wrote to Bucarely, forwarding a copy of Lacy's letter,
and ordering Bucarely to find out whether the Russians
were in fact advancing their explorations.[12]

Bucarely replied on July 27, showing no great anxiety,
but stating that he had already taken action. He referred
to a map printed at St. Petersburg in 1758 indicating that
two ships under Bering had explored the North American
coast between 55° and 60°, but he was inclined to doubt

[7] C-2038.
[8] C-1543.
[9] C-2162.

[10] Grimaldi to Arriaga, Apr. 6, 1773.
C-2209.
[11] C-2210.   [12] C-2211.

whether the land discovered was really part of North America. Lacy's letter showed, however, that the Russians had designs upon America, although their difficulties would be great, because of the scant population and the scarcity of supplies in Kamchatka, and because of the distance from St. Petersburg. Precautionary measures must be taken however, as the Russians might overcome the difficulties.[13] Referring to the Spanish situation in the Pacific, Bucarely said that the region between Cape San Lucas and Monterey had been occupied. There were no foreign establishments in that stretch, and no boats had been seen in recent years other than the Manila galleon and the ships that went to Alta California. San Diego and Monterey were the only ports, and were the only places with force enough to hold in check the innumerable Indians of Alta California. For reasons of economy the Alta California establishments had not been increased. The Department of San Blas was not capable of accomplishing much; skilled officers and pilots, supplies, and other things were needed before anything of much consequence could be done. Russian establishments in North America or those of any foreign country should be prevented, not that Spain did not have enough territory, for it had more than it could settle in centuries, but because any neighbors other than the Indians might prove dangerous. Although it would be hard for the Russians to establish themselves, it was a possibility, and if it were done would be to the disadvantage of Spain. For Spain to prevent their establishment would be easier than it would be for the Russians to undertake it, but it would cost Spain a great deal. Spain had the advantage of known ports and fertile lands, where settlements might be made, from which voyages could be undertaken. The best time to sail from San Blas was from the last of November to the end of January, and probably the same held true, north of Monterey. As Juan Pérez had signified a desire to make an expedition to the far north, Bucarely had given him secret instructions to draw up plans, and was now awaiting them. These

[13] For the map, cf. *infra* n. 34.

operations would be expensive, and would cost less if conducted from Manila.[14]

Despite the calm with which the viceroy viewed the situation and his underestimation of the danger, measures against the possibility of foreign aggressions were the keynote of his action from this time forth. In that same month a provisional *reglamento* for the Californias had been made. This will be taken up later in its local aspects, when it will appear that no point was made of a specific foreign danger. Yet, Bucarely wrote to his friend, General O'Reilly, July 28, 1773, that in forming the *reglamento* he had proceeded principally with a view to avoiding the ideas of the Russians.[15] Bucarely's lack of anxiety, however, is still further manifested in a letter to Arriaga one month later. Nothing further could be done about Pérez's voyage, he said, as that official had left for Monterey on his customary annual voyage with provisions, before Bucarely's letter to him had reached San Blas. He would therefore await Pérez's return.[16] An accident to Pérez's ship occurred, however, obliging him to put back to shore, and thus Bucarely was able to report, September 26, 1773, that Pérez had received his orders concerning the northwestern explorations sooner than he had expected.[17]

In his letter of July 27 Bucarely had requested that some naval officers be sent from Spain for use in Pacific coast explorations, and a royal order of August 24, 1773, informed him that six were being sent. Now that he was to have their assistance, Bucarely should be able to accomplish his purposes against the Russians, wrote Arriaga to the viceroy in a letter of December 23, 1773.[18] The order of August 24 had directed Bucarely to make settlements in ports south of San Diego, and to explore the whole coast and the neighboring islands in search of Russians, who were to be dislodged if found. Replying, November 26, 1773, Bucarely said that he had already taken steps for the departure of Pérez, and not only that, but the Anza expedi-

14 C–2337.
15 C–2342.
16 C–2365.
17 C–2397.
18 C–2456.

tion, the new *reglamento* for the Californias and San Blas, and certain orders given to Agustín Crame all bore on the question of checking the Russians. Crame had been ordered to explore the Río Coatzacoalcos, and report secretly to Bucarely. That river, being navigable up to Tehuantepec, had been used formerly for the transportation of artillery, and Bucarely wished to know whether it would still be easier and less expensive to send artillery to the Pacific by that route. Otherwise, the expense would be unendurable, or there would be the long delays incident to recourse to Manila. Pérez had been ordered to explore and take possession of only such lands as were not occupied by a foreign power, as he carried no force with which to dislodge an enemy. All of these matters must cost considerable sums that were not provided for by a fund, and would normally have to be granted by a *junta de real hacienda*, said Bucarely, but as these projects ought to be kept secret, he asked for authority to raise money by his own decree,[19] and his request was acceded to by the royal government.[20]

From March to May, 1773, Lacy in St. Petersburg was writing letters to Grimaldi about the Russian aggressions in North America. The dates of these letters, and those of Grimaldi's and Arriaga's letters in handling them are worthy of note, as they show a marked lack of anxiety on the part of those highest in authority, who often delayed action on Lacy's excited warnings. The Lacy letters referred to were dated March 19, April 23, May 7 (two), and May 11, 1773. The April 23 letter was a long one, possibly the most startling of all, but was neglected by the Spanish government for a year. It will be taken up in its place from the standpoint of action on it. The other four were acted on at the same time, although one of Lacy's May 7 letters may not have been forwarded to Bucarely. It had enclosed a map (in Russian) of Russian discoveries in Kamchatka, and a list of merchandise showing the kind of trade that the Russians were carrying on in that part

---

[19] C-2430.   [20] Revilla Gigedo, *Informe*, par. 47. C-5613.

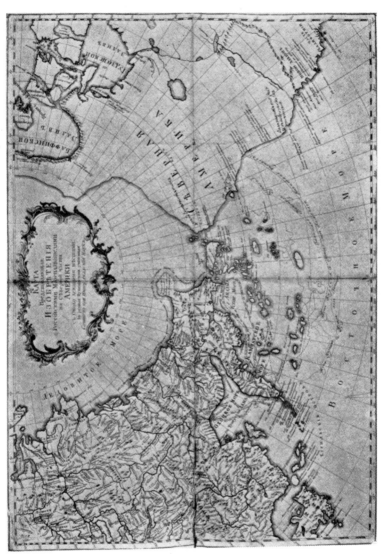

RUSSIAN MAP OF 1773 OF SIBERIA AND THE NORTH PACIFIC.

of the world.[21] Grimaldi forwarded this letter and its enclosures to Arriaga, June 13, 1773,[22] and the latter sent them next day to Jorge Juan[23] for an opinion.[24] Juan's reply does not appear, but the map at least was forwarded to Bucarely with Arriaga's letter of September 25, 1773, to be noticed presently.[25]

In his March 19 letter Lacy claimed to have made an important discovery. He had received a detailed report of the Russian expeditions between Kamchatka and America obtained by one who had handled and read the papers, which were sealed and deposited in the Russian archives. The report said that Bering and Chirikof in their voyages of 1741-42 had reached land at 60°, but they could not tell whether it was the continent or an island. In 1764, two ships went from Archangel under Estehacowy and Panowbafew,[26] and one from Kamchatka under Krenitzin. They joined, and explored the land from a little above 40° up to 75°, and reported it as part of the mainland. Between 235° longitude and Kamchatka the sea was full of islands, the inhabitants of which traded with the people of Kamchatka, wore the same kind of dress, and had the same manners and customs. They said that the land either joined Asia, or was not more than two hours away, as had been stated by Professor Steller who accompanied Bering. They believed the land to be the Californias, which in that case extended to 75°. It was a region of high mountains, with an agreeable, moist climate; it contained trees adapted for use as masts, for example, cedar; it had an abundance of copper, and signs of other metals; and it abounded in fur-bearing animals of the best quality of skins. In 1765-66 the empress authorized a company of Kamchatka business men to form an establishment, which they did on the mainland at 64°. There were twenty-four men in the company, employing two hundred Cossacks in hunting, making

[21] C-2250.
[22] C-2289.
[23] Juan was the celebrated Spanish mathematician, naval officer, and academician, who, however, is more famous to-day as joint author with

Ulloa of the *Noticias secretas* concerning affairs in the viceroyalty of Peru.
[24] C-2290.
[25] For the map, C-2126.
[26] I am unable to identify these names.

discoveries, guarding the establishment, and procuring the payment of tribute to Russia, and there were forty sailors and two ship-builders there. Members of the company were allowed to wear a gold medal with the bust of the empress, who had given to the company the privilege of trading in anything that it might see fit in that region. So far, they had traded mainly in furs, but also in walrus-teeth, whalebone, whale oil, and certain kinds of fish, and they planned to build up commerce with China and Japan.

They imported from Russia such goods as cloth, canvas, shoes, leather, wrought copper, and tobacco. Gold and silver they expected to find, and they had already found pearls, but pearl fishing had been discontinued, because of a certain disease of the fingers which it caused to those employed in it; a less harmful method of pearl fishing was being sought. Learned men of the Russian Academy were being sent out to discover mines.[27]

Writing May 7 Lacy said that Russia had formed a project of forcing the Great Wall and invading China with 25,000 men. They were also planning a naval expedition from Kamchatka against Japan under command of an Englishman, General Lloyd, although it would doubtless be postponed until the conclusion of the war with Turkey. He mentioned this as evidence of Russia's vast oriental projects.[28] In his May 11 letter he wrote that the empress had told Professor Haller of the Russian Academy about the discoveries in America, and that he had made a report to her, suggesting that part of the Russian fleet be sent around the Cape of Good Hope to Kamchatka, where it could refit and then go to America and make conquests. Haller said that Russia had more right to America than any other power, because the inhabitants of America came originally from Siberia, and had continued to trade with it; also, because the Dutch had made themselves masters of the Moluccas.[29] Lacy was sure that this report had been made, absurd as it might appear, and therefore thought it best to inform

27 C–2197.
28 C–2249.
29 It is difficult to see what the

Moluccas had to do with it, unless on the modern doctrine of "compensation."

Grimaldi, for nothing was deemed impossible by the Russians, however difficult or dangerous it might be.[30]

Grimaldi sent these three letters of Lacy to Arriaga on June 20, 1773. He had delayed after receiving Lacy's March 19 letter in expectation of a more detailed report which Lacy had intimated that he was about to send, but which had not come.[31] A few days later Grimaldi again wrote to Arriaga, sending him two letters of the Vizconde de la Herrería of the year 1764, when the latter was in St. Petersburg.[32] The letters contained notices about the Californias and information about Russian expeditions.[33] With them was a map of the year 1758, in French, made by the Imperial Academy of Sciences of St. Petersburg, showing the Russian discoveries in North America.[34] Arriaga was somewhat slow to act. Not until September 25 did he write to Bucarely, when he forwarded the documents which have just been discussed, and gave instructions for Bucarely to do what he should think proper to find out whether the Russians were advancing.[35] From another letter of Arriaga to Bucarely, January 24, 1774, we get a clear expression of the *ministro general's* views with regard to the Russian peril. "As for the Russian discoveries," he said, "they are still to me a very remote object of attention, and the present time seems much too early for them to be a cause for alarm. But as the preparations against them serve many other purposes, especially in that they conduce to the advancement of missionary work, and to the extension of the gospel, the more land we gain by discoveries, I am very well satisfied with all that has been done, for in this manner, by sea and land, we may proceed with our conquests to one place after another."[36]

Meanwhile, Bucarely had been making preparations for the Pérez expedition, his activity in this regard being in

[30] C-2252.
[31] C-2295.
[32] Grimaldi to Arriaga, June 28, 1773. C-2306.
[33] C-545, 561.
[34] C-442. The map was published in Müller's *Sammlung* (which I have

not seen), and appeared also in English in the English translation from that work of 1761, and in French in a French translation of 1766.
[35] C-2380.
[36] A.G.I., 146-4-2.

striking contrast to the delays of the administration in Spain. On July 18, 1773, Bucarely had ordered Pérez to draw up a plan for northward exploration, and Pérez's accidental return from his proposed Monterey voyage had enabled him to receive this order earlier than otherwise would have been the case, so that the plans were taken up at once. On September 1, Pérez completed his plan, which the viceroy approved in his order of September 29, making one change, — that Pérez must go north to 60° rather than to 45° or 50°, as that officer had suggested. There is no evidence to show that the *junta* was consulted.

The official instruction was not issued until December 24, 1773. It begins by declaring that the king had imposed a duty upon the viceroy of extending his dominions, as well as of preserving them, in order to bring the Indians into vassalage, and to spread the gospel among them. Therefore, the viceroy was ordering Juan Pérez to make explorations north of Monterey, in the frigate *Santiago*, otherwise *Nueva Galicia*, which was to carry provisions for a year. Pérez was also to take provisions to Monterey, but to stay there no longer than necessary to unload them, when he should again put to sea. He should reach at least 60° before starting back to Monterey, making a most minute examination of the coast upon his return, and landing, where possible without risk. He was to make no settlements, but might leave distinguishing marks at good sites, taking formal possession of them. If a foreign establishment should be discovered, he was to land north of it, and take possession, leaving evidences of his act. He must not communicate with such foreign establishment, but should view it from afar, getting in that way all the information that he could. He was to avoid ships that he might meet, or, if compelled to communicate with them, was to conceal his real objects. Indians were to be treated well, and their customs noted, especially in matters of government; likewise he was to note the productivity of the lands in minerals and agricultural products, and get data as to the animals, plants, and trees. He was to find out whether the Indians had ever seen boats before or any foreigners, and if they had, was to inquire about their visit there.   He might put into Monterey, if a storm or other accident should make it necessary, or if urgently in need of provisions, of which an extra supply had been ordered sent from San Blas. In entering Monterey or San Diego he was to hoist a certain signal, of which Rivera had been advised, so that he might know that Pérez's was not a foreign ship.   On no account was he to start hostilities with the Indians, remembering that his principal object was to explore the coast in search of foreign establishments, and to acquire information that might lead to a more thorough examination. Russian maps of 1758 and 1773 were being given to him, as possibly of some use, and, finally, he was assured that he would be rewarded according to his deeds.[37]

In answering Arriaga's letter of September 25, Bucarely wrote, December 27, 1773, enclosing a copy of the document just mentioned, and saying that the preparations for the voyage were already so far advanced that there had hardly been time to make a copy of the Russian map of 1773, and he had been obliged to send the map and Pérez's instructions by special courier. The instructions were secret, and were not to be opened by Pérez until after his departure from Monterey. He was to stop at Monterey to leave provisions, as the supply-ship *Principe* was laid up for repairs until February. Pérez himself had plenty of supplies, and a crew of his own choosing, and Bucarely hoped that some useful knowledge, at least, might result from the expedition.[38] A month later Bucarely wrote that Pérez and the *Santiago* had probably sailed already; he had heard that they were only awaiting a favorable wind in order to put to sea. Francisco Hijosa, the commissary of San Blas, had written, January 5, 1774, that the boat was provisioned for a year, besides carrying supplies for Monterey, and Bucarely had ordered the *Principe* promptly to San Diego and Monterey, so as to provide for every possible contingency that might cause Pérez to need more supplies.[39]

[37] C–2457.   [38] C–2464.   [39] C–2521.

Pérez had in fact sailed on January 24, as Bucarely soon
learned from Hijosa's letter of the 27th from San Blas. Up
to the Islas Isabelas, wrote Bucarely, soon afterward, the
voyage had gone very well, according to the letters sent
back from there by Pérez and by Serra, who was also on
board. Nor had the repairing and the provisioning of the
Príncipe for the voyage to Monterey been lost sight of by
Bucarely, who expected to hear, every instant, that the
boat had sailed.[40]

Reference has been made to a proposed exploration of the
Isthmus of Tehuantepec by Agustín Crame. This affair was
undertaken without delay. Crame was at first unsuccessful in his quest, informing Bucarely on December 28, 1773,
that he had not found a route across the isthmus suitable
for the transportation of artillery. Only a few days later,
however, January 2, 1774, he wrote enthusiastically of his
complete success. He had wandered in the hills, as if his
plan were to open a new way, instead of exploring what
he had been told was the old one, when by good luck he
hit upon a route which not only was suitable for transporting artillery, but which had formerly been used for that
purpose. The proof of this, which he regarded as incontest-
able, was that a way had been cleared to make a wide road,
something that would not have been done in this part of
the world for any other reason. As a result of this discovery it was clear that an excellent route existed, especially
if use were made of the rivers there ; it could be done wholly
by land, but at considerable labor and expense, as a stretch
of five or six leagues would have to be cleared. Crame had
a little more to do in order to complete his exploration, and
was making a map, so that his description of the country
might be more clearly understood.[41]

[40] Bucarely to Arriaga, Feb. 24,
1774. C–2551.

[41] C–2502. Crame referred also to
the possibility of an interoceanic canal
across the Isthmus of Tehuantepec.
This could be made, he said, by cutting
a space only eight or nine leagues long,
and making one tunnel, thus joining
two rivers flowing into opposite seas.
This led him to a consideration of the
ports of that country, of the possibility
of commercial development, and of the
advantages that would accrue, if trade
with Peru might avail itself of such
a canal, thus permitting the entire
commerce of both Americas to centre
upon one point. Crame had in mind,
no doubt, that, as things were, there
were two centres of trade, Vera Cruz
and Porto Bello, whereas the canal

The Crame Map of the Isthmus of Tehuantepec, 1774.

Evincing much pleasure over Crame's achievement, Bucarely forwarded his statement to Arriaga, January 27, 1774, again remarking that it formed part of a plan, along with the Pérez and Anza expeditions, to oppose superior forces to those which the Russians might create in the Pacific.[42] Writing again, March 27, 1774, Bucarely noted a new use that might be made of the Tehuantepec route, besides the one originally contemplated. Crame's map having been completed, he was forwarding it so as to show how easily goods might be carried that way both for use in Alta California and to assist in the explorations, or for other purposes, at less expense than the existing method by means of the Department of San Blas, and in less time than if reliance were placed on voyages from Manila. No authentic documents had been found to prove a former communication from sea to sea at Tehuantepec, but there were cannon at Vera Cruz which had been cast in Manila, Crame had found proofs of the use of the Tehuantepec route to transport cannon, and there was a tradition to the same effect in that country. Furthermore, Cortés had built ships there for voyages to the Californias, and he must have made use of the Crame route to transport his materials. All of these notices might be of some use in resolving what to do to check the Russians.[43] Crame's map will explain Bucarely's interest in the Tehuantepec route better than anything else.[44]

Between the departure of Pérez for the north and his return, late in 1774, there was a long gap when Bucarely's interest in the affairs of Alta California and its retention against foreign foes was more directly concerned with matters affecting an overland route, and with the development of the province, as by his projected settlement of San Francisco. He seemed willing to await the result of Pérez's voyage before engaging further in naval ventures. The authorities in Spain, however, were in a measure roused to a fear of both the Russians and the Eng-

would permit of there being one principal port as a base for both New Spain and Peru.

[42] C–2520.
[43] C–2597.
[44] For the map, A.G.I., *vitrina*.

lish by the resurrection of Lacy's April 23 letter of the previous year. This came about as a result of another letter from Lacy, January 25, 1774, which made references to the Russian discoveries in Kamchatka.[45] We may now take up the much neglected letter of April 23, 1773.

An emissary of Lacy's had come upon a civilized native of Kamchatka, then in St. Petersburg, and the latter had made the following statements: The Russians knew, as early as 1770, of the Spanish expeditions of 1769 to Alta California, and they were afraid lest Spain might threaten Russia's possessions. There was some talk of making an agreement with the English, who were also interested, to check Spain's advances, but when a report came that Spain had reached only 48° [sic], whereas the Russian possessions were in 64° and 65°, the Russians concluded that the Spaniards did not know of their settlements, and undertook no measures against them. The Russians had expected English help, because the Hudson's Bay Company was extending its possessions westward to the vicinity of the Russian settlements. The English company already had settlements all the way from Hudson and Baffin bays to the Pacific, and it was carrying on an extensive trade with the Indians. Its employes hindered everybody, even other Englishmen, from entering its territories, and the Russians had cause for complaint, because it won over tribes which had been disposed to join with the Russians, and overcame Russian efforts at winning the friendship of the natives, whenever they got too near the company's possessions. The Russians not only had a settlement on the American mainland, but also had several very large ones on different islands. The islands were part of a great archipelago extending southward to the equator, including the islands of Japan. This information, said Lacy, confirmed what he had said in his letter of March 19, 1773. Clearly, the Russians were already in the Californias, not far from the Spanish settlements, and he believed that it was a matter of the greatest importance to check them. On this point it might be well

[45] C–2514.

to know that the Russians had been obliged to abandon the land of the Yakutskis, because of the hostility of that people.[46]

Not until April 30, 1774, did Grimaldi take action on this letter, when he wrote to Arriaga that he was in doubt whether he had sent him a copy before. But, "considering the importance of these notices," he felt that he need not apologize for sending a copy again, if he had previously done so. He also enclosed copies of two maps sent by Lacy, one of which had been forwarded before in Grimaldi's letter of June 13, 1773, and another, in German, sent by Lacy with his letter of January 25, 1774.[47] The latter showed the discovery by the Russians of a new archipelago in the Pacific.[48] Arriaga acknowledged Grimaldi's letter of June 1,[49] and, two weeks later, forwarded copies of Lacy's letter and a translation of the German map to Bucarely, with instructions that the latter was not to lose sight of the Russian objects.[50] By another letter, June 25, 1774, Arriaga informed Bucarely that he still thought the danger of a Russian approach to the Spanish dominions in New Spain very distant. He had approved all of Bucarely's measures, but thought there would be time enough in which to check the Russians if Spain should proceed in the normal way. He specifically referred to the Crame and Pérez expeditions, however, as well adapted to procure the results for which they had been undertaken.[51]

Bucarely's reply of September 28, 1774, is further evidence to show in what estimation he held the reports of Russian and English aggressions, and shows also what he was doing to meet them. He was inclined to treat Lacy's report as absurd, as far as it dealt with the extension of the Hudson's Bay Company's possessions to proximity with

[46] C-2221. More likely the Chukchis were meant, rather than the Yakutskis.
[47] C-2615. Grimaldi said that the first-mentioned map had been forwarded in Lacy's letter of June 13, 1773. This seems to have been a slip for his own letter of that date. It will be noted that Arriaga did not at this time send Bucarely a copy of the map referred to, probably because it was the same

as the one already forwarded by him September 25, 1773. Bucarely's letter of September 28, 1774 (C-2732), remarks the failure to enclose the supposed Lacy map of June 13, 1773.
[48] The map is not in the file.
[49] C-2636.
[50] C-2649.
[51] A.G.I., 146-4-2.

those of Russia. This had the same appearances of in-
vention as the pretended voyage from Hudson Bay to the
Pacific about which so much had been published.[52] Referring
to his own letters about conditions in Alta California, the
voyage of Pérez, Anza's discovery of a route from Sonora
and his return, and the explorations of the Río Coatzacoalcos
to Tehuantepec by Crame, he repeated that all of these
activities had the same object. They were being executed
at the same time, and were evidence that his sole intention
was to prevent the possibility of foreign danger to Spain's
possessions of the Pacific coast. He was building a new
boat at San Blas, and planning a new expedition by way of
the Anza route to occupy the port of San Francisco. First,
however, it was necessary to consult with Anza, and to
learn the results of Pérez's voyage. He was also suspending
the change in location of the Sonora presidios, until he could
decide whether there should be one at the confluence of the
Colorado and Gila, in which case Sonora would require six
presidios instead of four.[53]

Meanwhile, preparations for a second expedition by the
Anza route to Alta California were going on, although not
much was done until after Anza's arrival in Mexico early
in November. At about the same time Bucarely got news
of Pérez's return, the *Santiago* having reached San Blas
on November 3. We have seen that Pérez had sailed from
San Blas on January 24, 1774, bound for Monterey. At the
same time, Anza was making the first of his expeditions to
Alta California. When Anza reached San Gabriel, March
22, 1774, he learned that Pérez was at San Diego, and therefore sent a force there to obtain provisions. One of the men
in that party was a soldier named Juan Bautista Valdés, who,
a little later, was sent back over the Anza route to Mexico
with Anza's despatches to Bucarely. Upon Valdés' arrival in
June, Bucarely ordered Melchor de Peramás to take a dep-

[52] This may refer to a voyage from
the Pacific by a transcontinental strait,
supposed to have been made in 1640
by an Admiral Fonte. Much interest
was taken in England, in the eighteenth
century, in accounts of this voyage,
and much was written, many English
writers believing that the voyage had
been made. It is now utterly dis-
credited.

[53] C-2732.

osition from him. Valdés stated that he had seen the
Santiago at San Diego, and had gone on board. All were
well. The boat had been there two weeks, having stopped
at Serra's request, he said, in order that supplies might be left
at the southern missions. Valdés seemed ignorant of the purposes of the voyage, stating that the *Santiago* had come to
bring provisions. New masts were being cut for the *Santiago*, the old ones being too high, although in other respects
the frigate was a good one. He had seen Serra, who was
well and had started overland for Monterey.[54] Writing to
Arriaga, June 26, 1774, Bucarely evinced displeasure at
the news of Pérez's stop at San Diego, because his orders
were against doing so, unless in great necessity, and it was
for that reason that he had caused the Valdés declaration
to be taken. The *Santiago* seemed to have had an easy voyage, and to have stopped either at Serra's request or because
of the excessive length of the mast. Serra had been willing
to be set down at Monterey when he started. Bucarely
was waiting to hear further as to the cause for this stop.[55]
By September 26, 1774, Bucarely had learned that Pérez
had started north from Monterey, and he so informed
Arriaga.[56]

Pérez had gone on to Monterey, reaching there May 9,
and setting sail again on June 11. He did not reach 60°
as instructed to do, but got to about 55°; he did not land
to take possession for Spain, nor was he able to make good
observations of the coast, due to bad weather and fog;
furthermore, he found no foreign establishments, nor proof
that they did not exist. He turned south, July 22, 1774,
reached Monterey on August 27, and left there for San
Blas on October 9. While Bucarely had not learned what
he had wished to learn, he considered that Pérez had gained
much useful information. Writing to Arriaga, November
26, 1774, he said that Pérez had reached 55° 49', where he
conversed and bartered with Indians who came to the ship
in canoes, and the same thing occurred in 49°. He had

[54] Valdés, *Declaration*, June 14, 1774.   [55] C–2656.
C–2648.   [56] C–2719.

been obliged to return because of fogs and cold, a fear that
the fresh water might give out, and his suspicion of an
unknown coast, but he had accomplished much more than
Bucarely had expected of a first expedition. The information
obtained would help in future voyages, and was some evidence
that there were no foreign establishments in the nineteen
degrees that he had covered, north of the Spanish settlements. The Indians seemed to have been the same as
those mentioned in the accounts of the Russian expedition
of 1741. They were docile, but more advanced than those
encountered hitherto by Spaniards; for example, they wore
clothes. He would immediately follow up this voyage by
preparing others, and he had already ordered the *Santiago*
to refit for another voyage. This time it was not to stop
at San Diego or Monterey. Bruno de Heceta was to be in
command, with Pérez as pilot and second in authority, and
with the same crew. Heceta was to bear similar instructions to those given to Pérez, particular stress being laid
upon his reaching a higher latitude, examining as much of
the coast as possible on his return, and taking possession for
Spain wherever he might land. After unloading provisions
at Monterey, Lieutenant Miguel Manrique, in the *Príncipe*,
was to explore the port of San Francisco, for, said Bucarely,
"I regard the occupation of this port as indispensable,
and to facilitate it I intend that Anza, who is now at this
capital, shall return to Sonora and make a second *entrada*." [57]
With this letter Bucarely forwarded a copy of Pérez's
diary and other documents emanating from those who had
taken part in the voyage.[58] In another letter of November
26, Bucarely was able to say that he had already appointed
a chaplain for the new voyage, and he was about to call
a *junta* to determine what fund should pay the expenses of
maritime expeditions of discovery.[59] Replying to these
letters, February 14, 1775, Arriaga gave his approval to
Bucarely's plans for a new voyage.[60]

Bucarely wrote yet another letter on November 26, 1774,

[57] C-2763.   [59] C-2765.
[58] C-2645, 2681, 2757.   [60] C-2848.

one to General O'Reilly, which merits particular attention. O'Reilly and Bucarely seem to have been warm personal friends. Evidence of this is to be found in two *legajos* of correspondence of the viceroy, now in the Archivo General de Indias (88–5–17 and 88–5–18). The first of these *legajos* is composed for the most part of the O'Reilly-Bucarely correspondence between 1769 and 1775, with scattering letters for other years. During this period each wrote to the other every month, and but few of their letters are missing. Bucarely's letters are *borradores*, or drafts, and O'Reilly's are signed with his name and rubric. In each case the body of the letter is in the hand of a clerk, with corrections by Bucarely or O'Reilly, but there are lengthy postscripts in their own hands and in some cases entire letters. Although intimately personal, they dealt mostly with the affairs in New Spain, O'Reilly's interest being explained by the fact that he himself wished to become viceroy, and Bucarely wished it no less. One of the most surprising disclosures of the correspondence, in view of Bucarely's remarkable activity and efficiency as viceroy, is the fact that he would have preferred to return to Spain from Havana instead of going to Mexico, and that he desired all along to retire, if his post could be obtained for O'Reilly. The correspondence is also of interest from the standpoint of the proportions given to the various affairs of the viceroyalty. From this we are able to see that Bucarely spoke the truth when he said that the matters having to do with checking the Russians were occupying his principal attention. Indeed events on the northern frontier and northwest coast were almost the only affairs of the viceroyalty that he discussed, and especially the matters dealt with most largely in this volume. One oddity may be noticed. O'Reilly never failed to inquire concerning his friend Hugo Oconor, and to urge that special favor be shown to him. Thus Oconor and his work get more space than any other single factor. O'Reilly's defeat before Algiers may explain why he failed to become viceroy of New Spain.

Bucarely's letter to O'Reilly of November 26, 1774, aside

from its paragraph about Oconor, is almost wholly devoted to his own activities against the Russians. Here again he speaks of having undertaken the Anza, Crame, and Pérez expeditions to counteract the Russian danger. Pérez had reached the very place where the Russians were in 1741. He had discovered some new tribes of Indians, and had ascertained that for four hundred leagues north of Monterey there was no reason to suspect the existence of foreign establishments. The rest of the coast would presently be explored, and Bucarely would lose no time in making fresh investigations which would make the path of glory easy for his successor.[61]

Notwithstanding the pressure of arranging for the second Anza expedition, Bucarely did not delay the preparations for new voyages of discovery. On December 27, 1774, he wrote several letters about the course of maritime exploration. In one he advised Arriaga that he was sending some articles which Pérez had obtained in trade with the Indians of 55° 49', enclosing an inventory of these goods.[62] These showed the Indians to be far advanced from barbarism; for example, the list included blankets, a fur cap, a woven hat, and a purse. Bucarely recommended that Pérez be promoted, as an incentive to others.[63] In another letter he wrote of his plan for the northward voyage of the *Santiago*. As in the case of Pérez's voyage, extra supplies were to be forwarded to Alta California to provide for the possible need of the *Santiago*. Pérez and Hijosa had suggested that it would be well for the *Sonora* to accompany the *Santiago*, and Bucarely had accepted the suggestion, asking Heceta of the *Santiago* to name a commander for the other boat from the naval officers sent from Spain. These officers were now in Mexico, but they would very soon be ready to start west. Bucarely was also hurrying forward a supply of arms and ammunition, by forced marches. Not only was Manrique to explore the port of San Francisco, but Heceta had also been ordered to do so upon his return, by

[61] C–2771. O'Reilly was expected to be his successor.

[62] C–2784 is the inventory.
[63] C–2783.

which time Bucarely thought that it might already be occupied by the troops that Anza was to conduct there. Heceta carried the same instructions as Pérez, except that he was not to stop at Monterey going north, unless in case of necessity. He was to reach 65°, if possible, before approaching the coast, and then explore as he came south. He was to avoid foreign settlements, if there were any, and to take formal possession elsewhere, when possible. Under no circumstances was he to make a settlement, but he was to get further information about the Indians found by Pérez, in particular whether they had any commerce, and whether the goods they exchanged with Pérez were of their own make or bought from others. Parties were to be sent ashore, but not inland nor in any way exposed to the treachery of the Indians. All that was desired was to accustom the Indians to good treatment by the Spaniards, and to get information from them.[64] The same day Bucarely wrote to O'Reilly telling of preparations for the voyages of discovery, again remarking that the northern lands would thus be explored for the benefit of his successor, and the Spanish court reassured concerning the explorations of the Russians.[65] Three months later, March 27, 1775, Bucarely wrote that the *Santiago* and *Sonora* had sailed for the north on March 16. With them went the *San Carlos* with provisions for Monterey, charged also with the duty of exploring San Francisco Bay.[66] Another letter of the same date advised that Manrique had gone insane, and had had to be put ashore, wherefore Ayala was succeeding him in command of the *San Carlos*, his place on the *Sonora* being taken by Bodega y Cuadra. All six naval officers sent from Spain, including Manrique, had thus far manifested the greatest zeal.[67]

Meanwhile, Arriaga seems to have become unusually excited over possible foreign establishments on the Pacific coast. Writing to Bucarely, December 23, 1774, he said that the king had directed him to give secret orders to the viceroy to dislodge any foreign enemies found on the coasts of the Californias. Bucarely was to ask them to go, and if they refused, he was to drive them away by force.[68] In reply Bucarely wrote, April 26, 1775, that Pérez's voyage had indicated that there were no settlements for twenty degrees north of Monterey, except of Indians who appeared less barbarous than those hitherto met with, but to make more sure, he had planned new expeditions. Anza had been directed to occupy San Francisco, and boats had been sent northward with provisions for Alta California, and to carry on explorations. He deemed it best to await the results of these expeditions, rather than engage in new ones which might be profitless without the information about to be gained, as well as expensive.[69]

Pérez's voyage had aroused considerable interest in Spain. Upon receipt of Bucarely's letter of November 26, 1774, Arriaga sent that and Pérez's diary to Vicente Doz,[70] June 1, 1775, asking his opinion relative to future discoveries, and how far away he thought the Russians might be.[71] Doz's answer shows a remarkable grasp of the situation. He had read of all the Russian voyages of discovery to North America, he said, especially the last one, that of Alexei Chirikof in 1741, which reached land in 55° 36′ latitude and 218° longitude, reckoning from Paris. Pérez claimed to have reached 55° 40′ latitude and $221\frac{1}{24}$° longitude. The difference in longitude stated was only forty leagues, and that might be due to an error in reckoning. Thus, they must have reached land at the same place. Pérez's men saw Indians with half of a bayonet and a piece of sword; doubtless these articles had belonged to some of the ten men sent ashore by Chirikof who did not return. Chirikof, being unable to land, had returned with the coast always in sight to a gulf in 51° 12′, which was only twelve degrees of longitude from Kamchatka. His and Pérez's diaries together proved therefore that the Cali-

---

[68] C-2777.   [69] C-2893.
[70] Doz was a Spanish astronomer who accompanied the Frenchman, Chappe d'Auteroche, to Baja California in 1769 to observe the transit of Venus from San José del Cabo. Humboldt, *Political essay*, I, liii and 222.   [71] C-2928.

fornias ran northwest by north up to 60° ; then west ; then south six hundred leagues to the said gulf, where America ended, one hundred fifty leagues from the Russian possessions ; then north and northeast, forming a channel with the eastern coast of Asia of not more than one hundred leagues in width in some places, according to some of the Russian voyagers. As to future discoveries, it would not be possible to pass 60°, unless a strait were found separating the land discovered by the Russians from the continent of America. The Russians had always been desirous of encroaching upon the Spanish domains in North America, but they had failed repeatedly in their attempts from Archangel, nor had their voyages from Kamchatka been altogether successful. Bering perished, and so did most of Chirikof's crew and the astronomer, De L'Isle. These misfortunes, the sterility of Kamchatka, and the slight civilization of the inhabitants of Kamchatka would protect Spain for the present. The English were quite as eager in seeking a northwest passage, as the Russians in their designs, nor had they suffered fewer misfortunes. Hudson and Baffin had proved to the English the fruitlessness of their undertaking, but a way to the Pacific might possibly be found, not by a strait, but by way of the rivers. The violent currents that Pérez encountered might come from some great river, and it might even be the one which the French reported as having its source near the Missouri River. De L'Isle thought that river might empty into the Pacific, and Müller reckoned its mouth as in the vicinity of the place where Pérez encountered the currents. It would therefore be well to examine that bay to see whether there might prove to be a passage. Although Pérez explored between Cape Mendocino and 50°, he had said nothing about the two entrances said to have been found by Aguilar and Fuca between 42° and 48°, which was some evidence that they did not exist, but as bad weather and fog had prevented Pérez's seeing a great part of the coast, it would be well to make a second exploration to uproot this preoccupation of the geographers.[72]

[72] Doz to Arriaga, June 21, 1775. C-2929.

R

On receiving this communication Arriaga wrote to Bucarely, June 23, 1775, approving all that he had done for the second voyage of exploration.[73] A few days later, July 8, he acknowledged receipt of the news of departure of the two boats for the north.[74] On receiving Bucarely's letter of April 26, Arriaga seems to have forgotten the approval recently given by him. Replying on August 26, he asked why the instructions to Heceta were at variance with his order of December 23, 1774, calling for the expulsion of foreigners from the coasts of the Californias. He was objecting to the paragraphs requiring Heceta to avoid coming in contact with foreign establishments or foreign ships other than to get information about them.[75] Bucarely's answer is not at hand, but he might have said that the order referred to did not reach Mexico until after the *Santiago* and *Sonora* had sailed, to say nothing of Arriaga's approval of June 23. However, it could not have been an issue of importance, because the viceroy was able soon to report the return of the two ships and that they had come upon no foreign establishments.

Before that time, however, Bucarely had made a report, August 27, 1775, as to the cost of the voyages. The Pérez voyage had cost 15,455 *pesos*, 4 *reales*, 11 *granos*, and the voyage then being made by Heceta and Bodega had called for 36,740 *pesos*, 2 *granos*, the total for the two being 52,195 *pesos*, 5 *reales*, 1 *grano*. San Blas had paid for all, although chargeable only with 20,000 *pesos*, wherefore Bucarely had ordered the additional sum returned to that department.[76] Both the expense and the method of satisfying it received the royal approval.[77] This matter is worthy of more than passing comment. Much has been said of the unwillingness or inability of the Spanish government to expend money. Yet for these voyages and the many other projects of Bucarely considerable sums were required. It shows either a more pronounced fear than appears from the

[73] C-2930.
[74] C-2951.
[75] C-2969.

[76] C-2978.
[77] Arriaga to Bucarely, Dec. 22, 1775. C-3050.

documents, or else a revival of energy based upon hopes from the future. The latter view impresses the writer more strongly. Arriaga had found a man who could get things done, things too that were worth doing, and he gave him free play. We have seen that the *Santiago*, *Sonora*, and *San Carlos* left San Blas for the north on March 16, 1775. The two former went in company until July 30, when they parted. Heceta in the *Santiago* went about to 49°, usually keeping near the shore and anchoring often. In the course of his exploration he came upon the mouth of the Columbia River. The sickness of many of the crew compelled his return, so that by August 29 he was already at Monterey. Bodega went nearly to 58°, made a thorough survey from the limit of Pérez's voyage, and landed twice to take possession. As usual on such voyages many of the crew were now sick with scurvy, and besides, provisions were failing. So the *Sonora* was turned southward, and, exploring the coast as best it could, made for Monterey and reached there on October 7. Neither vessel had found any Russians. Ayala in the *San Carlos* had in the meantime made a thorough exploration of San Francisco Bay, and returned to San Blas shortly before the other two vessels, while Heceta and Bodega got there on November 20. The results of these voyages were set forth at length by Bucarely in four letters of November 26, 1775, to Arriaga, all written before he learned of the arrival of Heceta and Bodega at San Blas, but based on reports which they had forwarded by Ayala in the *San Carlos*. In the first he wrote generally of all three voyages, telling of the latitude reached by them, and of Ayala's exploration of San Francisco Bay.[78] His second letter dealt with the voyage of Ayala.[79] Among its enclosures was a letter to him from Ayala, November 9, 1775, also about San Francisco Bay, saying that it was the best port that he had seen from Cape Horn north.[80] The third letter treated of Heceta's

[78] C-3032.
[79] C-3033.
[80] C-3028. The other enclosure was a report by José de Cañizares, September

7, 1775, of the exploration of San Francisco Bay, with a description of the bay. C-2985.

voyage,[81] and the fourth of Bodega's.[82] A month later, on
December 27, 1775, Bucarely informed Arriaga of the return
of Heceta and Bodega, and recommended the commanders
and pilots of all the vessels engaged in the recent explorations.[83] One of the pilots, whom Bucarely had also recommended in one of his November 26 letters, was no longer
alive to benefit by the royal favor. On the second day out
from Monterey, on the voyage back to San Blas, there had
occurred the death of Juan Pérez, This news was conveyed
by the same mail of December 27.[84] The promotions recommended were shortly afterward authorized.[85]

To return to the status of opinion in Spain: Doz's able
and complacent view of the situation in comparing the
Pérez voyage with those of the Russians may well have
lulled Arriaga into a feeling of security. Lacy in Russia
was far from that state of mind, however, and now bombarded
Grimaldi with a fresh series of letters about Russian activities in the Pacific. No evidencé has come to hand to show
that his communications were ever forwarded to Bucarely,
but they did reach Arriaga. They will therefore be re-
corded here.

In a letter dated April 31 [sic], 1775, Lacy wrote Grimaldi
that Pérez's voyage was causing some uneasiness at the
Russian court. If the Spanish ships were approaching
Kamchatka, he suggested that they get in touch with the
Chukchis, a people whom the Russians had not been able
to conquer, whose hatred for the Russians was so great
that they would be likely to give information to the Spaniards.[86] In a communication dated May 1, 1775, Lacy
enclosed a document tending to confirm what he had said
previously concerning Russian commerce and discoveries

[81] C-3034. This enclosed a number
of documents forwarded by Heceta
from Monterey. C-2816, 2967, 3003-5.
[82] C-3035. An account by Bodega
was enclosed. Bodega to Bucarely,
Oct. 13, 1775. C-3006.
[83] C-3057. With this letter he forwarded the diaries kept by the commander, pilot, and chaplain of each
ship. Another letter of the same date,
C-3058, forwarded the official acts of

Heceta and Bodega in taking possession
for Spain of places where they landed,
with maps of the ports entered. Most
of these documents enclosed in these
two letters are to be found in A.G.I.,
Estado, Aud. Mex., legajo 19.
[84] C-3062.
[85] Gálvez to Bucarely, Feb. 28, 1776.
C-3157.
[85] C-2900.

in America. He had also verified it through the statements of merchants engaged in the commerce of which the document treated, and by the most secret methods. Being "very much persuaded that these discoveries cannot do less than cause a notable revolution, in time, in the commerce of Europe," he would continue to be vigilant. The Russian government had learned of the Pérez voyage through an account in the Leyden Gazette of March 21, 1775.[87] The enclosed document stated that the Russians had discovered from the north of California to 67°. In 1763 a company of twenty Russian merchants was formed for trade with Kamchatka and the islands already discovered and those to be discovered. This company had two settlements in Kamchatka, and had come upon many populous islands in 1764 and 1766 on the western coast of America. The company's capital had increased from 10,000 rubles in 1763 to 60,000 in 1772,[88] and the furs and other products obtained by this company in 1773 [89] were valued at 300,000 rubles. Between 1768 and 1773 they sent seven frigates to the west coast of North America, one in 1768, two in 1770, one in 1772, and three in 1773; the boats of 1772 and 1773 had not yet returned. This company had no fixed settlement in America, but landed Cossacks there to hunt. The commerce of Kamchatka bore a considerable relation to that with America and neighboring islands, continued Lacy, and was therefore worthy of mention. In 1755 the Russian trade in Kamchatka did not exceed 10,000 rubles and it had already increased 300 per cent. They got cloth and other manufactured goods from Russia and Siberia. There were more than 3000 people in Kamchatka and dependent islands (exclusive of the newly discovered ones on the coast of North America), who paid tribute to the crown in furs of a total annual value of more than 20,000 rubles.[90]

Two months later, June 26, 1775, Lacy forwarded a map of Russian discoveries in America, being a copy made

[87] C–2901.
[88] At present a ruble is worth about 77 cents.
[89] Lacy probably meant those dis- posed of that year in Kamchatka, for the boats of 1773 had not yet returned.
[90] For the enclosure, C–2902.

by Müller, to whom Lacy referred as the head of the archive of foreign affairs in Russia, and a celebrated geographer of that empire. At the same time he enclosed a document relative to those discoveries, translated from the Russian into French by Müller, which gave information of all the islands of the archipelago in that part of the world.[91] Müller's note related to the Russian discoveries in the Pacific between 1764 and 1767. He commented upon the general awakening of European interest in the Pacific at that time, this being an important period for French and English discoveries farther south, while Russia was discovering new lands and inhabited islands in the north. The Russian discoveries began with Ivan IV (1533–84), who conquered Siberia, and sent an expedition to explore its northern and eastern frontiers, which returned in the next reign, having found the sea at both points. Müller had found documents in the Siberian archives showing that in a subsequent exploration along the Arctic coasts, one man reached Kamchatka. He must therefore have passed through Bering Strait.[92] Discoveries stopped during the troublous times of the usurpers, Boris and Demetrius, but were resumed in the reign of Peter I (1672–1725). He sent one body of explorers along the northern coast of Siberia, and others up the eastern coast of Kamchatka to see if they would meet, and to discover new lands and islands. It was not until 1728, however, that Danadisiki Bay in 66° was reached,[93] this being accomplished by Captain Bering. Later, Chirikof reached the coast of America, and Spanberg discovered the Kurile Islands, a great archipelago north of Japan. It was reserved for Catherine II (1762–96) to charter a company of Russian merchants to engage in commerce with the new islands and discover others. There were twelve in this company, to each of whom the empress had given a gold medal, while orders were given to her officers in Okhotsk to assist them in every way. Thus far, they had discovered a number of islands, from which came their

[91] C–2944.
[92] A reference, probably, to the Deshnef expedition, 1648–50.
[93] That is to say, America and Asia were proved to be separated.

principal profits in furs. In 1764 the company sent out ships from Okhotsk under Lieutenant Lynd, who discovered a number of islands between 56° and 57°, returning late in 1767. As a result a new map was published in 1768, which appeared again in the publications of the Academy of Sciences of St. Petersburg in 1773. Müller himself had made an even more striking map, showing all of the voyages and discoveries since the time of Bering, and the size, position, and in part the names of the islands. As regards products, dress, and speech, the islands and their inhabitants between 50° and 55° resembled those of the Kurile Islands; between 55° and 60° the people almost exactly resembled the natives of Kamchatka; between 60° and 70° they differed a little from the other sections. In all of these islands the people were very much like those discovered by the English and French in the middle of the Pacific. Beyond the islands discovered were others not yet occupied by the Russian argonauts, but a number of ships sent out in recent years had not yet returned. The present commander in Kamchatka, Timafey Tschemalow (Chemaloff) had 1120 men under his orders, as follows: 300 soldiers; 706 natives of Kamchatka; and 114 men in some of the Kuriles. A certain major, of Polish origin, in the government mining service of Siberia had informed Müller that the Russians had no settlements on the American coasts, although they were sending some vessels there every year, as well as to the new archipelago.[94]

These letters of Lacy were forwarded to Arriaga by Grimaldi in letters respectively of October 4,[95] and October 21, 1775.[96] It is strange if no copies were forwarded to Bucarely; if they were not, it is evidence of a lack of anxiety on the part of the Spanish government; if they were, Bucarely seems not to have become excited, or otherwise, some hint would have appeared in his letters on kindred matters.

With the return of Heceta and Bodega, whatever crisis there was had passed. Other voyages were planned, as will be pointed out, but they were not to be made until the

[94] C-2945.   [95] C-3002.   [96] C-3014.

situation had completely changed. In January, 1776, Julián de Arriaga died, and was succeeded as *ministro general* by José de Gálvez. Great as the latter had been as *visitador*, he was not to succeed equally well, in New Spain at any rate, as *ministro general*. His promotion meant the virtual removal of Bucarely from the direction of frontier affairs. Although this did not take effect until the end of 1776, that year marks a transition to a later period, as regards the northwest voyages, rather than the culmination of Bucarely's work. Discussion of such events for 1776, therefore, belongs more appropriately to that part of this work which introduces the new régime.

CHAPTER XI

SPANISH ATTENTION TO LOCAL PROBLEMS OF THE
CALIFORNIAS, 1773–1775

BUCARELY'S work of a more local character concerning
the Californias may be grouped under two principal heads:
the remission of supplies; and the matter of forming a
reglamento for the Californias. As to the first, it will be
shown that Bucarely's care and foresight narrowly averted
a possible failure of the Alta California establishments.
As to the second, a provisional *reglamento* was formed,
which with some modifications was to endure a number of
years, although at no time considered adequate. It was
sufficient, however, to bring order out of chaos. The matter
of the *reglamento* occupied considerable attention of the
Council of the Indies, being complicated by a consideration of Bucarely's division of the Californias between the
Franciscans and the Dominicans. Most active in the
discussion was José de Gálvez, whose opinions were able to
sway the Council. He opposed the division, and planned
a most ambitious programme of northwestward advance,
the central idea being the development and consequent
strengthening of the Californias, so that they might serve as a
secure bulwark for New Spain. In most respects he recommended sustaining Bucarely's action, and this was the only
practical result of his plans. The Californias remained divided, and Gálvez's plans seem not to have been put into
full effect. Bucarely's measures, however, were working
toward the same end.

One of the most important factors in the preservation of
the Alta California establishments was that of the annual

visit of the supply-ships from San Blas. An overland route was necessary, for the use of animals and settlers, and was contemplated for the sending of food-supplies as well, but as regards goods and effects the San Blas boats were for many years practically the sole support of the province. In the period treated here they were also the chief resort for food-supplies. If the overland route was a vital necessity in order to establish the province on a permanent basis, so also were these ships, without which Alta California must certainly have been abandoned.

As already noted, Alta California was barely saved in 1770, and again in 1772, by the timely arrival of supplies from San Blas. The same thing was to occur for the third time in 1774. Bucarely informed Arriaga, June 26, 1773, of the departure of the *San Carlos* with provisions for San Diego and Monterey. He planned to send another ship in November, although he understood that the Californias were already well provided with supplies.[1] A month later, July 27, 1773, when he had already received some of the reports about the Californias that he had asked for, he wrote of new arrangements that he had made for the voyages, the difficulty of navigation from the mainland to both Alta and Baja California having caused him to seek a remedy. From reports made to him he had learned that December or the beginning of January was the best season for voyages to Monterey, all the year except April to the middle of June for the voyage to San Diego, and all the year, but especially January, for those to Loreto. San Blas was too hot and damp a place in which to store maize, which formed the principal part of the supplies for the Californias, without exposing it to risk of damage, wherefore as crops were gathered in January, it would be best to put them aboard direct. The rest of the cargo could be gathered beforehand. Bucarely had given orders in accord with these conclusions, making provision also that boats should leave San Blas in January, if possible, or early in -February, at latest. This was to be not only for the year

[1] C-2304. Approved in C-2405.

1774, but also for ensuing years.[2] For these reasons and
also because of Bucarely's belief that the Californias had
abundant supplies, the November ship was not sent. Writing to Arriaga, September 26, 1773, he said that the *San
Carlos* had been unable to make the voyage to Alta California on account of the storms that it encountered in attempting to round Cape San Lucas. Having lost its rud-
der and sprung a leak, it put in at Loreto, discharged its
cargo there, and returned to San Blas for repairs. This
would have caused him anxiety over the needs of Alta California, had it not been that the pilots and the commissary,
Campo, informed him that Governor Barry had offered to
supply the northern establishments by land with as much
as they needed. Moreover, he had heard from Fages that
there was already enough to last for the rest of the year
1773.[3] Shortly afterward, Bucarely was confirmed in his
belief that all was going well by a letter from Father Verger
announcing progress in Alta California, saying that crops
were good, and that many converts were being obtained,[4]
which news Bucarely in turn transmitted to Arriaga,
November 26, 1773.[5]

On January 27, 1774, Bucarely wrote to Arriaga that
Pérez in the *Santiago* had probably started already on
his voyage of exploration to the northwest. Francisco
Hijosa, who had become the commissary at San Blas, had
written to him on January 5, that the boat was provisioned
for a year, in addition to supplies that it was carrying to
Monterey. In order to provide for every possible contingency, with Pérez's needs particularly in mind, Bucarely
had ordered the *Príncipe* to sail for San Diego and Monterey as soon as possible with more provisions,[6] and on
April 26, 1774, he was able to announce that it had sailed
on March 21. It had been delayed for repairs necessitated by the size of cargo that it was to carry; for, not only
was it to bear supplies for the missions and presidios of Alta
California, but also a copious store for the *Santiago*, in case

[2] C–2332. Approved in C–2447.   [4] C–2425
[3] C–2396.   [5] C–2441.   [6] C–2521.

that boat should be obliged to put back from its northwestward voyage, or for its use when it should return. Bucarely had ordered the repairs to be made promptly, so that the *Príncipe* might sail before the season of good weather should pass. Hijosa's letter of March 24 telling of its departure reported it to be laden with as much provisions as it could carry; so Bucarely felt sure that there would be enough to supply Alta California for many months, and to help Pérez's expedition, if needed.[7] In forwarding Palou's report of December 10, 1773, on the status of the Alta California missions, Bucarely wrote Arriaga, May 27, 1774, that he was much pleased with the progress of conversions, and manifested a belief that much more might be expected, since the natives were so numerous and the lands so fertile. The greatest obstacle had been a lack of provisions with which to maintain the Indians at the missions during the period of instruction. This lack should be remedied in a measure by the provisions in the *Santiago* and *Príncipe*, as also by the crops of Alta California. The anxiety of the missionaries should be relieved by the arrival of Serra, for he had been told that the needs of the missions would be supplied.[8] In another letter of the same date, Bucarely stated that he had ordered a new keel laid at San Blas, because it was too great a risk to rely on the frigate and two packetboats for the Alta California voyages.[9] It may be observed that the Palou memorial had not spoken of the danger of famine, although emphasizing the need for supplies.

While Bucarely rested secure in the belief that Barry would forward to Alta California the provisions which the *San Carlos* had left at Loreto, no such thing had in fact occurred, for lack of the means to convey them. As a result, the new establishments had to endure the worst famine of their history, lasting eight months, during which time milk had to serve as the principal aliment of the colonies.[10] At length, the *Santiago* reached San Diego, March

[7] C-2608.
[8] C-2625.
[9] C-2624.
[10] Palou, *Vida*, 153.

13, 1774, and was able to leave provisions enough to tide
over the situation until the arrival of the *Príncipe*. Other
missions had to wait several weeks longer, until the provisions could be distributed from San Diego and Monterey,
to which latter port Pérez arrived on May 9. To make
clear just how serious were the straits to which the settlements had been reduced it will be well to quote some documents of the period. Writing from San Gabriel, April 10,
1774, Anza told Bucarely that he had found a shortage of
rations at that mission, although it was accounted the
richest site in Alta California. Herbs and three *tortillas*
apiece daily were all that was to be had in the way of food
at that time.[11] Anza was himself in great need of provisions, but he was able to get little at San Gabriel.[12] He,
therefore, sent to San Diego for some, and procured a
supply, the *Santiago* being still at that port.[13] Equally
bad were conditions as regards food supply at the other
missions.[14] Nor was the want in Alta California solely a
matter of food. This appears, for example, in the letters
of Father Lasuén of San Gabriel to Franciscans at the
College of San Fernando. Lasuén had hoped to return there,
but was resigned to staying in Alta California, if required
to do so. He begged to be relieved, however, from the
great hardship that he was suffering for lack of wearing
apparel, which had already reached the point of indecency.
His clothes had been in continuous use for more than five
years. He had mended them, until they no longer ad-
mitted of it, and moreover, he no longer had materials for
sewing.[15] In another letter of the same date, April 23,
1774, Lasuén repeated the story of his needs. Perhaps it
was on that account, he said, that the Indians cared for
him so much, on the principle that like attracts like, for he
resembled them much in scantiness of wardrobe.[16] Writ-

[11] C–2603.
[12] Palou, *Noticias*, III, 158, says
that an animal was killed to provide
Anza with meat, but that the mission
could give him nothing else.
[13] Valdés, *Declaration*, C–2648 ; Anza,
Diary, C–2602.
[14] Palou, *Vida*, 158; *Noticias*, III,

148; correspondence and diaries of
Anza, Díaz, and Garcés.
[15] Lasuén to the Father Superior of
San Fernando, Apr. 23, 1774. M.N.,
Doc. Rel. Mis. Cal., v. II.
[16] Lasuén to Pangua, Apr. 23, 1774.
Ibid.

ing a general letter to his brethren of San Fernando, May 2,
1774, Lasuén said that Fathers Garcés and Díaz of the
Anza expedition had given him clothing, which would
cover his nudity for several months; the former gave him
a thin flannel undergarment and cowl, and the latter a
tunic and a pair of sandals.[17]   Two letters from Rivera
(successor of Fages) to Bucarely, June 16, 1774, show a
lack of military equipment and other necessaries at the presidios. In one of these letters he wrote that the forces at
San Diego were in need of thirty guns,[18] twenty small swords,
twenty knives, two cases of powder, one case of balls, one
case of munitions, and two packs of tobacco. Monterey
required twenty small swords, twenty knives, two cases of
balls, one case of munitions, two cases of powder, and
thirty guns. He wanted the guns to be examined before
sent, to make sure they were good.[19]   In the other letter he
complained that the things forwarded from San Blas were
not suited to the needs of the province. Articles asked for
were not sent, leaving the men entirely lacking in some
things that they needed, for which they had no other recourse, for example, in the matter of clothes. No corduroy
had been sent, although the soldiers liked to use it because
of its durability; nor had there been sent a cake of
soap or a handful of tobacco. There was a great need for
guns and small swords. Some soldiers entirely lacked
arms; others had the gun, but not the sword, or vice
versa.[20]

Rivera's requests were considered in connection with the
authorizing of a second Anza expedition, and Lasuén's
were a matter between him and his college. The general
scarcity, however, especially in food supplies, was met by
the arrival of the *Santiago*, followed a little later by the
Príncipe. Thenceforth, Alta California did not again suffer in that respect.[21]   Her relief had come not only from

[17] Lasuén to Franciscans of San
Fernando, May 2, 1774. *Ibid.*
[18] The word *escopeta* is equivalent
to-day to "shot-gun." In the latter
eighteenth century it seems to have
been used generally for such guns as

cavalrymen employed, and it hardly
seems likely that "shot-gun" would
be an accurate rendering.
[19] In C–2496.
[20] In C–2496.
[21] Palou, *Vida,* 158–59.

Bucarely's foresight in sending the well-filled *Santiago* and the *Príncipe*, in the face of favorable reports as to the situation in Alta California, but also because Bucarely never allowed of a relapse once he got actual information of the state of affairs there. As already noted, Bucarely learned from Anza of the scarcity of provisions in Alta California. Writing to Arriaga, August 27, 1774, he expressed an opinion that the cargoes of the *Santiago* and the *Príncipe* would relieve the immediate need. He realized that the question of supplies was one of considerable importance, as the ports of Alta California might serve to shelter and assist the boats engaged in northward exploration. It would be of great advantage to the royal treasury if the inhabitants might be given the means of sustaining themselves by their own industry. Hijosa had been ordered repeatedly to gather provisions at San Blas for their aid, and to this end he was then repairing two boats, which were to sail within a short time, one after the other.[22] A month later, Bucarely was able to say that Alta California's extreme need had been successfully met. The provisions of the *Santiago* had reached Alta California in time to relieve the sufferings of the missions, but they would not have done so, had it not been for the successful voyage of the *Príncipe*, which reached Monterey June 8, three days before the *Santiago* sailed. These provisions and the fertility of the soil would thenceforth insure the permanence of the colonies, and permit of further conquests. Such conquests would be easy, because of the docility of the Indians, if there were provisions enough to furnish them, for in that lay their attraction to vassalage and a knowledge of the faith. Rivera and Serra reported that all were content. The *Príncipe* got back to San Blas on August 30, and Bucarely had acquiesced in repairs proposed by Hijosa, tending to protect provisions from water; Bucarely realized the importance of sending supplies to Alta California, not only for its own subsistence, but also as stores for Pérez, in case of accident. He

[22] C-2706.

had therefore suggested to Hijosa that he repair another ship, and send the two with provisions in the coming January.[23]

Bucarely's plans matured, so that by February 1, 1775, the *Príncipe* left San Blas with provisions for San Diego. Due to the severity of storms it took seventy days to make the voyage, whereas the return occupied but thirteen, May 9 to 22. Quirós, the commander, reported that he saw the Indians of a whole village who had come to San Diego to ask for baptism, but it was denied them because there were not provisions enough to maintain all. It was believed, however, that the crops would be sufficient for their maintenance, despite the scant rainfall at San Diego.[24] The *San Carlos* under Manrique had tried to leave with the *Príncipe*, being destined for Monterey with provisions, but it ran aground in the port of San Blas itself. After getting it free, the officials of San Blas wished to unload, in order to see what damage it had suffered, which would have held back the voyage until March, but Bucarely ordered that it be reloaded with provisions for the families who were to go with Anza to found a settlement at San Francisco. The rest were to be left for the *Santiago*, in case there should be room for them in addition to those to be carried for its own crew in the new voyage of discovery that it was about to make. On February 24, 1775, the date of his letter to Arriaga, Bucarely had not yet heard whether such an arrangement was possible.[25] The *San Carlos* was in fact delayed until March 16, 1775, when it set sail, accompanied by the *Santiago* and *Sonora*, which were to make further explorations in the far northwest. This time, the voyage of the *San Carlos* was a success, for it delivered the provisions consigned to Monterey, was employed in exploring San Francisco Bay, and at length returned to San Blas.[26] Early in 1776 Bucarely again sent two provision ships to Alta

[23] C-2719.
[24] Bucarely to Arriaga, June 26, 1775. C-2935.
[25] C-2857. This letter states that the *Príncipe* had left on January 31. In C-2935 it is given as February 1.

Bancroft, *Cal.*, I, 241, says that the *San Antonio* or *Príncipe* left San Blas on March 16. This is an error.
[26] Bucarely to Arriaga, Nov. 26, 1775. C-3033.

California, the *San Carlos* and the *Príncipe*.[27] In August of
that year Gálvez, who had succeeded Arriaga, instituted
the *comandancia general* placing all of the frontier provinces, including the Californias, under a separate government from that of the viceroy, but he required that the
viceroy should continue to handle the matter of the supply-
ships from San Blas to the Californias,[28] a fortunate chance,
very likely, as the *comandancia general* was not a glittering
success in other respects. Thus, Bucarely informed Gálvez,
April 26, 1777, that the *Santiago* and *Príncipe* had set sail
with an abundance of provisions and effects for Alta California, as also the *San Carlos* for Baja California.[29] Further
than this we need not pursue this matter at this point, although more will be said later,[30] nor has it been thought
necessary to give in equal detail the measures for supplying
Baja California. It seems reasonably clear that the Californias owed much to Bucarely for his attention to the
supply-ships, and that under a less painstaking and watchful
viceroy disaster might have come to the new settlements
before they had a fair chance to become firmly established.
As will be pointed out hereafter, the material needs of Alta
California were a matter that occupied a large share of the
viceroy's attention, nothing in the affairs of the province
being regarded by him as of equal importance.[31]

Some of the action taken with a view to forming a *reglamento*, notably two memorials by Serra and the temporary
arrangement dividing the Californias between the Dominicans and Franciscans, has been discussed in another
connection.[32] A provisional *reglamento* was drawn up by
Juan José de Echeveste, at that time purchasing agent for
the Californias in Mexico City, the document being dated
May 19, 1773. This is the document which it became the

[27] Bucarely to Arriaga, Mar. 27,
1776. C–3185.
[28] The king (by Gálvez) to Teodoro
de Croix, Aug. 22, 1776. C–3293.
[29] C–3532.
[30] In chap. XVI.
[31] In an article entitled *The Alta
California supply-ships, 1773–76* (Southwestern historical quarterly, XIX,
184–94), I covered substantially the
same ground as that given here.
[32] In chap. V. It should be remembered that the Palou report, considered
with one of Serra's in chapter five, was
not before the *junta* at this time, but
was of later date, when conditions in
Alta California had improved.

habit to call the *reglamento provisional*, being accompanied
in later usage by the opinion of the *junta* and the decision of
the viceroy, modifying it in some particulars. It is hardly
what we would expect a formal instrument of government
to be, having numerous paragraphs of a temporary character, as well as the style of a recommendation for legis-
lation. It begins with an estimate of the number of men
and the cost each year of the Californias and San Blas.
For the two presidios and five missions of Alta California
Echeveste figured an establishment of eighty-two military
men and fourteen others, not including the missionaries.[33]
The salary roll would amount to 38,985 *pesos* a year, but
would in fact require an outlay of only 15,594 *pesos*, as all
but the officers were to be paid in clothing and effects at
an advance of 150 per cent, to cover the extra cost [especially
of transportation] to the royal treasury. For Baja California there were to be thirty-seven men, all military but one,
the commissary, at an annual cost of 16,450 *pesos*. As all
but the governor and commissary were to be paid in effects
at an advance of 100 per cent, the actual sum required was
to be 10,975 *pesos*.[34] The Department of San Blas was
considered under three heads: the department proper,
including the clerical, warehouse, and church officials;
the arsenal or ship-yard; and the fleet. The first named
should cost 8691 *pesos*, 4 *tomines*, 6 *granos*, including annual
rations for 127 men in the Californias;[35] the second, 12,355
pesos, 2 *tomines*, 6 *granos*, mostly for repairs to ships; the
third, 34,037 *pesos*, 5 *tomines*.[36] In addition, 2000 *pesos*

[33] The men required were the following: at Monterey, a captain, a
sergeant, two corporals, twenty-two
soldiers, two carpenters, two black-
smiths, four mule-drivers, and a store-
keeper; at San Diego, a lieutenant, a
sergeant, two corporals, twenty-two
soldiers, two carpenters, two black-
smiths, and a store-keeper; at the
five missions, five corporals, and twenty-
five soldiers.

[34] The men required for Baja California were the governor, a commissary, a lieutenant, a sergeant, three
corporals, and thirty soldiers.

[35] If the missionaries and the four

mule-drivers at Monterey were left
out, this would account for the entire
Spanish establishment of the Californias.

[36] The men required at San Blas
were the following: in the department
proper, a commissary, an accountant
(*contador*), a paymaster and store-
keeper, three scribes, an amanuensis,
a chaplain, and a sacristan; at the
arsenal, a master-workman (*mæstro
mayor*), a cooper, a rope-maker (*cor-
chador*), and a boatswain; in the
fleet: for the frigate, a captain and
pilot, a second pilot, a boatswain, a
boatswain's mate, a steward, a car-

would be required for the purchasing agent in Mexico City. Thus the total annual cost of the Californias and San Blas would be 92,476 *pesos*, 3 *tomines*. To pay this there was the yearly subsidy of 33,000 *pesos*, the product of the salt-mines near San Blas amounting to 25,000 *pesos*, and 10,000 *pesos* from the pious fund. The royal treasury would therefore have to make up the balance, 24,476 *pesos*, 3 *tomines*.

Then came the *reglamento* proper in seventeen numbered paragraphs, from which the following are the principal points. Neither the royal treasury nor the pious fund could give more funds for Alta California at the time; therefore, no further missions could be provided for, but all persons who wished to go there should be allowed to do so in the boats from San Blas. Such settlers ought to be granted rations for five years and a sailor's wages for two, and they could be used in raising crops, thus relieving the public treasury of expense. Each mission should get 800 *pesos* a year, with double rations to each missionary, including those awaiting assignment to new missions. These sums were in addition to those applied from the pious fund, but they were to stop in five years and were eventually to be repaid, for in five years the mission crops should be sufficient to maintain them. Salaries were to be discounted 50 per cent in Baja California, and 60 per cent in Alta California, and minute accounts of the cost of goods were to be kept.[37] The store-keepers of Monterey, San Diego, Loreto, and San Blas were to make an annual statement of the effects needed. San Blas was not to raise any crops, because it was difficult to do so there; the provisions both for San Blas and the Californias were to be purchased, and at the proper season, so that they might not suffer such damage as had resulted on previous occasions. As San Blas was not suitable for beasts of burden, the animals there

penter, a calker, two cabin-boys, six steersmen, twenty-seven ship's boys (*gurumetes*), and thirty sailors; for each of two packet-boats, a captain and pilot, a second pilot, a boatswain, a boatswain's mate, a steward, a car-

penter, a calker, two cabin-boys, six steersmen, ten ship's boys, and sixteen sailors.

[37] Note that salaries were to be paid in goods.

and their drivers should be sent to Baja California, and if
not needed there, to Alta California, while the cattle of
San Blas should be sold. The salt industry should be
managed by the commissary of San Blas, who should also
keep detailed accounts of all the business of the department. Similarly, accounts of all effects received should
be kept at Monterey, San Diego, and Loreto. The frigate
Santiago and the packet-boats *San Carlos* and *Príncipe*
should be used as provision-ships, and the packet-boats
Concepción and *Lauretana*, the sloop *Pilar*, and the schooner
Sonora should be employed on various commissions between San Blas and Baja California. The agent in Mexico
and the commissary of San Blas should buy goods that
were not only cheap but suitable, and after every remission
of goods, accounts should be sent to Mexico.[38]

On Bucarely's decree, May 24, 1773, the Echeveste *reglamento* was sent to the *fiscal*, Areche, for his opinion,[39] and he
suggested, June 14, 1773, that the administrators of the
pious fund be asked to pay more than the 10,000 *pesos*
required of them. He noted that Echeveste had failed to
provide for a surgeon, and had made no allowance for the
cost of powder; clothing, trappings, and arms might be
charged to the soldiers, but not powder. In other respects
he approved of the *reglamento*, for it would end the obscure,
improper methods employed at San Blas, Loreto, and
Monterey, which had been the cause of the confusion in
reports from the Californias. In closing he recommended
that the *reglamento* be sent to Mangino, director general
of the pious fund, for his opinion, and that it then be brought
before a *junta* for resolution.[40] On June 17, Bucarely ordered the *expediente* sent to Mangino.[41] Replying, June 19,
Mangino stated that the pious fund was contributing
14,879 *pesos*, 3 *tomines*, 6 *granos* to the missions of the
Californias.[42] Moreover, there were extraordinary ex-

[38] In C–2106.
[39] *Ibid.*
[40] *Ibid.*
[41] *Ibid.*
[42] To wit, 800 *pesos* to each of the
five Alta California missions, besides
1779 *pesos*, 3 *tomines*, 6 *granos*, for
their double rations, and 9100 *pesos*
for the thirteen missions of Baja California.

penses; for example, it had cost 6139 *pesos*, 5 *tomines*, 9 *granos* to get the Dominicans for the peninsula from Vera Cruz to San Blas. Consequently, it was difficult to estimate how much the proceeds of the fund would exceed expenses, and therefore, concluded Mangino, no additional contributions should be asked from it.[43] On receiving Mangino's report, Bucarely issued a decree, June 22, 1773, calling for a *junta*.[44] Of other matters that were to come before it, besides those discussed already, letters of January 27 and February 14, 1773, from Campo of San Blas are alone worthy of note. Campo complained that there were not enough funds even to pay the wages of the men.[45]

The decision of the *junta* is dated July 8, 1773. Taking the Echeveste *reglamento* as a basis it made the following recommendations. The beasts of burden at San Blas should be sold instead of being sent to the Californias, as the need of that province for such animals was not clearly known; and it would be best to sell the boats *Concepción, Lauretana, Pilar,* and *Sonora* for account of the royal treasury. The annual sum provided by Echeveste was approved, and in addition the amount needed for the pay of a surgeon. Funds needed in San Blas should be sent six months in advance. The governor and the commissary of the Californias, both residents of Loreto, might receive their pay at Mexico, and therefore without discount. For the year 1774 only, the pious fund was to contribute 10,000 *pesos* toward the expenses of the Department of San Blas. Particular attention was devoted to the methods of making accounts, and special note was taken of the need for sending funds to San Blas to cover expenses for the rest of the year 1773. As thus amended the Echeveste *reglamento* should go into effect in January, 1774.[46] Bucarely's decree of July 23 amounted to an agreement with the *junta* until the king should decide on a new *reglamento*. On July 27, 1773, Bucarely forwarded to Arriaga the five great *testimonios* to which references have been made bearing on San Blas and the

[43] In C–2106.
[44] *Ibid.*

[45] In C–2109.
[46] *Ibid.*

Californias, to which subject he said that he had devoted himself with the most painstaking care ever since he became viceroy.[47] The Echeveste *reglamento* and the *junta*'s decision should be taken in connection with the instructions to Rivera, August 17, 1773, when that officer was about to depart for Monterey to succeed Fages. Several paragraphs treat of the precautions to be taken against the entry of any boats other than those from San Blas and the Manila galleon, and others deal with the advancement of spiritual conquest, especially toward San Francisco. These paragraphs are taken up in more detail in other chapters, to which their subject-matter is more closely related.[48] The others may be briefly summarized here. The provisional *reglamento* and the decision of the *junta* of July 8 were attached. Rivera was named *comandante* for Alta California, and enjoined to maintain harmonious relations with the religious. He was to help them to reduce the Indians to mission control, and was to see that the latter were brought into villages, so that they might be civilized. Then follow several paragraphs about the selection of sites for mission villages, and details with regard to the plan of such settlements. Rivera was to remember that these towns might ultimately become great cities [it is noteworthy that such a possibility was contemplated]. Such matters as water supply, trees, the laying out of streets and squares (*plazas*), the raising of cattle, and the planting of crops, he was reminded, should command great attention, for much depended on what was done at the beginning. Lands might be assigned to the Indians, but they were to live at the missions, and similarly in the case of Spanish settlers, who were to live in the towns (*pueblos*), no scattering of habitations being permitted. In due season the missions might be converted into towns. In everything Rivera was to remember that the object of the Alta California establishments was to advance spiritual conquest, and, in consequence, to achieve an extension of the royal dominions, wherefore he was to

[47] C–2331.   [48] In chapter X and XIV.

propose from time to time such measures as he deemed of advantage to the colony. He was to maintain discipline, punishing infractions thereof, or sending incorrigibles to San Blas, where they should stay pending the viceroy's decision. This applied to other employes and to settlers, as well as to the soldiers. Rivera was to report to the governor of the Californias [then stationed at Loreto], but the latter was not to have power to change his measures [thus the virtual independence of Alta from Baja California was declared]. Communications with the peninsula were to be kept open, and Rivera was not to wait for boats in all cases by which to forward his mail. Great care was to be exercised not to molest the Indians along the route up the peninsula, and similarly in Alta California, especially when on expeditions of discovery. The right to correct baptized Indians belonged to the missionaries, as to the father of a family, and such had been the decision of a *junta* of May 6, 1773. The pilots were to decide all matters affecting the packet-boats, even the date of sailing, but they were not to carry any passengers without the permission of the *comandante* which was only to be given in very urgent cases. An instruction to Fages of July 26, 1773, was mentioned as binding upon Rivera,[49] as also the new *reglamento*. Rivera was to keep a diary of all that occurred in Alta California, sending it periodically to Bucarely. He was also to make inventories of the artillery, munitions, arms, and other implements there, stating their condition, and was to keep all records and papers carefully.[50] Bucarely forwarded a copy of the instruction to Arriaga on September 26, 1773. Serra and Rivera had already started for the Californias, he said, and other officials were soon to follow, and with them Francisco Hijosa who was to succeed Campo Viergol at San Blas.[51]

Arriaga sought the advice of Gálvez on these policies

[49] I have not found this instruction, but it is probable that it had some relation to the *reglamento*, which Bucarely had decreed three days before.
[50] C–2350.

[51] C–2391. Bucarely enclosed a list, drawn up by Melchor de Peramás, of individuals appointed to military and financial employments in the Californias and San Blas. C–2392.

that had been occupying the attention of Bucarely. Gálvez's memorials in reply form a complete review of the
situation by one who understood the conditions, and was
keenly interested in them. They in part touch on matter
that might properly have appeared in other chapters, but
as they bear primarily on matters discussed here, and are
so noteworthy in themselves, it seems best to take them up
in detail at this point. The first matter brought to his
attention was that concerning the division of the Californias
between the Franciscans and the Dominicans. On November 6, 1772, Fray Juan de Dios de Córdova wrote to
the king saying that twenty-seven Dominicans had started
for the Californias. In expectation of an abundant harvest of souls and to replace the missionaries who had died,
he now asked for twelve more.[52] This petition was acted
on by the Council of the Indies, February 6, 1773, and
denied ;[53] but the request was repeated, this time for twenty
more, the initiative coming from New Spain, and being
announced by Bucarely in a letter of May 27, 1773.[54] The
entire *expediente* about the division of the Californias
was thereupon sent to Gálvez, October 19, 1773.[55] Two
months later, on December 18, 1773, Gálvez returned his
report.

In a preamble he gave an account of the missions of Alta
and Baja California and Pimería Alta, telling of the slow,
expensive course by which they had been established in the
past, and of the good opportunity now for the rapid progress of conversions. He criticized the division of the Californias, which had been made, he said, with slight knowledge
of conditions there, calling attention to the interruption of
communications between Alta California and the peninsula
which was necessarily entailed.[56] He then proceeded to
make his recommendations.

A moderate settlement should be made on the largest of
the Tres Marías Islands, the one to the northwest, as had

[52] C-2056.   [53] C-2161.   criticism, Bucarely could not justly be
[54] C-2279.   blamed, because he had been ordered
[55] In C-2906.   by the king to grant a field in the Cali-
[56] Whatever the merits of Gálvez's   fornias to the Dominicans. C-1782.

been recommended in other years by Aysa[57] and Sánchez.[58] The garrison of Loreto might be placed there, for it was of no use where it was, Loreto being almost in the centre of Baja California, in a region long since reduced. Certain of the missions of Baja California [59] should be given over to the secular clergy under the bishop of Guadalajara, to whose jurisdiction the Californias belonged, and the same procedure should be taken successively with the other peninsula missions, thus freeing the pious funds now expended on them. The Dominicans should engage in active work of conversion [60] toward the north in the direction of the Colorado River, leaving the coast of Alta California to the *Fernandinos*. Gálvez called attention to the royal decree of August 19, 1606, requiring the Manila galleon to stop at Monterey on its annual voyage to Acapulco,[61] and suggested that it might carry goods to Alta California at less cost than under the existing system. In 1769 Gálvez had caused fifteen Sonora missions to be made curacies, but secular clergy had not been placed in charge. This ought to be done, the priests being named by the bishop of Durango, in whose diocese the province lay. The viceroy should be ordered to establish without delay five missions on the Sonora frontier among the Nixores, Opas, Yumas, and others who lived at the junction of the Gila and Colorado rivers and in its vicinity, and he should put them in charge of the *Queretaranos* under the direction of Father Garcés, who had repeatedly visited those lands and tribes. Orders should be given to Bucarely to let Anza make his proposed journey to open a route from Sonora to the Californias,[62] and he should also arrange, whenever he might deem it opportune, for two parties of cavalry to set out at the same time, one from New Mexico and the other from Monterey, and approach each other along the same line of

---

[57] Aysa to the king, Jan. 21, 1743. C–242.
[58] Sánchez to the king, Mar. 2, 1751. C- 308.
[59] Gálvez says, those missions comprising the first class in the *reglamento de sínodos* of November 30, 1768. This may refer to C–1118.

[60] The phrase is *en conversiones vivas* the implication being that missionary work in Baja California was not of an active or "live" nature.
[61] C–15, 16.
[62] Bucarely had already authorized it, over two months before.

latitude until they should meet, exploring the intervening lands, and noting their inhabitants, products, rivers, and especially the course of the Colorado River. The leaders of these expeditions should make exact reports of their journeys, so that fitting measures might be based upon them. Since converting the Indians to the faith was of primary importance, the viceroy should be ordered to avail himself of the funds taken from the expelled Jesuits to establish missions amidst the numerous peoples of Alta California, the Sonora frontier, and the other provinces of the frontier of New Spain. The royal treasury should not bear the cost, as it was already undergoing heavy expense to maintain the presidios and mission escorts, to the same end of advancing and sustaining conversions.[63]

Long before the Council arrived at a decision on Gálvez's plans, his opinions were sought with regard to the Californias' *reglamento*. Bucarely's letter of July 27, 1773, with its enclosures, was forwarded to Gálvez by Arriaga on December 22,[64] and that of September 26 on January 29, 1774.[65] Gálvez prepared a memorial covering both remissions, and sent it to Arriaga under date of March 8, 1774.[66] The memorial begins with a consideration of Serra's representations of March 13, 1773, commenting only upon such paragraphs as were "worthy of some notice or remark." Gálvez had not heard whether Bucarely had taken action on the proposed Anza expedition from Tubac to Monterey, or on Serra's proposal of an expedition to Alta California from New Mexico. He and Croix had favored such projects, and he thought that Bucarely should be charged to aid in bringing about the opening of communications from both Sonora and New Mexico, especially with the ports of Monterey and San Francisco, which ought to be made secure at all costs. The removal of Fages, without hearing from either Fages or Barry, he regarded as a mistake, but

---

[63] For the whole memorial, C-2454. Gálvez's words implying that conversions were the principal object of the government must not be taken unreservedly as he said them. As already pointed out, conversions were desired when they served to promote mundane ends.

[64] C-2455.
[65] C-2522.   [66] C-2566.

as it had in fact taken place, Fages might be promoted to
the command of a frontier presidio. Rivera could not
compare with Fages in spirit, resolution, and military
knowledge, wherefore Gálvez felt that the very important
Alta California establishments might be in grave danger,
since they had to confront a vast native population, and
were exposed to the repeated attempts of the Russians and
the subjects of other powers who had upon various occasions made land in those seas. Rivera had been captain at
Loreto in the time of the Jesuits, but the work there was
not difficult. It would be better to let him return to Loreto, and to send Barry, an experienced and warlike vet-
eran, to Monterey, which was the principal military post
and the most important centre of the new conquest. Gálvez did not favor certain of Serra's proposals relative to the
military escorts of missions, as for example one that each
missionary be allowed to choose a soldier to accompany him,
free from other obligations of the service. This request
had, very properly, been denied, and to have done otherwise would have meant that the soldiers would degenerate
from their profession. He approved Serra's recommendation of mixed marriages, but only by whites or *mestizos* [67]
with Indians, not by mulattoes; neither the *reglamento*
nor the *junta* had dealt with that point. Of Serra's other
memorials [68] Gálvez said nothing, except to refer slightingly
to the *Tribunal de Cuentas* of Mexico for having proposed to
abandon the Department of San Blas, adding that Bucarely
had caused Echeveste to draw up the *reglamento* instead of
the *Tribunal* because of the latter's lack of common sense
and its incapacity in practical affairs. The Department
of San Blas was indispensable, he said. Gálvez now took
up the provisional *reglamento*, which he felt should be approved, except as to a few particulars. Monterey should
have thirty-one soldiers instead of twenty-five since it was
the most important, the most advanced, and the most
exposed point on the northern frontier of the Pacific. San

[67] A *mestizo* is one whose blood is
part white and part Indian.
[68] Four memorials of Serra appear
in the *expedientes*, but only two have
been treated in this work, those of
March 13 and May 21, 1773.

Diego's twenty-five could be reduced to nineteen. The presidio of Loreto was useless, and there would be no danger if it were left without a garrison; at most seventeen soldiers and Captain Rivera would be enough, instead of the thirty-four allotted. The other seventeen, with a lieutenant, should be placed at Cape San Lucas, which was the most exposed point of that region and the key to Baja California. There lay the Bay of San Bernabé, of good depth and sheltered from all winds except those from the southeast. The Manila galleon came to San José del Cabo every year, and could have no protection unless a presidio were erected at that very important site. The salt-mines of San Blas, if well managed, would produce 30,000 *pesos* a year, and it might be worth while to offer the manager a percentage of the sales. Gálvez was opposed to the sale of the four boats, which the *junta* had recommended. They were necessary for carrying provisions from Sinaloa and Sonora to the peninsula. Moreover, in view of a decree of January 17, 1774, allowing freedom of trade between the Spanish kingdoms of the Pacific, these smaller boats would be very useful for carrying Chinese wares from Acapulco to the Gulf of California. Other matters in the *reglamento* and the decision of the *junta*, as well as Bucarely's instruction to Rivera, should be approved. One paragraph of the latter, however, would have to be amended as a result of the free trade decree, so as to permit other Spanish ships than those from San Blas and the galleons to receive help in Alta California, if they should be driven there by storm. This left one other matter upon which Gálvez wished to speak, the division of the Californias between the Dominicans and the *Fernandinos*. He and Croix had not wished to have the two orders in the Californias, but Bucarely had permitted the *Fernandinos* to be despoiled of Baja California, which cut them off from the peninsula as a base of supplies. By this measure, too, ministers with whom the Indians had already become satisfied were removed from their posts and supplanted by the Dominicans. On this matter, certainly, the decision should be reserved. As regarded all else

Bucarely should be thanked for his zeal, solicitude, and activity in fomenting and aiding the useful establishments of the Californias, for that province was a veritable bulwark for New Spain on the Pacific. Gálvez's recommendation that the decision as to the division of the Californias be reserved was adopted. Arriaga wrote Bucarely to that effect, March 21, 1775, saying that the matter was pending in the Council of the Indies. As the provisional *reglamento* had been made without the fullest information, the king ordered Bucarely to make a new one, when he should become sufficiently well informed, keeping specially in mind the situation which would result from Anza's expedition.[69]

Because statements were made that the provisional *reglamento* was formed without a sufficient knowledge of conditions, it must not be taken to mean that any criticism of Bucarely was intended. The *reglamento* was only provisional or temporary by reason of that very lack of information, and nobody realized this uncertainty more than Bucarely himself. Almost a year before Arriaga wrote the letter just referred to, Bucarely had written to him, May 27, 1774, that a new *reglamento* would be necessary. The provisional one had been formed without the information embodied in Palou's report of December 10, 1773,[70] and circumstances had changed as a result of the plans for northwestward voyages to verify the extent of Russian explorations, as also by the discovery of an overland route from Sonora to the Californias by Anza. In the same letter he said that he had informed the Dominicans of the abundant harvest [of souls] awaiting them along the Colorado River, hoping to inspire them with zeal to go there, and he had ordered Barry to lend aid to both orders in the Californias.[71] A year later, replying to Arriaga's letter of March 21, 1775, Bucarely wrote that he would await the issue of certain events before forming a new *reglamento*. He referred to the northwestward expeditions by land and sea,

---

[69] C–2872. The second expedition of Anza is referred to. The discovery of a new route by the first expedition was, however, one of the new facts calling for a change of *reglamento*.
[70] The Palou report has already been considered in chapter five.
[71] C–2625.

and to the decision whether the Department of San Blas should be moved to another port, since the one at San Blas was gradually filling in.[72] It was not until May 11, 1775, that the Council of the Indies reached a decision concerning the division of the Californias. In addition to Gálvez's opinion of December 18, 1773, and other documents already cited, it had meanwhile accumulated many more. On February 1, 1775, the Council decided to ask Arriaga for Anza's diary of the 1774 expedition to aid the Council in determining whether more Dominicans should be sent to Baja California.[73] The request was made[74] and the diary forwarded.[75] The other documents consisted mainly of reports concerning the peninsula.[76] At length, the Council proceeded to make its recommendation to the king. It began by claiming that Bucarely's division of the Californias was contrary to the royal orders, which had called for an establishment entirely separate from that of the *Fernandinos*, but had not contemplated depriving the latter of Baja California. The *fiscal* of the Council did not agree with this interpretation. Since the Father Superior of San Fernando had agreed to the division and no complaint had come from the *Fernandinos*, the division might be allowed to stand, although without approval, for it would cause inconvenience and expense to do otherwise.[77] The viceroy should be expressly directed, however, that the Dominicans were to make their establishments from San Fernando Velicatá eastward toward the Colorado, leaving the whole west coast to the *Fernandinos*, so that the two orders might not disturb or embarrass one another. The viceroy must also be careful that Alta California should not suffer harm from having been de-

[72] C-2934.
[73] C-2839.
[74] San Martín Cuato to Arriaga, Feb. 4, 1775, C-2840.
[75] Arriaga to San Martín Cuato, Feb. 13, 1775, C-2845.
[76] In C-2906 they are described as follows: Gálvez's statement of the number of Indians in Baja California missions when the Jesuits were expelled; a statement of the amount of the pious fund applicable to the Californias; the *reglamento* of *sínodos* of November 30, 1768; a diary of the expeditions of 1769–70 to Alta California; a map of the Californias; an opinion of the *fiscal*; a former opinion of Manuel Lanz de Casafonda.
[77] This, therefore, is an instance where the viceroy's action prevailed in the face of a contrary opinion of the Council. Cf. chap. VII, n. 63.

prived of support from the peninsula. Although it had
formerly denied them, the Council now granted the Dominican request for twenty missionaries, this decision being
reached as a result of Anza's discovery of a route from
Sonora. In order not to deplete the pious fund, the Council would authorize the viceroy to make curacies of all the
Baja California missions ready for that step, giving them in
charge of secular clergy, or in defect of these to religious,
who should be subject to ecclesiastical visitation and to the
rules of the royal patronage. The same might be done with
the older missions of Sonora. The five missions along the
Colorado and Gila rivers, repeatedly asked for by Gálvez
and the *fiscal* of Mexico, should be established, and later,
others should be erected among the friendly peoples made
known by Anza and the *Queretaranos*. The latter should
have charge of the new missions, and the cost of establishing them should be defrayed from Jesuit funds, the
royal treasury supplying whatever might be lacking. The
Council complained of the excessive allowance granted to
the Dominicans from the pious fund. Thenceforth, Gálvez's
arrangement of November 30, 1768, should be followed, the
amount allowed depending on relative distances and scarcity or abundance of provisions. For the greater security
of the missions and presidios of Alta California such cattle
and sheep as were needed should be sent, both from the
peninsula and from Sonora; there was an abundance of
these animals in Sonora, and they could be sent by the
Anza route. It would also be well to open a route from
New Mexico to Monterey, taking note of intervening lands
and the course of rivers. The viceroy should give fitting
orders to carry out these objects to the governors of the
Californias, Sonora, and New Mexico. The garrison of
Loreto should soon be transferred to the largest of the Tres
Marías, and Bucarely should call a *junta* to see about
settling those islands, so that they might be securely held
and serve to aid the Spanish ships obliged to put in there.
For the greater comfort and security of the Manila galleons
and to facilitate the development of Monterey, the king

should enforce the decree of 1606 requiring the Philippine boats to stop there. In reciting the advantages the Council quoted the decree of 1606 to the effect that Monterey was in 37°, almost at the halfway point of the voyage, and with an excellent and capacious harbor. It added on its own account that the galleon might bring such articles as were needed to develop the new establishments.[78]

It will be noted that Gálvez's recommendations had been adopted by the Council, substantially as he had made them. If these projects could have been executed in entirety, a tremendous advance would in all probability have followed, resulting in an increase of the white population of Alta California, and perhaps in the discovery of gold. What the effect would have been on the history of Alta California and of the United States is worthy of conjecture. If the Council's recommendation were embodied in a royal decree, no evidence to that effect has yet come to light, although shortly afterward, when Gálvez became *ministro general*, he gave orders which aimed to put most of these projects into effect. By the institution of the *comandancia general*, however, he prevented the successful achievement of the results desired. Until that time Bucarely was at work in harmony with the ideas of Gálvez and the Council, for, aside from the matter of the division of the Californias, he was in entire agreement with them. Had these projects been left in his hands they might have been brought to a successful issue, but Gálvez's appointee as *comandante general*, Teodoro de Croix, was not the man to carry them out. Great interest over the Californias had manifested itself in Spain in this period, but the government had actually done little more than to confirm Bucarely's measures. He it was who had saved the new establishments, and had placed the whole province on a sound basis.

[78] C–2906. There are ten signatures and rubrics attached to the document: Felipe de Arco; the Marqués de Valdelirios; Marcos Ximeno; Domingo de Trespalacios; José de Gálvez; Pedro Calderón Henríquez; Tomás Ortiz de Landazuri; Felipe Santos Domínguez; Manuel Díaz; José Antonio de la Zerda. This document amounts to a history of Dominican pretensions in New Spain, more especially as regards the Californias, from 1760 to 1775. Numerous documents are quoted and summarized before the part embodying the actual recommendation of the Council is reached.

CHAPTER XII

THE story of this chapter may quickly be told. Leaving Tubac on January 8, 1774, Anza made a successful march to Alta California without the loss of a man. There were thirty-four in his party, including Fathers Garcés and Díaz. The route led through Papaguería to the junction of the Colorado and Gila rivers, and across the Colorado Desert. The party was well received by the Indians en route, and especially so by the Yumas, who were exceedingly desirous of missions. On March 22 Anza reached San Gabriel, having proved the existence of a practicable route from Sonora, although not so good a one as could have been desired.[1] The entire expedition soon returned to Sonora, where Anza was prevented from going immediately to Mexico by orders of a superior officer. By November, however, he was in Mexico, and at once got to work with Bucarely to plan a new expedition. It was agreed that Anza should lead thirty soldiers and their families to Alta California for a settlement at San Francisco. Many domestic animals were also to be taken, so that the province might be placed on a permanent basis in that regard. The details of equipment, organization, expense, and minor parts of the plan were settled by Bucarely, Echeveste, and Anza, and the expedition was authorized by the first named, but

[1] The correspondence of Anza is my principal resort in this chapter for the details of the expedition, as that contains nearly all that is needed. I have made a preliminary translation, however, of two Anza diaries, the one sent back from San Gabriel and the diary of his return, and may eventually publish it. In that case the additional or varying details of the other diaries, on which I have taken notes, will accompany the translation. A consideration of the diaries of both Anza expeditions is given in an appendix.

a *junta* was called on December 16, 1774, to confirm what had in fact been arranged already.

So much for the externals. The key to these events, however, lies in the oft-discussed factor of precautionary measures against foreign aggression, particularly by the Russians. The documents used in this chapter make little allusion to that factor, but they must be read in the light of others, already or later to be discussed, which did so when dealing with the same events. The events treated here were only part of the larger plan which Bucarely had in mind, but of which others in New Spain were not fully cognizant. Some indications of this appear in the Bucarely correspondence of this chapter. For example, a letter of May 27, 1774, treats of the Anza expedition, of the possibilities for missions among the Yumas, of Rivera's expedition to Alta California, of the Alta California supply-ships, of Palou's 1773 report of conditions there, and of the voyages of exploration, for all were part of the same idea. Other Bucarely letters will yield something of the same, if viewed from this standpoint. The letters of other men must be construed more narrowly. One of the principal ideas of the time was the need of Alta California for overland communication with New Spain, a matter well understood by Alta Californians, and the principal import of the Anza expedition to them was that it seemed to supply this want. Palou's letter of April 22, 1774, most clearly presents this view.

As soon as he got word that his petition had been granted, Anza lost no time in making preparations for his expedition. On November 6, 1773, both he and Garcés wrote to the viceroy, the purport of their letters being that the expedition would start on December 15. They planned to take as northerly a route as possible, feeling sure that in case of need they could return to the Yuma country at the junction of the Colorado and Gila, and proceed from there to the Pacific without difficulty. This news was communicated to Arriaga by Bucarely on February 24, 1774, and was the

latest that he had been able to hear, owing to the great
distance of Sonora from Mexico City, but he felt certain
that the expedition had started.[2] Anza did not in fact
leave Tubac, the starting point of the expedition, until
January 8, 1774. Meanwhile, the existence of a route from
Sonora to Alta California was definitely proved. An
Indian, Sebastián Tarabal, by name, had escaped from
the San Gabriel mission, and had reached Altar, December 26, 1773. Four others who escaped with him, including
his wife and a brother, had died of thirst while lost in the
Colorado Desert. Tarabal alone reached the junction of
the Colorado and Gila, and came from there to Altar by
way of Papaguería.[3]

Originally, Anza had intended to go by way of the Gila
River to the Colorado junction, but he changed his plan,
choosing a route by way of Altar and Papaguería to the
junction of the rivers. Tarabal had said that that route
was a good one. Furthermore, the Apaches had made a
raid on January 2, stealing one hundred thirty horses, including many destined for the expedition. These could not
be replaced in that vicinity, and he did not wish to wait for
others to be sent, as the Apaches might capture some more.
He hoped to get more horses at Altar, having notified the
governor of Sonora of his need. Finally, he had decided that
it was better to ascertain the direct route from Pimería, as
that would be the only one by which produce could be sent
to sustain the Californias, as it was alone free from the
Apaches.[4] Garcés added that the Yuma chief, Salvador
Palma, who had accompanied Tarabal to Altar, said that
the Papaguería route was a good one.[5] It is probable that
the Apache incident was the determining factor with Anza.

[3] Noted in the diaries of Anza,
Garcés, and Díaz. Tarabal's career
of travel was a decidedly interesting
one. Originally he came from Baja
California, and in 1769 accompanied
Portolá. Later, he and his family
were brought to San Gabriel to live,
but he ran away, as observed above.
He accompanied Anza's first expedition
to Alta California, and was permitted
to return with it. Afterwards, he attached himself to Garcés, and thereafter accompanied him in his extensive
travels. Eldredge, in *Jour. Am. Hist.*,
II, 257. Diaries of both Anza expeditions. Fages, memorial of Nov. 30,
1775. C-3042.
[4] Anza, *Diary*, C-2503.
[5] Garcés, *Diary*, A.G.P., *Historia*,
v. 52.

The expedition left Tubac on January 8, 1774, reaching Altar a few days later. Writing to Bucarely from there, January 18, 1774, Anza said that Governor Crespo[6] had arranged to supply him with what he needed at Caborca, the last village through which he would pass in that district, at which he expected to arrive the following day. Despite the difficulty of procuring pack animals he was carrying four months' provisions. They would last longer, but for the necessity of making gifts to Indians en route. He was also carrying a quantity of baubles for them. These were rather scarce in Sonora, but for that reason they would be all the more valued by the Indians. The Indians of the Colorado River maintained communication and friendship with the Spanish post of Altar, in consequence of which Anza planned to send back letters of his journey, on arrival at the Colorado.[7] With this letter he enclosed a list showing the number of individuals and animals and the amount of provisions that he was carrying. Besides Anza himself, there were the two religious, Garcés and Díaz ; twenty-one soldiers, one of whom was Juan Valdés, the soldier from Alta California who was accompanying Anza in order to serve as guide when the expedition should reach that province ; Sebastián Tarabal, as guide from the Yuma country to the Pacific ; a Pima interpreter ; and eight other Indians, five as muleteers, two as servants of Anza, and one a carpenter. In all there were thirty-four persons. There were thirty-five loads containing provisions, munitions, gifts for the Indians, pioneers' tools, and other things, and there were sixty-five head of cattle, and one hundred forty horses.[8] Arrived at Caborca Anza did not find the expected number of horses promised by Governor Crespo, although he had included them in his count, and the few that he did get proved unfit to make the expedition.[9]

From Caborca Anza proceeded through sterile Papaguería to the junction, and crossed both rivers successfully. He wrote from San Dionisio at the junction, February 9,

[6] Successor to Sastre, who had just died.   [7] C-2506.   [8] C-2507.
[9] Anza, *Diary*, C-2503.

1774, telling how joyfully he had been received by the Yumas, although a portion of them had originally planned to oppose him. A Soyopa Indian had told him that there was a westward branch of the Colorado River, farther north, and the same Soyopa also said that the ridge to the northwest was impassible, because of its ruggedness and because of the lack of water and pasture. The Yumas must be very numerous, for Anza had seen about two thousand of them in the space of a league and a half, but they were not a people to be afraid of, even if they had been less friendly. He hoped to find more pasture during the rest of the march than he had encountered in crossing Papaguería. The Papaguería route was not a bad one, but he had had difficulties, due to his lack of acquaintance with it; in seasons of rain it would be an easy route for a party, however large Except for the soldiers who accompanied the Jesuits, no Spanish troops had ever penetrated so far as he then was, and his next day's journey would carry him beyond where they had gone.[10]   Anza's letter reached Altar in safety, and was forwarded by Captain Bernardo de Urrea of that presidio to Governor Francisco Crespo, and by the latter to Bucarely. Each of these officers added a letter to Anza's, having each received one from him. Urrea wrote, February 22, 1774, that a Yuma had brought Anza's letters so carefully that they appeared as if just written. He took occasion to praise Chief Palma of the Yumas, who had shown remarkable pro-Spanish proclivities on previous occasions, and who had now accorded Anza a good reception at San Dionisio.[11]   Crespo said little more than that Anza's march had fulfilled his own predictions.[12]

Bucarely forwarded copies of these three letters to Arriaga in his communication of May 27, 1774, calling attention to the parts that had impressed him. He took note of the large number of Indians, and their friendly reception of Anza; of Anza's well-founded expectation of finding a practicable route to Alta California; and of his report

[10] C–2533.
[11] C–2543.

[12] Crespo to Bucarely, Feb. 25, 1774. C–2554.

of a westward branch of the Colorado, which Bucarely surmised might be the river flowing into San Francisco Bay, as there were intervening mountains elsewhere. Bucarely had been very greatly impressed by the success of Anza's march to date, and by the delivery of his letters from the rivers, which facts he considered not less remarkable than the discovery of a route to the Pacific would be. If the route were found, it might in future conduce to the support of the new establishments of Alta California at slight cost, and might lead to a reduction to the church of vast numbers of Indians. Anza and Urrea had made presents to Chief Palma of the Yumas, of which Bucarely approved, and he had ordered Crespo to continue them to Palma and other Yumas at royal expense, but not to give them arms. He also referred to the Rivera expedition, the supply-ships, the voyages of exploration, and the Palou report of December, 1773, in this letter, showing that these events were connected in his mind with the Anza expedition.[13] In another of the same date he expressed a belief that Anza and Rivera might meet in Alta California, in which case there would be men enough to explore San Francisco and establish one or more missions there, something which Rivera had been ordered to do. Bucarely was hoping to hear that it had been done.[14] Two days before, in acknowledging receipt of the Palou report, he had expressed the same hope, and had asked for detailed information of everything tending toward such a result.[15] At this time also, May 27, 1774, Bucarely wrote to O'Reilly manifesting his satisfaction with the results achieved thus far by Anza.[16] Their importance appears from the prominent place that they occupied in the monthly extract of news from the frontier provinces, which contained detailed references to the Anza expedition.[17] This was forwarded to Arriaga in another Bucarely letter of May 27.[18] These letters show not only the broad standpoint from which Bucarely

[13] C–2624. Spanish official correspondence treated of but one subject in each letter.   [14] C–2626.

[15] In Palou, *Noticias*, III, 254–57.
[16] C–2634.
[17] C–2628.   [18] C–2627.

viewed the Anza expedition, but also his deep interest in it.

Meanwhile, Anza had encountered serious difficulty in his first attempt to cross the Colorado Desert. After spending a terrible day in the desert on February 15 in search of San Jacome, a village which later turned out to have been abandoned, he had been obliged to return to Santa Olaya near the Colorado River, because of the lack of water in the desert, and the exhaustion and rapid death rate of his animals.[19] He wrote to Bucarely on February 28 to forestall bad news, trusting to Chief Palma to attend to the delivery of his letter. He had descended the Colorado River, in order to go around the sands in which Tarabal got lost, when he crossed the desert. As a result of the failure of his first attempt, he had decided to leave behind a large part of his provisions and most of the animals, for the beasts were too weak to proceed. He would put all in charge of Chief Palma, in whom he had confidence, leaving also three soldiers and four muleteers, a proceeding which he regarded as safe, for the Yumas seemed to be even better disposed to the Spaniards than the Pimas and Pá-pagos of the reductions. Members of the two latter tribes often visited the Yumas, and they would see to it that no harm resulted. Farther on, there might not be another such favorable opportunity; yet, sooner or later, he would have had to leave some provisions behind, he said. On March 2 he would start with eleven packs, containing provisions for one month, enough at least until they should reach San Gabriel, according to Tarabal, who said that it would take only two weeks, or less, with good animals. After reaching the pass, at about a week's journey, there would be plenty of water, and there was some before there. So Anza and his men were expecting to complete their undertaking, and they would do it on foot, if necessary. He anticipated no trouble from peoples yet to be encountered, as he understood them to be as lacking in arms

19 Diaries of Anza, Diáz, and Garcés.

and spirit as the Yumas and Cojats.[20]   It might be two or
three months before he returned.[21]

Anza left Santa Olaya on March 2, traversed the desert
by a circuitous route, entered the mountains by way of the
San Felipe Canyon,[22] and reached San Gabriel on March
22. His letter to Bucarely from there, April 10, 1774,
gives the essential facts of his march after leaving Santa
Olaya, and accords high praise to the route discovered, as
a means of communication. His difficulties had been due
primarily to the weakness of his animals and his ignorance
of the country. Because of the former the soldiers had
been obliged to march most of the way on foot, and because
of the latter they had traveled more leagues than was
necessary. Where it had taken two hundred seventy-nine
leagues in coming, the return could be made in two hundred
leagues.[23] Monterey should be about three hundred leagues
from Tubac or Altar. There were no hostile peoples en
route; rather they were well disposed, and lacking in arms.
In five days' march from the Colorado River, Anza had
reached fertile lands with plenty of water, and the lands
thereafter were good. The route from Sonora was a very
good one, even suitable for wagons. Likewise, he expected
that that would be the case if a more direct route were
taken to Monterey, as by way of San Luis Obispo, which
he thought might prove to be the best route from Sonora
to Monterey. Lower Sonora could then furnish the necessary aid to Alta California; Pimería Alta could not, because of the Apaches. Due to a lack of provisions and the
exhaustion of his animals, he had not attempted to go directly to Monterey, as originally planned, but had come first
to San Gabriel, arriving there at the height of the great

[20] Díaz and Garcés say Cajuenches
for Cojats. Díaz, Diary, A.G.P., Historia, v. 396. Garcés, Diary, A.G.P.,
Historia, v. 52. Garcés adds that the
name Cajuenches extended as far as
San Diego.
[21] C–2560.
[22] Until recently it was believed that
Anza went through the San Gorgonio
Pass, the present route of the Southern
Pacific Railroad. Mr. Eldredge, Jour.
of Am. Hist., II, 521–23, was the first
to pronounce for the route up the San
Felipe Canyon. With more evidence
at hand than was available for Mr.
Eldredge, I have reached the same conclusion that he did.
[23] Based on the estimates of Anza
himself, the return was accomplished
in one hundred seventy-four leagues,
San Gabriel to Tubac. Anza, Diary,
C–2503.

famine. Being unable to get animals and supplies enough from there or San Diego, or even from the *Santiago*, then at San Diego, he had also been obliged to abandon his project of a direct return from Monterey. He had only sixteen days' rations for his troops, and had therefore directed most of his men to return to the Colorado by way of the route discovered, while he himself would go to Monterey before returning. He expected to be at Tubac by the end of May, whence he would proceed to Mexico in June to report there in person.[24] With this letter Anza enclosed his diary as completed to April 5. Díaz also sent his diary, with a letter of April 8, to Bucarely.[25]

Attention may be called to Anza's description of the route discovered as a good one entirely practicable for transmission of supplies. As regards that much of his account, at least, it would seem that Anza was unduly enthusiastic, even although he had just traversed this route without losing a man. At any rate, the enthusiasm of Anza's letter had due modification in the diaries of the expedition, those of Anza, Díaz, and Garcés agreeing substantially with the facts and with each other. As regards the Indians, those encountered between the Yuma country and San Gabriel had seemed to be of a very low grade of culture, and feeble in a military way. They were reported to be numerous, but along the route that Anza traveled, their numbers were not great. The Indians first encountered after passing the Colorado Desert, the Cajuenches, were of the Yuman family, and Anza records that they spoke the same language as the Yumas, although he also states that the Yumas were their enemies.[26] Next Anza came upon Indians of what we now call the Shoshonean family. Díaz remarked that the Indians met with in the mountains had a similar language to that of the San Gabriel Indians, basing his opinion on his own observations and on the fact that Tarabal, who had a slight knowledge of the San Gabriel tongue, was able to make himself understood by the mountain

24 C-2603.
25 A.G.P., *Historia*, v. 396.
26 Anza, *Diary*, C-2503.

Indians.[27] These family relationships might have become a matter of importance as affecting the future use of the route, but in fact they seem to have had no marked effect at the time. None of these Indians were so cordial to the Spaniards as the Yumas had been, but none of them had endeavored to impede the march. Finally, they were not considered by the expeditionaries as a serious military obstacle in any event, nor did they prove to be so in the few years during which Spaniards went back and forth along this route.[28] The Yumas, however, were a serious problem. They were more numerous than the mountain Indians, there being several thousand of them, and they were much more advanced in type of life, having good crops and better weapons, although not good enough to enable them to resist Spanish troops effectually. The remarkable cordiality of the Yumas seems rather to have deceived Anza at this time; his opinion may be summed up in his remark that there would be no trouble between the Spaniards and Yumas as long as Palma lived, but rather he and all his tribe would be well disposed and faithful to the king.[29] A warning note was sounded by Díaz, however. Unless some establishments were formed along these rivers, he said, the march through these lands would not be easy, for the inconstancy of the Indians was well known, and the passage of the river was difficult. If the Indians should become discontented or unwilling to coöperate in the passage of the rivers, or if they should try to hinder it, a large armed force would be required to conquer so vast a number of Indians, despite their low grade of culture.[30] This was in effect a prophecy of the disaster of 1781. The difficulty lay not alone in the numbers of the Yumas, but also in the necessity for their aid in crossing the Colorado River.

[27] Díaz, *Diary*, A.G.P., *Historia*, v. 396.

[28] For information about these Indians, see Hodge, *Handbook*, under "Cajuenche," "Serranos," "Shoshonean Family," and "Yuman Family," as also the map showing the linguistic families of American Indians. It may be remarked that if Anza had gone by way of the San Gorgonio Pass he would not have passed through tribes of the Yuman family on entering the mountains, which is further evidence, therefore, in support of Mr. Eldredge's contention for the canyon of the San Felipe.

[29] Anza, *Diary*, C-2602.

[30] Díaz, *Diary*, A.G.I., 88-1-22.

While Anza was hastening to Monterey and back, most of the soldiers, in charge of Father Garcés, made their way to the junction of the Colorado and Gila. On April 27 Garcés wrote to Bucarely from that place, detailing what had occurred on his march from San Gabriel. The return had been made between April 13 and 26. Garcés expressed much disappointment that Anza was to return by the same route, rather than seek a new one, as Garcés had desired, although Anza might have been compelled to take that course. He also regretted that no observations of latitude had been taken; the other religious had been ordered to accompany him to take observations, and not merely to give him counsel, but instruments and a knowledge of their use were lacking in Sonora. After Anza's departure for Monterey, Garcés had wanted the soldiers under him to wait until he or Díaz could go to San Diego for an instrument and instruction in its use, but they would not do so. Indeed, he was far from content with the achievements of the expedition, and his curiosity was still in many respects unsatisfied. Yet, Anza was worthy of praise for having undergone such great expense, and for the good conduct that he had shown; besides, his example might lead others to propose like undertakings. Reverting to his original complaint, he said that if he had gone to Monterey, he would have urged a direct return from Monterey, by a more northerly route. However, the conquests in Alta California would in time be attended to, as well as the establishment of less costly settlements on the Colorado and Gila. The latter was particularly important, he said, and it would be a matter for tears, if these numerous peoples, so well adapted for spiritual conquest, were lost sight of. With this letter he was forwarding his diary by the special courier who was also carrying the Anza and Díaz diaries and letters.[31] If Garcés' letter seems to give Anza scant praise, the concluding paragraphs of his diary are more liberal, referring specifically to Anza's good deportment toward the Indians, his kindly manner toward the soldiers, and his

[31] A.G.P., *Historia*, v. 52.

good treatment of the Fathers, to whom he gave not only necessaries, but also some luxuries. These good acts, thought Garcés, might have moved God to sustain the expedition in peace.[32]

A letter from Palou to the Father Superior at San Fernando, April 22, 1774, shows how important Anza's discovery seemed to Alta Californians. Anza had found that it was only one hundred seventy leagues from Tubac to San Gabriel, said Palou, through a fertile land, inhabited by peaceful people. Thus, in case of necessity, Alta California could receive help from Sonora. Six Alta California soldiers were to go as far as the Colorado with Anza to acquaint themselves with his route. Anza intended to propose further projects of conquest to Bucarely, which Palou hoped that the Father Superior might support. One of these was the establishing of a chain of missions from Sonora to Alta California along the route discovered. Another was for a mail service every two months, one courier to go from Alta California to the Colorado, receiving there the mail brought from Altar by another. A third project was that eight droves of mules, then idle in Sonora since the Cerro Prieto campaign, should be used for carrying grain and provisions to Alta California, four of them to go through Sonora to the Colorado, and the other four between there and San Gabriel. If that were done, Alta California would in a few years be able to maintain itself. A fourth Anza project was to bring settlers from Sonora by the new route, and he was quite certain that many would desire to come. Finally, he meant to propose that the Manila galleon be permitted to stop at Monterey or San Francisco. If the king might also permit it to land some of the goods that it brought from China, so that they might be used in trade with Sonora and New Mexico, that would cause this fertile Alta California to be settled, and would result in the reduction of the natives. Palou suggested that it would be a good time to ask of Bucarely that the horses and mules intrusted to the *intendente* of Sonora be sent to Alta Cali-

[32] Garcés, *Diary*, A.G.P., *Historia*, v. 52.

fornia, and likewise, every kind of cattle for breeding purposes. The missions might then reach a permanent basis, for with the good pasture, the abundant lands and waters, and the good climate of this country the animals would increase rapidly and aid greatly in the conquest.[33]

Reference has already been made to the arrival in Mexico in June, 1774, of Anza's courier, Valdés, and to the deposition made by him before Melchor de Peramás on June 14. Such of his answers as have not already been considered may now be taken up. He was one of those sent by Anza to San Diego for provisions. That port was said to be forty leagues from San Gabriel, but Valdés believed that he must have gone sixty, for it took him two days. He was in San Diego three days, and returned with laden animals, requiring four days.[34] The route was a good one, there being many small streams and three fordable rivers with tree-lined banks. The lands were fertile, for anything that he knew to the contrary, and there was much game, bears and birds, in that region. Monterey was usually reckoned to be sixty leagues from San Gabriel, but it was fully a hundred, as Valdés knew, for he had travelled that route four times. Anza had started for Monterey on April 11,[35] taking four of his own soldiers and two others from San Gabriel as guides. Díaz and two soldiers waited for him at San Gabriel while the others, twelve soldiers and two muleteers, left San Gabriel on April 18,[36] and returned to Sonora with Garcés, Valdés being one of this party. They went back by the same route, except for two short cuts by means of which they saved five days, experiencing no trouble with the Indians on this march, except that some Indians of San Sebastián killed a horse to get the meat. Palma received them joyfully, and ferried them across the Colorado on a raft that he had built for Anza's party. He had also kept Anza's provisions and animals without taking any, and the cows had even increased in number by the birth of some calves. The men whom Anza had left there had taken

[33] M.N., *Papeles de Lancaster-Jones*, v. 2.
[34] Anza stated that the provisions were of little account. Anza, *Diary*, C–2602. [35] April 10, in fact. [36] In fact, April 13.

the horses and returned to Altar, on hearing a rumor that misfortune had befallen Anza's party. Valdés and two other soldiers had gone from the rivers to Altar, while Garcés and the rest remained behind, and from Altar Valdés had proceeded to Mexico.[37]

Bucarely received the news of Anza's success with the greatest enthusiasm. He exhibits this in a long letter to Arriaga of June 26, 1774, announcing the discovery, and enclosing copies of Anza's San Gabriel diary, his letters of February 28 and April 10, and the Valdés declaration. Up to the Colorado the march had not been difficult, he said, but was so, afterward, although the mishaps encountered were only such as were natural when one was passing through unknown lands without guides who knew the way. So his animals became weak, and frequently he was unable to find good halting places with water and pasture. These great difficulties were overcome by Anza's good judgment, and by his own constancy and that of his troops. But for the failure of his horses, he would have reached San Gabriel with abundant provisions both for himself and the settlements there. His leaving some animals and provisions with Palma had involved some risk, but it had worked, and this appeared to Bucarely especially noteworthy, as also the courageous spirit with which Anza's soldiers had offered repeatedly to go on foot, if necessary. It was not strange that the march was not as direct as possible, since the route had never before been traversed by Spaniards. Anza's messenger said that five days had been saved on the return journey, and it was probable that more than a third of the distance would be eliminated when the route became better known. At any rate, there was no doubt but that it was better than the one from Baja California. The Indians along the route were reported by Anza as lacking in arms and peaceful. The Yumas were the most warlike, if any might be said to be so, and they were friends of the Spaniards. If they should retain this feeling, they might facilitate the erecting of missions and the establishing of peace

[37] C-2648.

in that country, for the Yumas wanted both, according to
Anza. Thus, there would be a secure route from Sonora to
Alta California. The sea route would always be necessary, but the new route would be a more important way for
assisting that land in a contingency, especially if Sonora
should prove able to grow all kinds of produce, and if cultivation continued to increase in Sonora as it was then doing,
according to the reports of Governor Crespo. As further
measures in connection with the new route required careful
consideration, he would wait until Anza reached Mexico
City, to which he contemplated coming upon his return.
Meanwhile, in order to retain the friendship of the Yumas,
Bucarely had ordered Crespo to keep on good terms with
Palma, and to cause others to do so. Crespo was to tell
Palma how pleased was Bucarely with his good faith, and
was to give him presents, although no arms or ammunition.
Thus he might be kept well disposed until such time as
missions could be established in his country, to facilitate
communication with the existing missions of Baja and Alta
California, and with others to be erected there. Garcés'
return to the Colorado was due, no doubt, to Anza's lack of
provisions, for Anza had left half of his with Chief Palma,
and there was a scarcity at San Gabriel. Anza's confidence
in Palma had proved warranted. The latter had built a
raft, thus fulfilling a promise to Anza, so as to enable Anza's
force to cross the river. More particularly did his good
faith show forth in the return of all the provisions, with an
increase in cattle. The peaceful character of the various
tribes, as appeared from Anza's accounts, persuaded him
of the importance of his discovery, and of the advantages
that might accrue, when communication should be established. Bucarely suggested that Anza be made a lieutenant colonel, and that each soldier be given an *escudo de
ventaja* entitling him to extra pay,[38] not only as a reward,
but also as an incentive to others to make explorations that
would bring the Spanish settlements into better communi-

---

[38] The soldier with an *escudo de ventaja* received an extra *ducado* per month.
Diccionario universal.

cation.[39] Bucarely evidently hoped that the Anza route would become the principal land route to Monterey, superseding the one from Loreto, while communication by sea would continue to be maintained. Nor did Arriaga fail to be impressed by Anza's achievements. He replied to Bucarely's letter of May 27, giving approval of what had been done, and making particular note of the attentions shown to Chief Palma.[40] He also procured Anza's promotion to lieutenant colonel, the royal grant bearing date of October 4, 1774.[41] He informed Bucarely of this in his letter of October 8, stating also that the *escudo de ventaja* requested by the viceroy had been granted to those soldiers who had so loyally accompanied Anza.[42]

The details of Anza's return journey require but little mention here. He left Monterey on April 22, going by way of San Gabriel and the route that he had discovered, saving time by cutoffs, much as Garcés had done. He reached the Colorado River on May 10, left there five days later, and proceeded by way of the Gila to Tubac, arriving May 26. From there he had intended to go at once to Mexico, but was prevented from so doing by orders of the assistant-inspector, Antonio Bonilla. Anza refers to Bonilla's act and tells of his return march to Sonora in a letter of June 8 to Bucarely. He would have gone immediately to Mexico, he said, but had been obliged to wait for a review of his presidio by Bonilla. Shortly after the latter's departure he sent Anza a secret instruction to proceed to Terrenate. Anza went there, and was placed temporarily in charge of the presidio until a new commander could be brought from Janos, which Bonilla had promised to attend to promptly. Referring to the events of his stay in Alta California, he spoke of a strange wreck that had been found at Carmelo. He had bidden Fages to send it to San Blas at the first opportunity, so that it might be examined there to see if it were the lost *San José*, and if not, as was likely, because it was of a type of construction unknown to those who had seen it, to de-

[39] C-2656.
[40] Arriaga to Bucarely, Oct. 2, 1774. C-2735.
[41] C-2737.
[42] C-2740.

termine to whom it had belonged. He remarked on the
scarcity of provisions in Alta California, but said that both
the troops and the missionaries were expecting early relief
through the coming of boats, and the opening of the Sonora
route. All the tribes in that country were maintaining absolute peace.[43]
Anza's detention in Sonora is more fully explained in a
letter by Bonilla to Hugo Oconor, July 16, 1774. Captain José de Vildosola of Terrenate had been arrested, following a riot of his troops due to graft indulged in at their
expense by the captain and *habilitado*. In this difficulty
Bonilla hit upon Anza as temporary commander, because
his ability and agreeable disposition, and his unusually
great knowledge of the character of presidial troops fitted
him to maintain order at Terrenate, and because he was
the only officer then in Sonora, for Captains Bernardo de
Urrea and Gabriel de Vildosola were habitually sick, and of
the subalterns there was scarce one capable enough to act
even as *habilitado*. Since Anza had the viceroy's permission to go to Mexico to report concerning his important
and felicitous discovery, an officer should be sent from
Nueva Vizcaya to relieve him, and Bonilla had taken it upon
himself to ask Governor Crespo to appoint Lieutenant
Pedro de Tueros.[44] This makes it clear that Bonilla's act
was not due to petty spite, such as Anza had to confront
on other occasions. Bucarely, however, was much dis-
pleased, although he may not have had full knowledge of
the motives that had prompted Bonilla. Writing to Arriaga, August 27, 1774, he said that he was persuaded that
nothing in the affairs of Sonora was more important than
what Anza had just accomplished, and as he had given
clear orders to Bonilla to have Anza come to Mexico, there
ought to have been no delay. Bucarely had notified the
inspector, Hugo Oconor, how objectionable Bonilla's act
was to him, and had ordered Governor Crespo to arrange
immediately for the relief of Anza, so that he might start
at once. By reason of this delay, Bucarely was unable to

[43] C-2642.   [44] C-2676.
U

give further details of Anza's achievement, other than
what Anza had said in his letter. He had spoken of the
distance saved on the return march, and of the lack of
incident in passing through the lands of the intervening
tribes.[45]

Shortly afterward Bucarely received Díaz's diary of the
return march. In his remitting letter, June 12, 1774, Díaz
explained that he was not coming to Mexico himself, as he
had originally planned. Referring to the expedition, he
said that the Indians of the Colorado and Gila were somewhat addicted to stealing, but they were very devoted to
the Spaniards, and, he believed, would gladly permit of
Spanish establishments in their territory. This fact was
due not a little to the Christian spirit, zeal, prudence, and
singularly good conduct of Anza, whose peculiar talents
rendered him deserving of the pious attention and patronage of the viceroy.[46] Copies of both documents were forwarded to Arriaga in Bucarely's letter of September 26.
Despite what Díaz had said, he had been ordered to come
to Mexico to report in person.[47]

Anza's diary of the events of his march from April 6 on
was not received by the viceroy until November, when it
was presented by Anza himself, for he had concluded it
after arriving in Mexico. A copy was forwarded to Arriaga
in Bucarely's letter of November 26. This letter was concerned largely with Anza's second expedition, which was on
the point of being ordered, but it had much to say about
matters related to the expedition just concluded. Bucarely
called attention to the merits of Chief Palma, and of the
Yumas and their neighbors; he noted the fertile lands,
hitherto unknown, which Anza had discovered; he spoke
of the opportunity for communication between Sonora and
Alta California; and he remarked on the well-grounded
hope that he had of extending the king's rule and the Catholic faith over the intervening tribes. Extension of the
faith, which in Bucarely's words "is the primary intention
of His Majesty and the only real object in the expenditures

45 C–2706.   46 C–2644.   47 C–2721.

that he makes,"[48] was to be achieved by establishing missions, which would be easy, in view of the friendship of the Yumas, that tribe being the most powerful of those en route, and the one by whose aid yet greater projects might be undertaken. Gifts and good treatment were the necessary means of preserving this friendship. Of Anza, Bucarely spoke in the highest terms. He thought that it would be a good occasion to stimulate other officers to like services if Anza were made a lieutenant colonel, and again suggested that an *escudo de ventaja* be given to each of the soldiers who had displayed such constancy in accompanying him.[49] Bucarely did not know that these last-named recommendations had already been acted on favorably by Arriaga in pursuance of an earlier suggestion by the viceroy. On learning of this Bucarely not only attended to the matter of Anza's promotion, but also gave fitting orders to the treasury officials so that the soldiers might receive the extra pay to which they were henceforth entitled for the rest of their lives. In order that the presidial troops might understand how the king rewarded those who distinguished themselves in the service, he had ordered the *comandante-inspector* to make this event known to all the troops, so that they too, inspired by this favor, might conduct themselves with activity and zeal on such occasions as they should have an opportunity to do so.[50] Seventeen men profited by this arrangement.[51]

Preparations for a new expedition began at once upon Anza's arrival in Mexico. Arriaga had announced the royal approval of the instructions given to Anza for his first expedition in his letter of March 9, 1774.[52] Bucarely

[48] It may again be insisted that statements of this kind are not to be taken seriously, although they might proceed from a pious motive, such as Bucarely himself might be expected to feel.
[49] C-2764.
[50] Bucarely to Arriaga, Feb. 24, 1775. C-2861.
[51] The list, C-2862, was enclosed in Bucarely's letter of Feb. 24, 1775, cited in the previous note. The men were: Corporal Marcial Sánchez; Juan de

Espinosa; José Marcos Ramírez; Juan Antonio Valencia; José Toribio Corona; Juan José Rodríguez; José María Martínez; José Pablo Corona; Francisco Figueroa; Juan Martínez; José Antonio Acedo; Isidro Martínez; José Antonio Romero; Pascual Rivera; Juan Miguel Palomino; José de Ayala; and Juan Ángel Castillo. One wonders what reward was accorded to that great traveller and worthy soldier, Juan Bautista Valdés.
[52] C-2567. Also in C-2496.

had already determined on a second expedition when he received this letter, and he ordered copies of it to be drawn up so that it might appear in the *expediente* on which the ultimate formal decision in favor of the new expedition should be based.[53] The expedition was virtually already ordered. The only remaining questions were: What preparations were necessary? What was the expedition to accomplish? These matters were allowed to wait, however, until Anza reached Mexico to give his advice in person. To the first question Anza made answer in his report to Bucarely of November 17. Judging from his report, he had already discussed the expedition verbally with Bucarely, for much appears without previous documentary warning. Regarding the forty soldiers who were to go with him to occupy the Río de San Francisco, men from Culiacán, Sinaloa, and Fuerte, Sonora, would be the best adapted and the most easily obtained without causing harm to the region where they lived, he said, and they would also receive more benefit than persons of other places. These people, whom Anza had just seen, were in a state of very great poverty and misery. In order to instruct recruits in military discipline, Anza wanted five presidio soldiers, to be chosen by him, to serve as sergeants and corporals. In order to equip his recruits with what they needed, he suggested that they be paid in clothing; if paid in money, they would waste it or lose it in gambling, a vice to which everybody in the frontier provinces was addicted. As the march to the Río de San Francisco was to be by way of Anza's route of 1774, it was indispensable to take along soldiers who knew both the land and the people, so as to aid Anza and to bring about the consummation of the expedition in peace. He, therefore, asked permission to take ten soldiers from Tubac of those who had accompanied him in 1774, their places at Tubac to be filled by five veterans from Terrenate and five recruits. January would be the best time to start, as the 1774 march proved, but it would mean too great a delay to wait until January, 1776, in

view of Bucarely's desire to advance this expedition with
all possible speed; so he thought that he might be able to
start from Sonora by September, 1775. There would then
have been some rain, which would result in there being
enough pasture up to the Colorado, and Alta California
would be entered at the beginning of the rainy season.
To arrive much after the rain had set in would be harmful,
because of the great number of mud-holes that they would
encounter. Provisions and pack-mules could be reckoned
on the basis of the 1774 expedition. They had enough
then for four months for the number of persons on that
expedition. The most difficult matter in the preparations
for a new expedition would be to obtain useful horses at
Culiacán or Fuerte, and to get them to Tubac, which was
about three hundred leagues from Culiacán. This could
be accomplished only by the viceroy's order to the *alcaldes*
requiring them to compel farmers to exhibit and sell their
horses. If only those for sale were to be bought, it would
take until July to get the necessary number. If Bucarely
should agree to pay recruits in equipment, the necessary
effects must be remitted without loss of time, so as to be in
Culiacán by the following March, when Anza expected to
get there; Anza might then distribute them. Not only
the recruits, but also their families would have to be supplied with everything, from shoes on their feet to ribbons
in their hair. As there might be some desertions, and as
Anza had found that judges rarely gave due assistance in
such cases, he asked Bucarely to give him special powers
in this and like matters. He realized that Bucarely was
very desirous that presents should be given to Indians, although this had rarely been done, and then only to some
Indians of Chief Palma's villages, wherefore it might be
well to grant Anza a supply of tobacco, and some blue, red,
yellow, and green glass beads, as presents in Bucarely's
name. That would make them attached to the Spaniards,
whatever might occur. Chief Palma's services were particularly deserving of reward by some mark of special favor,
as, for example, by the gift of a long coat and a cap.[54]

[54] In C-2496.

Plans for a second expedition now went on at a rapid rate. Bucarely was enthusiastic about it, expecting the most beneficial results for Alta California, as appears from the remarks already alluded to in his November 26 letter. Coming to his plans for a second expedition, Bucarely said in the same letter that it was advisable to explore the land about San Francisco, and to place a presidio there, for that site ought by all means to be occupied in order to advance the Spanish conquests. Therefore, he had planned a second expedition under Anza with a larger party, so that thirty men might be left as an escort and guard for two new missions that he planned to have there. Cows and horses would also be taken along, in order that, by their increase, the new establishments might be advanced. Referring to Anza Bucarely said that his presence, good judgment, and talents, which he had now experienced in person, confirmed him in the opinion that he had formed of Anza from the time that he had first proposed an expedition. Bucarely believed him a competent, suitable person for carrying out what he hoped to accomplish by the new expedition.[55] Two days later, Bucarely issued a decree authorizing the Anza expedition and settling many but not all of the details in connection with it. The authorization of the *junta* was not asked on this occasion. The following is a translation of the decree:

"The enlistments, by which it is believed necessary to increase [the force of] the presidio of San Carlos de Monterey in Alta California [56] are that of a lieutenant, a sergeant, and twenty-eight soldiers, so as to be able to detach from them, without prejudice to the existing force by which the missions [already] established are sustained, the number that may be needed for the two new missions planned for the vicinity of the port of San Francisco, establishing a port there, which may be marked for occupation, to be a base or beginning for future explorations. The lieutenant and sergeant are to be chosen from the presidial troops of

[55] C–2764.
[56] Called California Septentrional in the document.

Sonora, and the ıldiers who may wish to go voluntarily to that home are to be chosen from the same presidios, provided that their number may not exceed eight, because of the shortage that they might cause in their present home [if more should go]. The other twenty are to be recruited by Captain Juan Bautista de Anza, for it is he who is to perform this new service for the king, conducting them to Monterey by the route which, with so much glory, he discovered a few months ago; [he is] to deliver them to the commandant of those establishments, Fernando de [Rivera y] Moncada; [he is] to assist in the exploration of the Río de San Francisco, so that he may inform me of what he shall have seen, and [is] to return by the same route with the ten soldiers, whom he is to take, chosen from [those of] his presidio; besides [he is also to bring back] those that are permitted to come.[57]   In accordance with this resolution, Juan Bautista de Anza will arrange with Juan José de Echeveste to draw up as a continuation of this decree the estimate of expenses to which this measure will amount, so that whatever is most fitting to the service of the king may be determined, when this is considered in the *junta de guerra y real hacienda*. In addition to the estimate, they will make a note of what they believe conducive to supplying the stores that may have to be prepared. As ministers for the new missions to be established are in Monterey, there is no need to discuss taking missionaries or their supplies, but if it appear suitable that Father Garcés and another [religious as a] companion go with the expedition to the Colorado River, and [if it] seem well that they await there the return of Juan Bautista de Anza, as he [Garcés] did on the first expedition, this captain will set forth what shall appear most fitting to him on the point, etc."[58]

On December 1, in two communications to the viceroy, Anza nominated the men that he wished as lieutenant and sergeant. He proposed as his first choice for lieutenant,

---

[57] Probably this refers to those in Alta California who might gain permission to return from there.   [58] In C-2496.

José Joaquín Moraga,[59] who was in fact appointed,[60] and served on the expedition. Anza's first choice for sergeant was José Ignacio Espinosa; second, Antonio Bravo; and third, Pablo Grijalva.[61] Bucarely appointed Espinosa,[62] but Grijalva in fact went on the expedition. On December 5 Anza was ready with the suggestions that Bucarely had called for a week before, confining himself in his report to the statements in Bucarely's decree. He noted the number of soldiers that he was to take with him, forty in all, and he had already proposed for lieutenant and sergeant the only men that were suitable. The objection to taking eight such presidial soldiers as might volunteer was that the soldiers were so obedient to their captains that they would not volunteer without their consent, and the captains would not care to get rid of any but useless soldiers or those of bad habits, who would not assist Anza much in getting his recruits, and whose bad habits might defeat the objects for which they were intended in the new establishments. Anza, therefore, asked permission to choose these soldiers himself. The command and the duties imposed on him he accepted with the greatest pleasure. Echeveste and Anza had already conferred about expenses, and calculated them most minutely, estimating that they would amount to 21,927 *pesos* and 2 *reales*, of which the royal treasury had 6359 *pesos* and 4 *reales* in goods for the expedition and provisions for Monterey. That left a total of only 15,567

[59] In C–2496. Anza explained that Moraga was at the time *alférez* of Fronteras, and had seen eighteen years' service as a private soldier and *alférez*. He had fulfilled his duties courageously, and had the distinction of having a father who had been killed in action, while a subaltern at the same presidio. Moraga was especially desired because of his long service as an officer, his superior abilities, and his intelligence in writing. Anza's second choice was Cayetano Limón, *alférez* of Buenavista, who had seen over twenty years of service, working his way up from the ranks, and had been wounded at least twice in military actions. Moraga and Limón alone would fulfill the requirements; hence he made no further proposals.

[60] Bucarely, *Decree*, Dec. 30, 1774. In C–2496.
[61] In C–2496. Espinosa was a corporal at Terrenate. He had been seventeen years in the service, conducting himself gallantly in action, and had been wounded twice. Bravo of Buenavista had served ten years. Grijalva was another Terrenate corporal who had served about as long as Espinosa, and was of equal merit and wounds. Espinosa's long service and greater intelligence in it made him Anza's choice, although Espinosa did not know how to write and the other two did.
[62] Bucarely, *Decree*, Dec. 30, 1774. In C–2496.

pesos and 6 *reales*, even estimating the various items generously.[63] As to the collecting of stores, most of these were mentioned in the itemized note of expense. As for the provisions to be obtained in Sonora ready and fresh at the time of the journey, Anza suggested that Bucarely order the governor of Sonora to see that they were supplied from Horcasitas and the missions of Pimería Alta, those being the easiest places from which to get them. The missions could also sell cattle to the expedition. Anza would be too busy recruiting to attend to the collection of stores, and suggested the appointment of Miguel Gregorio de Echarri, who had served with credit in that capacity in Pitic during the military campaign in Sonora. Anza again requested that the lieutenant, sergeant, and eight presidial soldiers be chosen by him, this being an important preliminary step which would assist in recruiting. He suggested that Father Pedro Font go on the expedition instead of Garcés. The former was at one of the Sonora missions, and was said to know how to take observations of latitude. In case he were designated to go, would Bucarely please send Anza the necessary instruments.[64]

Matters were now nearly ready for presentation before a *junta*.[65] For its consideration, Bucarely ordered a number of documents added to the file of papers, to wit : the resolution of the *junta* in favor of the first Anza expedition ; the royal approval of that undertaking ; the diary of Anza for the expedition ; and four letters from Rivera.[66] All of these documents except two of the letters of Rivera have already been considered. Rivera had reached Monterey on May 23, 1774, and soon afterward took over the command from Fages. His letters of June 16 showing the military weakness of the colony have already been used in another con-

[63] A translation of the itemized account appears in an appendix to this work.
[64] In C–2496.
[65] The *junta*'s consent in this instance was probably little more than a mere formality. Bucarely had received permission to dispense with it, and had already ordered the expedition. Doubt-less, he felt quite sure of the result of its deliberations. Again, there being no mention in the documents of this file of the real relation of this expedition to foreign danger, there was no need for secrecy.
[66] Bucarely, *Decree*, Dec. 7, 1774. In C–2496.

nection.[67]   In one of them he stated that the founding of a presidio and missions at San Francisco, with which he had been charged, would be impossible without reënforcements. On October 8 Rivera again wrote two letters, even more to the point. In one of them he said that the families which he had left at Velicatá had not yet arrived, but that he was expecting them soon. Consequently, he was permitting five soldiers to return to San Blas. He was in doubt what to do with six deserters who had been captured, but he was inclined to give them their liberty, because the Indian women were very depraved, and they and the Indian men needed to be punished, Rivera's intimation being that that necessitated all the force that he could muster. He went on to say, that his troops were too few to found a mission at San Francisco unless the presidio were to be moved there; but if that were done there would be too long a stretch of country to defend, and it would be difficult to succor the missions left behind, when occasion should demand. The Indians, however, were quiet.[68]   In his second letter he expressed a desire to see an advancement of the establishments under his command, and said that he had written repeatedly to Bucarely that there must be new buildings and more laborers if it were to occur. There were only nine laborers at the time.[69]   On December 16, 1774, a *junta* considered the question of Anza's second expedition.[70] After reciting the various documents before it, the *junta* proceeded to its resolution, which amounted to a complete acquiescence in the plans of Anza and Bucarely.[71]

On receipt of a royal order of September 22, 1774, approving Bucarely's acts for establishing missions in Alta California, especially two at the port of San Francisco,

[67] *Supra*, chap. XI.
[68] In C–2496.
[69] *Ibid.*
[70] Of those in the *junta* of September 9, 1773, which had authorized Anza's first expedition, the following were present at this meeting: Bucarely; Valcárcel; Areche; Barroeta; Abad; Toral or Valdés; Gutiérrez; Mangino; and Arce. Mesia had been present at the *junta* of October 17, 1772, but not

at the one of September 9, 1773. Two new names appear: Antonio Villa-Urrutia, of the viceroy's council and *subdecano* in the *Audiencia* of Mexico; and Ignacio Negreiros, gentleman of the order of Santiago. José de Gorráez, the viceroy's secretary, also signed, although not a member of the *junta*.
[71] In C–2496. A translation of the document is given in an appendix.

Bucarely replied, December 27, 1774, telling what he had done to bring that about. Recognizing its importance he had planned a second expedition under Anza by way of the Gila and Colorado rivers. Anza was to take as many soldiers as were necessary for an escort to the two new missions, and was to erect a monument to indicate that the land belonged to the king of Spain. This matter, which Bucarely deemed indispensable, was about to be accomplished as a result of the resolutions of the *junta*, of which Bucarely enclosed a copy, that document showing that Anza was to get thirty recruits, married men, if possible, and to take them and their families to the port of San Francisco, with a view to founding a goodly colony there, not only to guard the land, but also to serve as a base for future settlements. For that reason, Bucarely had granted to these settlers the utensils, clothing, and other things which Anza represented as necessary. Anza would also take ten soldiers from Tubac, who would return with him by the same route as before, after which Anza would report in detail. Fathers Garcés and Font would go, — the former to the Colorado River, there to await Anza's return, and the latter all the way, to observe latitudes. Bucarely had left the erecting of missions at the port of San Francisco to Serra, and had instructed Rivera to lend his aid. He had also pointed out that a fort should be established at each of the new missions, not far from the coast.[72] The pious fund was to contribute 12,000 *pesos* to the Department of San Blas, of which 1000 each was for the two missions, and the treasury would have to pay the rest, which Bucarely had ordered. The ministers were to be taken from the supernumerary religious in Alta California. Strict expense accounts would be kept of the cost of the expedition.[73] Apprised of this new project, Arriaga replied sustaining Bucarely, as usual in his plans of conquest.[74]

With the authorization of the expedition, and Anza's

[72] In other documents Bucarely referred to a single fort, which he planned to establish between the two missions.

[73] C–2781.

[74] Arriaga to Bucarely, May 15, 1775. C–2912.

departure from Mexico City, little more could be done by Bucarely from the Sonora end relative to the objects to be accomplished by the expedition, for it would be nearly a year before it could start, and news of its departure would be several months more in reaching Mexico. Bucarely was able, therefore, to occupy himself in other ways conducing to the same end. This was the time when naval activities were especially prominent, some account of which was given in a previous chapter. Also there were affairs in the two Californias and in the frontier provinces, related more or less directly to northwestward advance, demanding his attention.

CHAPTER XIII

CONDITIONS IN SONORA AND BAJA CALIFORNIA, 1773–1776

BEFORE proceeding to the details of the second Anza and other expeditions having to do with the establishing of overland communications between Alta California and Sonora or New Mexico, it seems necessary to give an account of affairs in the regions adjoining the new province, for they have a bearing on the objects to be achieved by the Anza expedition. A full statement will not be attempted; rather, just enough will be given to indicate the course of events in those provinces which would tend to the disadvantage of Alta California, unless circumvented or controlled. In Sonora, affairs were unsettled throughout this period, both because of Apache raids from the outside, and because of minor internal uprisings. While the evils were not eradicated, and even tended to become worse, the province never got beyond control under Bucarely's rule. The interest in Baja California is in its material development, in order to judge whether it might have become a source of supply for Alta California in provisions, domestic animals, and men, or even have been able to serve as a suitable route to the new province. There is nothing in the history of the period, however, to show that the peninsula had changed. In fine, the need for an overland route, with all of the activity in Sonora and along the route, that its maintenance would involve, was as great as ever, if Alta California were to achieve a state of populous settlement.

Some mention has been made of the task assigned to Hugo Oconor to establish a line of frontier presidios, inspect those existing at the time, and combat the Apaches, matters which were the most important internal problem in the region from Sonora to Texas in the years 1773–76. It is not necessary to follow Oconor's course in detail. He began at the eastern end of his field and proceeded westward, although the whole frontier was under his rule. Continually annoyed by attacks of the Apaches, it was natural that Oconor should desire to chastise them; so, early in 1774, he informed Bucarely that he was going to sally forth against them, enclosing a plan of campaign. Bucarely replied, telling Oconor that he should complete the line of presidios first, that task taking precedence over any other, and should dislodge the Indians from the land intervening between the line and the Spanish towns; otherwise, Oconor's success on campaign would be doubtful, or if attained, might prejudice the results already achieved elsewhere by him. Moreover, if the enemy should cease to molest the provinces, a policy of kindliness and good treatment should be employed toward them, rather than offensive war. Nevertheless, Oconor went on with his preparations, and wrote to Bucarely on March 20 that he was going to Coahuila with fifty men, leaving Antonio Bonilla to inspect the presidios of Sonora. Afterward, they would meet at Carrizal, and agree on measures for a campaign, of the advantages of which he was unalterably convinced. Bucarely thereupon reiterated his commands, adding further reasons in support of them. After the Sonora presidios should be moved to the new sites that they were to occupy as part of the line, it would be well to await the results of Anza's expedition (for Anza was at this time engaged on his first expedition), so as to avail themselves of the information that he might supply, and so as not to put any obstacle in the way of his return, which might be the result, if the campaign were opened beforehand. Finally, Bucarely reminded Oconor that his commission had to do with all of the frontier provinces, and not merely with a small portion. A successful issue of the campaign would be more certain, if the line were occupied, when the pre-

sidial garrisons, freed from other tasks, might not only
defend their territory, but also take the offensive. Bucarely was especially insistent on his opinion because of the
expedition of Anza. He had learned of the coming of
Tarabal, which made it appear certain that Anza would
succeed, and he did not wish a campaign started before his
return, for fear that the enemy, by themselves or by stirring up others, might prevent the discoveries which seemed
likely to be made. Such was the tenor of Bucarely's letter
of April 26 to Arriaga, reviewing the whole matter,[1] and
the latter returned a specific approval of the instructions
given to Oconor checking his desire to go on campaign.[2]

The Apaches continued their bold attacks, even in Sonora.
A letter of Bonilla, May 3, 1774, said that large bands of
Apaches had recently entered that province, and they had
twice attacked a detachment of ten men going from Terrenate to relieve the garrison of Tubac. The Spaniards
had defended themselves in such a manner that they lost
but two horses, and one soldier was slightly wounded.
This account appeared in the report for June of news received from the frontier provinces,[3] which was forwarded
to Spain with the viceroy's letter of June 26.[4] The report
for August contained better news. Bonilla had reviewed
all of the presidios, and sites for the new line had been
chosen. The Apaches were giving no trouble, having withdrawn from the province.[5] Bucarely's letter of August 27
enclosed this report.[6] The same day he wrote another
letter in which he seemed now more ready to consider the
idea of a campaign. Everything was quiet in the frontier
provinces. Oconor was still running the line of presidios
in Coahuila and Nueva Vizcaya. If there were now no
enemies south of the line, an offensive campaign beyond
it might be considered in order to compel the submission or
withdrawal of the Apaches far into the interior, so that
they might not continue their assaults with such frequency.

[1] C-2607.
[2] Arriaga to Bucarely, Aug. 13, 1774. C-2705.
[3] C-2659. The monthly reports were summaries of the most prominent happenings of the frontier.
[4] C-2658.
[5] C-2708.
[6] C-2707.

Anza was coming to Mexico, and with the detailed account of his expedition Bucarely would know what changes were necessary in the *reglamento* of presidios, although Anza's report of the peaceful character of the tribes along his line of march led the viceroy to believe that very little or no change would be required. The reviews made of the Sonora presidios should contribute much to the final arrangement to be made. Bucarely closed, saying that among the duties of his command those concerning the frontier provinces held first place in interest.[7] Bucarely was mistaken as to the peaceful character of the Yumas, but he was not in error long, as is shown by his later recommendations for missions and presidios in that country.

The never-ending ebb and flow of the Apaches brought fresh danger to Sonora, early in 1775. Writing to Arriaga, March 27, 1775, Bucarely said that the Apaches of the Gila had merely pretended to make peace, and measures had been necessary requiring the troops to be on the watch to check their attacks.[8] Meanwhile, Oconor had to combat an enemy every bit as powerful as the Apaches, — graft. In this period occurred the incidents connected with the names of Captains Vildosola[9] and Tovar[10] already mentioned. The Tovar case arose as a result of Oconor's review of the presidio of Terrenate,[11] proceedings against Tovar being held,[12] and, as we have seen, his dismissal from the service recommended. The report for November, 1775,[13] forwarded by the viceroy in a letter of the 26th,[14] contained an account of the discovery of new mines at Cieneguilla. In another letter of November 26 Bucarely told of the measures taken by Pedro Tueros, in command at Cieneguilla, and by himself for the despatch of more troops to that place.[15] Gálvez approved, and suggested as an encouragement to miners that the duty on gold be lowered in Sonora and Sinaloa, and that a *junta* be called to consider granting this reduction.[16]

[7] C-2709.   [8] C-2878.   [13] C-3038.
[9] Referred to in chapters VI and   [14] C-3037.   [15] C-3039.
XII.   [10] Referred to in chapter VI.   [16] Gálvez to Bucarely, Mar. 22, 1776.
[11] C-2904.   [12] C-2933.   C-3173.

Indians living in Sonora caused some uneasiness in 1776. Writing, March 27, Bucarely said that Father Antonio Ramos of Saric thought that the Pimas were preparing an uprising, for they were having meetings and war dances. Governor Crespo was alarmed by these rumors, but neither Oconor nor Vildosola gave them credence, because no robberies or murders had been committed. Bucarely was persuaded by them that there was nothing to worry about.[17] Gálvez was suspicious, however, and wrote Bucarely, July 8, 1776, to watch the conduct of the Pimas.[18] The report for April,[19] forwarded by Bucarely the 26th of that month,[20] showed that a number of robberies had been committed, but held that no serious uprising was likely to occur. Referring to affairs at Cieneguilla in another letter of the same date Bucarely said that Tueros was clamoring for more troops. Oconor had promised to send twenty soldiers, and Bucarely had reiterated the necessity of so doing.[21] Gálvez's reply of July 26 charged the viceroy to exercise the greatest care to guard those dwelling at the mines of Sonora.[22] Tueros was continuing to call for more troops, wrote Bucarely, June 26, and as a royal order had required that he should have as many as he might ask for, Bucarely had given fresh orders to that effect to Oconor. Meanwhile, the presidios of Terrenate and Fronteras were being transferred to their new sites at Santa Cruz and San Bernardino, and it was expected that the change would check the excesses and robberies being committed, especially in the vicinity of Cieneguilla.[23] Gálvez's reply, October 18, 1776, repeated the royal order to supply troops to Tueros.[24] Tueros' apprehension seems not to have been shared by other officers on the frontier. Crespo wrote Oconor, July 3, 1776, that Tueros did not need the troops he was asking for, saying that the road from Cieneguilla to Horcasitas was entirely free from danger.[25] Oconor informed Bucarely, August 9, 1776, that he would send the troops asked for by Tueros, although he believed that they were not needed.[26]

17 C–3180.   18 C–3268.   22 C–3280.   23 C–3260.
19 C–3205.   20 C–3204.   24 C–3346.   25 C–3266.
21 C–3206.   26 C–3292.

x

This information was passed on to Gálvez by Bucarely's letter of September 26,[27] but did not change the opinion of the *ministro general*, who in due course forwarded his approval of what had been done in the matter.[28]

The Indian question, however, was gradually becoming more serious. Tovar soon achieved further discredit. He had already been removed as useless and prejudicial to the service, but was still in command at Santa Cruz (the new site of Terrenate), not having been relieved. Attacked by a band of Apaches, July 7, 1776, he ordered his troops to fight on foot, although the horses were in good condition. To this was ascribed the ensuing disaster, for Tovar and twenty-five others were killed, eight soldiers and one Ópata alone escaping. An account appeared in the report for September,[29] which was forwarded by Bucarely on the 26th.[30] Gálvez expressed great regret that the lack of skill and bad conduct of Tovar should have caused such loss of life.[31] In accord with Oconor's recommendation of July 6, 1775,[32] it had been decided to do away with Sonora's "flying company," but the Tovar disaster caused Bucarely to postpone such action for a time, lest the Indians might have become emboldened. Thirteen men had already been detached from it, and sent to Santa Cruz.[33] This decision received Gálvez's approval, with the condition, however, that the company be disbanded, as soon as the present exigency should pass.[34]

On receipt of Gálvez's letter of July 8, 1776, about the Pimas, Bucarely reasserted that there was slight foundation to expect an uprising at Saric. His chief concern in Sonora was to develop the province and to furnish it with protection from the Apaches.[35] He was mistaken, however, as to the Pimas. The report for the next month, November, contained news that certain Pimas were in revolt, although there was favorable news to counterbalance the bad. The

[27] C–3327.
[28] Gálvez to Bucarely, Jan. 12, 1777. C–3462.
[29] C–3326.
[30] C–3325.
[31] C–3403.
[32] C–2949.
[33] Bucarely to Gálvez, Sept. 26, 1776. C–3328.
[34] Gálvez to Bucarely, Jan. 9, 1777, C–3460.
[35] Bucarely to Gálvez, Oct. 27, 1776. C–3358.

Seris had attacked the rebellious Pimas and had killed two, while the Indians of Pitic had attacked a small group of Apaches and killed one. This was caused in each case by the rebellious Indians who stole horses from those who later attacked them. Less pleasing was the note that 1000 *pesos'* worth of damage had been caused by an Indian attack on the provision train going to Cieneguilla.[36] Bucarely forwarded the report on November 26,[37] and in another letter of that date commented joyfully on the news of the counter-attacks by Sonora Indians.[38] Indeed, it was unusual to find Seris fighting Spain's enemies. In the same month, November, the long-predicted outbreak in the vicinity of Saric occurred. A party of Seris, Pimas, and Apaches first wrought havoc at Magdalena mission and then at Saric, killing a number of persons, plundering and burning, and driving off cattle. The savages were pursued, but escaped.

It does not seem worth while to go into equal detail with regard to the affairs of New Mexico and the other frontier provinces as in the case of Sonora. In the first named, conditions seem to have continued much as before. In Nueva Vizcaya and the more easterly provinces Apache warfare went on as it did in Sonora. Sonora had experienced difficulties during the period of the Anza expeditions, but Bucarely and Oconor had been able to keep matters in hand. In late 1776 the situation was getting worse, but in all probability they would have handled it as capably as on previous occasions, without giving up projects of frontier extension to the northwest. These disorders, however, were to be a legacy to the *comandancia general*, established by the royal order of August 22, 1776.[39] Teodoro de Croix, the first *comandante general*, arrived in Mexico on January 22, 1777.[40] By that time the immediate effects of the Anza expeditions had been achieved. The question whether they were to be followed up, and related matters, like the

[36] C–3376.
[37] C–3375.
[38] C–3377.   [39] C–3293.
[40] Croix to Gálvez, Jan. 26, 1777.

Reference to the *legajo* of the Archivo General de Indias has been lost. Bucarely wrote on January 27 that Croix was already in Mexico. C–3469.

Indian wars of Sonora, were henceforth in the decision of Croix.

Baja California could not be other than the sterile peninsula that it always had been; yet, some advance in its prosperity may be noted in this period, although not enough to change the situation as regards the needs of Alta California for a better supply-route. As for the events of the period there is little beyond the persistent quarrels of the governor with the religious, and the installation of the Dominican order, in May, 1773, as successor of the Franciscan in mission work. The Indians continued to be as tractable as before, and very little show of military force was required. The principal interest in the province for our purposes consists in an indication of its material progress. At the time of the delivery of the missions to the Dominicans there were fourteen such establishments. With a letter of September 26, 1773,[41] Bucarely forwarded to Arriaga an *estado* showing the number of persons and domestic animals at eight of the missions at the time of the transfer to Dominican rule.[42] Two months later[43] he added like data for four other missions.[44] Not until September 26, 1774,[45] was he able to supply that information for the remaining two missions.[46] Having by that date information of the fourteen missions given up by the Franciscans, he enclosed an *estado* embracing all of them.[47] The figures follow:

From these figures it appears that there was a total of 4268 persons and 14,716 domestic animals in the Baja California missions in May, 1773. An estimate of the land under cultivation and the annual amount of the agricultural produce at the missions was not made at this time, but Bucarely's September 26 letter stated that orders had been given to include such information in future. The figures of the *estado* give some idea of the relative importance of the missions.

[41] C-2393.
[42] C-2394.
[43] C-2438.

[44] C-2439.
[45] C-2722.
[46] C-2724.

[47] C-2723.

MISSIONS	MEN	WOMEN	COWS	HORSES AND MULES	SHEEP	GOATS	PIGS
S. F. Javier Viaundó	139	140	89	115	498	195	13
N. S. de Guadalupe	96	73	120	178	396	500	4
N. S. de Loreto	103	84	0	170	0	0	0
Santa Gertrudis	462	338	196	253	110	320	0
Santa Rosalía Mulegé . . .	82	83	32	47	232	407	0
Purísima Concepción	89	71	64	117	243	193	2
San José Comondú	155	127	47	292	1413	249	20
San Ignacio	173	141	125	165	558	194	0
S. F. de Borja	533	467	648	387	2343	1003	0
San José del Cabo	34	17	64	143	63	51	0
Santiago de las Coxas . . .	47	28	22	257	90	75	0
N. S. del Pilar ó Todos Santos .	93	80	703	600	153	131	16
S. F. de Velicatá	176	120	78	13	71	89	0
Santa María de los Ángeles .	167	150	8	55	0	0	0
Totals	2349	1919	2196	2792	6270	3403	55

Before the end of 1773 Father Mora made a tour of the northern missions of his province,[48] inspecting them and leaving instructions for their spiritual and temporal management.[49] In reporting this to Arriaga, June 26, 1774, Bucarely remarked that it was clear from Mora's narrative that the regions visited by him were not so fertile and well favored as was the case with Alta California, but the missions were useful, for progress in conversions was being made. A new mission was planned by the Dominicans.[50] Arriaga expressed the royal pleasure at hearing this news and approved the plan to found a mission.[51] By the end of June, 1774, there were still fourteen missions. The total number of persons had increased in the course of a year, but that of domestic animals was less, the figures being 4340 and 14,558 respectively.[52] Bucarely announced this to Arriaga, February 24, 1775.[53]

In a letter of May 27, 1775,[54] Bucarely forwarded the monthly report, which in this case bore encouraging news of mission progress in Baja California. Before the end of the

[48] Diary, Nov. 4–Dec. 20, 1773. C–2424.
[49] For the instructions, C–2501.
[50] C–2657.
[51] Arriaga to Bucarely, Oct. 12, 1774. C–2745.
[52] From the estado, C–2859, and

extracto, C–2860, of Melchor de Peramás. Of the persons, 2428 were male and 1912 female. There were 2616 cows, 1896 horses, 839 mules, 6206 sheep, 2931 goats, and 77 pigs.
[53] C–2858.
[54] C–2919.

year 1774 Mora had selected Viñadaco, because of its fertility, as a good site for the new mission, and one religious had been sent there. Neve's letter of March 23 stated that a crop of 200 *fanegas* (320 bushels) of grain had been raised and 150 Indians brought under mission rule, and yet further progress was expected. A triumph had been obtained at Velicatá. The Indians of San Juan de Dios, near there, had always refused to receive the Christian faith, but recently the whole village of eighty persons had accepted conversion. Later, the chief of a coast village and fifty-two others had asked for baptism, and the chief had promised to bring in the rest of his following.[55] The viceroy's letter of February 26, 1776,[56] contained an *estado* showing in detail the persons, animals, and this time the crops at fourteen of the fifteen missions in existence at the close of June, 1775. Despite optimistic reports the province had remained practically stationary, although as before the number of persons had increased slightly, and that of the animals had fallen away. There were 4423 persons and 14,036 animals. Reports concerning agricultural wealth were received from only eleven of the missions. These had raised 2230 *fanegas* (3568 bushels) of wheat, while some of them had raised small quantities of other produce.[57]

Bucarely's letters of May 27,[58] and July 27, 1777,[59] may be taken together for data as to fourteen of the fifteen missions at the close of the year 1776. In the May 27 letter, which was the principal one, dealing with twelve missions, he complained of the lack of clearness in the answers received from the Dominicans. He was sending the information received to *Comandante General* Croix, to whose jurisdiction Baja California had been assigned. From the *estados* forwarded with each letter [60] we find that there were

[55] C-2920.
[56] C-3154.
[57] C-3152. Among other commodities were barley, maize, kidney-beans, chick-peas, grapes, wine, cotton, and wool, but only a few missions produced them, and then in small quantities, as a rule. San Ignacio was by far the most all-round productive mission, although least of the eleven in yield of wheat. San Francisco de Borja was perhaps richest, agriculturally, not only producing the most wheat, 460 *fanegas*, but also having over twice as much land under cultivation as any other.
[58] C-3563.   [59] C-3624.
[60] Respectively, C-3564 and C-3625.

at the fourteen missions referred to 5424 persons and 15,641 animals. In eleven missions giving figures the crops of wheat amounted to 3034 *fanegas* (4854½ bushels), and other crops had been raised in greater quantities than before, maize almost competing with wheat. At the same eleven missions there had been slightly more than 2250 *fanegas* (3600 bushels) of maize.[61] These figures show that some slight advance had been made by the Dominicans. Increase in animals, however, had been remarkably slight, as compared with similar advances at a later time in Alta California, after the latter province became securely established. In number of horses and mules, perhaps the most important class, because of their use as pack animals, the province had declined. Some animals, although not an appreciable number, had been taken to Alta California, as will appear in the next chapter.

Mention has already been made of the number of soldiers in the military establishments. In addition to the Spaniards in them and at the missions there were some miners and cattlemen in the peninsula, but their numbers were probably insignificant, and no statistics as to them or their possessions have come to hand.

Barry's quarrelling with the Dominicans was one of the reasons why Bucarely supplanted him with Felipe de Neve. Writing of this matter to Arriaga, December 27, 1774, Bucarely said that he had come to this conclusion, partially because of the repeated petitions by Barry himself to be relieved and permitted to go to Mexico, but also because the discord between him and the religious over questions of jurisdiction and other matters had reached an extreme point. Bucarely had ordered Mora to refrain from giving the least motive for complaint or resentment, as it might put back the service and render of no account the vast sums that had been expended there; this he did, he said, to prevent Mora from meddling in affairs of the royal

[61] Of the persons at the fourteen missions 2990 were male and 2434 female. There were 3537 cows, 1601 horses, and 736 mules. At twelve of the missions there were 5651 sheep, 3754 goats, and 33 pigs, to which should be added 329 sheep, goats, and pigs at the other two missions.

jurisdiction, which belonged to the governor. Moreover, he had written to the Dominican *provincial*, asking him to persuade Mora and the other religious to live in peace with the royal officers. At the time of his appointment Neve was sergeant-major of the cavalry regiment of Querétaro. Bucarely referred to him as a man of mature wisdom and prudence, but he had not failed to enjoin him to avoid quarrels with the religious. He had made him full governor (*en propiedad*), because he deserved it, both for his good qualities, and for his past services, especially for his handling of matters concerning the material wealth of the Zacatecas missions.[62] All of these acts of the viceroy were approved by Arriaga, April 26, 1775.[63] Neve departed at once for his province, and in March, 1775, relieved Barry, who, soon afterward, became governor of Nueva Vizcaya.

Neve, too, had difficulties with the friars. They resisted his attempts to make the Indians self-dependent, as had been the aim of Gálvez's regulation of 1768, whereupon Neve recommended that steps be taken with a view to secularization. This was not the only concern of the governor, for we find him complaining of want in ships, horses, clothing, and especially in arms. He also asked for more troops.[64] The last-named request was the subject of a letter by Bucarely to Arriaga, February 25, 1776. Both Barry and Neve had asked for additional troops, the latter for a sergeant and nine soldiers more. They were needed in part to escort the mails to and from San Diego and Monterey, and also because double escort was required when new missions were founded. On the authority of the royal decrees of September 6 and 16, 1775, requiring the Baja California establishments to be developed by all means possible, without sparing expense, Bucarely had acquiesced in Neve's request.[65] Gálvez approved.[66]

In fine, not enough change had occurred in the peninsula to enable it to contribute materially to the development of

[62] C-2792.
[63] C-2896.
[64] Bancroft, *N. M. St. & Tex.*, I, 740-41.
[65] C-3142.
[66] Gálvez to Bucarely, June 12, 1776. C-3248.

Alta California. Baja California continued to be held for
strategic reasons, and, besides, served as a convenient mail-
route between Monterey and Mexico, but in other respects
it was of scant economic or political importance. It is
not surprising that orders soon came for the governor and
lieutenant-governor to exchange capitals, the former going
to Monterey, and Rivera to Loreto.

CHAPTER XIV

PROBLEMS AND PROGRESS OF ALTA CALIFORNIA, 1774–1775

HAVING determined that Alta California must be developed in order to protect New Spain from foreign encroachment, Bucarely took steps toward that end by providing for an increase in the number of settlers and domestic animals, by sending guns and other needed articles, and by giving directions for promoting agriculture. Most important of his projects, perhaps, was the proposed founding of establishments at San Francisco, both to prevent that port and the so-called Río de San Francisco, which flowed into it, from falling into the hands of an enemy, and to serve as a base for further northward conquests. A proposal made at this time to move Monterey presidio to an inland point depended in a measure on the successful founding of San Francisco, but orders came from Spain not to change the site of Monterey. Bucarely's activities will be discussed in this chapter only in their local aspects, irrespective of relations with the outside world, but it must be remembered that the dominant idea was that of avoiding foreign danger.

The outstanding events of the two years treated here were Rivera's march to the province early in 1774, his expedition to San Francisco later in that year, Ayala's exploration of the bay at that port in 1775, and Heceta's overland trip to San Francisco in the same year. All of these bore on the coming of Anza with colonists for the proposed new settlements on the bay. These expeditions accomplished something, especially Ayala's, but more might have been done by Rivera if he had been more energetic in carrying out Bucarely's commands. Serra was an able, ardent supporter of the projects of Bucarely, although not equally interested in San Francisco, but the power to act did not rest with him. Of course, neither Serra nor Rivera appreciated the element of foreign danger as Bucarely did. To them Alta California was primarily a Spanish problem. Concerning local problems Serra certainly was competent to speak. More missions, more soldiers, and more domestic animals, the last named to come from Sonora, were the needs upon which he most insisted. As regards the importance of the military in maintaining the conquest there were memorials by Fages and the Franciscans of the College of San Fernando which presented even more compelling proofs than those offered by Serra, showing clearly the precarious footing of the province and that the soldiers were the backbone of the conquest. Progress in conversions, and increase of animals and crops went on at a normal and encouraging rate up to the close of the year 1775, although not fast enough to dispense with the need for more domestic animals. White settlement, however, had hardly begun by that date. In fine, Alta California was waiting for the one thing it needed to ensure its permanence, the coming Anza expedition of 1775–76.

Alta California's needs to the close of the year 1773 have been dealt with in earlier chapters, and the necessity for an overland route pointed out. So great was the destitution of the province, however, and so interested was Bucarely in the problem of meeting foreign danger, that it seemed best not to await the uncertain issue of Anza's search for a route, nor to rely wholly on supply-ships. Therefore, Fernando de Rivera y Moncada,[1] who was to succeed Fages,

[1] Rivera entered the service in 1742, working his way up from the ranks, and becoming captain at Loreto in the time of the Jesuits (C–2566). He accompanied Portolá to Alta California in 1769. In 1770 he wrote to Croix from Velicatá asking permission to retire, on the ground that his health was broken (Rivera to Croix, Mar. 2, 1770). Croix granted his petition (Croix to Rivera, Nov. 12, 1770). On receipt of this letter Rivera started south (Rivera to Croix, May 8), but was ordered back to San Diego by Governor Barry (Rivera to Croix, May 31, 1771). Permission to retire was again given by the viceroy, late in 1771 (Croix to Rivera, Sept. 12, 1771). Rivera then bought a farm in or near Guadalajara, but ran into debt, so that in order to provide for his family he had to re-enter the service. Called to Mexico he asked not to be sent to Monterey, as Bucarely had suggested, hoping that he might get the money to pay his debts in some other way (Rivera to Bucarely, undated, but probably early in 1773), but this request was denied. Rivera seems again to have asked permission to retire in 1775. Ortega wrote to

was given instructions, August 17, 1773, tending to the
relief of Alta California. So far as they dealt with precautions against foreign aggression and with general problems
of a religious, military, political, civil, and routine character, they have already been taken up.[2] Only a little remains for discussion here. Before proceeding to Monterey, Rivera was to recruit troops to replace those which
were to retire with Fages, and the recruits were to go with
their families, in order to make a beginning of effective
settlement. Single men should carry papers to prove their
status, so that the missionaries might perform the marriage
ceremony for them in Alta California without delay, in case
they should wish to marry. Rivera ought soon to examine
the site of San Francisco, if further examination were necessary, and to consult with Serra to see if a mission might be
placed there. They might also found other missions, if
the necessary escort could be obtained by withdrawing
troops from the missions that were on a solid footing.[3]　Gálvez's memorial of March 8, 1774, may again be quoted for
its insistence that a route from Sonora and New Mexico
should be opened, especially to Monterey and San Francisco, laying special emphasis on the importance of establishments at the last-named place.[4]

Rivera set out at once for Sinaloa to recruit the soldiers
and families for Alta California. On September 19, 1773,
Bucarely wrote to him that Anza had been authorized to
seek a route to Alta California from Sonora. Rivera was
ordered to detach exploring parties on arrival in order to
aid Anza's project.[5] Rivera replied from Guadalajara,
October 14, 1773, that he had been delayed, but would
obey Bucarely's orders. Anza might be expected to emerge
between San Diego and San Gabriel, he said, and Rivera
would have that region explored. As to Anza's proposal,

him that he regretted to hear of his
request, and told him that his great
services in the past were apt to stand
in the way of his obtaining permission
(Ortega to Rivera, May 5, 1775,
A.P.C.H., *Prov. St. Papers*, I, 161–64).
Rivera's misfortunes may help to account for the gloomy traits of character

that he exhibited while in Alta California. Except for the first reference and
the last the documents quoted above
are in A.G.P., *Californias*, 66.
[2] *Supra* chaps. X and XI.
[3] C–2350.
[4] C–2566.
[5] A.G.P., *Californias*, 66.

he regarded it as very important, because of the length of voyage to Alta California, and lack of provisions there. He himself had once planned to suggest such an expedition; therefore, Anza's undertaking gave him much pleasure. In conclusion, he said that he had tried to buy some mares and horses of Antonio de Ocio, who had them in Baja California, but Ocio would not sell, because he needed them at his mines.[6] Rivera recruited a force of fifty-one persons, of all ages, in Sinaloa. Most of the soldiers were married men with families, which, in accordance with Bucarely's order, were to accompany the expedition to Alta California.[7] Rivera reached Loreto in the middle of March. Lacking provisions for all of his following to make the march up the peninsula to Velicatá, he planned to go as quickly as possible with part of the men, so as to send back the necessary provisions from Alta California to Velicatá — an interesting proof of the insufficiency of Baja California as a base of supplies for the northern province. Therefore, he hastened to Monterey, reaching there May 23, 1774,[8] too late, however, to meet the Anza expedition, which was already well on its way back to Sonora.

The Rivera expedition and the founding of missions were involved in Bucarely's mind with the question of sending supplies to Alta California, for the progress of conversions depended on the missions having food for the Indians. Bucarely's activities in this regard have been taken up in detail in an earlier chapter, but should be borne in mind here. In a letter on the subject of supplies, May 27, 1774, Bucarely went on to discuss the founding of new missions. Serra had asked for several new ones, he said, and they should be established, but the two planned for San Francisco should be erected first. A fresh exploration of that port should be made, making use of the troops of Anza.[9] These plans were approved by Arriaga, September 22, 1774.[10]

[6] *Ibid.*
[7] I have found no roster of the expedition, but judge that the number of soldiers could hardly have passed twelve.
[8] Palou, *Noticias*, III, 150–51.
[9] C–2625. It is not clear whether

Bucarely was referring to the first Anza expedition which he hoped would join with Rivera to found the San Francisco establishments, or whether this was a reference by him to an already planned second expedition.
[10] C–2718.

A letter from Serra to the viceroy, June 22, 1774, is very important evidence as to the needs of the province. Referring to the departure of Fathers Crespí and Peña for Mexico, he said that they were not needed at the time, as there were enough religious for four new missions, which Serra hoped to see established. Speaking of the brilliant prospects of the colony, he said: "Live-stock is the only thing that remains to be desired, but it is enough for us that Your Excellency may know it; for in that case we do not doubt that you may remedy the matter, whether by commands to carry into genuine and due effect what has been agreed on and enacted for California, or by directing that the animals come by way of Sonora, for once they have been supplied, their increase is certain in lands so rich as these. No more will be necessary, although the conquests should penetrate many hundreds of leagues into the interior, for from here it will be possible to go on supplying the land farther on."[11]   This is most illuminating as to the situation, and prophetic so far as its claim goes that only a few would be required. With the same letter Serra enclosed a report of equal date, chiefly interesting for its comment on the Indians. They held the Spaniards in great esteem, or rather, awe, he said. At first they had thought the Spaniards to be children of the mules upon which they rode. Indians of Monterey had placed food and broken arrows around the cross left by Portolá, in order that it might not get angry with them. They also claimed to have noticed strange birds preceding the march of the Spaniards.[12]   Copies of these two documents were sent to Spain in a Bucarely letter of September 26, 1774. They confirmed Vizcaíno and Palou, said the viceroy, as regarded the fertility and richness of the land and the docile, tractable nature of its inhabitants. There ought to be a good-sized settlement at Monterey, so as to advance the conquest.[13]   This elicited from Arriaga, May 14, 1775, an expression of the king's gratitude for the zeal with which the viceroy was promot-

[11] C–2653.
[12] C–2654.

[13] C–2720.

ing objects which were among the principal cares of His Majesty.[14]

Another Bucarely letter of September 26, 1774, did not meet with the usual unqualified approval. A port on the Alta California coast had been sought constantly, since the conquest of the Philippines, said Bucarely, as a shelter and stopping-place for the galleons coming from Manila to New Spain. Lack of such a port might have been the cause for the loss of many boats in early times, and, at any rate, involved risks. Vizcaíno's discovery of Monterey gave rise to the idea of founding a colony there for the benefit of the galleon in case of accident, but his death put an end to that project. Despite some expensive attempts, later efforts had been unavailing until 1769, when a presidio was established. It was badly located, however, lacking fresh water, agricultural land, and timber, which it needed for houses. Rivera's letter of July 11 had proposed to transfer it to the shores of the Monterey River, a better site, and if the people of Monterey should wish to go, and it should turn out to be advantageous Bucarely intimated that he would rejoice at the change. He had planned to send two supply-ships to Alta California, instead of one, in the coming January, and as a result a brilliant town might be formed. In that case there needed to be left at the port of Monterey only a galleon to receive cargoes for the new town. The idea did not appear a bad one to Bucarely, in view of the fertility of the new site, and its greater nearness to San Francisco, but he would decide on nothing, until he had received more complete reports as to the advantages of the plan and until he might consult with Anza, whose presence was necessary before a decision could be reached.[15] Arriaga's reply, May 14, 1775, did not approve the proposed change of site. The presidio had been erected on the Bay of Monterey, chiefly in order that boats anchoring there might have prompt assistance from shore upon their arrival, and be guarded by the garrison and fort.[16]

14 C-2910.   16 C-2911.
15 C-2719.

Arriaga had reached this opinion after consultation with Gálvez, whose report will be taken up presently, for it dealt with other matters which may be treated more appropriately in another place.

Several of Bucarely's letters to Rivera may be quoted to show the variety and range of his interest in Alta California. The manifest idea in all of them is his eager desire for the advancement of the colony and the furtherance of the conquest. Although he did not express it in the letters, Bucarely himself had in mind safeguarding Spain's possessions against foreign enemies. Fages had asked Bucarely whether lands and cattle might be given to Spanish soldiers marrying Indian women. Bucarely's answer was directed to Rivera, September 21, 1774. After consulting with the *fiscal* he had decided that such marriages were conducive to advancing the settlements and that it was advisable to give lands in such cases, as this would extend the practice of cultivating the fields. So he would answer Fages' question in the affirmative. The Indians, too, ought to be instructed in tilling the soil; the missions and presidios would not lack for provisions, if that were done.[17] On December 15 he wrote that he had resolved to occupy San Francisco, which could serve as a base or beginning for future conquests. He had therefore ordered Anza to go there from Sonora with such provisions, domestic animals, and families of settlers as were needed to put the project into effect. After giving some details of the expedition he went on to say that he was sending by sea not only the usual supply of provisions, but also a year's stock for the settlers conducted by Anza, which was to be for them alone, and even Anza, if he should require anything for his return to Sonora, was not to levy upon that supply but was to get what he needed from the presidio or mission stock. These settlers would meet the lack of which Rivera had complained in his letter of June 16. Bucarely was also sending arms, as requested in Rivera's letter of October 8. Reverting to San Francisco, a further reason for occupying

17 A.P.C.H., *Prov. St. Papers*, I, 90.

it, he said, was to furnish irrefutable proof that the land
belonged to Spain. The best way to accomplish this, and
also to propagate the faith, would be to erect the proposed
missions; consequently, he had given appropriate instructions to Serra, whom Rivera was to aid to the extent that
might be necessary. The troops assigned to San Francisco
were to be under Rivera's command from the moment that
Anza should reach Monterey to deliver them, although
Anza was to assist in exploring the Río de San Francisco,
so as to be able to give information to Bucarely. In a
postscript, Bucarely repeated his comment on the importance of San Francisco from the standpoint of future conquests, and he charged Rivera to act in harmony with
Serra. He had heard that the Alta California crops were
abundant that year, and had urged upon Serra, who had it
in charge, to do everything possible to foment agriculture,
so that the religious conquest might be facilitated. The
presidio to be erected at San Francisco should be placed
near the coast between the two missions, in order to be able
to aid either, in case their escort of six soldiers each might
not suffice.[18] On the same day Bucarely wrote to Serra to
the same effect, with only such change of phraseology as
addressing another person required.[19] Shortly afterward,
Bucarely wrote to Rivera again, repeating his directions as
to the location of the fort at San Francisco and enclosing a
copy of the resolution of the *junta* authorizing Anza's expedition. He requested Rivera to keep an account of all
expenses in connection with the occupation of San Francisco.[20] In another letter, January 2, 1775, he took up
Rivera's proposal of moving the presidio of Monterey to a
better site a few leagues away. The plan did not appear
a bad one, but would better be delayed, because he had
ordered Manrique and Anza, and also Heceta on his return
from the north, to explore the port of San Francisco, which
might cause a change in plans; therefore, to avoid possible unnecessary expense, the proposed change of site was

[18] A.P.C.H., *Prov. St. Papers, Ben.*   [20] Bucarely to Rivera, Jan. 2, 1775,
Mis., II, 20–25.   A.P.C.H., *Prov. St. Papers*, I, 166–67.
   [19] A.P.C.H., *Arch. Mis.*, I, 49–56.

Y

to await further orders. Rivera might construct buildings, however, for the storage of cargoes arriving on the ships from San Blas.[21] On January 10 he wrote that the cattle and mules gathered in Sonora for the Elizondo campaign were to be turned over to Anza's expedition, now that they were not needed in Sonora. Except those which Anza might need for his return, these were to be delivered to Rivera for the benefit of the new settlements.[22] Bucarely seems also to have informed Neve that he contemplated conquests in the far north. This appears from a letter by Neve to Serra, April 8, 1775. The viceroy had written to him, he said, that the lands traversed by Anza in his first expedition might be taken from the Franciscans and awarded to the Dominicans, because he thought of using the former in a more northerly field, meaning the lands that might be opened up as a result of Pérez's discoveries.[23]

There was no doubt that the viceroy's plans for mission progress would find an ardent supporter in Serra. On September 9, 1774, he wrote to Bucarely complaining of Pérez and Rivera for not helping to found the two San Francisco missions at once. Serra had hoped to do so in October, when the families left by Rivera at Velicatá were expected to arrive, and Pérez had planned to wait and help Serra, but had changed his mind, and was resolved on an immediate return to San Blas. Nor was Rivera stirring himself in the matter. He claimed to be unable to act because of the non-arrival of the families left at Velicatá, and because Anza had left him no soldiers. He really intended to use the families at the presidio that he was planning, four or five leagues from Monterey, said Serra, and not at the San Francisco missions.[24]

The families from Velicatá reached San Diego, September 26. Some were despatched to Monterey by Lieutenant Ortega, *comandante* at San Diego, reaching their destination in November. Rivera now felt strong enough to

[21] A.P.C.H., *Prov. St. Papers*, I, 168–69.
[22] *Ibid.*, 171.
[23] M.N., *Doc. Rel. Mis. Cal.*, II.

[24] C-2716. Both the Spanish and a translation of this document appear in Historical Society of Southern California, *Publications*, II, 73–80.

attempt the oft-enjoined exploration of the port of San
Francisco. His party, which included Father Palou, left
Monterey on November 23. This time no attempt was
made to reach the old port at Point Reyes, but the expedition went up the peninsula to within the limits of the
modern city of San Francisco, placing a cross on the hill
overlooking the Seal Rocks. Nothing more was done because of the beginning of winter rains. The party returned
to Monterey, arriving there on December 13.[25] The expedition is described by Serra in a long letter to Bucarely
dated January 8, 1775. Palou had noted six sites between
Monterey and San Francisco suitable for missions, but
Serra did not want even one in that remote region without
a presidio. This, coming from so enthusiastic a missionary
as the Father President, is high evidence of the importance
of the military, but it will already have been noted that
Serra never failed to insist on the need for troops. Continuing, he said that he desired the conversion of those
lands, but before anything else (unless both things could
be done at the same time) four new missions ought to be
founded between San Diego and Monterey. That would
in a measure complete the chain of which there was so
much need. Above all, the two missions of San Buenaventura and Santa Clara [26] should be established. There
were plenty of provisions and religious for these two. He
repeated his former suggestion that the military establishment of the province should be increased from eighty to a
hundred men, the extra twenty to be used as the escort of
new missions according as he should decide. Unless
specific orders to that effect were given, the additional
number, if granted, would be used at the presidios. Referring to the existing missions, he said that an advance
had been made in all respects, as would appear from his
annual report, which he would send later. The Indians
continued to be docile, and a rumor that those of San Luis

[25] For the Rivera diary, C–2761;
for that of Palou, C–2762. The latter
is printed in Palou, *Noticias*, III,
261–316.

[26] Not to be confused with the site
of the later Santa Clara mission. Serra
referred to a place south of Santa
Barbara.

Obispo were planning to burn the mission had proved to be
groundless. The soldiers unfortunately killed a good Indian in connection with that event. The matter of a change
in site of the San Diego mission, crops there and at Carmelo, and his intention to bring mules and other animals
at Velicatá to Alta California missions were alluded to by
Serra. He then reiterated his proposal of two years before, that families of settlers be sent to Alta California.
Soldiers could be brought from Sinaloa, who should be of
good character, and some of whom at least should be married men and come with their families. There ought to be
two families at each mission, so that the wives might serve
to instruct the Indian women at the missions.[27]

On receipt of the news from Alta California, Bucarely
wrote to both Rivera and Serra on May 24, 1775. To the
former he said that he realized that his expedition to San
Francisco had occurred at a poor time of year for the establishing of missions, but he wished him to continue his
efforts to find sites. Serra and Palou had recommended
six new missions, several of them between Monterey and San
Diego, but the establishing of a fort and two missions at
the port of San Francisco was the most important thing to
do. Nor ought the missions proposed by Serra to be de-
ferred. Rivera was ordered to arrange for their establishment, therefore, provided they did not stand in the way of
the two at San Francisco, or interfere with the maintenance
of the existing missions and presidios.[28] Bucarely wrote to
Serra to the same effect, but in a different tone. Whereas
he had enjoined Rivera to help Serra, he now bade Serra
not to be too impatient for his missions. Bucarely realized
the advantages that would come from founding them at
the places named by Palou and Serra, but those at San
Francisco must come first. Therefore, he trusted that Serra
would be able to work in harmony with Rivera, who, he
believed, in view of Bucarely's orders, would contribute to
the establishing of missions. Resolutions would be taken

[27] C-2826. Appended to this, under date of January 10, is a list of the Alta California missions and the religious then serving them.
[28] A.P.C.H., Prov. St. Papers, I. 171-74.

in due time upon what Serra pointed out as necessary for
the propagation of the faith, and of these matters Bucarely
would advise Serra in season.[29] Writing to Arriaga of
these events, May 27, 1775, Bucarely blamed the weather
for the failure of Rivera and Palou to carry out his orders
and their own intentions. Nevertheless, they had advanced
Spanish knowledge of the vicinity of San Francisco, had
examined lands adapted for missions, and had beheld an
abundant spiritual harvest ready for the gospel — or, in
other words, had found numerous Indians. Anza and
Ayala had been given orders to occupy the port of San Francisco. As to Serra's request for the establishing of missions along the Santa Barbara Channel, he would tell both
Rivera and Serra to do what prudence might dictate, but
without prejudice to the new missions to be established at
San Francisco, or to the old missions and presidios. He
called attention to Serra's report of the increase in Christian converts. Similarly, the increase in crops gave promise that before long the new province might maintain
itself. From time to time, families might be sent, as Serra
had requested, and in case of urgency, Bucarely would
send the twenty additional recruits asked for, so as to run
no risk of losing the gains thus far made.[30] In acknowledging this letter, September 6, 1775, Arriaga took special note
of Serra's requests for families and more soldiers, approving
Bucarely's decision.[31]

We may now refer again to Rivera's plan to remove the
presidio of Monterey to a new site. Arriaga referred the
three Bucarely letters of September 26, 1774, already discussed in this chapter, to Gálvez for an opinion.[32] Gálvez
replied on April 15, 1775, looking with favor on all of Bucarely's measures, except the Rivera project. He did not
believe Rivera's allegations that Monterey lacked fresh
water, lands for crops, and lumber for buildings. Nobody
else had said so, and Costansó and Fages had reported the
contrary. He repeated his suggestion of the year before,

[29] M.N., *Doc. Rel. Mis. Cal.*, octavo
series.
[30] C-2916.   [31] C-2983.

[32] Arriaga to Gálvez, Jan. 27, 1775.
C-2837. The Bucarely letters are
C-2719-21.

that the governor of the Californias should live in Alta California.   He also urged that cattle be sent there from Baja California and Sonora, and that the missions be increased to as many as possible, making use of all the unemployed *Fernandinos* in Alta California, and of others from the College of San Fernando.   Finally, remarking on the importance of maintaining communication between that province and Sonora along the route discovered by Anza, and of advancing the mission conquest among the numerous and peaceful people that the expedition had made known, he said that these affairs were being discussed at the time by the Council of the Indies.[33]   Arriaga's letter to Bucarely need not be repeated.   In reply, August 27, 1775, Bucarely said that he had not ordered the change of site, although the project did not seem a bad one to him; he had told Rivera that the matter could not be determined until the results of the Ayala and Anza expeditions were at hand. Similar considerations had held back any change of the Department of San Blas; that would depend on whether Russian settlements should be found by the *Santiago*, in which case he implied that a better port would be necessary.   If a port were needed merely to assist the new possessions, San Blas would answer the purpose.[34]   Shortly after Gálvez's accession to power as *ministro general* he gave definite orders to Bucarely, April 10, 1776, forbidding the removal of the presidio of Monterey from the port, and requiring Neve and Rivera to exchange places.[35]   Bucarely's reply, July 27, 1776, stated that directions had been given accordingly.[36]

Reference has already been made to the Ayala expedition, its thorough exploration of San Francisco Bay, and the enthusiastically favorable reports of Ayala and Cañizares as to the merits of the bay.   Ayala left Monterey late in July, 1775, and was in the bay and its offshoots all of August and most of September, reaching Monterey on the return, September 22.   He had found that the bay had a practicable entrance, and not merely one port but many. Rivera had been ordered to coöperate with a land expedition, and the two were to erect buildings for the settlers coming with Anza, but as some of Rivera's troops were temporarily absent in the south, he was unwilling to withdraw any from his presidio. On the return of his soldiers he planned to send a party overland, but he did not do so before Ayala left the bay. Meanwhile, Heceta had endeavored to enter San Francisco on his return from the north, but had missed it in the fog. Arrived at Monterey, he procured soldiers from Rivera, those in the south having returned, and started overland for San Francisco, accompanied by Fathers Palou and Campa. The party left Monterey on September 14, and reached San Francisco on the 22d, just after Ayala's departure. Two days later, Heceta started back, and was at Monterey on October 1. Neither the buildings for Anza's settlers nor the missions had been erected, but there was no longer any doubt of the value of the port.[37] Ayala reached San Blas, November 6, 1775, and informed Bucarely of the result of the northward voyages. Of Ayala's exploration Bucarely wrote to Arriaga on the 26th, that the natives of San Francisco Bay seemed peaceful, the port good, and the place well adapted to settlement. There was plenty of fresh water, firewood, and stone; the climate was cold, but healthful, and free from the fogs that Monterey experienced.[38]

In another letter of November 26, Bucarely forwarded Serra's report of the progress made in 1774 by the five Alta California missions. Three other missions were about to be erected, one at San Juan Capistrano and the two at San Francisco.[39] The report showed a gain during the year of 62 marriages and 297 converts, the total neophyte population being 759. There had been an increase in domestic animals as follows: livestock, from 205 to 304; horses, 67 to 100; mules, 77 to 85; sheep, 94 to 170; goats, 67 to 95; swine, 102 to 131. The number of asses remained the

[37] Bancroft, Cal., I, 244–48.   [39] C–3036.
[38] C–3033.

same, to wit, 4.[40] In fine, the advance had been normal,
not enough to lessen in an appreciable manner the needs of
the province, but encouraging; to have held the province
at all, with the means at hand, was no small achievement.
Gálvez wrote to Bucarely, February 29, 1776, praising his
zeal for the distant province, as evinced by his measures for
its advancement, and approving what he had done, including the decision to found the three missions.[41]

Yet, in considering these figures, one must bear in mind
a latent factor, which if it knew its power, might possibly
have rendered everything without avail. The Indians of
Alta California have usually been accounted exceptionally
docile in their reception of Spaniards, and there are numerous documents which attest that view, based on the usual
conduct and the lack of military equipment of the natives.
Some hints to the contrary, notably in the letters of Verger
and Serra, have already appeared in this work. We may
now look into that matter a little more closely. One of the
most important documents that the writer has seen concerning conditions in Alta California is a report by Pedro
Fages dated November 30, 1775.[42] After being relieved of
his command by Rivera, he had departed for Mexico in
August, 1774. As might have been expected, Bucarely
had asked him to draw up a report concerning the far
northern province, of which Fages was competent to speak
by reason of five years' residence there, supplemented by
intellectual capacity of no mean quality. Fages describes
the land and the people from San Diego to San Francisco,
noting the progress made by the Spanish settlements and
the obstacles which they had to encounter. The natural
features of the route traversed in 1769 are given in detail,
that route being still in use in Fages' time for most of the
way. He tells of the products of the soil supplied by nature,
remarking that the land was much richer than it had seemed
at first, being perhaps the most fertile of any that had been

[40] C-2841.
[41] C-3162.
[42] C-3042. A free translation from a copy stated to be in the library of M. Ternaux-Compans is in the *Nou-velles annales des voyages et des sciences géographiques* (Paris, 1844), v. I (CI), 145-82, 311-47.

conquered. He speaks of the animals of the province, but most important of all, perhaps, is his description of the Indians, their barbarous traits, notably their religious customs, and their propensity to war, one village with another. On Spain's relations with the Indians depended the success of her establishments; it is natural, therefore, that he devotes to them the greater part of his account, dealing also with mission progress. Of the missionaries he speaks in terms of praise, a contrast to the way in which Serra was wont to speak of him. The most noticeable lack in the document is its failure to make any reference to affairs at the presidios, but the importance of the military appears frequently, showing that the oft-reported accounts of the docility of the Indians must not be overrated by us, just because no great disaster to the Spanish establishments in fact occurred. That none did, was due to the presence of soldiers, trained in frontier methods, and, it would seem, efficiently led. It is to this phase of the report that attention will now be directed.

After the overland expedition had left San Diego for the north in 1769, the Indians attacked the Spaniards remaining at that port, believing themselves sure of victory by reason of their superiority in numbers. Yet, although few Spaniards were able to bear arms, they killed three Indians, wounded others, and drove the enemy away. Thereafter, the Indians were not openly hostile, although at night they occasionally killed horses and other animals of the Spaniards, but more for the meat than as an act of hostility. In describing the traits of the Indians of San Diego and the region for thirty leagues north of it, Fages remarked upon their treacherous nature, saying also that they were not very friendly to the Spaniards.

The principal establishment of the next region described, embracing thirty-two leagues, was the mission San Gabriel. An impulse to mission progress there had been given by bringing five families of Christian Indians from Baja California.[43] These were acquainted with agriculture, and as

---

[43] Among these were Sebastián Tarabal and his family.

the site was good, they were able to grow sufficient crops to supply not only the Indians of the mission proper but the recent converts as well. The Indian problem, especially in the forty leagues and more between San Gabriel and San Diego, was no mean one. In that space the Indians were wont to show hostility whenever Spaniards passed without a numerous and formidable convoy. On that account Fages recommended establishing more missions with a due number of presidios, first making a thorough exploration of the region, however. As matters were, there was a great stretch of land in which nothing had been done to reduce it to the faith or to render it secure for whoever might pass that way. Every journey still had to be made with an armed force, just as on the occasion of Portolá's first march; the seeming docility of the Indians at such times was rather the result of their fear than of any feeling of friendship.

The next region discussed ran a distance of thirty-seven leagues, in part along the Santa Barbara Channel. There were no missions in that space, but the Indians were numerous and very different from the others in the province. They were of a good disposition and fond of work, but very avaricious, and displayed an aptitude for trade, being as Fages called them "the Chinamen of California." They were well disposed toward the Spaniards, but warlike with one another, an almost continuous state of war existing between the villages. They were too bold, however, for the Spaniards to count safely on their seeming affability and lack of good weapons. In fine, they were barbarians, and therefore capable of committing any kind of hostile act, if it should strike their fancy. It was for that reason that the mission of San Buenaventura, which the Marqués de Croix had decided to found there, had not been established.

The next region embraced thirty-three leagues and contained but one mission, San Luis Obispo. To this place also five families of Baja California Indians had been brought, for it too was a fertile site. San Luis Obispo and

San Gabriel together could in time supply all of the other missions without need of a recourse to San Blas for grain. The need for Spanish families in Alta California is apparent from a new point of view when we note the attitude of the Indians of San Luis Obispo. According to Fages they regarded the Spaniards as exiles from their own land, for they had noted that the newcomers had no desire to attack them, nor did they seem to wish to settle the country, since only men came. Therefore, they had reached the above-named conclusion, and consequently were a bit disquieted and lacking in confidence. Some of the soldiers at San Luis Obispo had offered to bring their wives and families to Alta California, which would certainly help, said Fages, to up-root the singular idea held by the Indians of that neighborhood. The Indians there and for twelve leagues around were affable and, except as already noted, friendly to the Spaniards. Reverting to the region of the Santa Barbara Channel, Fages recommended the establishing of missions there, under guard of a presidio of fifty or sixty soldiers. Such a number was necessary, because of the populousness of that district.

Between San Diego and Monterey the line of march lay either directly through or at least within gunshot of twenty or more villages. Along the march also were cliffs and other bad places where the natives might dispute and impede a passage, and instances had occurred when they had done so. At a village called Rincón they had stoned a party under Fages himself in the year 1772, while he was passing through a difficult place. No soldiers were lost, but it had been necessary to kill one or two Indians. This was apt to occur whenever small parties passed, and the only remedy for it would be the establishing of a mission and a presidio.

The fifth region taken up in Fages' report covered nineteen leagues, and contained one mission, San Antonio. The Indians were very friendly, being willing to give anything that they had to the Spaniards. From that region to San Francisco had been thirty-six and a half leagues by

Portolá's march, leaving Monterey to one side. There were no missions except San Carlos at Carmelo, near Monterey. The Indians of the mission and its vicinity were peaceful, but at Zanjones, six leagues away on the route to San Diego, the Indians had dared to attack couriers and other passers-by. No Spaniards had lost their lives, but they had killed a number of the Indians. Most of the Indians in the region beyond the sphere of mission influence were hostile both to the converted and unconverted of the mission region; before the founding of Monterey presidio there had been continual war, and fights still continued, especially in the groves where acorns were found, that article of food being the object in controversy. The presence of the Spaniards had served to check warfare, because of the fear on the part of outside Indians that the Spaniards would aid those who lived at or near the mission. This explained the great affection of the latter for the Spaniards, of whose aid and protection they stood absolutely in need.[44]

Quite a remarkable document of a different character is an account by the religious of the college of San Fernando of discoveries between 30° 26' and 57° 18' from 1769 to 1776. This was addressed to the king, although sent to Bucarely to be forwarded by him, and was dated February 26, 1776. The account was based on the diaries and other reports sent by the *Fernandinos* of Alta California to the college, with the conclusions of the writers with regard to the discoveries. The San Fernando memorial lacks the precision of the Fages document, a number of subjects being discussed with no apparent attempt at orderliness of arrangement. Yet this account, although perhaps less important than that of Fages, is not less interesting. After a few preliminary remarks it treats of the voyages of Heceta and Bodega is 1775. The principal point of this part of the document is an argument as to the probable existence of a strait through the continent, whether at Aguilar's

[44] A copy of this memorial was sent to Gálvez by Fages with his letter of March 25, 1776. C-3175.

River or at the Strait of Juan de Fuca, coming out possibly in Hudson Bay.[45] The latter part of the memorial
deals most largely with the expeditions to Alta California
of 1769–70. The importance of San Francisco, and especially of the so-called Río de San Francisco, is emphasized.
According to Father Crespí, who had accompanied the
expeditions of 1769, 1770, and 1772, to the vicinity of the
bay, San Francisco was in the midst of a vast country,
capable of maintaining many cities. The river was navigable for probably a hundred leagues, and might flow
near Pimería Alta and perhaps near New Mexico, and
would have plenty of timber along its banks with which to
construct boats. This made it appear how dangerous to
Spain it would be if another power should possess the
river and port of San Francisco; not only would that
check further northward conquest, but it would also mean a
loss of the prospective wealth of Moqui, and the endangering of the provinces already reduced.

After speaking of the hostility of the Indians between
Velicatá and San Diego, the memorialists went on to say
that from San Diego northward conditions were much
better. The land was better for agriculture and grazing,
there was an abundance of water and timber, and the
Indians had received the Spaniards in peace. This last
remark had to be qualified, however. A revolt at San
Gabriel, when that mission was founded, illustrated one of

[45] The argument for a strait is supported at great length, not merely by
the incidents of the Heceta and Bodega
voyages, but by a reference to the
Monarquía Indiana of the Franciscan
Torquemada (published 1615) and to
the career of the Spanish mystic, María
de Jesús de Ágreda, the celebrated
"Blue Lady" of the American Southwest. Torquemada had said that
Aguilar's River was understood to be
the Strait of Anian, joining the Atlantic
to the Pacific, and passing by a great
city which some Dutchmen had discovered when they went through the
strait, and he had expressed an opinion
that Quivira [at that time placed by
some maps on the coast of Alta Cali-
fornia] was in the vicinity of the river
discovered by Aguilar. Such a careful
historian as Torquemada must have
had authentic documents on which to
base his account, said the writers.
Would that he might be mistaken, for
great harm would result to New Spain
and to religion, if a Protestant power
should discover the strait and possess
itself of its mouths. The account of
Torquemada, however, had also the
support of María de Jesús de Ágreda.
This servant of God, said the writers,
was carried from Spain to the Indies
by the agency of the angels many times
between 1620 and 1631 to preach the
faith to the Indians, especially in the
provinces of New Mexico, Quivira, and
Jumanas. These visits had the high
proof of María's own account, to doubt
which was to doubt religion.

334 THE FOUNDING OF SPANISH CALIFORNIA [Ch. XIV

the causes of trouble with the Indians, for which the fault
lay with the Spaniards. Soldiers were wont to assault
Indian women, a practice prevalent at all of the missions,
and one which the religious had not been able to prevent
in entirety. This was not only scandalous but it involved
the province in very grave danger of being lost. The
Fernandinos had been able to check the evil in a measure,
and the Indians had remained at peace. Yet, such hostilities as had occurred showed that the missions could not
exist without the protection of a competent escort, to defend them in case of need, and to keep the converts in proper
subjection. Too much reliance should not be placed on
Indian docility and affability, for this might be feigned, or
more apparent than real, in proof of which an incident of
the Heceta voyage [omitted here] was cited. After describing native religions the memorial goes on to say that
the Alta California Indians had their false ministers or
priests, and the Spanish conquest meant depriving them of
employment. This might cause them to be discontented,
because of their loss of honor and profit, and might lead
them to stir up rebellion. If insults by the soldiery, such
as could not fail to occur, were added to the incitements of
these men, there would be great danger of an outbreak.
Moreover, the unconverted Indians near the missions had
threatened the converts, unless they should make an end
of the missionaries and soldiers. For these reasons it was
essential that there be a competent number of soldiers at
all missions, and that they be good Christians, in which case
more could be accomplished with a few soldiers than with
many whose manner of life was bad.[46] This is convincing
evidence that the military were the backbone of conquest,
at least until such time as a region became well settled by
Spaniards; missions were an effective and necessary agency,
but they depended on military aid. What is more to the
point here, this memorial helps to show how far Alta California was from being on a safe, well-settled basis.[47]

[46] For the memorial, C–3156.
[47] The memorial was enclosed with

a letter to Arriaga of the same date,
C–3155. Other enclosures were a

As the year 1775 drew to a close everything was ripe for the arrival of Anza's settlers, and the founding of the new missions at San Francisco. Until Anza should come, there would be delay because of Rivera's lack of troops. It was this which caused Rivera to write to Bucarely, August 8, 1775, that he intended to postpone exploring San Francisco until Anza's arrival, when he would erect the two missions and the fort. For the latter he intended to install two of the four cannon at Monterey. Bucarely replied, January 20, 1776, signifying his approval, and suggesting that the two cannon be carried from Monterey to San Francisco on the *San Carlos* when that boat should take the supplies that were to be given to the new settlements.[48] Meanwhile, not only Serra, but also the other *Fernandinos* in Alta California were impatient for new missions, there being more missionaries at the time than the existing number of missions required. Palou's letter of September 14, 1775, to Father Superior Pangua voices this eagerness of the *Fernandinos*. He wrote that he was only a supernumerary at San Carlos, but wished active service in this field of innumerable heathen awaiting conversion. Rivera was obdurate and immutable, however, being incapable of agreeing to anything that he had not first proposed, on which account Serra was not wont to insist very much, but gave Rivera mere hints, and said no more, if he got a negative answer. This was not altogether pleasing to Palou, who was impatient for new missions, and grieved to see so many Indians dying without baptism. Serra had not insisted more, as he did not wish to break with Rivera, whose help was important.[49]

An account of mission progress in Alta California during 1775 may now be given, although it was not until December 27, 1776, that Bucarely was able to remit this infor-

pamphlet of Father Alonso de Benavides of New Mexico in 1631, in which the incident of María de Jesús de Ágreda is discussed, C–28; Crespí's diary of the 1772 Fages expedition, C–1925; Peña's diary of the Pérez voyage of 1774, C–2640; Palou's diary of the 1774 Rivera expedition, C–2762; and Campa's diary of the Heceta voyage of 1775, C–2870.
    [48] A.P.C.H., *Prov. St. Papers*, I, 193–94.
    [49] M.N., *Doc. Rel. Mis. Cal.*, II.

mation to Spain.[50]   The following tables show the totals at
the end of both 1774 and 1775, and indicate the increase
in the latter year.

PROGRESS OF CONVERSION

	BAPTISMS	MARRIAGES	DEATHS	LIVING
1774	833	124	74	759
1775	1725	284	419	1280
Increase . .	892	160	345	521

DOMESTIC ANIMALS

	COWS	SHEEP	GOATS	PIGS	MARES	HORSES	MULES	ASSES
1774	304	170	95	130	31	69	85	4
1775	447	191	145	131	60	68	98	5
Increase	143	21	50	1	30 [sic]	− 1	13	1

CROPS [51]

	WHEAT SOWN	CROP	MAIZE SOWN	CROP	KIDNEY-BEANS SOWN	CROP	BARLEY SOWN	CROP
1774	22.5	475	103	540	13.5	40		
1775	34	1029	63.5	974	26	45.5	18	118
Increase .	11.5	554	40 [sic]	434	12.5	5.5	18	118

It will be seen that the year had been a good one from the
standpoint of conversions.   A striking feature was the pronounced increase in the number of deaths.   Was the inferior race already giving way in the presence of civilization?
The most important set of figures is the one concerning
domestic animals.   They were still too few to insure the
permanence of Alta California.   Crops had about doubled
as compared with the yield of the previous year.   In that
respect the province seemed well on the way to prosperity.[52]
There were still no settlers but the soldiers and friars and
the few families that Rivera had brought.

---

[50] C–3410.
[51] The amounts given are in *fanegas*,   a *fanega* being about 1.6 bushels.
[52] For the *estado*, C–3411.

CHAPTER XV

NOT content with the manifold activities that he had
already set on foot to insure the preservation of Alta California, — by an increase in number and efficiency of the
provision boats, by the voyages to the northwest coast, by
projects in relation to the Anza route for facilitating transmission of settlers and domestic animals and the occupation
of San Francisco, and by the Crame expedition to find an
easier route for the transportation of artillery from the
Atlantic to the Pacific, — Bucarely was meditating yet
other projects with the same object in view. One was the
discovery of new routes, a more northerly and more direct
route than Anza's from Sonora to Monterey, another from
New Mexico to Alta California, and another from Sonora
to New Mexico. Another project was to take the second
step in closing the gap between Sonora, the Californias, and
New Mexico by founding missions and presidios along the
Gila and Colorado rivers; this done, but little more would
be necessary before Sonora would become an interior province, with the two Californias as one fairly accessible,
natural frontier, and New Mexico another.

Steps were taken in 1775–76 with a view to the discovery
of routes. The New Mexico to Alta California route was
in fact discovered through the separate explorations of
Father Escalante from New Mexico and Father Garcés
from Alta California. Both reached Moqui. Escalante
and Domínguez attempted without success to find a more
northerly route from Santa Fé to Monterey. Proposals
were made for opening a direct route from Sonora to New

Mexico, but except for Garcés' journey by way of the Colorado, nothing was accomplished, and the same held true of the projected more northerly route from Sonora to Monterey. More was not done, because a second Anza expedition and the occupation of the Gila and Colorado were necessary preliminaries. The first of these projects was fulfilled, Anza going overland to Alta California with so many families of settlers and domestic animals that the permanence of the new establishments, although not on a strong basis, was assured. The expedition reached Alta California just in time to prevent the possible loss of the province as a result of a dangerous Indian uprising at San Diego. Furthermore, after Anza's departure, a settlement was made at San Francisco, an important step in Bucarely's programme of defence against foreign attack. Anza, Garcés, Díaz, Oconor, and Bucarely himself were among those who favored placing Spanish establishments at the two rivers, especially in the Yuma country. Anza's march, Garcés' stay at the junction and his explorations, Velázquez's discovery of a route from Baja California to the mouth of the Colorado, the visit of the Yuma chief Palma to Mexico City, and the child-like desire of the Indians for missions were factors tending to bring the event closer. Just as Bucarely was about to act, however, the new government of the *comandancia general* was promulgated, placing these matters under the direction of Teodoro de Croix.

Many proposals tending to the accomplishment of the projects which are the subject of this chapter had been made in years past, some of which have already been noticed. The success of Anza's first expedition led to a renewal of these suggestions. Anza is said to have proposed founding missions on the Colorado when he was at Mexico in 1774, but was opposed to such foundations on the Gila because of the danger from Apache raids. The establishing of missions on the Colorado, he had said, should be preceded by explorations, and a presidio should be placed there for their protection. A letter from Oconor to Garcés at this time indicates that official sanction had already been obtained for a transfer of the presidios of Horcasitas and Buenavista to the Gila and Colorado.[1] Bucarely's letter of January 2, 1775, to Garcés tended toward carrying out the suggestion attributed to Anza. Bucarely had just received the Garcés diary of 1774, Garcés having remained behind on the Gila, after Anza's departure, to make further explorations. In his diary Garcés had indicated a number of places where missions might be placed, the natives being ready for conversion. Bucarely said that he was particularly eager to found missions among the Yumas, who seemed so desirous of having them, and he informed Garcés of the plans for a new expedition on a vast scale under Anza's leadership, with Font to take observations of latitude. Believing that Garcés would like to have a part in it, Bucarely had already asked the Father Superior at Querétaro to allow Garcés to go. Bucarely desired him to go only to the junction of the Colorado and Gila, and there to await Anza's return. In the meantime he could explore that region, treat with the neighboring tribes, and find out their disposition for the catechism and vassalage to the king. He reminded Garcés that this would be an important service, because it might be the basis of future measures.[2]

Bucarely had written to Governor Crespo on September 21, 1774, asking his opinion with regard to the proposed Anza expedition. Crespo's reply, December 15, 1774, reached Mexico after the expedition had been authorized, and proved to have a more direct relation to the projects now being considered; the influence of Garcés' ideas is apparent throughout the letter. Crespo regarded himself as qualified to speak with some degree of authority, because he had made an exploration of the Gila River in the vicinity of its junction with the San Pedro, and had talked with Garcés. Such an expedition as Anza's was necessary to accomplish an extension of the faith, and for that pur-

[1] Bancroft, *Ariz. & New Mex.*, 390–91.   [2] A.G.P., *Historia*, v. 52.

pose he would place missions, not only at San Francisco, but also among the docile natives of the Colorado and Gila. This likewise would insure the route, would aid in supplying the Californias (for these regions were adapted to agriculture and stock-raising), would serve as a check against the Apaches, partially through the aid of the Indians of the two rivers, and would facilitate a passage to New Mexico and the reduction of Moqui. Coming more directly to the expedition, Crespo was inclined to disparage many of its projects. The presidio at San Francisco ought to be delayed until it could be learned where the best site for it would be, bearing in mind the possible establishing of communications with the east [New Mexico]. Much of the route discovered by Anza was a stretch of sand, impassable for large parties, because of the scarcity of water, and there was a like scarcity between Caborca and the Yuma country, on which account the expedition ought to go by way of the Gila River, cross the Colorado in the land of the Jalchedunes above the junction of the rivers, and from there take a direct route to Monterey. The passage of the Colorado might present some difficulty, but the rest of the march ought to be easy. The mountains were a guarantee of the existence of water, and the distance should not be great; Garcés had said that the Jalchedunes were accustomed to trade, through the agency of intervening tribes, with the Indians of the coast, which was four days' journey away. At any rate, it would always be possible to descend the Colorado to the junction, and proceed from there. Unless in case of raids of the Apaches, the proposed route was easy, as far as the Colorado River. The Apache danger could be remedied by establishing three presidios, one of which might be at the Colorado River. There should be two missions among the Pimas Gileños, who were eager for them, besides which their help against the Apaches could be counted upon. Following Anza's expedition the viceroy should await exact reports before taking further action, unless he should decide to establish the missions and presidios just mentioned, in which case, cattle and provisions might be sent there, but not settlers; the latter should wait until it could be ascertained how many would be needed. Although the route to Monterey, thenceforth, would be farther north, a mission might be erected among the Yumas for the sake of harmony. Coming then to the plan which seemed to him the most important of all, the exploration of routes to Moqui and New Mexico, Crespo gave a number of reasons why he thought it feasible. Garcés had obtained information from the Indians which seemed to indicate that Moqui was only about seven days distant from the Gila, and seven more from New Mexico. Further proof of a route to Moqui was that the Jalchedunes had dark woollen blankets of Moqui make. Above all, a Pima Gileño, captured by the Apaches three or four years before, had said that he was taken in five days to a place where he saw a religious say mass, and where there were Indians with Moqui blankets. He escaped, and got back to his tribe after seven days, travelling only by night. He must have been in New Mexico, thought Crespo. An expedition to New Mexico ought, therefore, to be attempted. In conclusion, Crespo remarked that he contemplated a different commander for this expedition, for extended explorations would be necessary, requiring an officer of particularly good qualifications and conspicuous talents. With an attempt at modesty, Crespo then offered his own services.[3] As immediately affecting the Anza expedition, Crespo's plans had no chance of adoption, even had they been received before that expedition was authorized. They involved considerable expense and delay in the Alta California settlements, which were at this time Bucarely's chief concern. Crespo, in Sonora, where foreign aggression was inconceivable, could not grasp the importance of founding San Francisco. In spite of Crespo's cool conceit, however, Bucarely gave his plans serious consideration, for in many respects they accorded with Bucarely's policy of northwestward advance. Crespo's projects found support, as might have been expected, from Garcés. The latte

[3] A.G.P., *Historia*, v. 25.

was on his way to Mexico to report in person to Bucarely, when he received a letter from the Father Superior of the college at Querétaro, informing him of the decision for the new Anza expedition, and the part that he was to play in it. Being at the time at the mission of Ures, Garcés got Father Díaz, who had accompanied him in the expedition of the previous year, to write a statement, March 21, 1775, of Garcés' opinions on the needs of the frontier. Díaz added that he too agreed with the recommendations of Garcés.

The new Anza expedition would serve a good purpose, they said, but they did not think that Anza, embarrassed as he would be by conducting families, could hope to make any new explorations. Yet, explorations were necessary, as the present route to Alta California had many difficulties, especially from lack of water. There ought, therefore, to be a separate expedition, designed to explore a new route to Alta California, and not only that, but also a route to New Mexico. If decided upon, it would be advisable to intrust its execution to Governor Crespo, who was well fitted for an undertaking of this nature. As to Bucarely's suggestion that Garcés explore the Colorado River with a view to founding missions there, Garcés was in full accord with the plan, but it was even more desirable to found them on the Gila, for the following reasons: the great desire of the Pimas Gileños for missions, as evidenced by their repeated petitions for missionaries; the aid which they had given in the past against the Apaches; their intelligence, in which respect they were in advance of the other Indians of that region; their ability to assure communication with both Monterey and New Mexico, better than the Yumas could; and the great fertility of their lands. The only objection would be the increased expense necessitated by some additional troops for the new foundations. That led the two Fathers to make a suggestion which if adopted would aid the provinces, and not greatly increase expense. The presidios as then arranged were not able to keep out the Apaches, being too far apart. Moreover, there were so many presidios with duties that had nothing to do with fighting the Apaches, that there was scarcely a soldier able to give his attention to punishing them, the time being taken up in guarding the horses of the presidio, escorting presidial property from place to place, and in other like duties.[4] It was possible to aid the proposed missions, without greatly increasing the forces, they said, by a change in the *reglamento* for the location of the presidios. Horcasitas and Buenavista might be suppressed, leaving detachments of ten and fifteen men respectively, as a check against the Pimas of Suaqui and the Seris. Altar might retain fifteen men, to attend to the Pimas Piatos and western Papaguería. San Bernardino, the site proposed for Fronteras in the *reglamento*, was a good location. That might have eighty men for use against the Apaches. Terrenate, ordered to Nutrias, would be better located at Santa Cruz, thirty-five leagues from San Bernardino; that, too, should have eighty men, attending principally to the Apaches. Tubac might be moved to the junction of the San Pedro River and Santa Teresa Creek, twenty leagues from Santa Cruz, rather than to Arivaca, as it was planned to do. That should have ninety men, in order to protect the Gila missions and punish the Apaches. Instead of placing Altar between Caborca and Bisani, as provided in the *reglamento*, it was most important that it be placed about thirty leagues northeast of the junction of the Gila and Colorado, with a garrison of fifty or sixty soldiers, to sustain the projected Colorado missions. These changes would not add greatly to expense. A hundred more soldiers in Sonora might be advisable; but they were needed anyway, if the effronteries of the Apaches were to be checked. The two Fathers mentioned six prominent advantages of their proposal, only one of which need be noticed here, — that it would be most helpful in assuring routes to Monterey and New Mexico. As to the objection that the Marqués de Rubí had studied the situation before suggesting the *reglamento*, times had changed matters, the discovery of a route to Monterey, the

[4] This seems to refer to the presidios as a kind of military ranch, — another indication of the graft from which the frontier provinces suffered.

suppression of the Seris and Pimas Piatos, and the new
missions proposed for the Colorado having presented a
situation, which the *marqués* himself would recognize as
different, if he were present.[5]

Bucarely wrote to Arriaga of the plan at considerable
length, May 27, 1775, saying that although he considered
it well thought out, he had said in reply only that he was
examining it to determine what was best to do. Oconor
was just about to enter Sonora to review the presidios, and
to treat of their changes of site; so Bucarely had sent him
a copy of the memorial with a request for his opinion, not
to be given, however, until after receipt by him of opinions
from Governors Crespo of Sonora and Mendinueta of New
Mexico. Bucarely was especially desirous of Oconor's
opinion as to the expense that it would occasion, saying that
although obliged to avoid superflous expenditure he would
not fail to assent to a necessary amount, once an evil situation demanded correction, until a remedy should be
secured. Until he should hear from Oconor he would do
nothing.[6] Arriaga's approval came in due course, dated
September 6, 1775.[7] Thus it was that the Garcés-Díaz
representation was marked "Suspended until the reports
of Oconor and Mendinueta come."

The writer has not seen memorials of Crespo and Oconor
concerning the Garcés-Díaz plan, but it is certain that
Oconor favored it, and probable that Crespo did, if we may
judge from his memorial already quoted. Oconor's report
recommended transferring the presidios of Horcasitas and
Buenavista to the Colorado and Gila rivers.[8] Mendinueta's opinion was influenced by the explorations and reports of a New Mexican friar, Father Silvestre Vélez de
Escalante. "In June 1775, or possibly 1774, he spent
eight days in the Moqui towns, trying in vain to reach the
Río Grande de Cosninas beyond. In a report to the governor he gave a description of the pueblos . . . and his

[5] A.G.P., *Prov. Int.*, v. 88.
[6] C-2917. [7] C-2984.
[8] Bolton, *Guide*, 102. Additional evidence of Oconor's opinion appears in

a Bucarely letter of March 27, 1776
(C-3180), and in Oconor's memorial
to Teodoro de Croix of July 22, 1777
(C-3606).

ideas of what should be done. He earnestly recommended
. . . that the Moquis should be reduced by force of arms and
a presidio established there. . . . As to the routes, Escalante thought from what he could learn by Indian reports
that the way from Terrenate by the Gila and thence north
to Zuñi would not be very difficult; that the central route
from the Colorado to Moqui would probably be found
impracticable; but that the best of all was one leading
from Monterey eastward in a nearly direct line to Santa
Fé." [9]

Mendinueta's report to Oconor, November 9, 1775,
begins by giving a description of the province of Moqui,
relying on Escalante's account. The Moquis numbered
about 7494 persons, and were prosperous, having good
crops of grain and a number of domestic animals, particularly sheep. Their government was in the hands of a body
of elders, who exercised absolute authority. They were
a peaceful people, engaging somewhat in trade, but they
were opposed to Christianity, and, moreover, were enemies
of the Apaches. They could not be conquered by force
of arms without endangering the Spanish foothold in New
Mexico, for it would also be necessary to fight the Yutas
and Navajós. The only practicable method of conquest
was by sending missionaries with gifts for the chiefs, who
might thus permit the Catholic faith to be taught. There
were evidences of the existence of a route to Sonora. Bernardo Miera, who took part in a campaign of 1747, said that
there was a route by way of the Río de San Francisco [10] to
the Gila. In that campaign the Spaniards from New
Mexico got within three days and a half of Terrenate, according to some Pimas whom they encountered. Marcial
Barrera, commanding an expedition of Zuñis against the
Apaches in 1754, captured a Christian *mestizo*, Manuel
Tomás, by name, who had been taken by the Apaches near
Terrenate, and carried to the place where Barrera came upon
him. Therefore, Sonora was not far away and communi-

[9] Bancroft, *Ariz. & New Mex.*, 260–
61.

[10] Not to be confused with the great
river described as flowing into San
Francisco Bay.

cations were not difficult, provided the Apaches might be pacified, but that was essential.[11]

Meanwhile, the second Anza expedition had started. Contemporaneous with it was another of lesser note, but worthy of record. The leader was José Velázquez, an *alférez* of Baja California. From a Bucarely letter of February 25, 1776, we learn that he was stationed along the northern frontier of the peninsula, and had been described by Neve as an useful officer.[12] An account of the Velázquez expedition appears in a letter written by him, December 8, 1775, to certain missionaries of the peninsula. Neve had ordered him to explore the northern coast of the Gulf, and a valley that had been observed near that coast, whereupon Velázquez left Velicatá on November 17, proceeded through the valley mentioned without encountering any obstacle, not even a small hill, and eventually reached the mouth of the Colorado. The Colorado came flowing through beautiful valleys, he said, so level and pleasing that he thanked God at seeing them. Only on the Sonora coast were there any hills. The lands traversed were suited to mission work, being well wooded, and having many streams of running water, much pasture, and many Indian villages. Seeing that there were only four in his party, some Indians at the mouth of the Colorado had threatened them, but desisted when Velázquez's men put hands to their weapons. The route had been north to east from Velicatá, and west, coming back. Velázquez did not know where he would come out on the return march, but he came upon the Alta California road between Santa Isabel and San Rafael, about sixteen leagues north of the new Dominican mission of Santo Domingo, reaching that mission on November 26.[13] The expedition is mentioned by Bucarely in a letter of March 27, 1776. He referred to Garcés' reports from the Colorado River of the inclination of the natives there to receive the faith, and said that he was also sending news of Velázquez's expedition, because of its immediate connec-

[11] A.G.P., *Historia*, v. 52.
[12] C–3142.
[13] A.G.P., *Historia*, v. 52.

tion with the accounts of Garcés. He then described the journey in almost the same terms that Velázquez had used in the letter just described. Consag in 1746 could not have seen the valley through which Velázquez travelled, said Bucarely, or he would not have described the land as lacking in inhabitants and full of sand-dunes, the contrary being the fact. This expedition proved that missions on the Colorado could be assisted from Baja California, as well as from Sonora, thus assuring, so much the more, the route to Alta California. He was in favor of serious attempts for a thorough occupation of the Californias, mindful also of the discoveries that might afterward be made between New Mexico and Alta California, a matter to which he was devoting much attention. In conclusion, he told of the remarkable progress being made at the new Dominican mission of Rosario de Viñadaco, 172 Indians having been converted since his preceding report.[14] This letter is noteworthy evidence of Bucarely's plans. All it drew from Gálvez, however, was an acknowledgement,[15] not that the new *ministro general* was not interested, but possibly because the affair had by that time fallen within the authority of the *comandante general*, replacing the viceroy.

We may now take up the Anza expedition.[16] The roster of the expedition as it left Tubac is worth quoting, as it bears directly on the objects which were intended to be accomplished :

Lieutenant-Colonel Anza	1
Fathers Font, Garcés, and Eixarch	3
The purveyor, Mariano Vidal	1
Lieutenant José Joaquín Moraga	1
Sergeant Juan Pablo Grijalva	1
Veteran soldiers from the presidios of Sonora	8
Recruits	20
Veterans from Tubac, Anza's escort	10

[14] C–3184.
[15] C–3274.
[16] This, like the first expedition, will be treated in summary fashion as regards events, except so far as they are discussed in the official correspondence. A consideration of the diaries of the expedition appears in an appendix.

Wives of the soldiers [17]   29
Persons of both sexes belonging to families of the said
    thirty soldiers [18]   136
Muleteers   20
Herders of beef-cattle   3
Servants of the Fathers   4
Indian interpreters   3
         Total   240

The vast total of 1050 domestic animals was taken, to
wit:

Mules with provisions, munitions, Anza's equipment,
    and gifts for the Indians   140
Mules carrying private effects of the soldiers . . .   25
Horses, including also some saddle-mules   500
Mares, colts, and asses   30
         Total of horses, mules, etc.   695

Cattle for subsistence en route and for the new settle-
    ments at San Francisco   325
Private cattle . . . .   about 30
         Total of cattle . . . .   [19] 355

Thus, not only was Alta California's population to be
vastly increased, with the element of which it stood most
in need, families of settlers, but its supply of domestic animals was to be nearly doubled. The mules, most of the
horses and cattle, and the very wearing apparel of the settlers were paid for at government expense. Families of

[17] Of the thirty soldiers who were to remain in Alta California, Moraga alone was not accompanied by his wife, for she was ill at Terrenate.

[18] Included in the group of 136 were some families of settlers, comprising, great and small, seventeen persons. This group also included three infants born during the march from Horca-sitas to Tubac. Later, five more children were born, and the wife of one of the soldiers died in childbirth, the day that the expedition left Tubac.

[19] Font, *Tubutama diary.* Anza

states the number of horses as 340, of cattle 302, and does not mention the 60 mares, etc., and private cattle. (Anza, Diary, A.G.P., *Historia,* v. 396.) Font's list was made after the expedition had started, for on October 22, the day before the expedition left Tubac, he writes that he did not set down the numbers of persons and animals of the expedition because he had not ascertained them. (Font, *Ures diary.*) As regards number of persons Font and Anza agree.

settlers, whether soldiers or not, were treated alike, "receiving pay for two years and rations for five. The expense of each family was about eight hundred dollars," [20] high evidence of the importance of the expedition, when we consider the state of the Spanish treasury.

A large part of the expedition had left Horcasitas on September 29, 1775. Anza did not consider himself as under way, however, until he left Tubac, on October 23, on which date he began his diary. The route led north to the Gila, and down that river to its junction with the Colorado, where the expedition arrived on November 28. It was everywhere well received, particularly by the Yumas and their principal chieftain, Salvador Palma. The more important facts of the march are presented in a series of letters to Bucarely by Anza, all dated December 8, at Santa Olaya, to which place Anza had proceeded shortly after arriving at the junction. In one of these letters he said that he had sent forward a party of soldiers before reaching the junction to see if they could find a better route across the Colorado Desert. They had rejoined him at the junction, and reported that they had found no water, and that conditions were not more favorable than those which had been known before. He would take the same route as before, therefore, but in three divisions, because of the scarcity of water. The divisions would march a day apart, uniting again at San Gregorio on the other side of the desert. This was a difficult stretch, and would cause a loss of some animals, for they were already weak from their long journey, and would have to go with almost no food for two days in crossing the desert.[21] In a second letter he said that he had met with delays which might cause him to change his original plan of seeking a direct route to Monterey, and go first to San Gabriel, being forced to this measure by a possible failure of provisions, because he had planned for only a seventy days' march. He might have to push ahead himself, therefore, leaving his sick at

[20] Bancroft, *Cal.*, I, 258. Cf. appendix IV.

[21] A.G.P., *Historia*, v. 396.

San Gabriel.[22]   A third letter explained why he had been delayed, despite the viceroy's order to hurry to Alta California.   It had been due to sickness of the expeditionaries. Usually about one-fourth of the expedition had been sick, and there were always two or three dangerously ill, as was the case at the moment of writing, but only one person, a woman, had died.   The greatest delays had been caused by the birth of children, in which event it was not possible for the mother to ride on horseback for four or five days.[23] The fourth letter related to the Indians.   So great was the docility and good-will of the Yumas, that thanks were due the Almighty.   In endeavors to please the Spaniards Salvador Palma had been and would always be, he thought, the model.   Anza had given to Palma the present which Bucarely had sent to him in the name of the king.   Palma had come out to meet Anza two days before his arrival. He wished Anza to reiterate his former request for missionaries, saying that he and all his people were desirous of being subject to the religion and the government of the Spaniards, and Anza had told him that he might expect the fulfilment of his desires in a very short time.   The fertility of the plains of the Colorado River was more evident at this season than on Anza's first visit, and he had learned that the Yumas numbered a third less than he had formerly estimated them.   The error had been caused by a failure to distinguish between inhabitants and visitors from outside coming to see his party.   The same held true of the Cocomaricopas and the Opas.   On his previous visit Anza had found these and other tribes engaged in a most devastating war, and he had bidden them in the king's name, to cease fighting.   Now they were at peace, and had thanked Anza for it.   The results were astonishing.   Formerly, Anza had been surprised at the barrenness of their river-plain; now it was the contrary that excited his wonder.   Moreover, clothing had become more prominently in evidence than at the time of his former march.[24]   The route from Tubac to the Gila went within three leagues of the

[22] A.G.P., *Historia*, v. 396.   [23] *Ibid*.   [24] *Ibid*.

Casa Grande, the ruin of a palace which the Aztecs were supposed to have occupied during their migration southward. In his fifth letter Anza told of going to explore it, and he enclosed an ichnographical description.[25] In his sixth letter, Anza said that he was leaving Garcés and Eixarch at the rivers, as Bucarely had planned. Palma had said that he would answer for their security while with the Yumas. They had three interpreters and four servants, and Anza enclosed a list showing the provisions and animals he had left with them; the list noted a goodly supply of food, gifts for the Indians, five head of cattle, and thirteen horses.[26]

Commenting on these reports in a letter of March 27, 1776, Bucarely said that he was only waiting to see what progress Garcés might make, and to receive news from Anza on his return, to resolve upon missions in the Colorado-Gila country, under the protection of presidios, for without them no progress would ever be made. With that idea in mind, as also that of facilitating communication later with Moqui and New Mexico, so many times recommended since the year 1702, a proposal of Oconor's to transfer the presidios of Horcasitas and Buenavista to the two rivers had seemed good to him. The Garcés-Díaz plan had been to the same effect, and had also asserted that such establishments would serve as a barrier against the Apaches, a point worthy of attention. Bucarely intended to await Anza's return, however, before taking action.[27]

One other fact worthy of note, not discussed by Anza in his letters, but referred to in the diaries of the expedition, was the problem of crossing the Colorado River, a much more serious matter than it had been with his light expedition of 1774. Font states that the ford by which Anza had crossed the river in 1774 no longer existed, for the current had deepened the river at that place. In spite of the fact that it was then the season when the Colorado was

[25] Ibid. Also C-3044. For the plan, C-3045.
[26] A.G.P., Historia, v. 396.
[27] C-3183. Acknowledged by Gálvez, July 9, 1776. C-3270.

at its lowest, it was impossible to cross the river there.[28]
Anza remarks that he at first planned to get the expedition
across on rafts, but the Indians told him that it would be
impossible, because the water was too cold [for Indians would
have had to swim with the raft to guide it], and, at any rate,
they could not get more than one raft across a day, and
even then there would be danger of its being upset. This
would have occasioned a long delay, and therefore Anza
himself spent the morning of November 29 in search of a
ford. He found one above the junction, where the river
divided into three shallow branches, but at a place impossible of approach on horseback because of the thickness of
the forest. Consequently, Anza had his men clear a way
that afternoon, and on the next day the entire expedition
crossed the river in safety.[29]

Anza left Santa Olaya on December 9, followed by Grijalva on the 10th, and by Moraga on the 11th. The
passage of the desert was successfully accomplished, but
Moraga's division endured great hardships. All were
reunited on December 17 at San Sebastián, whence they
proceeded together to San Gabriel, arriving January 4,
1776. The expedition had suffered greatly from the cold
en route, and had lost about a hundred animals, but no
human life. To have crossed such a stretch of territory,
including the Colorado Desert, with such a large party of
both sexes and all ages, and not to lose a life must indeed
be regarded as a remarkable achievement. The scores of
deaths among those attempting to follow the same route
in the days of the gold rush to California are testimony to
the hardihood and endurance of eighteenth century Spaniards of the frontier.

In fact the expeditionaries may have been in greater
danger than they realized. Garcés is authority that the
high regard in which Anza was held by the Indians was all
that saved his party from being attacked on the march to
San Gabriel. A rebellion had broken out at San Diego,

[28] Font, *Tubutama diary*.   [29] Anza, *Diary*, A.G.P., *Historia*, v. 396.

November 4, 1775, in which several Spaniards were killed. A Quemayá Indian brought word of the San Diego outbreak, said Garcés, who was at the junction of the rivers at the time, and reported that several tribes were already united to fight the Spaniards. They did not interfere with Anza's men, on the ground that they had done no harm, and because they were the Yumas' friends. It was easy to see, remarked Garcés, how important it was to have the tribes of the river friendly to the Spaniards, not only that the latter might go that way to Monterey, but also that the establishments of Alta California might continue to exist. Garcés ascribed the prompt pacification of San Diego to the failure of the Yumas to rise against the Spaniards at the time of the Quemayá's visit, and to the fact that the Quemayá had learned there of the good treatment that the Yumas had experienced at the hands of Anza.[30] This failure of the Yumas to join against the Spaniards is the more noteworthy in that they were kinsmen of the San Diego Indians. Garcés' opinion is even more emphatically stated by him in a letter (undated) to his Father Superior, Diego Ximénez. The letter was written after his return from his wanderings in 1776, and with it he sent, in advance of his diary, a summary of all that he had done, and made suggestions accordingly. The revolt at San Diego was no reason for not founding missions on the Colorado, he said, for there was no doubt that the Colorado Indians in great part caused the failure of that rebellion, and that their attitude prevented the occurrence of any mishap to Anza's expedition.[31] If Garcés' analysis of the situation was a correct one, then by his personality alone, Anza had rendered an inestimable service to Alta California, possibly saving the establishments there from destruction. Anza, however, knew nothing of this at the time, and did not perhaps appreciate the real seriousness of the San Diego revolt. To Rivera, who reached San Gabriel the day before Anza's arrival, the affair was all important. Anza

[30] Garcés (Coues ed.), I, 205-8, 257.   [31] C-3110.
Also C-3001.
    2 A

agreed to take seventeen men and to accompany Rivera to San Diego, for the time being suspending the projects that he had been ordered to accomplish. By January 11, when they reached San Diego, matters seemed to have quieted down.

If Garcés praised Anza's services in relation to the San Diego revolt from the standpoint of his influence upon the Yumas, Bucarely was equally emphatic as to the importance of Anza's presence in Alta California at the time that the uprising occurred. In a letter of March 27, 1776, he reported that Anza had reached San Gabriel without more serious misfortune than the loss of a few head of cattle and some horses. His arrival was indeed providential, for the San Diego Indians had just burned the mission there, and the aid of Anza's forces was just as if it had come from Heaven, changing the face of matters. At about the same time, the supply-ships San Carlos and Príncipe arrived. So the Indians, seeing forces coming from all sides, had become afraid that they were sent to punish them. Rivera had asked for twenty-five more soldiers, and Bucarely had ordered Neve to recruit them in Baja California. Some persons had made accusations against the Colorado River Indians in connection with the uprising, but Bucarely held them to be guiltless. "Of late," he concluded, "necessity makes clear that if those distant lands are to be preserved, a greater number of troops there is indispensable, and in consequence a greater expense from the royal treasure. All my plans are directed to this important end, for I know that it agrees with the plans of the king."[32]   Gálvez's reply, July 8, 1776, directed that Neve change his residence from Baja to Alta California as soon as possible.[33]

In the light of such documents as the memorials of Fages and the officials of the College of San Fernando concerning conditions in Alta California, the San Diego revolt and Anza's part in its suppression, even although he was not obliged to strike a blow, are worthy of special emphasis. Spain's retention of the province hung by a slender thread, and the San Diego affair had nearly snapped it. Its full import can be grasped by a comparison with the Yuma disaster of 1781, an event fraught with great consequences as we shall see. Yet the San Diego revolt was more widely planned, had fewer difficulties to encounter, and because of the distance from New Spain seemed more likely to be permanent in effect, if successful. As for the revolt itself, little need be said. On the night of November 4, 1775, the mission was attacked by hundreds of Indians. There were but eleven men there of Spanish blood, but they defended themselves bravely until morning, when the Indians retired. Two Spaniards were killed, including one of the missionaries, and all were wounded, one of the wounded men dying a few days later. The mission, as already noted, was burned during the attack. At the presidio, several miles away, there were but eleven soldiers at the time, of whom four were sick and two in the stocks. Indian plans to attack the presidio having miscarried, the soldiers fit for duty were able to aid the mission force on learning, next day, of the disaster. Subsequent investigation showed that tribes for miles around were in league against the Spaniards, the uprising being of a national character, out of fear lest the Spaniards should continue to be successful in making conversions, and should, therefore, subject the entire country. There was even some evidence of collusion on the part of the converts with the attacking party.

While at San Diego a quarrel developed between Anza and Rivera, the former wishing to proceed north to found the settlements at San Franiscoc, as ordered, while Rivera was unwilling to coöperate, feeling that the uprising had changed the aspect of affairs. After a stay of about three weeks at San Diego, Anza decided to wait no longer for Rivera, but to proceed with his expedition. On February 9, 1776, he started for San Gabriel, reaching that mission three days later. On the 21st he set out for Monterey, taking with him seventeen soldiers with their families, and six more soldiers of his escort, besides the religious, Font. The others were to follow in a few days under the command of Moraga, who was just then pursuing an Alta California deserter in the direction of the Colorado River. Anza arrived at Monterey on March 10, and Moraga came up soon afterward. While at the nearby mission at Carmelo Anza fell seriously ill, but, while still too sick to walk, insisted on returning to Monterey on horseback to prepare an immediate expedition to San Francisco. On March 23 he set out from Monterey, accompanied by Font, Moraga, eight of his own soldiers and three from Monterey. His exploration of the site of San Francisco, March 27 to 29, proved that everything needed for the new settlements was near at hand, even timber for buildings, which some previous explorers had not been able to find, although in 1770 Rivera had reported finding some. Anza then marched around the bay, and ascended the San Joaquin River a short distance. Thence, he crossed the mountains south of Mt. Diablo, and got back to Monterey on April 8. Shortly afterward, he parted from those whom he had brought to settle in the new country, leaving them at Monterey, and started for Sonora and the City of Mexico to report.

On August 27, 1776, Bucarely wrote that Anza had reached Horcasitas on June 1. His return had been accomplished without mishap, the Yumas according him a fine reception, and Chief Palma, to whom was due the success of Anza's two expeditions and the good-will of Indians of the Colorado toward Spaniards, was coming to Mexico with Anza to get better acquainted with Bucarely. Referring to Anza's explorations in Alta California, Bucarely regretted that the San Francisco settlements had not been made, due to Rivera's belief in the greater importance of the San Diego affair. Anza was not entirely blameless, said Bucarely, and he had written to both Anza and Rivera, telling them that they had acted improperly in not making a beginning of the settlements and fort at San Francisco. Neve's transfer to Alta California came in good time, he thought. He had told Neve that the San Francisco establishments were to receive his principal attention, and he had also written to him how annoyed he was by the dissension between Anza and Rivera, for that had been largely responsible for the bad outcome of Bucarely's measures. He felt that Neve would resolve the situation well, praising that officer highly. He closed saying that there was nothing to worry about, and that his own chief care was to find a way by new explorations for conducting provisions to those establishments, a matter that held precedence in his attention.[34] Bucarely seems here to be contemplating explorations for new routes to Alta California with a view to replacing the supply-ships. The Anza route was not good enough to replace them. This letter would indicate, also, that Bucarely did not know that frontier affairs were soon to be taken from his command. In acknowledging Bucarely's letter Gálvez ordered that Palma be tendered a good reception in Mexico, given presents, and in other ways distinguished.[35]

One incident of Anza's return helps to make clear why a new route to Alta California was desired, the difficulty experienced by Anza in crossing the Colorado River. He had arrived at the junction in June, when the Colorado is high, and although he now had but a small party and few effects it took him two days, June 13 and 14, to effect a passage. He was virtually restricted to crossing at a point where the river ran between hills for about a quarter of a league and was about a hundred yards wide, with a very rapid current and terrible eddies. There were other places of much greater width, where the river divided into branches, but they would have been impossible of passage owing to the vast mudholes and forests through which one had to go in order to reach the river. On the 13th he launched a raft at ten o'clock with part of his men and baggage, guided by twenty-three Yumas, but it was not until half past three that it got across. Another raft was launched, but it failed to reach the other side. The next day, small articles placed in large vases were carried across by the Indians, for the Yumas were expert swimmers.

³⁴ C–3301.   ³⁵ C–3404.

Finally, the rest of the men and the larger effects were put upon two rafts, and under the guidance respectively of thirty and about forty Yumas, made the passage in safety. On one occasion when it appeared that a raft might become submerged, over two hundred Indians threw themselves into the river in order to render aid if it should prove necessary. Commenting on his passage of the Colorado, Anza wrote: "On another occasion I have said that if the peoples who dwell along this great river are attached to us, we will effect its passage without excessive labor, and that if they are not, it will be almost impossible to do so." He went on to say that his present experience confirmed his former remark, for even with the aid of the natives, rendered voluntarily, it had taken him four days to cross the river,[36] and at no time in his journey had he been so fatigued by his efforts. Without Indian aid, it would have taken double the time. The river could not be forded, except from December to the middle of February, and then only by crossing both the Gila and the Colorado. At other times there would be a need of rafts, and the best place to cross would be at the place where he had done so. As to the rest of Anza's account of the return journey, it need only be remarked that he continued to speak well of the Yumas and the fertility of their lands.[37] In fine, if Anza's account of his first expedition was in some degree too highly colored, he had furnished a proper corrective in the account of his second journey. If he overestimated the constancy of Yuma friendship, he made it perfectly clear that a good disposition of the Yumas toward the Spaniards was a prerequisite to using the route that he had discovered. We have already seen that Bucarely understood the difficulties of the Anza route, and appreciated the Indian situation perhaps better than Anza himself.

Bucarely's attention to the Gila-Colorado country continued to be manifest in the correspondence of the latter

[36] On the 12th some preparations were necessary, and on the 15th a raft had to be sent for two soldiers and a boy, who had jumped off, the day before, when the raft seemed about to upset.

[37] Anza, Diary, A.G.P., Historia, v. 396.

part of the year 1776. We have already seen that since early in 1775, on receipt of the Garcés-Díaz plan, he had contemplated a transfer of Horcasitas and Buenavista presidios to the Colorado and Gila, and this project had received Gálvez's approval, February 14, 1776. A Bucarely letter of September 26, 1776, shows that he still viewed that project favorably.[38] On October 27, he wrote that Anza had arrived in Mexico, accompanied by Palma and three other Indians. Palma had asked that a mission and a presidio be established in the Yuma country, and Bucarely was in favor of it, because of the fruitfulness of that land in maize, kidney-beans, and wheat, with which it might assist Alta California, as also because such establishments would mean a reduction to the church of the vast numbers of Indians along the Colorado and Gila.[39] Bucarely's November 26 letter had more to say of Palma's visit. The three Indians with him were a brother and two other relatives. Palma had presented a memorial asking for missions, but seeking even more that he and his companions be baptized before leaving Mexico. Bucarely was favorable, regarding it as important for the extension of religion and the royal domain.[40] Palma's memorial bore date of November 11, being drawn up for him by Anza whose hand is also evident in the events and ideas set forth in the document. It recited the life of Palma, especially his relation to the Anza expeditions and his seven hundred league journey to Mexico. These achievements he offered as evidence of the sincerity of his petition for missions and his desire for baptism.[41] Gálvez's replies to the two Bucarely letters just referred to are worth noting. Answering the first, he wrote, February 10, 1777, ordering that the Yumas be given as many missionaries and presidial troops as might be required.[42] This was expressed in unequivocal terms, and the same words were used in a communication of equal date to Teodoro de Croix, in whose province the execution of the command then lay.[43] Only

38 C-3328.	40 C-3379.	42 C-3474.
39 C-3360.	41 C-3365.	43 C-3475.

four days later, in answer to the November 26 letter, Gálvez authorized the baptism of Palma and his companions, and "in its time" the founding of the missions and presidios asked for.[44] The order to Croix was in much the same terms, except that the settlement of the Colorado-Gila was to occur "in its due time."[45] Thus Gálvez undid the effect of his earlier order. With Bucarely in charge it would have made no difference, but Croix's interpretation of "due time" was apt to, and did, involve too great delay.

In November, 1776, Bucarely learned that San Francisco had been founded. Rivera had flatly refused to help Anza to explore San Francisco or to found the settlements that Bucarely had ordered, but later he changed his mind. While in San Diego he sent an order on May 8, 1776, to Moraga to proceed to San Francisco, and erect a fort. Moraga's force of soldiers and settlers and their families, accompanied by Fathers Palou and Cambón, reached San Francisco on June 27. They passed the first "Fourth of July" unaware how near they had come to selecting a resounding date for their arrival. Meanwhile, the preparation of buildings went on, and on September 17, 1776, a formal ceremony took place to indicate that the presidio of San Francisco had definitely begun its official existence. On October 9 there was another solemn function, this time to signalize the founding of the mission San Francisco de Asís, now more commonly called Mission Dolores. Bucarely had at length achieved one of the great objects for which he had been striving for more than three years. Although he could not have realized it at the time, he had also reached the culminating point in his achievements in behalf of the Californias, for the coming of the settlers and domestic animals with Anza and the successful founding of San Francisco mark the establishment of the Alta California settlements on a permanent basis.

Bucarely's plans, however, contemplated a much more pronounced development of the province, and it is to this part of Bucarely's programme that Garcés' activities of 1776

[44] C–3478.   [45] C–3479.

belong. Bucarely's instructions to Garcés had contemplated only the preparation of the Yuma and surrounding districts for the coming of missionaries, and subjection to the Spanish crown. On January 12, 1776, Garcés wrote to the viceroy from the junction of the rivers about the lower Colorado country. He had just returned from a trip to the mouth of the river, having travelled among various tribes. They received him better than he had expected, and he had even been able to end a war which the Yumas and two other tribes were waging against the Cucapás. All of these peoples were eager for the coming of Spanish missionaries and settlers. Their lands were suitable for every kind of seed, and in the main adapted to the raising of cattle and horses, especially along the river. There were not many sites for villages because of the floods of the Colorado, but there were some table-lands. Garcés expected equal success with the tribes up the Colorado, whom he planned to visit in a short time.[46] A month later, on February 14, Garcés started north. The idea occurred to him of attempting to reach Monterey by the northerly route, as he had wished to do at the time of the first Anza expedition, but he was unable to procure guides. He went instead to San Gabriel, finding guides for this route, which followed the line of the modern Santa Fé Railroad along the Mojave River and through Cajon Pass. He remained at San Gabriel from March 24 to April 9, when he set out in a fresh attempt to reach Monterey by an interior route. This carried him past modern Bakersfield to the vicinity of Tulare Lake, whence he turned back, and headed for the Colorado River at the point where he had left it. Not satisfied with what he had done, he resolved to attempt another of his favorite projects, — to reach Moqui from the Colorado. This he accomplished by July 2. Thence he retraced his steps to the Colorado, and proceeded to his mission of San Javier del Bac, where he arrived on September 17.[47] Thus another of Bucarely's great projects, although without his authorization, had been accomplished. It was

[46] A.G.P., *Historia*, v. 52.   [47] Garcés, *Diary*.

previously known that a route existed from New Mexico to Moqui; Garcés had proved that one might go on from Moqui to the Pacific coast. Bucarely's first information of Garcés' success seems to have come from New Mexico through a letter written from Moqui by Garcés, July 3, 1776, to the religious at Zuñi. He told of his arrival in Moqui, saying that the Moquis had not been pleased to see him; troops, Christian Indians, and gifts would be necessary, if they were to be subjected. He announced that he had found a route which could be used, following the establishment of a presidio on the Colorado, for communication and commerce with Sonora.[48] Bucarely commented on this letter in his communication of December 27, 1776, to Gálvez.[49]

Shortly after his return Garcés gave a general report, in an undated letter to his Father Superior, Diego Ximénez, of the results of his trip. The Pimas Gileños had never risen against Spain, he said, and they had recently asked for missions. Nothing would be more important in the service of God and the king than the founding of one or two establishments on the Gila, a comparatively simple task, too, because there were five villages in a distance of two leagues and a half, so that a few cattle and horses would suffice.[50] Garcés described his journey to Moqui and back, dealing primarily with the character of the Indians along his route.[51] When he got back to the Colorado-Gila junction the Yumas wished to detain him, believing that the missionaries and settlers were on the point of arriving, but he left them and returned by way of the Gila. He recommended missions among the Pápagos, as well as others on the Gila, for a post on the Papaguería route to the Colorado would be of value in case of uprisings of the tribes between Sonora and the rivers. Even without such a line of com-

[48] C-3265.
[49] C-3416.
[50] Garcés seems to have in mind beasts of burden, of which a smaller number would be necessary because of the nearness of the villages to each other.

[51] Moqui he described as the best Indian village that he had seen in New Spain, because of its excellent site, the height of the Indian houses, their doorways (which were accessible only by use of ladders), and the industrious character of the inhabitants.

munications, however, the Colorado settlements could be maintained by sea, being very near San Diego. "I am of the opinion," said Garcés, predicting in part what was later to occur, "that if the matter of missions on the Gila and Colorado is allowed to cool . . . there is danger that all will be lost, and that the Yumas may be the first to enter a league, and by their aid the Apaches can unite with the Pimas." Garcés rejoiced that the Apaches, who had recently sought an alliance with the Pimas, had treacherously killed some of the latter, for an Apache-Pima alliance would mean grave danger to the provinces, whereas Pima hostility to the Apaches would secure the Gila missions, if founded. After referring to the relation of the Yumas to the San Diego revolt in the terms already noted, Garcés added that if establishments were not founded on the Colorado within a few years, the Alta California settlements could not be maintained, even with two hundred more men than were there at the time. Settlers for the Colorado should not be taken from the frontier provinces, however, as these regions lacked a sufficient population. He had thought of recommending missions among the Jalchedunes, Jamajabes, and Yumas, but on second thought had decided for the Yumas, Cajuenches, and Cucapás, believing that if the Yumas were well secured, there would be no trouble with the settlements farther down the river. For the present, he did not recommend the use of routes from the Colorado to New Mexico or San Francisco and Monterey, because to march through tribes where there were no Spanish establishments would be pernicious in its effect, without any advantage whatsoever.[52] A copy of this letter soon reached Bucarely, who forwarded it to Spain with his communication of January 27, 1777. He regarded with favor the project for establishing presidios and missions on the Colorado, for not only did the security of the Alta California establishments, the route thereto, and perhaps the ability to send provisions there from Sonora depend on such establishments being made, but also the natives visited

[52] C–3110.

by Garcés as far as Moqui might be attracted to the faith, in which case it would not be difficult to effect their conquest.[53] Acknowledging this letter, May 3, 1777, Gálvez wrote that Garcés' account had given the king much satisfaction, and he directed Bucarely to extend to Garcés the king's thanks,[54] which the viceroy accordingly did.[55]

A copy of Garcés' diary was sent to Bucarely when completed, and another forwarded direct to Gálvez, April 18, 1777, by Father Ximénez.[56] Both Bucarely[57] and Ximénez[58] sent Gálvez maps covering the second Anza expedition and Garcés' wanderings of 1775-76 in entirety. They touch many phases of the subject-matter of this work, such as the prevailing ideas of geography and the names of places and people mentioned in written accounts.[59] Bucarely also sent a Font map covering the Anza march from Monterey to San Francisco.[60] Perhaps the most valuable part of Garcés' diary is that which contains his reflections, or conclusions. He begins with a list of the tribes he visited, giving in some cases, an estimate of their number, with other remarks concerning them. It need only be stated that the tribes were many, and that the total numbers of those along the Gila and Colorado in the regions that he visited were estimated as respectively 8000 and 16,500. Next, he takes up the question of their relations with one another. We may note that the Yumas were wont to be on good terms with the Jamajabes, Yabipais Tejuas, and Pápagos, and at war with the Cocomaricopas, Pimas Gileños, Jalchedunes, Jequiches, Jalliquamais, and Cajuenches. It would be necessary to rule over the tribes of the Colorado,

[53] C-3465.
[54] C-3540.
[55] Bucarely to Gálvez, Aug. 27, 1777. C-3655.
[56] C-3527.
[57] C-3431.
[58] C-3432.
[59] C-3432 is inserted in the text. A similar map appears in Garcés (Coues ed.), I, frontispiece, apparently a rather crude copy from this or from some other like map. For comparative purposes a Font map of the northwestern portion of the frontier provinces, including Alta California, is also inserted. This is in A.G.I., 95-7-21, and is referred to in Torres Lanzas, II, no. 349, at pp. 27-28.
[60] C-3430. This map is published in Pedro Font, . . . San Francisco Bay and California in 1776; three maps . . . with an explanation by Irving Berdine Richman. Providence, 1911. The other two maps show respectively the route of the entire march by Anza's expedition of 1775-76, and the entrance to the Bay of San Francisco.

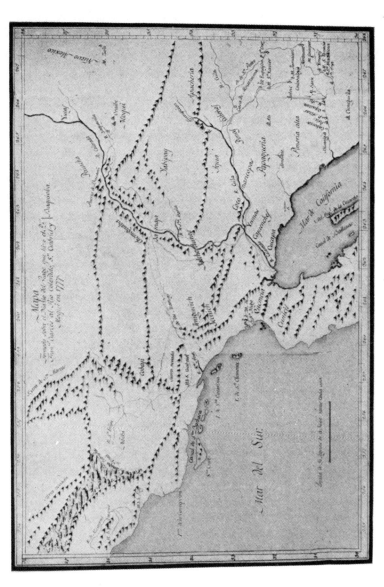

Map of 1777 of Garcés' Travels, 1775–1777.

he said, in order to render permanent the establishments of Alta California; otherwise, if these tribes were hostile and should join those of Alta California, that province could not be maintained, except at great expense. Conversely, anything expended on the conquest of the Colorado would lighten the burden of the Monterey establishments, and although the Indians of the mountains might remain unconquered, they were not a people to be feared, especially since help might be sent in case of need either from the Colorado or from Alta California. An occupation of the Colorado would facilitate conquering the Apaches, who, under existing conditions, were able to take refuge among the Yabipais Tejuas [61] and Chemeguabas. The Indians of the Colorado and Gila were ready to receive the faith, and Garcés named no less than fifteen sites where missions were needed. Supposing the king had already decided on two presidios of fifty men each, one on the Gila and the other on the Colorado, that would provide for four missions. If others were established, they should have an escort of ten soldiers each, and it would be well if the soldiers were married. The Gila presidio should be established some distance north of that river in the region between lands of the Pimas Gileños and the Moquis, for Garcés felt that he had proved that the latter were not far away. Three important advantages would result, besides the defence of the Gila missions: the Apaches would be cut off from their hiding-places in the lands of the Yabipais Tejuas and Moquis, and thus might be the more easily reduced; the presidio might serve as a base for opening communications with New Mexico by way of Moqui, and for subjecting the insolent Moquis; and finally, it would protect the route to Monterey, and especially a more northerly and better route, Garcés believed, than the one taken by Anza. Somewhat more than the number planned was recommended as the force for this presidio, to wit, fifty cuirassiers, eighty dragoons, and fifty convicts, and if there could be more,

[61] In one place Garcés says that the Yabipais Tejuas are friends of the Apaches; in another that the Yabipais are really Apaches.

so much the better.   In commenting upon a letter of Escalante, apparently written after Escalante's visit of 1775
to Moqui, Garcés said that one ought to be able to go direct
from New Mexico to Monterey or San Francisco, if it were
not for the tule-marshes.   An attempt to find such a route
would be advisable, however, as it might lead to discovering
a great river in the northwest, to which there had been
various references by early writers.   If this river were
found, it might be possible to descend it to the tule-marshes,
and go thence in small boats to San Francisco.   This route
might be used for supplying New Mexico with goods brought
to San Francisco from China, utilizing also the Mississippi
for transportation of goods from Spain.   Proceeding to
the matter of equipping the proposed Colorado River missions and presidio, Garcés was not inclined to favor using
the overland route for that purpose, giving as reason the
great distance from Mexico (over 600 leagues), certain
difficulties of the route itself, the possibility of uprisings
by intermediate tribes, and the expense involved in its use.
He therefore suggested two other routes, one by way of the
Gulf, and the other overland from San Diego, goods to be
sent to that port previously from Mexico.   The latter appealed to Garcés.   In case it were to be used, he said, the
San Diego colony should be under the commandant of the
Colorado River district.   San Diego, being nearer than
Monterey, would then be able to aid the Colorado establishments more promptly in case of need, and the Indians
along the route could be effectively controlled.   Also, the
friction that would almost inevitably arise if the establishments were under separate authority would then be avoided.

Bucarely's remitting letter was dated May 27, 1777.   He
praised Garcés' diary, and even more the reflections with
which he brought it to a close, referring specifically to some
of the suggestions that it contained.   Garcés had also
proved that the journeys of Father Juan de la Asumpción
in 1538, and Coronado in 1540 were not apocryphal, as had
been supposed.   The Indians that Garcés saw wore the
same style of clothing described in the early accounts, and

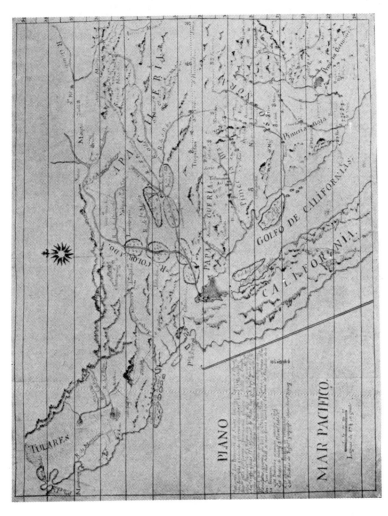

Font's Map of 1778 of the Regions Visited by Garcés.

he saw a town called Quivira with houses two or three stories high. Bucarely agreed with him as to the need for presidios and missions on the Colorado, for they would result in advancing the conquest, and would serve to protect Alta California. As this matter was now in the *comandante general*'s jurisdiction, he had sent Croix the necessary papers concerning it, for on this important matter depended checking the Apaches in that part of Sonora.[62]

One other expedition in line with Bucarely's projects had started before the new government of the frontier went into effect. This was the journey of Fathers Domínguez and Escalante of New Mexico in search of a route to Monterey. On July 29, 1776, the party, consisting of nine persons, left Santa Fé, going northwest rather than west, partially due to a belief that a better route would thereby be found. This took the party to northern Utah, whence it turned southwest in the direction of Monterey. Finding no indications of a route, and no knowledge of one among the natives, it abandoned the attempt and set out, October 11, to return to Santa Fé, arriving there on January 2, 1777. While on their return, November 25, 1776, the two Fathers wrote briefly to Governor Mendinueta of their journey to Moqui, as they called it, describing the country.[63] This letter soon afterward reached Bucarely, and was forwarded by him to Gálvez on February 24, 1777. The Domínguez-Escalante expedition, he said, bore a relation to his project for establishments on the Colorado and Gila, which were, in his opinion, a matter of very great importance, and all the more so now that Salvador Palma and his companions had been baptized.[64]

By this time, however, Teodoro de Croix, the first *comandante general* of the new frontier government, was already in Mexico. In his hands henceforth lay the development of the Californias, the founding of the Colorado-Gila establishments, and the opening of new routes. Bucarely turned these projects over to him with much already done, and the rest at the psychological moment for action.

[62] C-3562.   [63] C-3373.   [64] C-3494.

CHAPTER XVI

BUCARELY'S DIFFICULTIES IN MAINTAINING THE DEPARTMENT OF SAN BLAS, 1775–1777

MUCH has been said in this work about the problem of subsistence in Alta California, and not a little about the difficulties under which Baja California and Sonora labored in that respect. So far, not much attention has been paid to the Department of San Blas, which, with the two provinces just named, was Alta California's source of supply. The problem of supplying Alta California was complicated by the fact that San Blas, its main reliance for goods, effects, and food supplies, was in itself a knotty point in the many cares devolving upon the viceroy in matters of frontier advance. An understanding of these difficulties makes it the more clear to us why overland communication had been desired. With the growth of Alta California these troubles became worse, for San Blas lacked the necessary equipment to attend with ease to the added burden of supply, and it required all of Bucarely's diligence to supply the Californias at all.

Two other matters are also reviewed in this chapter. One deals with the orders sent out from Spain on receipt of news that the English navigator, Cook, was about to make a voyage to the Californias. The other takes up Bucarely's concluding measures in the year 1776 for the development of Alta California. Both are indirectly related to San Blas, as the steps ordered and taken in each case depended on the use of that department, but they are inserted here to round out the story of Bucarely's activities in northwestward advance, prior to considering the action of Croix. At least one measure of importance developed from Bucarely's attention to these matters, — the viceroy's instruction to Governor Neve, which was to be the actual basis for the administration of Alta California under the regime of Croix.

It had been intended to follow up the 1775 voyages of exploration to the far northwest with others, but even before the return of Heceta and Bodega it was clear that difficulties would be encountered. The Department of San Blas had exhausted its funds and had been obliged to borrow 7976 *pesos* because of the expense involved in fitting out the 1775 voyages. Bucarely more than made up the deficiency by remitting 20,000 *pesos* chargeable to explorations.[1] A more serious difficulty arose when the port of San Blas began to fill in. Bucarely referred to this in a letter to Arriaga of June 26, 1775, saying that the department might have to be moved to another port.[2] On August 27, he wrote two letters to Arriaga on this subject. In one, he said that he had directed Miguel de Corral, a lieutenant colonel of engineers, to make soundings at San Blas and other ports in the vicinity.[3] In the other, he implied that a better port than San Blas would be necessary, if Russian establishments were found in the northwest.[4] On July 27, 1776, we find Bucarely writing to Gálvez of measures that had been taken in view of the filling in of the port of San Blas. The nearby ports of Chacala and Matanchel had been explored, and there was something to be said in favor of moving the department to one or the other. Barring urgent necessity, however, no such course should be taken, he said, for, if the voyages of discovery to the northwest were to be continued, either San Francisco in Alta California, or Trinidad, Guatemala, would be a better site for a marine department.[5] Gálvez's reply of January 9, 1777, gave orders to continue the department at San

[1] Bucarely to Arriaga, May 27, 1775.   C–2923.
[2] C–2934.
[3] C–2975.
[4] C–2979.
[5] C–3288. Trinidad was suggested, it would seem, because more accessible by land from the Atlantic coast than was San Blas. For the same reason Bucarely had thought of making use of the Tehuantepec route, explored by Crame, to transport effects for Alta California. Bucarely to Arriaga, Mar. 27, 1774, C–2597.

2 B

Blas until its port should become wholly useless, and then to move it temporarily to Acapulco. Ultimately, it might be established in some good port of Alta California.[6] None of these plans for a change of site matured, however.

One of the greatest difficulties that the department had to encounter arose from a lack of enough boats with which to carry on its duties, despite the fact that there were five boats in the department in 1776. Several factors arose in that year to complicate this problem. One of these resulted from the development of Alta California, which made it necessary to send more supplies. The *San Carlos* and *Príncipe* had sailed on March 10, wrote Bucarely, on the 27th, fully laden with provisions, and yet it had, not been possible to avoid leaving behind some of the supplies needed at the missions and presidios. There was need for another boat.[7] The problem was accentuated by the receipt of orders for fresh voyages of discovery to the northwest, to be made in the year 1777.[8] In reply, August 27, 1776, Bucarely stated that such a voyage would be impossible before December, 1777, for the *Santiago* was the only serviceable boat then at San Blas, the *San Carlos*, *Príncipe*, *Concepción*, and *Sonora* being absent on provision voyages, the two former to Alta, and the two latter to Baja California. Moreover, a boat was necessary for Areche, the viceroy's *fiscal*, who had been appointed *visitador* to Peru, and Alta California had developed to such an extent that the *Santiago* was needed as an additional supply-ship. The two boats then in use had been obliged to leave behind many effects for which the missionaries were clamoring. Heceta and Bodega were eager to make the new expedition, but the first thing to do was to hold what had already been occupied.[9] A month later, Bucarely again referred to the uncertain status of the proposed voyages for 1777. He had arranged for calling a *junta* at San Blas to determine what boats were to be used for supplying Alta California and carrying Areche to Lima. He suggested that

[6] C–3457.
[7] C–3185.
[8] Gálvez to Bucarely, May 20, 1776. C–3223.
[9] C–3299.

two new frigates be built at Guayaquil.[10] The *junta* concluded that the voyages of exploration should be postponed for a year. At least two boats were needed on such voyages, it held, but it was impossible to procure them, because of the necessity of getting Areche to Lima and supplies to Alta California.[11] The boat situation did not improve. On November 26, Bucarely wrote that the *Príncipe* had just returned to San Blas. It had sailed from there in March, taking seventy days to reach Monterey. The *San Carlos* had sailed at the same time, requiring ninety-one days for the same voyage, and had not yet returned. Bucarely had hoped to send the *Príncipe* again, early in 1777, but as it was in need of repairs there was nothing to do but to wait for the *San Carlos*. Quirós had planned to take it to San Francisco with provisions, and this additional voyage might account for its delay. Its absence was unfortunate, however, because it was necessary to reckon on the *San Carlos* in deciding what steps could be taken.[12]

Bucarely prepared to follow the advice of the *junta*. On December 7, 1776, he gave orders to Arteaga, then head of the Department of San Blas, to take command of the *Santiago*, in which he had decided to send Areche to Peru,[13] and on the same day he gave instructions to Heceta, who was to succeed Arteaga at San Blas, in accord with the decision of the *junta*.[14] It was decided that a naval officer should go to Peru in order to solicit a frigate there for use in northwest explorations, Bodega being selected as the one to go, and measures were devised for hastening supplies to Alta California, for reports had come that the province did not have as much as it required. Bucarely purposed to send them first to San Francisco, for it was a new settlement, lacking in resources, and there were more soldiers and settlers at that port than elsewhere. He had feared, however, that he would be unable to send all of the supplies that Alta California needed, when the situation was changed

[10] Bucarely to Gálvez, Sept. 26, 1776. C-3331.
[11] C-3311. This was enclosed in a letter of November 23, 1776, by Ignacio de Arteaga to Gálvez. C-3370.
[12] C-3380.
[13] C-3390.
[14] C-3389.

by the chance arrival of a merchant ship at Acapulco, the *Fenix*, which had come from Guayaquil with a cargo of cacao. Writing of this event, December 27, Bucarely said that Areche could go to Peru in the *Fenix*, and the *Santiago* could be employed in carrying provisions to Alta California, enabling that province, he hoped, to receive a sufficient quantity. An extra frigate was still needed, however, and Bodega was to go to Peru to seek one. Only one more might now be required, instead of two, and it would still be possible to make the explorations of 1778, and to supply Alta California. If the *Santiago* and the *Príncipe* could not carry enough supplies, Bucarely would also send the *San Carlos*, thus enabling Alta California to be less embarrassed in 1778, while the voyages of exploration were being carried on. At all events, it was more important to supply that province than to make the explorations, for, otherwise, all gains thus far made might be lost.[15]

Bucarely's letters about the projected voyages were approved by Gálvez. A specific approval was given, December 24, 1776, to Bucarely's suggestion that two boats be built in Peru for use in New Spain,[16] and, the same day, orders were directed to the viceroy of Peru to construct promptly at Guayaquil two good frigates for use in northwest explorations.[17] On March 19, 1777, Gálvez approved Bucarely's letter of the preceding December,[18] and sent orders to the viceroy of Peru that only one frigate for Bucarely needed to be built, if Bodega should succeed in purchasing another.[19] Not to pursue this matter further it may be said that one boat was procured in Peru, and another built at San Blas, and the two left San Blas for the northwest coast in February, 1779.

It may be wondered why both ships were not built at San Blas. One reason was the inability of the department to procure the ordinary manufactured articles of which it stood in need, such as iron, tools, artillery, canvas, and tackle. In a letter of August 27, 1775, Bucarely asked of

15 C–3413.   17 C–3402.
16 C–3401.   18 C–3521.   19 C–3522.

Arriaga that a supply of iron and tools be shipped from
Spain to Vera Cruz for use at San Blas. He had already
asked for a supply of the other effects from Havana, he
said.[20] In a letter of September 26 he asked for 2500 binding plates (*planchuelas*) for use in making water-barrels for
the San Blas ships.[21] Grimaldi, acting for Arriaga, who was
ill, gave orders that the iron and other effects from Spain
be assembled at Cádiz for shipment to Vera Cruz,[22] and
that the materials sought from Havana be shipped from
there as soon as possible.[23] On the same day, December
22, 1775, he wrote to Bucarely reciting what he had done.[24]
There was a comparatively prompt response to the orders
as regards the effects sought in Spain. On April 9, 1776,
Ruiz informed Gálvez that they had been sent to Vera
Cruz.[25] The articles sought in Havana, however, were
not forthcoming. On October 21, 1776, Bonet the naval
commander at Havana, wrote to Castejón, of the ministry
of marine in Spain, that it was in the interests of the service
that the effects desired for San Blas be procured in Peru
rather than at Havana.[26] Castejón addressed Gálvez
about the matter on December 31,[27] and the latter wrote
to Bucarely[28] and to the viceroy of Peru[29] on January 4,
1777, to see if they might arrange as Bonet had suggested.
Bucarely replied, April 26, 1777, that he had written to the
viceroy of Peru, remarking also that it would be less expensive if the goods could be procured in that viceroyalty.[30]
Nearly two years had passed since he first asked for them,
and they seemed to be no nearer arrival than ever.

Not only effects but also men were lacking at San Blas.
A letter from two officers of San Blas, Diego Choquet de la
Isla and Juan de la Bodega y Cuadra, to Andrés Reggio of
Isla de León, Spain, dated February 13, 1775, recited some
of the needs of San Blas in this respect, telling also of the

[20] C-2976. He enclosed a detailed
list of the effects needed. C-2977.
[21] C-2998.
[22] Grimaldi to Felipe Ruiz, Dec. 22,
1775. C-3053.
[23] Grimaldi to Macuriges, Dec. 22,
1775. C-3052.
[24] C-3051.
[25] C-3191.
[26] C-3351.
[27] C-3423.
[28] C-3454.
[29] C-3453.
[30] C-3534.

unhealthfulness of the site and the disorderliness of ships'
crews.[31] The letter was forwarded to Arriaga,[32] who wrote
to Bucarely on November 3, 1775, requiring him to provide
San Blas with a surgeon and a chaplain, neither of which
it had at the time, and to send enough soldiers to compel
the crews to observe a proper respect for authority.[33] In
a letter of February 25, 1776, Bucarely spoke of a need for
carpenters, pilots, and a calker at San Blas.[34] Gálvez
seems to have taken up the matter with Castejón, for the
latter wrote to him on June 14 that two pilots, two carpenters, and one calker would be supplied for use at San
Blas.[35] Francisco Manxón of the Casa de Contratación
wrote to Gálvez from Cádiz on July 5 that he was awaiting
orders to send the calker and the carpenters, but that the
two pilots had not yet appeared.[36] Gálvez replied, July 12,
that these men and the pilots should be sent at government
expense on the first boat from Cádiz,[37] and on the same day
he wrote to Bucarely of the orders that he had given.[38]

It had been contemplated that the boats for the department should be built in the shipyard of San Blas itself.
However, if there were to be boats, there had to be men
who knew how to build them. Bucarely wrote to Gálvez,
on November 26, 1776, that a ship-builder, boatswain, and
other shipyard employes were needed at San Blas. He was
seeking a builder in Havana, but wanted one from Spain if
he could not get one in Cuba.[39] On December 27, he wrote
that Goya of San Blas had asked for eighty sailors, two
boatswains, twelve shipyard employes, four phlebotomists,
two light-tenders (*faroleros*), and two armorers. Bucarely
had ordered fifty sailors, a boatswain, and twelve shipyard
employes sent there, and had told Goya to try in future to
recruit men from the neighborhood.[40] By February 24,
1777, he was able to inform Gálvez that he had procured
twelve shipyard employes in Vera Cruz.[41] Bonet was un-

[31] C–2846.
[32] Reggio to Arriaga, Sept. 26, 1775.
C–3000.
[33] C–3026.
[34] C–3143.
[35] C–3252.
[36] C–3267.
[37] C–3275.
[38] C–3276.
[39] C–3382.
[40] C–3418.
[41] C–3496.

able to find a ship-builder in Havana,[42] but Gálvez wrote
to Bucarely on February 15 that one would be supplied.[43]
He took the matter up with Castejón, who replied on April
20 that José Chenard had been designated for the position,[44]
and Gálvez sent a letter next day to Bucarely to that effect.[45]
Bucarely wrote at length, May 27, 1777, reiterating the
need for a ship-builder,[46] for it was not until July that he
learned of the appointment of Chenard.[47] The latter did
not go to Mexico, however. On October 22, Castejón informed Gálvez that Chenard was unable to go, and asked
if there was still a need for a ship-builder at San Blas.[48]
Gálvez replied on October 27 that the king desired such a
man to be sent,[49] whereupon Castejón notified Gálvez on
November 22 that Francisco Segurola had been appointed
in place of Chenard.[50] Gálvez sent word to Bucarely to that
effect the following day,[51] giving orders at the same time to
one Francisco Rábago of Coruña to send Segurola by the
next boat.[52] This arrangement did not please Segurola,
who wrote to Gálvez on the 30th that his precipitate departure would compel him to leave his family destitute.[53]
Segurola's wishes seem not to have been considered, however, for we find a petition of Antonio de la Cuesta, dated
December 13, 1777, asking that Segurola's son Ramón be
allowed to take the next boat to Havana, in order to join
his father there,[54] a request which was granted through
Gálvez's letter of the 23d to Rábago.[55]

The above review is enough to give an idea of the difficulties experienced by the Department of San Blas. Bucarely did all that he could to repair the deficiencies, but
delays were unavoidable, for the men or commodities wanted
were not always at hand or readily assembled. Despite
these handicaps he had been able to sustain and develop
the Californias, and to carry on the exploring voyages to
the northwest coasts.

[42] Bonet to Gálvez, Jan 31, 1777.
C-3470.
[43] C-3481.   [44] C-3529.
[45] C-3530.   [46] C-3565.
[47] Bucarely to Gálvez, July 27, 1777.
C-3626.

[48] C-3676.
[49] C-3678.
[50] C-3687.
[51] C-3688.
[52] C-3689.   [53] C-3693.
[54] C-3697.   [55] C-3712.

At this place we may refer to a new factor in northwestward exploration caused by the news of an English voyage to the Pacific under Captain Cook. An exceedingly important letter of Bucarely's, June 26, 1776, sets forth the situation. It begins by quoting in full the royal order of March 23, apprising the viceroy of this matter. The king had certain information from London, said the royal order, that two frigates, the *Resolution* and *Discovery*, were being equipped for a voyage to the Pacific under Captain Cook, ostensibly for the purpose of restoring to the island of Tahiti in the south Pacific an Indian whom Cook had taken from there on a previous voyage. The real objects seemed to be for Cook to go over the route of the next Spanish fleet, to explore the Ladrones Islands, going on from there to the Californias with a view to establishing commerce with New Mexico, and to attempt to discover the famous northwest passage in order to gain the reward offered by the House of Commons. Although such a variety of objects might cause a doubt of the authenticity of the information, it was necessary, nevertheless, to exercise the greatest vigilance, lest the English should try any one of these projects. They had not lost hope of finding a passage, despite their repeated failures in attempts from the Atlantic side. The viceroy was ordered to take precautions requiring the officers in the Californias to be on the watch, and to bring about a failure of these projects, if possible, but without employing force. The English ships were to be checked by furnishing them sparingly with supplies, or in some other like way. Moreover, if either boat should come to the Californias, the officials there were to make inquiries to learn their objects and the instructions which they bore, practising all the formalities required by law in such cases, giving notice thereof to the viceroy, who would in turn advise the king.

In reply, Bucarely referred to an account of the voyages of Biron, Carteret, Wallis, and Cook, printed at Paris in 1774. There was nothing in that work about the coasts of New Spain, or concerning the recent Spanish explorations up to

58°. Nevertheless, it was clear that the English interest in discoveries was constant, and that the idea of finding a northwest passage had never been lost sight of by the English. The Bodega and Heceta explorations, which had been very carefully executed, made it appear improbable that such a passage would be found. Furthermore, Anson's voyage around Cape Horn and north to Acapulco was evidence of the difficulties to be encountered in a voyage to the Pacific coast of New Spain, even with a knowledge of the places in which Anson contrived to refit. Even if Cook could keep his ship in repair, he would be far from likely to succeed in his search for a passage; Spanish sailors had objected to transferring the Department of San Blas to Acapulco, because it was so far from Alta California, making it hard to send supplies there, and impossible to advance the work of exploration, but it was much more difficult in the case of Cook. Gálvez knew what great efforts had been necessary in dealing with the problems of the northwest coast, both before and after the expeditions which occupied Alta California, at the cost too of considerable expenditure. Bucarely then referred to no less than forty-seven of his despatches to the *ministro general*, showing the multitude of measures that he had taken to prevent possible Russian encroachments. It was for that reason that he had caused two expeditions to go from Sonora and one from Baja California to Alta California, brought about an exploration of the Isthmus of Tehuantepec, and despatched repeated expeditions by sea, all of these measures being intended to develop Alta California to the point which it had now reached.[56] Those letters would show what he thought, he

[56] The following are the serial numbers of the forty seven letters mentioned by Bucarely, followed in parenthesis by my *Catalogue* number, in cases where they have been used in this work. Of letters sent *vía reservada*, that is, to say, those about which there was more than ordinary secrecy as concerned who should handle them, there were the following: 1048 (C–2337); 1086 (C–2365); 1104 (C–2397); 1182 (C–2430); 1224 (C–2464);

1258 (C–2520); 1259 (C–2521); 1280 (C–2551); 1353 (C–2597); 1364 (C–2608); 1608 (C–2763) : 1639 (C–2780); 1640 (C–2781); 1641 (C–2783); 2031 (C–3032); 2032 (C–3033); 2033 (C–3034); 2034 (C–3035); 2073 (C–3057); 2074 (C–3058).
Others sent in the ordinary course were: 738 (C–2152); 1097 (C–2388); 1279 (C–2550); 1365; 1389 (C–2624); 1489 (C–2706); 1519 (C–2719);

said. His measures had been successful, and now that the coast had been explored as far north as 58°, there was very slight cause for fear. There would now be time to develop Alta California, so that it might sustain itself and furnish supplies to such more northerly settlements as might be established in future, as for example at the port of Trinidad, of which Heceta took possession.

Referring to the reports early in 1773 of a projected voyage by the Englishman Bings to the North Pole with a view to reaching the Californias, Bucarely said that such a voyage seemed to him less difficult than the one which Cook was undertaking. Cook was destined to suffer many disappointments, for even if he should reach Monterey and form a settlement (and in fact he could not sustain one if he did), the project of establishing commercial relations with New Mexico was fantastical. Bucarely had encountered great difficulties in his attempts to open communication from New Mexico, and had labored not a little to become acquainted with the intermediate lands, and to arrange that Monterey might count on assistance from New Mexico, Sonora, and San Blas. He was awaiting the return of Anza to treat further of the matter, and might decide to make Anza temporary governor of New Mexico in order to bring about the establishment of communications with Alta California from there.

Between the instructions of Bucarely for the treatment of boats arriving at the Spanish settlements and those given by Gálvez for observance with Cook, there was a wide divergence, said Bucarely. Without a display of force against him, Cook would not show his instructions, but if he himself were powerfully equipped, there was no corresponding strength either in the Spanish settlements or in the boats

1520 (C–2720); 1521 (C–2721); 1539; 1609 (C–2764): 1612 (C–2766); 1642 (C–2785); 1682; 1691; 1718 (C–2857); 1738 (C–2861); 1752 (C–2874); 1753 (C–2875); 1823 (C–2916); 1848; 1856 (C–2935); 1937 (C–2975); 1938 (C–2976); 1939 (C–2978); 1940 (C–2979); 2008 (C–3025). These documents are an exceedingly valuable list of materials bearing on the subject-matter of this work, but they do not include all that Bucarely wrote. For example, no. 1562, Bucarely to Arriaga, Sept. 28, 1774 (C–2732), used in chap. X), is an important letter directly in point. A great number of others, many of which I have used, are also directly or indirectly pertinent.

of San Blas with which to confront him, nor indeed was there a suitable supply of arms. Ship-commanders were at the time under instructions to avoid communication with foreign ships, and steps ought to be taken to apprise them, in case a new rule were to obtain, so that they might know what to do, if obstacles were to be placed in Cook's way, after his passage of Cape Horn. If it were decided to use force, it would be well to find out the strength of Cook's expedition, so as to make proper provision at Acapulco, and do what was possible at San Diego, Monterey, and San Francisco. Meanwhile, Bucarely would limit his measures to a literal obedience of the royal order, giving provisions sparingly, and indeed there would be few to give, and trying in a peaceful way to find out Cook's plans.[57]

At about the same time, to wit, on July 14, 1776, another royal order was directed to the viceroy, informing him that Cook's two ships had left London, and were believed to be bound for the northern coasts of the Californias. Appropriate orders should be given to the governors of coast provinces, especially to the governor of the Californias, to be on the watch for the English boats, and if the latter should approach land, to deny them admittance to Spanish ports. Quoting this order in his reply of October 27, Bucarely said that he had communicated it to the authorities at Acapulco and San Blas and to the governor of the Californias, charging them with exact fulfilment of the order, although he knew how slight a resistance could be opposed in the new settlements, and the port of Acapulco was hardly in a better state.[58]

On receipt of Bucarely's June 26 letter, Gálvez replied with a royal order of October 18, requiring that measures be taken in accord with his directions of March 23. The latter had been given in full knowledge of the weakness of the Californias, but if there should be force enough, owing to the diminished strength of Cook on arrival or for other reasons, proceedings were to be taken to detain, imprison,

---

[57] A.G.P., *Cor. Vir.*, series I, v. 12,   [58] *Ibid.*, no. 2534.
no. 2296.

and try him and his men as the laws directed. Following
the usual custom, Bucarely incorporated this order in his
reply, January 27, 1777, and announced that he would send
orders by the first mail to San Blas and Acapulco, calling
for an exact obedience to the royal mandate. As for the
Californias, he would send the royal order to the *comandante
general*, together with the one of March 23.[59]

This correspondence shows, in the first place, that Bucarely was not greatly alarmed by the news of the Cook
voyage, and secondly, that he saw no way of meeting a
strong expedition with the means at command. Nevertheless, although clearly out of sympathy with Gálvez's
order, he took the necessary preliminary steps to carry it
out, and might have done a great deal more, if the matter
had remained within his jurisdiction. The tone of his
letter of June 26, 1776, is almost identical with that of his
letter of July 27, 1773, three years before, which dealt with
measures as against possible English or Russian aggression.
Bucarely was sceptical then, but we have seen how much he
did, despite his own lack of worry. This time, however,
the matter was out of his hands.

The great significance of the second Anza expedition had
been that it had placed Alta California on a permanent
basis, although it was not at once apparent, nor was it possible to cease altogether to send aid. The situation as regards domestic animals had been greatly helped by Anza's
expedition, but there still seemed to be a need of animals
of the sort to provide for natural increase. In a letter of
August 27, 1776, Bucarely said that the animals sent to Alta
California had been bought in Sonora, and more were being
purchased there at the time for the same purpose, but the
cost of conducting them to Alta California was very great.
He had decided, therefore, to get what he needed from the
peninsula. Neve had written, May 9, 1776, that some animals could be furnished from San José Comondú, Guadalupe, San Ignacio, and San Francisco Borja. Not only

[59] A.G.P., *Cor. Vir.*, series I, v. 13, no. 2702.

were these missions near Alta California, but also they had found it possible to raise domestic animals, wherefore Bucarely thought of sending a number with the twenty-five recruits who were going north in consequence of the San Diego revolt. Neve was to distribute the animals as he saw fit, giving San Francisco the preference, however.[60] Bucarely enclosed a list showing the number and kinds of animals to be taken. They had been selected with a view to the procreation of more in Alta California.[61]

On October 27, Bucarely wrote that he had repeated his orders for Neve to transfer his residence to Monterey.[62] In another letter he told of measures taken to develop both agriculture and stock-raising in Alta California, with a view to providing the Manila galleon with supplies, that boat having been ordered, by a decree of May 16, 1776, to stop, in future, either at Monterey or at San Francisco.[63] A Bucarely letter of November 26 enclosed documents concerning the progress of Alta California, and in particular two letters of Serra, one dated June 27, 1776, about the founding of San Francisco,[64] and the other of October 8 about the work being done on the new mission at San Diego to replace the one destroyed by the Indians.[65] Bucarely complained of Rivera's letters, saying that they contained nothing but confused notices. He had learned, however, that San Diego was again at peace, and that the twenty-five soldiers recruited in Guadalajara and San Blas had arrived there. Serra said that ninety cattle and many provisions and effects had been taken along for the founding of San Francisco. With the San Francisco settlers, the twenty-five recruits just mentioned, and some sailors who had been left by the *Príncipe*, the province might be considered as having advanced and become better guarded,

[60] C–3300. Gálvez approved, C–3455.
[61] C–3070. The animals were as follows: 40 breeding mares; 3 stallions; 17 colts (*caballos orejanos*); 16 mules; 6 asses, 4 of them she-asses; 60 cows for breeding purposes; 4 bulls; 8 rams and he-goats; 60 lambs; and 60 goats. In all there were 274. There ought also to be, according to the writer of the document, 11 more breeding-mares, 1 more stallion, 1 ass, and 3 fillies.
[62] C–3357.
[63] C–3484.
[64] C–3262. The date of this letter is clearly wrong, possibly three months too early.
[65] C–3343.

but it had also made it necessary to send greater amounts of supplies, until such time as the soil should provide enough to free the royal treasury from this costly burden. If Rivera had devoted himself more to developing agriculture, as he had been instructed to do, the province would be much further advanced, and already there would be crops, perhaps, with which to maintain the settlers. Bucarely expected better results from Neve. As to new missions, Serra had convinced him that they were most needed along the Santa Barbara Channel; if some were founded there, it might make possible the establishing of a monthly mail service from Alta California by way of the coast of Sonora.[66]

On December 27, 1776, Bucarely announced the return of the *San Carlos*.[67] It had sailed from San Francisco, and brought news of the rapid progress of the newly founded settlement, but great as its progress had been, wrote Bucarely in another December 27 letter, he was taking no chance of a possible decline. He had ordered the purchasing agent of the Californias to seek a surgeon, a carpenter, a mason, and a smith in Mexico for San Francisco, and he was sending to San Blas by forced marches a quantity of clothing, tools, and other utensils and effects for San Francisco, those for agricultural uses being especially abundant. He was also planning new missions in Alta California to facilitate communication with Sonora and San Blas, and to permit, perhaps, of establishing a monthly mail service. Furthermore, cattle were being forwarded from Baja California. Having heard that there was a scarcity of provisions at San Francisco, Bucarely had ordered the *Santiago* to sail direct for that port, without a previous stop at San Diego or Monterey. With this letter he enclosed a copy of the instruction that he had given to Neve. Among other things, he had charged Neve to get on well with the missionaries, of whom he spoke in terms of the highest praise, for to them more than to anybody else he ascribed the preservation of the province, claiming that the governors had not developed the settlements under their command to the

extent that they should have. He expected good results
from Neve, however, because of his good conduct, experience, and moderation.[68]
The instruction to Neve was a document of twenty-seven
paragraphs, dated December 25, 1776, and it contained
orders of a temporary nature, as well as those of permanent
application, a practice that seems to have been general at
that time. [1] Bucarely acknowledged receipt of word from
Neve that he was gathering cattle to take to Alta California. [2] Rivera was then at San Diego being in fear of
another uprising, but his fears were silly, as the land was
at peace. [3] Bucarely announced the good news of the
founding of San Francisco. [4] Neve was to take measures
to restore the mission of San Diego, and to reëstablish a
satisfactory general situation there. [5] Punishment of the
San Diego chiefs was to be suspended, although Neve was
not to trust them, especially those who had rebelled.
[6] Two missions should be established along the Santa Barbara Channel at an early date, for they would serve as stop-
ping places for a mail service, which might be established
from Alta California either to Loreto, or, by way of the Colorado, to Álamos, Sonora, and thence by boat to San Blas.
[7] Neve was to proceed with erecting a mission at San Juan
Capistrano,[69] and there ought to be yet another between
San Gabriel and San Diego, and another at San Francisco
in addition to the one already there. [8] Bucarely praised
the missionaries, especially Serra, and told Neve to maintain proper harmony with him in extending the king's
domain. [9] There should be a mission between San Francisco and Monterey, but not until after the erection of the
others named. Santa Clara[70] and San Juan Capistrano
were to have the preference. [10] Instead of having nothing
to do, as heretofore, Spanish settlers should be given lands,
and encouraged to take up agriculture, for the soil was rich.
[11] Bucarely had sent some plough-shares and other uten-

[68] C–3412.
[69] This had previously been begun,
but had been suspended because of the
San Diego revolt.
[70] This migratory name referred in
this instance to the second San Francisco mission.

sils of husbandry, not only those that had been asked for,
but others besides. [12] Neve was to distribute the utensils and cattle under a condition of ultimate repayment to
the royal treasury. [13] Soldiers were to share in distribution of lands, but they could also have a vegetable patch
in common. [14] Then followed a paragraph about the
salaries of officers and men. [15] Rations were not to be
distributed equally, but according to whether a man were
married and had children, the amounts given being in proportion to the number dependent on him, [16] a method
that had been followed by Anza. [17] Not counting officers
and sergeants, Neve had seventy-five soldiers, including the
twenty-five sent in consequence of the San Diego revolt.
This excess number was to be used in the new missions,
with not less than six soldiers to a mission. [18] Reference
was made to the Rivera instruction, which was to be obeyed
as far as was consistent with later orders. [19] Bucarely
had received petitions from San Diego and San Francisco
for clothing and other effects, and had complied with these
requests. The same amount as was allotted to San Diego
was sent to Monterey, although no petition had been received from there. [20] Because of reports of scarcity, Bucarely had ordered the *Santiago* to San Francisco with goods
that were being sent from Mexico to San Blas by forced
marches, and the *Príncipe* was to follow with effects for San
Diego and Monterey. [21] An image of St. Francis was
being sent for use in the chapel of the fort at San Francisco.
A surgeon, a carpenter, and a smith from Mexico, and
a mason from San Blas were also being sent to San Francisco, both Moraga and Rivera having asked for them.
[22] Church utensils desired for San Francisco would be
forwarded as soon as possible. [23] Then followed a
paragraph concerning the building of houses and a warehouse
at San Francisco. [24] Bucarely doubted whether Hermenegildo Sal was competent to act as storekeeper at San
Francisco, and Neve was to appoint another to replace him.
[25] Bucarely insisted on steps for the economic development of Alta California, and the general measures of the

instruction to Rivera, little observed thus far, were to be put into effect. [26] The only way to win over Indians was by good treatment and gifts, which methods were preferable to more rigorous ones. Care of Indians was the specific work of the religious, and it was the duty of the troops to protect and aid them in this work. [27] As for the missionaries, Bucarely was so well content with the zeal and religious bearing of the Father-President and the other religious that he looked forward to happy results, if Neve should observe the instructions bearing on his relations with them.[71] With this instruction Bucarely's work for Alta California was well-nigh done, except for the matter of the supply-ships, which, fortunately, continued to be under his management.

[71] C-3406.

2 c

CHAPTER XVII

THE INCOMPETENT RULE OF CROIX, 1776–1783

THE year 1776 marks the culminating point in the north-westward movement as an effective force. By that time the northwest coasts had been explored, Alta California had been placed on a permanent although not very strong basis by the success of Anza's second expedition and the founding of San Francisco, the Colorado and Gila region had become well known, a route to Moqui had been dis-covered, Sinaloa had achieved a well-settled state, and Sonora seemed likely soon to do so. Thereafter, the proj-ects undertaken resulted, for the most part, in failure, due principally to the weakness of the Spanish Empire. Great rulers in New Spain had for a time achieved results out of all proportion to their resources, but Spain's need for funds now became so great that the government felt unable to incur more expense in North America on projects of frontier advance. Able rulers might still have accomplished some-thing, but a fatal move was made when Teodoro de Croix was named *comandante general* of a new government of the frontier provinces. To be sure, he not only had to face the problem of economy, but he also had serious Indian wars with the Apaches and others, — wars, however, of the same character that the viceroys had always been obliged to contend with. The task was a great one; but a Bu-carely could have managed it.

The *comandancia general* was established in August, 1776, and went into operation in the following January. Gál-vez's idea in founding the new government was that the northwestward advance should continue, and the importance of the Californias stood forth as almost the principal consideration in the document providing for the new government. But Teodoro de Croix, the first *comandante general*, was incapable of taking a broad view of affairs, never grasping the ideas of Gálvez and Bucarely with regard to the significance of foreign danger and the consequent need for advancing the conquest. Sonora he regarded as the most serious of his problems, but only because of the internal disorder there; its importance as a link in the chain of conquest seems not to have impressed him greatly. Yet, despite his solicitude for Sonora, he kept away from that province until late in 1779. He took little interest in the Californias and the proposed Colorado-Gila establishments, and he never understood their needs or their importance. Fortunately, the former had an able ruler in Felipe de Neve, who was able to accomplish many of the things that had been ordered prior to Croix's accession to power. Moreover, Croix approved anything that Neve actually did. The case of the Colorado-Gila establishments and the matter of routes from them to New Mexico, Sonora, and the Californias did not end so happily. Were it not for the orders given to him, Croix might never have thought of these projects. After a fatal delay, he at length founded weak settlements at the junction of the two rivers. Having little interest in the matter himself, he made economy the keynote of his policy for the new foundations. He himself had other things on his mind, as instanced by his voluminous memorials on the internal affairs of his government; one wonders if, after all, his mind were not primarily on the memorials themselves. The failure of the Colorado establishments was, under the circumstances, inevitable. It came with the Yuma massacre of 1781. On July 17 of that year the Spanish settlements were wiped out, and in January, 1783, a decision was reached to abandon the project of such establishments, and as a consequence, to give up the idea of overland communication with the Californias. Croix was at fault, but claimed falsely that Garcés and Anza had deceived him. Garcés having perished in the massacre, Anza was made the scapegoat. The achievements of Gálvez

and Bucarely, ably supplemented by those of Neve, were
not undone by the disaster, but their work suffered a permanent check. They had placed Alta California on an enduring basis, but it was settled on July 17, 1781, that the
province was not to develop at that time on a large scale.
Thus gold was to remain undiscovered for over half a century,[1] and the Pacific coast to be without sufficient allure-
ment to induce to its conquest by a strong power, until at
length the United States was in a position to be a decisive
factor. Had the Alta California settlements failed, England or Russia, presumably the former, might well have
occupied the territory. That Spain's establishments did
not fail was the work of Bucarely. That they did not become rich and populous was in large measure the fault of
Croix.

We have seen that the project of a separate government
for various portions of the vast kingdom of New Spain,
particularly of the frontier provinces, had long been advocated. Gálvez did not let much time pass, after he became *ministro general*, before he put his ideas on that matter into a royal order, dated August 22, 1776. The plan
itself was not bad ; the only objection that can be made was
to the man selected to carry it out. The entire northern
frontier, including the outlying Californias, New Mexico,
and Texas provinces, was included in the new government.
Arispe, Sonora, was to be the capital, on the ground that
it was midway between Nueva Vizcaya and the Californias,
although far west of the centre of the entire *comandancia
general*. The principal object of the government was to be
the "defence, development, and extension" of the territories comprised in it, but the most important of all (*motivo
principalísimo*) was to achieve the reduction to the faith
and to Spanish rule of the Indians to the north, to which
Croix was directed to devote his first attentions. Frontier
settlements were to be formed and explorations constantly

---

[1] Some gold was found before 1848, but not in sufficient quantity to produce
any marked effect.

undertaken. The preservation, development, and advancement of Alta California were depicted as important in the service of God and the king, wherefore Croix was ordered to visit that province as soon as possible and to secure its communication with Sonora. Moreover, a route was to be opened between Alta California and New Mexico by expeditions proceeding from both Monterey and Santa Fé. More settlers and cattle and whatever else might be needed were to be sent to Alta California from Sinaloa and Sonora to aid in the development and protection of the province. The San Blas supply-ships were also to be retained.[2]

This document shows that Gálvez had much the same ideas as those which Bucarely had been putting into practice, including a tendency to regard the Alta California settlements as extremely important. Whole paragraphs dealt specifically with Alta California, while not a single line referred exclusively to Nueva Vizcaya and the eastern provinces. A good illustration of Gálvez's attitude is shown in the concluding paragraph where he gives specific orders for Alta California officials to report anything of particular note, and then says generally that officials of other parts of the *comandancia general* are to do likewise. Quite as remarkable as Gálvez's interest in Alta California is Croix's lack of it and his failure to obey the instruction promptly or at all. Croix never visited Alta California, and his attention to the Sonora route was limited to the worse than useless attempt which was to provoke the disaster of 1781. Instead of proceeding to the northwest upon arrival, Croix went to Nueva Vizcaya and Texas, and did not reach Sonora until November, 1779. Further evidence that Gálvez had in mind his earlier projects is contained in a royal order of September 24, 1776, to Croix. The latter was ordered to fulfil the arrangements made by Gálvez in 1768–69, save such as time or other eventuality might have rendered undesirable, and in that case Croix was to write secretly to Gálvez of the matter.[3]

---

[2] C–3293. A notice to Bucarely, substantially the same as the preceding, bears the same date, C–3294. [3] C–3323.

Teodoro de Croix was a nephew of the former viceroy, the Marqués de Croix. He was employed by Gálvez, during the latter's residence in New Spain, and seems to have been an efficient subordinate, but that appears to have been the limit of his capacity. Serious-minded and industrious he certainly was, as is attested by the many voluminous, well-ordered reports that he made on the state of the frontier provinces, and also by the very tone of his letters. As a first assistant to somebody else, or even as ruler in a realm where there were no serious difficulties to encounter, he would have been a marked success, but as a leader in the frontier provinces of New Spain he lacked the broad vision to compass the whole range of his duties. While working hard to settle some one problem, he was apt to let the others take care of themselves, or try to have somebody else handle them, certainly as regards matters affecting northwestward advance. In fine, Croix was a hard-working, painstaking, well-meaning, but rather *stupid* man.

He remained in Mexico City from January to August, 1777, getting information about his government, and forming plans. The latter did not agree with those which Bucarely had followed and which in fact were in accord with the ideas of Gálvez. On May 17 Croix asked Oconor for information about the frontier provinces,[4] and the latter replied, July 22, with a long memorial of 245 paragraphs, giving an account of his own work since his appointment as *comandante inspector*, September 10, 1771, and making a number of general recommendations. He began by observing, in no friendly tone, that Croix's plans were opposed in every respect to his own. Among other matters referred to by him, he favored transferring Horcasitas and Buenavista presidios to the Colorado and Gila rivers, and maintaining routes to Alta California, provided the Yumas could be kept friendly. The Apaches he regarded as the only effective hostile force, and he made suggestions how to deal with them which showed that he had grasped the idea of the unity of the frontier. He himself had found the

4 C–3547.

provinces in a disturbed condition, but had left them in good shape for his successor.[5]

However Oconor may have left the provinces, there was certainly plenty to do in them at the time that he wrote his memorial, although perhaps no more than was usually the case. We may confine our attention to Sonora, remembering, however, that the Apache wars continued to be a factor embracing the whole frontier from Sonora to Texas. Late in 1776 the Seris with some Pima allies began again to burn, plunder, and kill, the missions of Pimería Alta being the particular object of their attacks. Writing of this to Bucarely, January 18, 1777, Governor Crespo expressed a fear that Sonora might reach a worse state than in the previous Seri war, for now the Seris might expect an alliance with the Apaches, which formerly they had lacked. Pimería Alta was in danger of destruction.[6] Croix appreciated the danger, he wrote to Gálvez, March 24, 1777, and since Crespo was coming to Mexico, he was sending Anza to put down the insurrection.[7] The Apaches, too, made sudden attacks in their customary manner, and one of them gave rise to a most spectacular incident in the military history of Sonora. On February 6, 1777, while at a place called Tinaja, four or five leagues from his presidio of San Bernardino, with his family, ten soldiers, and a few others, Captain Castillo was attacked by over four hundred Apaches. The battle lasted all day, every one of Castillo's party being wounded, but they at length escaped.[8] Another seat of perennial trouble, the rich mining-camp of Cieneguilla, appears frequently in the correspondence of this period. Tueros' letter to Croix of June 8 gives an idea of the situation. Cieneguilla was in a state of decline, not from any failure of its inexhaustible wealth, but because the miners were fleeing from the danger of Indian attack.[9] Four months later, Tueros wrote to Gálvez that Indian affairs

[5] C-3606.
[6] C-3464.
[7] C-3525.
[8] The account appears in Croix's monthly extract for April, 1777, C-3539, forwarded with a letter of April 26, C-3538. For his courage and skill on this occasion Castillo was made a lieutenant-colonel, C-3638-39.
[9] C-3574.

were getting worse, expressing an opinion that Croix
ought to come in person to punish the Indians as they
deserved.[10] With all this Indian trouble we also encounter
the old difficulty of graft at the expense of the presidial
troops.[11]

Anza had been appointed governor of New Mexico that
he might bring about communication between Santa Fé
and Monterey, but it is typical of Croix that he postponed
Anza's departure for New Mexico, using him instead to
combat the Indians of Sonora. By May 7, 1777, Anza was
at Horcasitas.[12] During nearly a year thereafter he faced
great difficulties and acquitted himself with credit. No
less than forty-one paragraphs of Croix's voluminous
memorial of October 30, 1781, treat of Anza's achievements
as military governor of Sonora down to March, 1778, when
Anza was succeeded by Tueros. Anza found the Seris in
rebellion, and there was a danger that others might rise,
especially the Pimas Altos and the Ópatas. Anza put
down the Seris, and the others kept at peace. He had not
been able to check Apache incursions, but that was excusable, said Croix. The province was in a much better
condition when he left it, but Tueros, his successor, was not
equally successful.[13]

Croix himself waited many months before venturing to
appear in person in the frontier provinces. In a long
letter to Gálvez, August 23, 1777, he sets forth his ideas.
He had at first planned to do nothing until he could visit
the provinces and verify personally the truth of the reports about them, but the Indian situation seemed so bad,
that he had decided to ask Bucarely for two thousand soldiers, making a total force of four thousand troops for the
frontier provinces. Sonora was then in the worst state of
all, and needed fifteen hundred men.[14] Croix had in
fact asked Bucarely for two thousand men, the day before,[15] but they were not granted to him. On October 16

[10] C–3671.
[11] C–3558, 3613, 3705.
[12] Croix to Gálvez, July 26, 1777.
C–3615.
[13] C–4430.
[14] C–3650.
[15] C–3641.

we find Croix asking Bucarely for the means with which to raise a thousand soldiers, at least, and meanwhile for the loan of a company of fusileers.[16] Commenting on this in a letter to Gálvez of November 24, Croix said that he believed that Bucarely would not give him more than two "flying companies," which he had already offered, but he hoped to get at least three such companies, which would serve the purpose until he could complete his tour of the provinces. He certainly was not going to Sonora until he might have enough troops to overcome the evils from which it was suffering. Yet that province was his most important consideration, and partly on that account he was going to Coahuila and Texas first, so that he might stay in Sonora, once arrived there. Meanwhile, Anza, to whom he took occasion to accord high praise, could keep things in hand until reënforcements could come.[17] Croix was doomed to disappointment. Gálvez wrote to him, December 29, 1777, that when he should obtain personal knowledge of the state of the frontier provinces, the king would determine the number of troops required.[18] The decision was not at all surprising. When the addition of from twenty to a hundred soldiers to such important establishments as those of the Californias could be debated, there was small likelihood of Croix's obtaining thousands, which would have enormously increased expense. It is also possible to detect in Croix a tendency to avoid responsibility, as witness his unwillingness to go to Sonora.

On July 31, 1777, Bucarely sent Croix sixteen letters from Rivera, Serra, and Neve which embodied important suggestions concerning Alta California. Croix was at that time on the point of leaving Mexico City for his journey to Texas, and so returned them to Bucarely, asking him to attend to them, although recognizing their importance. This called forth a reply from Bucarely, dated August 27. It was not in the power of either Croix or himself, he reminded the former, to change royal orders at will. Hence, since the Californias were in Croix's jurisdiction, he was

16 C–3673.   17 C–3691.   18 C–3719.

sending back the papers. He went on, however, to give Croix information about the Californias and to tell him what he himself would do, if still in charge. Neve's suggestions should be adopted, even although they involved additional troops and more expense, for these matters, in Bucarely's opinion, should take precedence of others in Croix's jurisdiction. There should be additional missions, too, in both Californias and along the Colorado and Gila rivers, so that there might be no gaps in the chain of communication with Sonora.[19]

Neve wished to erect a fort and three missions along the Santa Barbara Channel, to form settlements on the Santa Ana, San Gabriel, and Guadalupe rivers, and to increase the forces at San Diego, Monterey, and San Francisco. He wanted fifty-seven fully equipped soldiers, to be recruited by Rivera in Sinaloa, their equipment (which would include clothing, horses, and lesser effects) to be paid for by the *Real Caja* of Álamos. Many of the soldiers would be married men, and their families should come too. He also desired sixty families of laborers to be recruited, their numbers to include artisans of various kinds. In making these requests he gave a detailed account of the pay and equipment that should be given to each family, as also an account of things for general use at each settlement, including wages, rations, domestic animals, farming utensils, and weapons. The animals should come from Sonora, he said, and the other effects from Mexico by way of San Blas. In addition, he asked for more animals of a type likely to provide for an increase at the settlements already in existence. The Neve requests are stated in letters by Croix to Anza, Pedro Corbalán, and the *oficiales reales* of Álamos, all dated October 20, 1777, and all alike in phraseology.[20] With each he enclosed a note of the men, animals, and effects asked for by Neve.[21] He asked whether it would be possible to grant Neve's requests, without damage to Sinaloa and Sonora. Corbalán's reply, December 31, 1777, opposed Neve's projects, on the ground that the men and animals were needed

[19] C-3660.　　　　[20] C-3674.　　　　[21] C-3675.

in Sonora.[22] Anza wrote, January 1, 1778, that the men
and cattle should be obtained elsewhere than in Sonora,
but he agreed with Neve's plan.[23] Norberto de Corres,
answering for the Álamos officials, January 15, 1778, said
that Sonora had need of any surplus of men that Sinaloa
might have, but those wanted by Neve could be obtained in
Mexico. The animals could be purchased in Sinaloa and
Sonora.[24]

It was some time before Croix gave this matter any further attention. He had left Mexico in August, 1777, going
by way of Querétaro to Durango, which he reached in
October. From there he proceeded to Coahuila and Texas,
and did not receive the three letters just referred to until
March, 1778, when he arrived at Chihuahua, on his return
from Texas. It was not until September, 1778, that he
took up Neve's proposals again. On the 23d of that month
he wrote to Gálvez, enclosing the correspondence that has
thus far been cited, and exhibiting a degree of petulance and
lack of sympathy with the subject. He complained of
Bucarely's refusal to handle the Californias, and yet he had
not been prompt to authorize on his own responsibility
what Bucarely had suggested. He incorrectly quoted the
three Sonora officers as opposed to Neve's projects, and said
that he had read other documents about the Californias
sent to him from the viceroyalty, with the result that his
confusion had been only redoubled. No steps must be
taken that would take people away from Sonora, he said.
Nevertheless, he had approved Neve's projects, but would
wait until he got to Arispe, Sonora, before attending to them.
The animals and effects could be obtained from Sonora,
and the men from Sinaloa. Meanwhile, he had asked Neve
to make detailed reports of what was needed in the province, to take steps for the formation of a new *reglamento*,
and to send Rivera to meet Croix in Arispe.[25] Gálvez's
reply, April 19, 1779, bade Croix to take careful note of
Rivera's reports, when he should meet him.[26]

[22] C–3723.
[23] C–3741.
[24] C–3743.
[25] C–3880.
[26] C–3974.

Meanwhile, some advance in the affairs of Alta California had occurred, based on the earlier authority granted by Bucarely. In November, 1776, the mission San Juan Capistrano had been founded followed, in January, 1777, by the founding of Santa Clara. Neve was now in Alta California, having reached Monterey in February, 1777. In November of that year, he founded one of the settlements that he had proposed, apparently without any authority except that of his own initiative, San José de Guadalupe (modern San Jose), taking fifteen families from Monterey and San Francisco for this purpose. Neve told Croix about it in a letter of April 15, 1778,[27] and the latter replied, September 3, 1778, giving his approval.[28] Apprised of the matter by a Croix letter of September 23,[29] Gálvez also approved.[30] In another letter of September 23, Croix had forwarded an *estado* showing in detail the state of the missions and presidios of the Californias.[31] Gálvez's reply, March 6, 1779, indicated clearly that he was still of the opinion that the affairs of the Californias were the most important in Croix's jurisdiction. He bade Croix to view them with the preference and attention which, in view of their importance, they deserved.[32]

Although it was not until after his arrival in Sonora in November, 1779, that Croix was ready to give attention to Neve's requests of over two years before, Neve had continued to be busy. Before hearing from Croix on the matter he had begun to prepare a new *reglamento*, basing his action on Arriaga's order to Bucarely of March 21, 1775.[33] In a long report to Croix dated December 29, 1778, he showed what the existing *reglamento* provided, how conditions varied from it in fact, and what they would be if his recommendations were adopted. There was a vast difference between the amount stated as devoted annually to the Californias and the amount actually expended on them. Alta California soldiers were paid only forty per

[27] C–3791.
[28] C–3879.
[29] C–3882.
[30] C–3966.
[31] C–3881.
[32] C–3965. The whole document is given in an appendix.
[33] C–2872.

cent of the amount theoretically allotted to them, and those of Baja California and San Blas received fifty per cent only, paid wholly in clothing, effects, and provisions. Furthermore, goods were charged to them at an advance of a hundred to a hundred and fifty per cent to allow for the costs of carriage.[34] These goods were not sufficient to maintain a soldier in a fitting manner, and yet, the execution of the *reglamento* had been even worse than the law for in some years not even the meagre effects allotted had arrived in entirety. The men were often in deplorable need of both clothing and military equipment, for all necessities had to be brought at royal expense, there being no commerce with the Californias. If the present system of paying wholly in goods were employed, nobody would want to come there. Neve recommended that three-fourths of the pay be in goods and the rest in cash, and that the troops be paid more than at present, at least as much as those of the other frontier provinces. In that case they would be willing to remain, and others would be induced to come. Moreover, goods should be sold at their purchase price in Mexico, in which case salaries might be reduced twenty-five per cent. There was much else in this notable document, but it may suffice to recite Neve's claims that conditions would be bettered, if his plan were adopted, and that a saving of 4706 *pesos* a year would also be effected.[35]

Meanwhile, Croix had written to Neve, September 30, 1778, asking him to draw up a *reglamento*. Neve replied, March 31, 1779, saying that he would do so, making allowance for a new presidio, three missions, and a *pueblo*, to which Croix had consented in accord with Neve's suggestions.[36] By June 1, 1779, Neve's *reglamento* was ready. Interesting and important as it is, we may pass it by here, with the remark that it embodied substantially the suggestions of his December report.[37] In his remitting letter of the same date he stated that in view of the delays incident to the

[34] Thus, an Alta California soldier was supposed to receive but sixteen per cent of what his full salary would have purchased in Mexico.

[35] In C–3917.
[36] In *ibid.*
[37] C–3997. Also in Arrillaga, *Recopilación* for 1828, 121–75.

return of approval he was putting the *reglamento* into effect at once, subject to such changes as Croix might make.[38] Procrastination seems not to have been a Neve trait. On April 23, 1780, Croix wrote to Gálvez that he favored adopting Neve's *reglamento*, but it would depend on certain arrangements to be made with Viceroy Mayorga.[39] This referred to the preparations for the new establishments which Neve had recommended in 1777, Mayorga's coöperation being necessary, since many of the effects had to come from Mexico, as also the funds for administering the province.[40] Croix had written to Mayorga on February 9, 1780, that he proposed to found a presidio and three missions along the Santa Barbara Channel and a *pueblo* on the Porciúncula [Los Angeles],[41] and he had written again on the following day, telling of the help that he needed from the viceroy.[42] Croix reported this matter to Gálvez in a letter of February 23, 1780.[43] The latter returned a rather late approval February 8, 1782,[44] and on the same day wrote to Mayorga that he had approved the new establishments and the Neve *reglamento*, and that Mayorga was to furnish the assistance which Croix had asked for.[45] Mayorga replied, May 23, 1782, that he would furnish such help as should be necessary.[46] Before that late date, even Croix had had time to act, taking some steps with relation to the long-proposed establishments of the Gila and Colorado, for it was by that route that the new settlers for Alta California were destined to go.

Croix's intended policy with regard to settlements on the Colorado and Gila and related matters appears in his discussion of the Domínguez-Escalante expedition. He turned over the diary of that expedition [47] to Father Juan Morfi for an opinion. Morfi's memorial (undated but probably of July, 1777) is worth quoting in some detail. He began by comparing the diary with other accounts from Oñate's

[38] In C–3917.
[39] C–4131. Martín de Mayorga had succeeded Bucarely on the death of the latter in 1779.
[40] C–3293.
[42] C–4097.
[41] C–4095.
[43] C–4103.
[44] C–4492.
[45] C–4493.
[46] C–4633.
[47] For the diary, C–3291. Printed in *Documentos para la historia de México*, 2d series, I, 375–558.

time on. Domínguez and Escalante did not reach San Francisco or Monterey, because they mistook the route, he said; not knowing the situation of Monterey, they imagined it to be northwest, when in fact it was almost due west from Santa Fé, and they would almost certainly have reached there, had they gone in that direction. They merited thanks for their zeal, however, for they had made a journey of over 630 leagues in lands never before visited or known by Spaniards. Such missionary expeditions, made without due reflection, were rarely of great service, because of the impossibility of sending aid to such advanced posts, if they should be occupied. They advanced knowledge very little, for dependence had to be placed on diaries, and second expeditions over the same route had rarely been able to recognize descriptions in diaries of the first. Such expeditions even worked harm, because the missionaries told the Indians of the wealth of the king, and gave promises of Spanish friendship, when they themselves were almost nude and in need of Indian seeds. The Indians could not understand a Spaniard's descriptions of wealthy cities, never having seen any, and when nothing came of the promised gifts and friendship, serious consequences were apt to occur.[48] If the missionaries would confine their zeal for exploration to regions near or between the Spanish settlements, it would be better. For example, if the region between Pimería, the Colorado River, Nueva Vizcaya, and New Mexico had been explored, the Spaniards would at least know the haunts of the Indians and where they got their water, thus enabling war to be waged with some hope of success. The only Indians really hostile to Spain were the Comanches, who gave trouble to New Mexico and the El Paso district, and the various branches of the Apaches, of whom those of the Gila were a menace to Sonora, Nueva Vizcaya, and New Mexico, and the Natajés and Lipanes to Nueva Vizcaya, Coahuila, Nuevo León, and even to Texas. The Seris, Suaquis, Piatos, Pápagos, and Pimas would not

[48] These words might have been used to describe the cause of the Yuma massacre of 1781.

rise, unless the Apaches of the Gila gave them aid or a pretext, nor would the Taraumares, but for the Natajés and Lipanes. These hostile tribes ought, therefore, to be reduced or exterminated, and missionary activities should contribute to that end. This was not the time for new establishments, embarrassing the arms and occupying the attention of the government, just when active and continuous war was to be undertaken, because troops would be needed at such new missions and would have to conduct to the missionaries whatever they required. Money spent for the proposed missions among friendly Indians, such as the Yuma, Cucapá, Jalliquamay, Cajuenche, Jalchedún, Jamajab, Pima Gileño, Cocomaricopa, and Pápago tribes, would be wasted, if on the basis that these peoples give aid in war, for only the old, the children, and the women would remain in the missions, and they would be full of misgiving and little inclined to conversion. Anza had also expressed an opinion, he said, that these establishments would be inopportune, when with a delay of one, two, or at most three years it would be possible to make solid foundations. If Croix should achieve the pacification of North America, the Colorado and Roxo [Red] rivers should be taken as boundaries for the royal dominions, for it would seem from Escalante's map that these two rivers and the Río Grande had their sources within fifteen leagues of each other, and embraced a territory of great fertility. He then described the Colorado and spoke of the little known Roxo, or Colorado of the east, and of his project for settling the country between the boundaries that he had named, with all the lines of colonization centring on Chihuahua. Anza would soon have to go to his province, although his presence in Sonora might be more useful, and could be directed to go there by the northern bank of the Colorado to its junction with the Saguaguanas, which was the nearest point to tribes already annoyed by the establishments of Monterey. There he could meet Escalante, who should be sent there from New Mexico. Anza could then proceed by way of Moqui to New Mexico, taking note of good sites, and paying special attention to the Moqui and Navajó lands, with a view to their conquest, later. Escalante should explore the upper reaches of the Colorado, Roxo, and Río Grande before joining Anza. A shorter route than this between Monterey and Santa Fé might be found, but it would pass through a mountainous country lacking in facilities for its defence, whereas a line of presidios could be built along the Colorado. Although the Comanches were hostile to Spain, their aid might be obtained, because they hated the Apaches, and a man like Anza, skilful in dealing with the Indians, might handle this affair with good effect. Furthermore, granted peace or an alliance with the Comanches, an exploration of the Roxo by some religious would be possible. These plans would require neither troops nor expense. It would be well, too, to send Garcés and another religious to the Yumas, which would probably be enough for the present, since Palma and the warriors would have to join in the general campaign that Croix was planning; thus, few men would be left. Moreover, the two religious might serve to keep the neighboring tribes at peace. If Croix should be successful in his campaign, nothing would hinder the secularization of all of the missions of New Mexico, Nueva Vizcaya, Sonora, Pimería, Chinipas, Taraumara, and Nuevo León, and many of Coahuila and Texas. The native parishioners might then pay tribute to the king and tithes to the church, effecting a saving of 50,000 *pesos* a year, enough to support 166 missionaries at 300 *pesos* a year, and one schoolmaster at 200 *pesos*, besides the positive gain of the tribute and tithes. In conclusion, Morfi referred to the suggestion of Garcés, that the Pacific Ocean and Colorado River be used as a supply-route for the presidios on the one side, and the Atlantic Ocean and Roxo River on the other. Anza might examine the mouth of the Colorado, to see if this were practicable. As for the Roxo, Morfi knew only that it was a large river near its source, and that some Louisiana deserters in New Mexico claimed to have sailed on it.[49]

[49] C–3433.

2 D

The Morfi memorial, brilliant as it was in many respects, represented, nevertheless, the new way of doing things. Whereas Bucarely saw the need for extending the frontier as a measure of defence, and unostentatiously got things done, Croix was given to brilliant plans, which failed, however, to grasp the essential point, and were followed by dèlay of action. In a letter to Gálvez, July 26, 1777, Croix stated that all of Morfi's reflections seemed to him very well founded, and especially the parts concerning Anza's projected journey to New Mexico, the simultaneous explorations of Escalante, the proposed treaty with the Comanches, the exploring of the Roxo, and the sending of Garcés and another to the Colorado. These were, for the present, the best and only measures that could be taken for the success of the proposed Colorado-Gila establishments, for freedom of communication between Sonora, the Californias, and New Mexico, and for reducing the numerous tribes discovered, and punishing the Apaches. These matters were of such import, however, that he would not presume to give orders, without first consulting the viceroy, as also Anza, Mendinueta, Garcés, Domínguez, and Escalante.[50] Truly, the day of action had passed. Even those "best and only" measures of Croix were either not undertaken by him, or so long delayed that no advantage resulted.

Something was attempted eventually toward establishing communications with Sonora from New Mexico. Anza, who had at length been allowed to proceed to his province, although not by way of the Colorado, was in charge of the project. On November 9, 1780, Anza left New Mexico with a force of 151 men, and on December 18 emerged in Nueva Vizcaya, near the Sonora line.[51] Referring to this expedition in one of his long memorials, October 30, 1781, Croix said that the aim had been to come out by the presidio of Santa Cruz, Sonora, whereas Anza had appeared almost in front of Janos. It would therefore be necessary

[50] C–3619.
[51] Croix to Gálvez, March 26, 1781. C–4354. This is the principal document of a considerable file, which among other papers includes diaries of the expedition written by Anza, José de Vildosola, and Francisco Martínez, all in C–4244.

to repeat the expedition.[52]   Nothing further seems to have
been done, however, during Croix's regime.   Nothing was
accomplished as regards the Santa Fé-Monterey route,
despite Gálvez's instructions.   In the above-mentioned
Croix memorial of October 30, 1781, Croix said that the
discovery of such a route remained to be made, and it would
be well also to seek routes to San Antonio de Bejar, Texas,
and to the presidio of the Río Grande, Coahuila.[53]   Croix
does not appear to have considered making use of the Garcés
route to New Mexico, although, to be sure, there were steps
taken at this time with a view to converting the Moquis.

Not only had Gálvez's instruction of August 22, 1776,
called Croix's attention to the importance of founding establishments on the Gila and Colorado, but Gálvez had
repeated the statement in a royal order of February 14,
1777,[54] and Bucarely had turned over to Croix the file of
papers bearing on that project.   Croix decided, charac-
teristically, to postpone action until he should reach Sonora.
Until 1779 the matter was allowed to rest, although Chief
Palma of the Yumas continued to petition for missionaries.
On February 3, 1779, Pedro Tueros of the presidio of Altar,
Sonora, wrote to Croix of Palma's solicitations, and told of
the distinguished treatment which he himself had accorded
the Yuma chief.[55]   Croix, who had already heard of Palma's
renewed petitions, now decided to take action.   On February 5 he wrote to that effect to the *Queretarano* Father-
President, Francisco Barbastro, but said that he could
afford to send only two missionaries, of whom Garcés should
be one.[56]   On the same day he wrote to Garcés[57] and Pedro
Corbalán,[58] to the same effect, as also to Tueros on February 22.[59]   Corbalán replied that he would assist Garcés,[60]
and the other three announced their pleasure at Croix's
decision.[61]   A military escort had been promised to Garcés,
and the details left for Garcés and Tueros to arrange.   In a

[52] C–4430.
[53] *Ibid.*
[54] C–3478–79.
[55] In C–3924.
[56] In C–3925.
[57] In *ibid.*

[58] In C–3926.
[59] In C–3924.
[60] In C–3926.
[61] Tueros' reply is in C–3924; the other two in C–3925.

communication to the latter of March 23 Garcés made a
number of suggestions. His escort should be twelve soldiers, at least, and he named those that he wanted. There
should also be a carpenter. The soldiers should be accompanied by their wives, or everything might be lost.
Provisions for three months and gifts for the Indians should
be carried, the supplies to be furnished from Altar, the
nearest presidio. The soldiers should be instructed not to
hinder conversions, and especially to keep away from
Indian women. Both the soldiers and the settlers should
have domestic animals and crops of their own, and they
should be under the missionaries in everything except in
military affairs. Because of the danger from neighboring
tribes, other settlers from Sonora should be permitted to go
to the Colorado, if they should wish to, and some Nixoras
Indians, then in Sonora, should be taken along as interpreters. The commander at Altar should be ordered to supply
horses to transport the provisions and utensils.[62] Tueros
replied, April 14, granting Garcés' requests, or saying that
he would try to arrange for them, — with two exceptions.
He feared that the Indians might covet the soldiers' wives,
and so would not order that the latter go along, and he left
Croix to decide whether more settlers should be allowed to
go.[63] Both documents he forwarded to Croix in his letter
of April 29.[64]

On May 15 Corbalán wrote that a sum of 2000 *pesos* had
been advanced to Father Díaz, who was to accompany
Garcés, and charged to the *Real Caja* of Álamos.[65] This
sum did not last long. On July 8 Díaz rendered an account
showing that all had been spent, gifts for the Yumas being
prominent in the list, as well as mules and necessary effects.[66]
It was not until August that the tiny force started, and by
reason of the difficulties encountered, only Garcés and two
soldiers pushed on, at the time, for the Colorado. Shortly
after his arrival Garcés wrote to Corbalán, September 2,
that nearly all of his provisions were gone, and that he

[62] In C–3924.
[63] In *ibid.*
[64] In *ibid.*

[65] In C–3926. Approved by Croix
on July 28, in *ibid.*
[66] In C–3926.

needed a supply of gifts for the chiefs. He asked for 300
pesos to be expended for beads, shoes, cloth, and other
things that the Indians liked.[67]   Corbalán forwarded Díaz's
account and Garcés' letter to Croix on September 30.[68]
Croix, meanwhile, had changed his mind about the new
settlements, and seems to have issued an order on May 14
to abandon the idea, but the order reached Sonora too
late.

Conditions at the Colorado River are amply described in
three letters from Garcés to Croix. In the first, September
2, 1779, he announced his arrival, after a journey of some
difficulty through Papaguería. Because of the unusually
light rainfall, Garcés and two soldiers had pushed on alone,
leaving the rest of the party at Sonoita. The Yumas were
much scattered at the time, it being the season for planting,
but Garcés was in hopes that they would come together
soon, so that houses might be built and agricultural lands
made ready for the Spaniards. To avoid taking too much
land from the Yumas he hoped that a mission might be established among the Cajuenches, and that there might also
be missions among the Cucapás, Pimas Gileños, and Pápagos, all of whom were well disposed, although a bit jealous
of the preference shown for the Yumas. With a stronger
escort, missions might also be placed among the Jalchedunes
and Jamajabes. The presidio for their protection might
be postponed for a time, but certain expenditures, such as
those involved in erecting houses, paying interpreters, and
making gifts to the chiefs of the various tribes of the Colorado, were absolutely necessary. Muleteers and carpenters were more necessary than soldiers at present. Palma
was as cordial as ever. He had managed to keep the Yumas
at peace, although with difficulty, for they had wished to
make war, notably against the Jalchedunes.[69]

Garcés' second letter was dated November 6, 1779. Díaz
had arrived on October 2 with the soldiers. Garcés had
learned that the Jalchedunes, Cajuenches, and Cucapás
wanted missions, although from motives of self-interest, be-

[67] In *ibid.*   [68] In *ibid.*   [69] In C–4017.

lieving that they would receive all manner of material wealth
from the Spaniards. The same was true of the Yumas, who
had been spoiled by the good treatment accorded to them
and Chief Palma in the past. When Garcés arrived with so
little in the way of presents, he had found it difficult to get
even a little maize from the Yumas. In fine, the Yumas
were no better than the other Indians of the Colorado, and
it was not going to be so easy to convert them as Palma had
said. Too much reliance should not be placed on Palma
who was only one of many chiefs, and at the head of only
one very small village. Moreover, the chiefs had no real
authority, except in so far as the Indians wished to obey
them. Palma was certainly well disposed and seemed to
exercise much influence in matters of war. Presents were
an essential to success. If Corbalán should grant the 300
pesos that Garcés had asked for, the Indians might be persuaded to build a dwelling and a chapel and with what was
left a muleteer and two interpreters could be maintained.
Artisans were another necessity. The present settlement of
twelve men could not subsist by itself, wherefore there
should be other settlements among the Cajuenches and
Jalchedunes, thus allowing recourse to them in case of need,
for Sonora and Alta California were too far away to render
aid. Moreover, the Colorado-Gila establishment should
be increased, another mission founded, and more settlers
induced to come. In addition, if the soldiers were well
chosen from the standpoint of good character, and if some
financial aid were granted, success might be expected, for
the land was favorable for grazing and agriculture. The
Gila route was preferable to the one through Papaguería,
but its use would necessitate an establishment among the
Pimas Gileños and a military escort for the region between
Tucson and the Gila, because that section was much fre-
quented by the Apaches. The soldiers at the Colorado
should not be changed as Garcés had heard it was proposed
to do. Soldiers would not bring their families unless they
were to remain, and it was essential that they should bring
them, so that the wives could cook for the men and keep

them from such wrong-doing or desertion as had occurred in the case of the soldiers of Monterey.[70]

In his third letter, December 27, 1779, Garcés reported that affairs at the Colorado settlement were in a critical condition, and Díaz was leaving in order to see Croix to explain the situation to him. Corbalán had refused to grant the 300 *pesos* that Garcés had wanted. Garcés had word of Croix's decision to suspend the establishment, and rejoiced that it had not come in time; otherwise, Palma would have been murdered, both because the Yumas would have believed that he had deceived them and because he was hindering their going to war. Indeed, to keep the Indians at peace was a task requiring more ability than Garcés believed himself to have; more funds and more troops would be required.[71]

Arrived at Arispe, Díaz presented his petition to Croix on February 12, 1780. There should be missions among the Cajuenches and Jalchedunes, he said. The latter and the Yumas were bitter enemies, and if war should break out, the Spaniards might be obliged to help the Yumas, in which case the Cocomaricopas, the Pápagos of the north, and the Pimas Gileños would be estranged, for they were friends of the Jalchedunes. War between the Yumas and Cajuenches was also likely to occur. The two proposed missions could prevent these wars. Twenty soldiers should be added to the twelve now at the Colorado, to be under missionary authority as at present. For three years an allowance should be made to each mission for a good interpreter, a carpenter, a mason, a muleteer, and a farm-laborer, the last named to instruct the Indians in cultivating the soil. Each mission should have two religious. A second mission among the Yumas would be of advantage, with an additional ten men, in which case, although even then with difficulty, the Yumas could be made to keep the peace with their neighbors.[72]

Five days later Croix issued a decree providing for two

[70] In C–4017.
[71] In *ibid*. In this letter Garcés notes the arrival of a Monterey
deserter, José Hermenegildo Flores.
[72] In C–4017.

Spanish settlements among the Yumas. There were to be twenty-one soldiers in all, eleven at one settlement, and ten at the other, and thirty-two civilian settlers evenly divided between the two. Among the latter were to be artisans and interpreters for each place. The soldiers were to be married men and were to bring their families. Lands were to be divided among the Spaniards as the laws of the Indies provided, one portion being reserved for usage in common, and another for the benefit of the church. Croix planned for the Yumas to share in the lands, as well as the Spaniards, but was undecided whether they should be given individual plots or a larger area in common. He also doubted whether it was wise for the religious to manage the material wealth (*temporalidades*) of missions; he had intended to put that in charge of the commandant, but, in view of Díaz's objection, suspended his decision. The settlers were to receive pay and such other aid as they needed. Finally, there were to be two religious at each mission.[73]

Díaz was asked to comment on the decree and to add anything he thought necessary. He did so in a document dated February 19, showing that he was in substantial agreement with Croix. He called attention to the fact that the Yumas knew how to plant crops and were accustomed to individual property in land, wherefore those who wished to join the Spanish settlements could be assigned lands at an early date, for they would know how to manage them. He argued for missionary control of the mission wealth, because of the many expenses, incidental to mission work, but it would be even better if an additional fund of 200 *pesos* for these expenses might be granted.[74] On February 29, Croix's *asesor*, Pedro Galindo Navarro, gave his opinion on Díaz's answer. It would be against law and equity to dispossess the Indians of lands actually occupied by them, he said; therefore, matters had best be left as they were, as concerned the division of lands among them, until the Spaniards should become better informed. The importance of having Spanish establishments on the Colorado

[73] In C–4017.   [74] In *ibid.*

had been urged in several royal decrees, wherefore he favored granting the extra 200 *pesos* that Díaz had asked, for it was necessary to treat the Yumas well in order to attract them to the faith, and this expense would conduce to that end. Funds advanced to the settlements should eventually be repaid, on which account it would be well to set aside a portion of land for that purpose in each settlement. Such lands should be managed by a council elected by the soldiers and settlers from among their own numbers.[75] Croix gave orders, March 3, for the decree to be drawn up as modified by the *asesor*'s reports,[76] and this was done, the final decree being dated March 7, 1780.[77]

On April 23, Croix wrote at length to Gálvez, reviewing his action concerning the Colorado-Gila establishments, since taking charge of his government. His plan differed from that of Bucarely, he said, and he proceeded to argue its advantages. The former viceroy had wished to transfer Horcasitas and Buenavista presidios to the Gila and Colorado, and that had in fact been ordered, but it would not be possible to effect the transfer for many years, because of the Apache and Seri wars. The chief advantage of Croix's plan was in its economy. Temporarily, it would cost more than the Bucarely project, but not so much as it would have, if the presidios had been transferred, and their places supplied by others, as would have been necessary. His two colonies at the Colorado would attain the objects that Gálvez had desired. Croix's next task would be the matter of founding a presidio at the junction of the Gila and San Pedro with a view to securing the Gila route to the Californias.[78] With this letter Croix submitted two *estados*, one of which showed that the two settlements would cause an increase in expense of 4704 *pesos* a year,[79] and another showing that his plan would effect a saving of 9174 *pesos*, 6 *reales*, and eventually 13,878 *pesos*, 6 *reales*, over that of Bucarely.[80]

[75] In *ibid.*
[76] In *ibid.*
[77] In *ibid.*
[78] C-4128.
[79] C-4130.
[80] The figures in *pesos* were as follows:
Annual expenses of Horcasitas 18,998-6

Troops of the two villages   5120
Settlers ditto   2400
Twelve servants   2304
The two latter items were expected to cease. These figures did not mention Buenavista presidio.

So much then for the preliminaries of the ill-fated Colorado colonies. In one respect the documents exonerate Croix from charges that were made against him by contemporary writers who have been followed by later historians. The mixed character of his settlements resulting from the close association planned for missionaries, soldiers, settlers, and Indians was not against the wishes of the religious, but resulted primarily from their suggestions. Similarly, Croix had adopted Díaz's recommendation as regarded the mission property. The real criticism of Croix is because of his long delay in approaching the problem, which had resulted in a loss of the moment when the Yumas were most kindly disposed, and his false economy, when once he had decided on the establishments. Perhaps some idea of his attitude may be obtained by considering his long memorials, documents of very great value to historical scholars for conditions in the frontier provinces, which show, however, Croix's neglect of the Colorado-Gila country.

Croix seems to have acquired the taste for writing long memorials in one that he dated January 23, 1780, a document of 194 paragraphs or headings. This was wholly about his military policy, past, present, and future, but did not concern itself with the lands along the route to Alta California. He criticized the location of the line of presidios, and proposed a new line supported by a second line of settlements.[81] Croix now planned a monumental report in five parts, as follows: 1. the individual state of each province; 2. the most notable events during his rule; 3. his measures; 4. their results; 5. measures that should be taken in future. The first part was ready by October 30, 1781, a mighty document of 612 paragraphs, of which the affairs of Sonora formed the major part, and the Californias but little.[82] For the Californias he took Neve's suggestions, and it was well that he did. He showed a complete mis-

[81] C-4082. The copy that I used covered 248 pages of closely written manuscript.
[82] Texas and Coahuila required 120 paragraphs; New Mexico, 39; Nueva Vizcaya, 66; Sonora, 335; the Californias, 47. The document was 856 pages long.

understanding of the Gila-Colorado situation on the eve of
the calamity that was to happen there.[83] The most important feature to him was the saving that he was effecting.
His concern for Sonora was indeed greatest of all, — possibly
because he was then in that province. Yet his interest
was entirely local, based primarily on the Apaches, and to a
less extent on the Seris. His remedy was a fresh change
of presidial sites so as to form something like a half circle
around Janos, Nueva Vizcaya, as a centre. There was not
a word in the entire document about the larger projects
which had engaged the attention of Gálvez and Bucarely
— not a word about the possibility of foreign invasion of
the Pacific coasts, at a time too when this was more than
ever a probability.[84] In fine, if this document is a monument to Croix's painstaking thoroughness in matters of
detail which were before his eyes, it also bears the record
of his exceeding narrowness of vision.

Croix's remarks about the Colorado-Gila settlements
may be referred to a little more in detail. He approaches
this matter by giving an invaluable summary of documents
from 1735 on, concerning the location of frontier presidios.
Anza's discovery of a route to Alta California had caused
a change in the situation, as a result of which Bonilla,
Oconor, Crespo, Anza, Díaz, Garcés, and many others had
recommended that one presidio be placed at the junction of
the Colorado and Gila, and another at the confluence of the
Gila and San Pedro, so as to secure communication with
Monterey. Oconor had proposed that Horcasitas and
Buenavista presidios be transferred respectively to those
sites. Two of Croix's officers, Ugarte and Rocha, were
unfavorable to the location of a presidio on the San Pedro,

[83] The memorial is of later date than
the disaster, but clearly was written
before Croix had heard of it. Croix
got the news in August, but did not on
that account change his memorial.

[84] No attempt has been made to
record Gálvez's warnings to Croix concerning foreign danger, although it is
certain that they were made. A Croix
letter of July 27, 1778, refers to a secret,
royal order of March 22, 1778, concerning the movements of the English and
French. Croix replied that he had
given instructions to the governors of
Texas, Coahuila, Sonora, and the Californias about these movements. This
shows that some danger was threatening in the Pacific — possibly a reference
to Cook's voyage.

and Croix was of their opinion. He had also decided to
depend on his two settlements at the Colorado to hold the
ground there. Horcasitas and Buenavista could not be
moved, for the Seris were not sufficiently subjected, as
shown by their outbreaks in 1777 and more recently in 1780.
Croix spoke with enthusiasm of the brilliant prospects of
his Colorado settlements, and dilated upon the saving of
14,000 *pesos* a year that he was effecting by not placing a
presidio there.[85]

By April 23, 1782, Croix's second part was ready. This
filled 572 paragraphs, but was longer than the preceding.[86]
This did not follow his original plan, but dealt with his
military measures in the frontier provinces. It was intended to be general, for the whole government, whereas
the previous document was particular for each province,
but it included much detail about the different provinces.
The Californias alone were not considered, and were specifically stated as being outside the plan. The keynote of
the document, as might be expected, was the Apache wars.[87]
If Croix wrote any more long memorials, they have not
come to light. Events had occurred, meanwhile, which may
well have tempered Croix's fondness for indulging in these
reports, most prominent of which was the Yuma massacre
of 1781.

The two colonies on the Colorado were founded in the fall
of 1780, both on the west bank, Purísima Concepción near
the junction, and San Pedro y San Pablo de Bicuñer farther
down the river. Trouble began almost at once. The
Spanish paid small regard to the rights of the natives in
allotting lands, and their cattle ruined the Yuma crops.
In these and other respects the Spaniard of everyday life
lacked the halo with which the Yumas had surrounded the
transient gift-bearing visitors of other days. When provisions were exhausted, the Yumas refused to supply them,
unless at exorbitant prices, and the chiefs of the Yumas,
even Palma, began to incite their people against the set-

[85] C–4430.
[86] There was an even thousand pages in the document that I used.
[87] C–4568.

tlers. The storm broke in July, 1781. Rivera had arrived
in June with an expedition of forty recruits and their families, bound for Alta California, in fulfilment of Neve's
plan for developing that province. Having seen them
safely on their way, luckily for them, Rivera recrossed
the Colorado with eleven or twelve soldiers, and encamped
there in order to strengthen his animals before proceeding
himself to Alta California. Rivera's arrival had only added
to the discontent, for his cattle destroyed mesquite plants
of the Yumas, and he had not been liberal with gifts. On
July 17 the natives attacked San Pedro y San Pablo, killing
the two religious and most of the men, holding the women
and children as captives. The same thing occurred at
about the same hour at Purísima Concepción, although
Fathers Garcés and Barreneche were temporarily spared.
Rivera and his men were attacked, next day, and all were
killed, and the following day, Garcés and Barreneche were
put to death.[88]

Punitive campaigns were planned, and several expeditions made in 1781–82, but beyond ransoming the survivors
they accomplished little. Croix was not the type of man to
acknowledge blame. In casting about for a scapegoat he
hit upon Garcés and Anza, charging them with gross ex-
aggerations in praise of the Yumas and their lands. This
appears in his letter to Gálvez of November 4, 1782, in
which he announced that he was about to hold a *junta* to
decide whether a presidio should be established at the
Colorado River to keep communication open with the Californias.[89] The injustice of Croix's attack is apparent to
anyone who has read the Garcés and Anza memorials
and diaries. We have seen that Anza had said that his
route would be impracticable, if the Yumas should be hostile, or even if no more than unfriendly, owing to the difficulty of crossing the Colorado in seasons of flood, at which
time Indian help was necessary, and that Garcés had repeatedly recommended establishing a presidio at the Colo-

rado and Gila, while Croix's long memorial of October 30, 1781, quoted Anza to the same effect. The trouble was that Croix had not adopted their recommendations.

At the *junta*, held January 3, 1783, there appeared, besides Croix, Pedro Galindo Navarro, Pedro Tueros, Pedro Corbalán, and Felipe Neve, the last named having been promoted to be inspector general of the *comandancia general*. Neve had recently come from Alta California by way of the Anza route. He condemned the Colorado country, saying that it was a region of salt marshes and sand, with slight rainfall and scant pasture. Settlers would have to get everything from Sonora, he said. Others referred to the Seri and Apache wars, which required all of the troops to be used elsewhere, and also to the fact that it would be possible to use the route to Alta California in case of need, if thirty armed men were sent along, as the Yumas were weak foes. Therefore, as the settlements would cause heavy expense, and as in the *junta's* opinion they would do no good, it was held to be best to abandon them. These proceedings were reported in Croix's letter of January 27, 1783.[90]

The Yuma disaster was a severe blow to the career of that capable explorer, Juan Bautista de Anza, for now that Garcés was dead, Anza had to bear the brunt of the blame. Croix brought the matter up again in a letter of March 24, 1783, in which he described his military policy since entering office. It seems that Oconor had prophesied the Yuma disaster, whereupon Croix asserted that Oconor probably knew that it had occurred when he claimed to foresee it; anyway, it was not his fault, said Croix, but Anza's. Anza had misrepresented the country, he said, and it was that which had caused its occupation and therefore the disaster.[91] Late in the same year Croix was promoted to be viceroy of Peru — possibly a gracious way of relieving him from a task that had proved too big for him — and Neve became *comandante general*. The latter's bitterness against Anza is surprisingly great, and a little displeasing to the investi-

gator who has formed a high opinion of both. For example,
Neve told Anza to omit in future in his annual service report (*hoja de servicio*) to call himself the discoverer of the
route to Alta California, for not he but the Indian Tarabal
had discovered it. Similarly, Anza was not to lay claim
to having defeated the Comanche chief Cuerno Verde, for
that victory was due to Azuela, Anza's subordinate in that
fight. This and much else of the same character appear
in Neve's letter to Gálvez of January 26, 1784, and its
enclosures.[92] Some of the reasons for Neve's animus may
be conjectured with a fair degree of probability. It is not
likely that Neve took pains to read over the Anza diaries
and reports about the Colorado-Gila settlements, for the
idea had been abandoned before he became *comandante
general*, and naturally, he took the estimate of the em-
bittered Croix, eager to exculpate himself. The latter,
possibly by quoting certain portions of Anza's reports and
omitting others, made it appear that Anza had painted the
Colorado country as a kind of paradise and the Yumas as
having an angelic character. Neve had seen for himself
the falsity of such views, not realizing that if the whole
truth were known Anza would be found to have represented
the situation with substantial correctness. Moreover, the
disaster had checked a very great work in Alta California
that Neve had set on foot, and Neve seems not to have been
a man to be patient with failure, for which in this case he
wrongly blamed Anza. Finally, there seems to have been
some misunderstanding between them with regard to
affairs in New Mexico. Had Anza and Neve been personally acquainted Neve might have better judged his
man, but the evidence of their annual service reports would
tend to show that they never met.

Neve's successors tried to repair the injury done to Anza.
Neve had asked that Anza be relieved from the govern-
ment of New Mexico, claiming that he was incompetent.
A later *comandante general*, Jacobo Ugarte, wrote to Gálvez,

[92] C-4938. The enclosures consist of one letter from Neve to Bishop   Reyes, C-4935, and four to Anza, C-4915, 4932-34.

December 21, 1786, that Neve's opinion of Anza's administration in New Mexico had been founded on the incorrect
reports of Anza's opponents, and that Anza had merited
praise for his government of New Mexico rather than removal.[93] This was a courageous letter, in view of the fact
that Gálvez had already appointed a new governor. In
supporting Anza's petition for a province under the viceroy,[94] Ugarte warmly recommended him in a letter dated
February 1, 1787.[95] José Antonio Rengel, who a little
earlier had been temporary *comandante general*, and was
at the time inspector general and commander of the Nueva
Vizcaya-New Mexico district, wrote across Anza's petition
that he too indorsed it. Yet again, July 15, 1787, Ugarte
wrote to Gálvez in behalf of Anza. This time he urged
that he be made governor of Texas.[96] The result of Ugarte's
efforts has not thus far been revealed. Anza seems to have
been succeeded as governor of New Mexico by Fernando de
la Concha in 1788, after which no further record of his
career has yet come to light.[97]

Yet the career of Anza or of Croix is of slight account
compared to the tremendous importance of the Yuma disaster. That event checked the development of Alta California just at the moment when a great forward movement was being made. If measures are to be judged by
their results, perhaps, after all, Teodoro de Croix is deserving of a monument — but it should be erected by the
United States. And back of Croix lies Gálvez, who was
responsible for him. Investigation will likely prove that it
was due to the fatal weakness in Gálvez's character, which
made him work for himself above his country, that he chose
so inefficient an instrument as Teodoro de Croix to carry
out the projects which he himself had brilliantly inaugurated.

[93] C-5206.
[94] For Anza's petition, C-5204.
[95] C-5227.
[96] C-5244.
[97] Bancroft, *Ariz. and New Mex.*, 268, and Twitchell, *Leading facts*, 451, say that Concha did not succeed Anza until late in 1789. It is clear, however, that Concha was referred to as governor and was writing letters from Santa Fé in 1788. Twitchell, *Spanish archives of New Mexico*, II, 303, 308–10.

CHAPTER XVIII

THE AFTERMATH, 1783-1822

THE end of the Spanish northwestward movement had come with the Yuma massacre of 1781, but there were a number of contributory factors. A Spanish voyage to the northwest coast in 1779 failed to discover any Europeans; a series of voyages from 1788 on found too many, for English fur traders, following in the wake of Cook, had begun to come from China to the North American coast in 1785. Spain considered engaging in the trade herself, which she might have done to far greater advantage than her competitors, but she let the opportunity slip. The attempt to oust the English led to the Nootka controversy, by which Spain suffered a decisive check. Henceforth, the matter of expense, which had always been an important factor holding back the conquest, became a controlling element in considering such projects. The Anza route was officially abandoned; internal disorder continued to be a problem in the affairs of Sonora and New Mexico; and changes in jurisdiction in the frontier provinces became so frequent that a consistent policy of northwestward advance would in any event have been difficult to follow. In fine, Spain had taken the defensive, not the aggressive defensive of the time of Bucarely, but a waiting kind, the inevitable outcome of which was disintegration.

Yet, need for a route still existed, if Alta California were to become rich and populous, and despite its Indian wars Sonora could have supplied the sinews of development. Foreign danger, too, had become more than ever a fact in the northwest. Although Alta California had obtained a sufficient quantity of domestic animals, other needs were unsupplied or at the mercy of an enemy's ships. Goods and effects could come from San Blas or be smuggled in on foreign ships, and a few settlers could cross the Gulf and come up the peninsula. But unless there were some powerfully impelling motive, such as actually came with the discovery of gold in 1848, the province could only become populous by its own natural increase, which would have taken centuries, or by the use of an overland route. Fages, Borica, Arrillaga, and others favored reopening the Anza route or developing a route from New Mexico, but their proposals found scant response. Thus it was that Alta California settled down to an Acadian existence, able to live happily and well, and to keep out the casual foreigner, but not populous enough to thrust back up the river valleys where lay the magic gold, which, had it been discovered, would at once have changed everything. Meantime, the United States was pushing westward, not knowing that her advance was in fact a race with other powers for the Pacific before the discovery of gold. Unaware that they were doing an important work for an alien country, the Spanish Californians held the land, as it were in trust, for future delivery to the United States.

All along, the principal impulse for the Spanish advance had come from a fear of foreign encroachments, and heretofore, the promise of danger in the far northwest had been greater than the fact, but that had been enough to stir Gálvez and Bucarely to action. Henceforth, the actual peril was to be greater than it ever had been before, but it was not to rouse Spain to equal efforts with those of the past. We have seen that preparations for a new voyage were made after the return of Heceta and Bodega in 1775, and that this did not take place until 1779. In that year Arteaga and Bodega in the *Princesa* and *Favorita* made a careful exploration of the Alaska coast, but found no Russians, although at one time, near the actual Russian post on Kadiak Island. After their return a royal order was issued, May 10, 1780, calling for the discontinuance of

such voyages. Events were soon to cause a fresh attempt
however. Cook's voyage has already been noted. When
his ship brought some furs to China, a new force entered into
the history of the northwest. Captain Hanna, an Englishman, was the first voyager to follow up this phase of Cook's
discoveries. He was on the northwest coast in 1785, having
come from China, and he took back a cargo of furs. In the
next three years numbers of Englishmen followed Hanna's
lead. Meares, Tipping, Lowrie, Guise, Strange, Portlock,
Dixon, Barclay, Duncan, Colnett, and Douglas were leaders
in these voyages, some of them coming more than once.
Two American ships also came, Kendrick and Gray being
the commanders. Most of these boats came from China,
and made Nootka Sound, off Vancouver Island, their
rendezvous. In addition a French voyage of exploration
under La Pérouse passed along the northwest coast in 1786,
and reported that the Russians had several establishments
in the far northwest.

The Spaniards seem not to have participated greatly in
the rich fur trade of this period, but a very significant project for that purpose was broached from Manila by Ciriaco
González Carvajal, intendant of the Philippines. He had
heard of Hanna's voyage of 1785, and forwarded to Gálvez
a file of papers concerning it.[1] His own letter, dated February 3, 1786, recommended the establishment of a fur trade
by the Spaniards, who had the advantage of the ports of
Manila in the Philippines and San Francisco in the Californias to facilitate the trade. His idea was that the furs
obtained in the Californias (that is, the Californias considered as extending from Cape San Lucas to the extreme
northwest of North America) could be sold in China, and
that quicksilver might be procured in China to develop
gold mining in the Californias.[2] In another letter, on June
20, he suggested utilization of the port of Lampón (on the
eastern shore of Luzon, Philippine Islands) and one of the
ports of the far northwest discovered by Arteaga in 1779,
forming a settlement at the latter.[3] In September, 1787,

[1] C–5160. [2] C–5161. [3] C–5176.

the matter was referred to the directors of the Philippine Company for an opinion,[4] and when they neglected to reply, an order was sent to them in July, 1788, to hasten their answer.[5] The company replied on August 13 that González's ideas were not practicable; that there were not many furs in the Californias, or any knowledge of the way to catch the animals or cure the skins; and that quicksilver was very scarce and expensive in China. They were awaiting further reports from the Philippines, however.[6] The company feared, very likely, that this project might in some way injure its own trade. The Council of the Indies decided to await the reports referred to.[7] The matter came up again, however, as a result of a letter from the viceroy, January 12, 1790, which referred to the project as a possible means of occupying the northwest coasts, to the exclusion of foreigners, without incurring the great expenses hitherto undergone in the voyages of exploration.[8] In reply, July 29, 1790, the *ministro general* reserved decision.[9] As late as 1791, the matter was still being considered,[10] but at that point the evidence ceases. The interest in the file of papers is in the possibilities that might have resulted if the scheme had been tried. There certainly were furs and gold in the Californias.

Whatever the Spanish ministry may have thought about the projects of González, the reports of La Pérouse about the presence of Russians were not to be disregarded. Consequently, the *Princesa* and *San Carlos* were sent out in 1788 under Martínez and Haro. This time the Russians were found, and reports brought back that they intended to settle Nootka. Information of the English pretension to that port was also received. This caused Spain to take steps which brought on the Nootka controversy, of which little need be said here. Spain sent out an expedition which seized some English ships at Nootka in 1789, whereupon England threatened war. Spain appealed to France under

[4] C–5258.
[5] C–5297.
[6] C–5298.
[7] C–5302.
[8] C–5453.
[9] C–5458.
[10] C–5492.

the terms of the Family Compact, but the French National Assembly, then in control of the government, refused to live up to the treaty. Spain had to yield, acknowledging the right of English ships to trade and make settlements on the Pacific coast, north of the Spanish settlements, and even granting them a right to enter Spanish ports but not to trade.[11]

A Spanish interpretation of these events appears in a memorial of 278 paragraphs by Viceroy Revilla Gigedo,[12] April 12, 1793. This purports to be a history of the Department of San Blas and of the Californias (in the largest geographic sense of the term) since 1769. The keynote of the document is the matter of expense. Some of Revilla Gigedo's remarks on that subject are worth noting. It had been hoped, he said, that the salt mines of Zapotillo under royal administration might meet all the expenses of the Department of San Blas, but such a result had never been attained; rather, expense increased. He then showed how the projects of Bucarely had increased expenditure, such that the annual cost of the Californias had become nearly 60,000 *pesos* greater than it had been at the outset, without including closely related expenses, such for example as those incurred in connection with the Colorado River settlements. He praised Bucarely, however, and said that he might have achieved even greater results, if he had been able to make larger expenditures. After 1780 strict economy began to be practised, and in 1786 the salaries and gratuities of San Blas employes were cut down, but expenses soon became heavy again, because of a fresh series of explorations and the Nootka affair. Revilla Gigedo displayed some scepticism as to the existence of a passage from the Atlantic to the Pacific, but felt that the doubt should be settled, after which, voyages to the northwest should be abandoned. "From now on," he says, "every project which compels us to incur heavy expenses should be opposed, even if the

[11] The best account of the Nootka affair is William Ray Manning, *The Nootka Sound controversy.*
[12] The Conde de Revilla Gigedo was viceroy from 1789 to 1794. He was a son of the former viceroy of that name.

most positive assurances are made of brilliant results, because it is always understood that these results will be in the future, whereas the expenditures have to come out in cash from a treasury full of urgent necessities, and whose debts are increasing. Once the treasury funds and those of its money lenders [are] exhausted, the projects cannot be sustained, their advantages will vanish, the recovery of the money expended will be difficult, and it even may become necessary to continue in other and larger outlays with the very nearly certain risk of obtaining still worse results. During the period of twenty-five years, many millions of dollars have been expended in establishing and maintaining the new settlements of Alta California; in repeated explorations of its northern coasts; and in the occupation of Nootka. But if we persist in other still more distant and adventurous enterprises, then there will be no funds left to carry these on." [13]

With a complacency that would have been strange, twenty years before, Revilla Gigedo remarked that the Russians had establishments on the continent reaching southward almost to the vicinity of Nootka, but Spain had too few troops and ships of war, and too scant funds to dislodge them. However, there was plenty of time in which to perfect a defence both of the lands already possessed and of those that might be acquired in future, because it would be a long time before Russia could carry her intentions into effect. He saw more to fear in the English, not so much because of the fur trade, which he regarded as over-estimated or diminishing, but because they wished to engage in illicit trade with the Spanish dominions, and thus destroy the commerce between New Spain and the Philippines. This was why they disputed the ownership of Nootka, he thought, and why they claimed that San Francisco Bay should be the boundary of Spanish possessions, and that the region north of that be under joint English and Spanish occupation. The

[13] From the translation in *Land of sunshine:* cf. n. 15. I have changed "Upper California" and "Nutka" to "Alta California" and "Nootka." The word "these" in the last line of the translation refers to the lands already occupied by Spain, in particular Alta California.

same reason accounted for their desire to be allowed to fish at a distance of ten leagues from the Spanish coasts.

He proposed that expense should be limited to forestalling the English, after the existence or non-existence of an interoceanic waterway had been proved. To check them he recommended the following projects: the occupation of the port of Bodega,[14] and possibly the mouth of the Columbia River; the fortification of those points and the presidios of San Francisco, Monterey, San Diego, and Loreto; the transfer of the Department of San Blas to Acapulco; the conservation and development of the pious fund and the Zapotillo salt mines, so that fresh burdens of providing for missions in the Californias might not fall on the royal treasury. If the Columbia should prove to be an interoceanic strait, he would take possession and hold it for the king of Spain. If it were but a river, with its sources not far from its mouth, he would discontinue exploration, perhaps establishing a post there, in order to get a better title, and to remove the territory held in common by Spain and England to a great distance from the actual Spanish settlements. But if the source of the Columbia were near New Mexico, it would be necessary to occupy the river and the intervening territory with presidios and missions. The transfer from San Blas to Acapulco was recommended because of the superiority of the latter port. He made a long plea for the better management of the pious fund. The total value of the fund was 715,500 *pesos*, which should yield an interest of 35,575 *pesos*. Thus there should be a surplus, as the missionaries required only 22,000 *pesos* a year. These advantages had not been accruing, and the estates making up the fund were going to ruin. Similarly, the salt mines of Zapotillo ought to be more productive. His projects were not based on problematical future advantages, said Revilla Gigedo, but were merely to guard against the alienation of a territory which had cost Spain so much in life, hardship, and treasure. He was opposed to extending the Spanish dominion to the northern coasts,

14 Modern Bodega Bay, a few miles north of San Francisco.

as it involved a distant, adventurous, and costly enterprise. The retention of Nootka, or the occupation of any other distant locality would also be inadvisable because of the liability to foreign complications as well as the matter of expense. For his part, he would cede Nootka to the English, who seemed to desire it in a spirit of vainglory, to uphold a claim which had been controverted.[15] Clearly the Spanish Empire was on the defensive. An attempt to occupy Bodega was made, but failed, and the affair was permanently postponed. If anything else of consequence was attempted in fulfilment of Revilla Gigedo's suggestions, the writer has seen no evidence of it.

Other considerations contributed to check the Spanish advance, one of which was the failure to maintain overland communications between the Californias and New Spain. By a decree of 1786 even the punitive campaigns against the Yumas were ordered to be given up, until the Apaches should be conquered. The Indians of Sonora were periodically troublesome. Having re-acquired the habit of revolt in 1776, the Seris seem not to have lost it thereafter in the eighteenth century, for any great length of time. They were regarded as incorrigible, and various plans were put forth for banishing them altogether, or for segregating them on Tiburón Island. The Pimas and Pápagos planned an outbreak in 1796, but the plot was discovered in time to avert evil consequences. The Apaches gave trouble, of course, but in 1786 a new policy was inaugurated which proved successful; incessant war was to be waged against them, unless they would consent to make peace, and good treatment was to be accorded them if they would, in which event they were to receive gifts of articles which they themselves could not make, even guns and powder, although of inferior quality. They were also to be plied with liquor in order to demoralize them, and encouraged to make war on one another, the authorities hoping that in this way they might be exterminated. Furthermore, attempts to settle

[15] Revilla Gigedo, *Informe*. Also C-5613. Translation in *Land of sunshine* for 1899, v. XI.

Spaniards and friendly Indians on the frontiers were also
to be made. This policy seems to have been successful.
Between 1786 and 1797 peace with different groups of Apaches
was established, and was maintained for about twenty years
longer at an annual cost of 18,000 to 30,000 pesos. New
Mexico, too, had the usual Indian troubles. There was
scant hope of relief for the Californias from that quarter.

Yet, despite wars, and despite letters saying that no men
could be spared from the province, the state of affairs in
Sonora was not altogether unfavorable for a forward movement. In 1780 Sonora actually returned a profit to the
royal treasury, receipts in that year being 284,519 pesos
and expenses 278,703 pesos, leaving a balance of 5816
pesos. The figures are more striking when it appears that
Croix's salary of 20,000 pesos was charged against the
province. The largest item was that of the six presidios,
which accounted for 136,308 pesos. This information appears in an estado of September 14, 1781,[16] forwarded to
Spain in Croix's letter of September 23.[17] A summary, of
the same date, of receipts and disbursements in all of the
provinces of Croix's government, omitting the Californias,
showed 864,182 pesos received, as against 856,853 expended,
a profit of 7329 pesos.[18] The provinces of the viceroyalty
just back from the frontier were still yielding richly, however, as is evident from the accounts of the Real Caja of
Guadalajara. As for Sonora, full figures for other years
have not come to hand, but it is known that the mines
continued to yield richly. Further evidence of the well-
settled character of Sonora may be obtained from the statistics of population. Croix's great memorial of October
30, 1781, included a table of the population of Sinaloa and
Sonora by districts. The two provinces contained 87,644
persons, of whom 25,928 were men. From Fuerte de
Montesclaros northward, or about the equivalent of
modern Sonora, there were 52,228 persons, including
15,323 men,[19] the figures probably including all persons but

16 C–4406. The figures probably include Sinaloa. "Sonora" was often
used for both Sinaloa and Sonora.

17 C–4408.

18 C–4409.
19 C–4430. The whole table is given
as an appendix.

the unchristianized Indians. In 1793 the two provinces
had advanced to a total of 93,396 persons. At that time
the figures given for New Mexico were 30,953, and for
the two Californias 12,666. In 1803 Sinaloa and Sonora
had reached a population of 121,400. It would seem,
therefore, that Sonora could have furnished the sinews of
advancement.

Another factor tending to check an advance was the
rapid changes in government of the frontier provinces. In
1785 the *comandancia general* was split into three units only
partially under the *comandante general*, who himself ruled
Sinaloa, Sonora, and the Californias. The viceroy's superior
authority was at the same time restored. His power was
at first supposed to be only a special case due to the peculiar
ability of Viceroy Bernardo de Gálvez, a nephew of the
ministro general. After his death, late in 1786, the *comandante general* resumed full authority, but in March, 1787,
the power of the viceroy was in part given back. In the
same year the three *comandancias* were consolidated to form
two, one of the east, the other of the west, each ruled by a
comandante general, to some extent under the viceroy. In
1788 the full authority of the viceroy was restored, although
the two *comandancias* were retained for purposes of administration. A royal order of 1792 returned to the plan
of 1776, except that Nuevo León, Nuevo Santander, and
the Californias were to be under the viceroy. This went
into effect in 1793. In 1804 a decree called for the modification of this plan by dividing what then formed the *comandancia general* into two *comandancias*, respectively of the
east and west. This did not go into effect until 1812, but
remained thenceforth to the end of Spanish rule. It will
be noted that the Californias on the one side, and Sonora
and New Mexico on the other were in different governments
from 1793 on. This helps to account for the opposition of
later *comandantes generales* to reopening the Anza route.
It meant the making of an effort for the sake of regions beyond their frontiers, and a divided authority over any route
that might be opened. It must also have tended to make

local concerns seem to them of more account than the possibility of foreign danger.

The need for an overland route to Alta California still
existed, both from the standpoint of foreign danger and from
that of local progress. Enough has been said on the first
point. As to the second, one need had been successfully
met. The province could not well complain of want in
domestic animals, henceforth. Rather, their numbers began soon to outrun the requirements of the settlers. For
the rest, there were the usual difficulties with the old
routes. Manufactured articles and perhaps some agricultural products had to come by sea from San Blas, although
the need for food-supplies became less and less, and as time
went on, the supply-ships came infrequently. Then it was
that foreign traders were welcomed, despite the laws against
them. Alta California was also able to get all that it required of goods and effects, although at the risk of interruption of the traffic by the enemies of Spain. The greatest
need for an overland route was that more settlers might come.
A few persons came from Sinaloa in later years by way of the
peninsula, but the great majority of the settlers were those
who had come before 1782 and their descendants. This
could not permit of a growth in population great enough
to induce the inhabitants to leave the coast and go up the
river valleys where the gold lay in such abundance. On
the other hand, enough settlers had come to save the province from all likelihood of abandonment and to hold the
land for Spain against any but a strong attacking force.
The following table shows the state of the missions in 1790
and in 1800.

	Number of Missions	Crop	Large Stock	Small Stock	Christian Indians
1790	11	30,000	22,000	26,000	7,500
1800	18	75,000	67,000	86,000	10,700
Gain	7	45,000	45,000	60,000	3,200

The crop represents the number of bushels, mostly wheat, for the particular year, an amount which varied greatly in different years, but on the whole undoubtedly increased over a long period of time. Large stock includes horses, mules, and horned cattle; small stock, — goats, pigs, and sheep, although almost wholly the last named. These figures do not represent the total wealth of the province, although forming the greater part of it. The presidios and *pueblos*, particularly the latter, had considerable crops and large numbers of animals, but it is difficult to state figures with any degree of certainty. The number of presidios remained four, but the *pueblos* increased from two to three. The whites, including *mestizos* and mulattoes, may have numbered 970 in 1790, and 1200 in 1800, of whom most of the men were soldiers. The troops usually numbered 205, the quota allowed by the government. Most of the men were married, and their sons passed into the military forces, for no more troops were sent from New Spain. Alta California had already outstripped the peninsula in population and produce, the latter being retained, as in the past, for strategic reasons, and as a mail route to the northern province.

Proposals to reëstablish the overland route to the Californias were made several times in the closing years of the eighteenth century. For a time they were frowned upon, and in 1786 Viceroy Gálvez's instruction to Ugarte prohibited the reopening of the route.[20] Shortly afterward, the Apaches began to give less trouble, which may account for the comparatively favorable reception accorded to certain proposals by Pedro Fages in 1787.[21] The matter was explained in a letter of Viceroy Revilla Gigedo to the king, November 26, 1789. In 1784 the Dominicans had been ordered to add two missions to the three new ones that they had already built, the better to connect Baja with Alta California. San Miguel del Encino had been erected in 1787, but the other had been suspended on the ground that

---

[20] Gálvez, *Instrucción*, par. 115.
[21] Fages had been governor of the Californias since Neve's departure in 1782. This was the same Fages of earlier days.

it would have to be on a route toward the Colorado River
in order to avoid encroaching on the territory of the *Fernandinos*. Consideration of this matter led Fages to make
three proposals : that four new missions be erected between
San Diego and Santa Clara to complete the chain in Alta
California; that carpenters, smiths, masons, and other
artisans be sent to Alta California to instruct the Indians,
for that was the way to civilize them; that a presidio of a
hundred men be established at Santa Olaya,[22] from which
number twenty might be detached and placed at Sonoita,[23]
and twenty more in the valley of the San Felipe.[24] In this
way Alta California could be more securely held and the
160 leagues between San Diego and Altar protected, bringing Sonora and Alta California into communication. Fages'
plan was submitted to a number of persons for opinions.
The *comandante general*, Ugarte, favored it in all respects.
Miguel Costansó was not unfavorable, being especially
impressed, it would seem, by the project for sending artisans. The Father Superior of San Fernando discussed
the plan for new missions. Soledad and Santa Cruz were
the only sites that he knew of that would be suitable for
missions, he said, but he was ready to provide as many
missionaries as should be needed. If there were any intention of advancing northward from San Francisco to
Nootka, he would like to cede the present *Fernandino*
missions to the Dominicans, and take up the new territory.
Revilla Gigedo favored Fages' first proposal. He had
ordered two missions founded, he said, and a search for
sites for two others between San Diego and San Buenaventura. He was also taking steps to erect two more in Baja
California to fill the gaps there. He said nothing about
Fages' second project, although he probably favored it, for
the artisans were sent. He opposed the third. A mail
service had been established from Guaymas to Baja California, in part supplying the need for an overland route,
he said, and the advantages of the new presidio, he thought,

---

[22] On the west bank of the Colorado,
below the Gila junction.

[23] In northwestern Sonora.

[24] In Baja California, but along the
Anza route.

would not equal the cost. Furthermore, the multitude of Indians along the Colorado, whose power had been made evident in the massacre of 1781, was a factor making it advisable to suspend this project until a time of greater need.[25] Some action was taken, however, to found new missions. Santa Cruz and Soledad were founded in 1791. In 1797 San Fernando Rey was erected, followed in 1798 by San Luis Rey. Several other missions also date from this period, as also a settlement at Santa Cruz called the *villa* of Branciforte. The matter of the Santa Olaya presidio came up a second time in 1792, and again objection was made on the ground that Santa Olaya was surrounded by natives disposed to be hostile.[26]

In 1796 renewed proposals were made emanating from Borica and Arrillaga, respectively rulers of Alta and Baja California. Borica was influenced by a journey of exploration from Sonora to New Mexico by José Zúñiga in 1795.[27] He had heard that the journey was related to the fact that there were 1500 white persons in New Mexico without lands or work. He therefore sent for Garcés' 1776 diary and map, with a view to exploring a route from New Mexico to Alta California, in the hope that the latter might obtain the former's surplus of settlers. He urged his project in a report of October 2, 1796. It was received favorably by the viceroy and his *fiscal*, and the former proceeded to ask for reports. At about the same time, October 26, 1796, Arrillaga made his proposal, the same that had emanated from Fages several years before, of a presidio at Santa Olaya and garrisons at Sonoita and San Felipe. He suggested as an alternative measure a presidio at the mouth of the Colorado. Arrillaga's plan resulted from explorations by the Dominicans and himself toward the Colorado, the most important of which had been conducted by himself. Between June, 1796, and January, 1797, he made two journeys of

[25] C-5400.
[26] Borbón, *Parecer*, in A.P.C.H., *Prov. St. Papers*, XVIII, 37–44.
[27] For the instructions to Zúñiga, March 31, 1795, C-5711; for Zúñiga's diary, April 9 to May 29, 1795, C-5712; for the remitting letter from Chihuahua by Pedro de Rada to the Conde de Campo de Alange in Spain, July 9, 1795, C-5722.

exploration, and on one of them, in October, 1796, he reached the Colorado, where he had a fight with the Indians, and later returned by way of San Diego to Loreto.

Borica viewed Arrillaga's proposals with favor, although he wrote on September 4, 1797, that it would be unsafe for parties of less than thirty-five to follow Anza's route, for which reason he preferred Arrillaga's alternative proposal. Arrillaga did not make light of the Indian danger at Santa Olaya; it was on that account that he had made his second proposal, which he designed to be only a temporary measure. The presidio at the mouth should be on the western bank, he said, at a distance of twenty to twenty-five leagues from Santa Catalina, in northeastern Baja California, but he failed to point out a place for the location of the presidio. Borica thought it would be sufficient for the present to think only of gathering the Indians between Santa Catalina and the Colorado into a mission, treating them well, and procuring the cultivation of the lands and the increase of herds; the selection of a presidio site might come later, after careful explorations had been made.[28] An opinion was asked of the *comandante general*, Pedro de Nava, who wrote, on June 22, 1797, that he did not consider it difficult to open a route, but that its value for some time would be limited to traffic with the Indians. Even this would amount to little, unless the most detailed information were obtained of places, distances, and Indian customs. The settlers of the Californias and New Mexico were not in a position to carry on commerce with each other or to keep the route open, and they would not be so for many years. As to the proposal to take 1500 Spaniards from New Mexico to Alta California, it would be unwise to weaken New Mexico; these men could be used to good advantage, without removing them from their native soil.[29]

Favorable action was taken by the viceroy despite Nava's disapproval and the difficulties raised by Borica and Arrillaga themselves. The mission of Santa Catalina was

[28] Borbón, *Parecer*, in A.P.C.H.,   [29] *Ibid.*
Prov. St. Papers, XVIII, 37–44.

founded in November, 1797, but there the project rested for several years. In 1801 it came up again in conjunction with another proposition, that of the political separation of Baja from Alta California. Both of these matters were referred by the viceroy to Borbón, his *fiscal*. The latter replied, March 4, 1801. On the matter of the separation Borbón reported favorably. As to the establishing of communications between New Mexico and Alta California by way of the Colorado River, he took the opposite side. He gave a history of plans to this end since the massacre of 1781, laying particular stress on the disadvantages, and said that a more careful exploration of the lands would be necessary. Arrillaga himself had not been satisfied with the one he had made, he said, despite the care that he had used. Borbón thought it best to await the opinion of the new governor of Alta California, and the royal decision with regard to dividing the Californias, which would enable them to understand the matter of communication better. Meanwhile, he suggested that a copy of the papers on the subject be sent to Nava, and another copy to Arrillaga, then *ad interim* governor of Alta California, pending the arrival of Borica's successor. They should read the papers and state their opinions.[30]

Arrillaga's reply is lacking, but Nava's under date of July 20, 1801, is available. He adhered to the opinion expressed by him in 1797. A single post would not be enough for the passage of so considerable a desert, he said, while to withdraw so many persons from New Mexico would harm that province. True, there were 1500 persons in New Mexico without work, but they ought to be used in reëstablishing abandoned settlements between El Paso and Santa Fé; he had just arranged for that to be done. The advantages of reopening the Colorado route, said Nava, were reduced to two; the possibility of aiding the Californias, in case of a foreign invasion; and the benefits of reciprocal trade between the Californias and New Mexico. As to the first, if the necessity should arise, it would be possible

30 Borbón, *Parecer*, in A.P.C.H., *Prov. St. Papers*, XVIII, 37–44.

to send aid by land, if a considerable force went along; or
by way of the Gulf, unless that route should have been intercepted by the enemy. In the absence of a foreign attack, there was no need to keep the route open. As for
commerce, New Mexico was more advanced in settled life
than the Californias, but did not yield so many products
or manufactures that it required new outlets for its trade.
It had been accustomed to send all its surplus products to
Chihuahua, with an absolute certainty of being able to dispose of them, and to procure in return all that it needed.
It would be inadvisable to expose its scant capital to speculations of doubtful outcome, when because of distance the
expense would be so great. Moreover, it would be necessary to defeat the Indians opposing the passage, thus making
them hostile and increasing the burdens of the frontier. He
was not in favor of extending the line of presidios; not only
would that increase expense, but it would also make it more
difficult to defend the provinces, since they would embrace
a vast territory, which, much of the time, would serve no
good purpose.[31]

The opinions of Nava and Borbón prevailed. The
separation of the provinces was ordered in 1804, but the
matter of the route was not acted upon favorably. The
plan of developing Alta California by means of it had been
given up. Therefore, why use the route any longer? It
was there when the need should arise. A large body of
troops would have to be employed if the route were not kept
open, but in case of a foreign attack only a considerable
force would be of any avail to Alta California. Other
proposals to reopen the route may have been made, but no
attempt has been made to follow them; certainly nothing
came of these projects.[32] Fear of foreign aggressions in

[31] Nava, *Informe*, in A.P.C.H., *Prov. St. Papers*, XVIII, 34–37.

[32] One such proposal was made at the very inception of independent Mexican rule. Danger to the Californias from the Americans and the Russians was alleged. The Americans were feared along the whole northern frontier from Texas to the Columbia,

and the possibility of their descending the Colorado was mentioned. The Russian colony in Alta California, formed in 1812, a little north of San Francisco, was the cause of misgiving as to the Russians. A remedy was suggested in convict colonization, freedom of trade, and the establishing of communication between the Califor

2 F

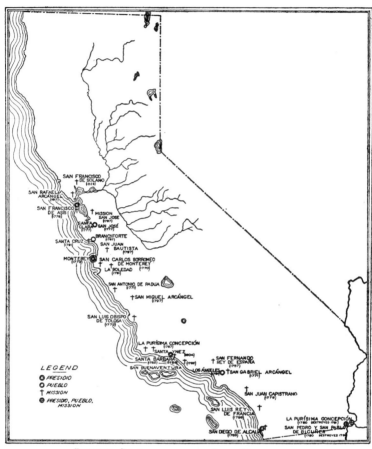

SPANISH SETTLEMENTS OF ALTA CALIFORNIA.

Alta California certainly continued, with ever-increasing justification,[33] but the day of action had passed.

The closing decades of Spanish rule in Alta California form one of those periods in the life of man which is the

nias, Sonora, and New Mexico. Tadeo Ortiz de Ayala, *Resumen de la estadística del imperio mexicano.* For another proposal at the same time, see Richman, 237, 470.

[33] With regard to foreign voyages on the Pacific coast of New Spain and,

particularly, voyages to the Californias the following thirteen *legajos* of the Archivo General de Indias are exceedingly rich in materials: *Estado, Audiencia de México,* 1, 4–15. I found nearly two hundred such documents in these *legajos.*

delight of the poet and romancer. "Life was one continuous round of hospitality and social amenities, tempered
with vigorous outdoor sport. There were no hotels in
California. Every door was open, and food, lodging, a
fresh horse, and money, even, were free to the guest, whether
friend or stranger. No white man had to concern himself
greatly with work, and even school books were a thing apart.
Music, games, dancing, and sprightly conversation — these
were the occupations of the time — these constituted educa-
tion. Also, men and women were much in the open; all
were expert horsemen, could throw a lasso, and shoot un-
erringly, even the women, accomplishments which fitted
their type of life, and made hunting a general pastime.
When foreign ships came, there were balls and the gayest
of festivals, nor were these visits the only occasion for that
type of entertainment." [34] In fine, here was an Acadia.
Life was less stirring than in other days, but infinitely more
agreeable. Yet, although the inhabitants could not possibly have known it, they were playing a part in history,
fraught with moment. They were holding Alta California
safe from foreign occupation, with its vast mineral wealth
undiscovered. Meanwhile, the United States was steadily
preparing to succeed to the rich inheritance which awaited
her on the shores of the Pacific.

[34] Chapman, *Spanish settlements on the Pacific coast.*

BIBLIOGRAPHICAL NOTES

I. Printed Works

THE number of works which at some point touch the field embraced by this volume is very great. A complete list would not only include very many narratives of the Spanish conquest, both by contemporaries, whether participants or not, and by writers of a later day, but would also give space to works on Spanish colonial institutions and Spanish colonization in general. Its value, however, in a work of this sort based primarily on manuscript materials, would be, at most, academic. Thus, a great number of works which I have actually employed in study surrounding my work will not be found in the list that follows. My bases for inclusion of titles have been: first, actual reference in my text to the works in question; or, secondly, in the case of a number of works not actually cited, a very intimate connection, nevertheless, with the field of this study. As for works in the first class, I have not included them where the reference has been incidental, without any necessary connection with the narrow limits of my field. As regards works of the second group, I have included outstanding works concerning the advance of the Spanish conquest up the Pacific coast toward the Californias and general histories of California. I have omitted works dealing with the period of Cortés, however, not alone because of their number, but also because their references to northwestward advance form only a meagre conclusion, as a rule, to their tale of Cortés' earlier conquests. Popular histories and references to repeated editions are omitted, an indication being given only of the edition used, or, in the case of works not cited, the first editions of works contemporary with my narrative and the latest editions of modern general histories. Distinction between primary and secondary materials has been abandoned, but it is believed that the object of that mode of arrangement has been attained by an index chronologically arranged according to the dates which the individual works represent as documents. Where publication followed promptly on completion of the work, the earliest date of publication is assigned; but where publication was delayed for many years a rough attempt is made to indicate the date when the writer completed his work. Comment on most of the items included in my list is unnecessary, but a few words may be said with regard to some of them.

Hubert Howe Bancroft's works have been used more than other printed materials in preparing this volume, especially the first volume of the *North Mexican States and Texas*, but except in the first chapter they have not been employed to any considerable extent. Of late it has been the fashion to pick flaws in Bancroft. Nevertheless, all students of Pacific coast history must begin with his works; they are the indispensable starting point.

Of early Spanish works treating of the progress of northwestward advance only those of Burriel and Palou have been drawn upon to any extent.   It may be said of all works of this class that they are useful primarily for events of the religious conquest, but rarely provide a clue to the causes of governmental action. These works should eventually take their place, therefore, as supplementary material, and the official correspondence should be substituted as the principal source on which investigators should rely for secular history.

Richman has been cited a number of times, usually, as it happens, in order to point out his errors. Nevertheless, there is much in Richman's work of value to the investigator, especially, perhaps, in his notes. Richman did not make adequate use of the materials that he cited, but unquestionably his is the best brief history of Spanish and Mexican California that has yet been written.

Father Engelhardt is doing valuable service in his work, not yet completed, in which he is bringing together a vast amount of data on the history of the Catholic missions of the Californias.

The *Colección* has been cited only once (chap. I, n. 11), but a few words about that set, based on my personal knowledge of some of the original documents from which the *Colección* was made up, and on general report current among workers at the Archivo General de Indias, may not be out of place. The *Colección* was compiled as a result of the Spanish government's desire to encourage the study of Spanish-American history, orders being given for the publication of documents. As an inducement to that end and to prevent delays a bonus was offered of so much for every printed page that should be published. The result in quantity was gratifying. To avoid slow, painstaking investigation the compilers drew very largely on *legajos* of the *Patronato Real*, a small group in the Archivo General de Indias which has been used more than others and was known to contain valuable materials about tne early explorers and conquerors. From these *legajos* they selected documents which were easy to read, choosing one or two in some cases from an *expediente* that contained twenty, and giving the title of the whole group to the one or two that they copied. Such, at least, was the case with certain New Mexico materials appearing in volumes fifteen and sixteen of the *Colección*.

Señor Torres Lanzas has contributed a valuable work, very well done, but it should be understood that it is by no means inclusive of all the maps in the Archivo General de Indias bearing on the regions named. Señor Torres Lanzas is gathering materials for a second and much amplified edition.

The work by N.N. deals with the entire Spanish domain in the Americas, not merely with the region which we now call the West Indies; indeed, that region gets very little attention. There are several chapters dealing with the northern frontier of New Spain, one of them being devoted wholly to the Californias.

Addison, Joseph. *Charles III of Spain.* Oxford. 1900.
Alegre, Francisco Javier. *Historia de la Compañía de Jesús.* 3 v. México. 1842.
Altamira y Crevea, Rafael. *Historia de España y de la civilización española.* 3 ed. 4 v. Barcelona. 1913–14.

Arlegui, José. *Chrónica de la provincia de n. s. p. s. Francisco de Zacatecas.*
México. 1737.
Arricivita, Juan Domingo. *Crónica seráfica y apostólica del Colegio de
Propaganda Fide de la Santa Cruz de Querétaro en la Nueva España.*
México. 1792.
Ascensión, Antonio de la. *Descubrimiento y demarcación de la California,*
in *Colección de documentos inéditos, relativos al descubrimiento, con-
quista y organización de las antiguas posesiones españolas de América
y Oceanía,* VIII, 537–74. Madrid. 1867.
Baegert, Jakob. *Nachrichten von der amerikanischen halbinsel Californien.*
Mannheim. 1772.
Bancroft, George. *History of the United States of America.* v. III–V.
New York. 1883–85.
Bancroft, Hubert Howe. *Works.* San Francisco. 1883–91.
    v. I. *The native races,* I. 1886.
    v. VI–VII. *History of Central America.* I–II. 1886.
    v. IX–XI. *History of Mexico,* I–III. 1886–87.
    v. XV. *History of the north Mexican states and Texas,* I. 1886.
    v. XVII. *History of Arizona and New Mexico.* 1889.
    v. XVIII. *History of California,* I. 1886.
    v. XXVI. *History of Utah.* 1889.
    v. XXVII. *History of the northwest coast,* I. 1886.
    v. XXXIII. *History of Alaska.* 1886.
    v. XXXVIII. *Essays and miscellany.* 1890.
Beaumont, Pablo de la Purísima Concepción. . . . *Crónica de la provincia
de los santos apóstolos S. Pedro y S. Pablo de Michoacán.* 5 v. México.
1873–74.
Bolton, Herbert Eugene. *Guide to materials for the history of the United
States in the principal archives of Mexico.* (Carnegie institution of
Washington. Publication no. 163. Papers of the Dept. of historical
research). Washington. 1913.
Bolton, Herbert Eugene. *The Spanish occupation of Texas, 1519–1690,*
in *Southwestern historical quarterly,* XVI, 1–26. Austin. 1912.
Bolton, Herbert Eugene. *Texas in the middle eighteenth century.* (Uni-
versity of California, *Publications in history.* v. III). Berkeley.
1915.
Bryce, George. *The remarkable history of the Hudson's Bay company.*
London. 1900.
Burpee, Lawrence Johnstone. *The search for the western sea; the story
of the exploration of north-western America.* New York. 1908.
Burriel, Andrés Marcos. *A natural and civil history of California . . .
Translated from the original Spanish.* 2 v. London. 1759.
Burriel, Andrés Marcos. *Noticia de la California y de su conquista temporal
y espiritual, hasta el tiempo presente. Sacada de la historia manuscrita,
formada en México año de 1739.* [!] *por el padre Miguel Venegas.*
3 v. Madrid. 1757.
Bustamante, Carlos María de. *See Cavo.*
Cardona, Nicolás. *Relación del descubrimiento del reino de la California*
in *Colección de documentos inéditos . . . América y Oceanía,* IX, 30–42.
Madrid. 1868.

Cavo, Andrés. *Los tres siglos de México durante el gobierno español . . . Publicada con notas y suplemento en 1836 por el licenciado D. Carlos María de Bustamante.* Jalapa. 1870.

Chapman, Charles Edward. *The Alta California supply ships, 1773–76,* in *Southwestern historical quarterly,* XIX, 184–94. Austin. 1915.

Chapman, Charles Edward. *Difficulties of maintaining the Department of San Blas, 1775–77,* in *Southwestern historical quarterly,* XIX, 261–70. Austin. 1916.

Chapman, Charles Edward. *The founding of San Francisco,* in *Grizzly bear magazine,* XVIII, nos. 3 and 4. Los Angeles. 1916.

Chapman, Charles Edward. *Importance of the military in early Spanish settlements of California,* in *Grizzly bear magazine,* XVIII, no. 2. Los Angeles. 1915.

Chapman, Charles Edward. *Spanish settlements on the Pacific coast,* in *Nature and science on the Pacific coast.* San Francisco. 1915.

Clavigero, Francisco Javier. *Storia della California.* 2 v. in 1. Venezia. 1789.

Costansó, Miguel. . . . *The narrative of the Portolá expedition of 1769–1770* . . . ed. by Adolph van Hemert-Engert . . . and Frederick John Teggart. (Academy of Pacific coast history, *Publications,* I, 91–159). Berkeley. 1910.

Costansó, Miguel. . . . *The Portolá expedition of 1769–1770; diary of Miguel Costansó,* ed. by Frederick John Teggart. (Academy of Pacific coast history, *Publications,* II, 161–327). Berkeley. 1911.

Coxe, William. *Memoirs of the kings of Spain of the house of Bourbon.* v. IV–V. London. 1815.

Croix, Charles François, *marquis* de Croix. *Correspondance du marquis de Croix . . . 1737–1786,* ed. by [a descendant,] the Marquis de Croix. Nantes. 1891.

Danvila y Collado, Manuel. *Reinado de Carlos III.* 6 v. (*Historia general de España escrita por individuos de número de la Real academia de la historia bajo la dirección del Excmo. Sr. D. Antonio Cánovas del Castillo*). Madrid. 1891–96.

Dellenbaugh, Frederick Samuel. *The romance of the Colorado River.* 3 ed. New York and London. 1909.

Doniol, Jean Henri Antoine. *Histoire de la participation de la France á l'établissement des Etats-Unis d'Amerique.* v. I. Paris. 1885.

Eldredge, Zoeth Skinner. *The beginnings of San Francisco from the expedition of Anza, 1774, to the city charter of April 15, 1850.* 2 v. San Francisco. 1912.

Eldredge, Zoeth Skinner. [*Studies of the Anza routes*], in *Journal of American history,* II, 38–42, 255–61, 521–26, 696–701; III, 103–12, 171–79, 395–403. New York. 1908–09.

Engelhardt, Charles Anthony, *in religion* Zephyrin. *The Franciscans in Arizona.* Harbor Springs, Mich. 1899.

Engelhardt, Charles Anthony, *in religion* Zephyrin. *The Franciscans in California.* Harbor Springs, Mich. 1897.

Engelhardt, Charles Anthony, *in religion* Zephyrin. *The missions and missionaries of California.* v. I–II. San Francisco. 1908–12.

BIBLIOGRAPHICAL NOTES 441

Espinosa, Isidro Félis de. *Chrónica apostólica, y seráphica de todos los Colegios de Propaganda Fide de esta Nueva-España.* México. 1746.
Fages, Pedro. . . . *The Colorado River campaign, 1781–1782; diary of Pedro Fages,* ed. by Herbert Ingram Priestley. (Academy of Pacific coast history, *Publications,* III, 132–233). Berkeley, 1913.
Fages, Pedro. . . . *Expedition to San Francisco Bay in 1770; diary of Pedro Fages,* ed. by Herbert Eugene Bolton. (Academy of Pacific coast history, *Publications,* II, 141–59). Berkeley, 1911.
Fernán-Núñez, Carlos José Gutiérrez de los Ríos, conde de. *Vida de Carlos III.* 2 v. *(Libros de antaño, nuevamente dados á luz por varios aficionados,* v. XIV–XV). Madrid. 1898.
Fernández Duro, Cesáreo. *Armada española desde la unión de los reinos de Castilla y de Aragón.* v. VII. Madrid. 1901.
Ferrer del Río, Antonio. *Historia del reinado de Carlos III en España.* 4 v. Madrid. 1856.
Fita y Colomé, Fidel. *Noticia de la California, obra anónima del P. Andrés Marcos Burriel . . . Datos inéditos é ilustrativos de su composición, aprobación y edición,* in Real academia de la historia, *Boletín,* LII, 396–438. Madrid. 1908.
Florencia, Francisco de. *Historia de la provincia de la Compañía de Jesús. De Nveva-España.* México. 1694.
Fonseca, Fabián de, and Carlos de Urrutia. *Historia general de real hacienda.* v. 1. México. 1845.
Font, Pedro. . . . *The Anza expedition of 1775–1776; diary of Pedro Font,* ed. by Frederick John Teggart. (Academy of Pacific coast history, *Publications,* III, 1–131). Berkeley, 1913.
Frejes, Francisco. *Memoria histórica de los sucesos más notables de la conquista particular de Jalisco por los Españoles.* Guadalajara. 1879.
Gálvez, Bernardo, conde de. *Instrucción formada en virtud de real orden de S. M., que se dirige al señor comandante general de provincias internas Don Jacobo Ugarte y Loyola para gobierno y puntual observancia de este superior gefe y de sus inmediatos subalternos.* México. 1786.
Gálvez, José de, marqués de Sonora. *Informe general que . . . entregó al excmo sr. virrey . . . Antonio Bucarely y Ursúa . . . 31 de diciembre de 1771.* México. 1867.
Garcés, Francisco. *Diario y derrotero que siguió el M. R. P. Fr. Francisco Garcés en su viaje hecho desde octubre de 1775 hasta 17 de setiembre de 1776, al Río Colorado para reconocer las naciones que habitan sus márgenes, y á los pueblos del Moqui del Nuevo-México,* in *Documentos para la historia de Méjico,* 2 sér., I, 225–374. Méjico. 1854.
Garcés, Francisco. *On the trail of a Spanish pioneer; the diary and itinerary of Francisco Garcés . . .* ed. by Elliott Coues. 2 v. New York. 1900.
Golder, Frank Alfred. *Russian expansion on the Pacific, 1641–1850.* Cleveland. 1914.
González Cabrera Bueno, José. *Navegación especvlativa, y práctica.* Manila. 1734.
Greenhow, Robert. *The history of Oregon and California, and the other territories of the northwest coast of North America.* 4 ed. Boston. 1847.

Hackett, Charles Wilson. *Retreat of the Spaniards from New Mexico in 1680, and the beginnings of El Paso,* in *Southwestern historical quarterly,* XVI, 137–68, 258–76. Austin. 1912–13.

Hackett, Charles Wilson. *The revolt of the Pueblo Indians of New Mexico in 1680,* in Texas state historical association, *Quarterly,* XV, 93–147. Austin. 1911.

Herrera y Tordesillas, Antonio de. *Historia general de los hechos castellanos en las islas i tierra firme del mar océano.* 8 v. in 4. Madrid. 1601–15.

History of California [by Clinton A. Snowden and others] ed. by Zoeth Skinner Eldredge. 5 v. New York. 1915.

Hittell, Theodore Henry. *History of California.* 4 v. in 8. San Francisco. 1898.

Hodge, Frederick Webb. *Handbook of American Indians north of Mexico.* 2 v. (Smithsonian institution. Bureau of American ethnology. Bulletin 30). Washington. 1907–10.

Hughes, Anne E. *The beginnings of Spanish settlement in the El Paso district.* (University of California, *Publications in history,* I, 295–392). Berkeley. 1914.

Humboldt, [Friedrich Wilhelm Heinrich] Alexander, [freiherr von]. *Essai politique sur le royaume de la Nouvelle Espagne.* 5 v. Paris. 1811.

Humboldt, [Friedrich Wilhelm Heinrich] Alexander, [freiherr von]. *Political essay on the kingdom of New Spain . . . Tr. from the original French by John Black.* 2 ed. 4 v. London. 1814.

Humboldt, [Friedrich Wilhelm Heinrich] Alexander, [freiherr von]. *Versuch über den politischen zustand des Königsreichs Neu-Spanien.* 2 v. Tübingen. 1809–14.

Lafuente y Zamalloa, Modesto. *Historia general de España, desde los tiempos más remotos hasta nuestros días.* 30 v. Madrid. 1850–67.

Laut, Agnes Christina. *The conquest of the great Northwest; being the story of the adventurers of England known as the Hudson's Bay Company.* New York. 1911.

López de Velasco, Juan. *Geografía y descripción universal de las Indias recopilada por el cosmógrafo-cronista Juan López de Velasco desde el año 1571 al de 1574.* Madrid. 1894.

Manning, William Ray. *The Nootka Sound controversy,* in American historical association, *Annual report . . . for the year 1904,* 279–478. Washington. 1905.

Mayer, Brantz. *Mexico, Aztec, Spanish and republican.* v. I. Hartford. 1853.

Mendieta, Gerónimo de. *Historia eclesiástica indiana.* México. 1870.

Mota Padilla, Matías Ángel de la. *Historia de la conquista de la provincia de la Nueva-Galicia.* México. 1870. [1871–72].

N   , N   , gent. *America: or An exact description of the West Indies: more especially of those provinces which are under the dominion of the king of Spain.* 2 pts. in 1 v. London. 1655.

Neve, Felipe de. *Reglamento é instrucción para los presidios de la península de Californias, erección de nuevas misiones, y fomento del pueblo y estensión de los establecimientos de Monterey,* in *Recopilación de leyes . . .*

de los Estados-Unidos Mexicanos . . . formada . . . por el lic. Basilio José Arrillaga, (Comprende este tomo de Enero á Diciembre de 1828. México, 1838), pp. 121–75.

Ortega, José de. *Apostólicos afanes de la Compañía de Jesús.* Barcelona. 1754.

Ortiz de Ayala, Tadeo. *Resumen de la estadística del imperio mexicano.* México. 1822.

The Pacific Ocean in history: papers and addresses presented at the Panama-Pacific historical congress . . . 1915. New York. 1916.

Palou, Francisco. *Noticias de la Nueva California.* 4 v. San Francisco. 1874.

Palou, Francisco. *Relación histórica de la vida y apostólicas tareas del venerable padre fray Junípero Serra.* México. 1787.

Pérez de Ribas, Andrés. *Historia de los trivmphos de nvestra santa fée entre gentes las más bárbaras, y fieras del Nueuo orbe.* Madrid. 1645.

Portolá, Gaspar de. . . . *Diary of Gaspar de Portolá during the California expedition of 1769–1770,* ed. by Donald Eugene Smith . . . and Frederick John Teggart. (Academy of Pacific coast history. *Publications,* I, 31–89). Berkeley. 1909.

Recopilación de leyes de los reynos de las Indias. 9 lib. in 4 v. 3 ed. Madrid. 1774.

Reglamento é instrucción para los presidios que se han de formar en la línea de frontera de la Nueva España, in *Recopilación de leyes . . . de los Estados-Unidos Mexicanos . . . formada . . . por el lic. Basilio José Arrillaga. (Comprende este tomo los meses de Enero á Diciembre de 1834.* Mexico. 1835), pp. 139–89.

Revilla Gigedo, Juan Vicente Güémez Pacheco de Padilla Horcasitas y Aguayo, conde de. *Early California. Unpublished documents — the viceroy's report,* tr. in *Land of sunshine,* XI, 32–41, 105–12, 168–73, 225–33, 283–89. Los Angeles. 1899.

Revilla Gigedo, Juan Vicente Güémez Pacheco de Padilla Horcasitas y Aguayo, conde de. *Instrucción reservada que el conde de Revilla Gigedo dió á su succesor en el mando . . . sobre el gobierno de este continente en el tiempo que fue su virey.* México. 1831.

Richman, Irving Berdine. *California under Spain and Mexico, 1535–1847.* Boston and New York. 1911.

Rivera Cambas, Manuel. *Los gobernantes de México.* v. I. México. [1873].

Rousseau, François. . . . *Règne de Charles III d'Espagne (1759–1788).* 2 v. Paris. 1907.

Serra, Junípero. *Letter of Fray Junípero Serra . . . to . . . Antonio María Bucareli y Ursúa . . . giving some account of the condition of the missions and complaining of the conduct of Captain Pérez and of the governor — dated 7th October, 1774,* Sp. and tr. in *Documents from the Sutro collection,* in Historical society of southern California, *Publications,* II, 73–80. Los Angeles. 1891.

Suárez de Peralta, Juan. *Noticias Históricas de la Nueva España.* Madrid. 1878.

Teggart, Frederick John. *The approaches to the Pacific coast,* in *Nature and science on the Pacific coast.* San Francisco. 1915.

Tello, Antonio. *Crónica miscelánea y conquista espiritual y temporal de la Santa Provincia de Xalisco.* 29 pts. in 1 v. Guadalajara. 1890–91.

Torquemada, Juan de. *Primera [segunda, tercera] parte de los veinte i vn libros rituales i monarchía indiana.* 3 v. Madrid. 1723.

Torres Lanzas, Pedro. *Relación descriptiva de los mapas, planos, & [!], de México y Floridas, existentes en el Archivo General de Indias.* 2 v. Sevilla. 1900.

Twitchell, Ralph Emerson. *The leading facts of New Mexican history.* 2 v. Cedar Rapids, Iowa. 1911–12.

Twitchell, Ralph Emerson. *The Spanish archives of New Mexico.* 2 v. Cedar Rapids, Iowa. 1914.

Vetancurt, Augustín de. *Teatro mexicano. Descripción breve de los svcessos exemplares, históricos, políticos, militares, y religiosos del Nvevo mundo occidental de las Indias.* 4 pts. in 1 v. México. 1698 [1697].

Villa-Señor y Sánchez, José Antonio de. *Theatro americano, descripción general de los reynos, y provincias de la Nueva-España.* 2 v. México. 1746–48.

Willson, Beckles, *i.e.* Henry Beckles. *The great company: being a history of the honourable company of merchants-adventurers trading into Hudson's Bay.* Toronto. 1899.

Zamacois, Niceto de. *Historia de Méjico.* v. V. Barcelona and México. 1878.

Zárate Salmerón, Gerónimo de. *Relaciones de todas las cosas que en el Nuevo-México se han visto y sabido . . . desde el año de 1538 hasta el de 1626* in *Documentos para la historia de México*, 3 sér., (4 v. in 1), IV, 1–55. México. 1856.

Chronological Index of Printed Works, Arranged According to Approximate Date of Completion of the Work

1574	López	1737–84	Croix	1775–77	Garcés
1589	Suárez	1742	Mota	1775–77	Garcés
1596	Mendieta		Padilla	1779	Neve
1601–15	Herrera	1746	Espinosa	1780	Beaumont
1615	Torque-	1746–48	Villa-Señor	1781–82	Fages
	mada	1754	Ortega	1783	Palou
1620	Ascensión	1757	Burriel	1786	Gálvez, B.
1626	Zárate	1757	Burriel	1787	Palou
1632	Cardona	1767	Alegre	1789	Clavigero
1645	Pérez	1769–70	Costansó	1789	Fernán-
1653	Tello	1769–70	Portolá		Núñez
1655	N.N.	1770	Costansó	1791	Fonseca
1681	Recopila-	1770	Fages	1792	Arricivita
	ción	1771	Gálvez, J.	1793	Revilla
1694	Florencia	1772	Baegert		Gigedo
1697	Vetancurt	1772	Reglamento	1793	Revilla
1734	González	1774	Serra		Gigedo
1737	Arlegui	1775–76	Font	1794	Cavo

1809–14	Humboldt	1891–96	Danvila	1911	Hackett
1809–14	Humboldt	1897	Engelhardt	1911	Laut
1809–14	Humboldt	1899	Engelhardt	1911	Richman
1815	Coxe	1899	Willson	1911–12	Twitchell
1822	Ortiz	1900	Addison	1912	Bolton
1833	Frejes	1900	Bryce	1912	Eldredge
1836	Bustamante	1900	Torres	1912–13	Hackett
1844	Greenhow		Lanzas	1913	Bolton
1850–67	Lafuente	1900–11	Altamira	1914	Golder
1852–74	Bancroft,	1901	Fernández	1914	Hughes
	G.		Duro	1914	Twitchell
1853	Mayer	1904	Manning	1915	Bolton
1856	Ferrer del	1907	Rousseau	1915	Chapman
	Río	1907–10	Hodge	1915	Chapman
1873	Rivera	1908	Burpee	1915	Chapman
1878	Zamacois	1908	Fita	1915	History
1883–90	Bancroft,	1908–09	Eldredge	1915	Pacific
	H.	1908–12	Engelhardt	1915	Teggart
1885	Doniol	1909	Dellen-	1916	Chapman
1885–97	Hittell		baugh	1916	Chapman

II. MANUSCRIPT MATERIALS

The bulk of the present work rests upon manuscript materials not hitherto used by historical writers. While a certain small proportion of the documents cited have been drawn on by others, notably by Bancroft, Richman, and Engelhardt, such materials, when employed here, have been utilized independently, and usually in a different way than in other works referring to them. Only a general description of manuscript material used by me can be given here.

A. *Documents in the Academy of Pacific Coast History, Berkeley, California.* These include local records, and copies from various archives of Mexico and Spain. Except for the documents referred to in paragraphs B, C, and D, I have drawn wholly on the Academy collection for manuscript materials. As regards material from the Archivo General de Indias, I used the Academy copies in many cases, but was able later to verify the references by comparison with the originals in the Archivo General de Indias, in which event citations are made by my *Catalogue* number to documents of the latter archive. In a few instances Academy copies from that archive were used of material that does not appear in the *Catalogue*. In those cases citation has been made to the *legajo* number of the Archivo General de Indias preceded by A.G.I., but it is to be understood that the Academy copies were used. The same practice has been followed with regard to copies acquired from Mexican and other Spanish archives by the Academy, that is, since the "Bancroft Collection" became the property of the University of California. A number of documents of the Archivo General y Público de la Nación (A.G.P.) and Museo Nacional (M.N.) of the City of Mexico have been referred to, and a few citations have been made to Mexican archives outside of the capital. Bolton's *Guide* (in-

cluded in my list of printed works) will supply any information that may
be lacking in my citations. Many of the copies thus far referred to were
part of Professor Bolton's private collection when I used them. A few
copies from the Archivo Histórico Nacional (A.H.N.) of Madrid, Spain,
have also been used. Other documents of the Academy have been cited
according to their location in volumes of the Bancroft Collection, preceded
by A.P.C.H. Special notice should be accorded to the James Bryce
Historical Essay manuscript of Mr. Karl C. Leebrick, used extensively
in chapter eight.

B. *Documents in the Archivo General de Indias, Seville, Spain.* These
have been by far the principal source for this volume. Out of the immense
mass of material in that archive bearing on the subject of this work I have
listed 6257 items. These in fact represent a great many more documents,
because *testimonios*, which often contain scores or even hundreds of separate
documents, were entered as one item. Thousands of items might have
been added had time permitted, but, as matters are, most of the documents
fall between the years 1760 and 1786. The entire list has been arranged in
chronological order with a view to possible publication, for the documents
are of value for far more than has been undertaken in this work. The
list alone would fill, if published, two or three octavo volumes. Reference
to such of these items as I have used has been made by a number preceded
by the letter C. The C stands for *Catalogue*, the first word of the title of a
manuscript list of the items in question ; the number is the serial number
of the document cited in a chronological arrangement of the list. Publication of the *Catalogue* is contemplated, but even if it shall not be published,
it will be accessible in manuscript at the Academy of Pacific Coast History.
It seems necessary, however, to supply information here regarding the
location of the documents cited by me, and such information is provided at
the end of this section. The material in Appendix I, referred to in chapter
three, was used at the Archivo General de Indias, although not entered
in my *Catalogue*. The same thing is true of the Crame map. Attention
may be called to the extraordinary wealth for the historical investigator
of the Archivo General de Indias. It is intended that all of the official correspondence of Spain's four centuries of over-seas administration shall
eventually be gathered into that one archive, and possibly half of all
materials on that subject now in Spain is already there. The advantages
of pursuing studies at one point, instead of having to visit the hundreds of
smaller archives in the Americas, are obvious. The materials are also of
the highest authority, being the official documents on which the Council
of the Indies and the *ministros generales* based their decisions. They consist chiefly of the following : originals (signed with the name and rubric
of the writer) of colonial officials writing to Spain ; copies, usually from
originals and usually certified, enclosed with documents of the first-named
class ; drafts, retained as the file copy, of replies, or orders sent from Spain
to the colonies; similarly, originals, copies, and drafts of inter-depart-
mental correspondence in Spain ; and finally originals and drafts of intra-
departmental correspondence, by means of which affairs were dealt with by
the *ministros generales* and the Council themselves. Cf. chap. VII, n. 63.

C. *Documents in the British Museum, London.* Considerable use
has been made in chapter five of an *expediente* in manuscript volume

13,974, section G., of the British Museum. These papers are not transcripts, but must originally have been deposited in the archives of the viceroyalty or of the College of San Fernando, probably in the former. Father Superior Verger's letters are signed with his rubric and marked duplicate. Those from Palou and others in the Californias to him are copies, often certified. In other words this is only the first remove from the technically best file, and lacks only the drafts of the *fiscal's* replies to Verger (which would almost surely appear in the original file) to be as useful as the principal *expediente*. These papers were purchased by the British Museum of "Tho. Rodd," March 11, 1843. How Mr. Rodd got them is not explained. A copy of the British Museum *expediente* now exists in the Academy of Pacific Coast History.

D. *The Biblioteca Nacional, Madrid.* The only document used independently of copies in the Academy of Pacific Coast History is the Cardona memorial, with maps, cited in chapter one.

In the list that follows of manuscript materials of the Archivo General de Indias used in preparation of this volume, the number at the left is the *Catalogue* (C–) number, followed by a reference to the location of the particular document in the archive at Seville. Where numbers are employed they represent (from left to right) *estante, cajón,* and *legajo* numbers. Documents in the *Papeles de Estado* group are numbered on a different plan. The following abbreviations are employed in citing them: Est, *Estado;* Am. G, *América en General;* A. G, *Audiencia de Guadalajara;* A. M, *Audiencia de México.*

15	104–3–4	46	"	186	"
16	"	47	"	187	"
17	67–3–27	48	"	188	"
20	67–3–28	49	"	189	"
21	67–3–27	50	"	191	"
24	"	51	"	192	"
26	"	52	"	193	"
27	"	53	"	199	"
28	104–6–17	54	"	201	"
30	67–3–27	55	"	202	"
31	"	56	"	203	"
32	"	57	"	204	"
33	"	58	"	205	"
34	"	59	"	207	"
35	"	60	"	208	"
36	"	61	"	212	"
37	"	62	"	213	103–5–25
38	"	63	"	217	"
39	67–3–28	65	"	219	"
40	67–3–27	66	"	224	"
41	"	177	67–4–45	225	"
42	67–3–28	178	"	228	"
43	"	182	"	231	"
44	"	184	"	232	"
45	"	185	"	236	67–3–29

239	103–5–25	337	"	395	"
240	67–3–29	338	"	397	67–3–31
241	103–5–25	339	"	398	104–3–4
242	67–3–29	340	67–3–31	399	67–5–3
243	"	341	"	400	"
244	"	343	103–6–23	401	"
245	"	344	"	402	104–3–4
246	"	345	103–5–20	403	"
249	103–5–25	348	67–3–31	404	"
253	67–3–29	349	104–3–4	405	103–3–6
254	103–5–25	350	67–3–31	409	67–3–31
256	"	351	"	411	103–6–23
259	67–3–29	352	104–3–4	412	"
260	"	353	67–3–31	413	"
263	"	354	103–3–6	415	"
266	"	355	67–3–31	416	67–3–31
272	"	356	104–3–4	417	"
274	"	357	"	418	67–5–3
276	"	358	104–3–5	419	67–3–31
277	"	359	"	420	67–5–3
278	"	360	"	421	103–6–23
279	"	361	"	427	"
283	104–3–4	362	"	428	"
286	103–5–20	363	"	429	"
287	"	364	"	431	67–3–31
290	"	365	"	432	"
291	"	366	"	433	"
292	67–3–31	367	"	434	103–6–23
295	103–6–23	368	"	435	"
307	67–3–29	369	"	437	67–3–31
308	"	370	"	438	104–3–4
310	67–3–31	371	"	440	"
311	"	372	67–5–3	441	"
313	67–3–30	373	"	442	Est, Am. G, 1
314	67–3–31	374	"	444	67–3–31
315	67–3–29	375	"	448	"
316	67–3–31	377	"	449	"
317	67–3–29	379	103–3–6	450	104–3–4
321	67–3–31	380	103–6–23	451	103–3–6
322	"	381	67–3–31	453	104–3–4
324	103–5–20	382	104–3–4	454	103–6–21
325	67–3–31	383	67–3–31	455	"
326	"	384	104–3–4	458	104–3–4
327	103–5–20	386	103–6–23	459	"
330	67–3–31	387	67–3–31	460	"
331	"	388	104–3–4	461	103–3–6
332	"	389	103–6–23	468	103–6–27
334	104–3–4	391	"	469	103–6–23
335	"	393	104–3–5	470	104–3–4
336	"	394	67–5–3	472	103–6–24

477	103–4–9	593	103–3–21	1271	104–3–2
478	"	596	104–6–13	1284	104–1–7
483	14–60–13	597	"	1290	104–3–2
484	"	598	"	1294	"
485	"	622	"	1305	"
486	"	628	103–3–21	1317	"
489	"	705	104–6–13	1348	104–1–7
492	103–6–24	706	"	1356	89–3–22
493	104–6–13	712	96–1–11	1365	Est, A. M, 19
494	Est, Am. G, 1	731	103–4–15	1384	89–3–22
495	103–6–24	735	96–1–11	1421	104–6–14
496	"	775	104–6–13	1434	104–1–7
499	104–6–13	811	104–3–2	1441	"
501	"	840	"	1447	104–3–4
502	"	842	"	1455	"
503	"	845	104–6–13	1460	"
511	"	880	104–3–2	1468	104–3–2
512	"	888	Est, Am. G, 1	1473	104–6–14
513	"	908	Est, A. M, 1	1504	104–3–4
518	"	930	104–6–15	1514	"
519	"	938	Est, Am. G, 1	1543	Est, Am. G, 1
520	"	940	104–3–2	1549	104–6–14
521	"	952	104–3–4	1553	"
524	"	954	104–3–2	1579	104–3–4
527	"	956	"	1583	104–6–14
528	104–1–6	961	"	1602	104–3–4
530	104–6–13	974	104–6–13	1712	103–7–1
531	88–5–25	977	"	1720	104–6–14
533	104–6–13	990	104–3–3	1725	104–3–2
540	104–5–19	993	104–2–13	1729	104–6–14
542	104–6–13	994	104–3–2	1731	104–3–2
544	104–5–19	1000	"	1735	"
545	Est, Am. G, 1	1001	"	1738	"
546	104–6–13	1002	104–3–3	1752	"
549	"	1014	"	1759	103–4–15
550	"	1051	104–3–2	1760	"
555	"	1066	"	1765	104–6–15
558	"	1068	"	1778	104–6–14
560	103–6–25	1069	103–3–12	1782	104–3–4
561	Est, Am. G, 1	1070	104–3–4	1783	104–6–14
562	104–5–19	1076	104–3–2	1792	"
564	104–6–13	1080	"	1799	"
569	"	1100	104–3–3	1802	"
571	"	1118	104–3–4	1806	"
572	"	1150	96–1–11	1807	"
573	"	1167	104–3–2	1810	104–3–2
574	"	1207	"	1813	104–6–14
582	"	1237	104–1–7	1820	"
590	"	1250	104–3–2	1821	"
591	"	1253	104–1–7	1834	Est, A. M, 15

2 G

1841	104–6–14	2197	Est, Am. G, 1	2394	"
1843	104–6–24	2199	104–6–14	2396	104–6–15
1850	104–6–14	2203	104–6–15	2397	Est, A. M, 1
1872	104–6–15	2204	"	2405	104–6–14
1895	104–6–14	2209	Est, A. M, 1	2424	104–6–15
1908	"	2210	Est, Am. G, 1	2425	104–6–14
1909	"	2211	Est, A. M, 1	2430	Est, A. M, 1
1910	"	2218	104–6–15	2438	104–6–14
1915	"	2219	"	2439	"
1922	"	2221	Est, Am. G, 1	2441	"
1925	104–6–17	2229	104–6–15	2446	104–6–15
1926	104–6–14	2230	"	2447	104–6–14
1931	"	2231	"	2454	104–3–4
1941	"	2233	"	2455	104–6–16
1959	104–3–4	2234	"	2456	Est, A. M, 1
1969	104–6–14	2237	"	2457	"
1983	"	2244	"	2464	"
1992	"	2246	"	2489	103–4–14
1993	"	2247	"	2496	104–6–16
1995	"	2249	Est, Am. G, 1	2501	104–6–15
2007	"	2250	"	2502	Est, A. M, 1
2010	"	2252	"	2503	104–3–4
2037	104–6–15	2254	104–6–15	2506	104–6–15
2038	Est, Am. G, 1	2270	104–6–14	2507	"
2045	104–6–15	2278	104–6–16	2508	104–6–16
2056	104–3–4	2279	104–3–4	2509	"
2058	104–6–14	2289	Est, A. M, 1	2514	Est, Am. G, 1
2060	"	2290	"	2520	Est, A. M, 1
2074	104–6–15	2295	"	2521	"
2077	"	2296	104–6–14	2522	104–6–16
2103	104–6–16	2304	"	2533	104–6–15
2106	"	2306	Est, A. M, 1	2543	"
2108	"	2324	104–6–14	2550	104–6–16
2109	"	2331	104–6–16	2551	Est, A. M, 1
2113	104–6–15	2332	104–6–14	2554	104–6–15
2126	Est, Am. G, 1	2334	104–6–15	2560	104–3–4
2137	104–6–15	2337	Est, A. M, 1	2566	104–6–16
2140	"	2342	88–5–17	2567	104–6–15
2149	"	2346	104–6–14	2597	Est, A. M, 1
2152	"	2350	104–6–16	2602	104–3–4
2161	104–3–4	2352	104–6–14	2603	"
2162	Est, Am. G, 1	2356	"	2607	104–6–15
2175	104–6–15	2365	Est, A. M, 1	2608	"
2177	104–6–16	2380	"	2615	Est, A. M, 1
2178	104–6–15	2388	104–6–15	2624	104–6–15
2180	104–6–14	2389	104–6–16	2625	"
2185	"	2390	"	2626	"
2186	"	2391	"	2627	"
2195	"	2392	"	2628	"
2196	"	2393	104–6–14	2634	88–5–17

2636	Est, Am. G, 1	2792	104–6–16	2976	"
2640	104–6–17	2816	Est, A. M, 1	2977	"
2642	104–6–15	2826	104–6–16	2978	104–6–16
2644	104–6–17	2837	104–6–17	2979	104–6–17
2645	Est, A. M, 1	2839	104–3–4	2983	104–6–16
2648	104–6–15	2840	"	2984	"
2649	Est, A. M, 1	2841	104–6–17	2985	Est, A. M, 1
2653	104–6–17	2845	104–3–4	2998	104–6–17
2654	"	2846	104–6–18	3000	104–6–16
2656	104–6–15	2848	Est, A. M, 1	3001	104–6–18
2657	"	2857	104–6–16	3002	Est, A. M, 19
2658	"	2858	"	3003	Est, A. M, 1
2659	"	2859	"	3004	"
2676	103–4–14	2860	"	3005	"
2679	104–6–15	2861	104–6–15	3006	"
2680	"	2862	"	3014	Est, A. M, 19
2681	Est, A. M, 1	2870	104–6–17	3019	104–6–17
2705	104–6–15	2872	104–6–16	3025	"
2706	"	2874	Est, A. M, 1	3026	104–6–16
2707	"	2875	"	3028	Est, A. M, 1
2708	"	2878	104–6–16	3032	"
2709	"	2885	104–6–17	3033	"
2716	Est, A. G, 1	2893	Est, A. M, 1	3034	"
2718	104–6–15	2896	104–6–16	3035	"
2719	104–6–17	2900	Est, A. M, 19	3036	104–6–17
2720	"	2901	"	3037	"
2721	"	2902	"	3038	"
2722	104–6–15	2904	104–6–17	3039	"
2723	"	2906	103–3–13	3042	"
2724	"	2910	104–6–17	3044	"
2732	Est, A. M, 1	2911	"	3045	"
2735	104–6–15	2912	104–6–16	3050	104–6–16
2737	"	2916	"	3051	104–6–17
2740	"	2917	"	3052	"
2745	"	2919	"	3053	"
2757	Est, A. M, 1	2920	"	3057	Est, A. M, 1
2761	104–6–16	2923	"	3058	"
2762	"	2928	Est, A. M, 1	3062	"
2763	Est, A. M, 1	2929	"	3070	104–6–18
2764	104–6–15	2930	"	3110	"
2765	Est, A. M, 1	2933	104–6–17	3142	104–6–17
2766	104–6–16	2934	104–6–16	3143	"
2771	88–5–17	2935	"	3152	"
2777	Est, A. M, 1	2944	Est, A. M, 19	3154	"
2780	"	2945	"	3155	"
2781	104–6–16	2949	104–6–17	3156	"
2782	88–5–17	2951	Est, A. M, 1	3157	Est, A. M, 1
2783	Est, A. M, 1	2967	"	3162	104–6–17
2784	"	2969	"	3167	"
2785	104–6–15	2975	104–6–17	3173	"

3175	"	3365	"	3527	"
3180	"	3370	"	3529	"
3183	"	3373	"	3530	"
3184	"	3375	"	3532	"
3185	"	3376	"	3534	"
3186	"	3377	"	3538	"
3191	"	3379	"	3539	"
3193	"	3380	"	3540	"
3204	"	3382	"	3547	"
3205	"	3389	"	3558	"
3206	"	3390	"	3562	"
3223	Est, A. M, 1	3394	103–1–13	3563	"
3248	104–6–17	3401	104–6–17	3564	"
3252	"	3402	"	3565	"
3254	96–1–12	3403	"	3574	"
3260	104–6–17	3404	"	3606	"
3262	104–6–18	3406	104–6–18	3613	"
3265	"	3409	"	3615	"
3266	"	3410	"	3619	"
3267	104–6–17	3411	"	3624	"
3268	"	3412	"	3625	"
3269	"	3413	"	3626	"
3270	"	3416	"	3638	"
3272	"	3418	"	3639	"
3275	"	3423	"	3641	104–6–17
3276	"	3430	"	3650	"
3280	"	3431	"	3655	104–6–18
3285	"	3432	"	3660	103–4–12
3288	104–5–24	3433	103–6–8	3671	104–6–18
3291	104–6–18	3453	104–6–18	3673	"
3292	"	3454	"	3674	103–4–12
3293	103–3–13	3455	"	3675	"
3294	"	3457	104–5–24	3676	104–6–18
3299	104–6–18	3460	104–6–18	3678	"
3300	"	3462	"	3687	"
3301	104–6–17	3464	"	3688	"
3311	104–6–18	3465	"	3689	"
3319	96–1–12	3469	"	3691	"
3323	104–7–33	3470	"	3693	"
3325	104–6–17	3474	"	3697	"
3326	"	3475	"	3705	"
3327	104–6–18	3478	"	3712	"
3328	"	3479	"	3719	104–6–17
3331	104–6–17	3481	"	3723	103–4–12
3343	104–6–18	3484	"	3741	"
3346	104–6–17	3494	"	3743	"
3351	104–6–18	3496	"	3791	103–4–9
3357	104–6–17	3521	"	3879	"
3358	104–6–18	3522	"	3880	103–4–12
3360	"	3525	"	3881	103–4–17

3882	103–4–9	4330	"	5160	104–5–19
3917	103–4–19	4354	"	5161	"
3924	104–6–19	4406	103–4–24	5176	"
3925	"	4408	"	5204	103–5–5
3926	"	4409	"	5206	103–5–6
3965	103–4–9	4430	"	5227	103–5–5
3966	"	4492	103–4–13	5244	103–5–6
3974	103–4–12	4493	"	5258	104–5–19
3997	103–4–19	4514	104–6–19	5297	"
4017	104–6–19	4541	103–4–14	5298	104–5–24
4082	103–3–24	4568	103–3–24	5302	104–5–19
4095	103–4–13	4633	103–4–13	5399	105–1–25
4097	"	4727	103–5–2	5400	"
4103	"	4767	104–6–20	5453	104–5–19
4128	104–6–19	4793	103–5–3	5458	"
4129	"	4915	103–5–4	5492	"
4130	"	4932	"	5613	Est, A. M, 2
4131	103–4–19	4933	"	5711	103–5–11
4189	103–7–7	4934	"	5712	"
4190	"	4935	"	5722	"
4244	103–4–14	4938	"		

APPENDIX I

The following table was prepared by the writer from materials in *legajos* 104-3-9 and 104-3-21 in the *Archivo General de Indias*. The three sets of figures given in each column are for *pesos, tomines* or *reales,* and *granos,* respectively. Remissions were made to the *caja real* of the place named. Percentage is reckoned on the basis of the proportion of the amount remitted to the amount of receipts. These figures are commented upon in chapter three.

Years	Receipts	Disbursements	Remissions Mexico	Remissions Álamos	%
1743	255,183-2-4	37,119-4-10	218,063-5-6	—	85
1744	234,952-0-3½	36,825-2-3½	198,126-6-0	—	84
1745	227,650-1-8½	31,082-6-6½	196,567-3-2	—	86
1746	200,050-0-9½	33,621-5-6½	166,428-3-3	—	83
1747	213,648-5-5½	35,775-5-5	177,873-0-0	—	83
1748	256,947-2-9	37,970-5-0¾	218,976-5-8¼	—	85
1749	244,502-4-10	58,531-0-2	185,971-4-8	—	76 [1]
1750	346,357-4-0	32,513-6-8	313,843-5-4	—	90
1751	344,796-4-1	39,370-7-3	305,425-4-10	—	88
1752	279,934-3-5	34,576-7-9	245,357-3-8	—	87
1753	381,447-3-1	36,755-5-7	344,691-5-6	—	90
1754	248,254-1-3½	35,259-0-4½	212,995-0-11	—	85
1755	281,326-1-4	32,841-2-3½	248,484-7-½	—	88
1756	253,962-1-10½	34,430-0-7½	219,532-1-3	—	86
1757	263,468-0-5½	34,215-3-2½	229,252-5-3	—	87
1758	302,522-1-9	34,001-0-1½	268,521-1-7	—	88
1759	304,736-2-11	34,638-4-2	270,097-6-9	—	88
1760	277,108-1-3	35,630-2-6½	241,477-6-8½	—	87
1761	321,828-6-2½	36,527-5-5½	285,301-0-9	—	88
1762	348,568-1-2½	36,074-6-8½	312,493-2-6	—	89
1763	410,041-5-5	37,544-1-6	372,497-3-11	—	90
1764	354,940-3-8	42,299-3-0	312,641-0-8	—	88
1765	418,981-6-11	46,353-2-9	372,628-4-2	—	88
1766	514,073-7-0	36,864-3-11	477,209-3-1	—	92
1767	425,691-5-0	43,014-7-10	382,676-5-2	—	89
1768	453,036-5-1	53,756-5-7	399,279-7-6	—	88
1769	432,699-5-9½	44,961-7-1½	387,737-6-8	—	89

[1] The amount remitted in 1749 would have been eighty-four per cent, if disbursements included the *situado* for a presidio, as seems likely.

Table Showing Total Receipts and Disbursements of the Real
Caja of Guadalajara in Each Year from 1743 to 1781. *Continued*

Years	Receipts	Disbursements	Remissions		%
			Mexico	Álamos	
1770	344,667–6–9	43,322–7–8½	301,344–6–½	—	87
1771	344,608–6–10	49,148–0–4	295,460–6–6	—	85
1772	382,643–1–3	56,915–1–11	314,930–1–0	—	82 [2]
1773	540,986–6–4	58,086–1–4	376,940–1–7	91,995	86 [2]
1774	510,874–1–4	70,030–0–6½	324,479–1–6½	104,493–1–0	84 [2]
1775	524,422–5–9½	64,553–0–10½	316,991–4–2	132,991–2–0	85 [2]
1776	496,383–6–11	60,591–0–9	314,027–1–3½	110,000	85 [2]
1777	450,317–7–6	92,883–6–8½	290,486–1–0	50,000	75 [2]
1778	567,368–1–8	97,337–6–4	350,030–3–4	120,000	82
1779	628,338–7–5½	15,668–4–2½	312,670–3–3	200,000	81 [3] [4]
1780	526,072–2–5	70,146–7–0	307,806–6–0	140,000	85 [2]
1781	717,847–7–10½	81,516–1–6	436,475–1–8½	130,000	79 [2] [4]
	14,631,242–6–½	1,892,757–1–6¼	11,505,995–4–11¼	1,079,479–3–0	86

[2] The discrepancy between totals for these years is due to the fact that small amounts were kept on hand, *e.g.* in 1772, 10,797–6–4.

[3] The total receipts in 1779 were 948,338–7–5½, but of this amount 320,000 had been sent from Mexico.

[4] In the columns for remissions to Álamos, San Blas figured twice. In 1779, San Blas got 80,000 from Guadalajara, and in 1781, the full 130,000. In fact, San Blas got 400,000 in 1779, but that sum included the 320,000 sent from Mexico (*supra*, n. 3). Of this amount 150,000 was for the Philippines.

APPENDIX II. SPECIMEN TABLES OF THE REAL CAJA OF GUADALAJARA, SHOWING RECEIPTS AND DISBURSEMENTS, ITEM BY ITEM, FOR EACH OF TWO YEARS

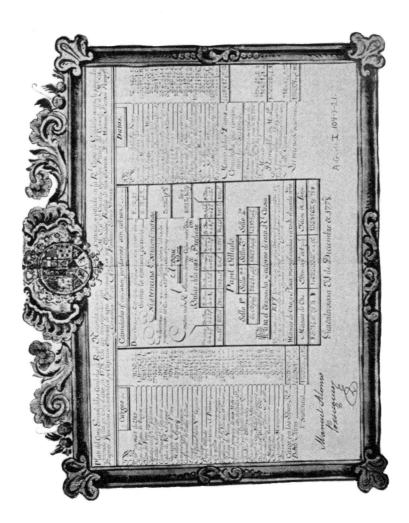

APPENDIX III

DIARIES OF THE ANZA EXPEDITIONS

IN recent years many copies of different diaries of the Anza expeditions have been procured by American libraries, and a number of them have been translated and published, so that most are accessible. It would not be worth while to attempt to make a list of all such copies, but there is a real value in pointing out the location of original diaries, or, where that is not known, of such contemporary copies as were used by the government at that time as a basis for action. It is still far from possible to provide a complete list, but I shall point out as many of the diaries as I have been able to get trace of, giving also a brief indication of their content and use. I shall eliminate variants, rough drafts, and extracts. All of the diaries mentioned, except the larger Font, exist in some form in the Academy of Pacific Coast History.

I. The Expedition of 1774

A. 1774. Jan. 8 to Apr. 5. San Gabriel. Juan Bautista de Anza. *Diario de la Ruta y operaciones que yo el infrascrito Capitán . . . hago y practico en solicitud de abrir camino de dhã Provincia* [Sonora] *á la California Setemptrional.* Certified copy, June 26, 1774, México. 120 pages, 21½ by 31 cm. A.G.I., 104–6–15; another, A.G.I., 104–3–4. C–2503.

B. 1774. Apr. 6 to May 27. Dated Nov. 13, México. Juan Baupᵗᵃ de Anza. *Continuación del Diario del Capitán . . . Anza . . . que . . . comprehende su regreso hasta . . . Tubac.* Certified copy, Nov. 26, 1774, México. 23 pages, 21½ by 31 cm. A.G.I., 104–6–15; another, A.G.I., 104–3–4. C–2602.

C. 1774. Jan. 8 to May 27. Dated Nov. 13, México. Juan Bapᵗᵃ de Anza. *Diario de la 1ª Expedición q practicó por Tierra el año de 74 el Tenᵗᵉ coronel . . . Ansa á los Nuevos establecimᵗᵒˢ de la California.* Original. [A.P.C.H. copy, 92 pages, 21 by 27½ cm., typed.] A.G.P., *Historia,* v. 396.

D. 1774. Jan. 8 to Mar. 22. San Gabriel. Juan Díaz. *Diario, que forma el Padre Fr. Juan Díaz . . . en el viage . . . para abrir camino desde la Provincia de la Sonora á la California Septentrinal.* Original. [A.P.C.H. copy, 33 pages, 21 by 27½ cm., typed.] A.G.P., *Historia,* v. 396.

E. 1774. May 3 to May 26. Tubac. Juan Díaz. *Diario que formó el P. Fr. Juan Díaz . . . en el Viage, que hizo desde . . . Sⁿ Gabriel . . . hasta . . . Tubac.* Certified copy, Sept. 26, 1774, México. 19 pages, 21½ by 31 cm. A.G.I., 104–6–17. C–2616.

F. 1774. Jan. 22 to Apr. 26. San Dionisio [near the junction of the Gila and Colorado rivers]. Francisco Garcés. *Diario de la Entrada que se practica . . . para los nuevos Establecimientos de San Diego, y Monterrey.* Original. [A.P.C.H. copy, from an unnamed source in Spain, 52 pages, 23 by 33 cm., typed]. A.G.P., *Historia,* v. 52.

The latter part of *C* is the same as *B,* but the earlier part of *C* differs substantially from *A.* The paragraphing is the same, but in *C* remarks are added or left out and the Spanish phraseology is improved. *A, D,* and *F* were carried to Mexico by Anza's courier Valdés, being delivered to Bucarely early in June. No continuation of Garcés' diary has been found, nor any complete Díaz or Garcés diary like the *C* of Anza. Garcés probably wrote a continuation, and this seems the more likely since he remained in one of the Cocomaricopa villages of the Gila, after Anza's expedition had departed.[1] The significance of the opening and closing dates of the diaries is explained in a note.[2]

A, B, and *C* are fullest in details, and perhaps had most weight with governmental officials of the time. *D* and *E* are brief, and much like *A, B,* and *C* in matters of route, but add something in other respects. *F* is strikingly original, good on matters of route, and teeming with Garcés' ideas concerning the advancement of the conquest. *D* and *E* are in excellent Spanish; the Spanish of *F* is so bad as to be at times almost unintelligible;[3] and *A, B,* and *C* are a readable medium between them.

II. The Expedition of 1775–76

G. 1775, Oct. 23, to June 1, 1776. Horcasitas. Juan Bap^{ta} de Anza. *Diario de la Rutta y Operaciones que Yo el Infrascripto Theniente Coronel . . . practico segunda vez . . . á la California Setemptrional.* Original. [A.P.C.H. copy, 142 pages, 21 by 27½ cm., typed]. A.G.P., *.9ai,.osritv36H*

H. 1775, Oct. 21, to Sept. 17, 1776. Dated Jan. 3, 1777. Tubutama. Francisco Garcés. *Diario que ha formado . . . en el viage hecho este año de 1775 . . . con . . . Anza, y . . . Font . . . acompañándolos hasta el río Colorado.* Certified copy, May 31, 1777, México. 215 pages, 21½ by 31 cm. A.G.I., 104–6–18; another copy, not certified, in the same *legajo.* C-3001.

[1] Garcés was desirous of finding out whether he could get a letter through to New Mexico from that point.

[2] January 8, the expedition leaves Tubac; January 22, the departure from Caborca, after which point the march was to proceed through lands not nearly so well known as those between Tubac and Caborca; March 22, the arrival at San Gabriel; April 5, Anza decides to send back part of his forces to the Colorado River and ends diary *A,* in order to send that with the returning party, and thence to Mexico; April 6, while still at San Gabriel, Anza begins a new diary; April 26, the party sent back to the Colorado under Garcés reaches San Dionisio, near the junction; May 3, the remainder of Anza's forces leaves San Gabriel for the return to Sonora; May 26, Anza and Díaz reach Tubac ahead of the expedition; May 27, the expedition reaches Tubac.

[3] I am inclined to believe that Garcés' bad Spanish is in some measure the fault of copyists. Garcés refers to the illegible character of his penmanship in Garcés to Bucarely, Mar. 8, 1773 (In C–2113).

I. 1775, Sept. 29, to June 2, 1776. Dated June 23, 1776, Ures. Pedro Font. *Diario que forma . . . del viage que hizo á Monterey y Puerto de S.ⁿ Francisco.* Original. 79 pages, 15½ by 21 cm. A.P.C.H.
J. 1775, Sept. 29, to June 2, 1776. Dated May 11, 1777, Tubutama. Pedro Font. *Diario que formó . . . en el viage que hizo á Monterey.* Original. 336 pages, 14⅘ by 20 cm. John Carter Brown Library, Providence.[4]
Father Eixarch accompanied the expedition as far as the junction of the Gila and Colorado rivers, but no diary by him has been found. *J* is an expansion of *I*, the two being identical except for the extensive insertions in *J*.[5] Although there are wide differences in the Garcés diaries that have come to light, it is probable that they are but variants from the same original.[6] The opening and closing dates of the diaries are explained in a note.[7]

H is an exceptionally important document, but not so valuable for the Anza expedition as the others, since Garcés did not go on with Anza when the latter departed from the Gila and Colorado junction on December 4. Further references to the expedition appear, however, in entries of later date. *H* was accorded prominent attention by the governmental authorities, but more particularly for its testimony concerning the region of the Colorado and Gila and the route to Moqui. For the expedition proper, *G* was the most important diary from the standpoint of official use. The style and the Spanish of *G* and *H* are similar respectively to *A, B, C,* and *F* of the 1774 diaries. *I*, the official Font diary, is a meagre account, not comparable with *G* in value, except for information regarding the exploration of San Francisco Bay, in which case the story is given by it in detail. *J* seems not to have been written with a view to being submitted to the governmental authorities, nor have I seen any reference to it in official correspondence. For the facts of the expedition, however, it is a noteworthy supplement to *G*, and for information about the lands and peoples along the march it is very valuable, mentioning details not occurring in other diaries of the two expeditions, *e.g.* descriptions of *flora.* Although something of a pedant, Font perhaps had a greater fund of learning than

[4] Mr. Champlin Burrage, librarian of the John Carter Brown Library, very graciously supplied me with the technical data concerning diary *J.*

[5] The Font accounts are considered in Pedro Font, *The Anza expedition of 1775–1776; diary of Pedro Font,* edited by Frederick J. Teggart, in A.P.C.H., *Publications,* III, 3–5. Berkeley, 1913. In the same work, pages 6 to 131, the Spanish and an English translation of *I* appear. Of the four accounts mentioned there, one seems to have been a report by Font to his college, not a diary, and another was the rough draft that he made in course of the march.

[6] A consideration of three Garcés diaries is given in Garcés (Coues ed.), I, *Introduction.* Coues surmised that all three were based on the same origi-nal. Cf. n. 3. *H* was not known to Coues. It would seem to be nearest to the original, in point of date of certi-fication, of any Garcés diary at present known. Coues translated into English one of the versions that he refers to. Another appears in Spanish in *Docu-mentos para la historia de México.* 2d series, I, 225–374.

[7] September 29, 1775, the expedi-tion leaves Horcasitas; October 21, Garcés goes from his mission of Bac to Tubac, to join the expedition there; October 23, the expedition leaves Tubac; June 1, 1776, arrival at Hor-casitas on the return; June 2, still at Horcasitas, where Font makes an astronomical observation; September 17, Garcés reaches Bac on his return.

the other frontier missionaries whose diaries have come to my notice, and he does not fail to display his knowledge in diary *J* whenever occasion offers. Much space is devoted also to the expression of his petty and rather harmless spite against Anza. From the trivial details which he cites in this connection, however, and so too from other portions of his account, one gets such an intimate view of the march as rarely appears in official diaries. From the standpoint of interest as a story, I have never read a diary that compares with the *J* of Font.

APPENDIX IV

THE ECHEVESTE-ANZA CALCULATION OF THE PROBABLE COST OF THE SECOND ANZA EXPEDITION

IN course of the preparations for Anza's second expedition Anza and Juan José de Echeveste were asked to draw up a minute calculation of the probable cost of the expedition. A translation of their calculation is given below, partly because it bears a relation to the northwestward movement, showing in one instance the expense which the government was ready to undergo, but more because of its interest from the standpoint of individual equipment, wages, and prices at that time. The estimates are in *pesos* and *reales*, eight *reales* being worth one *peso*. The present value of a *peso* would be fifty cents. I have seen copies of this document in three *testimonios* concerning the preparations for the second Anza expedition. The location and nature of the three *testimonies* are as follows:

A. Certified copy, dated December 24, 1774, México, in A.G.I., 104–6–16. (C-2496.)

B. Copy in A.P.C.H. of a certified copy, dated January 18, 1775, México, in A.G.P., *Californias*, v. 72.

C. Copy in A.P.C.H. of a certified copy, dated March 20, 1777, México, in A.G.P., *Californias*, v. 35.

The original is probably in A.G.P., *Provincias Internas*, v. 134, a volume which contains the originals of other documents in the file of papers concerning the authorization of the second Anza expedition. José de Gorráez certified that the copies mentioned in *A* and *B* conformed to the original, and Melchor de Peramás did so for the copy referred to in *C*. There are some differences in the three. *B* employs abbreviations of words, while the words appear in full in *A* and *C*. Certain obvious errors or omissions in some of the copies are corrected by use of the others. The translation is based on all three, with an indication in notes of some of their difficulties and differences.

"Minute calculation of the cost that it may amount to: for the wardrobe of thirty recruits, their wives, and the garments adequate for one hundred and eighty children, six for each one, half for males and half for females; for the arms, riding-horses, rations, and baggage for the service and transportation of all, from the province of Ostimuri to the presidio of San Carlos de Monterey, namely:

461

" Wardrobe for a Man

Item			Pesos
3 shirts of good Silesian linen	at 18 reales		6 pesos 6
3 pairs of underdrawers of Puebla cloth [1] of 4 varas,[2] each one	" 2 "		3 " 0
2 cloth coats which with their lining and trimmings are worth			9 " 3
2 pairs of trousers, ditto			5 " 3
2 pairs of stockings	" 2 "		0 " 4
2 pairs of chamois-skin boots	" 10 "		2 " 4
3 pairs of gaiter shoes [3]	" 5 "		1 " 7
1 cloth cape lined with thick flannel			11 " 0
1 hat			0 " 6
2 Puebla powder-cloths [4]	" 2 "		0 " 4
1 ribbon for the hat and hair			0 " 4
			42 pesos 1

" Ditto for a Woman

Item			Pesos
3 shirts	at 4 pesos		12 pesos 0
3 pairs of white Puebla petticoats	" 12 reales		4 " 4
2 pairs of petticoats, some of silk serge, others of thick flannel, and an underskirt, all at a cost of			16 " 0
2 varas of linen stuff for two linings	" 5 "		1 " 2
2 pairs of Brussels stockings	" 4½ "		1 " 1
2 pairs of hose	" 2 "		0 " 4
2 pairs of shoes	" 6 "		1 " 4
2 women's shawls	" 12 "		3 " 0
1 hat			0 " 6
6 varas of ribbon			0 " 6
			41 pesos 3

For 30 wardrobes of men and women at 83 pesos, 4 reales   2505 pesos

" Clothing for Ninety Boys

Item			Pesos
5 pieces of cloth containing 180 varas	at 12 reales		270 pesos 0
12 pieces of Puebla cloth for linings and white trousers	" 6 pesos 4 reales		78 " 0
270 varas of linen stuff for shirts of about 3 varas	" 5 "		168 " 6
50 hats [5]	" 4 "		25 " 0
8 dozen shoes for children of various sizes	" 4 "		32 " 0

[1] The Spanish is *Manta de la Puebla*. *Manta* is a coarse kind of cloth.

[2] A *vara* is equivalent to 2.78 feet.

[3] *B* has *zapatos abotonad^s* which might be rendered "button shoes." *A* and *C* have it *zapatos abotinados* (or *avotinados* in *C*), which might mean black shoes or gaiter shoes as rendered above.

[4] This is a doubtful translation for *Paños de Polvos Poblanos*.

[5] Possibly the fifty hats were only a reserve supply, as the boys might be expected to have a hat apiece to begin with. Certainly fifty hats could not be divided among ninety boys.

" Clothing for an Equal Number of Girls"

270 *varas* of linen stuff for shirts	at 5 *reales*	168 *pesos* 6
4 pieces of Puebla cloth [6] for petticoats and linings	" 6 *pesos* 4	26 " 0
90 cloths for women's shawls of all sizes	" 10 *reales*	112 " 4
2 pieces of thick flannel for little petticoats	" 45 *pesos*	90 " 0
4 pieces of cloth of about 34 *varas* for undershirts	" 12 *reales a vara*	204 " 0
12 pieces of ribbon for bands		20 " 0
16 ditto of fine rope		5 " 0
8 dozen shoes for girls of various sizes	" 4 *pesos*	32 " 0
120 blankets, single bed size for all	" 15 *reales*	225 " 0
120 shepherds' [7] blankets	" 5 "	75 " 0
		1532 *pesos* 0 [8]

" Arms"

20 saddle-tree guns [9]	at 12 *pesos*	240 *pesos* 0
20 cases of those that they call *fundas ordinarias* [10] of good timber	" 15 *reales*	37 " 4
20 swords		85 " 0
20 lances		40 " 0
22 [11] leather jackets [12] of about 7 *ases* [13] each a *vara* and a quarter in length	" 24 *pesos*	528 " 0
30 shoulder-belts with the name of *San Carlos de Monterey*	" 11 *reales*	41 " 2
20 cartridge-boxes with 14 bullets	" 10 "	25 " 0
		996 *pesos* 6

" Horses and Trapping for a Man" [14]

60 horses, 2 for each recruit	at 8 *pesos*		480 *pesos* 0
20 saddles	" 9 "	4 *reales*	190 " 0
20 pairs of spurs	"	7 "	17 " 4
20 fine mule-bits	"	11 "	27 " 4
20 pairs of pads	" 2 "		40 " 0

[6] *Manta* is rendered "Puebla cloth," although *de la Puebla* does not appear in this case.

[7] For *Pastoras*, a word that does not appear in the Spanish dictionaries. Probably it was made from the noun *Pastor*, meaning "shepherd." Blankets worn to-day by shepherds in Mexico have a hole in the centre through which the wearer puts his head, leaving the blanket to fall naturally about his shoulders.

[8] Thus it appears that the wardrobe for each man in terms of American money, if a *peso* is reckoned as fifty cents, was to cost $21.03; each woman, $20.59; each boy, $4.02; and each girl, $4.48.

[9] *Escopetas de Arzon* means literally "shot-guns of saddle-tree," probably referring to the guns used by cavalry-men, which are attached to the saddle-tree. The word "guns" is used instead of "shot-gun" because *escopetas* was frequently used in documents of that time, as if it were the general word for "gun."

[10] *Fundas ordinarias* is equivalent to "ordinary cases."

[11] Eight of the thirty soldiers were to be veterans; therefore but twenty-two were necessary.

[12] *B* has *cuerdas* which would mean "ropes," "cords," or "halters," clearly an error for *cueras* which *A* and *C* have.

[13] An *as* is a measure of weight amounting to eleven ounces. Therefore, these jackets would weigh four pounds and eleven ounces each.

[14] This paragraph was omitted in *A*, an error of the copyist, for these estimates of expense appear in the totals.

"Ditto for a Woman and Family

60 mares	at 8 pesos	480 pesos	0
30 saddles	" 9 " 4 reales	285 "	0
30 fine mule-bits	" 11 "	41 "	2
		1561 pesos	2

By 60 rations, 3 [15] each family at 1½ reales in 40 days which is reckoned as the duration of the march, with the necessary delays, in the 200 leagues from Álamos [16] to the presidio of Tubac .... 450 pesos 0

"Baggage and Beasts of Burden

20 mules	at 25 pesos	500 pesos	0
20 instruments and things in connection with them	" 4 " 2½ reales	86 "	2
30 chamois-skin gripsacks for the soldiers and their families	" 2 "	60 "	0
		646 pesos	2

By 3 months' pay in advance to the lieutenant, sergeant, and 28 soldiers: the first at the rate of the enjoyment of 700 pesos a year; 450 to the second; and one peso daily to each soldier .... 2807 pesos 4

10,498 pesos 6

"Collection of stores at the presidio of Tubac necessary for the expedition, of useful articles necessary for it, of cattle, provisions, and their conveyances, to ration all its people, reckoning 70 days' march, including rests, for 122 individuals, to which its number reaches, the expense of everything in detail and that of the aid [in useful articles] which it is bearing to the presidio of San Carlos de Monterey, namely:

1 flag with the royal coat of arms		12 pesos	0
11 tents for cavalry of bramant linen, with wooden frames from those that the factory of the royal estate [17] possesses, and [of a kind] that shall be fit for use,[18] 10 for the 30 families and [the other] for the Father Chaplain	at 27 pesos	292 "	0
4 Biscayan hatchets well strengthened with iron	" 3 "	12 "	0
4 spades ditto	" 9 reales	4 "	4
4 shovels ditto	" 3 pesos	12 "	0
1 small crow-bar	"	.5 "	0
10 ball cartridges		0 "	0
40 sole-leather powder-flasks for blasting	" 4 reales	20 "	0
Carry forward		345 pesos	4

[15] This should be two rations a day for each family, because there were thirty families, and, in fact, but two meals a day were taken during the march. It is written "3" in B and C, and "tres" in A.

[16] B has los bams. Álamos was in fact the vicinity where Anza intended to recruit his force.

[17] Real Hacienda, referring to the board of finance in Mexico.

[18] B and C omit the part of this sentence after "possesses" through "use."

Brought forward			345	*pesos*	4
8 iron pans [19]	at	2 *pesos*	16	"	0
10 copper campaign kettles	"		75 20	"	0
12 large chocolate-pots ditto	"		6	"	0
1 case of iron pieces [21] well adapted and arranged; ⅔ for horses and ⅓ for mules; with a duplicate key	"		82	"	0
1 tool-chest [with the instruments] for shoeing horses			10	"	0
2 blank-books for military registers	"	2 "	4	"	0
			550	*pesos*	4

"Cattle and Provisions to Ration the People of the Expedition

				pesos	
100 head of cattle, one for each day	at	8 *pesos*	800	*pesos*	0
30 loads of flour for *tortillas* [22]	"	8 "	240	"	0
60 *fanegas* [23] of *pinole* [24]	"	18 *reales*	135	"	0
60 *fanegas* of kidney-beans	"	5 *pesos*	300	"	0
6 cases of ordinary chocolate			225	"	0
2 *tercios* [25] of white sugar with 6 [26] *arrobas* [27]	"	2 "	12	"	0
12 *pesos* [worth] of soap			12	"	0
3 barrels of *aguardiente* [28] for necessities	"	71 "	213	"	0
			1957	*pesos*	0

"Table for the *comandante* and chaplain about which Echeveste is making a statement to His Excellency the viceroy against the objection of the party concerned [Anza].

				pesos	
1 case of beans [29] with 7 *arrobas*	at	5 *pesos*	35	*pesos*	0
25 pounds of pork-sausage	"	1 "	25	"	0
6 cases of biscuit			96	"	0
1 ditto of fine chocolate with 7 *arrobas* at 3¼ *reales* [30]			82	"	0
1 barrel of wine			65	"	0
6 *arrobas* of cheese	at	2 *pesos*	12	"	0
4 pounds of pepper	"	5½ *reales*	2	"	6
½ pound of saffron			3	"	0
4 ounces of cloves	at	6 *pesos* a pound	1	"	4
4 ditto of cinnamon	"	9 " " "	2	"	2
Carry forward			223	*pesos*	4

[19] *Comales*, or flat pans, used in cooking corn-cakes.

[20] *B* and *C* have 15 *pesos*, but the 75 of *A* is in accord with the totals and with the normal price.

[21] The Spanish word is *herreaje* in *A* and *errage* in *B* and *C*, for what is now *herraje*. The literal translation has been preferred rather than "shoes" or "horseshoes," which the writers probably meant, that word being *herradura*.

[22] A kind of pan-cake.

[23] A *fanega* is equivalent to about 1.6 bushels.

[24] A kind of cereal meal.

[25] A *tercio* is one of the packages of a mule-load.

[26] *A* has 16, but 6 seems to be right.

[27] An *arroba* is equivalent to 25 pounds.

[28] A spirituous liquor.

[29] In *A* it is *jamones*, or hams.

[30] The extension for the amount and price stated is wrong, but some small measure seems to be contemplated. At 3¾ *reales* a pound the extension would be correct and more in keeping with the price that we would expect.

Brought forward			323	*pesos* 4
1 jug [31] of [olive] oil	at		4	" 2
1 ditto of vinegar			5	" 0
For the freight of all the pieces reckoned at 500 *arrobas*		" 28 *reales*	750	" 0
For sleeping-mats,[32] *guangoches*,[33] large sacks and plaited bass-ropes			78 [34]	" 6
For 140 leathern sacks for the provisions		" 4 *reales*	70	" 0
			2232	*pesos* 4

"*Beasts of Burden for Carriage* [*of Freight*]

4 divisions composed of 132 mules	at 25 *pesos*	3300	*pesos*
100 complete harnesses for the 4 divisions	" 6½ "	650	" 0
20 mule-drivers with their respective monthly salaries from 8 to 14 *pesos*, reckoned for a journey of only 2½ months		540	" 0
		4490	*pesos* 0

"*Provision and Aid for the New Establishments*

200 head of cattle: bulls and cows	at 6 *pesos*	1200	*pesos* 0
6 Indian cowboys at 1 *real* each day		52	" 4
		1252	*pesos* 4

"*Gifts for the Indians*

6 cases of glass beads that contain no black and abound in red, with 600 war-clubs	at 8½ *reales*	637	*pesos* 4
1 sleeveless cloak of blue cloth lined with gold	"	20	" 0
1 coat and trousers of chamois-skin	"	13	" 0
2 shirts [35]	" 4 *pesos*	8	" 0
1 cap with its coat of arms like that of dragons		5	" 0
2 *tercios* of highest grade tobacco containing 350 lbs.		262	" 4
		946	*pesos* 0
[Total]		21,927	*pesos* 2

" As appears in the margin, the calculation of the outfit of the 30 recruits with their families and wardrobe, the arms, horses and trappings, baggage and beasts of burden, and other expenses of the second expedition of Captain Juan Bautista de Anza, from his presidio of San Ignacio de Tubac to that of San Carlos de Monterey, [amounts to] *21,927 pesos, 2 reales,* in which quantity is included the estimated value of the effects at present in the royal estate here and at Álamos, to the end that one may at once gain a clear knowledge of the total cost of the expedition." [36]

[31] *Botija*, a round, earthen, short-necked jug.

[32] The word is *petates*, which might also be rendered "luggage" or "baggage."

[33] *Guangoches* is the Mexican word for a certain kind of thick, coarse cloth.

[34] *B* and *C* have 18 *pesos*, but the 78 of *A* accords with the totals.

[35] *B* and *C* omit this item. By in-cluding it the total becomes a *peso* too high, but without it would be 9 *pesos* too much. The shirts, as also the cloak, coat, and trousers, were for a gift to Chief Palma of the Yumas.

[36] The signature of Juan José de Echeveste alone appears on all three copies, but it is clear from other documents that Anza helped Echeveste to draw up the document.

APPENDIX V

RESOLUTION OF THE JUNTA OF DECEMBER 16, 1774, CONCERNING
AUTHORIZATION OF A SECOND EXPEDITION BY ANZA TO ALTA CALIFORNIA

THE following literal translation was based on a copy in the Academy of Pacific Coast History from the original resolution, signed with the names and rubrics of the members of the *junta*, in A.G.P., *Provincias Internas*, v. 134. This was compared and found to agree substantially with copies *B* and *C*, referred to in Appendix IV. The document is also in copy *A* of Appendix IV (C–2496). It is referred to in the text in chapter XII, where the names of the signers are given, in note 70.

"It was resolved by common agreement : that, for the new expedition or sally which Captain Don Juan Bautista de Anza is to make from his presidio of San Ignacio de Tubac to that of San Carlos de Monterey and to the two new missions which are to be established, everything be done as he has proposed for the accomplishment of so laudable an enterprise, to which effect and as regards enlistments of those [soldier-settlers] whom His Excellency deemed necessary to accompany him, let there be issued by the said Excellency the suitable decrees for appointments of a lieutenant and a sergeant from one of the subjects proposed for each position by Captain Anza, leaving to his [Anza's] judgment the choice of ten soldiers that he needs to accompany him [to Alta California and back], and granting that he himself may recruit the rest to his satisfaction. And to this end, and that such desertion as may occur may be checked, let His Excellency despatch the strictest orders to the respective courts of justice, that they on their part may aid Captain Don Juan Bautista de Anza on this and other matters which may present themselves in the accomplishment of this undertaking, until [he may go] by way of the same route that he discovered, deliver his people to *Comandante* Don Fernando de Rivera y Moncada, and assist in exploring the Río de San Francisco, and thereupon be able to inform His Excellency of what he may see there, and return with the ten soldiers accompanying him. And let him be accompanied, as on the first expedition, by Father Garcés who will wait for him on the banks of the Colorado until his return ; and besides the said Father, he shall be accompanied also by *Fray* Pedro Font on all the journey, so that [the latter] as one skilled in these matters may observe latitudes. And to this effect let there be sent to him by the hand of Captain Anza the instruments which he may need, and for this matter [about Font] let the fitting official letter of request and command be despatched by His Excellency to the Reverend Father Superior [of Querétaro].

"And having noted the total of expense to which this expedition amounts, and that Don José de Echeveste and the captain himself took things into consideration in detail in order to form it,[1] and as this royal *junta* has considered the matter with exceeding particularity, it was resolved with

---

[1] This refers to the itemized list of expected expenditures. See Appendix IV.

468   APPENDIX V

respect to these affairs, that from the pious funds employed for propagation of the faith in the Californias there be spent 10,000 *pesos* of the treasure at present in the money chest assigned for its custody, to which end the director [of the pious fund] shall put at the disposal of the royal officials of this court 10,000 *pesos* for the expenses of the new expedition, which sum they shall deliver to the *factor* Don Manuel Ramón de Goya, and they shall do the same with whatever more may be required to be spent for it, and whatever it shall be, let it be charged to the account of the royal treasury. Let 2000 more *pesos* from the same funds [be delivered] to the syndic of the College of San Fernando, a thousand for each of the new missions which are going to be established at the Río de San Francisco or in its vicinity, it likewise remaining in the duty of His Excellency to despatch the corresponding official letter to the Reverend Father Superior [requiring him] to put in them the missionary Fathers of his [college] who are now in Monterey. And [let] 10,000 *pesos* [be employed] to assist in expenses of the Department of San Blas, which amount, conformably to the royal *junta* of July 8 of last year, is due to be supplied with despatch for the first named [San Blas], and for this once only, from the pious funds of the treasure which is in the aforesaid chest, and still this amount has not been paid. And finally, as to what Don Juan Bautista de Anza set forth about not being able to gather by himself the things for provision of the individuals of the expedition, because he has to be occupied in recruiting the new troop in different places, to this effect His Excellency named a person who may do it, or rather let it be Don Miguel Gregorio de Echarri,[2] whom the said captain proposes, and of whom he says that he managed these matters with credit in the barracks of Pitic during the military expedition in those provinces, or [let it be] another, whoever shall be to his will, as a favor that is due to him for his work, and let the person that he shall be pleased to appoint keep an account and explanation of what he shall spend so as to present it to the *intendente* or royal official of Álamos.

"And for everything, let there be drawn up sworn copies [*testimonios*] of the explanation of costs and [of the proceedings] of this *junta*: one for *Comandante* Don Fernando [Rivera y] Moncada; another for the *factor*, Manuel Ramón de Goya; another for the *Tribunal y Real Audiencia de Cuentas* [tribunal and royal court of accounts]; another for the royal officials of this count; and another of the same and of his representations of the 17th ultimo and 5th instant, for Captain Don Juan Bautista de Anza, and let the latter, the *factor* Goya, and *Comandante* [Rivera y] Moncada, and in the same way the missionary Fathers make separately a formal and approved account of their respective expenses to remit to His Excellency, as soon as their distribution and employment have taken place. And finally, let it be drawn up in triplicate so as to give an account to His Majesty of everything new that has been done up to now since [the time of] the royal order with his approval, for he has already had a report of what happened before that.

"Thus, this is agreed upon, and the gentlemen who composed it [the *junta*] signed."

[2] This wording of the resolution is some evidence to show that Bucarely was the real ordering authority. It looks as if the *junta* momentarily for- got its rôle of appearing to order the appointment, and then in language corrected itself. Cf. chap. VII, n. 63.

APPENDIX VI

THIS document is the draft, retained for the *ministro general*'s file, and consequently not signed, of a letter of the date mentioned from Gálvez to Teodoro de Croix. It is to be found in A.G.I., 103–4–9, (C–3965). The phrase *Por Dup^{do}* indicated that both an original and a duplicate were to be presented to Gálvez for his signature and both mailed to Croix. The document, used briefly in chapter XVII, is here inserted entire:

Ha entendido el Rey los progresos que los PP^{es} Misioneros han con-seguido en las Misiones y Presidios de Californias, assí en la extensión de la Religión Católica, como en el beneficio y Cultivo de aquellos Terrenos: lo que ha sido mui del agrado de S.M. y me manda que reitere á V.S. el encargo de q mire p^r aquellos Establecimientos con la preferencia y esmero q^e merece Su importancia, como S.M. lo espera del zelo de V.S. cuya vida g^{de} Dios m^s a^s El Pardo á 6 de Marzo de 1779. S^r D^n teodoro de Croix. Por Dup^{do}

469

APPENDIX VII

THE status of settlements in Sinaloa and Sonora was a fact of great importance at all times in its bearing on matters of northwestward advance. In the table following there appears for the year 1781, an important date in the history of Spanish conquest in the direction of Alta California, more complete data than is usually available for the eighteenth century. The table shows not only the total population, but also its distribution by districts, distinguishing, too, according to sex, and as between adults and children. The figures may be taken to include the entire Christian population, without distinction as to blood, but they probably did not include unconverted Indians. The table appears in paragraph 227 of Teodoro de Croix's long memorial of October 30, 1781, (C–4430) of which the original is in A.G.I., 103–4–24. This table is referred to in chapter XVIII.

DISTRICTS	MEN	WOMEN	BOYS	GIRLS	TOTALS
Real del Rosario . . .	1546	1868	1217	996	5627
S. Juan Bautista de Maloya	629	568	283	270	1750
S. José de Copalá . .	2725	2274	1657	1715	8371
S. Miguel de Culiacán .	3234	3254	2055	1947	10490
Sinaloa	2471	2531	2144	2032	9178
Fuerte	2376	2172	897	706	6151
Cosalá	1184	1055	685	595	3519
Álamos	2055	2005	2107	1670	7837
Ostimuri	3477	3564	3058	3581	13680
Sonora	6231	6052	4495	4263	21041
Totals	25,928	25,343	18,598	17,775	87,644

INDEX

Academy of Pacific Coast History, 445, 446.

Academy of Sciences of St. Petersburg, 247.

Acapulco, 7, 8, 40, 58, 194, 265, 268, 370, 372, 377, 379, 380, 423. *See* Manila galleon.

Africa, 174, 179.

Agriculture. *See* Crops, Food supplies.

Aguilar, 241.

Aguilar's River, 58, 332, 333.

Álamos, 48, 131, 383; *Real Caja* of, 52, 53, 88, 131, 132, 140, 394, 395, 404, 455, 456, 468.

Alarcón, Hernando de, 7, 9.

Alaska, 176, 177, 418. *See* Californias, North America, Russians.

Alberoni, 22, 23.

Albuquerque, 39.

Aleutian Islands, 176–78.

Algiers, 199, 237.

Almodóvar, Marqués de, 61.

Alta California, VII–XII, 7, 8, 13, 24, 34, 57, 59, 60, 68–70, 80, 84–88, 91–94, 96–115, 118–30, 143, 145–47, 149, 151, 153–56, 158–61, 167, 179, 217–19, 222, 231, 232, 234, 238, 240, 244, 249–80, 283–90, 293, 294, 298–301, 308, 309, 311, 313–38, 341, 342, 346–48, 350, 352–57, 359, 360, 363–72, 377–90, 393, 396–98, 406, 410, 411, 413–15, 422, 427–35, 467, 470. *See* Baja California, Californias, Colonization, Crops, Deserters, Domestic animals, Expense, Food supplies, Foreign danger, Gifts for Indians, Gila and Colorado, Gold, Goods and effects, Indians, Junction of the Gila and Colorado, Laborers, Land route, Mails, Manila galleon, Military, Military equipment, Northwestward conquest, Pious fund, San Blas, Sea route, Settlers, Supply ships.

Altamira, Marqués de, 43, 44.

Altamirano, Pedro, 56, 61.

Altar, 44, 48, 61, 89, 132, 134, 135, 137, 156, 164, 167, 275–77, 280, 284, 286, 343, 403, 404, 429.

Altar River, 13, 19.

Alva, Duque de, 77, 78.

Amarillas, Marqués de, 62, 63, 85, 150.

Amarillo, Río, 65.

America, 188, 190. *See* American colonies, Americans, Americas, Brazil, North America, South America, Spanish America, United States.

American colonies, 188, 194, 197, 200, 203–15.

American Revolution. *See* American colonies.

Americans, 183, 186, 208, 419. *See* American colonies, United States.

Americas, 82, 174, 179. *See* America, Spanish America.

Anian, Strait of, 8, 26.

Anson, George, 30, 60, 73, 75, 181, 377.

Antilles, 204.

Anza, Juan Bautista de, (Jr.), 14, 24, 90, 92, 115, 127, 130, 145–60, 162–70, 217, 218, 223, 231, 234, 236, 238–40, 253–56, 265, 266, 269–71, 273–304, 307, 314–17, 319–22, 325–27, 335, 337–42, 346–61, 364, 365, 378, 380, 384, 386, 387, 391–95, 400–2, 411, 413–18, 426, 431, 457–68.

Anza, Juan Bautista de, (Sr.), 24–29, 47, 157.

Apachería, 43, 64, 66, 135.

Apaches, 3, 13, 16, 18, 26, 28, 29, 34, 35, 37, 39, 41–50, 54, 61, 65, 66, 69, 78, 79, 91, 130, 132–37, 139, 140, 144, 147, 149–52, 156, 157, 162, 164, 275, 280, 301–4, 306, 307, 338, 340–43, 345, 346, 351, 363, 365, 367, 386, 390–92, 399–402, 406, 409, 411, 412, 414, 424, 425, 428.

Aragón, Pedro de, 49.

Aranda, 188, 192, 193, 195, 196, 198, 201–4, 206–11, 213.

Arce y Arroyo, 62.

Archangel, 225, 241.

Archivo General de Indias, 446.

Arctic Ocean, 176, 186, 246.

Areche, 155, 156, 159, 167, 168, 260, 370–72.

Argentine, the, 216.

474 INDEX

476 INDEX

Ferrelo, 7.

Finances, 25, 46, 51–53, 69, 71, 76, 78–80, 90, 190, 261, 266, 268, 401, 425, 455, 456. *See* Expense, *Junta de guerra y real hacienda,* and names of *cajas reales.*

Finland, 198.

Fiscal, 39; of Mexico, 43, 62, 271, 320, (*See* Areche, Borbón, Casafonda, Goyeneche, Rebolledo) ; of the Council of the Indies, 28, 31, 42, 63, 117, 270.

Florence, 94.

Florida, 5, 6, 189, 190, 211.

Floridablanca, 188, 211–14.

Font, Pedro, 151, 297, 299, 339, 347, 351, 355, 356, 364, 459, 460, 467.

Food supplies, for Alta California, 59, 93, 96–102, 107, 113, 119, 124, 125, 160, 161, 235, 240, 249–57, 259, 260, 280, 281, 284, 289, 317, 320, 331, 340, 357, 359, 368, 370–72, 381, 382, 427. *See* Crops, Domestic animals, Supply ships.

Foreign danger, 3, 16, 32, 38, 53, 58–61, 63, 65, 73–75, 82, 83, 85, 86, 92–94, 113, 116, 117, 129, 146, 167, 173–75, 187, 188, 192, 216, 217, 219, 220, 228, 229, 235, 236, 238–40, 242, 274, 314, 315, 320, 338, 341, 387, 411, 417–20, 427, 432–34. *See* Americans, Dutch, English, French, Portuguese, Russians.

France, 55, 66, 75, 174, 187–89, 191–98, 201–14, 420, 421.

Franciscans, 12, 23, 34, 70, 102, 104, 112, 116, 117, 249, 253, 257, 264, 308, 315, 322 ; of Jalisco, 72, 88. *See* *Fernandinos, Queretaranos,* Querétaro, San Fernando.

French, 3, 5, 16, 36–41, 43, 55, 60, 65–67, 75, 179, 181, 183, 184, 186, 241, 246, 247, 419.

Frobisher, 184.

Fronteras, Corodeguache de, 16, 19, 24–26, 29, 48, 54, 132, 134, 135, 150, 305, 343.

Frontier provinces, 1–13, 43, 44, 65, 66, 73–81, 87, 92, 237, 248, 257, 266, 301–4, 307, 308, 410–12, 417, 433. *See* Alta California, Apaches, Baja California, Californias, Chihuahua, Coahuila, *Comandancia general,* Durango, Moqui, New Mexico, Nueva Vizcaya, Nuevo León, Nuevo Santander, Pimería Alta, Sinaloa, Sonora, Texas.

Fuca, 241.

Fuenclara, Conde de, 31, 34.

Fuerte de Montesclaros, 13, 47, 292, 293, 425, 470.

Funnel, 180.

Fur trade, 75, 175, 177, 178, 182–86, 225, 226, 245–47, 417, 419, 420, 422.

Gage, General, 204.

Gali, Francisco, 8.

Gallardo, José, 35, 54.

Gallo, 4.

Gálvez, Bernardo de, 426, 428.

Gálvez, José de, VIII, 45, 51–53, 67–71, 73–89, 91, 94, 97, 105, 106, 108, 110, 113, 116–18, 141, 143, 145, 153, 154, 161, 179, 190, 219, 248, 249, 257, 263–72, 304–6, 312, 316, 320, 325, 326, 328, 347, 354, 357, 359, 360, 362, 364, 367, 369, 372–80, 386–93, 395, 396, 398, 402, 403, 409, 411, 413, 415, 416, 418, 419, 469.

Garcés, Francisco, 70, 145–49, 153–59, 162–67, 169, 218, 254, 265, 273–76, 281, 283–88, 295, 297, 299, 337–44, 346, 347, 352–54, 359–66, 387, 401–7, 411, 413, 414, 430, 458, 459, 467.

Garnier, 201, 204, 205.

Gente de razón. See "Civilized people."

Georgia, 59.

Gibraltar, 51, 189, 213, 214.

Gifts for Indians, 106, 107, 124, 132, 133, 166, 276, 287, 291, 293, 348, 350, 351, 357, 362, 385, 404–6, 412, 413, 424, 425, 466.

Gil de Bernabé, Juan Crisóstomo, 133, 158.

Gil Samaniego, Manuel, 89.

Gila and Colorado rivers, region of the, 14–20, 22–25, 28–35, 37–45, 47, 50, 53–55, 57–59, 62–64, 66, 88, 89, 92, 118, 145, 146, 150, 153, 162, 164, 166, 168, 271, 283, 290, 299, 337–44, 351, 353, 358–60, 364–67, 386, 387, 390, 394, 398–415. *See* Colorado River, Gila River, Junction of the Gila and Colorado.

Gila Mountains, 19, 148.

Gila River, 7, 13, 19, 20, 24, 26, 29, 33, 47, 76, 79, 91, 117, 130, 146–48, 275, 288, 304, 345, 349, 350, 358, 362, 363, 406, 409, 411.

Gold, in Alta California, V, VI, VIII–X, 272, 388, 418–20, 427, 435. *See* Precious metals.

Gonzaga, San Luis, 67.

González Cabrera Bueno, 37, 84.

González Carvajal, Ciriaco, 419, 420.

Good Hope, Cape of, 179, 226.

Printed in the United States of America.

Filibusters and Financiers

By WILLIAM O. SCROGGS, Ph.D.

Professor of Economics and Sociology in the University of Louisiana

Cloth, 8vo, $2.50

Professor Scroggs has written a very valuable supplement to American history in this account of the activities of William Walker and his associates in the filibustering activities of the mid-nineteenth century. Nothing but scant notice has ever been accorded by historians to Walker's exploits in Central America and consequently one has never been able to form a just appreciation of the Latin-American attitude toward the United States. Walker and his band were Americans, and it was as Americans that Nicaraguans and Costa Ricans came to distrust and fear them.

The author in his preface says, " The part played in Walker's career and in Central American politics by American financiers and captains of industry; the designs of Walker upon Cuba; his utter repudiation of the annexation of his conquests to the United States; the appeals of Central American governments to the leading European powers for deliverance from the filibusters; the thinly veiled machinations of Great Britain, Spain, and France against the American adventurers — these are some of the facts, hitherto overlooked or ignored, which it is here sought to set forth in their true light."

The Pacific Ocean in History (*Preparing*)

Papers and Addresses Presented at the Panama-Pacific Historical Congress

EDITED BY HENRY MORSE STEPHENS

AND

HERBERT E. BOLTON

THE MACMILLAN COMPANY

Publishers   64–66 Fifth Avenue   New York

The German Empire Between Two Wars

By ROBERT H. FIFE, Jr.

Professor of German at Wesleyan University

Cloth, 8vo, $1.50

This is not a "war book" and yet one of its several interests undoubtedly arises from the application of the matters which it discusses to present events. The author writes impartially; he is not pro-German but treats Germany sympathetically as well as critically. In the first part of the volume he considers the relations of Germany with foreign powers from 1871–1914, after which he takes up internal politics during the same period. He then presents a view of the Germany of to-day, giving special attention to the government of the rapidly growing cities, the school systems, the church, and the press.

Japanese Expansion and American Policies

By J. F. ABBOTT

Of Washington University

Cloth, 12mo, $1.50

Here Professor Abbott sums up dispassionately and impartially the history of the diplomatic and social relations of Japan with the United States, and in particular gives the facts that will enable an American to form his own opinion as to the possibility of future conflicts between these two countries.

THE MACMILLAN COMPANY

Publishers   64-66 Fifth Avenue   New York

Travels in the American Colonies, 1690–1783

EDITED BY NEWTON D. MERENESS

Under the auspices of The National Society of the Colonial Dames of America

Cloth, 8vo, $3.00

This book consists of eighteen hitherto unpublished narratives, some written originally in English, others being translations from the French or German. They give accounts of travel on the Atlantic slope from Savannah to Albany; from Albany to Niagara Falls, Quebec, Hartford, and Boston; through the Great Lakes from Detroit to Chicago; up the Mississippi from New Orleans to St. Louis; down the Ohio and the Mississippi from Pittsburgh to New Orleans; up the Tennessee; through the country of the Choctaws, the Creeks, and the Cherokees and through the backwoods from Pennsylvania to North Carolina.

The Mastering of Mexico

BY KATE STEPHENS

Cloth, 12mo, $1.50

The conquest of Mexico by Cortes in the sixteenth century was one of the most thrilling and picturesque exploits in all the annals of the art of war. ' The stern and hardy explorer and his few hundred heroes who led Europe's quest for the treasure-land of the new world, left behind them memories full of adventure more stirring than the strongest fiction. The tale of one of these adventurers, Bernal Diaz del Castillo, with a genial spirit which we are not apt to attribute to men of his time, has left for us the picture of this little band of Spaniards triumphing over a militarized nation of fierce warriors, sweeping through Mexico on foaming horses from the sea-board to the Aztec capital, with the glory of conquest blazing in their eyes through the glitter of swords and the flash of muskets and the gleam of the southern sun. In retelling Diaz' narrative for modern readers Miss Stephens has lost no particle of that astonishing visualization of the deeds and sufferings of Cortes' intrepid conquerors, and none of the impression of sturdy, single-hearted faith in comrades and captain which so richly pervaded the original.

THE MACMILLAN COMPANY

Publishers   64–66 Fifth Avenue   New York

The Life of Andrew Jackson

By JOHN SPENCER BASSETT, Ph.D.

WITH ILLUSTRATIONS. NEW EDITION. TWO VOLUMES IN
ONE

Cloth, 8vo, $2.50

This is a one-volume edition of a biography that has since its first publication several years ago, come to be regarded as one of the most faithful stories of Jackson's life and of its effect on the nation that has ever been written. Professor Bassett has not slighted Jackson's failings or his virtues; he has tried to refrain from commenting upon his actions; he has sought to present a true picture of the political manipulations which surrounded Jackson and in which he was an important factor. The volume contributes largely to a clearer realization not only of the character of a great man but also of the complex period in which he lived.

The Writings of John Quincy Adams

VOLUME VI. EDITED BY

WORTHINGTON C. FORD

Cloth, 8vo, $3.50

This volume brings Mr. Ford's remarkable series up to the year 1821. Mr. Adams's last dispatches from London, while minister there, deal with the matters left undetermined by the Treaty of Ghent and with his association with the English reformers of the day.

THE MACMILLAN COMPANY

Publishers   64–66 Fifth Avenue   New York